*Books by Germán Arciniegas which
have been published in English:*

THE KNIGHTS OF EL DORADO (*1942*)
GERMANS IN THE CONQUEST OF AMERICA (*1943*)
THE GREEN CONTINENT: *A Comprehensive View
    of Latin America by Its Leading Writers*
    (selected and edited by Arciniegas, *1944*)
CARIBBEAN: SEA OF THE NEW WORLD (*1946*)
THE STATE OF LATIN AMERICA (*1952*)
AMERIGO AND THE NEW WORLD: *The Life and
    Times of Amerigo Vespucci* (*1955*)
LATIN AMERICA: *A Cultural History* (*1966*)

THESE ARE *Borzoi Books*
PUBLISHED BY *Alfred A. Knopf* IN NEW YORK

LATIN AMERICA

A Cultural History

Latin America:
A Cultural History

by Germán Arciniegas

TRANSLATED FROM THE SPANISH BY
Joan MacLean

New York : Alfred A. Knopf : 1967

THIS IS A BORZOI BOOK
PUBLISHED BY ALFRED A. KNOPF, INC.

To Gabriela

Paris, 1964

Acknowledgments

When I signed a contract to write the present book, the task ahead looked easy because I had been dealing with its subject matter in my classes at Columbia University. But when I began the actual writing, I saw that to condense so vast a subject into one volume would by no means be simple. In any case, Alfred A. Knopf had asked me to write the book, and I am grateful to him for that invitation.

I profited from opportunities to give lectures on related materials to many organizations in Italy. In those lectures I developed the work chapter by chapter, beginning with the introduction. Later I condensed it for a course given at the Institut des Hautes Études de l'Amérique Latine of the University of Paris.

In the preparation of the manuscript Gabriel Giraldo Jaramillo gave me valuable suggestions out of his profound knowledge of Latin American art and travel documents. The editors and expert readers of the Sudamericana publishing house of Buenos Aires helped me to correct many points when preparing the Spanish edition. For the English edition I received opportune suggestions from Mrs. Joan MacLean, the translator; from Herbert Weinstock, my editor at Knopf; and from Mrs. Harriet de Onís.

Many persons helped in collecting and choosing the illustrations, but I want to make special mention of Graziano Gasparini, architect and writer, whose work on Venezuelan art has been outstanding and whose valuable collection of photographs of pre-Columbian and colonial architecture, covering all of Latin America, he generously placed at my disposal; most of the illustrations in this book are from his collection. The Mexican poet Carlos Pellicer was kind enough to write the sonnet that strikes a note of beauty at the opening of the book.

I have set down these few names as examples of the good fortune with which this book has met and which has brought it into the reader's hand as it appears now.

July 1966   German Arciniegas

Toda, América Nuestra

Medio cielo y dos mares y agua buena.
Tierra altísima y baja; sol de soles.
El hombre cóndor y sus arreboles.
El hombre azul y la noche serena.

La Historia en el diamante y en la arena.
Silencioso rumor de caracoles.
Tiempo y eternidad en sus crisoles
de antigua juventud hacen cadena.

Los tres reinos devoran despilfarro.
La mano modeló cantante barro
y en toda destrucción la geometría

deja sus huellas. Tierno está el olvido.
Campanario a pirámide se alía
y se espera en la Luz nuevo sentido.

Carlos Pellicer
Tepoztlán, México, junio de 1965

(Half sky and two seas and good water. High land and low; sun of suns. The condor man and his sunset reds. The blue man and the serene night. History in the diamond and the sand. The muffled murmuring of sea shells. Time and eternity are linked in their crucibles of ancient youth. The three kingdoms devour wastefulness. The hand, singing, modeled clay, and in all destruction geometry leaves its traces. Forgetfulness is tender. Bell tower and pyramid are allied and await new meaning in the Light.)

Contents

Introduction: The Four Americas   XV

I   America's Old World   3

II   The America of 1500   27

III   What the Spaniards Brought to America   38

IV   The Birth of a Literature   64

V   Don Quixote and the Conquest of America   76

VI   Green Brazil   88

VII   The Spanish Colonies   123

VIII   The Convents and the Missions   143

IX   A First Inventory of Spanish-American Literature   168

X   The Arts in the Spanish Colonies   193

XI   The Enlightenment   230

XII   The Scientific Missions   264

XIII   Independence   286

XIV   Romanticism and Liberalism   314

XV   Civilization and Barbarism   351

XVI   From Utilitarianism to Positivism   378

XVII   Brazil from Colony to Empire to Republic   404

XVIII   Haiti in Black and White   442

XIX   From *Modernismo* to *Anti-Modernismo*   461

XX   Between Ariel and Caliban   487

XXI   Appointment with Necromancy   523

Chronological Table   551

Bibliography   571

Index   *follows page* 594

Illustrations

following page 288

1. GUATEMALA. *Antigua: Palace of the Captains General*
   Foto Graziano Gasparini

2. GUATEMALA. *Guatemala City: Mayan Bas-relief*
   Foto Unesco—Albert Raccah

3. MEXICO. *Teotihuacán: Pyramid of the Sun and Roadway of the Dead*
   Foto Graziano Gasparini

4. MEXICO. *Uxmal: Quadrangle of the Nuns*
   Foto Graziano Gasparini

5. MEXICO. *Tepotzotlán: Façade of the Convent*
   Foto Graziano Gasparini

6. PERU. *Arequipa: Façade of the Church of Yanahuara*
   Foto Graziano Gasparini

7. PERU. *Macchu Pichu: The "Torreón"*
   Foto Graziano Gasparini

8. DOMINICAN REPUBLIC. *Santo Domingo: Porch of the Cathedral*
   Foto Graziano Gasparini

9. DOMINICAN REPUBLIC. *Santo Domingo: Gothic Vaulting in the Cathedral*
   Foto Graziano Gasparini

10. ECUADOR. *Quito: Façade of the Church of the Compañía (Jesuit)*
    Foto Graziano Gasparini

11. BRAZIL.   *Congonhas do Campo: Prophets by Aleijadinho*
                Foto Graziano Gasparini

        12. BRAZIL.   *A Prophet by Aleijadinho*
                Foto Graziano Gasparini

        13. BRAZIL.   *Rio de Janeiro: Copacabana*
                Foto Graziano Gasparini

        14. VENEZUELA.   *The Church of Santa Ana
                de Paraguaná (1681)*
                Foto Graziano Gasparini

15. VENEZUELA.   *The Church of Clarines (restored, 1963)*
                Foto Graziano Gasparini

        16. VENEZUELA.   *Carora: The Calvary Chapel (1787)*
                Foto Graziano Gasparini

        17. PUERTO RICO.   *San Juan: The Fortress of El Morro*
                *Economic Development Administration,
                Commonwealth of Puerto Rico*

                18. BOLIVIA.   *Church in the Highlands*
                        Foto M. Chamudes

        19. COLOMBIA.   *Mompox: Church of Santa Bárbara*
                        Foto Nereo

                20. COLOMBIA.   *Bogotá: Detail of a Retable
                        in a Colonial Church*
                        Foto Germán Téllez

                21. COLOMBIA.   *Popayán: Pulpit Stairs,
                        Church of San Francisco*
                        Foto Hernán Díaz

        22. PANAMA.   *Old Panamá: Ruins of the Cathedral Tower*
                        Foto Graziano Gasparini

Maps

Planned and executed by Theodore R. Miller

MEXICO (7)

CENTRAL AMERICA and PANAMA (11)

SOUTH AMERICA and the CARIBBEAN (17)

INTRODUCTION
The Four Americas

In common parlance, a European is a European, as an African is
an African. But an American is not always an American. When
people say that Americans are rich, or that the Americans have an
army that rivals Russia's, this has nothing to do with the Paraguayans, a poor nation, or the Costa Ricans, who have no army.
And yet a Paraguayan is as at least much an American as a New
Yorker, and Costa Rica was a part of America a century before
the Pilgrims on the *Mayflower* landed at Plymouth.

Newspapers in the United States are becoming more and more
accustomed to referring to the inhabitants of "Latin America"
simply as "Latins." When a news story in *The New York Times*
announces that a plan to aid the "Latins" is being drawn up in
Washington, everyone knows that the writer is not talking about
the Italians or the French, the Portuguese or the Spanish, but
about the people of the republics south of the Rio Grande. What
is so Latin about these republics? Where do you draw the lines
that divide the Anglo-Saxon, the Latin, and the Indian? New Orleans is much more Latin than Cuzco in Peru, than Otavalo in
Ecuador, than Pátzcuaro in Mexico. The very names Cuzco,
Otavalo, and Pátzcuaro are as authentically of the America south
of the Rio Grande as that of Boston is of the United States. New
Orleans, Latin though it is, is incorporated in the world of the
United States body and soul, and if the descendants of Italians

now living in the United States were considered Latin Americans, their number would exceed the population of several of the republics south of the Rio Grande.

The confusion over the name "America" has no parallel in any other portion of the globe. Over a period of three or four centuries, the Spaniards were determined not to adopt the word: they spoke always of the "West Indies." They called the inhabitants of the New World "Indians" because Columbus believed that he had landed on one of the islands of the East Indies, a belief that became so firmly implanted in the minds of the monarchs of Castile that once the name "Indies" had taken hold, it could not be displaced from either the popular or the scholarly vocabulary. By the time it had become clear that the discovered land was actually a new continent, or a New World, it was too late to rectify the error, or else there was no particular reason for doing so. The name simply became the "West Indies." America as a word rang with too much independence; it connoted a revolution that the writers of treatises felt impelled to reject. Charles V gave to the first statutes drawn up during his reign the title "Laws of the Indies," from which title came the term *"Derecho Indiano,"* meaning the law in force over the Spaniards in America. Even in this century, a child born in Cuba to Spanish parents is called an *"indiano."* The word *indiano* is still defined by the *Dictionary of the Spanish Academy* as: "A national, but not a native, of America. . . . Also applied to one who returns wealthy from America."

The "Black Legend" established against Amerigo Vespucci has prevailed since the time of Bishop Fray Bartolomé de Las Casas. It caused the name "America" to seem specious because it derived from that of Amerigo Vespucci, in whose honor the canons of Saint-Dié, in Lorraine, were inspired to coin the word. The suspicion bred by Las Casas persisted to so great a degree that Emerson wrote in *English Traits:* "Strange . . . that broad America must wear the name of a thief, Amerigo Vespucci, the pickle-dealer at Seville . . . whose highest naval rank was boatswain's mate in an expedition that never sailed, but who managed in this lying world to supplant Columbus and baptize half of the earth with his own dishonest name." Emerson died without realizing who Amerigo Vespucci really was, and never knew of his four voyages to the New World or that the monarchs of Castile had made him chief pilot, thereby bestowing on him a rank higher than that of any of the Spanish pilots. Columbus died unaware that a new continent existed, still firmly convinced that he had reached Japan and that the islands in the Caribbean were a Japanese archipelago.

Further to complicate this comedy of errors, the group of philosophers[1] who met in Philadelphia to draw up the Federal Constitution after the colonies had won their independence did not think to give the new nation a name of its own. As a consequence, the United States is the only country in the world without an unmistakable name. To say "united states" is to say federation, republic, or monarchy. The United States of the North is not the only United States of America, for there are the United States of Mexico, the United States of Venezuela, and the United States of Brazil. But if Brazil is Brazil, and Mexico is Mexico, and Venezuela is Venezuela, each of them is as much a part of America as the republic in the North. In an unusual book on the nomenclature of America—that is, of the geographical names adopted in the United States—George Stewart says that the generic name United States was accepted as a provisional denomination after the search in Philadelphia for a suitable name to give the new republic had been postponed. Later a plan was formulated that would give the country the name "Columbia" or "Colombia" in honor of Columbus. But for once matters moved slowly in the north, and

---

[1] In Latin America, the framers of the Constitution of the United States and of its Declaration of Independence are often referred to as "philosophers" because they did much to mold the new political philosophy of the late eighteenth century. Of the four figures especially so designated—Franklin, Adams, Jefferson, and Madison—all were members of the five-man committee that drew up the Declaration (Jefferson preparing the actual paper), except for Madison, who was, however, responsible for so much of the actual Constitution that he is often referred to as its "author." Although Jefferson and Adams were abroad during the Constitutional Convention of 1787, representing the United States in France and England, respectively, their influence in the Constitutional Convention was still very strong, and Jefferson, when he returned, was, along with Madison, instrumental in remedying the principal defect of the 1787 document—its lack of a bill of rights—by working to bring about the adoption of the first ten amendments to the Constitution. An American historian of philosophy, Herbert W. Schneider, in his *History of American Philosophy*, says of these men (p. x): "It is somewhat embarrassing to the historian of philosophy to point to John Adams, Benjamin Franklin, Thomas Jefferson and James Madison as cosmopolitan and distinguished expressions of the philosophy of the Enlightenment and to be compelled to admit that their writings are full of commonplaces and their minds full of confusions. They had no systems of thought and they consciously borrowed most of the scattered ideas which they put into action. They are poor material for the class room, but they are, nevertheless, still living as well as classic symbols in American philosophy."

in the meantime the old viceroyalty of New Granada in the south took the name "Colombia," invented by Miranda in 1806. Bolívar adopted the title Great Colombia for the country that combined New Granada, Venezuela, and Ecuador. This made it impossible for the United States to call itself the United States of Columbia. Someone then suggested as a substitute "Freedonia," which combines the Anglo-Saxon root *frēo* with a Greco-Latin ending, in order to christen it the country of freedom. At about that time, some wag wrote a letter to a newspaper in the south pointing out that "donia"—that is, *doña*—means lady in Spanish, and that the republic was considering calling itself the country of "free ladies. . . ." That was the end of that. The debate dwindled away and the country was left without a proper name. The consequence is that less than half of the people living on the American continents call themselves "Americans."

Actually, however, there are four Americas that represent four historic zones, four experiences, four styles, four characters, each in search of self-expression, of a culture. They are the Hispano-Indian America, the Portuguese America (Brazil), the English America (the United States), and the Anglo-French America of Canada. Each of these Americas has an area more or less equal to that of the others. Hispano-Indian America covers 3,800,000 square miles; Canada, 3,400,000; Brazil, 3,200,000; and the United States, 2,900,000. The history of each of these Americas begins at a different date, even in different centuries.

Apart from the fact that the America of the Quechuas, the Aztecs, and the Maya is very ancient, the intimate bond between the New World and Spain was formed in 1492. After 1500 the Conquest expanded so swiftly and the colonies were founded so soon that any of the Hispano-Indian nations can say that its post-Columbian history goes back four and a half centuries.

Portuguese America, unlike the others, has no recorded pre-Columbian history. Its indigenous cultures were rudimentary; the aborigines never managed to create a civilization. Brazil has no pre-Columbian city (neither had Canada). The Portuguese never hurled themselves into any venture as the Spaniards plunged into the Conquest. They arrived later and penetrated the land more slowly. Bahia, the oldest city in Brazil, was founded in 1549; Rio de Janeiro, in 1567. By comparison with Mexico City or Lima, both were minuscule. Not until the capital of the Portuguese empire was transferred temporarily from Lisbon to Rio de Janeiro early in the nineteenth century, when the Braganzas left Portugal

to escape falling into Napoleon's hands, did Rio de Janeiro acquire
the brilliance of a city. Following that event, the families of the
early settlers who, until then, had been living in their mansions on
their estates, moved into the capital. As a matter of fact, the
capital of Brazil has a history of migrancy. The first was Bahia,
which ceased to be the capital in 1763, when the government
moved to Rio de Janeiro; nowadays the capital is Brasilia.

Compared with these two Americas colonized by people from
the Iberian peninsula, which for the sake of simplicity we call
Latin America, the northern Americas seem young. Canada's
history began in 1541 and 1542, nearly half a century later than
that of Hispano-Indian America, when Jacques Cartier claimed
"New France" on his second voyage of discovery. Quebec was
founded by Samuel de Champlain in 1608, but the settlement
grew so slowly that half a century later its inhabitants barely
numbered twenty-five hundred. The cultivated land amounted to
only thirty-five hundred acres—an area less than that of a typical
big estate in Mexico.

The last of the settlers to arrive were the English. They
founded the Jamestown Colony in 1607. In view of the fact that
John Cabot had explored the northern coasts for Henry VII of
England a hundred and ten years earlier, one must conclude that
the children of Great Britain had many reservations about cutting
all ties and crossing the sea to settle as colonists in the New
World. The Pilgrims on the *Mayflower* overcame their reservation because their desire for religious freedom was stronger than
their doubts.

All in all, the Americas brought to world culture a new concept
of civil life. The development of a new political philosophy, which
came to rule much of the world in the course of time, was some-
how overlooked by Giovanni Papini, so alert to everything and so
curious—but so arbitrary, too—when he wrote the famous indictment of Latin America in which he refused to grant that portion
of the world any gift to the Occident. Nevertheless, with the
United States, Latin America did give the Occident a new dimension that it had been unable to attain under the hierarchies established by kings. Long before the French Revolution or the
Encyclopédie, before Rousseau and Montesquieu, the Europeans
who had left the Old World to settle in the New had acquired a
feeling for liberty—which they won, more or less; and for democracy—which they practiced, more or less, and by means of which

they laid the foundations of a new political philosophy and thereby altered the traditional bases of political science. On this point, white man, Indian, and Negro were in agreement. At the time when the old rules for colonial government were in crisis, what everyone thought but did not say became obvious. Adams exclaimed: "I do not wonder that suddenly all the sons of these English colonies declare for independence, because they had already declared themselves upon taking ship in European ports to find a land of their own in America!"

While Rousseau was still a humble engraver's apprentice about to run away from his master's atelier to experience the gamut of spiritual adventure that he records in his *Confessions* (written thirty years before *The Social Contract*), two Panamanian Creoles, José de Antequera and Fernando Mompox, settled in Asunción, Paraguay, where they practiced a doctrine that antedated the Genevan's. Antequera said: "The people may oppose the Prince who does not proceed *ad aequa et bone*. Not every mandate of the Prince need be carried out. In order to reserve to themselves the rights that have been made express, the people created and deputized the town governments to speak in the name of the people." According to Mompox, the power of the common people of any republic, city, village, or hamlet is greater than that of the king himself; the people have the power to accept or reject any law or governor they desire, for "even though [that law or governor] be given by the Prince, if the common people do not wish it, they may properly resist and fail to obey."

Five years after Antequera had been defeated in 1725 by authorities in Asunción loyal to the Crown, a new movement to oppose bad government was born, thanks to Mompox. Father Lozano reports that when the *comunero* militia entered the city, "the chief justice went out on the balcony to speak to them and exhort them to retire in good order to their homes. A voice interrupted him: 'Señor Provisor: what does *Vox Populi vox Dei* mean? You can answer that any way you like, but you can be sure that it means the common people.'"

The word "republic" does not mean the same thing as the word "democracy," nor does "monarchy" necessarily mean the absence of representation in the government. England became both democratic and representative earlier than France. And her colonies in America were both, too. New England had the representative system of the town meeting, which meant a measure of self-government, a kind of social contract, at a time when the philosophers of the Old World were only beginning to formulate their theories. I need hardly say that I am referring to the modern Old World. The world of Athens and ancient Rome belongs in another historical category. But if what happened in the eighteenth century was in a sense a Renaissance modeled to some degree on Athens and Rome, that Renaissance was cradled in America.

How was America able to anticipate the Europeans in proclaiming those precepts which are universally familiar today? The answer is simple: the force of political circumstance. The more deeply a European country was rooted in history, the greater difficulty it had in arriving at democratic formulas. The Americas never had to struggle to overthrow monarchies, never had a powerful nobility. The people of the Americas were commoners— plain Pérezes in the Hispano-Indian colonies, plain Smiths in the English. Europeans who had been docile vassals in Europe emigrated to America as bold adventurers.

But what might seem an aspiration common to the Western hemisphere was worked out on the field of action by many different means and methods. Such differences serve to demonstrate the four sets of circumstances that explain four different cultural characteristics.

Brazil and Canada won their independence without exchanging a shot with their mother countries. Hispano-Indian America and the future United States were forced to fight years of bloody wars to accomplish the separation.

When Canada became an English colony and a member of the British Commonwealth (which functions today as a "club" of nations), the transition was made through a gentleman's agreement, an English gentleman's agreement. Everything was done in a parliamentary, phlegmatic British "club" atmosphere, in which the speeches were well spoken, and gazettes were read while smoking a pipe in a velvet armchair under the tranquil gaze of an understanding monarch. Today, when the Queen of England visits Canada, it is not as Queen of England, but as the Queen of Canada. Thus one free and democratic American country has remained loyal to the Crown that all the others have rejected; but that crown does not lie heavy on Canada.

The story of how Brazil gained independence is a world wonder. The country passed from colony to independent nation with a gentleness and serenity that might have been expected of Canada, where the cold freezes even the formidable channel of the St. Lawrence River, but not of a green tropical paradise in which the sun and the music might have been expected to stimulate more hot-blooded solutions. The transition was made with great ease during the period of Dom Pedro's rule as regent in the name of the House of Braganza. Some of the gentlemen in the government went to the prince and explained that the nation would like to become independent. All of formerly Spanish America already was independent; the United States was independent; and therefore it was absurd that Brazil should continue dependent upon Lisbon. In short, they said to Dom Pedro: "Would you like to be our emperor?" Dom Pedro accepted, saying: "Independence or Death." And without more ado the country became independent. The change-over gave the people a reason for celebrating, the army a holiday, and everyone an excuse to parade. Nothing was heard from the armed forces, except band music.

Sixty-seven years went by; then the Brazilian empire made an equally smooth transition to a republic. Dom Pedro II was the last of the great enlightened monarchs. A founder of academies and libraries, philosopher, scholar, friend of the most illustrious men of Europe. But still an emperor. The republicans went to call on him. "Your Majesty," they said, "what Brazil wants is a republic like the republics all over America." His Majesty could find no objection. "So be it," he said. The gentlemen who had come calling escorted Dom Pedro to the port, accompanied him to his stateroom, a luxurious one, and bade him godspeed as they waved their handkerchiefs on the shore. Dom Pedro spent the rest of his life quietly in Europe, highly respected by the Brazilians. The republic was proclaimed in a box in a newspaper. Another holiday for the people. The soldiers, like the great philosophers they were, celebrated their own little revolution in the military college by reading the works of Auguste Comte and by placing on their nation's flag the two magical words "Order and Progress."

In more recent Brazilian history, Getulio Vargas committed suicide; Janio Quadros, another kind of suicide, relinquished the presidency; but the waters of the Amazon still run to the sea unstained by blood, whereas elsewhere in the world, Amazons of blood have been shed over changes of government. In Cuba, for example, matters have been quite otherwise, and Cuba is in America, too.

Any book on the history of a Hispano-Indian republic will demonstrate to the reader that its national development can be divided into four periods: the discovery, the conquest, the colony, and independence. If we consider these four large divisions, we shall see how their development flowed naturally from the discoveries that began with the landing of Columbus to conquest by such redoubtable captains as Cortés and Pizarro, who subjugated them; to the colony, in which they absorbed the essence of the Spanish world; and finally to the period when, in gaining their independence, they were made resplendent by men like Bolívar and San Martín. The history of the United States could be divided into the same four periods, but in reverse order. The first step was independence; then came the colony; then from colony it went on to conquest; and finally from conquest to discovery. This strange inversion of the historical process explains the deep differences between these two Americas better than anything that could be said about climate, race, or religion.

When the *Mayflower* sailed from Plymouth in 1620, the hundred Pilgrims who embarked did so in a kind of romantic demonstration of independence. They had not come in order to discover the land, which had been known for some time, or to carry out a conquest of the interior. The people of the Plymouth Colony were not soldiers; they were a group of families—men, women, and children—only forty-one of whom were adults. The *"Mayflower* Compact,"* which those forty-one adults signed before they sailed, states:

> We, whose names are underwritten . . . Do by these Presents, solemnly and mutually in the Presence of God and one another, covenant and combine ourselves together into a civil Body Politick, for our better Ordering and Preservation and Furtherance of the Ends aforesaid; And by Virtue hereof do enact, constitute, and frame, such just and equal Laws, Ordinances, Acts, Constitutions, and Offices, from time to time, as shall be thought meet and convenient for the General Good of the Colony.

Clearly, the Pilgrims intended to establish a government of their own and to enjoy the freedom needed to worship according to their belief, a desire that had already forced many others to leave the British Isles and settle on the continent of Europe.

Thus having declared their right to make their own law, the people of the *Mayflower* and those who followed them founded colonies on the eastern coast of North America. They organized themselves as bourgeois companies not unlike corporations. Their charters stipulated that they were not to settle beyond a certain number of miles inland, lest they expose themselves to Indian raids. Yet they were not to cling too closely to the shore, where they would be open to hit-and-run attacks by pirates. Their local laws were passed by city council or town meeting. The colonists elected their own local officials and governed themselves. The English governors appointed by the Crown were there on sufferance: the colonies fixed their salaries. The colonies expanded to such an extent that they were obliged to keep moving the frontier westward, not with the intention of conquering the West, but with that of acquiring living space for their increasing populations. Washington, as commander-in-chief of the armies that fought the war for independence, which merely confirmed the already existing independence, fought over a territory that seems minuscule to the Hispano-Indians by contrast with the ground that Bolívar covered. At a considerable distance east of the Mississippi, the tiny theater of war embraced only a portion of the original thirteen colonies of the union, which were, themselves, but a small portion of the fifty states that form the present United States.

The real conquest began with the word that gold had been discovered in California. This came in 1848, that is, three hundred and twenty-four years after Giovanni da Verrazano had touched land on the spot where New York now stands, three hundred and twenty-nine years after the conquest of Mexico, and three hundred and twelve years after the conquest of Peru. Complete control over the western half of North America was completed only a little more than a hundred years ago, in the middle of the past century, during a stampede accompanied by gunfire and turning wheels as in a faithful moving picture of the "Far West." So swift was this rush to the west that such vast tracts as Nevada and Oklahoma were really discovered years later.

Three centuries earlier, the Spanish Conquistadors, who looked as if they had stepped out of a medieval tapestry, explored and conquered Mexico and Peru in armor and coats of mail, sometimes on horseback, but mostly on foot and defending themselves from the Indians with dogs as often as with sword and gunpowder. They explored some of the mightiest rivers in the world—the Amazon and Paraná, the Magdalena, and the Pánuco—founded cities on the Caribbean coast, along the Atlantic shore, at the mouth of the Río de la Plata, on the Pacific coast of Chile—and at an altitude in the Andes of ten to twelve thousand feet. They accomplished this fabulous adventure in the space of thirty years. The conquest of Mexico was finished in 1519; Santiago, Chile, was founded in 1548. Of course, the Conquistadors could not have done what they did if they had brought families who clung to their hands as the families of *Mayflower* Pilgrims did, or had brought even a single woman. After years of incredible forced marches through unknown jungles, over freezing mountain peaks, through green hells, at a seemingly infinite distance from their own land, they took to themselves Indian women, whom they could not exterminate if for no other reason than that of the natural relationship between man and woman, a bond that failed, however, to restrain the Anglo-Saxon men to the north, who wiped out the Indian tribes along the frontier. That human patch with a new color, born in the south, is much the more extensive today, for it has bred many more children than the descendants of the thirteen colonies.

By the end of the Spanish Conquest, colonies were being established in the cities, but as colonies they had no government of their own. Spain appointed the viceroys who represented the king; the archbishops and bishops who represented the Spanish Church through the Crown's right as guardian; the judges of the Royal Audiencia, or supreme court; and the officials, major and minor, all of whom were selected in Spain and left the Peninsula not to labor as colonists, but to govern. At the end of the War of Independence, the colonies became republics without having known the experience of self-rule, for the colonists had never elected their authorities or drawn up their own laws. The Spaniards who left Spain had not migrated initially in an act of independence; they came to America in the service of the Crown and the Church.

The independence proclaimed in the *Mayflower* Compact of 1620 was not formulated in Hispano-Indian America until 1810. Yet, however strange it may seem, the people of Latin America offer the one instance in world history of so great a human mass that has lived largely in peace for three hundred years. While blood was spilled again and again in Europe during that same span of time, the blood of Europeans and Indians was quietly mingling in the America south of the Rio Grande.

While they were gaining independence—a historical process that began before the war in 1810 and is still uncompleted—the people of Hispano-Indian America had to create everything anew. For that reason, we who live in the South view the work of the

Constitutional Convention in Philadelphia as only another stage in
the development of something that had already existed viably in
the colonies, whereas in the South it had to be violently revolutionary, somewhat in the style of Europe, which could not pass
from empire to republic without rivers of blood flowing through
the streets.

When the four historical processes of the four Americas are explained in this summary manner, a better understanding of their
differences and likenesses is possible. Because of a long series of
experiences, the inhabitants of Hispano-America express themselves in Spanish, and along with their language they have retained the Catholic religion, Roman law, and a tendency toward
quixotic flights of fancy. The free fusion of bloods has created in
them a certain instability, which was augmented by the profoundly revolutionary rupture of 1810, when the spirit of repub-
licanism rebelled against the centuries-old tradition of powerful
hierarchies that had kept the colonies under the rule of a remote
power. Since then, the Spanish language in America has taken on
the ring of an aggressive idiom.

The people in the Portuguese America of Brazil have come to
speak Portuguese with a caressing, delightful, almost danceable
accent, warm and bright with sun and carnival. While others
were spending their time thinking of armaments, the Brazilians
were devoting their time to study. Once having spanned their
Amazon of politics with bridges of intelligent and peaceful agreement, these people are replete with good sense and serenity that
have given their language a tinge of philosophical humor.

The people of the English America of the United States have
expanded their language into a lively, constructive idiom as rich
as their country, precise, unambiguous, spread over an America
that has broadened as the contours of a prosperous democratic
empire have expanded, one in which complications and difficulties
arise only when races and traditions other than those of the white
men of the thirteen original colonies come into play. This is a
country in which religious freedom is practiced in many accents
and with a tradition of work that has made its factories and its
New York of steel-and-glass skyscrapers outstanding in the world.

The people of the Anglo-French America of Canada now speak
both English and French. The two languages are not separated by
an English Channel. The images of the saints in the Catholic
churches are not decapitated. Canada, almost as large as all of

Spanish America, contains fewer inhabitants than Colombia and
Ecuador combined. It developed in peace; while others were
spending their time winning independence through warfare, the
Canadians were busy establishing industries, felling pine forests
to make paper, trapping beavers for fur coats, and converting
waterfalls into electric energy. History has frozen there in the
winter since the days of the Vikings. But when the snow melts,
the eighteen million Canadians come forth and start back to work.
A third of them speak a somewhat archaic French.

To us, these four Americas are four great provinces on a continental mass, moving along their separate paths in search of the
same thing: freedom.

The preceding observations have not deterred the author from
writing this book on "Latin America." If the expression must be
accepted, however conventional and to some degree false, nevertheless it corresponds to a political reality of our time and is in
general use. To introduce another term would mean to range one's
self against a concept that the world accepts.

Furthermore, there is a unity in the Latin American republics.
They constitute a bloc with a spirit all its own. José Martí, who
was never inclined to use the expression "Latin America," spoke
of "our America," a cordially definitive term that often is chosen
to convey a more intimate vision of this geographical zone.

If this be true, why do we offer the point of view of four
Americas in this introduction? Because it will serve as an exposi-
tory means of clarifying the differences and contrasts that explain
a good part of the history and the styles of the Western Hemisphere. The author has used this method in his professorial chair
to make the exposition easier, and perhaps it may prove as useful
to the reader as it has been to him.

LATIN AMERICA

A Cultural History

I: *America's Old World*

¶ THE VENUS OF TLATILCO

In his letter announcing that the newly discovered land formed no part of Asia but was a continent separate from the three already known, Amerigo Vespucci requested that it be called the "New World." The expression became the accepted one from that moment. His report bearing the title *New World* was published in Venice in 1507, and the expression is still in use today. What was actually new, however, was not the world that for the first time lay open to the exploration of Europeans. Only their seeing it was new. The people of the Western Hemisphere beheld a new era opening before them in 1492. But this does not mean that the Aztecs and the Incas had had no history before that date. The year that Columbus set foot on American soil drew a line through America's chronology not unlike the one drawn through Europe's reckoning of time by the birth of Christ. Christ was revealed to man in America in 1492, and for him the Christian era began with that year. Yet great civilizations, which we would term pagan, had flourished earlier under other gods, and an acquaintance with them is essential to the interpretation of the rest of history. A study of pre-Columbian life is as necessary to America as a knowledge of the pre-Christian civilizations of Assyria, Egypt, Greece, and ancient Rome is to the other hemisphere.

Some twenty-three hundred to three thousand years before the arrival of Columbus, a small terra-cotta figurine was modeled. Now known as the Venus of Tlatilco, it represents a nude woman with elegantly dressed hair, a wasp waist, and massive thighs and hips. Its contours are similar to those modeled by the British sculptor Henry Moore, in our own day, to express feminine beauty. Henry Moore created those same contours for women some three thousand years later than the potters of Tlatilco, whose work could be likened, in turn, to the Greek figurines made in Crete and Mycenae fourteen centuries before Christ. Because they were tinted, the Tlatilco figurines, like the Greek, had an additional quality that Moore's lack. The colors of the Tlatilco Venus, applied in decorative geometrical lines, also similar to some present-day work, traced a transparent garment over the nude woman. Her face wears an expression of wit and irony. The anonymous artist who modeled and painted this figure, possibly as an amulet, must have sought that expression as a partial fulfillment of its magical functions. Whether the Tlatilco figurine was meant to carry a message to the gods of the harvest, a petition, or a religious summons to fertility, the modeling of the clay obeyed a transcendental impulse, at once ingenuous and mystical. The figurine was made expressly to be *enchanting*. Hence the enduring freshness of its impact. But it is not unique. This Venus is one among a thousand discovered in an archeological deposit near Mexico City. All the figures demonstrate that the year 1492 was not a point of departure but a dividing line. After the arrival of Columbus, art in the areas colonized by Spain was Hispano-Indian; it could only have been indigenous before him.

Not many years ago, the pre-Columbian nations were scarcely mentioned in studies on the culture of Latin America. Nevertheless, a radical change has occurred. Between 1950 and 1963 an exhibition of Mexican art traveled all over Europe. Hundreds of thousands of people saw it—in Stockholm, Brussels, Zurich, Cologne, The Hague, Berlin, Vienna, Moscow, Leningrad, Warsaw, Rome, Paris. . . . All the critics pronounced it one of the most comprehensive and revelatory art exhibitions ever assembled in this century. Revelatory because none of the monumental works on ancient art published in Europe before then had given much space or consideration to the ancient cultures of America. Archeologists had learned a great deal about those cultures during the first half of the twentieth century. But some critics found fault with the Mexican exhibition on the ground that the space allotted to Spanish American colonial art was meager by comparison with the thirty-odd galleries exhibiting that of the pre-Columbian civilizations. The Olmecs, Teotihuacáns, Zapotecs, Mixtecs, Huastecs, Toltecs, Maya, and Aztecs were represented by nearly nine hundred artifacts, whereas the Spanish American works numbered fewer than forty. What had brought about this disproportion? Not only the fact that the three thousand odd pre-Columbian years embrace a range of cultures in Mexico difficult to compress within the narrow confines of an exhibition hall, but also that those cultures were original, the source from which everything sprang, which is what interests the scholarly European. This is not to deny the value of the three hundred years of the Spanish colonial period, itself very rich in Mexico, but to explain the growing interest in the pre-Columbian, which is as evident today in bibliographies all over the world as it was within the Mexican exhibition. To the European in the street, the Mexican exhibition was like a second New World unfolding before his eyes. The first was announced by Amerigo Vespucci in his letter of 1503.

¶ ONE WORLD UNKNOWN

The acceptance of the designation "New World" by sixteenth-century Europe marked a step forward in geographical knowledge from that available at the time of Columbus. In his day America was completely unknown. The voyages of the Vikings to Labrador and Greenland, lost to memory, had left no open route to and from the north of Europe; indeed, they were not accepted as fact in geographical literature. On the other hand, Africa and Asia, although largely unexplored, were imbedded in European tradition. Some of the most stirring chapters of European expansion had been written on those continents between Greek and Roman times and the Crusades.

The physical characteristics of Negroes and Mongolians were not strange to Europeans. The Italian cuisine was spiced with pepper from Java and cloves from Ceylon. Alexander the Great had led his conquering armies as far as northern India, thereby opening the door to ideas, religions, gods, and philosophies from remote lands. The Caesars brought back from Egypt obelisks to adorn Rome. The mosaics in baths and palaces were designed by artists from Alexandria. Roman emperors built the *thermae* in Rome and the temples of Baalbek in Heliopolis (now Lebanon) during the same period. The story of Christianity, which placed in the hands of Europeans the books of the Old Testament, with

its memories of the Queen of Sheba, has as its base the exodu.
of the Jews from Egypt to the Promised Land. In those days, the
continent was not so much Europe as it was the land bordering
the Mediterranean Sea. Europeans, Asiatics, Africans built along
its shores the civilizations that formed the nucleus of the ancient
world. The Arabs spread over the coasts of Spain and Italy; the
Romans fought in Carthage; Christianity emerged in Asia. The
narrow fringes of Africa and Asia bordering the Mediterranean
were history's *terra firma*, and the sea, like a lake, was their common life force. The cities that gave ancient civilization its significance rose along those shores. The one absolute unknown was
America. Atlantis was no more than a myth: the fabled island
vaguely bruited in legend and believed to be sunk forever in
the Atlantic.

The reason for America's isolation is obvious. Except for Australia, it is the only part of the world surrounded by ocean. The
Atlantic and the Pacific defied seamen for centuries. Indeed, the
European of the final years of the fifteenth century and the early
years of the sixteenth hardly dared try to cross them. Even England waited until the seventeenth century before sending her most
venturesome colonists to the opposite shore. Because of the most
extraordinary circumstances the caravels that brought Columbus
to Guanahani sailed under the standard of the least nautical
kingdom in Europe: Castile.

¶ THE MAYA

Civilizations much older than those of Europe, although less
ancient than those in Asia, were flourishing in America. The
Venus of Tlatilco symbolizes them. The British Isles and the
Scandinavian countries, in fact, all of northern Europe, were still
living on a primitive level when, fifteen hundred years before
Christ, an important nation based on the cultivation of corn was
born on the plateau of Mexico. The clay figurines, among other
things, bear witness to that nation. They represent men and
women of delicate and elegant outlines, caricatures of fat men, and
grotesque hunchbacks that probably were thought to bring good
luck. All of them are notable in that they seem to be intentionally
expressive. The feminine beauties of the time are portrayed in
yellow, red, white, and violet, colors corresponding to the hues
of corn, according to the archaeologists. And strange women with
two faces, like those created by Pablo Picasso.

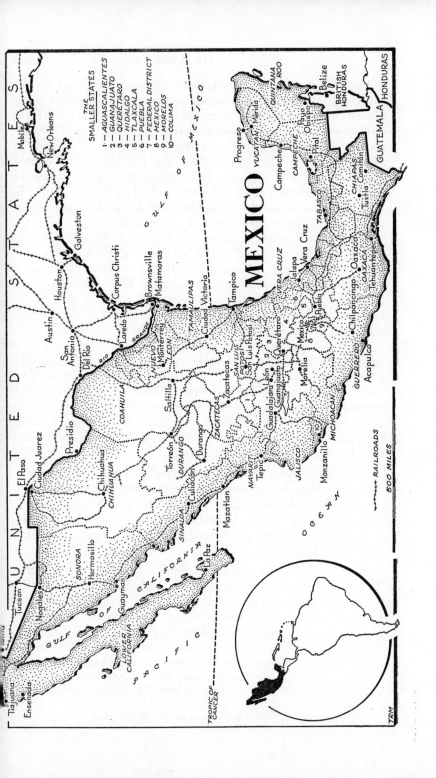

In addition to the figurines, there are many indices of the advancement attained by our distant ancestors. The invention of the Mayan calendar must have occurred in about 360 B.C. The Mayan civilization covers two thousand seven hundred years of history, starting from 1000 B.C. Its territory embraced the present-day Mexican states of Campeche, Yucatán, Chiapas, and Tabasco, and the territory of Quintana Roo; the entire area of Guatemala; parts of Honduras and El Salvador; and all of British Honduras —in all, an area of about two hundred forty thousand square miles, slightly more than that of Italy, including its islands.

The Maya invented a hieroglyphic writing, the oldest known texts of which correspond to the beginning of the Christian era. They used a very advanced numbering system, superior to Europe's because it made use of the zero. This enabled them to leave an accurate chronology in their codices. Their year of 365 days was divided into nineteen months: eighteen of twenty days each, and one of five. Their metric system was vigesimal, that is, it was based on the number twenty. They used their calendar to advance their knowledge of astronomy more than to record their political history. The Mayan manuscript known as the *Dresden Codex* is an almanac for divination. The date with which their chronology begins must be a reference to a myth of the creation of the world. The Mayan priests recognized the difference between the year of 365 days and the solar year, and remedied the difference by means of a secondary series.

> Indeed the calendar-correction formulae worked out by the ancient Maya astronomer-priests at Copán, back in the sixth or seventh century of the Christian Era, were slightly more accurate than our own Gregorian leap-year correction, which was not introduced until nearly a thousand years later, in 1582 by Pope Gregory XIII.[1]

Such advances were not the accomplishment of a single nation. The Olmecs, who lived within the boundaries of present-day Mexico, (800 B.C. to A.D. 800) and moved along the Gulf Coast to the present United States boundary, kept abreast of the Maya, and even preceded them. "The knowledge of the Maya concerning mathematics and writing came through perfecting the discoveries of the Olmecs: numeration, zero, and the vigesimal system. But the Maya knew better how to turn these discoveries to their advantage than did other groups of Central Americans who were

[1] Sylvanus G. Morley: *The Ancient Maya*, pp. 304-5.

also heirs of the Olmecs" (Fernando Gambos). Unfortunately, the Conquistadors, in their zeal to exterminate non-Christian creeds, made bonfires of most of the Mexican manuscript volumes. The few surviving codices are now in European museums and are most important auxiliaries in the rediscovery of America. The *Popul Vuh* and the books of *Chilám Balám*, collected after the Conquest, reveal the poetic ideas of these nations concerning the creation of the world and the magic in their traditions.

Of the Mayan cities known to us by their ruins, the most extensive is Tikal, in Guatemala. It covered an area of nearly two square miles. Six pyramids dominated the city, varying in height from Temple II, which rose to about 145 feet, to Temple IV, some 230 feet high. The altar at the apex of each pyramid was an architectonic triumph. Thus, by climbing the ritual stairway, one could arrive at a marvelous belvedere. The doorways were adorned with elaborately decorated wooden carvings, as the depictions of them in the Dresden Museum testify. But the pyramids were not a uniquely Mayan invention. They were common to all the great Mexican civilizations. The culture of Teotihuacán (300 B.C. to A.D. 1000) has been named "the culture of the pyramids." Their ruins are the symbolical center of ancient Mexico. The Pyramid of the Sun, 211 feet in height by 650 at the base, is the largest that survives from pre-Columbian America. The pyramid of Cholula, now in ruins, was larger than that of Cheops in Egypt. As Cholula is contemporaneous with the pyramids at Teotihuacán, these two sites in Central Mexico are twin peaks of Mexico's ancient grandeur. The Spaniards were privileged to see in all their splendor the pyramids in Mexico City—then Tenochtitlán—and the Conquistadors described them accurately.

If Tikal was the greatest of the Mayan cities, Copán, in Honduras, was their seat of learning, their university city. Imposing in itself, with its squares and colossal platforms crowning flights of stairs, it has immeasurable value because it preserves in its ruins the most complete inscriptions in Mayan hieroglyphics. Astronomical knowledge reached its highest point of development in Tikal. The temple containing the hieroglyphics dates from the year 756; the one dedicated to the morning star (Venus), from 771. At Chichén-Itzá, also in Mexico, the eleventh- and twelfth-century temples have, as unusual features, columns portraying the plumed serpent. The circular tower of the astronomical observatory, nearly 43 feet high, with its famous interior spiral staircase, is also there, along with the pelota courts with massive

walls and stone rings for playing a kind of basketball dating back
a thousand years. The most extensive court is more than 540 feet
long by 224 wide. The balls were of raw rubber; the first Spanish
historians' description of them brought to Europe the earliest
knowledge of this elastic gum. The hundreds of ranked columns
in the temple are reminiscent of the cathedral at Córdoba in Spain,
once a mosque.

No less impressive than the ruins of Chichén-Itzá are those
of Uxmal, with its cloister, its witches' house, and its monumental
staircase and platform of decorated stone, and those of Kabah,
a little over nine miles from Uxmal, which include a palace of
masks. Of even greater interest to archaeologists is Uaxactún,
because it is the most ancient monument discovered in the Mayan
territory, built in 328 B.C. At Uaxactún were found the most
beautiful of the polychrome ceramics, the first astronomical observatory, and a fresco that foreshadows those of Bonampak.
Another sacred city, fully as famous, is Palenque, interesting for
its pyramids decorated with polychrome stucco and stone reliefs
which give the measure of the refined elegance of the Mayan art.

The monumental sculpture of the Maya, with its gods, warriors, serpents, and jaguars, is as majestic as their architecture.
Equally notable is their ceramic art. The evolution of the Maya
and the influence of their culture as it spread by conquest of their
neighbors may be traced through the forms, drawings, and colors
of their pottery. The arts of weaving and featherwork were widely
practiced; their jewelry in gold and carved gems was beautiful.

That scattering of dead cities is not all that is left us of the
Maya; there are living men, too. In Guatemala, weaving is still
done in the Mayan way, and the Indians there retain a touch of the
old magic in secret references to their ancestors. The continuity
of their art is also evident on more exalted levels.

The "House of Colors" in Bonampak was discovered in the
chicle forests of Yucatán in 1946. Until that time, no white man
had ever set foot there. When Bonampak's interior frescoes,
ranked with those of Teotihuacán as among the most beautiful in
pre-Columbian art, were revealed, scientific expeditions were organized in Mexico and the United States to ensure their preserva-
tion and to make known to the scientific world this unsurpassable
document of Mayan life in the eighth century of our era. A prince,
warriors, courtiers, musicians, prisoners, and dancers are shown
on the walls of a small temple, where the blues, greens, reds,
grays, and yellows are still vivid. The palace scene depicts a

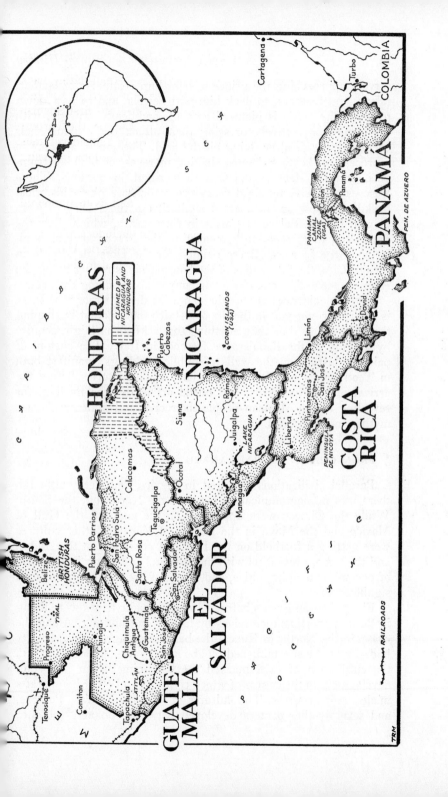

servant approaching the prince to offer him vestments of leather, fabric, and feathers, to deck him with jewels, and to bow down to him. The battle is pictured as a life-and-death struggle, with the conquerors actively pressing their attack and leaving their enemies lying dead or dying on the field. The musicians play in a procession, beating drums, shaking maracas, or blowing trumpets, and the dancers perform their ritual in motions. These frescoes of twelve hundred years ago, which are like a historical backdrop, show an unexpected similarity to those Diego Rivera painted for the Palace of Cortés in Cuernavaca, which show the Spanish soldiers seemingly reenacting the Mayan scenes. Similarly, in the frescoes Rivera painted for the Hotel del Prado in Mexico City, the fat toadies of the bourgeoisie, strolling along the Alameda, echo the courtiers of Bonampak approaching the prince.

Such coincidences across the centuries demonstrate that there is an artistic constant in the life of Mexico more potent in shaping the artist of our time than anything that a Mexican might acquire by a study of the Renaissance frescoes in Italy. The custom of painting history on the walls of public buildings, manifest both in Teotihuacán and Bonampak, dates back centuries before the arrival of the Spaniards, and mural art is still the medium for revealing to the Mexican people their civil and military history, myths, and traditions.

¶ FROM CHAVÍN TO TIAHUANACU

Parallel civilizations emerged in Mexico and Peru, although there was no communication between the North and the South. While the Olmecs were appearing on the coast of the Gulf of Mexico and the Maya in the jungles of Yucatán, other cultures were getting a foothold on the Peruvian coast and in the Andes, and they, too, present us with monumental testimony in the form of pyramids, temples, cities, and works of art that have universal significance.

Eight thousand years before Christ, nomadic tribes were living in Peru supporting themselves by fishing and hunting. Along the coast, in the North, in Huaca, the basis of an agricultural society had already been established by about 2550 B.C. About 1250 B.C. the cultivation of corn marked the beginning of an important development in the course of which ceramics and other handicrafts made great progress. The cultures of Chavín, Huaraz, Paracas, and several other centers developed between 800 and 300 B.C.

Another city, Tiahuanacu, built on the shore of Lake Titicaca, 12,500 feet above sea level, is one of the great mysteries of archeology. Its monumental ruins offer one of the most awe-inspiring sights in America. They belong to a civilization that emerged before the time of Christ and reached its apogee in A.D. 500, according to some scholars, while others claim that it lasted until 1000.

Traveling across the plateau of Bolivia toward the source of a small tributary of the Amazon, one arrives at the area explored in 1919 and 1943 by the famous Peruvian archeologist Julio C. Tello (1880–1947). There he discovered the remains of a sacred city built in a certain style, later called the Chavín style, after the name of the place, Chavín de Huántar. Archeological science today considers this the most ancient style among Peruvian cultures. The pottery found at the bottom of most archeological deposits in Peru always bears the characteristics of the Chavín style. All that survives as architecture in the ruins of Chavín de Huántar is the so-called Castle, the oldest building in Peru. This castle rises to a height of three stories from a base measuring 246 by 236 feet. Like the great temples and palaces built later in several parts of Peru, it is constructed of dry stone fitted together without mortar. Its interior is a veritable labyrinth of rooms, corridors, and ramps, through which fresh air circulates constantly. On one of the galleries an enormous carved stone was found, known as the Goad. How could such a temple, with such proportions, have been built in the eighth century on a site that was the goal of pilgrimages rather than a city, properly speaking? The answer is to be found in an institution called the *minga*, which still lingers among the Indians of Peru and Ecuador. The *minga* brought them together to carry out great collective undertakings.

Wendell C. Bennett, an archeologist who devoted the greater part of his brief life to a study of ancient Peru, writes: "During one or more weeks of the year many people made a religious pilgrimage to Chavín de Huántar. When they had gathered together in great number, they collected construction materials and erected stone walls. Under this system, they set some immense slabs of stone in place. At the conclusion of the religious ceremony and after the pilgrims had returned to their distant land, building specialists in their turn worked with squads of masons, living on the site and completing the construction." This explanation uncovers the secret of many constructions, including those at Tiahuanacu, which John Alden Mason justly compared with the Temple of Karnak.

The ruins of temples and palaces at Tiahuanacu are spread over an area measuring 3280 by 1471 feet. The plaza of Calasasaya alone measures 442 by 426 feet, and its colonnade of huge square-cut monolithic blocks seems to indicate that it was used for ceremonies where thousands of pilgrims came together, some coming from the plateau and the mountains, some from across the lake by raft, and all of them united in a religion so well established and revered that it could summon them over great distances through the highest ranges and plateaus in America in which man has created a civil society. As in Chavín, and in many settlements on the plateau extending from Mexico City to Yucatán, the people coming there were peasants who carried on their agriculture and industries in their villages. They used their city only as a center for religious and civil ceremonies, and perhaps as a market. If Tiahuanacu stood on the shores of the lake, from which the waters have retreated so far now that its banks and the ruins are widely separated, it must have been a remarkable sight in the days of its flowering when it was full of color and life. The entrance to the enclosed precinct known as the plaza of Calasasaya, the most famous of the group of structures at Tiahuanacu, is the Sun Gate, one of the most beautiful decorative monuments of ancient America. The Sun Gate is very small by comparison with the immense columns; it was carved from a single stone slab and weighs about ten tons. Above the geometric trapezium of the gateway is the image of a god, possibly Viracocha, whom forty-eight figures of warriors and priests are approaching to pay homage. The figures are incised in the polished surface of the stone. Perhaps they were inlaid with gold at one time. The eyes are represented by semi-precious stones. Such luxury was appropriate to a city that must have been like an altar erected on the heights of the Andes, where the sky seems widest, the air thinnest and most transparent.

The quarries from which the massive blocks were cut for all the buildings lie no less than three miles from Tiahuanacu, which implies that many gangs of well-organized workers were employed to quarry the stone, transport it, and set it in place as geometrically ordered columns impossible to move even today without great difficulty. A single monolithic sculpture now decorates a square in La Paz. Discovered by Wendell C. Bennett in 1932, it stands nearly 244 feet tall and represents the finished art of sculptors who conceived the figures of their deities in a rigid, austere, hieratic style befitting people who live on those heights in the Andes.

There will always be gaps in the reconstructed history of Tiahuanacu, as in that of other civilizations that developed in South America, beginning with Chavín. Written matter is lacking. The story of San Agustín, in Colombia, is as obscure as, or even more obscure than, the background of Tiahuanacu, for at the time of the Spaniards' arrival San Agustín was already in ruins. San Agustín, named for a neighboring village, may have reached its meridian toward the end of the eighth century of our era, but its monuments were lost until the beginning of the nineteenth century when Francisco José de Caldas (1770–1816) mentioned them. The Italian geographer Agostino Codazzi speaks of them later, in 1857. The first great scientific work on this culture was written by a German, K. H. Preuss, in 1914. By now some three hundred monolithic sculptures have been uncovered; some are monumental, with certain similarities to those of Tiahuanacu. San Agustín lies in a hidden fold of the Andean cordillera, at an altitude of 4534 feet above sea level. Like Tiahuanacu, it may have been a sacred place. Around it are no remains that might indicate the existence of a city. In Lavapatas, at the foot of the mountain, a series of canals and dams cut from the living rock and a number of stone images of serpents and lizards offer evidence of some sort of water-worship.

Even longer unknown than San Agustín, Machu Picchu, in Peru, was lost until 1911, when the world heard of it through its discoverer, Professor Hiram Bingham. Machu Picchu was equally well hidden in the mountains. It stands upon a rock like a fortress, some 2,000 feet above the bed of the Urubamba River, which flows through a valley. A much-traveled road passes through this valley, used constantly by the Peruvians who never suspected that those ruins, now famous, were standing above them. It is certainly one of the most extraordinary monuments of ancient Incan architecture. Steeply rising stairways cut from the living rock lead in a tight spiral to the summit, which is crowned with an array of buildings and a circular "observatory," like a truncated cone. No ruin is more photogenic.

Chavín, Tiahuanacu, San Agustín, and Machu Picchu are sanctuaries in stone which trace an ideal gridwork extending from Colombia to Peru and Bolivia. Over a period of centuries parallel cultures in those separate communities could have arisen under an influence circulating among them by roads that still wind their serpentine way across the high plateaus and through the folds of the Andes. The faces and postures of the sculptured figures in San Agustín are the same as those in Tiahuanacu. The kingdom of the Incas was founded on the slope descending from the high plateau between Bolivia and Cuzco, and Machu Picchu belongs to the Incan culture. But Chavín and Tiahuanacu strongly influenced its pottery.

¶ THE POTTERY OF ANCIENT PERU

More important than the stones, more significant than the palaces, the statues, and the sacred cities as a means of reaching the heart of South America's Old World are the potsherds, the remains of textiles, and gold. The most finished expression of those cultures, the measure of the artistic sensibility that produced work of such refinement, is to be found in painted vessels for cooking and jars modeled with great ceramic art, in finely woven, multi-colored textiles, and in gold, which became a ductile metal in the hands of the Andean Cellinis who made the amulets and magical vessels of that long-past age.

Pottery and weaving attained in Peru a perfection never surpassed. Between the years 300 B.C. and A.D. 500, these crafts reached their height in Moche, Paracas, and Nazca. We know by the scenes painted on vases that hunting was a favorite sport of the aristocracy, that they fought their wars with lances and shields, that the wounded were removed from the battlefield by a system that was a precursor of the Red Cross, that prisoners were classified to differentiate the conquered captains from the common soldiers (on one vase a dead warrior is shown being transformed into a bird that is flying away with his lance and shield), that medicine had solved such problems as bone surgery, that trepannation and circumcision were practiced, and that written communication and mail may have envolved to the point where beanlike seeds bearing written messages were sent by post. We see how the men and women dressed—the men always more luxuriously—and that they wore a caste mark of some sort on their garments. We know their musical instruments: drums, timbrels, flutes, and a kind of bagpipe. One scene shows a prince, seated on his throne, receiving distinguished visitors carried on litters by hard-working servants. That picture might have been painted on a Greek drinking vessel. A marsh scene is rendered on a Moche vase. Some little birds perched on the reeds, two herons, one at

each side of the scene, and a fish beneath are all as finely drawn and decorative as the figures on a Japanese screen. Even more remarkable are the sculptures, the portraits on earthenware jugs, which, like the English Toby mugs, show us the types characteristic of that old society: haughty heads of princes or warriors, hieratic priests, women. . . . The pottery depicting jaguars, birds, llamas, or fruits equals this anthropomorphic pottery in realism and decorative design.

To attain so great a power of artistic expression, the ancient Peruvians had to solve all the technical problems of modeling, kiln-baking, coloring, and glazing. The Nazca pottery was particularly successful in its painting of scenes on the smooth surfaces of the vessels. "As many as eleven harmonizing colors can be found in the painting of a single vase: black, white, violet, gray, flesh-pink, two separate hues of red, yellow, and burnt sienna. The absence of blue and green is worth noting" (Mason).

¶ PERUVIAN TEXTILES

Peruvian textiles compare favorably with the most nearly perfect ever produced. The spinners drew their threads to extreme fineness, the weavers wove a very close web on their primitive looms, and they used colored threads to work out designs of birds, llamas, fish, and stylized jaguars. Their fibers were from the llama, the alpaca, and the vicuña. They made lace and veils. According to Mason:

> The use of colouring materials certainly long preceded the manufacture of textiles, and their application to cloth was a natural extension of an age-old practice of painting. Most of the dyes were probably of vegetable origin, such as indigo (*Indigofera suffruticosa*) for the blue, and achiote (*Bixa orellana*) for red, but products of the animal world were known, and possibly mineral colours also. The red insect cochineal (*Coccus cacti*) was cultivated for this purpose, and probably a purple colour was obtained from *Purpura* molluscs, as it was by the natives of Central America. A related shellfish produced the famed Tyrian purple of classic Mediterranean dyes. Pigments were mixed to obtain a great variety of tones; O'Neill distinguished one hundred and ninety hues in the textiles of the Paracas necropolis, though doubtless many of these may be ascribed to differ-

ential fading. In addition, of course, there were the natural variations in the tones of cotton, white or brown, and those of llama, alpaca, and vicuña wool.

The necropolis of Paracas is situated on a sandy desert never touched by rain. There the illustrious dead were buried several yards deep, dressed in their finest mantles, which the dry sands preserved intact throughout the centuries. When the tombs were opened not many years ago, the colors of America's Old World were revealed with a brilliance startling in that abode of the dead. It would seem that no people ever departed this life better dressed than those of pre-Columbian Peru.

Peruvian civilization was so permeated with the arts of spinning and weaving that even its writing was entrusted to strands of yarn with knots in them, which were called quipus. The Incans wore their records of the salient deeds in history, of astronomical observations and the like, hanging from a narrow woven sash, with the dates marked by the knots, or quipus. The length of spaces between the knots indicated time. A scholar who investigated the quipus believed he had discovered a calendar in the prototype preserved in the Musée de l'Homme in Paris. Quipus and their use as means of intercommunication continued for centuries. In 1781, news of the uprising of Tupac Amaru in Peru came to Copacabana through the Indian Tomás Callasaya, who arrived in the public square of the city, took out his quipus, and showed them to the Indians. The Indians "read" the message and rushed to join the rebellion.

¶ GOLD AND EL DORADO

Gold was another matter entirely. From Peru to Central America, goldsmithery became a highly developed craft that reached its peak in Colombia, the legendary seat of El Dorado. Indeed, gold work was that country's authentic form of expression, even though Colombia served as a bridge linking the cultures of North and South, even though the stone sculptures of San Agustín are reminiscent of those in Tiahuanacu, and though traces of Peruvian pottery remain in the Valley of the Cauca and the mountain ranges, and the small ceramic heads at Tumaco must be ranked alongside those at Esmeraldas in Ecuador.

The legend of El Dorado confirms Colombia's leadership in gold work. It is said that the priest of Sogamoso, or Sogamuxi,

went every year to the Lake of Guatavita to obtain the favor of
the gods, and that there he threw gold dust over his body, which
was coated with some kind of pitch. Then he bathed, like a shining, living statue. The Indians tossed into the lake small idols,
called *tunjos*, modeled in the shapes of amphibians such as frogs,
serpents, and small lizards, creatures most appropriate to the
commingling of earth and water and for harmonizing the elements
needed for agriculture. The *tunjos* that have been salvaged now
form a part of the collection in the Gold Museum of Bogotá. The
sun was the god to whom the temple of Sogamoso was dedicated.
This wooden structure roofed with straw was lavishly adorned
with strips of gold leaf, as were the standards that fluttered in
the breeze outside the temple. Word of all such marvels spurred
the Conquistadors in 1538 to advance to the heart of the kingdom
of the Chibchas, some 10,000 feet above sea level on a summit
of the Andean cordillera. Owing to the carelessness of some soldier, the temple of Sogamoso burned to the ground after the
arrival of the Spaniards.

The Indians worked pure gold or gold mixed with other metals
in an alloy called *tumbaga*. The *tunjos* made of *tumbaga* were
placed in a bath of pure gold, with the juice of certain plants
acting as a mordant. The gold was pounded with a stone hammer,
melted down, cast in forms in the lost-wax technique, and reduced
to sheets or threads soldered with absolute perfection. The products of this craft can best be appreciated by visiting the Gold
Museum in the Bank of the Republic in Bogotá, which contains
the richest collection in the world, totaling several thousand artifacts. The styles of the regions that comprise the gold map of
Colombia can be studied there: Calima, Quimbaya, Darién, Sinú,
Tairona, Chibcha, and Tolima.

¶ THE MOUNTAIN CIVILIZATION

Anyone who studies the geographical map of the pre-Columbian cultures, from the Sierra Madre of Mexico to the southern
Andes, will find that their first distinctive characteristic was the
migration of peoples from the coast to the interior, to the mountains. At the same phase of Europe's development people were
gravitating to the shores of the Mediterranean Sea. In America,
the people's primary impulse led them to scale very lofty mountains and settle the high plateaus, obeying an instinct to rise that

finally found its appropriate symbol in the temples crowning pyramids. Meanwhile, across the Atlantic, people felt the urge to sail: the Phoenicians sailed, Homer's characters sailed, Aeneas sailed. But America began with the burning of boats. Such radically opposed attitudes inevitably brought the Europeans and the Americans to where they were in 1492. In that year, as never before, the Europeans demonstrated their passion for sea travel: the Italians, the Portuguese—even the Castilians were voyaging! And in that year, the Aztecs still were sacrificing on the tops of their pyramids. Mexico City, Tenochtitlán, was not to know that white men had sailed to the Antilles until twenty-seven years had gone by.

The expanse of land bordering the great American civilizations on the two continents was still desert. Neither Brazil, nor the Argentine pampas, nor the vastnesses of present-day Canada and the United States kept back the people who, after leaving the plains and low-lying woodlands, climbed the highest mountains in order to build sacred cities. Similarly, the Caribbean was also a seedbed of savage nations from which groups migrated to the continent, climbed the mountains, and became civilized . . . just as the emigrants did from the Amazon region and from the jungles of Brazil. Quite possibly man may have come to America from Asia or Polynesia at some very remote time, and may have crossed the land that is now Canada and the United States in his wanderings; he may even have reached Brazil by traveling upstream along the courses of the great rivers. He may have entered southern Chile on his way to Peru. Another hypothesis is that man may have emerged in some corner of America at some phase of evolution. An analysis of archeological deposits, ascertaining the percentage of carbon 14, the radioactive isotope of carbon, contained in them, provides grounds for the deduction that human beings were present in Lewisville, Texas, thirty-seven thousand years ago, and in Tule Springs, Nevada, about twenty-three thousand years ago. Yet neither the first primitive men nor those who came later ever founded in the territory now the United States any nation that can be compared with the Maya, the Aztecs, or the Incas. The people in the North, like those of the Argentine pampas and the jungles of Brazil, never evolved beyond the nomadic life of the hunter. Enclosures such as corrals, or palisades carved and painted with magical emblems, which lend the redmen and their kind a vestige of tribal picturesqueness, were rare among them. The same thing was true of the cannibals of Brazil, described by Vespucci on his third voyage of exploration to the New World, and of the Tierra del Fuegans of Patagonia.

What circumstances determined the location of the great civilizations in America? How did the nomad of the plains make the transition from the primitive life of hunter and fisherman to the settled life of farming on the heights of mountains? How did it happen that Columbus, the navigator who cruised the coasts of the mainland and the islands, saw only naked Indians living in primitive huts? The answer lies in a single word: corn. The great history of the American Old World comes out of a kernel of corn. Our book of Genesis might well open with these words: "In the beginning was corn."

¶ IN THE BEGINNING WAS CORN

As rice is to the Orient, as wheat is to Europe, so is corn to America. Corn grouped men and held them together, whether in Peru, Mexico, or Central America. The sowing, harvesting, grinding, and consuming of corn, either in bread or in fermented drinks, meant agriculture and industry. Because of corn the Americans learned to classify and cultivate plants. Because of corn the development of an empirical astronomy began, and it culminated in the Aztec, Mayan, and Incan calendars. Corn kept the tribe in one region and laid the foundations of a nation, of an empire. Corn was adored as a god, and out of the magical invocation of the gods came the complicated religious systems that determined the construction of temples and offered an outlet for the creative genius of the architect. It stimulated the sculptor, whose skill advanced from the modeled clay of the time of the Venus of Tlatilco to the huge stone sculptures of Palenque.

The *Popul Vuh*, the sacred scripture of the Quiche Maya and one of the few surviving Indian codices, contains a compilation of the religious ideas, the history of the migrations, and the poetic accents of the most powerful nation that settled on the Guatemalan high plateau. Its author was one of the first of the primitive Indians to learn from the missionary monks how to write his own language in Roman characters. This Indian gathered together the traditions of his people and the myths that prophesied the coming of the white men with their new religion. The creation of man is set forth in the *Popul Vuh* as follows:

In the darkness of the night there was naught but silence and stillness. The Creator, the Shaper, Tepen, Gucumatz, the Progenitors, were alone in the waters, surrounded by light. They were hidden beneath green and blue plumes, and that is why they were called Gucumatz. And so it was that the sky came to be, and the Heart of the Sky, for this is the name of God and the name by which he is called.

Then in the darkness, in the night, Tepen and Gucumatz came together, and the word was revealed unto them, and accordingly Tepen and Gucumatz spake one to the other. They spake and talked together, consulting each other and meditating; and they reached agreement with each other, joining together their words and their thought.

And behold, they saw clearly, as they were meditating, that with the coming of the dawn man must appear. And they turned to their labor of creation and to the growing of the trees and the reeds, and the birth of life and the creation of man. . . .

And when the labor of creating all the four-footed creatures and the birds was done, the Creator and the Shaper and the Progenitors spake to the birds and bade them: "Talk together, utter your cries, warble, call, speak, each one according to his kind, according to the variety granted to each of ye!" And they spake the same words to the deer, the birds, the lions, the tigers, and the serpents.

"Speak ye then our name. Invoke Huracán, Chipi, Caculhá, Raxa-Caculhá, the Heart of the Sky, the Heart of the Earth, the Creator, the Shaper, the Progenitors: speak, invoke us, adore us," they said unto them.

But it was not granted to them to speak like men: they could do naught but screech, crow, and croak; for the form of their language had not been revealed unto them, and each one cried out in a different manner. . . .

And so it was that the Creator, the Shaper, the Progenitors had to try once more to create and shape man.

"Try once more! Now Daybreak and Dawn are drawing nigh; let us make him who will sustain and nourish us. How shall we labor that we may be invoked, that we may be remembered upon the earth? Now have we come forth with the fruit of our first labors, our first creatures; but it was not granted unto us to succeed in making ourselves praised and venerated by them. Therefore let us try once more to create obedient and respectful beings who will sustain us and nourish us."

Then was man created and shaped. Of the earth, of the mud they made his flesh. But they saw that he was not good, for he became unmade, he was soft, he had no movement, he had no strength, he fell, he was turned to water, he did not move his head, he turned his face aside, his vision was veiled, he could not see behind him. In the beginning, he did speak, but he had no understanding. In the waters he became saturated straightway and could not hold himself upright. . . .

And thereupon they destroyed him, they undid their work and their creation. And straightway they said, "What shall we do that our work may be perfect, that our adorers may come forth well made? . . ."

"Cast now your lots with your seeds of corn and of *tzité* [a tree used in the country for enclosures, which bears a pod containing red seeds]. Do thus and it shall be known and shall show forth whether we shall mold or carve his mouth and his eyes from wood." These words were told to them by the soothsayers.

And forthwith they made their divination and cast their lots with the corn and the *tzité*. And behold, the augury was good! A creature! . . .

And they began their divinations by speaking thus: "Join ye together, couple! . . . Thou, corn; thou, *tzité*; thou, good fortune; thou, creature: unite, increase ye!" they said unto the corn, the *tzité*, unto their auguries, unto the creature. . . .

Then they talked one to the other and spake the truth: "Your puppets made of wood will come out well; they shall speak and they shall endure upon the face of the earth."

"Amen!" they answered when they spake.

And straightway they carved puppets from wood. They looked like man, they spake as man, and they peopled the face of the earth. . . .

Legends equally poetic were born all over America. They are pictured in relief on the sculptures at Palenque and in the statues of stone and clay. The Musée de l'Homme in Paris contains at least one beautiful written copy, which the poets of today cherish and exalt. Luis Cardoza y Aragón, a Guatemalan poet, wrote in 1902:

The Supreme Creator brought us the kernels of corn. Everywhere he gave them water, like a benediction, on the cold peaks and the warm plains. The gods of wind and rain, the gods of sky and sea on the Mayan Olympus, embodied their wishes, reached the epiphany of their divine agrarian dream in the spindle of the ear of corn, in the jade green of the corn patch, upon which the Indian smiles at last. In the center of Guatemala, where the telluric star of the navel glows, an immense stand of corn rises to lend us its swaying and murmurous shade.

The umbilical cord of the Maya child was cut with an obsidian knife. The ear of corn was anointed with his blood and the seeds were planted for the child until he was able to sow them himself; and thus he would live a long, strong life. "They laid out their dead," Landa says, "by filling their mouths with the ground corn which is their food, and with a drink they call *koyem*, and beside the body they laid some pebbles they used as money, so that in the afterlife they would not lack for food."

In their folk tales, children drop kernels of corn so the hero may not lose his way. In the jungles it is impossible to light one's path with fireflies, or to orient one's self by them, for their clusters of stars are variable and flickering. And if the night is blind, like the ebony night when witches do their work, only the little kernels can show the way home. Only the little kernels maintain their milky way, their constellation, along the black road of the child who, sleeping, dreams.

The night sky is peopled with corn. Itzamná sows it broadcast from open hands to the six points of the compass. No hero has ever lost his way; he always comes home.

Where corn was first found and where its culture started are moot questions; no one knows whether it started in Mexico and Central America, or in Peru, or in Paraguay. The oldest archeological date established by carbon 14 in some deposits found in Puebla, Mexico, is roughly 5000 B.C. Peruvian agriculture began with corn and was later enriched with the potato and other produce. But the influence of corn in America has spread over such an immense territory and has been so consistent that even today one of the hardest-working groups of people in Colombia, people who follow the old ways, call themselves "*maicero*," because they pride themselves on being "entirely of corn." In Mexico, corn is the essence of the tortilla, which was the staff of life long before the arrival of the Spaniards. Such a great variety of breads, soups, *chichas* and other beverages, savories, and desserts are made from the many varieties of corn, indeed there are so many regions in which neither rice nor wheat has ever displaced corn, that in this fundamental custom, at least, the American has remained loyal to his traditional culture.

II: *The America of 1500*

¶ ANCIENT AMERICA TURNED ITS BACK TO THE SEA

Columbus carried in his mind a picture of the Indies, the bright
and fabulous goal he was seeking, that was like the picture of
Cathay depicted in Marco Polo's book *The Million:* mandarins
robed in silk, cities with graceful marble bridges, gilded temples,
and forests of cinnamon. What he found was some poverty-
stricken islands peopled by naked Indians. To his amazement he
saw forests of unknown trees, which added color to his account.
He was more blessed with parrots than with gold. He never discovered a single city on any of his four voyages to the Antilles and
the continent. The world he had known in his youth, the Mediterranean world, looked out upon the sea from three continents and
contained very wealthy cities, centuries old. To him, the New
World seemed barbaric and primitive by comparison with his
memories of his old, known world. The experience of Amerigo
Vespucci (1451–1512) was much broader, much stranger than
his. In his exhaustive reconnaissance, Vespucci cruised along almost the entire Atlantic border of the continent and visited the
Caribbean, the coast of Brazil, and the Argentine coast as far
south as Patagonia. Everywhere it was the same: no ports, no
cities. Naked Indians.

From the very beginning, the culture of the New World seemed strange and mysterious, the reverse of European cultures. Instead of clustering along the coasts, it flowered on the peaks of the cordilleras; the great nations of America were not maritime, but inland, by a tradition dating back centuries that was deeply rooted by 1492. The two great empires that flourished at the time of the arrival of Cortés and Pizarro—their European discoverers—were those of the Aztecs of Mexico and of the Incas of Peru, each completely unknown to the other. If they had established any relationship with each other, they might have grown to new and greater dimensions through trade, industry, and warfare. The Western Hemisphere could have been a magnificent theater for the struggles, contradictions, stimulations, and interminglings of the two civilizations. But in that part of the globe the wheel, the ship, and gunpowder were unknown in 1500, and America's lack of them explains her limitations vis-à-vis Europe. To be sure, some Aztec toys suggest that the wheel was known, but in any case it was not developed because there was little need for it. In America, there were no draft beasts, neither ox, nor horse, nor donkey, nor mule. Someone has said that the wheel was to the Americans as gunpowder to the Chinese: they were acquainted with it only as a means to enliven their leisure, but they never suspected that it could be used for warfare. The wonderful pavements laid by the Incas were meant to be traversed on foot. No ship ever sailed the Caribbean, but there were canoes, which made such an impression on the Spaniards that *canoa* was the first American word to enter the Castilian dictionary. If a Peruvian ship was ever seen in the Pacific, it proved nothing but the ability to construct it, for ships were not necessary as a means of transportation in a world without seaports or "international" trade. When Cortés dumfounded the Mexicans by a shot from a firearm, they believed he was holding in his hands some object with the power to produce lightning.

And yet the grandeur of Tenochtitlán and Cuzco held the Spaniards spellbound. Their cities in Spain were small and unimpressive compared with the majesty of the Mexican capital. Hernán Cortés likened Tenochtitlán to Seville and Córdoba, but declared that the former's main square was about "two times that of Salamanca, completely surrounded with gateways where upward of seventy thousand souls come and go every day, buying and selling." Bernal Díaz del Castillo, to whom Tenochtitlán was something out of a tale from *Amadís de Gaula*, said that the movement and noise in the main square of the Aztec capital might be compared with the bustle in the squares of Constantinople or

Rome. Yet Mexico's wealth never equaled that of the Incan empire, and the gold that the Pizarros sent to Spain eclipsed what
Cortés took out of Mexico. The expression "worth a Peru" has
survived to describe an immense treasure.

¶ TENOCHTITLÁN, A GREAT CITY OF THE SIXTEENTH CENTURY

Tenochtitlán, the capital of the Aztec empire, became Mexico
City after the Spanish conquest, the capital of the first viceroyalty.
Originally the Conquistadors named the country "New Spain."
This Spain in America, a land of deep rivers, virgin forests, vol-
canoes, and gold and silver mines, was the reverse of the Spain
in Europe. The high plateau of Mexico, the Valley of Anáhuac,
covered with green fields and lakes, and the abstract silhouettes
of cacti, composed a picture bearing no resemblance to Castile's
plains, golden with wheat fields.

The Mexican capital rose from water like a gigantic lotus
blossom of stone lying 7800 feet above sea level, "where the air
is most transparent." Two large lakes, one brackish, the other
fresh, were separated by a dike not high enough to hinder the
mingling of their waters in a tidal rhythm. The city itself was
an island that the Aztecs had enlarged by building the banks outward with gardens and trees that were held in place by the mud
as it solidified to form small islands like those in the "floating
gardens" of Xochimilco today. The Aztecs had built paved causeways across the lake as access routes that could be broken by
destroying the bridges, thus protecting the city in much the same
way as the moats and drawbridges of Europe protected the castles.
Happy in their initial victory, Cortés's horsemen entered the city
along these causeways, and they fled by the same route after their
first defeat.

Cortés, a scrupulously objective writer, begins his description
of the great city of Tenochtitlán with these words "It is built on
the salt lake, and from the mainland to the main part of the
said city, it is two leagues from whichever direction you wish to
enter it. It has four entrances, all paved with stones cut by hand,
as broad as two knights' lances."

Perhaps the Orient of 1500 may have had cities larger than
Tenochtitlán, but Europe did not. Oddly enough, neither Cortés
nor Bernal Díaz del Castillo, nor any of the first men who described it, compared it with Venice. That may have been be-

cause there was no square in the Venice of 1500 as large as the
main square in the Aztec capital. But in Tenochtitlán, as in
Venice, half the streets were on land, half were canals alive with
canoes—the gondolas of America. The population of the city
was a floating population in another sense, too, for most of them
came from nearby regions to market their grains, fruits, birds, fat
puppies, wood, blankets, and so on.

One of the finest descriptions of Tenochtitlán appears in a
letter by Cortés: "All the streets are open here and there so that
the water may cross from one to another, and all these apertures,
some of which are very wide, have their bridges, constructed of
very broad, very heavy joined beams, sturdy and well wrought;
so that ten teams of horses would be able to cross many of them.
Seeing that if the natives of this city wished to perform some
treacherous act, they were well prepared for it, the said city
having been built in the manner I speak of, and if the bridges
and the entries and exits were taken away, they could leave us
to starve to death, for we would be unable to go out onto the
land, therefore after I had entered the said city I made great
haste to have four brigantines built, and I had them made in
a very short time, large enough to convey three hundred men to
land and to carry the horses any time we should wish it. This
city has many squares where continuous markets and trade in
buying and selling go on. It has another square twice as large
as the one in Salamanca, all surrounded by gateways where up-
wards of sixty thousand souls buy and sell every day; where there
is every kind of merchandise to be found in any land, staples as
well as viands, jewelry of gold and silver, of lead, of brass, of
copper, of tin, of stones, bones, oyster shells, snail shells, and
feathers. Cut stone as well as stone to be cut is sold, along with
sun-baked bricks, kiln-baked bricks, and wood, both carved and
ready to be carved in numerous ways. There are streets full of
game, where every breed of bird on earth is sold, including hens,
partridges, quail, wild duck, flycatchers, widgeon, turtle doves,
doves, little marsh birds, parrots, owls, eagles, falcons, sparrow
hawks, and kestrels, and the skins of some of those birds of
prey with their plumage, heads, beaks, and claws. They sell
rabbits, hares, venison and small dogs, which they raise to eat.
There are streets of herbalists where there are all the roots and
medicinal herbs to be found anywhere on earth. There is a
house like a druggist's where prepared medicines are sold, both
those to be taken inwardly and those used in unguents and

plasters. There are houses like barbershops, where heads are washed and shaved. There are houses where food and drink are provided at a price. There are men like those called porters in Castile, for carrying loads. There is much wood, charcoal, braziers of clay, and many kinds of mats for beds, and other thinner ones for sitting on and for hanging in drawing rooms and bedrooms. . . . Finally, as every kind of thing to be found on earth is sold in the said markets, there are, in addition to those of which I have spoken, so many, and those of so many qualties, that owing to the abundance of them, and because it did not occur to me to commit so many to memory, and even because I do not know what names to call them, I do not mention them. Each type of merchandise is sold in its own street, with no other merchandise whatsoever placed amid it, and in this they keep great order. Everything is sold by count and measure, except that up to now I have not seen anything sold by weight."

The cities of America were political centers where the great civil ceremonies or demonstrations of military might were performed, religious centers where sacrifices were conducted, and marketplaces that brought people together from the farthest points of the country. The sixty thousand Indians whom Cortés saw going and coming in the main square of Tenochtitlán were from the country; they had come to sell and buy. The media of exchange were coins, grains of cacao, grains of gold, gold dust carried in the quills of feathers, and disks of tin. The most impressive sights in the city were the square, the temples, and the emperor's palaces. The great pyramid dominated the city, the valley, and the mountains. When the Cathedral of México was built, although it is one of the largest in the world, its base barely covered one section of the space occupied by the pyramid that had stood there when Cortés arrived. The view from its top embraced the entire city in all its grandeur. There were a hundred and fourteen steps to climb before reaching the top. Today it is difficult for us to grasp what that massive construction, nearly two hundred feet high, looked like, with its white-stuccoed sides broken by ornamented terraces and crowned by a small temple decorated with fabulous sculptures. Moctezuma took Cortés up to this belvedere of his empire, pointed out the size of his palace at the foot of it, his subjects hard at work, the lakes, and the white contours of Popocatépetl and the Sleeping Princess in the background, sharply defined in air like crystal. To a Spaniard, a sight like that could never even be imagined.

No city in Europe had lines like that, a landscape like that, a style like that. If it was a New Spain, the old Spain cast over it only a single shadow—the shadow of Cortés and his army. At any rate, that is how it must have seemed to Moctezuma's nephew, Cuauhtémoc.

¶ CUZCO, CAPITAL OF THE INCAS

If Tenochtitlán, the city of the lakes, was a watercolor of white pyramids splashed with the bright tones of the Indians' blankets, Cuzco, the city of the heights, built in the cyclopean style at an altitude of 11,207 feet in the South American Andes, was a masterpiece of Cubist architecture. The palaces and temples, built from enormous blocks of unmortared dark stone, had at their feet terraces covered with gardens. Another style, another manner, another conception of government and of life. Although the greatness of the Incas was not expressed in the city but in the empire itself, for Cuzco is the center of a star from which paved roads shoot forth to the outer edges of the empire, its dimensions were nevertheless awe-inspiring to Europeans. Karsten says that "in the number of its houses, its streets, its markets, and its type of life, not only was Cuzco the equal of most of the medieval cities in Europe, but in many respects it surpassed them." Pedro Sancho, who went to Peru with the Pizarros, wrote:

Cuzco is so large that it would be worth seeing even in Spain, and all filled with the palaces of lords, for poor people do not live in it, and every lord builds his house in it, and likewise all the *caciques* [chiefs], though the latter do not live there continuously. Most of these houses are of stone, and are built in very good order, with broad streets in the form of a cross, very straight, all paved with stone, and through the middle of each runs a water pipe reinforced with stone. This city is located on the height of a mountain, and there are many houses on its side and others lower down, on the plain. The plaza is square and level, for the most part, and paved with cobblestones; there are four gentlemen's houses around it, belonging to the principal lords of the city. The houses are painted and their stone is carved, and the best of them is Huaina Cápac's, and the door is of white marble and colored with other hues, and it has other buildings with flat roofs, very well worth seeing.

Cuzco was not exceptionally large. Its population is estimated not to have exceeded fifty thousand. The city must have been about a mile and a half long and a little less wide. But it was so solid that the Spaniards were not able to raze it; in the end, they preserved some of its streets and built their churches on the foundations of the old palaces. The austere Incan line contrasts sharply with the rich decoration of Tenochtitlán. Present-day visitors to Cuzco echo the question voiced by the Spaniards on the day of their arrival: "How did the Incas manage to reduce these enormous monoliths to geometrical shapes, and to fit them into their walls with such accuracy that the blade of a knife cannot be inserted between one stone and the next?" The Incas knew nothing about mortar: the blocks are joined dry, each face flush with the face of its neighbor. To the Peruvian, stone was the symbol and the substance of his mountains, but inside the palaces it was covered with gold leaf. The sun was his god, and visible; he worshipped his god in the palace through an astronomy in which the sun outshone everything else in his planetarium, and he carried his god on standards of gold. If Tenochtitlán rose from the lake dressed in color like a stone lotus blossom, Cuzco, with its walls and ramps, from the lower part of the city to the fortress of Sacsa-Huaman—a crown of cliffs reduced to a cyclopean order —seemed to embody the soul of the Andes, monumentally carved by a people who approached their gods by the path of geometry.

When Pedro Sancho says that "poor people did not live" in Cuzco, he strikes the keynote of the pre-Columbian American city. People who worked lived in the country; they wove their blankets and made their pottery outside the city. The greatest difference between Cuzco and Tenochtitlán was in the market-place. The Incan system, communist in its general outlines, never inspired people to make money; it produced nothing like the dealers in the Aztec capital whom Cortés and his soldiers observed. Peru had no coinage. In all the descriptions of the conquest of Peru, the absence of money in Cuzco's market square was noted. It never existed in Cuzco. The nobles, the *amautas*, were both masters and teachers, and the craftsmen attached to the court worked in precious metals to beautify the capital of an empire more inclined to peaceful conquest than to war. Those were the people living in the city. The Spaniards found a garden of gold, with plants made in their natural size. Indeed the gold that poured into Spain from Peru was what gave the conquest the colossal dimensions of limitless wealth.

The city was divided into Upper Cuzco and Lower Cuzco. Its two sections joined at the center in the great palace—Coricancha —built on the site where the tribe of the "Quenti-Cancha" (the "Hummingbird Circle") had lived in times long gone. The Quechua word *cancha*, which has passed into the sports parlance of our day, was used by the Incas to describe the circle of fields around the city. José Uriel García tells of the wealth that dazzled the eyes of Pizarro and his comrades in the following words:

. . . in the rear courts and outbuildings of the Coricancha the work centers functioned, shops for manufactures destined especially for the consumption of ideological necessities. *Ahuacpintas*, textile shops; *corihuayrachinas*, smithies and foundries for gold, silver and other metals. Goldsmiths and silversmiths who forged the architectonic ornamentation for the large cluster of buildings: plinths of columns that linked 'Heaven' and 'Earth'; pilasters, cornices, in short, the portals to each sanctuary. Perhaps, if a few more years had elapsed before the Spaniards conquered these people, they would have found some monuments in the Coricancha more fully covered, or completely covered with sheets of gold and repoussé work of even more fantastic proportions, providing there had been room for it, than in the Coricancha that was sacked in 1533. If that had been so, the gold of the Incas would have covered over completely the magnificent work of the architects of the period when the city arose.

The metal workers made tools of *champi*, the Andean bronze, especially for the technical phases of general labor. Lapidaries and miniaturists, burinists who engraved precious stones, such as jade, obsidian, emerald, and alabaster, were working to fill the niches designed to hold the symbols of the productive forces with votive and other offerings. Builders and stone cutters, carvers of andesite, granite, and basalt, pounded stone endlessly to broaden the galleries and mansions of the monumental Quechua "university." The garden of gold, correctly named, which occupies the outside terraces and is visible to all men, also demanded unceasing effort, never-ending labor on the part of the goldsmiths, for to some degree the famous "Garden" was a copy of the "Garden of the Incas," of the corn patches, of the most characistic Andean flowers, of the flocks of *auquénidos* [llamas and vicuñas] on the high plateaus, each with its own shepherd

brandishing his sling to keep them in line. Coricancha reproduced life itself in all its fundamental aspects through
the work of the goldsmiths and all-around metalworkers.
The material and social structure of the world was explained
through the medium of all those plastic images, resplendent
in gold, for the enlightenment of the existing generations
and those to come; through the postures of the gods or the
mummies, through the foreshortening of the images sym-
bolizing the productive forces—sky, earth, water, plant-life,
animals, and men. Even to us, their descendants of the
twentieth century, the Quechuan *amautas* explain that "history is nothing more than human production through labor;
or, if you like, the development of nature by man.

When the Spaniards first saw Tenochtitlán in 1515 and Cuzco
in 1538, those cities were to them the most original in the known
world. All the cities of Europe, from the time of the Roman
Empire to the Renaissance, from Italy to the British Isles shared
styles more or less widespread. The Romanesque, the Gothic,
and the Italian Renaissance styles were expressed in remarkable
cathedrals and palaces built above the tight cluster of the medieval
city and entirely enclosed within defensive walls. The style of
the pyramids and temples in America had never been seen before,
and whether they were in Tenochtitlán in the North or Cuzco in
the South, they were distinctive and exotic from root to crown.
But even more amazing than those great cities of the Aztecs and
the Incas was the desolation surrounding them, the absence of
bonds that might have united these civilizations. The Americans
had never bothered to open sea lanes, but obviously they had never
been linked by land either. Dead cities were far more numerous
than live cities in the America of 1500. For this reason the scope
of American culture was mysterious and remains so. The mere
thought that Tiahuanacu, Palenque, Uxmal, San Agustín, and
Machu Picchu were but the fleeting shadows of an ancient
grandeur implies that the America of legend must have been
infinitely greater than that which has survived would indicate.
To move from Tenochtitlán to Guatemala, Alvarado and Cortés
had to travel through the world's most extensive virgin regions.
To reach the wild coasts of Venezuela, or Santa Marta at the
tip of the Andes, where the mythical capital of El Dorado was
located, Federmann, for one, and Jiménez de Quesada, for another, were forced to go through the most appalling jungles.

Orellana and Lope de Aguirre were able to reach the headwaters of the Amazon only by making their way through regions that had swallowed up armies. Belalcázar crossed hundreds of leagues of bleak and desolate plains. As troops ascended the estuary of the Plata to the upper end of Potosí, where the Plata mines were situated, their number kept dwindling and years went by without bringing them to their longed-for goal. Valdivia traveled from Lima to Chile, passing the bones of many of Almagro's comrades who had died while crossing the bleakest deserts ever seen by man.

The Mexicans were not acquainted with the potato, which had been domesticated by the Incas; the Incas did not know the tomato, which was Mexico's. The tropical forests, the frozen peaks of the mountains, and the deserts reduced the inhabited settlements to archipelagos on the mainland, and the pride of the empires only made the solitude of the largest and most beautiful islands stand out more clearly.

The natural ebb and flow of human masses through most of Mexico's territory determined the expulsion of the most ancient nations as they were forced to surrender their field to newer, more aggressive nations. The invaders set themselves up as lords over the land from which the conquered had fled in disarray, but they did not destroy. The traces of successive occupations may be found today in a single pyramid. The conquerors never razed the pyramid on which their predecessors had worshipped the sun and sacrificed their victims; instead, they set a new layer of stones on top of it to stand as something new and even more imposing. Soon the enjoyment of their possessions restrained the impulse to conquer, and the jungle fixed an insurmountable boundary.

Other nations all around the Aztec empire tried to seize the capital, but in the meantime they did not trouble themselves to build rival cities, so that from Veracruz, where Cortés disembarked, to the capital, the Spaniards found no cities of any size. The idea of building along the shore of the Gulf made no sense to people who had never grasped the fact that the sea could be a road of a thousand lanes. Thus the contrast between the civilized city and the rude backlands was always much sharper in America than in the European world.

In 1500 the expanse of empty land, much larger than all of Europe, made as deep an impression on the Spaniards as the few great cities. North America was vacant; Brazil was vacant.

The men who moved across that immense stage were living more or less in a state of savagery, on the fringe of any civic development. The accounts of Ponce de León or Hernando de Soto's comrades who adventured through Florida and the Mississippi basin leave an impression that deepens as the narrative unfolds. Wilderness lay all around them; whenever they chanced to meet a man, he was a primitive man, a naked hunter, an elemental man. A gap of centuries of culture yawned between the hunter of those regions and the courtier in Moctezuma's court. The hunter was forced to sustain himself on roots, small wild fruit, and raw meat at a time when the Aztec already had his bread and his cookery. The market of Tenochtitlán becomes all the more fabulous if we compare its produce with the potluck of the savage lost in the basin of some river such as the Mississippi, the Magdalena, the Orinoco, the Amazon, the Pánuco, or the Plata.

Even from the point of view of man's enemies, the scenario of America is most extraordinary. The great beasts of Africa and Asia that elevate the human drama to the plane of mortal combat did not exist here. No traces of elephants, lions, tigers, hippopotamuses, giraffes, or hyenas have ever been found in America . . . only the small ocelots, which the Aymarás, high in Peru, domesticated like the llamas. The cougars, small lions that never bore the stamp of the royal beasts of India, were timidly democratic little lions. On the other hand, we did have mosquitoes, chiggers, poisonous spiders, scorpions, little creatures that get between the nail and the flesh, as annoying for their buzzing as for their bite, and which attack the child more often than the man. And unlike Europe, with its forests of pines, its dry plains, its orderly seasons, its seldom turbulent rivers, its more refined geographical background, America lived in a kind of ecological disorder, the vegetation alternating between the mad growth of jungles and the spare harshness of deserts, as twentieth-century man sees it.

And to round out the picture America has earthquakes; as Cardoza y Aragón said in describing his country: "In Guatemala, is there a place to go where the ground would not tremble?"

III: *What the Spaniards Brought to America*

¶ THE HORSE, THE COW, THE DONKEY, CHICKENS, AND MICE

The conventional picture of the Conquistador shows him astride his horse, an armed medieval knight with lance at rest, his sword at his side, and his helmet like a metallic distortion of his head. The likeness is true, for pieces of armor have been dug up in Santiago, Chile, as excavations were made preparatory to paving San Isidro Street. A helmet, steel greaves, and a Toledo sword were uncovered. Only the heat of the tropics could force that hero to exchange his cuirass for a padding of quilted cotton. The soldiers marched behind their gallant captain, shouldering their harquebuses, the most modern of the Castilian weapons of the day. All such things as the horse, steel, and gunpowder were new to America, however.

But to portray the Conquistadors as traveling only with their horses, lances, swords, harquebuses, and armor is to show only a fragment of the picture. Gonzalo Jiménez de Quesada, for example, took a hundred and eighty men and one donkey with him to found his colony at Sabana de Bogotá. Not long afterward, Nikolaus Federmann, a German adventurer, arrived in Venezuela with as many soldiers and some hens. Later Sebastián de Belalcázar came from Peru with some pigs. His forces had been reduced to one hundred and eighty men. And from then on, the new creatures that were to complement the three cook stones in the house of the poor peasant—all of them hitherto unknown to America—met after months of sea travel in that remote corner of the Andes.

Later, the Spaniards imported fierce dogs, which Balboa set upon the Indians. Yet before long every Indian had his dog, and the poor conquered fellow had found a faithful friend. Near the middle of the century mice came. In the early days of the Colony, a friar wrote:

Although in Lima (because it is a land more warm than cold) there are loathesome creatures, none of them is dangerous, for even the scorpions do no harm and the vipers and serpents do not secrete venom. No dog has even turned rabid; no noxious grasses have grown. The first mice ever seen in Peru arrived in the year 1544, the year that the ship sent by Don Gabriel de Carvajal, Bishop of Plasencia, to cruise the sea of the North and the South, made port and entered Callao by way of the Straits of Magellan. So testifies Agustín de Zárate, the Auditor of the Emperor's Council, whom the Emperor sent to be Auditor of Wages to this High Court of Lima in that same year of forty-four. He says in his book that the ship brought the first mice, which went ashore among the clothing. And until then they had never been seen in those lands of Peru. Presbyter Gómara says the same thing; and others prove it was so by the name the Indians have given mice, which is *hucuchoca*, corrupted to *hucucha*, meaning that the mice came from the sea, and averring by this name that this vermin came in that ship from the sea. But Garcilaso says that the mice brought by that ship were the big rats which we call *pericotes* [horse rats], three times as big as the ordinary ones, and that the other, small ones, many of which breed in the putrefaction on the land, were already on the plains and in the mountains in great abundance. I hold this to be true, and that the ones that ship brought were those huge field rats which have multiplied to such an extent on these plains, they being offensive to an extreme; the cat that will attack them is a rare one, and rare indeed the one that can catch them, but no species of these carries poison, while those in Europe and Asia, as Aristotle declares and Bercorio believes, can kill in three ways, by their pestiferous venom, by their urine, and by the touch of their tails, and wherever they bite they leave poison and kill; here none of them kills or secretes poison.

If the Spaniards brought mice, they also brought cats. Or, to put it more precisely, the Spanish men brought dogs, and the Spanish women cats. Every ship was a Noah's Ark. Pairs of animals crossed the Atlantic, and they multiplied unbelievably in America. Horses, bulls, and dogs bred like mice in the pastures. Creatures that had been kept as domestic animals in Spain went wild, became *cimarrones*, in many places. In Buenos Aires, sheep were disappearing at such a rate that the infant wool industry was being ruined as the wild dogs destroyed the flocks. Posses were formed to hunt and kill the dogs. The historian Guillermo Gallardo in "The Wild Dogs" recounts the efforts made by the colony to correct this evil:

> A small notebook of the eighteenth century, preserved in the General Archives of the Nation, tells a curious story. An account was kept in it of the number of tails from dogs that had been killed, and of the bounty paid for them at the rate of half a *real* for those from big dogs and a quarter *real* for those from the small ones. The slaughter was confined to dogs in the city, and from July to October of 1790, the number reached a total of 768, both large and small. Sergeant-Major de Areco states that on the basis of the bounty paid in the spring of that year, 2,437 dogs had perished there in one big round-up. . . . By 1796, the warfare had become broader and better organized, in spite of the resistance of the militiamen, who detested the absurd nickname they were acquiring everywhere of *dog-killers*.[1]

The maverick cattle on the pampas were common property. The gauchos would take private possession of them by hunting them and branding them with their own brands. The wild horses became a menace, and Negroes were assigned the task of wiping them out by a knife-thrust in the belly. The wounded animal would drag its entrails as it moved and the wild dogs would devour it.

Donkeys and mules were exempt from attack. Mexico took a great interest in the increase of the burros. Humboldt reports a hundred thousand mules in Veracruz and thousands of calèches drawn by mules in Mexico City and Havana. Roads for

---

[1] *Cuadernos*, Paris, June, 1963.

shod beasts were built through the Andes, and all the goods of trade were moved along them in the care of drovers and muleteers. Salta, Tucumán, and Potosí were the great mule markets for the traffic between Upper Peru and Buenos Aires. Concolorcorvo (1715?–78?) paints an excellent picture of those markets at the end of the eighteenth century in his *Lazarillo de Ciegos caminantes*.

Some of the routes the creatures followed to reach the New World were very long. The silkworm arrived in Spain from China, together with the mulberry tree that fed it. The Moors brought it with them and made Granada a center of the silk industry. The silkworm and the mulberry tree moved on to Mexico in the time of Hernán Cortés, thus completing their tour of the world. Neither wars nor explorations could stay the quiet work that went on in the cocoons. Three centuries after Cortés, Hidalgo, the father of Mexico's independence, put the Indians in his parish of Dolores to work planting mulberry trees to feed his silkworms.

The Spaniards brought some camels to Peru in the hope of making available a beast of burden more rugged than the llama. The last camel died in 1615 without having succeeded in endowing America with its offspring.

¶ SUGAR, FRUIT, VEGETABLES, AND HERBS

The Arabs brought sugar cane from India to Spain and the entire Mediterranean. By the sixteenth century, Egypt, Sicily, and Andalusia all had their canefields. In 1420 the Portuguese planted sugar cane in the Azores and the Canaries. When Columbus landed in Cuba, that mysterious island where tobacco grew and men breathed smoke, the Admiral carried with him the first sugar-cane seeds, and thereby set the island's future course. Cuba was to become the land of Havana cigars and the world's sugar mill. The cradle of Cuban independence would rock to the roll of tobacco leaves in Tampa, and as her sugar mills ground cane, the republic would link itself first to the United States and later to Russia.

Bananas had never been grown in America. In 1516 Fray Tomás de Berlanga, who died in 1551, brought to the Antilles a species that had originated in Guinea and had been acclimated in the Canaries, Tunis, and Algiers. These bananas were known as *guineos*. Berlanga moved from Santo Domingo to Mexico, from Mexico to Panama. He served as provincial of the Dominicans in Santo Domingo, and as bishop in Panama, but history remembers him for the banana, which brought the poor country people of the hot lands a notable change of diet. In the course of time, the banana plantation developed from the banana tree, and centuries later the banana groves came under the house flag of the United Fruit Company. The so-called banana republics brought a little progress to Central America, accompanied by a loss of independence, as the banana became the fodder of dictatorships. As these developments met the eyes of the field workers, they had their first intimations of just how "broad and alien is the world."

The journey of rice to the New World was as long as those of silkworms and of sugar cane. It moved from India to China and Japan, and the Arabs brought it from India to Spain. The Aragonese carried it to Naples fifty years before the discovery of America, and Columbus took it across the Atlantic with him. Rice came to mean comfort to the poor. The biography of Columbus might sound more inviting if it began like this: "Once upon a time there was an admiral who carried some grains of rice on his ships. . . ."

Now and again the paths of the fruits may have crossed. Pineapples were mentioned by Peter Martyr as follows:

> The invincible King Ferdinand has eaten of another fruit which they bring from those lands. That fruit has many scales, and in appearance, form, and color it resembles the cones from the pine trees; but in softness it resembles the melon, and in taste it excels any fruit with a stone, though it is not a tree but a herbaceous plant very similar to the thistle or the acanthus. The King himself accords it first place.

The mango came to America from India in exchange for the American pineapple. The tree with its delicious fruit and dense foliage also became a favorite among all the species of plant life adopted by tropical America.

García Mercadal, who made a brief inventory from notations by the early chronicles in his *Lo Que España Llevó a América* (*What Spain Brought to America*), quotes Acosta:

> The common peach and its close relatives, the red-stone peach and the apricot have done very well, especially the latter, in New Spain; in Peru, such fruits are scarce, except for the common peach (brought later), and still scarcer in

the Islands (The Antilles); apples and pears do only moderately well; plums grow rather scantily; figs, abundantly, especially in Peru; quinces, everywhere, and so well in New Spain that fifty choice fruits may be bought for half a *real;* and pomegranates, well enough, though they are all the sweet ones; the sour ones have not prospered. In some places the red-stone peaches are very good, as in Tierra Firme and parts of Peru. Neither sweet nor sour cherries have thus far had the luck to get a foothold in the Indies; I do not think this is because of the climate, for it is of all kinds, but rather for the lack of care or skill.

Among odoriferous things the Spaniards brought the garlic and the onion. The monks specialized in the aromatic herbs: balm gentle (or common balm), mint, sweet basil, marjoram, thyme, and rosemary. The herb gardens of the Franciscans are still preserved in California, where collections of these plants are treasured as if they were small medicine chests. García Mercadal makes this basic inventory of the plants America received from Spain:

wheat, barley, rice and rye; beans, chickpeas, lentils, and red beans; almond, mulberry, and cherry trees; walnut, chestnut, medlar, and jujube trees; flax, hemp, alfalfa, and canary seed; quince, apple, and apricot trees, and almost all the small fruits with a stone; oranges, limes, lemons, citrons, grapefruit, pears, and plums; rosemary, osiers, broom, and various other aromatic herbs; rosebushes, lilies, and a great variety of flowers.

The life story of the flowers in America verges on the miraculous. Thirteen years before the birth of St. Rose of Lima, a Greek named Miguel Acosta planted the first rosebush in Lima, in the garden of the Espíritu Santo Hospital, behind the house of St. Rose's father, Gaspar Flores. When the first rose bloomed, the enthusiasm of the people was so great that they carried it in a procession to the cathedral where Brother Jerónimo de Loaisa laid it at the Virgin's feet. St. Rose was christened with the name of Isabel, but an Indian woman who came up to look at her as an infant was so struck by her beauty that she said: "She is a rose." From that day on, the child's mother called her Rose. It is said that when the first move to canonize Rose was made, the Pope remarked: "To be a saint, lovely, and a Liman is as paradoxical as if it were raining roses now." And behold, a rain of roses fell.

Father Bernabé Cobo lists the following vegetables that were brought to America from Spain: cabbage, lettuce, endive, borage, asparagus, spinach, celery, parsley, and wild marjoram.

¶ WHEAT, OLIVES, AND HIDES

When Pedro de Valdivia left Cuzco to begin the conquest of Chile, he took a Spanish woman with him, a very rare occurrence in those early conquests. Later the Licentiate La Gasca, who had been sent to Peru to establish order, ruled that Valdivia was committing a sin by traveling with a woman not his lawful wife. Nevertheless, the couple accomplished their objectives: Valdivia founded Santiago with Inés Suárez. Inés had brought with her a handful of wheat, some chickens, and some sheep. One day while Valdivia was absent, the Indians burned the infant city. Single-handed, Inés rescued the settlers from a defeat that seemed inevitable and saved the chickens, the sheep, and the wheat as well as the men. Valdivia wrote to the king: "And a rooster and a cockerel were saved by their mistress who was with us: and so the number of chickens has been greatly multiplied."

Bernal Díaz del Castillo was among the soldiers with Cortés during the conquest of Mexico. After many years of hard and heroic effort, Bernal Díaz settled in Guatemala and wrote his *Verdadera Historia de la conquista de la Nueva España* (*True History of the Conquest of New Spain*). He also left another and no less welcome remembrance of himself. He brought seven orange seeds to Mexico, and it was he who opened the doors of the continent to the orange. The Spanish orange came before 1514. Later, in 1520, another variety, perhaps the mandarin orange, entered from the Philippines, for Spain had flung a bridge across the Pacific from Mexico to the Philippines, in this case a bridge of oranges.

The Spanish people took with them to America that phase of their culture which was certain to put down the deepest roots in the New World: farming. The importation of wheat for seed meant the start of another way of cultivating the fields and gathering the harvest. Planting the wheat, winnowing it, converting it to flour in a grist meal, making the flour into dough, and bringing forth a loaf of baked bread spelled a new way of life. Perhaps the Indians thought the Spaniards were right to pray for their daily bread and to seek the body of their God in it. The wheatfields clothed the landscape in a new and more refined manner. The land changed color as it was worked by the new methods. First it was dark from the plow, then as the new shoots appeared, it turned an emerald green, and as the wheat ripened, it changed to gold, thus marking the rotation of the months like a new calendar. Though wheat could not displace the cultivation of corn, and though wheat would remain the mainstay of the white man rather than of the Indian, its coming brought a new style of life to America, and it changed the landscape.

The entry of wheat into Mexico reads like a fairy story as López de Gómara tells it:

> A Negro with Cortés, who was named Juan Garrido, I think, planted in a garden patch three grains of wheat that he had found in a bag of rice. . . . Two of them sprouted, and thus he had a hundred and eighty grains. He planted these grains in their turn, and little by little, an infinity of wheat came to be.

For Chile to become a country of miles of vineyards, as it is today, the first grapevine had to be planted, and this was done within three years of the founding of Santiago. The olive tree was a late arrival and a novelty. Encinas says:

> Don Antonio de Rivera brought a shipment of a hundred olive seedlings to Lima from Seville, ninety-seven of which dried out in the crossing, which took nine months. Of the surviving three that were planted in Lima in 1561, one mysteriously disappeared. Neither threats nor excommunications were of any avail. But before the end of the century, Chile was exporting olive oil to Peru.

Clavigero notes: "In America there were no lemons, oranges, figs, peaches, grapes, melons, olives, sugar, rice, or wheat."

Although the names "Eagle Knight" and "Jaguar Knight" were given to some pre-Columbian sculptures, the truth is that the New World had no knowledge of the knight, that is, of a man on horseback, before 1492. In times of war, every man was a foot soldier, even the captains and the princes, as the frescoes of Bonampak testify. Unless he wanted to walk, the ruler, whether Aztec or Incan, had to be carried on a litter, which his courtiers and servants bore on their shoulders. The only beast of burden, the llama, has always been the judge of his own capacity, thus determining the exact weight of the load he will carry. If the load is even a pound overweight, the llama will not take a step and will spit at the man who tries to abuse his willingness to work. The animal has his own work rules and abides by them. The Indian was the beast of burden that carried the heavy loads. But with the arrival of the horse, and later the mule and ox, the Indian ceased to be the principal beast of burden.

With the horse came the blacksmith to shoe him, the harness maker and saddle maker to accouter him, and the groom to care for him, provided that the master did not serve as groom. A new feeling of hierarchy came, too: the horse was for the cavalier, the knight. The man on foot was the servant with "his hoof to the ground." At best, he was the squire who rode on a donkey, like Sancho Panza, behind his lord.

With the coming of the blacksmith, the natives of America learned of a new metal and became acquainted with such equipment as the anvil and the forge. The hammer with which the smith shaped the rough ingots plucked from the white-hot fire with tongs a yard long, rang through the village like a bell with an insistence greater than that of the church bell. The sight of a shod animal—and horses and mules were both shod—was also something very new, and their rhythmic tintinnabulation rang along the stone roads, awakening echoes never previously heard, for the tread of the barefoot Indians on the pavements of Peru was almost inaudible. Indeed, there were roads of flowers in Paraguay that the Guaranís could travel without crushing the blossoms.

Leatherwork became so important that one could speak of the age of leather in Montevideo. Before Columbus, leather was used rarely, either for clothing, drumheads, or sandals. A hide was usually the trophy of a fight with a jaguar. Before the coming of the Spaniards, the only sources of hides besides the jaguar were the deer and the llama. The Spaniard added new leathers: cowhide, sheepskin, goatskin, pigskin, cordovan, and mulehide. Saddles, reins, cinches, straps, boots, doors, beds, wall hangings, trunks, windows, lines, portfolios, notecases, blacksmiths' aprons, riding habits, sleeping mats for travelers, and awnings over carts were all made of leather. Hides represented such great wealth that the cattle were slaughtered on the Argentine pampas for their skins alone; the flesh was left for the crows. In the end, leather was exchanged for pounds sterling in gold, and the stock market of England entered the countries along the Plata River through a door of leather.

In time the crafts of ironworking and leatherworking made

their appearance. The smith moved on from making horseshoes to forging branding irons, keys, locks, keyholes, door knockers, bolts, and hinges—all the things needed to safeguard the white men's big houses—and the craftsman developed his work into a decorative art employing Arabian motifs and figures, shaping the keyhole in the form of a pomegranate or an eagle or a man on horseback, the knocker representing a cat or a small hand squeezing an apple, keys with heads like lacework, and beautifully wrought bridles. And the same thing was true of leather: tooled leather for saddles, painted leather on tabourets, leather worked in the Cordovan style for monks' saddles, leather braided in reins, and leathern trunks with gold initials and traced designs of musical instruments. Little by little, the Indians, and especially the *mestizos*, began to find work in the harness makers' and shoemakers' shops, in the smithies, and in the locksmiths' booths. They learned their crafts and gave everything a new and indigenous twist.

❡ THE WHEEL AND THE SHIP

When the ox arrived in America, the wheel came too. The wagon changed life in certain parts of America to such a degree that it was generally regarded as a symbol of the pampas in the Argentine and Uruguay. One of the most beautiful and significant monuments in the world is a tribute in bronze to the wagon which stands in Montevideo. The wagon was no less effective in the tranformation of Brazil. An exhaustive work has been written there showing the evolution of rural society owing to the wagon.

The Spaniard brought the plow along with the ox; from then on, breaking ground ceased to be quite so laborious and elemental a task, and it was no longer necessary to sow the kernel of corn by poking a hole in the earth with a pointed stick. Almost all the village churches in Colombia contain an image of St. Isidore the Farmer guiding his plow, which is a kind of talisman that marks the transition from the planting stick, a forward step as important as the move from the mule to the airplane in modern times.

To every American of today, the Nativity scene, with its Infant Jesus on a cradle of straw and the donkey and ox in the background, is a natural and immediate part of his life. But if the American of 1500 had looked at a scene like that, it would have seemed to him highly unnatural, with its nonexistent animals and the strange kind of chaff on which the Child lay.

America had no ships, in the strict sense of the word, before the Conquest. Rafts of reeds or branches of some very light woods were used under mast and sail on Lake Titicaca. As many as fifty men could be accommodated on that type of raft, it is believed, and in fact Thor Heyerdahl proved by crossing the Pacific on the *Kon-Tiki* in 1947 that the mythical voyage of the Topa Inca might have been made. But the ship as such, the ship that links nations in the maritime trade, did not exist. If the history of the ships built in the America of 1500 is ever written, it will make a tale as stirring as that of the Conquest. For ships had to be built in the very theater of adventure and they played their part in the discovery and exploration of America. Balboa could not proceed with his exploration of the Pacific without ships, and he had them built in the jungle of Panama. His men carried them out on their shoulders, no less, to an anchorage in the Pacific. Don Pedro de Alvarado built ships in Guatemala in order to accomplish his planned conquest of Quito. When the time came to conquer Peru, Francisco Pizarro had ships built in Panama which were larger than those Columbus managed to acquire from Spain for his first voyage. But Columbus had the help of the queen, of Italian bankers, of wealthy men in the port of Seville in assembling his three caravels and his hundred and twenty men. Pizarro built *three* ships in 1524 in Panama, where ships had never been built before, or even known, with the help of the soldiers who had been in the Conquest from the beginning. The vessels were designed to carry 114 soldiers and a number of Indians. By 1531 he set sail with 180 men and 37 horses, in the Panamanian ships.

The Europeans never quailed at the thought of destroying their ships when their adventure demanded it, for they knew they could build others. On his first voyage, Columbus broke up the useless hulk of the *Santa Maria* with a volley of shellfire, and Cortés burned all his ships to force his soldiers to advance to the heart of Mexico. On his Amazon expedition, Orellana sailed the river until he came out at the Atlantic, and Lope de Aguirre, who left the Amazon along the Casiquiare branch, came to the Orinoco, entered it, and followed it as far as the island of Margarita in the Caribbean. Orellana's and Lope de Aguirre's ships were built in the jungle's green hell. Cortés built shipyards on the banks of Lake Tenochtitlán for his final assault on the capital of the Aztec Empire, situated in the middle of the lake. The ship

El Comunero was built in Asunción, Paraguay, as far inland as a city in America could be, and Governor Núñez Cabeza de Vaca returned on it to Spain. The vessel and all its cargo docked in the port of Cádiz in perfect condition.

Who built those ships? Men who had never before seen a shipyard. The story of the adventurers who were shipwrecked on the coast of Florida, where they were forced to build a boat or die, is a famous one. The men who sawed down trees and made them into planks with a minimum of tools had never worked in a carpenter shop. They fashioned the bellows for their forge from their horses' hides and used the horseshoes to make nails. Their caulking came from the resin of plants. Their lines were strips torn from their shirts, the sails any available cloth. A man who had spent his childhood in a village where trees were sawed to make the ribs of ships, where iron was beaten on an anvil, unconsciously carries in his memory some knowledge of such things and can apply it to his own needs when he is beset by bad luck even though he may never have been a helper in any carpentry shop or smithy. That even one ship was built in raw, virgin Panama for Balboa's venture into the Pacific—a ship comparable to that in which Columbus crossed the Atlantic—seems almost miraculous. But it happened. A thousand things never beheld before were being seen in the New World: a new style in houses and temples, tabourets, tables, trunks, and chests. When furniture was decorated, when altars were raised, the cabinetmakers came into their own, and wood was shaped to modes of expression and uses never before known. As the Indians worked at the craft, they began to blend their idiom into the decoration of the altars, almost furtively, almost as contraband, almost unintentionally. First they helped as apprentices, but as they gained skill, they became master craftsmen. Thus a *mestizo* art, a Hispano-Indian art was born and was acclaimed in the churches of Arequipa, Quito, Tunja, and Mexico City. And in the process a people's university was created as another of Spain's gifts to America.

¶ LANGUAGE, RELIGION, THE ALPHABET, LAWSUITS,
GUNPOWDER, AND SLAVES

To an Indian living in Otavalo, Ecuador, the mountains of Peru, the south of Mexico, Guatemala, or the rural regions of Bolivia, the donkey, the hen, and the pig are more potent testi-

monials to the arrival of the Europeans than the Spanish language,
now that four and a half centuries have passed. The people still
speak their Maya, Quechua, Guaraní, or Aymará. The animals,
often the only trace of Europe to be found in their huts, are
what they owe to their masters, who brought them. But they
could not deny that the Spaniard also passed on to them his
language, rooted in Latin, Greek, and Arabic, a language with
all the strength of the century in which Spain was most vigorous
and rich, most creative and poetic, most heroic, mystical,
theatrical, and juridical—in short, most universal—her Golden
Age, the century of Cervantes, St. Teresa, Lope de Vega, and
Quevedo. Bards were singing their ballads in Castilian; Alfonso
the Wise had promulgated his laws in that tongue in the thirteenth
century, and subsequent history was written in it. In the New
World the flow of language had been dammed by isolation; there
was no lingua franca to help the traveler moving southward from
Central America, but within a short time after the discovery, a
common language that made communication possible between
all the colonies, from Mexico to Chile and the Río de la Plata,
was introduced by the Spaniards. Each new capital of a viceroyalty, each governmental unit, each little village became Spanish-speaking in time. Most of the newcomers were illiterate, but
they knew by heart the Castilian ballads as well as snatches from
the works for the theater by Lope de Vega or Calderón, Quevedo's
couplets, and most of the rich literature of chivalry, which they
had learned by ear and passed on orally. The few who knew how
to read would entertain those who had never been exposed to a
primer, reading aloud to them. Almost everyone learned in this
way the tales from *Amadís de Gaula* and the plot of *La Celestina*.

The Spaniards introduced a new religion, too, a different moral
code from those which had prevailed in the various regions of
America previously. Baptism, the Mass, churches, images, bells,
religious celebrations, prayers, new principles of good and evil,
heaven and hell, the concept of the Crucified Christ, the Virgin
and the saints, and the constitution of the family all brought
changes in the general tone of life and in its very foundations. If
the Church, imbued with the missionary spirit, had not moved
into the most remote regions of the Americas, the Conquest might
have ended at the point of the Conquistadors' farthest thrust. A
new division of time, the week, was introduced, with Sunday the
day not so much of rest as of rejoicing. Sunday, the day of the
Mass and the market, also became the day when dwellers in

villages and open country met in the town square, when scattered families were united, when they exchanged news, some good, some bad, when the illiterate Indian was able to read a newspaper of his own that was printed on the air. After a while the Indians made it their habit to follow this exchange of news with a visit to an inn where they could forget their servitude for a moment, freeing themselves from it by drinking. Through the religious celebrations the Indian learned the innocent uses of gunpowder, and to him it seemed sublime.

The Church brought the school. The priest and the monk typified the literate phase of the Conquest. To be sure there were men of letters, like Jiménez de Quesada, Bernal Díaz del Castillo, and Cortés among the Conquistadors, but many of them were barely able to mark their names with a cross. Among the monks, however, there were distinguished writers, although their curriculum for the Indians was confined largely to Christian doctrine and labor, taught them, not infrequently, in their own language. Only very exceptional natives ever went as far as the university. But for all that, an alphabet, and later the printing press, came to America through the efforts of the Church.

The first act of the Church, supported by the Conquistadors' strong arms, was to expel the ancient gods, to relegate everything connected with the American's religious world to the realm of heresy. The art that had built the pyramids of Mexico and the temples of Cuzco and had achieved mastery among the potters of the Incan Empire and the goldsmiths of the Quimbaya nation was restricted by the authorities of the new religion. The new Christian art was substituted, and the Indian was forced to play a secondary role, insinuating himself into the white man's work, injecting into it a clandestine mixture of white and Indian that revealed in a subtle way the hidden genius of the anonymous artists.

The arrival of the new religion and a new civic life made an end to human sacrifice and cannibalism wherever they were practiced. The American was not necessarily a better man for that; rather he was a warier and more malicious man. The missionaries have left us copious notes in very high praise of the Indian they found in America, emphasizing his honesty, cleanliness, and innocence. The new religion infused the fear of a new God who, like the old gods, favored the ruling class. It brought the terror of hell and of the new authority, of Spanish justice. The American in the new society had to renounce all his freedoms—such as they were—and fear rushed in to fill the vacuum. On the other hand, the Laws of the Indies were promulgated at about the same time to afford the Indian protection and to enable the Church to cover him with a mantle of motherly charity, but laws could not banish the ever-present master. The Indian had become the servant of the Spanish Empire and a member of the Church's flock.

With Spanish law came the lawyer; with the lawyer, the lawsuit and the vice of litigation. Bernal Díaz del Castillo said that the Conquistadors petitioned the king "not to send lawyers, for when they enter the land they will introduce rebellion, with their books, and there will be lawsuits and dissension." One Conquistador, Jiménez de Quesada in New Granada, held a degree in law and knew lawyers like the palm of his hand, but he wrote in his recommendations for the good government of the Indians that "no official of Your Majesty, nor any person who may hold a degree, nor any other powerful person, whosoever he may be, now holding any office of justice whatsoever" should be allowed to enter his name or take any part in the drawing of lots to elect or appoint ordinary mayors.

The new law was formulated first in the so-called *repartimiento*, or "division," and later in the so-called *encomienda*, or "complimentary grant." Under the *repartimiento*, the Spaniards were able to divide up the Indians and to make use of them as though they were cattle. Consequently, the Indians worked the mines, built the cities, and cultivated the fields. When the Crown modified its system through the *encomienda*, it granted land and the Indians on it to some of the Conquistadors and gave the latter the right to exact tribute, but it required them to teach their Indians Christian doctrine.

To a certain extent, the Spaniards brought paper. Before their arrival it had been made in Mexico, but exclusively for the sacred scrolls. Anyone wishing to send a written message to Moctezuma painted images on a piece of cotton. This was the medium that conveyed to the emperor the news that Cortés had landed on the Gulf Coast. The scriveners who worked for the lawyers came to America with Spanish paper, which they covered with legal verbiage as destructive to the Indian as the imported diseases that refused to respond to his traditional herb medicines. In some regions more Indians died of the measles than of wars. They were defenseless against syphilis—"the French disease." Maladies hitherto unknown in Europe were brought from America, and vice versa, and spread freely in the new-found world, although in the case of syphilis no one knows whether it traveled from Europe to America or from America to Europe. In any case, people who were virgin to a new disease had no idea how to fight it.

Hand in hand with paper came the convent, the university, and music. To be sure, the Incas in Cuzco already had their convent and university, and music had existed in America as far back as its nations had memory. What the Spaniards brought was their version of each. In music, song, and dance this was rich and complex, an admixture already old in the Peninsula. This included the writing of music, instrumental music and vocal music. The instruments included many types of drums, horns, and trumpets, timbrels and pipes, flutes and reed flutes. These were made of bamboo, bones, baked clay, or brass, depending upon the stage of development in the art of instrument-making on the continent. The Spaniards brought the harp, which became popular in Paraguay, Peru, Chile, Colombia, and Venezuela. This instrument was similar to the so-called "old harp," without pedals. The violin, trumpet, and clarinet also became popular and soon took their place in regular orchestras like those in Mexico City. The guitar, which had come to Spain from the Orient, begat a whole family of instruments both large and small, such as the Mexican guitar, the *charango* of Argentina and Bolivia, the *cuatro* of Venezuela, and the *tiple* and *requinto* of Colombia. Then the tambourine arrived to play an essential role among the percussions, in the family meeting and mingling of native and imported instruments. American musicians found a new range in the European flute. In time, the accordion became the people's instrument in Buenos Aires and on the Guajira Peninsula of Colombia, home of the half-savage Guajiros. The marimba came later, from Africa.

In the earlier civilizations music had been correlated with popular functions. The Spaniards brought the elements of the European song and dance to create a new expression as, little by little, *mestizo* or Creole music evolved with the colony and gave rise to new forms that developed and were diffused within definite limits. From the simplest kind of secular song and plain chant to the most complex compositions for the instruments of the time, this musical current flowed and spread. Out of all this variety, however, some new variations came. For example, though the *cueca*, a courting dance, retained its basic characteristics everywhere, it was called the *marinera* in Peru, the *zambacueca* in Argentina, the *cueca* in Bolivia, and the *cueca nacional* in Chile. The *bambuco* of Colombia has an African name. And as time passed and music came from everywhere, the *tango* became the specialty of the Argentine, the *rumba* of Cuba, the *cumbia* of Colombia, the *galerón* of Venezuela, the *jarabe* of Mexico, and so on.

Spain itself had assimilated Oriental music, especially Arabic and Hebrew chant, as well as the gypsy dances and flamenco airs. All of them, including Gregorian chant, she carried to America; then she opened the doors to African music and everything else that has come out of the musical New World. Afro-Cuban music alone provided Fernando Ortiz with the material for his admirable studies.

Spain brought another coinage, although Mexico had a medium of exchange in the form of cacao seeds and of little cylinders containing gold dust. The Chibchas used small gold-plated discs for trading. But the coinage of the king of Spain was like another invention. Originally the Indian had to pay his ransom in measures of gold; later he paid his tribute in hens, eggs, corn, or sacks of potatoes.

The white European brought another exotic newcomer to America—the African Negro. In this way, the Indian made the acquaintance of the African slave, even worse off than he was. Before Columbus there had been neither white nor black men in America.

To what degree has all that came from Europe between the sixteenth and the twentieth centuries—from wheat to the Mass, from the horse to Roman law, from the hen and the donkey to the alphabet and gunpowder—made an impact on the ancient American peoples? What do we find of Europe in a hut perched on the Ecuadorean cordillera or in the slum shanty of today? These questions are hard to answer. Spanish America has registered the presence of the European man *en masse* longer than anywhere else outside Europe itself; the blood of the Occidental has mingled for centuries with that of the native in prodigal reciprocity; the religion of Christ has replaced the ancient creeds more radically than in any other non-European lands. And yet . . .

For the most part, the white people have clustered in the capital cities and have relegated the ancient peoples to a second-class status. The European has been content to take ownership of the land and to exploit the despoiled Indian as a laborer not far removed from the medieval serf. Throughout vast areas of America, the poor rustic still lives in a hut that contains little the Indian had not previously known: some iron implements, such as a knife, some chickens, some pigs, a dog, a burro, and the image of a saint. The European plays the role of boss in the fields. In the cities the boss lives amid the furnishings, machinery, comforts, and luxuries of the Western world. When he takes any part of all that to the country with him, he emphasizes the difference between his level and that of the local people. What Europe has sent to America adds up to thousands of items, from the carriage to the cigarette lighter. All together, they represent the city man's wealth, and they also highlight the differences between levels.

The *mestizo*'s situation is not the same as the Indian's. The *mestizo* received no more than half of the things that came from Europe—everything about him is by halves. He is a native product, and an illegitimate one to boot, born of the contact between the white man and the Indian woman, an under-the-counter product, as it were. If he was a child of love, he enjoyed some consideration on that account. But the social background from which he was born, with a right to it that was never complete, made him a rebel, or a difficult man at best. Here and there the alphabet reached the *mestizo*, and even before the time of his country's independence, he was delegated some degree of authority. Such advantages made him a man more real to himself, a man with the possibility of acquiring value and of making himself valued. And the *mestizo* had his horse, though the Indian had only his donkey. The *mestizo* even held one advantage over the white man in that he was able to live as well in the country as in the city. He never lost his intimate contact with the lowly people and the earth. In the main, he lived in villages. To a lesser degree than the white man, he turned the things from Europe to good account, but to a greater degree than the white man, he utilized the things of America advantageously.

All in all, substantial changes occurred in everyone, some through travel, others through everyday contact. The white man in America became profoundly American. Almost without knowing it, he had brought "his democracy" from Europe. "His democracy" was a repudiation of the society he left behind him in Europe. The Spaniards had a name for their wanderers, their displaced persons. They called them *indianos*, a word meaning that they were born in Spain but had moved to the Indies and identified themselves with their new home. The son of the *indiano* was the Creole, whom centuries of colonialism transformed into a revolutionary.

The circumstances of day-by-day living decreed that the two

Americans—the white man and the Indian—had to be separate types. Two radically opposed types at times. To the white man religion is either the Spanish Catholic Church or the freethinking of the nineteenth century; to the Indian it is an inextricable and incomprehensible tangle of magic and superstition hidden beneath the sign of the Cross. To the white man law is a right and the beginning of liberty; to the Indian it is a source of obligations and the beginning of fear. And so it goes in everything. Europe's intrusion among the masses and in the jungles of America has been disconcerting and inconsistent. For this reason the march of culture through the lands conquered and colonized by Spain has taken unusual turns.

The first prophetic passages in the books of *Chilám Balám* reveal the perplexity and fear aroused in the land of corn tortillas by the sight of the European with his loaf of wheat bread:

The 11 ahau [which fixes the date] is the date that begins the tale, for the Katun was transpiring when the strangers came, those who brought Christianity and made an end to the power in the East and caused the heavens to weep, and filled the bread of corn with heaviness. The Jaxal Chuen will be beheaded, the Great-Monkey artificer, Ixkanyulta, and Precious-throat. The women who sing and the men who sing, and all who sing will be scattered across the world. The child sings, the old man sings, the old woman sings, and young man sings, the young woman sings. . . . When your Elder Brothers arrive, the accursed strangers will change your belt-braces, they will change your clothing, they will change the whiteness of your belt-brace, they will change the white colors of your clothing. . . . Their priests will adore a Red God. . . . His head will be the jaguar, his body the stag. Throughout all the land of the peoples the harmful government will begin in Ichcaansiho, Make-the-birth-of-the-sky.

With such words, the sorcerers nourished the traditional magic of the Indians.

¶ THE VILLAGE AND TRAVELING PLANTS

In spite of all the foregoing evils, the Spaniards' presence in America yielded some positive good. The most important was that they carried the new civilization to regions where the Maya, the Aztecs, and the Incas had never set foot. The Spanish Empire embraced a territory many times the area of any of the earlier empires, and if the colony introduced a new concept of political, religious, and domestic life to the Aztecs and the Incas, it also represented the first example of organized government in the Antilles and the jungles. Other remarkable changes were accomplished by the new rulers, such as the elimination from the Aztec religion of human sacrifice and the abolition of cannibalism in the most primitive regions. (Vespucci had encountered it, as we have seen, on the coast of Brazil.)

The Spaniards also introduced a most important new scheme of life by establishing the village as they conceived it, with its priest and church, its mayor and town hall, and its gentlemen's houses of adobe and tile. The village became a new stage for celebrations enlivened with such innovations as bells, fireworks, and bullfighting. It also provided a show window that was slowly being enriched by the importation of plant life. From the time of the founding of the colony until today, the peasant, the Indian, has gone to the village, irresistibly drawn there—even at the risk of colliding with the law or being drafted into the army—by the market, where all the news is known. The village is his school, his club, his social life. Only the truck, and to a lesser degree the radio, have wrought as great a change as the village in the life of the Indian.

Another event on the positive side, which has never lost its effect, is the green revolution, the botanical revolution. Even to our day, the endless wanderings of plant life still go on in an endless interchange between America and the far corners of the earth. Coffee was brought from Ethiopia to Brazil, and from Brazil to the rest of tropical America and the Antilles. The eucalyptus, originally from Australia, has spread all over America. It is the only giant tree found on the high plateaus of the Andes. Sugar cane came from Asia to blanket Cuba. Alexander von Humboldt, a German, introduced the willow to America. Antonio Nariño brought clover to Colombia in the boxes that held his books. Fodder, flowers, and fruits have traveled unceasingly through the centuries, to the benefit of mankind. America's gardens are bright with roses, azaleas, lilies, and dahlias, each of which has a personal history that begins something like this: "When Don Camilo Restrepo went to Europe in the seventies, he brought back this rose. . . ."

¶ WHAT WENT TO EUROPE FROM AMERICA?

Gold was not America's greatest export. To be sure, it had real value; it was dazzling in its very abundance at the moment when the output of the mines in Africa was dwindling. But smoke proved more potent than gold. Tobacco smoke. Tobacco changed the customs of Europe. It came like the work of magic. In England, where Queen Elizabeth looked upon it with loathing and forbade it in her court, it played an indirect part in Sir Walter Raleigh's trial, which cost him his head. Raleigh introduced London to tobacco, and gave the name Virginia, for his virgin queen, Elizabeth, to the section of America best known for its tobacco. The thought of a London club of our day without tobacco, of a girl without cigarettes, of a Churchill without his cigar is enough to prove the extent of the change in Europe's environment caused by the tobacco leaf from America. Before the voyages of Columbus, soldiers preparing for a campaign used to pack some garlic in their knapsacks on the theory that an army felt more energetic and aggressive after eating it. Centuries yawn between the troops who reeked of garlic and those who smoke in their moments of idleness.

The man who orders beefsteak and potatoes in a Paris restaurant and has it served to him surrounded by slices of tomato, eats food entirely unknown to Europeans during the first sixteen centuries of the Christian era. Potatoes and tomatoes came from America. The feat of initiating Europeans to the taste of the potato called for valor, and the men who performed it, such as Parmentier in France, are commemorated as the heroes they were. Today almost everyone eats potatoes. But people in some places cannot yet conceive that any creature save an animal could eat corn. In Italy it is disrespectfully called the "Turkish grain." On the other hand, the whole world enjoys chocolate from the cacao tree, which, like corn, originated in America.

The transition from iron-rimmed wheels to rubber tires is only one of many improvements in the life of Western man for which caucho, the native American rubber, can be thanked. The variety of American plants in the pharmacopoeia is infinite. The discovery of cinchona, the source of quinine, which took place in the eighteenth century, opened a new horizon to medicine. On the other hand, the coca leaf, despite its great usefulness, engendered a vice through its misuse. Balsam of Tolu, ipecac, jalap, guaiacum (a resin obtained from the lignum vitae tree), sarsaparilla, vanilla, campechy wood for dyeing, quebracho bark for tanning, and polisander, as well as the sweet potato, the alligator pear, the pineapple, chili, and red beans, or *frijoles*, all traveled to Europe after the sixteenth century. Perhaps the showiest flower that America gave to Europe is the one brought to Paris by Louis de Bougainville: the gardens of Switzerland and the Côte d'Azur owe much of their beauty to the bougainvillea.

The American vegetable world is still a fountain of healing drugs, medicines, beauty, and vice. For example, the poisonous hyacinth of the Amazon, the orchids of the Andes, and the chicle of Yucatán are worth a passing mention. Wealthy America paid Africa for the people stolen from her with some of the foods Africans eat today: corn, peanuts, cassava, sweet potatoes, and cacao.

A rapid glance at the catalogue of the fruits in America, which are the envy of the world, shows that only a small proportion of American trees made the journey westward. However many the fruits of European origin displayed in an American market, they are few compared with those of native origin. The avocado is rare in Europe, and the chirimoya, the papaya, and the curuba, unlike the pineapple, have never successfully crossed the sea. American trees have not always been lucky in the eternal adventure of travel. Vegetable life runs as great a risk in changing habitat as does man. The most famous and successful transplants are quinine, rubber, and coffee.

¶ RUBBER GOES TO ASIA VIA KEW GARDENS

La Condamine did not so much discover as rediscover rubber in the last days of the colony. Its use had already spread all over the world to the extent that when the old colonies gained their independence, they regarded rubber as one of their mainstays. Brazil tried jealously to hold it in America by prohibiting the export of hevea seeds. In 1870, at the behest of the governor of India, an Englishman named H. Wickham managed to smuggle out seventy thousand seeds as "botanical specimens." The three thousand that survived the voyage were acclimated in Kew Gardens near London. From there, the seedlings were shipped to a more propitious climate: the botanical station of Henaragoda in Ceylon. By the end of the century, the rubber plantations in Ceylon, Sumatra, Malaya, Borneo, India, Burma, Thailand, and

French Indo-China were in full production . . . and Brazil, Colombia, and Peru were temporarily ruined. Since then Latin Americans visiting the beautiful Kew Gardens are reminded of dismal days.

The Indians knew a great deal about quinine. In Loja, Peru, a Spanish Jesuit and a governor learned from them that it was effective for reducing fevers. The Countess of Chinchón, wife of the viceroy of Peru, was cured by quinine, and the fame of her recovery grew so great that quinine entered the pharmacopoeia under the name of Cinchona bark. In Peru, it is simply called "the Countess's powder." The Jesuits spread the knowledge of its virtues through Europe so efficiently that it was known as "the Jesuit's powder" in Rome. Cardinal Juan de Lugo, a Jesuit who directed the college of pharmacy in Rome, was so enthusiastic over quinine that it acquired still another name, "the Cardinal's powder." Treatises on quinology were written; every variety of the plant was studied; and a scientific specialty evolved in which such men as José Celestino Mutis and Ruiz and Pavón distinguished themselves. Also, the "Indian powder" or "Peruvian febrifuge," to use a pharmaceutical term, was known everywhere. But the commercial name became "cascarilla." Like raw rubber, cascarilla proved to be one of the achievements of the Enlightenment in the last days of the colonial period, but when the republics of Colombia, Ecuador, and Peru were being born, their trade in cascarilla bark was slowly waning. About 1849 the French carried samples of cinchona bark to Algiers; the Dutch sent a botanist named Haskarl to Peru to dig up shoots destined for Java. Another Dutch businessman, named Ledger, took samples from Bolivia. The English brought seeds to Ceylon. The result of all these transplantations was that the infant republics lost what then seemed their only source of wealth.

Now and again the journeys of plant life have been accompanied by situations almost fictional. The adventures of the Spanish navigator, Alvaro de Mendaña (1549–95), discoverer of the Solomon Islands, are connected with the importation of coconut palms to Mexico from the Philippines via Colima in 1569. The palm trees changed the landscape as they spread from Colima and brought a new beverage, coconut milk, to the Mexican table. Encouraged by the success of that venture, Mendaña again hoisted sail and discovered the island of Santa Cruz in 1595. He lost his life on that voyage, but his wife, Isabel Barreto, sailed on and discovered the Marquesas and eventually delivered the survivors of the expedition to Manila in safety.

Culture has moved hand in hand with plant life, bringing the learned men of the two worlds into closer contact. A Sevillian physician, Nicolás Monardes (*c.* 1493–1588) founded a museum of America's native products in his city, and wrote the *Historia Medicinal de las Cosas que se traen de nuestras Indias Occidentales (Medicinal History of the Things That Are Brought from Our West Indies)* in 1574. His botanical knowledge gave him a deep insight into the effects of herbs; he identified diphtheria as a disease, and his name is still carried by plants of the genus Monarda, which was christened by Linnaeus. Philip II's physician, Francisco Hernández, sailed to Mexico in 1570 to study its native plants for a period of seven years. Later he brought out his monumental *Historia de las Plantas de la Nueva España.* The pages of the *Historia del Nuevo Mundo,* by the Jesuit Bernabé Cobo (1582–1657), who moved to Peru in 1596, are bright with descriptions of flowers in minute and touching detail. One of these is the passion flower. Since those days seeds, shoots, and plants have moved from place to place, always facilitating the dialogue between the two worlds with the language of flowers, roots, and fronds. An odd but not unusual instance of this was the description of the flowers of New Granada given by a doctor from Santa Fe de Bogotá to the Empress of Russia during the century of Linnaeus.

¶ EUCALYPTUS MIGRATES FROM AUSTRALIA TO
THE NEW WORLD

The country that benefited least from the plants of America was Spain, partly because the great awakening in botany began with the decline of the Spanish Empire in America toward the end of the brilliant eighteenth century, as the world was beginning to communicate with greater fluidity. To be sure, plants and seeds were delivered to the botanical gardens of Madrid as well as to those in Sweden and Austria. But Spain's botanical gift to America was much greater than America's to Spain. Even today most Spaniards will not eat cornbread as readily as Americans eat wheat, rice, and bananas. And Spain ceased to be the middleman in the exchange of plants after the wars for independence. A man touring the savannah of Bogotá today finds a landscape that is a natural part of the people's life, the landscape sung by the poets, a part of the Bogotan's soul from childhood. It is dominated by great eucalyptus trees that tower above the ranch house, willows that lean over the turbulent waters of the Funza River, and clover that covers the pastures for the nourishment of Normandy cattle and English bulls. The features of this landscape have all been created since the days when the Indians were left to themselves, since the colonial period. Eucalyptus trees were imported from Australia in the nineteenth century during the term of the radical president Manuel Murillo Toro (1815–80); the willows brought by Humboldt provided the green branches proclaiming independence; clover arrived with some French books belonging to the trail-blazer Antonio Nariño, who took ship for Bogotá after escaping from prison in Spain. Such things were happening all over America. The trees, crops, and animals in the fields, as well as the houses and their gardens, are sometimes more closely related to those of Europe than the men are. The earth received some investitures that man did not. In this sense, the American is closer to the European than the European to the American. The European feels the presence of America only when he is at table, if indeed he realizes it then, as he enjoys tomatoes, avocados, and potatoes, and smokes his cigar.

In the history of vegetable travel, coffee made the round trip that most deeply affected America. It was imported to America where it flourished so rampantly that the names of Brazil, Colombia, Central America, and the West Indies came to dominate the world's coffee market, and its Arabian origin was forgotten. On the eve of Africa's independence, some Europeans conceived the idea of revitalizing that continent by transplanting products that had brought wealth to Latin America. Coffee was first on the list. The success of the venture ushered in another period of crisis in America, following the pattern of caucho and cascarilla.

¶ POLITICAL IDEAS ALSO TRAVEL

But the conclusive gift from all the Americas is a political virtue that stimulated the great European movements of modern days, from Romanticism to liberal democracy, moved the writers of the eighteenth century to exalt the ideal of the noble savage, and eventually resulted in the toppling of crowned heads as the people strove to achieve a more liberal world. The idea had already sparked the revolt of the *comuneros* in Paraguay and New Granada, and it culminated in the revolution of the English colonies and the birth of the United States. Republican government, which traveled to France from America, became the ideal of other states.

When the ephemeral First French Republic fell, leaving the field open for Napoleon's empire, republics were being born in Latin America. Much has been said of the instability of Latin America in defiance of the fact that fifteen of its republics date from the early 1800s.

IV : *The Birth of a Literature*

¶ COLUMBUS WRITES THE FIRST PAGE

The first page of Spanish American literature was written on October 13, 1492. An Italian, Christopher Columbus (1451–1506), wrote it in the Castilian language. This is the only case in history in which the exact date, almost the hour, of the birth of a literature can be pinpointed. On that day, a European tongue, a Romance language—was used for the first time to describe the American landscape and to paint a picture of its people. While Columbus was on board ship, he kept a journal of the incidents of his voyage—one of the most dramatic in history. On the night of October 11, he saw the first signs that he was nearing the west coast of the Atlantic. The wondrous idea propounded by the Florentine Toscanelli, that the Orient could be reached by sailing westward, was about to be verified. The notes in Columbus's journal evoke the emotion of that moment which was to mark such a radical change in the dimensions of the world.

Fray Bartolomé de Las Casas acquired a copy of the journal and made an abstract of it in which he included long quotations. This abstract, used by Las Casas in writing his *Historia de las Indias (History of the Indies*—not published until 1875), is a manuscript of 76 folios in the historian's own hand. It was discovered shortly after 1790 in a Spanish Library (that of the Duque del Infantado) by Martín Fernández de Navarrete (1765–1844), a retired naval officer commissioned by Carlos IV "to collect documents bearing upon the history of Spanish navigation and discovery" (S. E. Morison). The work is entitled *El Libro de la Primera Navegación (The Book of the First Voyage)*.

From various complaints by Las Casas about the scribe who had made his copy of Columbus's journal, as well as from obvious copyists' errors of the type common in manuscripts of the time, one must conclude that even the quotations are not always exactly the words Columbus wrote. Nevertheless, such an acute historian as Samuel Eliot Morison is convinced that they are largely the explorer's own words. Admiral Morison's translation of the original Las Casas manuscript is the source of the passages below. Passages quoted by Las Casas directly from the journal are enclosed in quotation marks.

The abstract of Columbus's entry for Friday, October 12, 1492, begins as follows:

At two hours after midnight appeared the land, at a distance of 2 leagues [six miles]. They handed [lowered] all sails and set the *treo*, which is the mainsail without bonnets, and lay-to waiting for daylight Friday, when they arrived at an island of the Bahamas that was called in the Indians' tongue *Guanahaní*. Presently they saw naked people, and the Admiral went ashore in his barge, and Martín Alonso Pinzón and Vicente Yáñez, his brother, who was captain of the *Niña*, followed. . . .

Once ashore they saw very green trees, many streams, and fruits of different kinds. The Admiral called to the two captains and to the others . . . and said that they should bear faith and witness how he before them all was taking, as in fact he took, possession of the said island for the King and Queen, their Lord and Lady, making the declarations that are required, as is set forth at length in the testimonies which were taken down in writing. Presently there gathered many people of the island. What follows are the formal words of the Admiral, in his Book of the First Voyage and Discovery of these Indies:

"I," says he, "in order that they might develop a very friendly disposition toward us, because I knew that they were a people who could better be freed and converted to our Holy Faith by love than by force, gave to some of them red caps and to others glass beads, which they hung on their necks, and many other things of slight value, in which they took much pleasure. They remained so much our [friends] that it was a marvel, later they came swimming to the ships' boats in which we were, and brought us parrots and cotton thread in skeins and darts and many other things, and we swopped them for other things that we gave them, such as little glass beads and hawks' bells. Finally they traded and gave everything they had, with good will; but it appeared to me that these people were very poor in everything. They all go quite naked as their mothers bore them; and also the women, although I didn't see more than one really young girl. All that I saw were young men, none of them more than 30 years old, very well built, of very handsome bodies and very fine faces; the hair coarse, almost like the hair of a horse's tail, and short, the hair they wear over their eyebrows, except for a hank behind that they wear long and never cut. Some of them paint themselves black (and they are of the color of the Canary Islanders, neither black nor white), and others paint themselves white, and some red, and others with what they find. And some paint their faces, others the body, some the eyes only, others only the nose. They bear no arms, nor know thereof; for I showed them swords and they grasped them by the blade and cut themselves through ignorance. They have no iron. Their darts are a kind of rod without iron, and some have at the end a fish's tooth and others, other things. They are generally fairly tall and good looking, well built. I saw some who had marks of wounds on their bodies, and made signs to them to ask what it was, and they showed me that people of other islands which are near came there and wished to capture them, and they defended themselves. And I believed and now believe that people do come here from the mainland to take them as slaves. They ought to be good servants and of good skill, for I see that they repeat very quickly whatever was said to them. I believe that they would easily be made Christians, because it seemed to me that they belonged to no religion. I, please Our Lord, will carry off six of them at my departure to Your Highnesses, that they may learn to speak. I saw no animal of any kind in this island, except parrots." All these are the words of the Admiral.[1]

[1] Passages from the Journals of Columbus are quoted by permission of Samuel Eliot Morison, editor and translator of *Journals and Other Documents on the Life and Voyages of Christopher Columbus* (New York: The Heritage Press; 1963).

The passage from which the foregoing was translated reproduces, word for word, the beginning of Spanish American literature, preserved for us by the diligence of Las Casas. It conveys clearly the impression that America—albeit an island peripheral to the continent proper—made upon Columbus and his men.

This first impression of America was to endure for a long time as the synthesis of everything that first met the eyes of Europeans. Amerigo Vespucci was so taken with the parrots of Brazil and he described them so well that on the first maps the southeastern portion of the continent was called "the land of the Parrots." Columbus never abandoned the idea that he had reached Japan, though perhaps the only touch of the Orient he found in the Antilles was the parrot. When he returned to Spain to convey the news of the islands he had discovered, he took parrots with him as talismans, and they attracted more attention than the gold and as much as the Indians.

The hunger and thirst for gold are reflected in Columbus's journal and letters better than in any other contemporary document. Finding it became an obsession with him. Guanahaní was only a barren islet, without a grain of gold. Although it is hard to imagine how Columbus and the Indians communicated, how they understood one another, Columbus wrote on the October 13:

> . . . I was attentive and worked hard to know if there was any gold, and saw that some of them wore a little piece hanging from a thing like a needle case which they have in the nose; and by signs I could understand that, going to the S, or doubling the island to the S, there was a king there who had great vessels of it and possessed a lot. . . . I decided . . . to go to the SW to search for gold and precious stones. . . . [However,] here [on Guanahaní] is found the gold that they wear hanging from the nose. But, to lose no time, I intend to go and see if I can find the Island of *Cipango*.

In the mind of Columbus, as in the geography of his day, Cipango (Japan) lay within that Asiatic world of great nations that was commonly designated as the "Indies," the Ganges Indies, Indo-China, and so on. To Columbus, Japan, the Orient, Asia were the Indies, and his conviction that he had reached the Indies brought a long train of consequences. Spain named America the West Indies and its inhabitants Indians. The first code of laws drawn up for Americans was "The Laws of the Indies." The Spaniards who struck it rich in America were called *indianos*.

American law was *Indian* law. Father Las Casas never agreed
to the adoption of the name "America," for he had elected himself
counsel for the defense of Columbus, and he chided the Admiral's
son for his failure to inveigh against Vespucci in the book on
his father's life. Las Casas believed that Vespucci had invented
the name America.

Columbus spent his youth either in Italy or sailing with his
countrymen and Frenchmen. Later he settled in Portugal, where
he married. By the time he arrived in Castile, in the waning of
his youth, he was full of plans for convincing the Catholic
Monarchs to aid him by financing a voyage of exploration westward across the Atlantic Ocean. Until that time, he must have
expressed himself in Italian, French, or Portuguese. Yet from the
time of his arrival in Castile, his written and spoken language was
Castilian. If the conjecture were correct that he belonged to a
family of Spanish Jews who had sought refuge in Italy, this
would explain how he was able to express himself precisely in
Castilian from the beginning. His diction is popular and rich.
Menéndez Pidal, who made a study of it, found traces of languages
other than Castilian in it, as might be expected of a man who
traveled in foreign lands. But the structure and color of the writings of Columbus are entirely Castilian.

¶ VESPUCCI, OR THE RENAISSANCE

A new literature, not only Spanish-American, but world wide,
came to life with the discovery. Other contemporary accounts
were written in other languages. Verazzano's letters on his explorations are in Italian; Federmann, who explored Venezuela
as an agent of the Welsers, and Schmidt, who covered the Río de
la Plata and the Paraguay, both wrote their books in German.
Amerigo Vespucci's letters addressed to Lorenzo di Pierfrancesco
de' Medici, or to Piero Soderini, Gonfalonier of Florence, were
written in Italian and were promptly translated into Latin and the
other living languages of Europe (for at that time Latin still was
a living language). With the letters of Columbus and Vespucci,
a dialogue began which echoed all through the Western world, and
of which the central theme was the New World.

Columbus proved what others had predicted, what had generally
been sensed in advance: the possibility of crossing the Atlantic.
But his news of the islands of Japan fell short of rocking Europe
to its foundations. The reports of Portuguese navigators who had

sailed around the Cape of Good Hope to the wealthiest countries
in Asia were more attractive. Then Vespucci announced the
existence of another continent and his news eclipsed all previous
reports. His announcement was based not on intuition or on the
hearsay of other navigators, but on experience. By chance, he had
explored, during three of his four voyages, the coast of the mainland of South America, from the Caribbean to the South Atlantic
—from Venezuela to Patagonia. Nothing he found on that immense
continental land mass, which Columbus never had the chance to
see, bore any relation to Marco Polo's descriptions of Asia.
Vespucci was therefore able to state that those lands were not in
Asia, nor in Africa, nor in Europe, but were a new continent.
This was the outstanding news of the century. It explains why
the canons of Saint Dié, a body of learned geographers, took the
initiative and named the New World America, in homage to
Amerigo Vespucci, who had announced it.

Although Vespucci and Columbus were close friends, they
represented opposing positions in the thinking of their time, when
the Renaissance was struggling to overthrow medieval traditions.
Columbus, even though he had opened the way for the greatest
conquest of modern times, still adhered to the medieval texts.
Vespucci represented the Humanism of the Renaissance.

Columbus was bound by the official thinking of the Castilian
Crown. He attributed his feat to the work of Providence, to the
fulfillment of the words of the prophets. He declared that the
dictates of science—that is, the maps of the world—had been of
no use to him, and toward the end of his life he indulged in some
wild conjectures recorded in his *Book of Prophecies*. His arrival
at the mouth of the Orinoco became the subject of a scientific-moral
essay on the Garden of Eden, based on the texts of the Holy
Fathers. He believed that his ships were guided by the hand of
God to the precise spot where the Earthly Paradise was situated.
His last letter, dated July 7, 1503, written in Jamaica, told the
Spanish monarchs that he had spoken directly with the Lord and
that the Lord had said to him:

> "O fool, and slow to believe and serve thy God, the God
> of every man! What more did He do for Moses or for David
> His servant than for thee? From thy birth He hath ever held
> thee in special charge. When he saw thee at man's estate,
> marvellously did He cause thy name to resound over the
> earth. The Indies, so rich a portion of the world, he gave thee

for thine own, and thou hast divided them as it pleased thee. . . ."

Columbus wrote in Castilian, Vespucci in Tuscan. The two languages represented at that moment two different attitudes toward the world and its problems. Whereas Columbus said that maps had been of no use to him at all, Vespucci constructed a globe showing the discovered lands to the Humanists of Florence. Columbus based some of his fanciful prophecies on lyrical passages in the Bible; Vespucci used some of the most beautiful of Dante's verses to help him describe the southern stars in his letters, and his paragraphs on nature in Brazil are reminiscent of the stanzas Politian dedicated to Simonetta Vespucci, Botticelli's model who inspired him to paint the Primavera. Columbus, with his tragic sense of life, said truly that no one had wept so much as his eyes had wept in the fury of the Caribbean tempests. And in his letter from Jamaica, his words rang like a Jeremiah's. Vespucci, however followed a school of literature running from Boccaccio's *Decameron* to Lorenzo the Magnificent's carnival songs as, in his letters to Lorenzo di Pierfrancesco de' Medici, he described the pleasures offered by the Indian women at the Yucatán "court," and the glory of sleeping in hammocks. Columbus launched the fable of the Amazon women, which captured the imagination of the Conquistadors, already stimulated by books of chivalry. Vespucci's description of the giants of Curaçao reduced them to the size of Francesco degli Albizzi of Florence, and explained in passing that they looked enormous to the Indians because they were overcome by fear. Columbus ended his days still fighting lonely battles for recognition of his titles of Viceroy of the Indies and Admiral of the Ocean Sea; Vespucci spent his old age in his office tracing on accurate maps and navigation charts the discoveries announced by the first explorers. Columbus was driven by his search for the phantom of gold. When Vespucci was told that there was gold in the interior of Brazil, he remarked: "There may be, but I shall not believe it until I see it; I belong to the school of St. Thomas." Columbus possessed the superlative daring that was needed to set forth in search of the other shore of the Atlantic. Vespucci followed the road already opened, studied from the bridge of his ship the safest means of navigating, and in so doing, made a great scientific discovery. Columbus was a mystic; Vespucci a Florentine.

In the final analysis, this duality of the Medieval and the Renaissance man, which is like the great dialogue in the Spanish theater at the beginning of the sixteenth century, constitutes the first chapter in the contradictions surrounding the birth of the New World's culture. Spain herself was engaged in a struggle between the new spirit from Italy and the old spirit of Castile. One of the most famous of the Conquistadors, Gonzalo Jiménez de Quesada, was inspired to undertake the conquest of El Dorado, but he whiled away the night watches in the encampment in the marshes and jungles covering the valley of the Magdalena River by discussing poetry and defending the ottava rima of Spain's traditional ballads against the hendecasyllabic verse of Petrarch's sonnets, which either the priest or his captains championed. From the earliest voyages, when mad adventurers and illiterates sailed with Columbus, all of them knew by hearsay both the "mendacious stories" of the Amadises and the doctrines of the Erasmists, who were seeking a new light by which to renew the teachings of the Gospel. Father Las Casas, the most impassioned champion of Columbus against Vespucci in a fictive argument created by his heated imagination, includes in his general history of the Indies a treatise on magic. When he was planning an experiment in Utopian colonization in South America, he promoted the formation of the "order of the Knights of the Golden Spur." Diego Méndez, one of the men most loyal to Columbus, rescued his Admiral from the useless *Gallega*, marooned off Jamaica, and later made a hazardous journey by dugout to report the Admiral's plight. The only legacy left by this hero were the books of Erasmus.

¶ LAS CASAS, A MAN WITH A MISSION

Two books by Fray Bartolomé de Las Casas (1474–1566) are essential to an interpretation of the great fresco of America's discovery. These are his monumental *Historia de las Indias*, and the *Brevísima relación de la Destrucción de las Indias* (*Brief Account of the Destruction of the Indies*). Las Casas was a soldier when he came to the Antilles, but he took holy orders there after he had seen the abuses committed by the colonists. A man of great vitality, inspired with a sense of mission, he crossed the Atlantic time and again to promote his campaign on behalf of the Indians. His report on the destruction of the Indies is so exaggerated that his readers might well believe that the Spaniards were determined, like the non-Spanish colonists of North America, to leave not one Indian alive. The impassioned indictment penned by Las Casas gave rise to the "Black Legend" that accused the men from Spain of genocide. But for all its exaggeration, this list of grievances bore good fruit in the Laws of the Indies, promulgated by the Spanish Crown to protect the Indians as pitiful creatures deserving of mercy. That the Spaniards did not exterminate the Indians, whom they needed as a source of tribute and common labor, is proved by the masses of their descendants, who still populate the immense territory of America.

Las Casas rescued from oblivion documents such as the logs and diary of Columbus, which are the incunabula of American literature and all histories of the discoveries. And he himself wrote his colorful report of the conquest, containing pages of great importance to American letters. As one instance, he left a great picture of the dramatic and heroic acts that occurred during the first uprising against the Spaniards of the Indians led by the Indian chief, Enriquillo, who ruled the province of Baoruco. Three hundred years later, Manuel de Jesús Galván used this report as a source for the most important novel of the Caribbean, *Enriquillo*, written in 1882.

Las Casas lived to the age of ninety-two with never an idle moment, so dedicated was he to his moral and literary enterprises, which are amazing in vehemence and scope. He wrote the greater part of his works in America, where the pen was as hard-working as the sword in those years, the most stirring recorded by history. Such things were characteristic of the Spaniards.

¶ CABEZA DE VACA, OR SHIPWRECK IN BOTH AMERICAS

High adventure, hardship, shipwreck, and discovery were not solely the prerogative of Christopher Columbus. He opened an era in which a generation of bold Spaniards hurtled into the most fabulous and fearful undertaking of centuries. Columbus died in 1506 knowing only a part of the land around the Caribbean: Cuba, Santo Domingo, Trinidad, Jamaica, Curaçao, the Lesser Antilles, and a strip along the coasts of Venezuela, Panama, and Honduras. Vespucci cruised the coasts of Central America and the Gulf of Mexico and the Atlantic littoral from Colombia and Venezuela to Patagonia between 1497 and 1502. But the Spaniards, for the most part, put aside mere exploration to move toward the interior. Their discoveries, made by shank's mare and vagrant sail, almost defy belief.

From 1513, when Balboa crossed the Isthmus of Panama and discovered the Pacific Ocean, to 1520, when Magellan passed through the straits that bear his name, the ships navigated by people who had never been seamen covered more blue water than the ships of Venice, Genoa, or the ancient Phoenicians. Between 1519 and 1521, as Magellan was making the first voyage around the world, Cortés was conquering Mexico. The year after Balboa reached the Pacific, Ponce de León discovered Florida as he was exploring the Caribbean. But the second period of these adventures, the twenty years from the day in 1521 when Hernán Cortés made Tenochtitlán the capital of New Spain until Valdivia founded Santiago, Chile, in 1541 were years of human restlessness during which Spaniards covered ground that neither they nor anyone else had trod in fifteen centuries. Their exploration of the great rivers alone could have been the subject of a continued story in some imaginary newspaper covering the five adventurous years between 1536, when Gonzalo Jiménez de Quesada entered the Magdalena, and 1542, when the Amazon was navigated. A dramatic appendix to the story of the Amazon was added by the cruel and rebellious Lope de Aguirre, a tragic figure in the fabulous early history of America, who explored the Orinoco. Others were following the Plata and its tributaries, the Paraná, the Uruguay, and the Pilcomayo upstream during the same period.

Anyone reading the books in which the adventurers tell the story of their exploits in their own words is lost in admiration, quite unable to say which is the more surprising—the discoveries they made, or the quality of the discoverers. The literature begun by Columbus spreads outward into much vaster panoramas, and brings to life more fully the notes that the Admiral set down in his melancholy correspondence. *Los Naufragios* (*The Shipwrecks*) and the *Comentarios* of Alvar Núñez Cabeza de Vaca (*c.*1490–*c.*1557) are models of this type of reading. This luckless hero, the first to traverse the entire southern territory of what is now the United States, from Florida to Mexico, and who later took part in the conquest of Paraguay, saw with his eyes as many lands as Marco Polo had seen. They were not the lands of mandarin silks, however; they were hostile lands of jungle and swamp without orderly civic life. The saga of Cabeza de Vaca exemplifies the turns and twists of fortune. In the end, he was treated more cordially by the savages than by his own compatriots. One of the high points of his story came when he and his men were shipwrecked off Florida. They were huddled naked over a fire "praying to Our Lord God for mercy and forgiveness for our sins, shedding many tears, each one pitying not only himself but all the others, too, for they all saw one another in the same state," when some Indians came upon them by surprise. They might have eaten the Christians. But no:

> When the Indians saw the disaster that had struck us, and the disastrous state we were in, so full of misfortune and misery, they sat down among us, and with great sorrow and pity . . . they all began to weep copiously and so genuinely that they could have been heard from afar. This went on for more than a half hour; and in truth, the sight of these men, so unreasoning and so crude, like brute beasts, bewailing our fate so lustily, caused the emotion and the contemplation of our bad luck to increase in me and the others in the company. . . . I begged the Indians to take us to their houses. . . . They showed by signs that they would be very pleased to do so. . . . We went to their houses. As it was very cold indeed, and they feared that some [of us] might die or faint along the way, they provided four or five very large fires to be lighted at intervals, and they warmed us at each of them.

How different this was from Cabeza de Vaca's experience, years later, when he went to Asunción, Paraguay, with letters from the king. Far from welcoming him, his fellow countrymen threw him into prison until they could send him back to Spain on a ship made on the spot—in what kind of shipyard? It was named *El Comunero*, meaning "a member of the party upholding freedom against the encroachments of Charles V," rather than merely "a comrade," and later signifying "a revolutionary." For all that, the ship docked safely in Cádiz.

But in 1528 Cabeza de Vaca was one of the four survivors of the abortive expedition that Pánfilo de Narváez led to Florida. For eight years, until the skeleton-like wanderers reached Mexico City in 1536, he and his three companions made their uncertain course through vast wildernesses on both sides of the Mississippi, earning the trust and good will of the Indians by his acting as a healer—a medicine man—almost as a sorcerer, adapting himself to the prevailing customs. When he rejoined other Spaniards at last, they took him for an Indian. His former comrades, who recognized him, thought him a ghost come back to life. His written record of his experiences abounds in episodes worthy of a motion picture scenario—shipwreck, ambushes, flight, starvation, and sorcery.

Sometimes his account touches on the picaresque; at other times, on the miraculous. But the account of his heroic victory over starvation and death is given without heroics. One simple episode from this extraordinary book epitomizes the laborious effort put forth over many years:

> As we saw that we were provided with fish and roots and water and whatever other things we could lay hand on, we agreed to embark again and continue on our way. We dug the boat out of the sand into which it had sunk. It was necessary for all of us to take off our clothes and we had to work very hard to launch it in the water. . . . And being thus launched and some distance out, we were struck by such a great wave that we were all soaked. As we were naked and the weather was very cold, we were forced to let the oars fall from our hands, and the sea gave another surge and capsized the boat. The quartermaster and two others grasped it to save themselves, but the reverse happened; the boat carried them under and they were drowned. As the coast is very wild, the sea cast up all the others on the very shore of the island in one tumble, enveloped in sea water and half drowned, and all but three had been carried under by the boat and drowned. Those of us who had escaped were as naked as the day we were born and had lost all we had taken with us; although altogether it was of little value, at the moment it was of great value to us. And as it was then November, and the cold very intense, and ourselves in such a plight that our bones could be counted without much difficulty, we had become the very picture of death.

Discovery was indeed a life-and-death adventure, and when conquest came later, death was always in view. A very Spanish theme for a writer, and quite a natural counterpoint to the Spanish popular philosophy. Hence Cabeza de Vaca and his shipwrecked men provide a fitting chapter to open the great volume of the new literature of Spaniards in America.

V : *Don Quixote and the Conquest of America*

¶ THE IMPORTANCE OF AMADÍS DE GAULA

The Spaniards used gunpowder and steel, horses and dogs to conquer the Indians. These auxiliaries were enough to subdue people who did not possess them. But gunpowder and steel, horses and dogs, the common patrimony of all Europeans, cannot in themselves explain the surge of Spain's advance through the virgin lands and the ancient seats of civilization in America. Bernal Díaz del Castillo says that, after God, his compatriots owed their victory to their horses. Granted this was true in battle. But what about the jungle? And the desert? And the sea? And the mystery? Something more than arms was needed to grapple with such forces. What moved the Spaniards to embark on their great adventure at all? What spurred them on? What gave courage and spirit to the hallucinated rabble that left the Antilles for all the corners of the earth?

In part, it was the elemental magic of the books of chivalry, still working like yeast in a people in love with superhuman exploits. Superstition is perhaps more potent than economics in the history of a people without a middle class and all that it implies. The conquest of America was the last heroic fresco, and the most grandiose, ever painted by a medieval hand to chronicle the race. The life of Amadís de Gaula, the hero of one of the most famous of the books of chivalry, inspired men to step aboard the caravels.

Then, strangely enough, the literature of chivalry revived and took a new lease on life after the discovery of America. Plato was reborn during the Renaissance in Italy. But Amadís was obviously the hero due for rebirth in Spain. In his *Books of the Brave*, Irving Leonard studies these matters in detail. His work is of great value for the compilation of curious news items it contains and for the accuracy of its notes and comments.

From 1500 on, books of "mendacious tales" were reissued, rewritten, and invented. Some were supplemented with new adventures and were widely distributed, fresh and throbbing with immediacy, on both sides of the Atlantic. The few who knew how to read, read them aloud to the wandering, embattled, and illiterate crowd surrounding them. They delighted everyone; they made it seem there was something in the Conquest that might have occurred in the days of fable. Bernal Díaz del Castillo reports the Spaniards' first glimpse of the city of Mexico in these words: "And from the moment we saw so many cities and inhabited villas in the water, and other large towns on firm land, and that pavement so straight and level that led to Mexico, we were wonder-struck, and we said it looked like some work of sorcery told about in the book of Amadís."

Henry Thomas has catalogued forty-nine books of chivalry published in Spain between 1508 and 1602, covering the century preceding the publication of *Don Quixote*, the century of the conquest of America. Among these books were: *Amadís de Gaula* (1508), *Las Sergas* [*Adventures*] *de Esplandián y Florisando* (1510), *Lisuarte de Grecia, Leoneo de Hungría, Amadís de Grecia, Florisel de Niqueda, Lidamor de Escocia* [*Scotland*], *Lucidante de Tracia* [*Thrace*], *Palmerín de Inglaterra* [*England*], *Foramante de Colonia* [*Cologne*], *Febo de Troya*, and *Clarisal de Bretanha* [*Brittany*]. An entire geography of the imagination cloaked in heroic legends. Why did nobody write something new, like *Cortés in Tenochtitlán, The Pizarros in Cuzco*, or *Orellana in the Amazon*?

In the *Sergas de Esplandián*, a sequel to *Amadís de Gaula*, Garcia Ordóñez de Montalvo describes the encounter between the knight Esplandián and King Armato which occurred when all the pagan princes were trying to wrest Constantinople from the Christians. Armato's retinue included a tribe of Amazon women whose queen came from the island of California. The queen led her woman warriors and some man-eating griffins. This imaginary island inhabited by the woman warriors was what Cristóbal de

Olid (*c.* 1492–1524) believed he had discovered when he sighted
in the distance what is now Lower California. As a consequence,
the map of the United States and Mexico testifies to that fantastic
spirit, that Spanish madness, which led to discovery.

❡ CANNIBALS, GIANTS, AND PYGMIES

Were the books of chivalry pure imagination? Not at all. Adventure apart, they were the sum of a geography and a history
that navigators, astronomers, naturalists, poets, and philosophers
accepted. Many of the legends were taken from the Greek.
Columbus hoped to find Atlantis; instead he blundered into the
Sargasso Sea, where the seaweed aroused such terror in the crew
that they were on the point of mutiny. Would they ever find winds
to blow their ships back to Spain? Columbus was able to reas-
sure his men, for Theophrastus had written in his *Historia
Plantorum* three centuries before Christ: "Beyond the Pillars of
Hercules, marine algae of extraordinary size may be found, it is
said, broader than the palm of the hand. These algae are carried
by currents from the outer to the inner sea." Columbus reasoned
that if Theophrastus was able to supply this information, it must
mean that the Greeks had reached that sea and turned back. Now,
after eighteen centuries, men had returned to be perplexed once
more by the same conditions.

Columbus was certain that he had reached the Indies. No one
could move him from that belief. The Indies were the continent of
Sinbad the Sailor and Marco Polo: whatever Sinbad had imagined,
Marco Polo had verified, and the trade carried on by the Venetians,
Florentines, and Genovese since his day offered final proof. Prester
John had established his kingdom in those lands. And now the
Portuguese were visiting that legendary twelfth-century kingdom
in ships much like those of Marco Polo.

The Amazon women who figured in the *Adventures of
Esplandián* already had appeared in books by the Greeks. In
mythology, Bellerophon had gone forth to do battle with them on
his air-borne steed, Pegasus; Theseus had had to fight them later
when he invaded Ithaca. And even though Homer sang of actual
events, such myths passed into his epics. Pliny the Elder used
Homer as his authority for several chapters of his natural history.
The name *Amazon*, meaning "one breast" was given to the woman
warriors because they were described as having cut off or cauter-
ized a breast in order to be able to handle their bows more freely.

The Guaranís told the German explorer Schmidt much the same tale.

The fabled wanderings of Ulysses were a prologue to the voyages of Columbus. Ulysses visited the land of the Lotus Eaters, the island of the Cyclops, the island of the winds, and the lands of the huge cannibalistic Laestrygonians, of the sorceress Circe, and of the Sirens. Inevitably the discoverers of the Antilles looked for those isles. Pliny the Elder mentions the pygmies who had been brought to the Indies from Africa; he describes the Astomi, men without mouths who fed themselves by drawing the perfume of the fruits and flowers into their nostrils, and, of course, giants. Federmann saw pygmies on his search for El Dorado, Vespucci the giants of Curaçao. Pliny also describes the Monocoli, one-legged men who shaded themselves from the sun by lying down and raising their single enormous foot over their heads. Pigafetta reports that in the south Magellan found giants with abnormally large feet whom he named Patagonians. Peter Martyr confirms the report. Thus, as the fables of California and Florida marked the extreme northern point of Spanish exploration, that of the Monocoli —Patagonians—marked the extreme south. The America being born could trace many of its names back to a map of Greece.

And to a map of Arabia, too. The tales of the thousand and one nights were nowhere more clearly stamped on the popular mind than in Spain. The adventures of Sinbad the Sailor were told to Sinbad the Landlubber on at least a thousand and one nights. Sinbad found the Island of Paradise in the Orient. Columbus rediscovered it in the Antilles and believed himself both discoverer and rediscoverer.

One legend of Prester John locates his kingdom in the Far East. "Sir John Mandeville," another great spinner of yarns, who is believed to have been born in Liège and christened Jehan de Bourgogne, wrote fictive accounts of travels to the Orient and Near East. He had killed an adversary in a duel, the story goes, and had made a pilgrimage to the Holy Land to do penance for his sin. The many stories he wrote concerning that alleged trip made up a book of chivalry. As the scope of Portuguese travel widened, Henry the Navigator, Cabral, and many others including even Magellan, followed the threads of Prester John's and Mandeville's yarns to the actual countries of camphor and pepper, nutmeg and pearls, alabaster and carpets.

Pizarro believed he had identified a cinnamon tree in the Amazon jungle and concluded he had reached the land of cinnamon.

Columbus and Vespucci both fished for pearls off Cubagua, thinking it the Gulf of Ophir, and perhaps expected to see Mandeville's dogs with human faces or men with dogs' tails.

¶ GERMANS AND SPANIARDS IN SEARCH OF AMAZONS

The warp and weft of the Conquest was the conflict between fantasy and reality. If fantasy ran unbridled, reality, in all its brutality, had the last word. One of the greatest of the early historians was Gonzalo Fernández de Oviedo, a man who had firsthand contact with events in America, and who, in his monumental *Historia Natural y General de las Indias*, set himself the task of presenting an accurate picture of the birth of the Spanish Empire in the New World. Anderson Imbert says:

> He had a taste for literature, so that it seems his first published book, which he translated rather than wrote, was *Claribalde* (1519), a novel of chivalry and adventure. Later, under the influence of Erasmism, perhaps, he was ashamed of such light fiction and condemned in harsh words the novel as a genre. From then on, his life was guided by an imperious ethical feeling, and what was of greatest value to him was the truth of history, not the beauty of fantasy."

Bernal Díaz del Castillo reports that in the thick of one of the battles during the conquest of Mexico, the soldiers saw the Apostle James charge onto the field of battle on a sorrel horse, thereby assuring their victory. "What I saw," the historian says dryly, "was So-and-So astride his sorrel."

Another realist was Hernán Cortés (1485–1547), and his letters, which constitute one of the basic books of the period, reveal his political realism. He took an objective view at all times and managed to avoid any eulogy of himself in his reports to Charles V. His war against Moctezuma was a masterpiece of calculation, coolness, and political good sense. He set aside all scruples to achieve his objective of conquering the Aztec Empire. But he could not altogether step out of the magic circle surrounding him. In the articles he signed with Diego Velázquez, the Governor of Cuba, which placed him in charge of the Conquest, he was warned to be careful, "for they say there are people with great, wide ears, and others who have faces like dogs, and likewise (I found out) where and in what region the Amazon women dwell,

who . . . these Indians say, are not far from there." After reaching
the heart of Mexico, Cortés sent Cristóbal de Olid out to explore.
Olid brought back the legend of California, which Cortés reported
to Charles V:

> [Olid] brought me word of the lords of the province of
> Ciguatán, which, it is often declared, is entirely populated
> by women, without a single man, and that at certain times
> men go there from the mainland with whom they have con-
> gress, and who leave them pregnant, and if female children
> are born, they keep them, but if they are males, they cast them
> out of their company.

The Spaniards in America were not alone in falling under the
spell of fable. The Germans were equally susceptible; indeed it
would be hard to judge which were the more credulous, the
agents of the Welsers of Augsburg (bankers to Charles V), or
the sons of Spain who knew nothing about bourgeois finance.
Nikolaus Federmann (1501–42), born in Ulm, went to Venezuela
as governor soon after Charles V had granted his German banking
house the administration of that region. Always lured on by the
legend of El Dorado, Federmann crossed plains, jungles, and
mountains in his search, and when he wrote the book of his adventures, published in German, he confirmed the story of the
kingdoms of pygmies and Amazon women. Ulrich Schmidt, another German, who took part in the conquest of the lands along
the Plata and Paraguay rivers, traveled to the home of the Xaray
Indians. He reported that the chief

> began to speak to us about the Amazons, and he gave us to
> understand that they possess great wealth. We were very
> glad to learn it, and our commander asked him immediately
> if we could travel that far by water, and at what distance
> they were to be found. The Indian answered that we could
> not reach them by water, but should have to go by land and
> to travel for two months. We decided on the spot to go to
> where they were. . . . These women, the Amazons, have only
> one breast, and the men are with their women only two or
> three times a year. If the woman made pregnant by her hus-
> band gives birth to a man child, he is sent to the father; but
> if it is a girl child she keeps her and cauterizes the right breast
> so that it will not grow any more. The reason is that in this
> wise she will be able to handle arms and bows; for these

women are warriors and they fight continually against their enemies.

If the Italians, Spaniards, and Germans, from Columbus and Cortés to Federmann and Schmidt, were always seeing woman warriors on the horizon in the course of the great Castilian adventure, it is no wonder that the men in the camps of the Pizarros in Peru, the hard and illiterate, daring and credulous, realistic and fantasy-ridden soldiers, saw them, too. Indeed Hernando Pizarro, Francisco's brother, left the encampment to go with Francisco de Orellana and Lope de Aguirre to search for the Amazons, whose base Orellana thought he had found in the green hell of the jungle through which the mightiest river in America flows. Some famous chronicles of that exploration—for example the book by Gaspar de Carvajal (1504–84)—still remain, and the name Amazon will endure.

¶ THE FOUNTAIN OF YOUTH

The legend of a republic of women exercised a universal fascination. Another, concerning a fountain of youth, was no less alluring to the Conquistadors, and it, too, left its mark on the map of the United States. Spain lost Florida's green peninsula, with the most delightful beaches in the New World, through the Treaty of 1821. And in time Florida became a veritable fountain of eternal youth to the Republic of the North. The name Florida is shortened from *La Pascua Florida*, meaning Flowering Easter, the predestined day when the Spaniards rejoiced in the sight of its beaches, and it carries the connotations of the Fountain of Youth that Ponce de León was seeking. Juan Ponce de León (c. 1460–1521) believed that he had understood the Indians to say that the fountain of eternal youth was on the island of Bimini. He obtained an appointment as governor and sailed away to discover a peninsula where, instead of a smiling paradise, he found death. Hernando de Soto (c. 1500–42) and other men inherited his madness and it throve in them. Their conquests were remarkable enough in themselves, but the story of their adventures along the way, as told by the Inca Garcilaso de la Vega (1539–1616) in his book *La Florida del Inca*, makes up one of the most beautiful works ever written in America. The Inca, son of a famous Spanish captain related to the great Spanish writer, and of a princess of the royal Incas of Peru, also wrote *Los Comentarios Reales (Royal Commentaries)* in Spain. This history of the Incas has never been superseded; it is the most important book left us concerning an American dynasty and nation. Not for nothing did its author carry ancient tradition in his blood. In the moments of his greatest poetic inspiration, he interrupted this exhaustive study to compose *La Florida*. He said: "I wrote the chronicle of Florida in a truly florid manner, not in my dry style, but with the flower of Spain."

The Inca was one of the great *mestizos*. In his veins the haughty blood of the Conquistador and the noble blood of the Indians struggled for mastery. His dual aim was to extol the greatness of men like his father, who had left the Peninsula, and to defend the traditions of the indigenous kings who made Cuzco "the Rome of the New World." His song of the heroic feats performed during the military expedition into Florida reads almost like a novel of chivalry. The Inca had been sprinkled at the baptismal font with the Romantic impulse, for the man who held him in his arms, his godfather, was Diego de Silva, the son of Feliciano de Silva, author of *Don Florisel de Niquea*, one of the books that made the blood of the Conquistadors course faster. *La Florida* has withstood the passage of centuries much better than *Don Florisel*, however, and even in its day the Inca was caught on the horns of a dilemma, like Don Quixote, but in the reverse sense. He changed from an enthusiast of the books of chivalry to an opponent appalled by them. As Irving Leonard has noted: "A long time afterward, he admitted to being ashamed of his early fondness, which changed to aversion, as he announced, after reading the scathing denunciation of this literary genre by Pedro Mexía in his learned *Historia Imperial*."

¶ SPANIARDS, GERMANS, AND ENGLISHMEN
SEARCH FOR EL DORADO

The Conquistadors who searched America for El Dorado were seeking something more positive than legend. Their thirst for gold raged unslaked from that October 13, 1493, when Columbus tried to find it in the Bahamas, to the nineteenth century, when from all over the United States the sons of the English colonists hurled themselves into the gold rush to California. The most dramatic and continent-wide episode of the search came during the first half of the sixteenth century in South America.

An incident in the childhood of St. Teresa of Jesus illustrates how legend could set the Spanish mind afire. Her biographer,

Francisco de Ribera, wrote (in a passage quoted by Irving Leonard, but here translated from the original Spanish):

> She gave herself to these books of chivalry, if not of illusions, with great pleasure, and she spent much time on them; and as she had an excellent wit, she so drank in their language and style that within a few months she and her brother, Rodrigo de Cepeda, wrote a book of chivalry, its adventures and tales, and it came out in such a way that a great deal came to be said about it. . . .

The Saint herself tells how she spent many hours of the day and night reading books of chivalry and fought mock battles and abducted ladies beside her brothers on the vacant land around their house. They slew monsters and freed captives as they dreamed of becoming the heroes of such tales. When they grew up, she accomplished in Spain the herculean task of reforming the Carmelite order while her brothers went to America, to the Río de la Plata, to Quito. They tried to wrest from the Conquistadors enough gold to help Teresa complete her reforms. In 1582 Agustín de Ahumada, Teresa's brother in Quito, wrote to the viceroy:

> I stay in this city, treating with the Royal Audiencia, that I may win their favor and help to leave this city with a hundred men or so in order to go and see a certain province which some citizens under this government came upon, which, from what they tell, and the directions they give, is believed beyond a doubt to be El Dorado.

El Dorado was a will-o'-the-wisp that lured both saints and devils. Agustín de Ahumada searched for El Dorado in the hope that he could help the wise woman of Ávila with her plans to release her nuns from the cells where their virtue was withering away and prepare them for their heavenly mansions. The rebel Aguirre looked for it with a satanic pride that led him to turn traitor to his king. El Dorado was on every tongue and its capital in many places from the Río de la Plata to Coro, Venezuela, and Santa Marta on the Colombian beaches. And everywhere, with malice aforethought, the Indians directed the Spaniards to distant provinces where they said gold might be found. The object was to get the white men off their land.

The most famous of the Conquistadors who explored for El Dorado was Don Gonzalo Jiménez de Quesada (1500–79), the

Knight of El Dorado. He had served as a soldier in the wars in Italy and had taken part in all the battles that finally delivered Francis I of France into the hands of Charles V. But Quesada was more a man of letters than a soldier. A graduate in law, he was always known as "the Licentiate." He knew Italian and Spanish poetry. He read all the books written on the Italian wars. He was a graceful, ironic, and patriotic writer, with no ambition for power but great zeal for justice. To him El Dorado had the force of legend rather than the allure of riches. Before Cervantes had thought of writing *Don Quixote*, Quesada was quixotic. He performed the most extraordinary feats of daring. Unlike Cortés, who advanced from the Gulf Coast to the Aztec capital in a few months through territory peopled by great nations, Quesada spent two years fighting his way from the Coast of the Caribbean to the presumptive capital of El Dorado on the crest of the Andes. He crossed the rawest, hottest, and loneliest jungles by forced marches, and his story as reported by his historian, Fray Pedro Aguado (who died after 1589), can stand comparison with the most dramatic passages in certain novels of our own time, such as *The Vortex*, by José Eustacio Rivera (1889–1928). When Quesada and his soldiers reached the summit of the Andes, they found nothing but a high green plateau dotted with lakes, not even a llama. The trees were dwarfed. The Indians dealt in salt, which they mined from the entrails of a mountain. El Dorado's gold was found only in some little lizards and toads and miniature chieftains made of gold which passed from hand to hand. The natives themselves had obtained them by bartering salt. Those amulets, or *tunjos*, were tossed into the sacred lake on days of important ceremonies. The Indians were savages who cherished their gold frogs as coin that pleased the gods of rain and the harvest. Unlike the Aztecs, they had no intention of cutting out their prisoners' hearts with obsidian knives.

Yet Jiménez de Quesada founded the New Kingdom of Granada upon the fugitive image of El Dorado. Before returning to Spain to converse with the Emperor about his conquests, he made Santa Fe de Bogotá the capital. Catching up on his reading at home, he learned that one of the greatest of the Humanists, Paolo Giovio, had written a chronicle filled with lies about the conduct of the Spaniards in the Italian wars. He returned to his own people and upheld the nobility of the Spaniards as compared with the Italian soldiers, baring the facts of the battles mentioned and adding luster to the name of the Emperor and to the courage of

his soldiers. With this book still in the planning stage, he went
back to Santa Fe de Bogotá, where he wrote it. Thus was born
a work unique in the history of the world: the *Anti-Giovio*, a book
rich in style, ridicule, and irony. This mad licentiate meant to destroy the good name of one of the great men of the Italian Renaissance through this work, but it was not published until four
centuries later.

In addition to his *Anti-Giovio*, Jiménez de Quesada wrote a
number of books on history which have been lost, a treatise on
good government for the Indians, and sermons to be read by the
priests on feast days of the Virgin. And, as his quixotic drive
could be extinguished only by death, a few years before yielding
his soul to God, he organized a new expedition to search for El
Dorado, which, he guessed, was located in the wilds of Venezuela.
Defeated by the elements he returned to Santa Fe, but he was not
yet ready to retire, for he headed a war against some savage Indians. By that time, he could not even climb up on a horse. But
he fought. He died old, poor, and sick, leaving the heritage of the
Governance of El Dorado to his niece and his library to the convent. The niece and her husband spent three years in an attempt
to claim that fantastic government, haunting the anterooms where
Miguel de Cervantes Saavedra also waited. Cervantes had come
home from his captivity in Algiers, and was petitioning for a
position in America—in Guatemala or Peru, or in Cartagena,
where Jiménez de Quesada had served as governor.

The fabulous story of Quesada's life may very well have been
the genesis of the great novel by Cervantes. Cervantes himself
said that Don Quixote was a gentleman by the surname of Qui-
jano, or Quijada, or Quesada. The flesh-and-blood Quesada of
America's epic was the last prototype of those gentlemen who had
seemingly stepped out of, and now stepped back into, a Gobelin
tapestry of the Middle Ages, never to return to a world where
they had lived lives of protean adventure. And Don Quixote was
among them, a shadow of a shade. The Colombians believed that
he lay buried in Popayán.

At about that time, Sir Walter Raleigh was languishing in the
Tower of London at the will of his Majesty, James I. Raleigh,
the great Humanist who wrote his *History of the World* in
prison, had read every book and document he could obtain
on the discovery and conquest of the New World. By tactics in
no way mysterious—that is, by boarding the ships en route to
Spain from America—Englishmen learned what was going on in

the colonies from letters and papers they seized. Some letters from the Governor of El Dorado, Don Antonio Berrío, who was married to Quesada's niece, fell into Raleigh's hands. He petitioned the Crown to let him out of the Tower under pledge to conquer that illusory realm of the quixotic founder of Santa Fe de Bogotá. The allure of El Dorado was felt in the Tower of London and the English Court. Raleigh organized his expedition and sailed for the Caribbean with some fellow countrymen as credulous as himself. They reached the mouth of the Orinoco and found nothing but beckoning death. Raleigh's son was drowned in the river and he himself never succeeded in penetrating the jungle that was to inspire William Henry Hudson, centuries later, to write *Green Mansions*. Raleigh went back to London, and the ax of the executioner cut off his head. For the moment, the history of knight errantry seemed to have closed in the capital city of England.

Don Quixote and quixotism fared better in America. Irving A. Leonard has proved that the first editions of the novel, exported in boxes, like crackers, to Lima, Cartagena, and Mexico City, were consumed as avidly there as they were in Spain.

The first part of *Don Quixote* was published in 1605, and in 1607, long before the second part appeared, a masked Knight of the Rueful Countenance frolicked in the carnivals of Lima. Everyone in the city square recognized the figure. In 1621 people dressed as Don Quixote, Sancho Panza, and Dulcinea paraded through the streets of Mexico City, and others representing characters from the novels of chivalry paraded with them. Cervantes himself hoped to go to America, and he had a clear idea of the place where he wanted to go.

VI: *Green Brazil*

¶ VAZ DE CAMINHA AND VESPUCCI INITIATE
BRAZILIAN LITERATURE

Seldom has chance turned out so happily as on the day when first the Pope, and later the monarchs of Castile and Portugal, agreed to divide South America along an imaginary meridian. Experience has shown that the east side, over which the flag of Portgual was to fly, was one thing, and the west side, over which the banner of Castile flew, another and very different thing. Two colonial styles born of the laws of nature evolved in response to the two realities. The immense area of Brazil, extending over almost half of the total territory of South America, held no civilization comparable with that of the Aztecs, the Maya, and the Incas at the time of Columbus. There are no indications that anything at all resembling the life west of the meridian ever had developed there. Throughout the vast expanse of the Amazon and Orinoco river basins, the hunters and fishermen living in villages had not advanced beyond the dart and the dugout, which still survive. They had never used a stone to carve an idol; metal was conspicuous by its absence. These people, who had settled there many centuries before, maintained a magical relationship with their gods of the jungle. They could find no open land where they could group together to build a city or locate a seat of government. Even today, they are scattered through a limitless jungle of gigantic, varied trees. Through it deep rivers roll silently and tangled streams form lagoons better suited to caymans than to men. The descendants of the early Omaguas paddle tens of leagues in their dugouts to meet once a year for ceremonies around a sacred fire, the only fire amid that green of foliage, near that running or stagnant silent water, under the tropical sun that they and the panthers and enormous serpents of the jungle know only as a greenish light filtering through damp leaves. Plants climb the trees in search of full sunlight, forming networks of lianas which the monkeys use as ladders.

The Indians who live on the plateaus of the center and south never have learned the art of navigating the rivers. Solid land was more important to them than currents of water. The Tupi-Guaranís, who extended the realm of their nakedness as far as the hidden Paraguay, were the noble savages, living in close touch with nature, whom Montaigne admired. How far they spread and to what extent they united with the aborigines of western South America remains a problem for anthropologists. Whatever inter-minglings there were took place in times that present-day science never has been able to explore. The nomadic Araucos, or Arawaks, who moved along the coasts, may have reached the Caribbean to form a family unit during the long history of their wanderings. Other migrants from Brazil may have scaled the Peruvian Andes. And, like the Caribs who followed the rivers upstream and climbed to the tops of the mountains, they may have adopted cloth-ing because the cold forced them to. They must also have seen stone idols for the first time: solid, hard idols (harder than the wooden fetishes they had carved in the forest), and there also they saw their first massive constructions.

The oldest reports on Brazil were made by Pedro Vaz de Caminha and Amerigo Vespucci. Pedro Vaz de Caminha accom-panied Álvares de Cabral in 1500, and on May 10 of that year he wrote the first page of Brazil's literature, a page in the Portu-guese language as priceless as the page in Spanish written by Columbus on October 13, 1492. In that same year, 1500, Amerigo Vespucci wrote a letter in Italian to Lorenzo di Pierfrancesco de' Medici from Seville in which he mentioned another region of Brazil: the northern coast which, with the Guianas and Venezuela, he visited on his second voyage. Later, in reports on his third and fourth voyages, from 1503 to 1505–6, Vespucci related his experi-ences as he cruised the coasts stretching from Cape San Agustín to Patagonia, with more ample references to nature and man in

Brazil. The reports by Vaz de Caminha and Vespucci agree and complement each other.

The papers from America and those which reached him from the other hemisphere enabled the King of Portgual to form some idea of the relative value of the discoveries being made by the Portuguese. His ships sailed to both the Orient and the West Indies, a coverage that no other nation could match. Before him, as before no other sovereign, lay a world perspective of the seaways. Everything indicated to him that he must stress his Oriental enterprises, and this he did, but he knew that he must also reserve to himself all rights to future settlement in that America which might be another pathway to the Orient. Vaz de Caminha's letter shows why the King organized the exploratory expeditions with which Vespucci, then a mature man, sailed three years later as an expert who had completed two voyages in the service of the Spanish monarchs. What better man could the Portuguese monarch call upon to verify the first data? Out of that voyage came the first definitive revelation that America was a separate continent.

Vaz de Caminha's letter contains one of the liveliest reports written during that epoch. It describes a very brief experience and his enjoyment of every moment. Each day, from April 25 to the first of May, he set down his account of the Portuguese sojourn in brotherly contact with the aborigines. The Indians met the Europeans with bow and arrow, but as soon as they saw that the white men were not intent on war, they laid down their arms and approached the sailors, coveting the glass beads and red caps for which they gladly traded their dearest possessions. When the Europeans asked them by signs and by pointing to the jewels they were wearing whether there were gold and silver in their land, the Indians pointed to the interior. But they gave no evidence of it, for they were naked. "The innocence of this people, Lord, is such that Adam's could not have been greater." Vaz de Caminha considered the women, naked as they came into the world, better made than those in his own country. The men, slender and strong, wore green stones of a good size in their lower lips, which had been pierced by a large needle. The greatest natural wonder, next to the women, was the parrots. They were mentioned again and again. On the other hand, the letter records:

> We showed them a sheep, but they paid no attention to it. We showed them a hen and they were almost afraid of it; they did not want to touch it. Later they did so, but as though

fearful. We gave them bread to eat and boiled fish, preserves, little cakes, honey, and dried figs. They hardly wanted to taste any of them, and if they did take something into their mouths, they spat it out. We offered them wine in a cup, but they barely touched it with their lips; they did not like it and did not want any more.

He says in another passage that there was neither ox, nor cow, nor goat, nor sheep, nor hen, nor any other animal habituated to living with man. Their only food was yams. As the Indians watched, the carpenters made the cross that they intended to set in the ground in memory of the arrival of the Christians. The Indians followed the work with the closest attention. "I believe they did so to see the steel tools rather than the cross."

Dancing was their great delight. Caminha's picture of a festive evening foreshadows the modern Brazilians' love for dancing.

Beyond the river, many of them were moving about, enjoying themselves and dancing, some of them facing others without joining hands. And they did it well. Then Diego Dias crossed to the other side of the river. He was a royal tax collector, a graceful, pleasure-loving man. Our piper accompanied him on the bagpipe. And he mingled with the dancers, taking them by the hand. They frolicked together and laughed, and followed the music of the pipes very well. After they had danced together, Diego Dias performed many leaps and turns for them, and the royal leap, which astonished them, and they laughed and played a great deal.

Vaz de Caminha's practical conclusion was: "The best fruit that can be gathered there, it seems to me, is the salvation of these people. This is the most important seed, which Your Majesty must sow here . . . as he yearns so much for the increase of our faith."

Vespucci's letters are in the Italian or, more precisely, the Florentine style. If compared with the descriptions by the Spaniards of the cities of Tenochtitlán and Cuzco, his reports read as though written from another world, as indeed they were. In them, he proved that the expedition had not found either China or Japan:

This land is very pleasant, and full of an infinity of trees, very green and very tall, and they never shed their leaves, and all of them have a very soft aromatic odor and yield a great many fruits, many of them good-tasting and healthful to the body, and the fields bear abundant grass and flowers and very soft, good roots, so that at times the sweet scent of the grass and flowers and the taste of those fruits and roots is so wondrous that I could think myself close to paradise on earth. What shall I say about the number of their birds and the variety of their plumage and color and song and their many species, and of their beauty? I do not wish to expatiate on this, for I doubt that I would be believed. Who could count the infinity of the woodland animals, such an abundance of tigers and ounces [panthers] and other felines, not of Spain now, but of the antipodes, so many lynxes, baboons, and monkeys of so many species and many of them so large, and we saw so many other animals that I think so many kinds would be able to enter Noah's Ark only with difficulty, and so many wild boar, and small goats, and deer, and hind, and hares, and rabbits; but we never saw one domestic animal.

Let us turn back to the rational animals. We found the whole land inhabited by completely naked people, men as well as women, with nothing to hide their shame. They are well set up in body, and well proportioned, white in color, with black hair and a scanty beard or none. I strove mightily to learn their way of life and customs, for I ate and slept among them for twenty-seven days, and what I learned about them follows immediately hereafter.

They have no law nor creed and they live in harmony with nature. They know nothing of the immortality of the soul, they have no private property among them, for everything is held in common; they have no boundaries to their kingdoms or provinces; they have no king; they obey nobody; each man is his own master. [They know] neither friendship nor gratitude; indeed those are not necessary to them, for greed holds no sway among them; they live in common in houses made in the manner of very large communal cabins, and their cabins, or rather their houses, may be considered marvelous for people who have no iron nor any other metal whatsoever, for I have seen houses 220 paces long and 30 wide, and cleverly constructed, and one of these houses would hold five or six hundred souls. They sleep in nets woven of cotton, hung in the air, and without any covers; they eat sitting on the ground; their foods are the roots of herbs, very good fruit, an infinity of fish, a great quantity of shellfish, and crustaceans from the sea—oysters, lobster, crabs, and many other things the sea yields. As a rule, whatever flesh they eat is human, as will be told. When they can have other flesh of animals and birds, they eat it, but they hunt little, for they have no dogs, and the countryside is thickly covered with forests, which are full of cruel wild beasts, and for that reason they are not accustomed to entering the woods, except with many other people.

The men customarily pierce their lips, their cheeks, and in the holes they make, they place bones, and stones, and do not think they are small, and most of them have at least three pierced holes, and some seven, and some nine, in which they place stones of green and white alabaster which are half a palm in length and as thick as a Catalonian plum, something that seems beyond the natural; they say they do this to make themselves seem fiercer, but, after all, it is a brutal thing.

These first pages of Brazilian literature reveal the obvious differences between Spanish and Portuguese America. The Incas kept domestic animals such as the llama, and interpretations made by some scholars of the decorations on the Sun Gate in Tiahuanacu indicate that the Aymarás may even have tamed the wildcat. The Mexicans kept fat dogs, which appear as familiar motifs on surviving examples of their marvelous pottery. In Brazil, only birds, mainly parrots, were domesticated for enjoyment.

Throughout the Andean world, agriculture was highly developed in the cultivation of corn, potatoes, and cacao. The Indians knew how to terrace, as the old plantations in Cuzco indicate, and their irrigation system and use of manure were amazing. Farming in Brazil, however, was a mere matter of removing the poison from the yam and making bread with the flour from it. Root vegetables and wild fruits were the staff of life, augmented by the products of hunting and fishing, and in some places by coca.

Vespucci noted that in wartime the men fought naked, without any armor. In the oldest of the Mayan sculptures, the war scenes are like adaptations of those done by the Greeks. The best of them are in the frescoes at Bonampak, a document of those centuries in color. Vespucci wrote, with a Florentine elegance reminiscent of Petrarch:

They are a warlike people, and very cruel among themselves, and all their arms and their blows are, as Petrarch says, *entrusted to the wind*, for they are bows, arrows, darts, and stones, and they are not accustomed to wearing defenses on their bodies, for they go about naked as they were born.

In another letter, he notes: "They live according to nature, and might more properly be called Epicureans than Stoics."

¶ THE PORTUGUESE IN AFRICA, ASIA, AND THE NEW WORLD

A curious parallel can be drawn between the colony that the Portuguese ruled and Portugal itself, owing to the situation of both on the sea, with all the advantages of access to coasts on both sides of the Atlantic. Portugal was a Brazil on a Lilliputian scale, in a sense. The coast of Brazil is the longest and most populous in South America. As a coast, however, it was little more than a promise then, lacking any trade or maritime civilization. The American civilizations in full flower, the populated nations, lay beyond the western slope of the cordillera. Portugal, on the Iberian Peninsula, was a balcony overlooking the sea, whereas Castile was a landlocked kingdom, a feudal country cleaving ever more closely to its traditions and maintaining a style of living in sharp contrast with that of the exuberant Italian cities of the Renaissance. Portugal, a second Venice, built its greatness and based its hopes on the sea. Henry the Navigator developed in his school of navigation the systematic study of geography and navigation which would permit the Portuguese in his time to sail ships of discovery even to China and Japan. A summary of such great exploits demonstrates as in a motion picture sequence what the Portuguese accomplished as compared with the Spaniards. Ten years before the departure of Columbus for the New World, Portugal had founded San Jorge de Mina, the first European colony of modern times in Africa, in order to defend the gold of Guinea. An expert Portuguese seaman, Diego Can, sailed from that outpost, crossed the Gulf of Guinea, entered the Congo River, and discovered the Kingdom of the Congo. Immediately afterward, King John II sent two emissaries to Cairo to learn what they could about the legendary kingdom of Prester John in the Indies. The King hoped to make that realm his base for colonizing Africa and expanding through Asia. In 1488 Bartolomeu Dias rounded Cape Storm, now the Cape of Good Hope, and entered the Indian Ocean. In 1494 the Portuguese monarch and the monarch of Castile entered into negotiations concerning the demarcation line drawn by the Pope to divide whatever lands might be discovered in the western hemisphere. The line was later rectified and moved westward under the Treaty of Tordesillas, which fixed the line of demarcation three hundred and seventy leagues west of Cape Verde (the westernmost point in Africa—now Cape Vert, in Senegal). Thus Brazil, then unknown, was reserved to the crown of Lisbon. Did Lisbon have some secret knowledge of the New World? If not, such foresight smacks of genius. In a determined move not to jeopardize her right to keep a foot on the other side of the Atlantic, Portugal had acted instantly to claim land beyond that agreed upon with the Pope.

But Portuguese discoverers felt a stronger pull toward the Orient, and four years after the Treaty of Tordesillas, Vasco da Gama reached the Malabar coast of India. Pedro Álvares de Cabral, en route to India in 1500, touched the coasts of Brazil as if by inadvertence, as if some error in routing his round trip had taken him across the Atlantic. He was really on his way to Calcutta to set up bases for trade on the seas opened by the Portuguese. Cabral's stay on the coast of Brazil lasted from April 25 to May 2, 1500. The flag of Portugal was planted then on the soil of America, and with this act, Cabral founded a settlement that he called Vera Cruz. On the expedition that carried Amerigo Vespucci three years later, that ceremony was repeated again and again in an ever-quickening tempo. But naturally, the attention of the Portuguese remained fixed on the Orient because they knew that great nations, prosperous cities, and commercially valuable goods awaited them there. In 1505 Francisco Almeida went to India as viceroy. Alfonso de Albuquerque succeeded him, and organized the Portuguese Empire in the East, which was based on three conquests: Ormuz in 1507, Goa in 1510, and Malacca in 1511. Portuguese ships discovered Japan in 1515. (At that time, Cortés was still four years away from his Conquest.) In 1520, Portugal sent an ambassador to Peking.

This sequence of maritime adventures gave the little kingdom the glory of world-shaking discoveries in Africa and Asia, continents already famous for gold, spices, silks, pearls, carpets, and the whole array of fabulous wealth reported in Marco Polo's book *The Million*. Their American adventure would come later. Already the reports of Vaz de Caminha and Vespucci had proclaimed this section of the new continent to be full of cannibals and parrots. Whether Vespucci ever reported directly in writing to the King of Portugal we do not know, but it may be inferred that he gave at least a verbal account to the man who had engaged him.

The first engraving made of an American subject showed the Brazilians practicing cannibalism as Vespucci had described them. What gave Brazil its present name was a kind of wood—the *brasil* or brazilwood, a red dyewood. Names such as those given to Argentina—the Silver Kingdom, because at that time it was entered by the Río de la *Plata* (Silver River), and *Castilla del Oro*, or Golden Castile, as New Granada was called because it was El Dorado's legendary kingdom—ring with a modulation which contrasts with the humble name "Brazil."

Years before the first great wealth from Mexico and Peru had begun to arrive in Spain, the flow of riches from the Orient into the port of Lisbon was so copious that Venice feared to be outstripped by this new center of trade as she saw the privilege she had previously enjoyed slipping through her fingers. The Orient was beginning to be reflected in every aspect of life. The new styles were reminiscent not only of Turkey and Persia, both relatively near, but also of more distant nations. The columns in the Church of Madre de Deus, Lisbon, carved like Indo-Chinese ivories, provided the model for the architectural style called *Manuelino*, after King Manuel I (1495–1521), during whose reign it flourished throughout Portugal.

Calmón notes:

> The spices bought in Alexandria and Beirut by the Venetians carried heavy duties that were paid in the course of the voyage, so that what cost a ducat at its original source, finally came to 60 or 80 ducats. After the arrival of Da Gama's fleet, the possibility that the same product could be sold in Europe for 30 or 40 ducats was realized. Martino Sanuto reports in his Diary that in 1503 the Venetian merchants petitioned the Senate to order a turn-around of the ships en route to pick up their cargo in Egypt, because they did not wish to "order spices bought very dear and sold very cheap, as they would have had to do owing to the great abundance of those commodities found in the market in Lisbon at low prices." In 1503, Vasco da Gama's armada transported 35,000 hundredweight of pepper, cinnamon, ginger, and nutmeg, not to mention precious stones and pearls, to the value of a million

ducats (the expenses of the expedition being no more than
200,000 ducats). In 1504 spices were sold in Lisbon for one
fifth the price in Venice. The profits of the private individuals
who had contributed to the expenses of the armada were almost double the money advanced.

¶ SUGAR AND NEGROES

The Portuguese Empire of the fifteenth century created something original, with no Venetian antecedents: the exploitation of
the land by plantations. The Portuguese were not content to open
the high seas to commerce; they also organized agricultural enterprises based on slavery. The idea that the sugar-cane establishments should pay the expenses of the fleets went back to the days
of Henry the Navigator.

In 1445 the Venetian Cadamosto visited the island of Madeira
and found four towns there—Funchal, Machico, Santa Cruz, and
Câmara au Lobos—and eight hundred settlers, of whom two
hundred owned horses. The island produced 468 hundredweight
of sugar, though one of its principal sources of wealth was its
woods. The Portuguese ships, the caravels, were the best vessels
of their time. This island, settled a hundred years before Brazil,
was an operation in miniature of the plan adopted for the Portuguese colony in Brazil.

The counsels of Prince Henry had worked out so well that in
1499, before Portugal had started to make good its claim to Brazil,
the court was beginning to feel some alarm at the excessive sugar
production, which was threatening to lower the price on the
European market. The island of Madeira alone had sold 60,000
arrobas (150,000 pounds) in one year. Until then, sugar had
been so precious that it was sold in pharmacies, weighed out like
gold dust. No market existed for the products Brazil could offer
its discoverers—manioc, millet, and brazilwood—except for the
dyewood. The mines were opened much later. Indeed, news of
them came two centuries after the discovery of Brazil. A start had
to be made with sugar. In 1516, when the crown first began to
think of colonizing, its first act was to look for a practical man
capable of setting up a sugar mill. Seven years later, a French
pirate, Jacques St. Maurice, hijacked several chests of sugar off
some ships coming either from the Madeiras or from Brazil.

Actual colonization in Brazil started with Duarte Coelho in

1532. This pioneer was a seaman who had gone to India as a very young lad, had acted as an emissary to the King of Siam, had become acquainted with China, had traded in pepper, and had visited the coasts of Africa. After his appointment as one of the original twelve captains whom the Crown chose to penetrate Brazil, his first enterprise was to try to plant canefields and set up sugar mills in Pernambuco, or New Lusitania. He took with him as settlers six hundred Portuguese, many of them jailbirds, many new Christians (converted Jews), and the rest adventurers. And most significantly, he brought Negro slaves, trained to working with sugar cane. The real history of Brazil was about to begin with these words: In the beginning was sugar.

¶ CAPTAINCIES AND PLANTATIONS

As no large indigenous city existed in the interior of Brazil to attract expeditionaries and lure them through the jungles, and as the legends of El Dorado and the White King circulated outside the radius of Portugal's land, no figure emerged like that of the Conquistador who dominated the history of Spanish America, no human type comparable to Cortés, Pizarro, Quesada, or Valdivia. Neither was there any conquest. As in the lands settled by the English in the north, the dominant idea was to establish a colony on the coast and then to push the frontier slowly toward the interior. On that frontier the first heroes of the Brazilian drama appeared: the standard-bearers, the *bandeirantes*.

The king appointed such men to captaincies and granted each of the twelve men so favored a strip of land along the coast. In this way he divided his American territory into more or less equal parts, from the mouth of the Amazon to the vicinity of the Plata. The captains and their heirs kept up a sustained movement inland, pushing back the frontier and hunting Indians, and the spread of the plantations kept pace. The cities were feudal citadels rather than urban settlements; the monasteries were also much like feudal forts. The Monastery of Carmen in Bahia was used as the headquarters of Fradique de Toledo in 1625.

However, there was a vast difference between the frontier as the English in North America understood it and the Portuguese frontier. Not only had the Portuguese settler brought with him the experience of working in tropical climates, not only did he introduce an Afro-Asiatic culture rather than a European one, but he was also much closer to exotic types, for his own blood had been crossed, much to his liking, with that of Moorish women in his own land. He did not scorn Negro women and he coupled joyously with Brazilian women. Nor was he the sort to bother his head about the Jewish question as the more fanatical Spaniards did.

Portugal's population was very small, hardly enough to hold an empire scattered over the four continents of Europe, Africa, Asia, and America. Consequently, from the beginning, the Crown encouraged mating with people of other races and drew up special decrees to further its ends. Women were permitted to play a direct role in the new civilization, and to say women is not to exclude the natives. "The dark woman," Gilberto Freyre says, "has been the one preferred by the Portuguese for love: at least for physical love." The blondes were the "pale virgins," the "fair damsels" whom literature had raised to an almost metaphysical plane. But, after all, the so-called non-discrimination of the Portuguese settlers was nothing more than the result of historical necessity if the Portuguese family was to develop naturally.

The one thing the Crown demanded of those who were emigrating as colonists was that they be Catholic. Englishmen, Italians, Germans could and did join in the colonizing enterprise, but they had to be Catholic. Yet Catholicism, to the Portuguese, was an elastic religion, less harsh and more human than it was in Spain.

In the new society, the African was better able to withstand the work on the plantations and in the sugar mills than the European or the Indian. He introduced his own cuisine, his culture, and his work techniques. All in all, he fed himself more appropriately than the natives and even more substantially than the white man. As Freyre says:

> The indigenous cultures in America, even the least backward of those found by the Portuguese, cultures of which some remnants still exist on a brute level, were inferior to that of most areas of African culture, from which pure Negroes and those of mixed blood were to be imported later for the sugar plantations.

The natural propensity of the Portuguese to unite with the American natives was already evident among some men who had been shipwrecked or marooned in the first expeditions and who had lived with the Indians. They became the first "tongues" able to facilitate the dialogue between the captains' men and the natives. Cabot, Diego Álvares, and Martín Alfonso found Portuguese men at several spots along the coast after they had long been given up for dead. They were safe and sound, however, with wives and children, a good command of the native idiom, and trusted by the Indians. They seemed almost to have been born and reared in that land. Thus shipwrecked men held living professorships in Tupi-Guaraní, the language that the Jesuits later recorded in orderly and methodical grammars.

The political and social world of Brazil, unlike that of Spanish America, had no city or village square to use as a proscenium. Its world was born of the twelve captaincies, and it would develop in the feudal manner on the plantations and in the mills, where the dialogue between the people in the big house—the masters, the lords—and the occupants of the slave quarters began. The tools of the new culture were those brought in almost equal proportions by the Negroes from Africa, who were set to work on sugar cane, and by the whites from Portugal, who established their religion and customs. The king and the laws of Portugal fade in the distance. Then came the Jesuits. The Jesuits played an infinitely more important role in the creation of Brazil than the religious men of any other order, primarily because, in the beginning, the monks could not function effectively as missionaries to a world that kept broadening its frontiers to make room for the spread of the green patches of sugar cane. In the second place, because Portuguese colonization came later than the Spanish, at a time when a considerable effort was being made to give momentum to the colony and when the Jesuits had just been recognized as an order by the Pope. And in the third place, because the King of Portugal made haste to recognize the Jesuits and to lend them his support even before the Pope had given his approval to the Company of Jesus.

The experiment of the captaincies was short-lived. It began in 1532; by 1549 it was considered a flat failure. Some of the captains were eaten by the Indians; others never reached their destination. But as soon as colonization started, the planting of sugar, the work of refining it, the arrival of the Africans, and the mixing of bloods also began. A new life for the colonist opened out. He had to defend himself, for he had little to do with the king and would not suffer his supervision. An enterprising agricultural middle class emerged, its wealth based on slave labor but not dependent on tribute from the Indians as was that of the Spanish *encomenderos*. Little by little Brazil affirmed its nationality, its industry, its independence. Later the colonists would have to defend themselves from attack by pirates and from invasion, for they could not hope that the mother country would come to rid them of marauders.

First the captains, and later the feudally organized colony responded to a singular system of exploitation which kept gaining ground with time, an original system, unique in America. The Brazilian way of life became so deeply rooted that the Philips were never able to modify any part of it during the years when the Spanish monarchy ruled Portugal (1580 to 1641); nor could they introduce there the style they had set for their own American colonies.

¶ A FRENCH KING IN RIO DE JANEIRO

At the time when the captaincies were struggling to get a foothold in Brazil, the King of France was coming to the conclusion that the Pope's decree dividing the land of the New World between Spaniards and Portuguese was without justification. Francis I said: "The same sun shines on me as on the others, and I should like someone to show me the stipulation in Adam's will which says I am excluded from the partition of the world." The King's attitude was echoed by French writers from that time to the days of the Encyclopedists. Indeed the interest that France maintained in the New World was no last-moment whim. The name of America had been taken to heart by the canons of Saint-Dié, and Montaigne conceived the idea of the noble savage, which he developed in the pages of his *Essais*, as he watched the arrival of a group of Guaranís in Rouen.

The King of France issued letters patent to privateers who were more than willing to attack Portuguese ships as they flew his flag, and he showed favor to anyone wanting to settle in Brazil, for he claimed that the land was open to everyone. Nicolas Durand de Villegaignon, Knight of Malta and Vice-Admiral of Brittany, a distinguished man, a valiant soldier, and a good seaman, offered his services. This archetype of the idealist and adventurer became a protégé of the King. He conceived the idea of establishing Plato's Republic in those regions of America which Vespucci had described as an earthly paradise. At about that time, Thomas More's *Utopia* appeared in French translation, and it, too, must have made a deep impression on his mind. Like the bold knight he was, Villegaignon had only recently escorted to France her future queen, Mary, Queen of Scots, in defiance of His

Britannic Majesty's fleet.

King Henry II's son, who later became Francis II, and the latter's wife, Mary Stuart, were pleased when, in 1555, Ville-gaignon recruited his volunteers for the French colony in Brazil from the streets of Paris. He crossed the sea with his fellow adventurers and established himself on the island he named Coligny. There he assumed the title of *Rex Americae*. For nearly twelve years this "King of the Americas" reigned over his island, even obtaining the help of some Swiss Huguenots with whom he had been conducting a theological dialogue that was to be renewed later in France. One of his correspondents was a fol-lower of Calvin named Jean de Léry who wrote an interesting book entitled *L'Histoire d'un Voyage Fait en Terre du Brésil Autrement dit l'Amérique*, which inspired Montaigne.

De Léry's book was not the only one to come out of Ville-gaignon's adventure. A Franciscan monk and cosmographer named André Thevet traveled with the knight and later wrote works entitled *Cosmographie Universelle* and *Les Singularités de la France Antarctique*. In the latter, one finds vivid pictures of that section of Brazil.

The famous King of America observed that his field of action kept shrinking constantly until little by little he became con-vinced of the impossibility of maintaining his kingdom. Finally, in 1567, he surrendered to the governor, Mem de Sá. At least his life was spared and he was permitted to return to his own country.

¶ THE FIRST GOVERNOR

The Villegaignon episode showed the Portuguese how exposed to invasion their coast was. After the French came Englishmen— Fenton, Sir Richard Hawkins, Withrington, and Thomas Caven-dish—and then the Dutch. Portugal's empire in America was in reality only a narrow strip of land with two fronts: one on the Atlantic in danger from corsairs and pirates, the other facing the green background of wilderness, open to adventure and to Indian fighting. The *bandeirantes*, who were pushing the frontier inland in order to open their sugar mills, were men cut out for combat, the stuff of legends, stout men whose deeds cover half of Brazil's history.

To give his colony some substance, the king decided it must have a governor general, and in 1549 he appointed Tomé de

Souza to that position. His fleet carried a crew of three hundred
and twenty, and the passengers who came with him to settle were
six hundred men recruited mainly from the jails. Many new
Christians went along, too, and their presence was to prove of
great importance to Brazil. Six Jesuits, the nucleus of the order's
future missions, were aboard. Five horses and two donkeys.
Citron, orange, fig, and lemon seedlings for green Brazil. The
lemon on a field of green, symbol of her future flag as well as
symbols of order and progress. Then came cows and young bulls,
some pigs, goats, and mares. After 1551 shiploads were sent
of "women of good quality, suitable for marriage." They arrived
in 1552, 1553, and 1557. John III, who had spent his money
freely on his overseas enterprises and had gone through serious
financial difficulties, could do no more.

Farmers, blacksmiths, carpenters, and harness makers began to
arrive with their tools to go to work in Bahia and in the mansions
on the plantations. These were the good things brought by the
Europeans. Hand in hand with the good came the bad, including
diseases such as syphilis, which became a scourge during certain
periods of Brazil's development. Freyre has characterized it by a
play on words—"Civilization equals syphilization."

The governors initiated a more highly co-ordinated and trained
soldiery to defend the only existing source of wealth, the plantations, against the pirates and corsairs, who generally kept hands
off the cities. Only the Dutch tried to take possession of the land
and to found a colony; their efforts led to better results than did
those of the French. The English were content to seize the sugar
that the caravels carried.

Meanwhile the sugar industry was developing steadily, to the
extent that in 1628 Fray Luis de Sousa said there were no fewer
than three hundred and twenty-five sugar mills. Any development, apart from that, was a pipe dream. Calmón sums up as
follows what he labeled the varied production of Brazil:

Nothing is of much account after sugar, and the other
products of the land only began to amount to something
during the following century, except for brazilwood, the red
dyewood with which Brazil's trade had got its start. The
Indians spun some cotton, but only for cord and nets. The
colonists brought the ancient art of weaving cloth, along
with their looms. Tobacco, or *yerba santa*, was used as a
medicine; theologians argued over the question of smoking

it freely. In Spain it was condemned by an ecclesiastical
junta in 1616. The Jesuits found it of use against the rigors
of the climate, and in the end, innocuous. Nobrega reported
in 1550: "All the meals are hard to digest, but God sent
a remedy for this in an herb, whose smoke greatly aids
digestion and other bodily ills."

¶ THE JESUITS COME

The founding of the Company of Jesus was associated intimately with the history of Portugal and her colonies. Diogo
Gouveia, a protégé of King John II, with a doctorate from the
Sorbonne, who later became rector of the University of Paris, was
the first to discover in his friend Ignatius Loyola a vocation for
sainthood. Gouveia, Ignatius Loyola, Francis Xavier, and Simão
Rodrigues, the immediate adviser of St. Ignatius, all were students in the secondary school of St. Barbara in Paris. They pon-
dered the question of becoming missionary priests in the period
of the great discoveries. Gouveia, who had come to Paris to complete his humanistic studies, also served his king in political and
cultural matters, particularly in the school of St. Barbara where
the King supported fifty scholarships for Portuguese students.
He pointed out to King John that the Jesuits, then in their
fledgling phase, would be able to play an important part in the
missions to India. The monarch grasped the idea so firmly that
even before the Pope had approved the order's rules, Loyola's
men were negotiating with the King to found colleges in Portugal
and launch their missionary work. The Ambassador to Rome received orders from the King to recruit the Jesuits on his behalf.
He said: "There can be no part of the world better suited to what
they desire than my conquests." Pope Paul III echoed his words
on approving the Company of Jesus, saying that the Jesuits must
go wherever the pontiff should order them "be it that he command
them to where the Turks are, to the lands of other infidels, or
be it to the parts that are called India, as also to the countries
of heretics and schismatics."

The Jesuits were soon installed in the convent of St. Anthony
in Portugal, their first house in the world, and, with royal
permission they established secondary schools in Coimbra, Evora,
and Lisbon, and then moved on to Brazil. Almost no one of any
other religious order was then in the colonies.

Gilberto Freyre (1900–   ), who has subtly comprehended the

social development of Brazil, concludes that the militant order of
the soldiers of Christ adapted itself readily to the colonial development for unusual reasons: "It seems as if Loyola must have assimilated African origins into his own spiritual exercises."
Elsewhere he writes:

> The very system of the Jesuits—perhaps the most effica-
> cious force that worked toward technical Europeanization
> and intellectual and moral culture among the indigenous
> population—achieved its greatest success during the first
> centuries in Brazil in the mystical, devotional, and festive
> phases of the Catholic creed. In the Christianization of the
> catechumens through music, through singing, through the
> liturgy, the processions, festivals, religious dances, mystery
> plays, and comedies; through the distribution of religious
> medals like the Agnus Dei, which the catechumens hung
> around their necks and from their belts, and the rosaries;
> through the adoration of relics of the True Cross and of the
> heads of the Eleven Thousand Virgins, many of which ele-
> ments, then serving the work of Europeanizing and Chris-
> tianizing the natives, were impregnated with an animistic
> or fetishistic power that was, perhaps, derived from Africa.

If the Jesuits were offered greater opportunities in Brazil than
any other order, and became an essential element in the formation of the country, they still had to undergo tests that brought
about a temporary eclipse of their order. They tried to free the
natives from exploitation by the Portuguese, whom they called
"Mamelukes." The rivalry that sprang up between the Jesuits
and the Mamelukes assumed the proportions of a civil war. The
Jesuits had a center for expansion in São Paulo, their own creation. This expansion took them, like the *bandeirantes*, so deep
into the interior that they reached Paraguay, and they formed
a so-called empire. The Bishop of Tucumán invited them to in-
filtrate the Spanish colonies, and the general of the order, Father
Aquaviva, established the province of Paraguay for his soldiers.
In his turn, the governor of Madrid assigned them an immense
zone that included part of the territory of present-day Uruguay
and Paraguay—except for the lands granted the *encomenderos*—
and lands in the Spanish colony as far north as the borders of São
Paulo. An empire of such size was bound to awaken the jealousy
of the Mamelukes. And for their part, the Jesuits were not nig-
gardly with the verbal ammunition they fired at both Mamelukes

and *encomenderos.* Father Angulo wrote to Archbishop Tomás de Morgrovejo telling him that "there is no slavery nor captivity in Borneo nor in the Turks' galleys that subjugates more" than that enforced by the *encomenderos.* The Mamelukes, who had been hardened by the violent life of the frontier, decided to attack. In 1628, nine hundred white men and three thousand Indians, commanded by Manuel Preto and bearing on their flags the words: "Indians! Gold! Jewels!" hurled themselves against the missions. The catechumens working on the plantations were taken prisoner. The priests abandoned the small villages. The Mamelukes burned some of the mission buildings and profaned the churches. "The Jesuits took desperate measures," Calmón says, "abandoning the hamlets of Encarnación, São Paulo, Arcangeles, and Santo Tomás Apostol and dispersing the people, and they sent Fathers Maceta and Mansilla to São Paulo and Bahia to beg for the release of the prisoners, whose number, as far as anyone knows, amounted to upward of twenty thousand."

Under such circumstances, the defense of the missions called for a military organization. The Jesuits obtained royal authorization to arm the Indians; they trained a Guaraní militia that became famous in history. The Indians, mounted and armed with harquebuses, acquired a skill sufficient to defeat the Mamelukes. By so training them, the Jesuits contributed to the development of a new type of man, the *gaucho,* who looms large in history and fiction, in poetry and the romances of southern Brazil, of Uruguay, Argentina, and Paraguay. "With their harquebuses sloped, drawn up in straight lines, loyal to the priests, they were no longer the poor catechumens of yesterday. They attacked with manly vigor. As they became habituated to riding horseback and wielding the lance, to fighting in swift, death-dealing engagements as they sped across the pampas, the fatalistic Indians, oscillating between obedience to the parish priest and fear of the *bandeirante* vanished to make way for the campaigner of the *coxilhas* [militia], the Guaraní emerging as the *gaucho.*"

Thus by force of circumstance, the holy empire of the Jesuits came to resemble a temporal arm of the Church in America, and as such it incurred the normal consequences of participation in political life. Then, too, other orders arrived late in Brazil. To be sure the Franciscans, Capuchins, Dominicans and Carmelites lacked the lively, even bellicose, organization of the Jesuit missions. By the time the other orders arrived in Bahia, between 1665 and 1693, a century and a half had passed since the first monks had stepped ashore in the Antilles and Mexico. Gilberto Freyre considers the Jesuit system less adapted to local needs than the Franciscan. He supports his thesis by the observations of Gabriel Soares, author of the *Tratado Descriptivo do Brasil en 1578* (*Descriptive Treatise on Brazil in 1578*), a famous book that came out of the sixteen years that Soares spent in the country, where he married and owned a sugar plantation. Freyre says:

> With the wisdom of the practical man, Gabriel Soares introduces the catechumens he met on his first voyage as "clever enough to retain whatever the white men taught them" except for precisely those exercises in memory-training, reasoning, and abstraction that the Jesuit fathers insisted upon teaching in their secondary schools as a matter of principle. . . . Reading, counting, writing, singing by note, and praying in Latin were the very endeavors that the natives showed no taste for learning, and it is easy to imagine the boredom which study in the fathers' schools aroused in them—a boredom scarcely mitigated by lessons in singing and music, by miracle plays and religious functions, and by having to learn one or another of the manual trades. Anchieta bases his judgment of the natives' "lack of skill" on this, and Gabriel Soares himself describes the Tupinambas as "very barbaric" in intelligence. . . . Gabriel Soares found the same Tupinambas "very well disposed toward the Franciscan monks" who owned everything in common. But their aptitude for manual work was matched by their distaste for too much learning. The native of Brazil was the very type of neophyte or catechumen who, judged by the light of catechization, did not fit into the Jesuit ideology. An enthusiast of the Franciscan order could defend this thesis: The ideal missionary for a people communal in their inclinations and rebellious toward intellectual learning, such as the people native to America, would have to be a Franciscan. A Franciscan in theory, at least: that is, an enemy of intellectualism, lyrical in his simplicity, fond of the manual arts and light industry, and almost animistic and totemistic in his relationship with nature and with animal and vegetable life.
>
> According to St. Francis, two great evils afflicted the Christian world of his time: the arrogance of the rich and the arrogance of the erudite. He is reputed to have said

upon learning that a certain Parisian doctor, one of those
refined subtle men, had entered the convent as a brother:
"These doctors, my children, will be the destruction of my
vineyard." The Jesuits did, in fact, become the scholars of
the Church through their keenest intellects, their great men
of science. . . . Certainly their greatest failure was what
happened in America. In Paraguay. In Brazil. It appears
that the orientation of the Franciscans in their missionary
teaching would have been of greater benefit to the Indians
of Brazil.

¶ CONTRABAND COFFEE

Acclimating the products of Africa and Asia in Brazil proved
easier than establishing plants from Europe. Geography was
inimical to the imports from the temperate zone. While Argentina
became rich by blanketing the pampas with European wheat,
Brazil ended up by becoming dependent on coffee, which originated in Arabia. Raising livestock turned out to be difficult: rivers
overflowed their banks and flooded the pastures; solid ground like
that of the pampas was scarce. In the Argentine, flocks of sheep,
herds of colts, and packs of dogs multiplied in wild, prodigal
profusion. Even today, in spite of technological progress, the
Amazon jungle remains defiant.

A century after the discovery of raw rubber, *caucho*, by La
Condamine during the eighteenth century, the rubber forests had
become the green hells of fiction, where the rubber worker toiled
like a galley slave under the hard hand of a diabolical foreman.
Cassava bread was still the colony's loaf, and is today; wheat gave
only a very small portion of the population its daily bread. Someone has said that wheat flour was used only to make the Host for
Catholic worship. The theory of the geopolitics of hunger, based
on a study of the still unconquered earth of Brazil, has been out-
lined in our time by the Brazilian Josué de Castro. The only cereal
found in Brazil was millet.

Europeans had been in Brazil for two centuries before it be-
came known that some coffee plantations had been started in
Surinam (Dutch Guiana) and later in French Guiana. Those
same Dutch who had been expelled from Brazil had moved into
Guiana, where they conceived the brilliant idea of bringing to
America the bean that already was beginning to be popular in

Europe, and that was destined to become one of the great riches of the New World. The Turks had brought coffee to Vienna; from Vienna it traveled to Venice. By the end of the eighteenth century, the coffeehouse was a meeting place, the forum of the politicians, the artists, the people of high society, and the Encyclopedists.

The cultivation of coffee in the Guianas was kept a secret, and great and jealous care was taken to prevent the Brazilians from carrying off any beans. In 1727 Maia da Gama, then governor, sent Sergeant-Major De Melo Palheta from Belém to the authorities of Cayenne on a diplomatic mission concerning the boundaries between Guiana and Brazil. His duty was to carry out his political mission and combine it with espionage. The governor had also instructed him that "if he had occasion to enter an orchard, or garden, or clearing where there is coffee, you will see whether, under the pretext of trying some beans, you cannot hide a few, and with all possible dissimulation and caution, you must send them straightaway." The ambassador accomplished his task so well that he subtracted, not a couple of beans as the governor expected, but a couple of thousand, plus five seedling plants. From his theft another empire, never before imagined, was born: the Brazilian coffee empire, safer and sounder than that of the Jesuit fathers.

Vespucci said in his letter of discovery that he had not seen any gold, that the natives had told him he would find it in the interior, but that he, being a Florentine, doubted it. "I am of the school of Saint Thomas." He had to see in order to believe. But two centuries later, in 1700, the rumor of mines in the interior began to spread. To reach this section of Brazil, the *bandeirantes* first had to break the resistance of the Jesuit state. They did so and pushed ahead. The next hundred years brought a mineral production of sixty-five thousand hundredweight. Brazil's treasure reached Europe almost two centuries after the gold of Peru. The next big strike came in California after another century and a half.

¶ THE COSMIC RACE

When José Vasconcelos visited Brazil, he was inspired to write his book, *La Raza Cósmica* (*The Cosmic Race*), by what he saw there. No other country has fused colors and cultures so lovingly from the beginning, for Brazil was thus advancing along a course set by Portugal herself. The Arabs, whether in Portugal or in Spain, introduced the best agricultural techniques. Out of them, Portugal retained the Arabs' mills and glazed tiles, copied in Brazilian churches from those in Lisbon's churches, and many of the customs and crafts of their everyday living: baths, carpets, and divans; cookery using sugar, cinnamon, spices, egg yolks, almonds, and preserves; cleanliness and poetry. The Jews made a cultural contribution that was equally beneficial: they brought their medicine, science, and the art of managing money. The social position of the Jews was so high that a match between a nobleman and a wealthy Jewish lady was considered ideal. All of these things inundated Brazil, along with the cultural contributions of Africa. The slave, although bound to hard labor, found enough freedom to make his music and perform his dances, thereby preserving his magical religious memories. The Negro women lived in the heart of the family. Their children, fathered by the landowners, were allowed to climb the social ladder. The Negro found his defenders in Brazil sooner than elsewhere in America. The Jesuit priest Antonio Vieira wrote chapters that were forgotten by Father Las Casas when he defended the Indians and asked for African slaves. At the crest of the flood of slaves from Ethiopia, Father Vieira delivered himself of a long sermon in Bahia. Its tone may be judged from these few lines:

> Oh, that inhuman traffic wherein the merchandise is man! Oh, that diabolical trade wherein the traders steal the souls from others and jeopardize their own! Here we behold happiness and misery in one and the same theater. The lords are few and the slaves many; the lords in gala dress, the slaves naked; the lords at their banquets, the slaves perishing of hunger; the lords swimming in gold and silver, the slaves loaded with chains; the masters treating them like brute beasts, the slaves adoring and fearing them as gods; the masters standing erect and quick with the lash, like statues of arrogance and tyranny, the slaves prostrate, with their hands bound behind their backs like the vilest image of servitude.

The Indian turned out to be made of a soft and malleable substance. The famous cannibal of the first accounts was happy to eat yams after all. His physical vigor on the sugar plantations was far surpassed by that of the Africans. But he knew herbs and their medicinal value. Where the Indian was not working in the mines or cultivating cane, he was practicing other crafts, such as weaving hammocks. The Indians taught the vice of the coca leaf, and in the South they introduced the Europeans to *yerba maté*. Their resistance to disease was very low. Measles, never known until the Europeans came, wiped out entire tribes, especially in the Amazon region. In the struggle between the *bandeirantes* and the Jesuits, they lined up now on one side, now on the other in mobile corps. Finally they were able to build their own striking forces of extraordinary strength, but only where the relative purity of their race had been safeguarded in the Guaraní missions. Their cunning aided them and doubled the efficiency of their arms.

During Brazil's early years so little could be realized from the products of the earth that in the sixteenth century a ship from France paid the costs of its voyage with six hundred parrots, worth their weight in gold because they learned, during the trip back, to swear in French.

¶ THE MANSION AND THE SHANTY

In Brazil, the "big house" is something more than the heart of the plantation. It determines a way of life for the family and the economy, a social organization, an exploitation of slavery, and the pre-eminent power of the masters. It is a tight colony, with its own jail and church, its cemeteries and its nurseries for children of all colors. There slavery is deepened and softened. The master becomes hard and he falls in love. With its enormous kitchens and storerooms, workshops and stables, the big house bears a remote resemblance to the old monasteries of Europe. Like the convent, the big house served as hospital, inn, bank, and school. But this was not entirely by coincidence, for the big house is *sui generis*. It has a quality of human intercourse not found in the plantation mansions of Louisiana and the Carolinas. A new and strictly functional architecture characterized it, for everything that came from Europe with the masons and carpenters, the locksmiths and harness-makers, with all the concomitant crafts of building walls, roofing, making doors and locks, cabinet-making, and curing leather, was directly associated with life in the country, where the man and the ox drew closer, like the woman and her chickens, the children and the pigs, the family and the water flowing in the river. This fief was more like a corral than a walled castle, for it smelled of the herds and the sugar cane going through the crusher. The families of whites and Negroes lived separate lives there, but were no more strangers to one another than the families of servants and masters. The master let the African share, to some extent, his free life and his Catholicism, allowed the natural development of the young African children, and was tolerant of fetishism. Gilberto Freyre writes:

> The big house, complemented by the slave quarters, represents an economic, social, and political system for production (the one-crip agriculture of the *latifundio*); labor (slavery), transport (the ox-cart), the *bangüê* [stretcher from which dead slaves were buried], the hammock, and the horse; religion (the family's Catholicism, with the family priest subordinate to the *paterfamilias*, and the cult of the dead); sexual and family life (patriarchial polygamy); physical and household hygiene (the bath, the dip in the river, the hip bath, the sitz bath, and the foot bath); and politics (government by cronies). In addition, it was fortress, bank, cemetery, inn, school, poor house and old people's home, refuge of widows, and orphanage. An admirable example of that absorbing patriarchy of the big house in colonial days was that of the Norwegian engineer in Pernambuco, with his house full of parlors, bedrooms, and corridors, as well as two convent kitchens, a dispensary, and a chapel.

An entire life of work, pleasure, multiplication of the species, and close relationship between the races moved and had its being within this small world, the only one that those who dwelt within it ever knew; far from any king, in a lonely spot where authority is born, grows, but does not die in the hands of the master who is a patriarchial chieftain. Many such houses were equipped to put up a hundred guests. Baths were set up in the bedrooms on large stands, and the Negro women stood by to help a child to bathe by pouring the water over him from a porcelain basin. The same Negro women helped him to eat at the table and put him to bed at night, taught him to walk, and told him hair-raising stories. Dozens of people belonging to the household sat down at table, and a large staff of Negroes was needed to do nothing but serve so many. The kitchen and work areas looked like paintings by Brueghel. Some people kneaded bread, others carried pans to the oven, others ground meal in stone mortars, others brought in lambs for the spit. The storerooms were like the domains of army quartermasters. The chapel adjoined the bedroom of the *paterfamilias*. The priest tailored his sermons to the master's tastes, baptized the children, and conducted the funeral services. A short distance away, at the river, the laundresses kept coming and going with clothes baskets on their heads. A little farther away was the sugar mill, the vats where the sap was boiled, and the storerooms where the great sugar loaves were kept. And everywhere ox-carts went their lumbering way. A thick volume has been written to illustrate what the ox and wagon meant to Brazil during the two centuries of its evolution.

Great estates have flourished in other parts of America, but only in Brazil was the estate a colony in itself. And it was a source of great power for a hierarchy that derived its life from the streams of a feudal world, but from a feudal world that was peculiarly Brazilian in style.

¶ THE THEATER, POETRY, NATURAL HISTORY

If the development of Brazil is compared with that of the Spanish American colonies, Brazil's shows a blank in the field of literature, the Spanish side being filled with the great works of the sixteenth century, the period of the conquest. But later on Brazil developed a genre unknown to Spanish America: a literature of the frontier, of the *bandeirantes*, whose multifarious exploits continued almost to the present day. The literature of the missions was sparse. In Brazil there was not the diversity of orders which graced the Spanish scene. On the contrary, the Jesuits held the predominant place. Nor did Brazil have a variety of civilizations or any great cultures. Among languages, only Tupi-Guaraní became a specialized language, and as such, played a major role in the Jesuit missions.

The Portuguese never concerned themselves with founding universities when the colony was established, unlike the Spaniards, who made a great effort to endow the New World with other Salamancas. True, Bahia had a secondary school that included a seminary where Latin, the arts, theology, and "matters of conscience" (casuistry, in the strict sense) were taught, and where, by 1572, a course in Philosophy and Sciences was offered, including an approximation to the study of physics. Diplomas were awarded "as is the custom in the academies of Europe." And what was true of Bahia was also true of Pernambuco, Rio de Janeiro, Maranhão, Santos, and São Paulo. But what a far cry from the University of Mexico!

The fathers of the Company of Jesus adopted some of the functions developed by the Franciscans, Dominicans, and Augustinians in Mexico. Among these was the theater. At that time the theater was a part of the religious festivals, and in America it was ingeniously adapted to attract and amuse the Indians. From the beginning, music and dances of Indian or African origin were blended into the mysteries of the new religion, resulting in a hybridization, a transculturation that left a deep imprint on the popular development of the country.

Arthur Ramos, who has traced the course of folklore in Brazil, notes that the African element entered the colonial theater. He finds conspicuous examples of it in the mysteries, the dances of shepherds and martyrs' lives used by the Jesuits in their labor of propagating the faith. They altered the pageants of medieval origin to bring into them African and Indian elements. According to Ramos:

> The most characteristic of those church presentations, as far as we know, is a succinct description that appears in the work of Pereira de Melo on the music of Brazil. It has to do with the Mystery play of Jesus in which characters from Christian hagiology and from the heroic history of the Iberian Peninsula, such as St. Lawrence, St. Sebastian or the guardian angel and others such as Nero, Diocletian, and Valerian meet face-to-face with characters from the Amerindian myths and totemic survivals like Savarana, Gaixara and Aimbiré, or Pijori and Cupié the Crow, Urubu, Tuaurana the Sparrow Hawk, and the Big Dog.

The purely African communities instantly accepted the school of the Jesuit theater and learned from it. Pereira da Costa found in his search for ancient documentation particulars of the festival that the Sisterhood of Our Lady of the Rosary put on in Iguaraçu, in the region of Pernambuco. The pageant was a version of the Portuguese monarchy, with the king, the queen, the secretary of state, the general of the armies, ladies-in-waiting, marshals, brigadiers, and colonels. Each head of a parochial district chose its king and queen, who were crowned on the day of Our Lady of the Rosary. Usually the parish priest placed the crowns upon their heads, a ceremony entirely European, done in black. Dances from the Congo and from the Malabar coast followed the coronation.

Those presentations were repeated for centuries and became the hardiest graft of Negro culture onto the colony, the empire, and the republic. The congas were born of it. Even the poetry of our day echoes the magical and musical elements of songs that are a blend of African and Portuguese voices in a fraternal chorus unimaginable in the South of the United States. Deep inside Brazil the thought of a Negro king marrying his daughter to a crown prince of Castile could be entertained without a qualm, as in the following song:

> *Long live our King,*
> *A black of Benguela,*
> *Who married off his princess*
> *To the Infante of Castile.*

The arrival of the Negroes seemed to them the work of some diabolic sorcery that had accomplished a broad jump from Africa to America:

> *I'm the King of the Congo:*
> *I want to make a leap—*
> *I just got here*
> *From Portugal.*

The chorus, in no wise Greek, intoned magic words to accompany such performances:

> *E . . . e . . . Sambangolá!*
> *Sambangolá . . .*
> *I just got here from Portugal.*

The saints in the play could perform the same tricks of levitation. St. Lawrence would fly from Europe to the Brazilian Congo. The festivities started with an invocation to the Virgin, in whose honor dances from Africa were enacted to the beat of drums and cymbals and hands clapping furiously to double the roll of the drums. Bare feet slapped the earth softly in a rustling echo of the beat. They saluted the saint not with the "Ave Maria" but with a Congolese chant. Then St. Lawrence came on stage:

> *Oh, my lord Saint Lawrence*
> *Comes to bring us consolation.*
> *He calls the devout together*
> *To dance in our procession.*
> > *Turu, turu,*
> > *Zipretinho,*
> > *In this kingdom*
> > *of the Conga.*

Father José de Anchieta (1543–97), a native of Tenerife and a member of the Company of Jesus, holds a high place in the literature of his day as an author of church pageants and mystery plays. He wrote with equal fluency in Portuguese, Tupi-Guaraní, Latin, and Castilian. The *auto*, or mystery play, he composed on the *Universal Pregasão* (*Universal Sermon*), first in Portuguese, then in Guaraní, went on for three hours. It was the first dramatic work to be written in Brazil. Anchieta's poem *De Beata Virgini* (*The Blessed Virgin*) comprises 5,786 verses. His *De Gestis Mendi de Sáa* (*The Deeds of Mem de Sá*), dedicated to the governor who earned his glory by expelling the French from Rio de Janeiro, was meant to be Brazil's *Aeneid*. But it would seem that the literary merits of Father Anchieta fell somewhat short of his Christian virtues, and though his works are no longer read, efforts have been made to canonize him, so that his image may some day appear on altars.

Like other Jesuits, he had heard the call to carry on the profession of literature in the Portuguese colony. His writings included poetry, essays, natural history, and linguistic studies; and his letters, written in Latin, are valuable for his descriptions of the flora, fauna, and races of Brazil. He composed biographies of the Jesuits who had most distinguished themselves in Brazil and embodied them in his sermons. Another Jesuit, Father João de Azpilcueta Navarro, distinguished himself like Father Anchieta, in the study of Tupi-Guaraní. He translated excerpts from the Bible into the native tongue and also left some of the famous Jesuit letters, written about the year 1550.

Like Anchieta, Bento Texeira Pinto (1540–after 1618) was a poet. His poem in honor of the governor of Pernambuco, Jorge de Albunquerque, comprising ninety-four stanzas, is believed to be the first written by a son of Brazil, although some modern scholars argue that the honor belongs to a man named Pinto, from Portugal. The truth is that the deeds of the governors so honored were not the matter for great epic poetry. For all their heroic persistence, the *bandeirantes* and their adventure were blurred by the conditions of their struggles with the jungle in the interior of Brazil; they lack the splendor of wars against great empires. Consequently, they did not beget great poetry. On the other hand, natural histories and essays of immense interest could be written on that virginal and unknown Brazil which flaunted a wealth of flora and fauna as rich as they were exotic.

Father Fernão Dardim (*c.* 1540–*c.* 1625) wrote *Do Principio e Origem dos Indios do Brasil* (*The Beginning and Origins of the Indians of Brazil*) and *Do Clima e Terra do Brasil* (*Concerning the Climate and Land of Brazil*), combined and reissued in our day by Afranio Peixoto under the title of *Tratados da Terra e Gente do Brasil* (*Treatises on the Land and the People of Brazil*). These works abound in observation and anecdote; they have contributed to the creation in Europe of the notion that Plato's Republic had been established by the Jesuits in the New World's Garden of Eden. Authentic treatises on sociology and natural history were complemented by the *Jesuit Letters*, considered the first essays in Brazilian literature. Pedro Calmón says: "If the topical or historical matter is taken out of the letters, what is left in these extraordinary documents is an attitude that remains like a constant in Brazilian literature until the nineteenth century: a poetic exaltation of the countryside, a dithyrambic form that carries on the Biblical idea of Paradise." The initiator of this epistolary literature was Father Manuel de Nobrega (1517–70). The letters were read widely through many editions, and even before Nobrega died they had been translated and published in Spanish, Italian, and Latin.

An author whose body of information has never been superseded and who is praised today for his style was Gabriel Soares de Sousa (1540–91). He has already been mentioned in these pages, and his work is one of the main sources upon which Gilberto Freyre has drawn in his studies. The author of a book entitled *Diálogos das grandezas do Brasil* (*Dialogue on the Grandeurs of Brazil*) whose correct name was verified only recently by Capistrano de Abreu and Rodolfo Garcia, was Ambrosio Fernandes Brandão, a man of great knowledge who went to Brazil as a new Christian. Pero de Magalhanes Gandavo, a noted Humanist of the sixteenth century, born in Ghent and a friend of Camões, wrote a eulogistic prologue to his book *Tratado da Terra do Brasil* (*Treatise on the Land of Brazil*) in *terza rima* in 1576.

A great part of the Spanish literature on the discoveries and conquests was written by the king's chroniclers or by historians who never left Spain but gathered their data viva voce from the men who had returned from America, or from reports to the Crown. In Portugal that type of literature was not common, for the Brazilian enterprise was less spectacular and the native civilizations were far from dazzling. The Orient and Africa were overriding considerations owing to Portugal's achievements there. To the poets and other writers in the kingdom, Africa came first because the Portuguese had discovered kingdoms like the Congo, had explored the barbaric coasts, and even had rounded the Cape of Good Hope. Next came the east coast of India, distant China, and fabulous Japan, each rich in gold, spices, pearls, silks, and carpets. Compared with them, Brazil was a wilderness. Alonso Ercilla wrote the great Spanish epic of his time about Chile, because, in a sense, Chile was Spain's greatest exploit. Portugal's most miraculous feat was to sail around Africa and across the Indian Ocean to India. Consequently, Camões chose Vasco da Gama as the hero of Portugal's great epic, *The Lusiads*.

From time to time writers came to Brazil from other nations, and thanks to the generosity of the Crown in opening its doors to Catholics all over the world, foreign writers compensated for the absence of Portuguese chroniclers. One of these, Hans Staden, born in Hamburg, arrived in Lisbon in 1547 and later led a life of adventure in Olinda. His *Viagem ao Brasil*, originally published in German in 1557 under the title *Warhaftige Historie und Beschreibung einer Landtschafft der Wilden*, later was translated into Latin, French, and Portuguese. The engravings that illustrated the early editions of this book reflected life in Brazil as Europeans imagined it, with its Indians engaged in warfare and human sacrifice, maltreating prisoners, or working for the Christians. That was how sixteenth-century Europe imagined Brazil. The picture would soon show a modification made by the Dutch, whose coming gave Brazil a strange experience that the Spanish colonies never knew.

¶ THE ENLIGHTENED RULE OF THE DUTCH

The Dutch stepped onto the stage of Brazil during the period when the kingdoms of Portugal and Castile were both governed by the Philips of Spain. Castile's harsh policy toward Jews and foreigners created situations that had not arisen previously among the more flexible and outgoing Portuguese. Although they were devoutly Catholic, the monarchs of Portugal were more tolerant of Jews and offered their new Christians wider opportunities. In part, Brazil was developed by the new Christians, and sugar circulated freely in the channels of European trade because nuclei of Jews living on the mercantile triangle of Brazil, Amsterdam, and Lisbon had stimulated commerce. A great many of the Jews expelled from Spain had found a refuge in Amsterdam, the great market and emporium of northern Europe.

Meanwhile Philip II was tightening the ring around the Jews and ordering the expulsion of foreigners from Brazil while

Holland, a bitter rival and opponent of Spain, was becoming
more aggressive. The Dutch East India Company had already
been formed and the Dutch West India Company followed, to
the immediate interest and delight of all the bourgeoisie, especially the Jews. Before long, it occurred to the Dutch that instead of making piratical hit-and-run attacks on shipping, they
might do better to plant the Dutch flag in Brazil and found New
Holland. A large fleet was fitted out. A company was organized
in 1621, and by 1623 a fleet of twenty-six ships sailed, half of them
armed. The first assault was made. From that, it was but a step
to landing troops and settlers, dispatching governors, and captur-
ing sugar mills. Bahia fell to the invaders, and a large portion
of the colony came under the Dutch flag, which flew until the
House of Brabant ascended the throne.

The Dutch colony reached its zenith under the rule of Count
Joan Mauritz van Nassau-Siegen (1604–79), a brilliant and
progressive prince descended from William the Silent. He held
degrees from the universities of Basel and Geneva, had been tem-
pered in the wars against the Spaniards in Flanders. He intended
to surround himself in Brazil with a group of scholars, and although he failed to persuade his friend Piet de Groot, the son of
the legal philosopher Hugo Grotius, to join him, he succeeded
with other scholars, painters, and poets. He built a Flemish-style
fortress (which eventually became a convent for Carmelite nuns),
acclimated seven hundred specimens of fruit trees in his botanical
gardens around the palace, and made his court an academy for
painters, naturalists, and physicians. Franz Post, born in Leyden,
one of the best artists, introduced oil painting to Brazil and left
documentary canvases of the greatest importance depicting man
and nature in the colony. Some of his works are in the Louvre.
Sixteen compositions by Albert Eckourt, a Fleming, are hung in
the room named for him in the Copenhagen museum. Eckourt's
portraits of African and Indian types mark him as a forerunner
of the ethnographic artists. Another seventeenth-century man of
many talents, Zachariah Wagener from Dresden, became governor of the Dutch Indies and distinguished himself in feats of
arms. He was also a designer.

Pedro Calmón notes that the artists "attempted to document
their work by reproducing what was characteristic of the country: the people—incuding Indians and colonists, cannibalistic
Tapuyas and Negroes from Guinea—their customs, and the landscape with its fauna and flora. They also painted panoramic views

of São Francisco, La Guayana, Olinda in ruins, the big houses, and the mills which evoke the old patriarchy. Hundreds of cartoons and drawings, canvases, studies, and sketches done by first-class Dutch artists revealed Brazil to Europe as it was captured by Flemish brushes in all its raw, bright color. When the Count offered the paintings of Brazil to Louis XIV he said: 'They show all of Brazil in pictures, and that means the nation and the inhabitants of the country, the quadrupeds, the birds, fish, fruits, and grasses . . . and also the current situation of the country, its cities and fortresses.' " Desportes designed cartoons for French tapestries from some of these canvases. A portrait of America war thus presented through the graphic arts, beginning with a profusely illustrated book by the Dutch poet and historian Caspar van Baerle (1584–1648). They showed all the human types resulting from crossbreeding, the gentle fields covered with sugar cane, the surprising coexistence of the races, war and peace, and certain features of a rural beauty that was growing as the fields of the preceding century were being built into pleasant suburbs, smiling valleys, and cultivated meadows. That picture was an appendix to history; in a sense, it anticipated history.

Scholars came with the artists, among them Willem Piso and Georg Marcgrave, natives of Holland whose studies of the flora and fauna complemented the Portuguese books. They were pioneers in tropical medicine, which eventually would constitute Brazil's greatest modern contribution to world science. Marcgrave was also an astronomer, mathematician, and cartographer. Piso and Marcgrave collaborated on the *Historia Naturalis Brasiliae*, published in Amsterdam in 1648. Piso alone wrote *De Medicina Brasiliensi*.

The great poet of Nassau's period was Elias Herchmans, also a theologian. His poems in the Dutch classic style may be read in anthologies.

¶ THE DARING OF FATHER VIEIRA

The Dutch had been in control for nearly thirty years when Father Antônio Vieira (1608–97) attacked them in 1640 in one of the most audacious sermons that has come down in Christian oratory. At that moment, people had just been imploring divine protection for Portuguese arms by a fortnight of prayers in the church of Our Lady of Succor. Father Vieira, a member of the Company of Jesus whose fame was already world-wide, delivered the invocation that closed the ceremonies. Unlike his predecessors, he called the Lord to account, instead of beseeching aid. "So convinced am I of Thy mercy, O Lord, that even though we are the sinners, Thou must be the penitent." The Jesuit went on to indict the Lord for permitting the heretics to take possession of the lands conquered for the Catholics. If God had tolerated them, His was the blame:

> And so, my God, I have every right to expect that Thou wilt leave this sermon repentant, for Thou art the same as Thou wert, and no less a friend now of Thy name than in times past: *Propter nomen tuum.* [For the sake of Thy name.] Moses said unto Thee: *Ne quaeso dicant:* Hear now, my Lord, what they say. The heretics insolently say now that Thou givest or permittest them to prosper from their deeds; they say now that since their so-called religion is the true one, therefore God aids them and permits them to conquer, and that because ours is wrong and false, Thou showest us Thy disfavor, and we are the conquered. So they say, and that is what they preach, and if they do evil, it must be because someone abets them. Is it possible then, Lord, that Thy permissiveness may be used as an argument against Thine own faith? Is it possible that blasphemies against Thy name may arise from our punishment? That the heretic—the tongue falters before speaking his name— that the heretic may say that God has become a Dutchman? Oh, permit not such a thing, my God, as Thou art who Thou art! I speak not for us, for it matters little that Thou shouldst chastise us; I speak not for Brazil, for it matters little that Thou shouldst destroy it; I speak for Thee and for the honor of Thy most holy name that is openly blasphemed with such impunity. *Propter nomen tuum.* And now that the perfidious Calvinist may base his religious argument on the victory that he has won solely for our sins, and boasts, and blasphemes saying that his is the true one, make him see, by the turn of the wheel of fortune, on which side the truth lies. May the very winds and storms that break up and destroy our armadas defeat and rout theirs; may the illnesses and pestilences that diminish and weaken our armies scale their walls and strew ruin through their quarters.

That was the substance of the prayer by this singular orator who had come to Brazil as a child, had become a Jesuit in Brazil, and would return to Portugal a famous man. He became a counsellor to King John IV (called "The Fortunate"—1605–56, reigned 1640–56), and during the ninety years he lived in full activity, he defied the powerful, confronted the Inquisition, fought for the new Christians, denounced the misery of the Negroes and Indians, rose up in arms against the rich, and left a row of books containing sermons, arrogant yet Christian in tone, which strike the sharpest note in all the Jesuit preaching in Brazil. Yet proud as Father Vieira was, he was humbled by the sensitive Mexican nun Sor Juana Inés de la Cruz, who spoke out on behalf of Christian meekness.

The eventual overthrow of the Dutch lent Father Vieira's sermon the virtue of prophecy, and from the point of view of its national development, Brazil profited from the Dutch defeat. The victory did not belong to the Portuguese, however. The colonists, the Indians, and the Negroes united as Brazilians to win it for themselves. Vieira went to Portugal and obtained from the king a decree that placed the Indians under the same safeguards as the slaves. He intended thus to prevent the landowners from conducting manhunts to round up slaves for labor on their plantations. His speech in Lisbon on the question of Negro slavery has already been quoted in these pages.

Another of Father Vieira's campaigns was fought on behalf of the Jews, for he believed that the new Christians should be assimilated. This priest, whose character was a blend of the practical man, the ardent political man, and the Utopian revolutionary, was the most eloquent spokesman of the period whose fervent voice gave the Portuguese colony a new tone.

VII: *The Spanish Colonies*

Who can say which is stranger and more astonishing—the Conquest, one of the greatest in European history, which brought the Spanish people across the ocean and to the New World within a span of forty years, or the period of colonies, where that same people who had once moved with such momentum marked time for three centuries and never took another forward step? The Spanish troops fought tirelessly to reach their ideal goals in Mexico, Peru, New Granada, Chile, and Paraguay, explored and reconnoitered within a radius of hundreds of leagues around them, discovered rivers, jungles, and mountain ranges—and conquered, only to stay almost motionless thereafter in cities, villages, and *encomiendas*. The Conquistador turned almost overnight into a master who oversaw the labor of his Indians while riding on horseback over the land given him by the lottery luck of the *repartimientos*. He never dreamed of crossing the sea again, nor did his sons and grandsons. The Conquistador presided over a huge family with blurred outlines like concentric circles of color radiating from the white center of the legitimate scion through many variations of the coppery and dark tones of bastardy, marking the successive conquests of body by body in a human expansion that defined the circumference of a small personal empire.

For seven centuries the Christian Spaniard had never relaxed his crusade through the Peninsula, had never deviated from his objective of forcing back the Moors and advancing at lance point from the North to the South as he drove out the invaders. This was the type of man who later took the tremendous leap that established new frontiers on the remote continent stretching to the waters of the Pacific. Then came the pause while he enjoyed his latest acquisitions. The mercantile spirit had never developed in him as it did in the Italians, who spread their commercial nets throughout Asia, Africa, and northern Europe. He lacked the seafaring spirit of his Portuguese brothers. The Spaniard came to America as a conqueror. He was born in a kingdom where the lords of the earth—who were few, and of whom he was not one—had seen that their power was dwindling outside the cities. In America, where he could become a lord, he gave the feudal way of life a new color as he acquired land generously apportioned to him by the Crown. The miracle of the multiplication of his servitors was wrought and his power as an *encomendero* was buttressed. Those moves created the most important, indeed the decisive differences in political culture which separated the English colonies of the North from the Spanish colonies of the South. In the North, middle-class Puritans landed in America as members of egalitarian companies with instructions to settle along the coast far enough from the shore to avoid exposure to attacks by pirates, but not so far inland as to be helpless against Indian raids. Those colonies were meant for trading. They were small nuclei, with no gold mines and no servants, which at first made a living from the fur trade with Europe.

In Spanish America the port was only a doorway to be entered before heading to the heart of the country. When Cortés burned his ships, he symbolized the prevailing attitude, and it was a curious coincidence that the idea of the Spaniards matched those of the Indians in that the Spaniards moved from the coast to the crests of the mountain ranges, just as the Indians had done. The Spaniards intended to build New Castiles where no maritime temptations could reach them. During the longest period of the colonies' development, an inert king, Philip II, occupied the throne. He reigned for forty-two years, from 1556 to 1598, and spent a good part of those years sitting on a monkish rawhide chair. A result of this strange transition from a mad rush across half the world to a long hibernation, Spanish America presented a unique and improbable example, the only instance in history of a vast ter-

ritory living beneath a European flag for three centuries of unbroken peace—except for attacks by the Drakes and Hawkinses,
who could do no more than scratch the skin. Cartagena in the
Caribbean and Veracruz and old Panama City were like castles
built to contain the virgin colonies behind padlocks of stone.

The greatest Conquistadors, Cortés and Pizarro, longed to
crown their lives with the title of marquis, to become lords. Their
ambition for power was rewarded with enormous inland estates
and the thousands of Indians living on them, who were obliged
to pay them tribute. Later their rule was reinforced by the labor
of slaves brought from Africa, as if they had placed a black collar
around their holdings. The fabulous *encomienda* expressed as well
as gold did the wealth and grandeur of the New World. The
encomienda granted Cortés contained a hundred thousand Indians.
The entire territory of the Kingdom of Quito was divided among
Belalcázar's captains at the time of its founding. Pizarro rewarded his men equally well. Jiménez de Quesada issued land
titles to his captains, writing them on deerskin with bixin wood
sap for lack of paper or ink and thus legally dividing the fruits
of New Granada among them into *encomiendas*. As those
surveyors of areas large enough for Pantagruel smoothly and
simply divided up the map, the *repartimiento*, or partition,
came first, followed by the formula of the *encomienda*, which included the territory so partitioned together with all its inhabitants,
who were bound to the *encomendero*. At least one village was
granted to each Conquistador fortunate enough to become an
encomendero. In this way the Crown created many feudal lords
and gave them a human herd of Indians who were obliged to pay
tribute in fruit, livestock, or gold, and, above all, in services and
labor. The Crown laid upon the *encomendero* the duty of making
every Indian a Christian—the salvation of their souls was "com-
mended" to him—and he unfailingly taught them the *Pater Noster*
and the *Ave Maria*. But the daily bread mentioned in his "Our
Father" was eaten by the *encomendero*, and the "Hail Mary" expressed the Indian's astonishment and horror at every outrage
committed by his master. The Indian would exclaim "*Ave María
Purísima*" and cross himself. Some of the *encomiendas* originally
granted only for life were passed on from father to son for several
generations, although most of them were not hereditary. Not an exceptional case was an estate sold in Bolivia, together with a number of Indians living on it, as late as the first half of the twentieth
century.

The great estates in Mexico were outgrowths of the *encomiendas*. When the colony ended, all the land used for grazing was owned by some five thousand big ranchers. In 1789, when O'Higgins decreed the end of the *encomiendas* in Chile, only three large *encomenderos* were left to oppose him; ranchers owned the rest of the land. In Argentina, Viceroy Avilés reported early in the nineteenth century that some ranchers were attempting "to expand their possessions to infinity." Juan Sagasta had already pointed out in 1783 the wisdom of breaking up the estates because some of them covered six, twenty-four, fifty-four, ninety-six, a hundred and fifty, or even two hundred and sixteen square leagues. The land in Quito was divided into twenty-three *encomiendas* in the sixteenth century, Guayaquil into thirteen. In New Granada, a royal cedula of 1601 proclaimed:

> I have been informed that in that Kingdom and the provinces of its regions, there are many hereditaments and estates . . . and that many Indians occupy them and are held prisoners on them without freedom or doctrine, and the owners of them hold them as slaves, and when they sell, barter, or convey the said hereditaments and estates to other persons, they transfer the Indians with them, and they are always kept in servitude.

The Spaniard who did not obtain the grant of an *encomienda* was forced to live in discreet obscurity. He became the village blacksmith, or harnessmaker, or carpenter. Perhaps he painted images or made jewelry. But the people in that middle zone understood and shared more charitably the troubles of the Indians.

Great wealth accumulated in a few hands, including those of the Church. In Mexico, when Miguel Lerdo de Tejada (1812–61) succeeded in winning approval of the land laws, the Church and the religious orders had to relinquish any land of theirs not being used for religious worship, and that meant half of the arable land. The *encomenderos* lived a crude sort of life even though they were rich. Their background had never taught them how to cope with luxury and splendor. On the other hand, the Church delighted in building great temples of stone, housing altars that looked like gold foam.

To preserve the luster of El Dorado, the goal of the Conquest, Negroes were imported to work the mines and the *mita* was adopted. The *mita* was a system of labor gangs which the mine owners utilized to demand that the Indians work underground a certain number of months. The period of service in the mines

VII: *The Spanish Colonies*

was obligatory: the Indian could not escape it. He was torn from his family and taken to distant, unhealthful regions where his period of backbreaking labor might cost him his life. In 1575, Viceroy Toledo assigned ninety-five thousand men in labor gangs to the mines of Potosí. One of several eloquent testimonials to the *mita* as a source of abuses has come down to us through the *Memorias Secretas* (*Secret Memoirs*) of two engineers, Don Jorge Juan and Don Antonio Ulloa, who visited Potosí as envoys of the king late in the eighteenth century. All the facts they report in their famous book were results of firsthand observation.

Under this medieval system and its concept of life, the miserable Indians alternately received the protection advocated by some Christian souls and were exploited as slaves by Spaniards who had profited from the Conquest. This capricious treatment left scars that are still visible in many parts of America. In Peru today, the powerful oligarchy that became the heir of the Crown lives apart from the poor Indian masses, who can only dream of St. Martin of Porres, the patron saint of the humble.

While these practices were in operation in the Spanish colonies for three centuries, the middle-class North American colonists were prospering and gaining a mercantile experience that enabled them to lay the foundations for a highly developed industrial structure, the United States. And a movement toward rebellion was gaining momentum in the Spanish colonies. This was not a Renaissance movement, but something much older, a rebellion against injustice, against inhuman exploitation, which was deeply rooted in Christianity. Monks who thought like Bartolomé de Las Casas headed it. They won laws that protected the Indians—and infuriated the *encomenderos*—while at the same time they initiated theological debates that enlisted other humanitarian monks to do battle with the crude opportunists who were bent upon making history by way of a materialistic interpretation. The high point of those debates was reached in the lesson taught by Father Francisco de Vitoria, which became one basis of modern international law.

All in all, unjust as it was, the colonial system bore good fruit. Gold was discovered. The wealth of America became legendary and the mines were the nest from which the gold fledglings escaped to Europe, leaving those less fortunate to stay at home in the New World and chew on their ironical thoughts. Fray Antonio de la Calancha (1584–1654), a Peruvian monk, wrote in his *Crónica Moralizadora del Orden de San Agustín en el Peru* (*Moral Chronicle of the Order of St. Augustine in Peru*):

In order to realize how much Spain owes to these Indies, you must compare the greatness it has today with the poverty it used to have, the regal pomp it flaunts with the miseries it used to endure. In chapter ten of the fourth part of the *History of Spain* written by King Alfonso the Wise, he says: "King Alfonso IX of Leon made war on his son Fernando the Saint, and the son, seeing the great harm done, sent to know of his father what was the cause of such a bloody war in order that the latter might inform him and recommend what he should do about it, and his father replied in writing that he was making war because his son had not paid him ten thousand maravedis that he owed to him: whereupon he paid it and the war ceased." The amount was thirty-six pesos and six reales and four maravedis. A father against his son and a Catholic kingdom against its neighbor tried to kill each other for thirty-six pesos and six reales, which a porter would spend today in providing a repast.

¶ THE FOUR VICEROYALTIES

The areas of colonial administration were set up according to the divisions among the indigenous empires and nations. In the beginning there were only two viceroyalties, corresponding to the two great empires: the Aztec and the Inca. The site in Mexico where the Aztecs had located their capital became the new capital. The Catholic Monarchs had thought in advance of appointing viceroys over the imaginary lands that Columbus would discover and had granted him the titles of admiral, viceroy, and governor of all the lands and seas he might claim for Spain. When Columbus died, his son Diego became viceroy of Santo Domingo. But those arrangements were all ephemeral, almost fictive. The viceroyalty as an institution with teeth came with the conquest of Mexico and Peru.

Spain followed a recent precedent in establishing viceroyalties in the ancient kingdoms, whether conquered or acquired. In 1503, thirty years before the Mexican overseas government was established, Gonzalo de Córdoba expelled the French from Naples, and through the "logical necessity of things" as Benedetto Croce says, the ancient kingdom of Naples, threatened by the Turks, became a viceroyalty under the protective mantle of Spain. The song that begins: *"Son quel Regno Sfortunato . . ."* ("I am that unfortunate realm . . .) dates back to then. At the beginning of the fifteenth century, Sicily and Sardinia were ruled by Aragonese viceroyalties.

The first viceroy of Mexico was Antonio de Mendoza, appointed in 1535; the first in Peru, Francisco de Toledo, appointed in 1569. Nearly two centuries went by before the Spanish government decided to establish two additional viceroyalties. The first of these was New Granada, created in 1717, with Santa Fe de Bogotá as its capital. It was abolished in 1724, then re-established in 1740, after which it lasted only seventy years. The last was the viceroyalty of the Plata, established in 1776, with Buenos Aires as its capital. It lasted thirty-four years.

The viceroyalty of New Granada embraced what had been the kingdom of the Chibchas and extended almost as far as the legendary realm of El Dorado, including Ecuador to the south and Venezuela to the north as far as La Guayana. The viceroyalty of the Plata covered present-day Bolivia, Paraguay, and Uruguay and included the region of the legendary White King, or King of the Plata. Thus the viceroyalties symbolized gold and silver respectively; they were the late-born children of the two myths that lured the Spaniards to bring about the conquest of the South.

Wherever the viceroyalties had no jurisdiction, the *audiencia*, or high court, ruled; within the viceroyalties themselves, *audiencias* operated as supreme courts of justice. But outside the boundaries of the existing viceroyalties, *audiencias* performed governmental functions in Santo Domingo (starting in 1511), New Galicia, now the state of Guadalajara (1548), Santa Fe de Bogotá (1549), Charcas (1559), Quito (1563), Santiago de Chile (1609), Buenos Aires (1661), Caracas (1786), and Cuzco (1787).

By the end of the eighteenth century, the four viceroyalties and the missions theoretically took care of the entire colonial empire—that is, everything that the Conquistadors had won, or the explorers claimed, or the missionary orders of monks had proselytized. Only Brazil, desert Patagonia, Canada, and the small part of what is now the United States which included the thirteen original colonies lay outside the map of Spain in mainland America. In the Antilles, Cuba and Santo Domingo were Spanish, but a few of the other islands were held by the French, English, Danes, and Dutch, who had established themselves sporadically or permanently. Those islands were the stamping ground of filibusters, corsairs, and buccaneers; although they had a scattering of regular settlers who were not Spanish.

Owing to the immense difficulty of communication, the viceroys turned over portions of their vast domains to the administration of presidents, or governors, or captains general. As a consequence, the presidencies of Guadalajara and Cuzco, and the governancies or captaincies of Quito, Caracas, and Chile came into being.

Distance was always master. The Crown created ways of controlling the men in charge of government, but with dubious success. The trail-blazers—the men who arrived in America *before* the Conquest—like the "forerunners" in Spain of the period of the Reconquest from the Moors, were check-reined, in theory, by the governors. But Cortés, who was answerable to the governor of Cuba, and Jiménez de Quesada in New Granada, who was answerable to the governor of Santa Marta, rebelled and became uncontrollable when they were separated from their governors by the sea or the jungle. As rebels, they rendered their accounts directly to the king. They laid their conquests at the feet of the monarch in token of their submission and fealty to him, and to him alone. Like the viceroys themselves, the governors were under the control of the royal *audiencias*, but as often as not the justices were mere licentiates, corruptible and dilatory; indeed they were often the butt of ridicule as they brandished their ordinances, for heroic deeds overrode the law. Lazy settlers also could control and intimidate the viceroys through the law of residence, which they used to register endless statements with the scribes in the hope of seeing buried beneath mountains of paper a viceroy who had failed to win them over.

Within this minute clockwork that gradually wore out in the New World, there were some progressive viceroys and governors who accomplished all the positive good discussed in later chapters of this book; there were also incompetents, or simply vain men, and there were arbitrary and petulant men. The colony reflected administrative incapacity wherever it existed. Spain never succeeded in constructing a strong and dominant state out of her empire. If inefficiency reigned where the king was present, what could correct it in the gigantic American empire, where the king was an almost illusory shadow?

¶ THE CITIES

The Spaniards founded many cities in a very few years. Among the first of these were Santo Domingo (1494); San Juan, Puerto Rico (1508); Santiago, Cuba (1514); Havana (1515); Veracruz (1519); Panama City (1519); Antigua, Guatemala (1524); León, Nicaragua (1524); San Salvador (1525); Santa Marta (1525); Coro (1527); Maracaibo (1529, later abandoned, rebuilt in 1571); Puebla de los Angeles (1531); Cartagena de Indias (1533); Guadalajara (1533); Quito (1534); Lima (1535); Quayaquil (1535); Buenos Aires (1536, abandoned, refounded in 1580); Popayán (1536); Cali (1536); Asunción, Paraguay (1537); Santa Fe de Bogotá (1538); Caracas (1536, soon abandoned, refounded in 1567); Saint Augustine, Florida (1565). A single Conquistador like Belalcázar might establish several settlements: he founded Guayaquil, Quito, Popayán, and Cali and helped to found Bogotá. Cuzco, the oldest city in Peru was superposed on the Incan capital. Mexico City merely changed its name and master.

Mexico City was the richest, largest, and most beautiful metropolis on the continent until early in the nineteenth century. The novelist Fernández de Lizardi (1817–77) wrote of it: "I was born in Mexico City, the capital of southern America." And it was still known as the real capital of southern America when the English colonies gained their independence to create the United States. In 1803, Humboldt gave it a population of 183,000 inhabitants. At that time New York had 80,000; Philadelphia 42,000. Boston grew from 18,320 in 1790 to 61,392 by 1830, and Washington from 14,093 in 1800 to 51,687 in 1850. Humboldt said that no other city had academies, schools of higher learning, or artistic riches like those of Mexico City. The Plaza Mayor is still one of the largest and most beautiful squares in the world, and the cathedral, which was built on the site of the great Aztec temple, the *teocalli*, ranks among the first of the Catholic faith. The governor's palace, once occupied by the viceroys, on the other side of the square, was built where Moctezuma had his own dwelling. The College for Indians, founded by Peter of Ghent, had chairs in religion, Latin, music, painting, sculpture, and divine service. The University dates back to 1553, and Francisco Cervantes de Salazar (born before 1515, died after 1575) the Humanist who wrote Latin dialogues in the manner of Vives, was a professor there at its opening. In addition to his *Crónica de la Nueva España* [*Chronicle of New Spain*], he left a description of the city, its environs, and life at the university which endows his dialogues with major historical interest. Even before the university was founded, there was a printing press in Mexico City; it was introduced in 1535. Some books bearing its colophon and dated 1539 are known.

These dates stand out in contrast with 1638, the year when the first printing press arrived in the English colonies of North America. All these facts explain why Mexico City was called the Athens of the New World by the end of the sixteenth century.

As the city grew, the lakes were drained to allow more room. But in the eighteenth century canals still gave certain parts of it a Venetian touch. If the descriptions of Tenochtitlán, the Aztec city of the sixteenth century, as it appeared to Cortés and Díaz del Castillo are matched with pictures of the Spanish city of the eighteenth century, two great metropolises are seen, each as rich in color and movement as the other.

The markets of Moctezuma's time were opulent bazaars stocked by the industrious and hard-working Indians who crossed the lake in canoes, then paddled along the canals. During the vice-royalty, the products of the New World were traded at fairs and the display of merchandise was doubled by imports from Castile. Tomatoes, tortillas, red beans, and cacao were piled beside wheat, rice, and oranges. Venison and fat puppies were no longer the only meats, for beef, lamb, and pork had been added. The fabrics made by the Indians were still being sold, but there was woolen cloth from Córdoba, too. Newly opened stalls selling sheet tin reflected faces peering at themselves. Glass and tile decorated the store fronts. Gone were the princes and courtiers who, with their feathered head-dresses, seemed to place the court of Moctezuma under the wing of a *tzenzontle*, the sacred bird. Their bright plumage was replaced by the habits of monks and nuns, the gowns of canons and justices, the laces, velvets, and breastplates of soldiers, the gala dress of captains, so that all the colors in the *zócalo*, as the main square was commonly called, had not perished. How had the Plaza Mayor of Mexico City come to be known as the *zócalo?* Because for many years the monument to Charles V did not advance beyond the socle, or "*zócalo.*" This statue, now on the Paseo de la Reforma, came to be known as "the little horse" when the republic was created. Times changed—from the native city to the Spanish, from the Spanish capital to the Republican—but the brilliance of the metropolis never diminished. The little horse has been kept because it was a fine bronze statue, but no one ever mentions that the horseman is Charles. The king and all he signified died in the hearts of the people, but the "little horse" lived on.

At about the middle of the seventeenth century there was one city in America more populous than Mexico City, busier and wealthier than any other in the hemisphere. That was Potosí, now in Bolivia. At that time its population numbered 160,000. It was also one of the highest cities in the world, at an elevation of 13,000 feet above sea level. Potosí, built at the foot of a hill that contained the richest silver mine recorded in history, was planned and settled by Spaniards. Sixty million pounds of gold and silver, worth four hundred million dollars in the money of our time, were extracted from the hill in fifty years. The silver was for export. Local industry smelted it, and it was used to make silver dinner services, altars, picture frames, saddle mountings, even chamber pots. The Spaniards had come to Potosí in answer to the alluring legend of the White King, ruler over the realm of the white metal. Hence the name of the Río de la Plata (Silver River) and Argentina, the Silvery Republic. At the peak of the mine's production, churches, convents, and palaces were built which made Potosí, now a ghost city, one of the most beautiful sights in Spanish America. When the richest and most accessible lodes had been worked out, Potosí was almost abandoned: by 1950 its population was less than a fifth of what it had been in 1650.

The queen of the South American colonial capitals was Lima. Pizarro selected for his capital a site near the sea on which, to judge by some extensive ruins, a town of some size may once have stood, instead of building upon Cuzco, the seat of the Incan Empire high up in the mountains, in the manner of Cortés in Mexico. Arturo Jiménez Borja says:

It is probable that amid the verdure of the valley the Spaniards may have glimpsed the shining masses of native palaces and temples painted in brilliant yellows and reds, along with cultivated fields of corn, manioc, yucca, or potatoes, with the Limans of that day going and coming along the roads or bent over their labor in the fields.

Whatever they may have seen or fancied they saw was an optical illusion, for the buildings lay in ruins. Jiménez Borja recalls the words of a man of the time, Miguel de Estete: "It must have been very ancient, for there are many fallen buildings, and the town must have been walled, although at present most of the enclosures have collapsed." Alfonso Reyes reminds us that Mexico City was born "in the most transparent region of the air," but Lima lives beneath a cloudy sky, where rain never falls, where the *garúa* prevails, a stubborn drizzle that dampens clothing but never forms a driving rain against which the Liman could defend himself with an umbrella. Drizzle and earthquakes have been the city's devices, as it were. On that land, which time had rubbed to a blank sheet, and upon actual paper, the Conquistador traced the map of the city as a chessboard pattern, dividing it into a hundred and seventeen "islands" or blocks. Each block contained some 16,000 square yards and was subdivided into four lots. A great plaza was set aside for the cathedral and Pizarro's palace. A major portion of the wealth from Peru and of the silver from Potosí poured into Lima. Earlier, the Pizarros had seized Atahualpa's treasure in Cajamarca. Lima built with it a society composed of noblemen, a swarm of monks, and a clutter of poor Indians. By the first half of the seventeenth century, Lima had 26,441 inhabitants, of whom a tenth belonged to religious orders. Juan María Gutiérrez says that Lima was an "immense monastery of both sexes." Jorge Basadre remarks: "In time Lima held the excessive number of twenty-two convents, fourteen monasteries, and four nunneries. According to the census figures quoted in the memorandum of Viceroy Avilés, 1,135 of the 3,941 houses in the capital were the property of convent communities or were institutions for pious works." On the other hand, there were more than two hundred large coaches "trimmed with gold and silk, and of great beauty" in the city in 1619. After the processions, fervent prayers were said, asking for silks, laces, diamonds, and a thousand luxuries before mentioning food. The first university in Lima was flanked by two preparatory schools for it, the Real y Mayor de San Felipe, and the San Martín.

The following description by the engineer Amédée François Frézier, who visited Lima in 1713, if correct, justifies evaluating Lima as "worth a Peru":

Since in the cities of Europe carriages are counted as the index of their magnificence, Lima can number some four thousand calèches, the common carriages of the country drawn by two mules; but to give some idea of the opulence of this city, suffice it to report the exhibition of wealth put on by the business men of Lima about 1682 to greet the Duke of Peralta's arrival to assume control of the city: they paved the expanse of two streets—Mercedes and Mercaderes, through which the Duke must enter the Royal Plaza, where the palace stands—with ingots of silver called *quintados*, each of which usually weighs about two hundred *marcos*

[1 *marco*=8 oz.], twelve to fifteen inches long, four to five inches wide, and two to three inches deep, all of which would add up to a sum of eight hundred million *escudos*, or about three hundred twenty million pounds in our money at its present value. Lima is truly the depository of the treasures of Peru, in a manner of speaking. . . . The men and women are alike in their taste for magnificence in dress: the women, not content with the richness of the most beautiful fabrics, trim them in their fashion with a prodigious quantity of lace, and they are insatiable for pearls and precious stones, bracelets, earrings, and other adornments, the crafting of which absorbs them greatly and ruins their gallant husbands. We have seen ladies wearing seventy thousand *piastres* worth of jewels on their persons, that is to say, jewels worth more than two hundred forty thousand pounds.

The sumptuary grandeur of the Spanish cities in America explains in part their incapacity to match the momentum of the cities in the United States, which surpassed them in a few years of progress during the Industrial Revolution. The manner of America's discovery and Spain's colonial exploitation of it delayed the birth of a middle-class spirit, and by the time the mother country made an effort to slough off the stasis of three centuries under despotic monarchs, it was too late. Extant descriptions of the cities of Mexico, Potosí, and Lima convey something of the medieval tone that stifled the culture of colonial Spanish America and kept it out of the stream of progress. The English colonies, with their small cities, conserved their energies and grew into modern life in a way that the great Spanish metropolises in America which came into the nineteenth century virginal, without one real school of commerce and industry, never knew.

❡ THE PLAZA AS A SCHOOL FOR RICH AND POOR

The cities, towns, and villages founded by the Spaniards followed a civic organization and pattern quite unlike those of their older counterparts in Spain. The Spanish streets and alleys twisted and turned and crisscrossed like tree branches as they grew slowly through the centuries. They had not been built to follow an original plan; indeed, no geometric plan had ever been drawn. In America, however, the vacant expanses of naked earth were divided into rectangles and the streets laid out in straight lines.

In the center was the rectangular plaza, perhaps the most perdurable feature that Spain brought to America, perhaps more important to everyone than the Spanish language itself. In the United States, where rapid growth became a stampede, where there was no time for anything but joining the rush westward, the main artery was a "Broadway" or a "Main Street," a freeway. In Spanish America the colony sat down. The plaza was the setting for the fairs, the center of life and leisure, the stage for religious and civil functions. In the shade of the trees on the plaza petty plots were woven, politics was conducted, justice and injustice were done, and people dreamed. The fruits of the earth were sold and butchers spread their awnings. Bullfights were held, bonfires were lighted on the Eve of St. John, and fireworks hailed the New Year. The processions of Holy Week and Corpus Christi filed through the plaza, and the town crier announced proclamations, the levying of tariffs and fines, war with the English, the death of the king, and the birth of a prince—this after such news was read from the balcony of the town hall: the broadcasting system that gave reports from overseas, both bad and good, directly to the people. If a prince was born, the town rejoiced in a fiesta with fireworks. Old friends met in the square; families gathered there. The poor people got drunk after the market closed. Independence was declared at an open meeting in front of the town hall. Later, the men of the republic spoke from the same balconies, when they incited the populace to civil war. If the United States had built plazas like those in Spanish America, it might have produced more politicians, men more unstable, more anarchical, less bourgeois. Spain built plazas instead of providing schools for the people. And the people acquired whatever education they got in the plaza, and found a wide theater for their culture there.

The main square of the capital was the colony's stage for the display of extravagant luxury. When the great personages of the day—the viceroys, justices, marquises, archbishops, bishops, nuns, friars, captains, soldiers, scribes, and men of the guilds came and went in a kaleidoscope of colors, they composed a varicolored scene of the Middle Ages. The colors in the square changed after the revolution, but the plaza took on new life. In some cases, it was renamed for a revolutionary or for the revolution itself: the *plaza mayor* of Bogotá became Bolívar Square; the one in Buenos Aires became the Plaza de Mayo, for May was the month of the revolution.

¶ THE CHURCH AND THE TOWN HALL, FACE TO FACE

The two buildings on the colonial plaza directly opposite each other—the church and the town hall—were the principal symbols present there. Which of the two powers had the greater influence? Which was the stronger? After Spain was united by the Catholic monarchs, the centralization of the monarchy's power and the strengthening of the hierarchy of the Church spelled great changes in the political philosophy and governmental practice of the late fifteenth century, the time when the colonial empire began.

The fall of Granada came soon after the kingdoms of Castile and Aragon were joined by the marriage of Isabel of Castile to Ferdinand of Aragon. For the first time in the history of the Peninsula, a royal couple was able to extend its rule over all of Spain, with such success that Macchiavelli, then searching for such national solutions, chose Ferdinand the Catholic as his model for *The Prince*. After Isabel's death, Ferdinand became the first monarch to assume sole command of the country. Castile next became the center of the empire of Charles V, and a great national army overran the earth of Flanders, put the Pope to flight, and captured the King of France at Pavia. Once the Jews were expelled and the Moors driven out, the monarchs were granted the right to increase their powers and privileges by dispensing benefices, which meant that the Pope handed the Crown the freedom to choose the bishops. The sum of all this was a concentration of authority in Spain so formidable that it reduced to a whisper the former power of the feudal lords. In America all power was centralized, for each official functioned as a direct representative of the king. Government was by royal cedula. Viceroys and governors alike officiated in the name of the king, but that no one might imagine that authority had been delegated blindly, a judicature in residence was established. Even Columbus, Admiral of the Ocean Sea and Viceroy of the Indies though he was, felt this control so stringently that he was sent back to Spain in irons by the judge then presiding in Santo Domingo.

Essentially, however, the Spaniards in America had brought with them certain libertarian impulses, and though they always paid their king the reverence due him, they formed their own town corporations, which sometimes ignored the authority of the governors and elected their own captains. Solitude and distance favored such measures, indeed made them necessary.

Balboa took the bold step of appointing himself leader of his people in Urabá. Cortés followed his example in Veracruz, as did Quesada when leaving Santa Marta. Irala and his *comuneros* in Asunción, Paraguay, dared to put Governor Cabeza de Vaca on a ship and send him back to Spain. Aguirre went even farther in the Amazon: he rebelled against his command and declared himself "traitor to the king." Such acts established a historical precedent for the habit of rebellion which still persists in Spanish America. But once the colonies were firmly established, the town governments dozed. In the end, positions in the town corporation were put up for sale and the independent spirit of the civic life cells lay dormant not to awaken again in open town meetings until three centuries had passed.

The Laws of the Indies were promulgated as an instrument to protect the aborigines. By their enactment, the king draped a mantle of charity over his image, but the environment still ruled all things, as though the jungle could swallow up even the law. During the war of the *comuneros*, a group that lived communally and upheld the liberty of Spaniards against the encroachments of Charles V, people commented on the irony of remote rule in the words of a ballad: "But the king is very far away." The Americans expressed their gratitude to the paternal but impotent figure of their monarch with the shouted words: "Long live the king, and death to bad government."

The town hall on the plaza, with the jail in its basement, symbolized the colony's ambivalence.

¶ A CATHOLIC, APOSTOLIC, SPANISH CHURCH

The Church that was implanted in America was responding to the atmosphere of the Catholic Reform. The Spaniards were no less ready than the Calvinists or Lutherans to condemn the abuses in Rome which outraged Christian humility. But the Church in Spain undertook to accomplish her own reformation from within instead of founding a separate church. The small reform group in Rome made a passionate plea to throw the blame for corruption in the Vatican on the Spanish Pope, Alexander VI—Rodrigo de Borja, or Borgia—while another Borgia, Francisco, was following the path to sainthood within the strict military order of the Jesuits. The founder of the Company of Jesus, Ignatius Loyola, was himself a Spaniard, and the great Humanist and prime mover of the Spanish church and state, Cardinal Cisneros, lived the life of a Franciscan ascetic and ordered the poetic books of the Moors to be burned. Saint Teresa of Ávila, aroused to action by the scandalous laxity of the Carmelite nuns, was canonized for her stern and resolute efforts to restore the old, strict rule. Thus the Church of the sixteenth century was orthodox, imbued with a crusading spirit; it proved much more active and imaginative than the Crown, and ultimately more resourceful than the Crown in America. The missionaries went where the officers of the Crown could not go and pushed ahead from where the Conquistadors stopped.

The Church was plainly visible everywhere. Its bells convoked all the people. Its towers and spires rose high above the cities and villages. The priest spread the doctrine of conversion to an entire race as he carried out his "conquest" of the Indians. He taught them the Catechism and put them to work in the convent shops, which were their *workhouses*. The members of the Franciscan and Jesuit missions were all things to all men—the government, the machinery for the propagation of the faith, the school, and the fountain of original creativeness. The Church held in its hands many of the functions that belong to the state in the modern world. Education, including the university, public charity, hospitals, and banks—all were administered by religious orders. Censorship of books, control of customs (to keep out unsuitable books and other items), and application of the immigration laws to debar Jews and Lutherans all came under the jurisdiction of the ecclesiastical court of the Inquisition. Secular Spain defended herself against the English for reasons of state, and against the Jews according to the new policy inaugurated by the Catholic monarchs, but Catholic Spain regarded an Englishman as a Protestant, first and foremost, and a Jew as an enemy of Christ.

The Inquisition established to some degree a reign of terror in America. It quashed intellectual movements and committed excesses, but its acts were not very different from those of other states in other parts of the world. Salvador de Madariaga said that the English executed thirty to fifty times as many persons for witchcraft as the Spanish Inquisition sent to the stake in the Indies. Mariano Picón-Salas sketched a picture of the Spanish Inquisition in America, showing the reality of it by bringing it down to everyday dimensions:

As Lutherans and Jews were not always available, the most frequent occupants of the Inquisitorial jails were the native people, and more than one rogue, whether Spanish or Creole,

exploited the credulity of the village in the disguise of a
priest; many a clergyman of scant intelligence and loose
morals rampaged through the native villages, and the
'*beatas*' [holy women] and '*beatos*' [holy men]—the famous
Angela Carranza in Córdoba for one, and Francisco Ulloa in
Santiago, Chile, for another—acquired a considerable religious following and enjoyed a bogus halo of sainthood with
their poorly assimilated books on mysticism and all the ingredients of superstition that an autochthonous environment
breeds. There were innumerable trials of poor "blasphemous"
Negroes, servants in some rich household who often felt the
master's lash and often sought an outlet for their woes by
"denying God and the saints" with the most desperate Castilian abjurations. Such charges of blasphemy were punished
by pilgrimages, night vigils, candles, the rope and the gag,
the recantation of Levi, and two hundred lashes.

Not infrequently the Inquisition concerned itself with
matters as trivial as that of a Negro woman who "talks
through her chest," which many considered a proof of diabolical intervention. The court sentenced her masters, after endless papers had been drawn up in the most priestly prose, to
sell her and get her out of the confines of Mexico in a peremptory number of days. The devil is a familiar character in the
Inquisitorial records, a devil barbarized by the American
environment who had learned the crudest kind of tricks from
his dealings with Indians and Negroes. The simple *mestizo*
or *zambo*, unlike Dr. Faustus, needed no help from the devil
to state a metaphysical problem or to grant him eternal youth;
he needed help only for his most concrete wants. A case in
point was that of the Mexican *zambo*, Francisco Rodríguez,
"aged forty-three years, a coachman and cattleman by trade,"
who was tried by the Inquisition on the 6th of April, 1646,
on the charge of "having made a pact with the devil, to render
him adoration, and he made him a pledge in writing of
slavery for nine years at the completion of which he would
carry him off to hell." According to the Inquisitors' records,
what Rodríguez had obtained by that supernatural deal (in
testimony of which the devil had offered him "an image of
himself, stamped on parchment") was "to be able to fight with
a thousand men; to win all the women he wanted, however
painted they might be, the power to fight bulls and ride
horseback at no personal peril whatsoever; to go in one night

to this city and elsewhere and return, however great the distance, and other atrocious and very felonious acts, unworthy of mention so as not to offend Catholic ears."

The case of Rodríguez, which modern justice would have settled by sending him to a sanitarium, was important enough to draw from the Mexican Inquisition a sentence that included an exhibition of the penitent with "a green candle in his hands, a rope around his neck, a white garment, the recantation of Levi, two hundred lashes," and acquaintance with hell on earth at the oars of the galleys of Terremate.

¶ THE FLEET AND THE CORSAIRS

The conservative spirit of the empire and the determination to prevent the entry into the colonies of Europe's reform notions and its vices moved Spain to isolate "her" America, to keep it behind a curtain of suspicion. America began with the Pyrenees, and independence found its first outlet in smuggling. The doors to the colony were all on the shores of the Caribbean, and each entrance was walled and reinforced with forts and castles built by liberal use of slave hands. Veracruz, Cartagena, Panama City, Puerto Cabello, Havana, and San Juan, Puerto Rico, became monuments to military defense. Buenos Aires was still a phantom city without a port open to commerce. Traders who wanted to take their merchandise to Buenos Aires or Montevideo were obliged first to travel to the other side of America, to Peru or Panama. The sea, especially around the great entrances to the Caribbean, was alive with privateers sailing under French, English, Dutch, or Danish flags. They and the pirates, the buccaneers, and the freebooters were prosperous and thriving. To go by ship from Cádiz to the Caribbean ports was a highly dangerous adventure, as risky at the end of the sixteenth century as in the days of Columbus, for man has always been an enemy more deadly than nature. In self-defense the Spaniards worked out a system of sailing in fleets with men-of-war as escorts for the merchant convoys. Yet for all the sea castles and walls, the colonies inland, behind this picture-book display of flags and adventures, were lapsing into ever-deepening silence. The only capital cities raided by the bold "great pirates" were those in the Antilles and Lima, which, being close to the sea, were exposed to their outrages.

The colonies remained subject to the evolution of the Crown's internal policies, and their fortunes slowly fell or rose according to the decadence or prosperity of the reigning families, whether Austrians or Bourbons. As all administration originated in Spain, the colonies' lights grew dim under the inept monarchs and brightened under the enlightened ones, the brilliant ones. The history of Latin American culture during the three centuries of Spanish rule is identical with the life processes of Spain as reflected in the far-distant mirror of the colonies. The convent was its cradle and it matured with the awakening of the mind that came during the enlightened despotism of Charles III.

VIII: *The Convents and the Missions*

¶ THE TOWER OF BABEL AND LANGUAGE LESSONS

As the monks pursued their course toward civilizing the colonies, they acquired a function more complex and difficult than that of the Crown authorities. A viceroy, a governor, or a justice was an official empowered to apply the royal ordinances without moving from his desk, merely by following a routine that in the end anesthetized all initiative. Only the first viceroys, men like Antonio de Mendoza in Mexico or Francisco de Toledo, themselves the creators of the colonies, were able to play major roles by laying the foundations of the two great viceroyalties. Two long centuries went by after that before the viceroys of the "enlightened despotism" renovated the intellectual pattern and economic bases of administration; by then the Spanish empire in America was approaching its end. But even in the days of the first two viceroys, the civil authorities administered the law of Conquistador or king in the Spanish language and used the power granted by the Crown to govern nations of conquered Indians apportioned among the colonists in *repartimientos* and *encomiendas*. The monks, on the other hand, had to enter the mysterious minds of the Indians, learn their languages, bury themselves in jungle or desert, and complete a much more difficult and complicated conquest there. The conquest in the missionary field stretched over two centuries, and the arms at the command of the monks in no way resembled those by which Cortés and Pizarro slashed their way. Only the Spaniards, the Portuguese, and a few French religious men undertook the missionary conquest of the Western Hemisphere. As they were only a handful, carrying on a hard struggle in remote spots and never engaging in warfare, history does not mention them with the verve that brightens other chapters, though theirs was no less heroic.

Within the Church itself, wide differences separated the religious orders from the parish priests. The secular clergy was appointed to parishes on the basis of the calculated value of their incomes and their exploitation of the Indians. The monk or priest who built his mission beyond the regions governed by the immediate authority of the Crown was another breed of man. The monastery of sixteenth-century America was a fountain of adventure unlike anything the religious orders in Europe had known. Instead of living the secluded life of the cloister, the monks in America had to go out to face all the dangers that can beset wandering discoverers and hunters of souls. That their purpose became twisted and corrupted in time does not change the picture. Historical fact shines forth in all its truth when the mystery of the old American nations is investigated today. The information in published books is augmented by the vast unpublished archives of the monasteries, and the total testifies to the immense amount of work done in every field by the religious organizations.

Their first problem was language. The monks decided that it was much safer and simpler to study the languages of the Indians than it would be to teach them Spanish. In Mexico, the official language spoken throughout the Valley of Anáhuac and among some of the conquered tribes was Nahuatl. Robert Ricard says that Nahuatl had spread as far as Tlaxcala and a part of the present states of Jalisco, Colima, Nayarit, Aguascalientes, Zacatecas, and Sinaloa. There were other languages: Maxtec and Totonac on the Gulf Coast, Otomí in the north, Mixtec and Zapotec in the south, Tarascan in the west. What occurred in Mexico was true of all the colonies as far south as Chile, Argentina, and Paraguay. Nevertheless, the monks had come there to teach a new religion, with all its mysteries and its complicated theology of a God-Man born of a virgin, and a Father, Son, and Holy Ghost who were three separate persons in a single true God. How could such things be preached unless the native languages were mastered? The confusion was compounded when the confessor had to talk with the Indian in the confessional. In the beginning, confessions were heard through an interpreter, but this could be only a temporary expedient, because it violated the intimacy of the sacrament that, by its very essence, must observe the strictest confidence and secrecy. A single language was of no use in preaching a sermon, which had to be repeated, as often as not, in three or four languages during a single mass. The convent perforce became a university for language study. Vocabularies and grammars had to be compiled as tools. Only a few of those texts, the greater number of which remained unpublished because they were meant solely for the use of the convent, have come down to our day. They are invaluable to the anthropologists. As for matter printed in America, Mexico alone could list a hundred and nine items in ten different languages during the earliest period—that is, before the arrival of the Jesuits. A span of only a few years stretched betweeen the day when the monks had to deliver their sermons in sign language and the time when they were able to address the Indians in their own tongues.

Learning the native languages hastened beyond all expectations the interchange of cultures. Fray Toribio de Benavente, who died in 1569, made a great name for himself in colonial literature under the pseudonym of Motolinía, meaning "the poor man" in one Indian language. Fray Toribio explained his pen name by saying: "This is the first word I learned of this language and it will be my name henceforth, that I may not forget it." Perhaps his most famous work is the *Historia de los Indios de la Nueva España* (*History of the Indians of New Spain*).

Like many another monk, Motolinía sponsored theater. He staged mystery plays in the language of the Indians, adopting a familiar and humorous tone as he presented scenes from sacred history. So great was his success that the Indians flocked to one show in such numbers that they knocked down the stands for the audience. The number of conversions multiplied as candidates for baptism came in crowds: according to Motolinía, five million Mexicans were baptized between 1524 and 1536. Archbishop Zumárraga said in a letter to the main chapter in Tolosa that between 1524 and 1531 the Franciscans alone had baptized a million Indians. The Franciscans favored mass conversions. The Augustinians, who came later, went about their task more formally so as to do things more conscientiously and to differentiate themselves, as they put it. Adults were baptized, amid impressive ceremonies, only four times a year.

Fray Bernardino de Sahagún (1500–90) was a disciple of

Fray Antonio de Olmos (1500–71), who had collected a good
deal of data on the Aztec traditions in his *Pláticas de los ancianos*
(*Old Men's Talk*). While Sahagún was rector of the convent
of Tapeapulco, he established a school for teachers in the Nahuatl
tongue and turned to the work of making a systematic collection
of the Indian traditions and of the Aztecs' descriptions of the
arrival of the Spaniards, with special emphasis on the greatness
of the native heroes. Out of that came his *Historia General de
las Cosas de la Nueva España* (*General History of the Things
of New Spain*), which he wrote entirely in Nahuatl and later
translated into Spanish. He dedicated his life of arduous toil and
heroic endurance to this enterprise. Not all the superiors of his
order understood the life of the Indians as well as he did, and
the moment came when it was considered dangerous to bring the
indigenous traditions into books lest they jeopardize the unity
of the dogma. An order went forth to call in Sahagún's manuscripts. He was forced to await better days before he could
recover them. Thanks to the persistence of this great scholar,
however, minutely detailed information has survived to help
reconstruct the picture of the Aztecs' culture. Through Father
Sahagún we know something about their customs, their industries, the very complicated process of making feather cloaks,
details of their rituals and creeds, and the chapters of the conquest as they were seen through the eyes of the Indians, such
as the siege of ancient Tenochtitlán ordered by their priests, the
slaying of the priests at Alvarado's command, and many other
scenes that take on the accents of poetic greatness in the telling.
The images, the emotions, the original colors give these reports
a tone never found among the Spanish historians.

The work of the great historian Fray Pedro Aguado, author
of the *Conquista de la Nueva Granada* (*Conquest of New Granada*), fared worse than Father Sahagún's. His books were seized
by the Inquisitors in Spain and were so ill treated that entire
volumes were lost. The censors cut out the sections in which
Aguado denounced the Conquistadors for the wrongs they had
done. Even so, Aguado's history is the basic work from which
later historians reconstructed the earliest history of what became
Colombia and Venezuela. One can only imagine what a monument
of Spanish American letters it might have become if it had been
preserved in its entirety.

¶ THE PURIFYING FIRE

If we look at the reverse side of the coin, we must remind our-selves of the great complexity of the moral problems that the monks had to grapple with. According to their philosophy and beliefs, expressions of aboriginal culture and its great artistic monuments were the work of the devil. The missionaries approached the Indians lovingly, to be sure, but trembled for their own souls. The razing of temples and the destruction of idols was a spiritual exercise that grew into a competition between the Franciscans and Dominicans. In 1525, Fray Martín de la Coruña destroyed all the temples and idols in Tzinzuntzan, the holy city of Michoacán. Peter of Ghent (1486–1572), who founded the first school for Indian children in 1523, who taught thousands of them the manual and decorative arts in his forty years as a missionary, and whose school graduated the first native craftsmen to be employed in the churches, said in a letter written in 1529 that one of his pupils' major occupations was knocking down idols and destroying temples. Zumárraga confirms this and points to the satisfactory total of more than 500 temples and 20,000 idols demolished. The Spaniards believed that the Catholic Church could stand only upon the ruins of pagan temples. This belief had been common in Europe from the time of Constantine, and was expressed among the Mexicans themselves as one nation fell and another seized the power. "To preserve the temples, which Cortés wished to keep as memorials," Robert Ricard says, "would have been [considered] madness; to found a museum would have seemed even more fantastically absurd at the time: it would have been viewed as a sign of respect, which could serve at that juncture only to strengthen the Indians' adherence to their ancient religion."

The native manuscripts suffered the same fate. Very few of the codices were rescued from the fury of destruction. A recon-struction of many chapters in the history of Mexican culture can-not be made because what was then thrown into a bonfire will be forever missing. Book-burning was not unusual in that period, however, for Cardinal Cisneros, famous in the history of culture for his zeal to destroy, consigned the Arabs' volumes of poetry and science to the flames. Indeed such acts were the keynote of the times, which the Old and the New World struck in unison. Luther's works were burned in Louvain, Cologne, Paris, and Rome.

The missionary tried to come close to the Indian and to win his confidence insofar as he did not endanger his own soul by so doing. To fix a boundary line between charity and conscience was a problem that might compromise his very salvation. But it was generally agreed that the missionary might adopt the language, the dress, and the customs of the catechumens to the extent that they did not conflict with Christianity. Christian sanctuaries were built where the Indians had established their places of worship. Even today the Indians make pilgrimages to render homage to the Virgin Mother of Jesus on the very spots where their remote ancestors had congregated to adore their gods and a goddess who resembled a primitive version of the imported Queen of Heaven. The veneration of the image of the Virgin of Guadalupe in Mexico blends with the people's most deep-seated traditions, which is why her standard was flown as the flag of the revolution for independence. The first Mexican evangelists hit upon the idea of calling the Virgin by the name of the goddess Tonantzin, whose sanctuary stood where the Basilica of Guadalupe rises today. Ricard numbers fifteen temples built upon ancient native places of worship in the section of Mexico that he chose for his study of the missions. This figure increases all along the line of the routes taken by the missionaries through the rest of America. The sanctuary of the Virgin of Chiquinquirá, in Colombia, stands on the spot where the Chibchas worshipped the deity Bachué. Bridges could be built easily between the American religions and the creed introduced by the Spaniards to link what the newcomers were about to cancel with what they were trying to implant. According to the missionaries, the Aztecs be-believed in the sign of the Cross because it was the symbol of the four points of the compass, and also the conventional emblem of the rains and the winds. And their great God, Huitzilopochtli had been born of the virgin goddess Teteoinan.

Father José Acosta (1539–1600), the famous Jesuit author of the *Historia Natural y Moral de las Indias* (*Natural and Moral History of the Indies*), whom Feijoo called "the Pliny of the New World," compiled his *Doctrina Cristiana y Catecismo* (*Christian Doctrine and Catechism*) in Spanish, Aymará, and Quechua. He believed fervently that man in America had a soul like the European's, and in defense of the Indians, he said: "In Spain and Italy tribes of men are found who, but for visage and figure, have nothing else like men." But at the same time, he warned the missionaries to be on the alert for whatever the devil in America would do to try to make himself like God by imitating the sacrifices, religion, and sacraments of the true Catholic religion. In several chapters of his history he speaks of monasteries of maidens built by the devil on the same plan as the convents of Catholic nuns; of the penances and mortifications mimicking the Christian sacrament which Satan taught the Indians; of his duplication in Mexico of the feast of Corpus Christi, and his imitation of the mystery of the Most Holy Trinity in Peru.

Such scruples gave rise to impassioned debates inside the convents. In opposition to those who defended the Indians, some monks, among them Domingo de Betanzos, who died in 1538, maintained that they were bereft of reason. Caught between their evangelical zeal for spreading the Gospel and their suspicion that they might be working in an atmosphere impregnated with sulphur by the devil, the monks became the victims of an inner conflict that never reached such dramatic intensity in the consciences of the laity.

To appreciate the point of view of many members of religious orders, we must read this description of the Indian written by Fray Tomás Ortiz, a Dominican monk who was in Santa Marta in 1524:

The men on the mainland of the Indies eat human flesh and are more sodomistic than any generation. There is no justice among them, they go about naked, they feel neither love nor shame, they are asses, stupid, mad, insane; to kill or be killed is all the same to them; they have no truth in them unless it be to their advantage; they are inconstant; they do not know what counsel is; they are ingrates and fond of novelties; they boast of their drunkenness; they distill wine from various herbs, fruits, roots, and grain; they also get drunk on smoke and on certain herbs that steal away their brains; they are bestial in their vices; neither obedience nor courtesy do the young boys show to the old, nor sons to their father; nor are they capable of learning from doctrine and punishment; they are treacherous, cruel, vengeful, for they never forgive; extremely inimical toward religion, idlers, thieves, liars, and poor and mean in judgment; they keep neither faith nor order; men do not stay faithful to their wives, nor wives to their husbands; they are sorcerers, soothsayers, and necromancers; they are as cowardly as rabbits, as dirty as pigs; they eat lice, spiders, and raw worms wherever they find them; they have neither the art nor the dexterity of men; when they forget the matters of faith they have learned, they say that such things are for Castile and not for them, and they wish not to change customs or gods; they are beardless, and if some beard hairs sprout, they pull them out; they treat the sick with no pity at all; even though they be neighbors and kinsmen they leave them helpless at the moment of death; or else they carry them into the wilderness to die with a sup of bread and water; the older they grow the worse they are; up to the age of ten or twelve years, it seems to me they come forth with some breeding or virtue; from then on they become as brute beasts. In short, I say that God never created people so steeped in vices and bestiality, with no leaven of goodness or politeness.

¶ THE UNIVERSITIES

The first monks to arrive in Mexico, as in the rest of America, were Franciscans. Later the Domincans appeared. In Mexico, the Augustinians came third. In Santo Domingo, the Brothers of Mercy followed the Dominicans. The convents of those orders had been established for many years throughout America by the time the Jesuit order was founded in 1540. Still more time went by before the Jesuits sent missionaries to Spanish America, although they had come to Brazil earlier, during Tomás de Souza's term as governor (1549–53).

The Franciscans arrived in Santo Domingo in 1502; in Darién, Colombia in 1509; in Mexico in 1523; in Quito in 1534; and in Bogotá in 1549. The Dominicans reached Santo Domingo in 1510; Mexico in 1526; Santa Marta and Venezuela in 1529; Quito in 1541; and Bogotá in 1549. The Brothers of Mercy established themselves in Santo Domingo in 1514, and from the moment they set foot on the island they went to work to save the Indians from the destruction inflicted upon them by the Conquistadors. They founded Indian villages and gathered in the natives. The first step in their "spiritual conquest" was education. By 1513 the Crown had ordered the teaching of Latin to Indians who showed outstanding aptitude for learning. The first secondary school was founded by the Franciscans in Santo Domingo in 1505. The other orders followed their example. In 1538 the school of the Dominicans was authorized to carry the title of university. It became the University of St. Thomas Aquinas, the first in the New

World. The University of Santiago de la Paz, founded in 1540, was an outgrowth of a secondary school started by Bishop Ramírez de Fuenleal some years earlier.

In 1553 the Universities of Lima and Mexico were opened. These institutions were natural consequences of an intense intellectual movement that had arisen in the monasteries. The first rector of the University of Mexico was the Augustine monk and teacher of Sacred Scripture, Alonso de la Vera Cruz, who had taught philosophy for years to the students of the secondary school at Tiripitío in Michoacán province, and who may be considered the father of all philosophical study in America. Three of his books were published in Mexico: *Recognitio Summularum* and *Dialectica Resolutio*, both in 1554, and *Physica Speculatio* in 1557. He was a product of the best school in Spain, the University of Salamanca, where he attended the classes of Francisco de Vitoria and Fray Luis de León. The inaugural oration delivered at the opening ceremonies of the University of Mexico was by Francisco Cervantes de Salazar, who became a follower of Erasmus through his friend Luis Vives. Later he became the professor of rhetoric. Although not all the colonies could claim such eminent men, their number was relatively large. The monasteries provided laboratories for linguistic studies, which were often linked to studies of the indigenous society made with correct academic accuracy and thoroughness. Thus schools assumed a very great importance in the Spanish colonies, as they supplanted the armies of the Conquest. Original methods were invented to deal with situations unknown in Europe. Vasco de Quiroga, for example, tried out the Utopia of Thomas More in an experimental version in Michoacán.

Pedro Henríquez Ureña gives a picture of the university schools that emerged in the colonies:

> Adding together all the institutions with university prerogatives, or to which those were attributed, even though for only a few years, the sum comes to twenty-six (although all of them were never in existence at the same time because some of their prerogatives were revoked): two in Hispaniola (both in the city of Santo Domingo), one in Cuba (Havana), three in Mexico (one in Guadalajara, one in Mérida, Yucatán, and one in the capital), one in Nicaragua (León), one in Panama (the capital), two in New Granada, now Colombia, both in Bogotá), two in Venezuela (one in Caracas, one in

Mérida), four in Ecuador (all in Quito), four in Peru (one
in Lima, two in Cuzco, one in Huamanga), one in Upper
Peru, now Bolivia (Charcas), two in Chile (both in Santiago), and two in Argentina (both in Córdoba del Tucumán). The most important of these were: St. Thomas
Aquinas in Santo Domingo, to which students came from
Cuba, Puerto Rico, and Venezuela for three centuries; the
University of Mexico, which granted more than fourteen
hundred doctorates; San Marcos in Lima; San Carlos Borromeo in Guatemala, founded in 1676 with a legacy from
Pedro Crespo Suárez; San Jerónimo in Havana, established
in 1728; St. Rosa in Caracas, opened in 1725; the Dominican University in Bogotá, founded in the seventeenth
century; San Gregorio Magno, founded by Jesuits in Quito in
1620; St. Francis Xavier, founded by Jesuits in Charcas in
1624; and St. Ignatius Loyola, founded by Jesuits in Córdoba in the seventeenth century.

The trail-blazer for studies on American society was Fray
Román Pane, of the order of St. Jerome. He came to America
with Columbus, either on his second or his third voyage. A remark like a sigh may be found among the writings of Columbus
as transcribed by his son Ferdinand: "I have grown weary of
trying to find out what it is that they [the Indians] believe." Fray
Román proposed to find out for Columbus what he wanted to
know. The good monk stayed in the islands for several years
and finally went to live with the Franciscans. He succeeded in
mastering at least one of the native languages, and supplied in
his short treatise of twenty-six chapters the first written information extant regarding the religious concepts of the Indians—how
their women were created in their book of Genesis, how men
transformed themselves into animals, and so on. Fray Román
describes the ceremonies that accompanied the making of magic
medicine and notes the appearance of some diseases, such as
the "French disease" (syphilis). He reports that they have
"their laws set down in ancient songs through which they rule,
as the Moors through their scriptures. And when they wish to
sing their songs, they play a certain instrument that is called
the *maiohanan*."

Fray Román's treatise concludes with an account of the first
Indians converted to Christianity. He mentions the oratory that
was built as a place where the first seven converts could adore

Christ and says that when the subjects of Chief Guarionex profaned it, the lieutenant-governor of the island, Bartholomew Columbus, acting in the name of the Admiral, "brought suit against the evil-doers, and when the truth was revealed, he had them publicly burned." Fray Román's treatise gives a crude picture in miniature of what later was learned in the large during the conquest of America. Ferdinand Columbus copied the incident in his book *La Vida y Hechos de Cristóbal Colón* (*The Life and Deeds of Christopher Columbus*).

¶ THE JESUITS

The Company of Jesus was founded as the order of the soldiers of Christ. A religious group so constituted was bound to play a major role in the missionary field. Half a century went by between the founding of the order and its establishment in that part of Spanish America where its work would become famous. When the Jesuits arrived in Mexico, they found the Franciscans, Dominicans, and Augustinians already firmly installed. The same held true of South America. In 1560 the king had decreed: "We do not consent to have monasteries of the Trinity nor any other order in Peru except those of St. Dominic, St. Francis, and St. Augustine." By 1572, Philip had changed his mind, and the Jesuits were admitted with permission to share the missionary work in the colonies with the three above-mentioned orders. The decree was amended to read:

> What is asked is that in the Indies there be no monasteries nor religious men if they be not of the four orders of St. Dominic, St. Francis, St. Augustine, and the Company of Jesus; for these four orders are well approved there, and the others are likely to cause scandal among the Indians and Spaniards, but above all because until now there have been only these and the Order of Mercy.

An Augustinian friar, Agustín de la Coruña, had insisted most strongly that the Jesuits be admitted to Spanish America. He had been in Mexico; then, in 1564, he was appointed bishop of Popayán in New Granada. Fray Agustín petitioned the Crown so urgently to send Jesuits to South America that as he later wrote to St. Francis Borgia: "I begged those gentlemen so often and sent them so many petitions in which I asked favor for the Holy Company of Jesus, that, as they did not grant it to me,

I have unburdened my own conscience and laid the burden on the royal conscience." His efforts bore fruit, however, in 1566 when the first three Jesuits were dispatched to Florida. Eight were sent to Peru in 1567, three to New Granada in 1589. These fourteen missionaries were a token force in the second half of the sixteenth century. None of the three Jesuits who landed in New Granada was there at the end of ten years. By 1604 the priests had barely got a foothold in Santa Fe de Bogotá. Venezuela received its first Jesuit in 1628. The order arrived in Santo Domingo in 1650, nearly a century and a half after the Franciscans.

The Order's stay in America was cut short and its work interrupted in 1767, when the Jesuits were expelled from Spain and her dominions during the reign of Charles III. But though their stay was relatively brief, they left a deep imprint on colonial life, and their missions were built in some of the most forbidding regions. They founded colleges all over Spanish America; some of their churches are famous, in particular the Church of the Company in Quito. The order flourished during a period when the other orders had lost their original fervor and had become deeply involved in a fierce struggle with one another. The Jesuits were forced to cope with the most trying situations in their dealings with the authorities and the rival orders. But the kings of the House of Austria stood staunchly behind them.

The Jesuits began their work on a very modest scale, as the small number of fathers in the first missions indicates. Their first steps in learning the indigenous languages recall the difficulties that faced the Franciscans in Mexico. Juan Manuel Pacheco, S.J., reports the experiences of the first Jesuits in New Granada in these words:

> Father Medrano preached in Castilian against idolatry, but upon observing that many Indians did not understand a word, he arranged for a priest who knew the Muisca language to accompany him and translate what he was expounding. The Indians, impressed and fearful, handed over more than three thousand idols, which they had kept hidden underground and concealed in the roofs and walls of their houses. Other idols made of varicolored feathers were cast into the fire as they sang "*Confundantur omnes qui adorant sculptilia*" ("Let all who worship graven images be confounded"). The gold idols were melted down and the precious metal was used in the construction and decoration of the churches.

Some non-Spanish religious orders introduced a new element into the missions. Except for Flemings like Peter of Ghent in Mexico and Jodoko Ricke in Quito, the Spaniards had been practicing a kind of missionary nationalism.[1] The Jesuits were an international apparatus, for the fathers came from many nations and kept moving all over the map of Europe so as to achieve the widest religious coverage. In 1601, Father Diego de Torres, who had been in Peru, moved to Rome and published there a small work in Italian showing that the Jesuits' work was bearing fruit in Peru. The booklet was reproduced in Milan and translated into Latin, German, and French. Immediately thereafter, many Italian Jesuits volunteered to go to America. But Spanish law forbade any foreigner to take part in the missions. Father Torres begged fervently for the repeal of this law, and was seconded by the Portuguese priest Alonso de Castro. Eventually the pressure of the Jesuits brought about the issuing of individual permits to priests of foreign birth. Hungarian, Polish, and German Jesuits then went to Paraguay, where they changed the tone of the missionary enterprises. Among the twelve Jesuits who arrived in New Granada to lay the foundations of the Company's province were three Italian priests, Dadey from Modovi, Coluccini from Lucca, and Grossi from Naples. Father Lamberri was French. Even the Spaniards who went with them had a European cast. One of them, Father Funes, had entered the Company in Salamanca, was ordained in Lloret, was transferred to Germany and Hungary, and taught in Graz and Milan. His *Methodus practica aurei libelli Thomas de Kempis de Imitatione Christi* (*Practical Method of the Little Golden Books of Thomas à Kempis's Imitation of Christ*) was published in Cologne and was translated into French and Italian and his books on theology appeared in Graz and Milan.

The Jesuits of Santa Fe de Bogotá chose two Spaniards, a German, and two Flemings to conduct a mission among the plains people in the hope of bringing the Gospel to the Orinoco. Radiel, the German, was drowned while crossing a river; Beck and Theobast, the Flemings, were murdered by the Carib Indians; Fiol, the Spaniard met the same fate. The only one who lived to tell the tale was the other Spaniard, Father Vergara, who spent a

---

[1] Jodoko Ricke brought the first wheat to Ecuador, taught the Indians the use of the plow, opened the first school of native children, and initiated them into Castilian songs and dances. With another Fleming, Egas, he built the church and covent of Saint Francis, a jewel of the purest Baroque style.

hundred and fifty days traveling from the Orinoco to Casanare with his pupils. During all that time they ate meat only once. In spite of their first failure, however, the Jesuits returned to the region with reborn zeal.

¶ FROM THE EMPIRE OF PARAGUAY TO THE EXPULSION

The greatest Jesuit experiment was made in Paraguay. In 1607 the General of the Company resolved to make the missions of Paraguay completely independent of those in Peru. Earlier they had covered a vast region containing parts of present-day Paraguay, Brazil, Bolivia, and Argentina. The original idea was to group the Indian population around the communities of new converts in the care of cells under Jesuit rule. They proselytized in ever widening areas, initiated the catechumens into the arts and crafts, and developed a comprehensive plan of colonization. During the eighteenth century, the communities of converts expanded to the number of thirty. One hundred and five thousand native colonists lived in this communal republic, which the Jesuits kept jealously isolated from the surrounding Spanish and Portuguese colonies. The colony was an actual state, governed by not more than four hundred members of the Company. The Jesuits were attempting by this means to provide the Indians with a shelter against the power of the white laymen who were exploiting them on the *encomiendas*, and as long as the Crown sponsored them, they were able to evade any interference from the Spanish authorities.

Each community was like a small municipality containing houses for the Indians all built according to the same plan, common workshops for handicraft, schools, and a staff of *corregidores* and native officials who were themselves supervised and directed by the priests of the Company. The system must have been inspired, at least in part, by the Incan plan for its indigenous communities rather than by any European scheme. Most of the converted community was under the *Tupa-Mbae*, meaning God's share, whereby all the Indians had to work a certain number of days each week, as a kind of tithe, to defray the general expenses of the community. Tools, seed, and animals were owned in common. Handicraft from the workshops of the community was handled in the same way. The printing press was introduced in the communal missions of Paraguay earlier than in Argentina, and the books in the Guaraní language that came off the press were printed from wooden fonts carved by the Indians themselves. Guaraní was the spoken language, but the hymns and prayers were in Latin. As the Indians returned home in the afternoon from their work in the jungle on rafts steered along the great rivers, they sang in Latin to the accompaniment of a harp. The harp became the instrument of popular music, and remains so in Paraguay today. The ruins of the churches and workshops still bear witness to the scope of this experiment, during the time of which Utopia came true for a century and a half.

The missions in Paraguay made such an impression in Europe that writers as astute as Montesquieu never shied away from their belief that Plato's Republic had been built on that spot in America. Articles in Montesquieu's *Encyclopédie*, published before the expulsion of the Jesuits from France, described the missions in the most laudatory terms.

Yet the missions had not made an easy start. First they had to fight the Indians. Fathers González de Santa Cruz and Rodríguez y del Castillo died the death of martyrs in 1628 and were beatified during the papacy of Pius XI. Later they had to stand off the Paulistas and the Mamelukes, who were spreading out around São Paulo in Brazil and had destroyed several communities of converts. For all that, the fathers managed to keep their republic under firm discipline until 1767, the year of their expulsion. To be sure, they protected the community so paternally that none of their villages was capable of governing itself, and when they left, the jungle grew up behind their footsteps. But the idea that the missions should be set apart and sheltered against the surrounding whites sank into the Paraguayan mind. When the country gained its independence under the dictatorship of Dr. Gaspar Rodríguez Francia, it freed itself from Argentina and Uruguay rather than from Spain, and if the Paraguayans no longer had to fight the Spaniards after that, they certainly had to do battle with the Argentines, the Uruguayans, the Brazilians, and the Bolivians. Rodríguez Francia's chief aim was to keep the Paraguayans from contact with their neighbors and by so doing to shield them from contamination by ideas which, in his opinion, would corrupt the purity of his republic.

The Paraguayan experiment is not comparable to other missions in Spanish America. In the first place, the land in the rest of the colonies was already held by the Spanish authorities or by other religious orders, so that no territory as large as that which the Jesuits controlled in Paraguay could be isolated. In Mexico, Peru, and New Granada the Jesuits were in constant conflict with the other orders and with the authorities. The Company's stay in Chile is summed up in these lines from the history by Encinas:

> The predominant duality in the character and spirit of the Company of Jesus—that is, their enlightenment combined with their practical exercise of great economic aptitudes and their political sagacity and cunning—stood out in high relief in Chile. Their development was very rapid, for when their final hour struck in less than twenty years, they held more power than all the other forces in the kingdom together. Their prodigious sense of hierarchical organization and their discipline, together with the flexibilty of their conduct, impelled them to mold themselves to the new environment in which they were to carry on their activities. This was polarized in five definite directions: first, the reform of the creed and religious practices; second, the conversion of the Indians through religious instruction, with the moral and material aid of kings and governors; third, to keep the Araucanian War under control for the better development of their evangelical labors; fourth, the vigorous drive toward intellectual progress—within the most rigid orthodoxy, of course; fifth, their basic contribution to the economic progress of the country, which they knew how to implement with laudable dexterity in agriculture and industry alike.
>
> Except in the anomalous case of Father Valdivia, the Jesuits in Chile put into practice, with astonishing perfection, the political tactic of governing indirectly through pressure upon the men in authority and dissimulating that influence, insofar as possible, in order to escape suspicion and envy and to evade responsibility. At all times, the Jesuits here, as in the rest of America, defended the concept of equality between the spiritual natures of the aborigine and the Spaniard, and their attempt to reproduce the Paraguayan experiment in Chile failed, not so much through the progress of the incipient Spanish colonial society as through the contumacious resistance of the Mapuches, who rejected Christianity with even greater violence than they did personal servitude, and who tried to preserve the purity of their

blood and their spiritual heritage. When Father Valdivia, carried away by unheard-of heterodoxy, applied the mystico-practical particularism of the Jesuits precisely, by tolerating the practice of polygamy by the Indian chiefs, he found out for himself that Mapuche resistance was bone deep, not limited to transient circumstantial concessions. Nothing can express better this attitude of stubborn rebellion in the Araucanian than the dialogue that took place between Pedro Riquelme, a great friend of the Indians, and the chief Vilumilla, whom the Spaniards solicited to send his sons to the Jesuit school of Chillán to be educated. "It will make men of them," they told the chief. To which Vilumilla answered in the name of all the chiefs: "Will knowing how to read and write change their copper color? . . . Did our ancestors need to know how to read and write? Did they need the priesthood to become men and to be respected by the Conquistadors themselves? No, certainly not. We know how to defend our freedom and our customs without literacy and without the priesthood." Father Rosales reports that he usually encountered stiff resistance against baptizing Indians condemned to death, "Saying that if they were not to live, why should they be baptized?" The evidence is beyond question and most copious: as a race the Mapuches faded away because they mixed their blood without ever accepting Christianity.

In 1767, the year of the expulsion of the Jesuits from the Spanish dominions, the number of the Company's members in all Spanish America barely totalled 2,200; yet they had 700,000 Indians in their care. They owned schools, hospitals, dockyards, and workshops where they trained the Indians to spin, tan, and make pottery. They had accumulated immense wealth. No other order had received as many legacies as they received during the last century of their stay in America, or held so much land. When the Company fell into disgrace with the monarchs and lost the favor of the papacy, the other orders, already jealous, joined in the effort to have the order suspended throughout the Catholic world, which meant also that they themselves would automatically fill the vacuum left in America by the expulsion. Once the Jesuits had gone, education took on new life under the Enlightenment, employing the instruments and ideas of "enlightened despotism."

¶ THE NUNS AND ENLIGHTENED WOMEN

The convents for religious women in America began differently from those for men. The Conquest was of, by, and for men, after all. Women were only a hindrance to the males going forth to explore an unknown continent peopled by nations of savages, monsters, and mysteries. Rare indeed was the woman with a spirit of adventure strong enough to succeed in breaking through the circle and mingling with men in an enterprise so eminently virile. But there were some, for the Spanish woman has always shown great spirit; and, like most women, she loves danger. Two examples will prove the point. Inés de Suárez went to the conquest of Chile with Pedro de Valdivia and played an important role in it, for she was responsible for the introduction of chickens and wheat into Chile and her defense of the city of Santiago was what saved the first colony. But a clerk of the court, one Licentiate La Gasca, was so horrified by her participation in the political life of Chile and in the infant Chilean civic society that he forced Valdivia to send for his lawful wife in Spain. Doña Inés de Suárez was forced to end her days as a cloistered penitent.

At about the same time, the bishop in Guatemala suggested to the king that Don Pedro de Alvarado, the founder of the colony, should not be permitted to return from Spain except "with the stipulation that he come back married." In 1539, Don Pedro informed the town corporation from Puerto Cabello: "I can only say that I am coming married, and Doña Beatriz is very good: she is bringing twenty maidens, very gentle women, the daughters of gentlemen, and of very good lineage; I well believe this is merchandise that will leave me nothing in the store, and will repay me well, for otherwise I must be excused for speaking of it." Doña Beatriz and her twenty damsels all perished two years later during an earthquake that destroyed the city. But in her two brief years as a wife, Doña Beatriz proved that she was a fearless and formidable woman.

The Crown tolerated adventuresses in the Conquest. But the colonies felt otherwise. A woman who came to America was expected to soothe and calm the men and to persuade them to settle down in the cities or on the *encomiendas* and have nothing more to do with the Indian women. Her duty was to keep the bloodline clear and to rear a Spanish Christian family. The ideal woman would either have a large family or would devote herself to prayer. Not adventuresses but serene mothers were wanted.

The house should be a miniature cloister to enfold the women and keep them safe from the lust of the men. Difficult goals to attain in a society whose masculine element derived from the mighty Conquistadors and the proud *encomenderos*. The convent became the only truly safe refuge for scrupulous women, the only place where they could feel protected and secure against the temptations of the flesh. Unlike the missionary monk, a man of extraordinary mobility and inventiveness, which he translated, at times, into great Utopias, the nun shrank into mystic contemplation. She knew how to read, and sometimes she wrote.

The first religious woman to attempt poetry was Doña Leonor de Ovando, who lived sometime before 1609, and who said in referring to the "divine spouse of my soul,"

> He suffered that I might be given life
> and I know that he would have suffered for me alone
> and would have given redemption to me alone
> had I been born into this world alone.

Leonor de Ovando was born in Santo Domingo. The first Spanish American woman poet, she wrote verses which, in the opinion of Max Henríquez Ureña, were in an elegantly involved and refined style related to that of the Spanish poet Luis de Góngora y Argote.

The colonies were no longer in their infancy when the nunneries were established. Both Saint Rose of Lima (1586–1617) and Mariana de Jesús (1618–45), "the Lily of Quito" (for some unexplained reason never beatified), were possessed with the most passionate mystical fervor, but neither ever entered a convent in her life. Saint Rose ran the whole mystical scale; she espoused herself to the Lord and lived like a recluse. She was dedicated to the worship of divine love, answered successfully the interrogations of the theologians, and was canonized. As she was dying, she asked to be buried where the Dominican monks rested. Saint Rose was the rose of Lima; Mariana of Jesús was the lily. Both holy women were accompanied from childhood by singing birds. Legend records that Mariana stopped an earthquake and was a pillar of the church in Quito. She had a dream of a convent to be built in Quito, and one was constructed later precisely as she had pictured it. These mystical women were the forerunners of the convent women who took their vows and became famous in Spanish American literature: Sor Juana Inés de la Cruz, the tenth muse of Mexico; Mother Castillo of Colombia, who wrote the *Afectos espirituales* (*Spiritual Passions*) in

Tunja; and Sor Catalina de Jesús, an Ecuadorian, whose auto-biography, *Secretos entre el alma y Dios* (*Secrets Between the Soul and God*) is impregnated with divine love.

The religious woman whose life was the greatest inspiration to the mystical corps of women who founded the nunneries was Saint Teresa of Ávila. She set them an example that they followed in administering their covents and restoring discipline during the autumn of the colonial age, which was marked by laxity among the orders of religious men and women. Saint Teresa left a model for spiritual perfection in her *Moradas* (*Mansions*) and her *Vida* (*Life*), a history showing how the declining orders must strive to restore themselves to their original freshness. Her name, inter-woven with the history of America, joined the Spanish people of Spain to the Spanish people of America in a firm bond. Saint Teresa's brothers came to America, took part in the conquests and the colonization of the Río de la Plata, Peru, and Quito, and even contributed gold to help his sister with her reform of the Carmelites in Spain.

As the "Lily of Quito" had dreamed, the first Carmelite con-vent was founded in the house of Saint Teresa's brother, Lorenzo de Cepeda, with Saint Catherine of Siena as its patron. In front of the house a fountain invited the neighbors to drink its water, water that belonged to Don Lorenzo by the grace of Philip II and had been donated by him to the public use. Don Lorenzo also wrote religious poetry, and as one critic has written:

> must be considered chronologically not only the first poet but also the first biographer of the colony in Quito on account of his *Vida y Virtudes de Doña Juana de Fuentes* (*The Life and Virtues of Doña Juana de Fuentes*). This lady, Cepeda's wife, was first on the roll of the saints of Quito, the first blossom of the flowering of piety that began in her time, a model of meekness and familial love. Don Lorenzo encouraged his daughter Teresa to love literature, too, and in time she became the first Creole woman writer in the colony.[1]

Teresa de Cepeda was also the first Ecuadorian Carmelite nun.

When the mystical women's movement in Ecuador was still far in the future, the Carmelite nun Sister Magdalena Dávalos, a sculptress, made some of the statues that later decorated the convent church.

[1] Jorge Carrera Andrade, *Galería de Místicos y de Insurgentes.*

Oftentimes society women sponsored the founding of convents, even in the days of the orders' decadence. The famous Teaching Convent in Santa Fe de Bogotá was established in 1765 under the patronage of Doña Clemencia Caycedo. At that time there was not a single school for young girls in the city; women who knew how to read and write were rare, and the only prospect before a daughter of the people was to work as a servant in the house or in the fields. Señora Caycedo donated to the founding of the school a gold mine she owned, her thirty-four slaves, the tools for building, a cattle ranch, cacao plantations in the vicinity of her mine, and, as the site of the convent, her enormous house in the capital.

None of the convents produced a saint. Such famous nuns as Sor Juana Inés de la Cruz and Mother Castillo, both of whom wrote with distinction, testified in their biographies that the inner life of the communities was petty and rife with plots to which they themselves inevitably fell victim. The convents were little hells. The monasteries, on the other hand, molded militant clergymen whom the church recognized by conferring on them the titles of Venerable, Beatified, and Saint. But the list of saints is short in proportion to the number of religious men who led heroic lives. Doubtless many more of them might have won a place on the altars if the stage for their exploits had been Europe. The list of American saints includes: Toribio Alfonso de Mogrovejo, Juan de Palafox, Francisco Solano, Luis Beltrán, Pedro Claver, Felipe de Jesús, and Martín de Porres. The last-named, who was canonized during the reign of Pope John XXIII, was a mulatto monk who founded the first orphanage in Lima and taught agriculture. The most eminent was Saint Peter Claver, a Jesuit who dedicated his night vigils to the slaves in Cartagena and attained such a height of heroic virtue and humility in the service of the Negroes that he has come down in history as the slave of slaves.

¶ LAXITY

In the course of three centuries of heroic struggles and petty disputes, the religious orders lost much of their original fervor. They grew rich and they relaxed. Rivalry among the orders reached extremes of bellicosity. The men under the rule of the seraphic Saint Francis of Assisi made war in Santiago on the nuns of Saint Clare of Assisi, thereby rejecting the meekness of the two saints and the mystical love between Clare and Francis.

The entire Franciscan cell attacked the nuns "with weapons, and pushed them about rudely, dragging them along the ground, and when they covered their faces with their hands, they pulled them along by the hair." But such scandalous behavior as that pales when compared with the out-and-out warfare between the same Franciscans and Clares in Cartagena. The nuns there were trying to free themselves from their long obedience to the monks and to place themselves under ordinary ecclesiastical jurisdiction. The nuns' allegations of ill-treatment and injury suffered at the hands of the friars were accepted and their petitions were granted. At about that time it was learned that a monk with five sisters who were all Clare nuns had been elected regional head, or provincial, of the Franciscans, and that his sisters preferred the earlier regime. The dispute grew hotter and hotter. The bishop ordered the sequestration of the abbess and her community. The nuns everywhere ranged themselves on one side or the other.

Then the Franciscans entered the lists. Their entire community mobilized against the bishop and they attacked the nunnery. Grott reports in his *Historia Eclesiástica y Civil de la Nueva Granada* (*Ecclesiastical and Civil History of New Granada*):

> The Franciscans, their monastic order of life already violated, were reinforced by the laity and other clergymen. In defiance of censure by the Church, they passed beyond the bounds of modesty and respect for society and rioted through the city, shouting and stirring up feeling against their prelate. They threatened him with punishment and warned the nuns that they would break up their cloister and tear down their doors. . . . And they did not stop with threats, but proceeded to carry them out, for they had already made lists of the officials and locksmiths and carpenters who were to force the locks. Thereupon the bishop declared them publicly excommunicated; he read the interdict to them, and posted notices of excommunication and censure on the doors of the cathedral and the convent. . . . The monks paid no attention whatsoever. Determined to make light of the censure, and with their plot against the prelate already ripe, they gathered men together in the barracks, and with every sort of weapon and tool they marched to the beat of the drum to the nunnery of Saint Clare, bent upon breaking down the cloister.

In retaliation for their excommunication by the bishop, the monks declared the bishop excommunicated. They rang the bells for the interdict. The city was split into two factions and was put on a war footing. Letters were dispatched to the Pope and the King.

> They laid siege to the convent and began to shout at the doors very stridently and to yell threats. The nuns, who were ready for them, replied with stones thrown through the grilles and windows, while each party kept insulting the other. The monks started to take the locks off the doors of the church, and when they had removed the hinges from the door called the *rule*, they burst into the cloister. Meanwhile the nuns in the convent kept them away from the entrance with a shower of stones; but the owners of the church, the governor, the lieutenant governor, and the monks and priests stayed in the cloister, eating and drinking in splendor, as if they were in their own homes. The superiors became convinced of the impossibility of conquering by main force and affixed new locks to the door, locked it, and turned the keys over to one of the monks. Immediately thereafter the town crier broadcast a ban that forbade any person, under heavy penalties, to communicate with the nuns by word or writing, even to the very servants of the convent, who must not help them or serve them food or render aid of any kind, even such absolute necessities of life as water, bread, medicines, and so on.

The next events of this story would fill a fat novel. In other nunneries, the women took sides and formed into parties over the dispute, and the laity and the civil authorities did likewise. The siege of the convent lasted six months. No one could imagine how the nuns were able to withstand it. Then someone discovered that the underground sewers, large enough to permit a man to walk freely through them, provided an open route by which food was being brought to them. The sewers were closed. The nuns still held out. The governor took a step toward peace by begging them to take their case to the Pope and the King for a final decision. But that meant only a truce. The bishop of Cartagena excommunicated the bishop of Santa Marta as punishment for helping the nuns. The bishop of Santa Marta countered by excommunicating the bishop of Cartagena. The Franciscans appealed to the governor, petitioning him to force the nuns into obedience. Once more the nuns refused. The convent was besieged again. The hinges were forced from the doors with iron bars. The nuns broke out of the cloister and ran into the church. The mob entered the church. The nuns fled through the streets to seek refuge in the bishop's palace.

Somewhat similar events took place in Quito. Fighting among the orders came out in the open. The laxity was incredible. In the Convent of the Conception a hundred and fifty nuns kept five hundred maid servants. Archbishop González Suárez wrote: "The greatest calamity to our society in the days of the Colony was undoubtedly the scandalous laxity of the monks; laxity that was merely scandalous? No, scandalous to the point of cynicism." The Jesuits did not escape criticism by the illustrious archbishop: "Among the aberrations into which the Jesuits in the ancient province of Quito have fallen," he said, "as a consequence of their excessive wealth, two are undoubtedly the most deplorable—the distillation of rum and the purchase of Negroes to become slaves on their estates."

The most impressive evidence of this decadence in the convents is given in the aforementioned *Memorias secretas* of Jorge Juan and Antonio Ulloa. Both were learned men and acute observers. The fresh breezes of the Enlightenment stimulated them to make a most valuable and realistic study of American society, especially in Ecuador and Peru, in addition to their work in geography. Their pages on the convents and the deplorable practices and vices into which men in religious orders and secular priests alike had fallen offer prima facie evidence regarding the colonial church in the period of its decadence. The Indians apportioned to the religious bodies eventually had to pay tributes as high as those set by the *encomenderos*. As for the Franciscans, examples such as the following are given:

> During our residence in Quito, the time came to hold a meeting of the chapter on the religion of Saint Francis, and that was our reason for living in that particular quarter, and we had the opportunity at least to see what was going on. For two weeks before the meeting was held, we were amused to see the religious men coming to the city with their concubines, and for a month or more after the meeting was concluded, it was equally diverting to watch them leaving to return to their new appointments. On that same occasion, it so happened that while a monk was living with all his family across from the house where one of us was lodging, a child of his chanced to die. At two o'clock in the afternoon of that same day, the whole community went to sing a

responsory for him, and afterward each one of them of his own accord came to condole with him in his sorrow.

Another time we found ourselves passing near one of those monasteries on our way from Cuenca to Quito, and we went into it to pay our respects to some monks we knew: when we arrived at the first one's cell, we found three women in it, all nice-looking girls. We also found a couple of the other religious whom we had been coming to visit, one of whom was in bed having a seizure and quite out of his mind; the women were plying him with fumes and endeavoring to bring him to. We asked the other monk the cause of the seizure, and in a few words he informed us that one of the three women, she who was most solicitously attending the sick man and showing greater signs of emotion, was his mistress with whom he had had a quarrel the day before, and he being angry with her, this girl went indiscreetly to place herself in front of the church of a nunnery where he was preaching at that hour; and he flew into such a rage at the sight of her that he suddenly had that seizure, for he fell down in the pulpit and had been unable to go on with his sermon or to return to his senses. This gave the other monk cause to deliver a long speech on the passions of life, which he concluded by informing us that one of the two other women present belonged to him, and the other to the father superior of the community.

The authors of the *Memorias secretas* tell equally damning stories about the convents of nuns.

What was actually dying in the convents was the colony, which had grown corrupt and soft. When we examine the work of the orders over three centuries and consider, on the one hand, the architecture of the churches, the development of painting, the study of the Indian languages, the heroic examples of the saints, and, on the other hand, such scenes as those in the convents of Cartagena, we see a historical development, a human one, in a time of struggle and passion, for which the Church was largely responsible. On the eve of Independence, the same virtues and the same vices came to the fore again. As for the Jesuits, their expulsion from America kindled in the exiles a passion for study that was shared by those who were struggling to destroy the Spanish Empire in America.

IX: *A First Inventory of Spanish=American Literature*

¶ THE CONQUISTADORS

The rapid growth of the map of the Spanish Empire and of the information unfolding before the eyes of the Conquistadors inspired a new literature in Spain. Its authors were men who had collected the data pouring in from America, but who had never themselves crossed the Atlantic—that is, they were men who got their material by communicating with the recent discoverers and Conquistadors. New Spain, New Granada, and Castilla de Oro doubled the realms of the Catholic monarchs and prolonged the heroism of the great captains. Some of the men who exploited those themes wrote in Latin, others in polished Castilian.

Peter Martyr of Anghiera (1457–1526) was an Italian historian and geographer who wrote in Latin. He was in touch with Vasco da Gama, Vespucci, Hernán Cortés, and Magellan, and witnessed the welcome given Columbus in Barcelona after his first voyage. He may have known Columbus in Granada. Peter Martyr was one of the universal men of the Renaissance. His earliest written work describes a diplomatic mission to Egypt. Later, in the first of the works he called "decades," he concentrated on the phenomena of America, and his sole theme thereafter was the New World. He sent copies of everything he wrote to Pope Leo X. After nearly thirty years of work, he compiled his remarkable *De Orbe Novo Decadas* (*Decades on the New Globe*).

Antonio de Herrera (1559–1625), a prolific Castilian historian, was appointed chronicler of the Indies and Castile by the Crown. Although he wrote in Castilian rather than Latin, he, too, called his work "decades": *Decadas o Historia General de los Hechos de los Castellanos en las islas y terra firme del Mar Océano* (*Decades, or General History of the Castilians in the Islands and on the Mainland of the Ocean Sea*). Antonio de Solís (1610–86), who was Chief Historian of the Indies after 1661, and also a poet and playwright, wrote the *Historia de la Conquista de México* (*History of the Conquest of Mexico*). Another chronicler, Francisco López de Gómara (1511–66?) was the author of the famous *Historia General de las Indias*, (*General History of the Indies*) which Montaigne often consulted for data on America which he included in his *Essais*. López de Gómara was personally acquainted with Hernán Cortés; he was his chaplain, and the Conquistador was the source of most of his information on the Conquest of Mexico. That circumstance might suggest that he was biased, but his accounts demonstrated that he was no blind worshipper of Cortés. Not at all. Like the excellent writer he was, he left a good likeness of Cortés, a portrayal so human that it may be compared with the best Spanish portraiture. The Cortés whom López de Gómara pictured was a devout Catholic and a womanizer, a gambler and a man of high courage, a politician and a shrewd leader.

Bernal Díaz del Castillo (1492–1581), one of the old soldiers who had fought beside Cortés kept himself busy in his old age by writing for posterity a most unusual history that recorded the living memory of his life as a soldier and Conquistador in the army of Cortés. He felt that his own merits had been passed over, that he should have had more than he had been given: at times he grumbled. But his sketches are always entertaining, and he had a genius for remembering everything in colors undimmed by age. He kept writing in no particular haste until López de Gómara's book came into his hands. He read it and was outraged. It seemed to him that the chronicler had worked from what he had heard back in Spain and that he was more interested in flattering Cortés than in giving enough credit to his soldiers. Díaz del Castillo was nearing ninety at that time, and his pen trembled in his hand. Nevertheless, he decided that he was the man chosen to right that wrong and incidentally to do justice to himself. He would bring the forgotten soldiers into the spotlight, those courageous anonymous men to whom, except for God and their horses, all the credit for victory was due. He hastened to explain that he knew no Latin—thus launching a shaft directly at Gómara—but that he was going to write as one of the common people. And in truth his language is as rich as the popular idiom that Saint Teresa used in telling the story of her life. His book, picturesque and cinematic, mocking and just to all, is never less than lively. It is the first Gobelin tapestry of the Conquest, even though it is not always scrupulously accurate. His pages that picture the city of Mexico are immortal; his remembrance of the colors and acts of each gentleman, and of the number of steps up the pyramids of Tenochtitlán, is incredible. Best of all, Cortés comes out covered with glory. The opening passages, which seem to threaten an implacable demand for punishment and a belittlement of Cortés, are followed by a text that reveals the simple attitude of a man who, as a soldier, respects and admires his captain. He talks his story more than he writes it, like an old man yarning with his friends. And like other old men's story-telling, his has the charm of memories evoked beneath the tree gilded by twilight. Its merits have made his *Historia Verdadera de la Conquista de la Nueva España* the favorite history of the period. He wrote it on his estate at Chamula—he was not as poor as he said he was—and entitled it a "true history," as Cervantes was to speak later of the "true" adventures of Don Quixote.

¶ THE COLONIES AS SOURCE BOOKS FOR HISTORY

Like Díaz del Castillo, the monks and soldiers living in the colonies were pricked by the desire to write as they gradually quieted down. They set themselves to compiling either general histories of America or particular histories of the conquests. As we have seen, Fray Bartolomé de Las Casas already had been so moved. Other examples abounded, and the harvest was so great that a brief catalogue will serve to show that no corner of America was without its writers.

Gonzalo Fernández de Oviedo (1478–1557) started his massive *Historia Natural y General de las Indias*, already summarized (p. 80), when he was lieutenant governor in Darien; he continued it as governor of Cartagena, and completed it in Spain after he was appointed Chronicler of the Indies. In Mexico, Francisco Cervantes de Salazar (1514–75), a professor who was the rector of the University of Mexico, was named historian of the city and wrote his *Chronicle of New Spain* there. Fray Bernardino de Sahagún got material for a dictionary of the Nahuatl language from his conversations with the Indians, and had time to write his monumental *Historia General de las cosas de la Nueva España.* Fray Toribio de Benavente—"Motolinía"—wrote his *Historia de los Indios de la Nueva España* while deeply involved with his great work of educating the Indians. Fray Juan de Torquemada (*c.* 1563–1624) collected a mass of documents for his *Monarquía Indiana*, although he is not an original writer. More vivid, richer in data, and saltier in language, *Historia de las Indias de la Nueva España* (*History of the Indies of New Spain*) was the work of Fray Diego Durán (1537–88), who lived in Texcoco from childhood. José de Acosta (1539–1616), more daring and ambitious, made his famous *Historia Natural y Moral de las Indias* a classic study of the ideas of the colonial period and of the American world. Jerónimo de Mendieta (1525–1604) wrote the *Historia Eclesiástica Indiana*, an ecclesiastical history that supplemented Acosta's natural and moral history of the Indies. Juan de Cárdenas (1636?–?), a physician, was the author of *Primera Parte de los Problemas y Secretos Maravillosos de las Indias* (*First Part of the Problems and Marvelous Secrets of the Indies*). Everything mentioned thus far was written in Mexico.

Other writers besides Bernal Díaz del Castillo were at work in Guatemala. Antonio de Remesal, who came to America as a missionary in 1613, reported the conquest of Guatemala by Pedro de Alvarado and the beginnings of that colony in his *Historia de la Provincia de San Vicente de Chyapa y Guatemala.* Francisco Jiménez also composed a work entitled *Historia de la Provincia de San Vicente de Chiapa y Guatemala*, and Francisco Vásquez (1647–1714) wrote the *Crónica de la Provincia del Santísimo Nombre de Jesús de Guatemala.*

From New Granada came Fray Pedro Aguado's *Historia de Santa Marta y Nuevo Reino de Granada*, as well as his *Conquista de la Nueva Granada.* Brother Pedro left Spain in 1560 and died sometime after 1589. His book, although pitilessly multilated in Spain, still stands as one of the important works of the period. Fray Pedro Simón (1574–1630) wrote *Noticias Historiales de las Conquistas de Tierra Firme en las Indias Occidentales.* The *Epitome de la Conquista del Nuevo Reino de Granada*, by the Conquistador Gonzalo Jiménez de Quesada, was used by other historians as a sourcebook before it disappeared. Fray Reginaldo de Lizárraga (1539–1609) wrote the *Descripción y Población de las Indias* in Quito, and Fray Gaspar de Carvajal (1504–85) wrote the *Relación del Descubrimiento del Gran Río de las Amazonas* in the same city. The latter is a book closely related to several other books: *El Marañón y el Amazonas* by Father Manuel Rodríguez (1628–84), the *Nuevo descubrimiento del Río Amazonas* by Fray Cristóbal de Acuña (1597–1676), and *Noticia y Relación de Quito y del río de las Amazonas* by Licentiate Toribio Ortiguera, a mayor of Quito, who was living there in 1569 with his Indian wife, Isabel Guachay.

These American works, taken together, give a full account of one of the most extraordinary adventures in the discovery of rivers, an epic as stirring as fiction, which combines great battles, the wildest jungle settings, and utter savagery. Speaking of Ortiguera's book, Carrera Andrade says:

> It has the breathlessness of a great novel of adventure, full of extraordinary happenings, stories about *entrepreneurs*, Indian uprisings, and volcanic eruptions. He tells of the expedition led by Gonzalo Pizarro and Francisco de Orellana into the country of cinnamon as they were searching for the mines worked by Huayna Cápac; the itinerary and death of Pedro de Ursúa in the Amazon jungles; the delusions of grandeur of Lope de Aguirre, who tried to establish a kingdom in the very heart of equatorial America . . . the rebellion of the Indians, and the destruction of the cities of Quechidona and Ávila, which had been built in the heart of the jungle.

Literature got off to an early start in Peru and developed very richly. It was not the fruit of a monastic peace. The struggle against the Indians was made longer by civil wars among the Spaniards, the Pizarros against the Almagros. Francisco López de Jérez (1504–39) wrote the *Verdadera Relación de la Conquista del Peru y Provincia de Cuzco* (*True Report of the Conquest of Peru and the Province of Cuzco*) in 1534; Juan de Betanzos (1510–76) the *Suma y Narración de los Incas* (*Compendium and Account of the Incas*); Pedro Cieza de León (1518–1560) the *Crónica del Peru* (*Chronicle of Peru*); Pedro Sarmiento de Gamboa (1530–92) the *Historia Índicao de los Incas* (*History of the Incas*); Juan Polo de Ondegardo (who died in 1575) the *Información sobre la Religión de los Incas* (*Information on the Religion of the Incas*): Agustín de Zárate, who died sometime around 1560, the *Historia del descubrimiento y conquista del Peru* (*History of the Discovery and Conquest of Peru*). Pedro Cieza de

León, who took part in the conquest of New Granada for a time, joined Licentiate La Gasca in the expedition to pacify Peru after the Pizarros' civil wars were over. Later he wrote his book on the civil wars, along with several other works on Peru. Pedro Sarmiento de Gamboa (*c.* 1530–*c.* 1592) was present at the discovery of the Solomon Islands, visited the Straits of Magellan, carried on a campaign against Tupac Amaru, pursued Sir Francis Drake, and wrote his own *History of the Incas* (*Historia Indica*).

In Chile, Diego Rosales (1603–77) wrote the *Historia General del Reino de Chile* (*General History of the Kingdom of Chile*). Pedro Hernández (who died about 1513) wrote his *Comentarios al viaje de Alvar Núñez Cabeza de Vaca al Paraguay* (*Commentaries on the Voyage of Alvar Núñez Cabeza de Vaca to Paraguay*) in Buenos Aires. Fray Bérnabe Cobo (1528–1627), a wanderer who visited the Antilles, Venezuela, Quito, and Mexico, packed his *Historia del Nuevo Mundo* (*History of the New World*) with information on the American flora and very good descriptions of the colonial customs.

¶ THE POETS

The names of many poets are listed among those of the Spanish-born men who wrote in America. The saga of the conquest called for verse. A work that contributed not a little, perhaps even too much, to the awakening of the nascent lyricism, a work above all the others, is *La Araucana*, by Alonso de Ercilla y Zúñiga (1534–94). Ercilla served as a soldier and courtier in his youth and traveled in the suite of the crown prince of Spain to the courts of Italy, Germany, Austria, and France. He walked with the young Philip through the fields and cities of Flanders, and was chosen a member of the entourage that arrived with him in London for his marriage to Mary Tudor. By that time, Ercilla had had his fill of court life and had decided to try America. He sailed for Peru. The capital of the new colony did not suit him and he elected to move on to Chile, where he fought in the wars against the fierce Araucanians. He admired his haughty adversaries, for they were highly skilled warriors, firmly resolved to defend their land, and as resourceful militarily as the Spaniards. When Ercilla sought to balance the drive and courage of each against the other, his scales trembled now and again. This one-time courtier, soldier, and traveler finished his career as a poet in Chile. He may well be called the father of poetry in that kingdom, for *La Araucana*, his epic, still stands as the greatest heroic narrative of America written in Spanish. Yet Ercilla's epic is not dedicated to the exploits of any one hero. He did not recognize any Cid Campeador or any fabulous and knightly captain in the Chilean war. He saw two antagonists meeting in a struggle to the death, and thereby discovered one of them, the native. Yet he could not fully understand why those people attracted him. In fact, the land, the men, and the circumstances all together captivated him. Ercilla himself was conquered by America, and he sang not to a conquered Chile, but of a conquered Spain, his Spain, as he surrendered himself to contemplation. The title of the epic tells this; it is so American, so Chilean, so Araucanian. At one point the poet asks himself:

> *Who was it that cast you in an ocean of woes*
> *Deafened by the throbbing of drums and brasses*
> *As you longed to be one with the tree and the rose,*
> *Plucking their blooms in sweet-scented masses?*
> *Who ever ensnared you in trouble and sin*
> *Lies, fictions, fables, affairs with loose lasses*
> *When you'd rather be feeling the breeze on your skin*
> *And I'd run to meet you with a joy that surpasses?*
> *Must living be ever constricted by war,*
> *Hatred, resentment, senseless desire,*
> *Discord, enmities, rivers of gore,*
> *Outrage, folly, uncontrolled ire,*
> *Dark vengeance, brute deeds—can life hold no more*
> *Than destruction, cruelty, killing, and fire?*
> *They reduce even Mars himself to disgust—*
> *His tolerance, greater than mine, they exhaust.*

Who got you into it? he asks, and answers himself in a stanza like a muted hymn to the Chilean nation:

> *Chile province fertile and renowned*
> *Provides the famed Antarctic with a shore*
> *Good seed has burgeoned from its ground*
> *In proud and gallant people, fond of war.*

The fidelity with which Ercilla recaptures the Araucanians' love of liberty makes him the first poet to isolate the germ of American independence in a verse like a rallying cry of 1810, the year the colonies began their struggle against Spain. He puts the following words into the mouth of the Chilean:

By all the powers of hell I swear,
If I'm not among the dead next year,
I'll drive from Chile the rule of Spain,
Cost what it may in bloodshed and pain.
Nor cold, nor heat, nor fear shall shake me,
My steadfast purpose won't forsake me.
For deep in the twilight of my realm
No Spanish hand can hold the helm.

A work so famous could not be written without some effect. Soon many versifiers were following the footsteps of the successful poet, hoping to write cantos that would equal his. Another Chilean, Pedro de Oña (1570–1643) composed the *Arauco domado* (*The Araucanian Tamed*), a poem in fifteen thousand verses intended to clothe the wars, the life, and the courage of the Araucanians in new arguments. Martín del Barco Centenera (1544–1605) wrote what is known as the Argentine Epic, an abbreviation of a very long title: *La Argentina y Conquista del Río de la Plata con otros acaecimientos de los reinos del Peru, Tucumán y Estado del Brasil.* Of all those imitators and followers, only the Chilean achieved some felicitous moments. Some of the verses in the *Arauco Domado* ring with authentic beauty, exemplified in the passage in which Caupolicán meets Fresia as she bathes in the river that runs through the forest. Oddly enough, Oña's scene might describe a meeting between Hercules and Aphrodite, as Alone (Hernán Díaz Arrieta) remarks in his commentary:

In this warm, southern forest of Chile—described by Oña— we would look in vain for oaks, mañíus [a tall tree of Chile], elms, or towering pines; the European species that had not yet reached the country are there: the poplars, the willows, the live oaks, the cypresses. Beneath their leafy branches wild boars and leopards roam. Nightingales sing in the glades. Is this meant to belittle the original flora and fauna? Or is it timidity at using words not consecrated to poetic custom? Or mere blindness to the sight of a new reality? Probably a little of each.

Caupolicán and Fresia chase each other, embrace, delight in the water. Their play is described in the following passage:

And now the knot's untied,
And she, pretending dread
Though secretly enraptured,

Ran, fleet of foot. He swifter sped,
With hands outstretched, and captured
A foot that would the snow enhance.
The water in its upward dance
Fell back into its silv'ry bed
The turtledove with envious sigh
Looks on, and breathes her avian cry.

Oña also wrote a long poem, *El Vasauro*, that remained unpublished for nearly three centuries. He completed it in 1635, but the full text was not issued until 1941. Only a fragment had been known until then.

But to return to the poets born in Spain: Juan de Castellanos (1522–1606), a priest of Tunja, New Granada, though inspired by *La Araucana*, composed in his own style, quite distinct from Ercilla's. He also wrote in verse the *Elegías de Varones Ilustres*, (*Elegies to Famous Men*), and the *Historia de la Nueva Granada* (*History of New Granada*), which together constitute the longest poem in the Castilian language. The critics saw fit to dismiss it and to censure the poet for crudeness and vulgarity. True, he forced events to fit his verses, and was guilty of such odd barbarisms as altering dates to make the rhymes he needed for the hendecasyllabic meter he employed. But he wrote some delightfully fresh scenes with touches of humor, vivid reconstructions of Columbus and the discoverers, admirable pictures of the Conquistadors' marches through jungles and swamps, and portraits of such characters as Drake and the tyrant Aguirre. He is a mine of information and intimate detail that might be sought in vain in other books and that all historians have drawn upon.

Some of Spain's great poets settled in America. Bernardo de Balbuena (1561–1627), author of *Grandeza Mexicana* (*The Grandeur of Mexico*), the first lyrical poem in Mexican literature, only can be classified as great. In the words of Alfonso Reyes, Balbuena "is proud of his two countries; he is a superior poet, and we appreciate in him a monument to that modern Alexandrinism which everyone labels Baroque. . . . His is not a tropical, ardent poetry, as it has been called now and again, but rather it is urbane, polished, and even geometrical. The *Grandeza* is a mural of Mexico City in graceful tercets, with horses, monuments, theater, literature, elegance, crafts, and so on, carefully drawn and illuminated by a sunny palette."

There you will find in gifted bands
The masters of the world of learning

> *In numbers like the Ganges' sands*
> *More godlike than mundane at turning*
> *A phrase alike profound and clever*
> *Themselves forever with the truth concerning.*

Balbuena found his inspiration for the composition of a pastoral novel, *Siglo de oro en las selvas de Erífile* (*The Golden Age in the Erífile Jungles*), in the Italian poets. But his Renaissance approach did not detach him from the medieval world around him, as he showed in his poem *Bernardo o la victoria de Roncesvalles* (*Bernard, or the Victory at Roncesvalles*).

Cervantes said that America was the refuge of thieves and rascals . . . yet he asked the king to appoint him to a position in Guatemala, Cartagena, or Chuquisaca. Only God knows whether *Don Quixote* would ever have been written if he had obtained what he asked for. Something about America lured all the writers in Spain. The New World—an earthly paradise and a lethal jungle—contained the Fountain of Youth and El Dorado. Legends about them filtered like gold dust through the literary foliage of the century. Lope de Vega praised the poets of America and dedicated one of his works to denouncing Drake for his raids, for Drake was the dragon that led the hosts of the anti-papist English and infested the seas around America. This epic, *La Dragontea*, was also inspired by Lope's experience with the Spanish Armada. But the episode did not quench his interest in America. His American discovery was a woman whom he called Amaryllis, but whose real name may have been María Gómez de Alvarado. We do not know whether Amaryllis was born in Bogotá or in Lima, but at any rate she sent him a letter composed in meter which was the opening of a correspondence with the great Spaniard. They wrote to each other in verse and Amaryllis proved herself a poet as ingenious as the Phoenix (as Lope was called). In one of his replies, Lope said:

> *I like to fancy, and I'm sure I am right*
> *That when I am gone, you'll not cease to send,*
> *My New World Amaryllis, letters written in light*
> *To wherever I'll be, in that mystery-filled realm.*

Tirso de Molina (pseudonym of Gabriel Téllez, 1571?–1648) was more resolute than Cervantes or Lope, in his wish to make a direct acquaintance with America; or perhaps he was luckier. As a monk in the order of the Brothers of Mercy, he was able to go to Santo Domingo when he was forty-four years old. By his own account, at that time he had written nearly three hundred comedies. During the three years he was in Santo Domingo, he occupied the chair of theology at the university and breathed the new society's atmosphere, which, according to some scholars, modified his later work. The experience was a happy one for him. The opposite was the fate of the poet Gutiérrez de Cetina, who composed the most beautiful madrigal in the Spanish language, which begins: "Clear, serene eyes, if praised for your sweet glance . . ." He went to Mexico and met his death there in an obscure nocturnal encounter before he could leave any written traces of his life in America. All he left was allusions in his prose work, *Paradoja en la alabanza de los cuernos* (*Paradox in Praise of Horns*) and some influence on his friends in Mexico. The Sevillian poet Juan de la Cueva (1550?–1610?) spent three years in Mexico. He left Spain in dire poverty. In his treatise on poetry, he followed the line of Horace and leaned toward Italian verse. Those inclinations may have planted a seed in Mexico, according to the poet Francisco de Terrazas (1525–84), who wrote many Petrarchian sonnets. At that time a sonnet in the style adopted by Terrazas was unusual. It began as follows:

> *Lay down the mesh of gold you weave*
> *To hold my soul in thrall*
> *Take back the roses' hues and leave*
> *Them like the snow's new fall.*
> *Give back the coral, pearls and all*
> *That makes your lovely mouth so sweet*
> *And to the envious solar ball*
> *Return the stolen light that made it grieve.*

¶ AFTER THE SPANIARDS THE CREOLES

The Creoles, like Terrazas, were creating their own literature. Creoles wrote everything—prose, poetry, plays, history, chronicles, and pages of pure mysticism. Juan Suárez de Peralta (1537–91), the son of a brother-in-law of Hernán Cortés, left vivid pictures of Mexico in his *Tratado del descubrimiento de las Indias y su conquista* (*Treatise on the Discovery of the Indies and Their Conquest*). Alfonso Reyes described him as

an obscure Mexican Saint-Simon who knew the palace and its secrets and who doubtless saw more than he tells. In the idiom of good colonial society, without great art, but with a touching naturalness and candor, he brings to life before our eyes the conspiracy of Martín Cortés (the Conquistador's son, drunk with longing to rule over an independent Mexico), the trial of the Ávilas, and an episode involving the English corsairs who put into port at San Juan de Ulúa.

Another Mexican, Pedro Gutiérrez de Santa Clara (born before 1570), wrote a work entitled *Historia de las guerras civiles del Peru* (*History of the Civil Wars in Peru*).

A godson of Jiménez de Quesada named Juan Rodríguez Freile (1566–c.1640) brought to life in New Granada a picaresque literature developed, so to speak, across history. He ignored the heroic phase of his godfather's life and gave free rein to a satirical spirit, perhaps born of the cold and snow on the Bogotan heights, a spirit that can be traced through later literary chronicles of the city. His manuscript bore the long title *Historia de la conquista de la Nueva Granada*, but it became famous under the familiar title of *El Carnero* (*The Sheep*). Bound in sheepskin, the manuscript was passed from hand to hand for some two centuries. Instead of recording the exploits that brought fame to Quesada, this delightful book tells about witches who flew from Santa Fe de Bogotá to Santo Domingo, about infidelities in the new society, about the remarkable case of Doña Inés de Hinojosa, who traveled from Venezuela to Tunja in New Granada, switching husbands along the way by inducing each new lover to murder the incumbent. In the end the law caught up with her and she was hanged from a tree. Everything in this diminutive anthology of tales and intrigues was in a similar vein. Perhaps that is why the manuscript was more popular and welcome than many of the flamboyant histories.

Another Bogotan, Juan Flórez de Ocariz, who died in 1692, wrote the monumental *Genealogías del Nuevo Reino de Granada* (*Genealogies of the New Kingdom of Granada*). He succeeded in publishing only the first volume (Madrid, 1674). The second vanished as mysteriously as if in a tale from *The Sheep*, for as the story goes, some family stole it lest it become known that their family tree was not well planted in the heraldic garden of Flórez. It would seem that similar reasons prompted the disappearance of the second volume of the *Historia de la Conquista y Poblaciones de la Provincia de Venezuela* (*History of the Conquest and Towns of the Province of Venezuela*) by José Oviedo y Baños (1671–1738). What survived is one of the most beautifully written works of the period. All in all, it is entirely possible that the lost works of all the writers may exceed in number those that have been preserved. Of those rescued, many have been discovered in the archives of Spain after two or three centuries in oblivion.

The kingdom of Quito produced some outstanding writers. First among them was the Augustinian monk Gaspar de Villarroel (1587–1665), whose *Govierno Eclesiástico Pacífico, o Tratado de los dos cuchillos* (*Peaceful Ecclesiastical Government, or Treatise on the Two Rights of Governing*) is highly regarded. Jorge Carrera Andrade ranks Fray Gaspar

> among the most distinguished cultivators of Castilian prose, and one of the best Humanists of the seventeenth century. The rich, heavy texture of his style cannot veil the light of his irony, which illuminates the roughest and most winding trails, hitherto untrodden, in the colonial system, and points out the defects and viciousness of the monarchy and the clergy.

Fray Gaspar traveled from Quito to Spain, where he became such on outstanding preacher to the Court that he was appointed to the see of Chile. From there he went to Chuquisaca, where he died. Everywhere he left the stamp of his genius and his goodness.

Gaspar de Escalona y Agüero traveled in Villarroel's footsteps. He was born in Riobamba, studied first in Quito and then in Spain, returned to America, lived in Chuquisaca and became an *oidor* (justice) of the *audiencia* in Santiago de Chile, where he died. He wrote a book that treated the economic history of America: *Gazophilatium regium pervianum*, published in 1647, and later the compendium, *Ordenanzas Generales para los Oficiales de las Indias*, a handbook of rules for officials.

Francisco Núñez de Pineda (1607–80), author of the *Cautiverio Feliz o Razón de las Guerras Dilatadas de Chile* (*Happy Captivity, or the Reason for the Long-Drawn Wars in Chile*), was born in Peru. His narrative was so vivid, fascinating, and well-written that Anderson Imbert characterizes it as the forerunner of the novel in America. But Pineda was a poet above everything. He left many ballads and sonnets, and his *Captivity* mingles prose with verse.

Fray Antonio de la Calancha (1584–1654) came from Chuquisaca in Upper Peru, now Bolivia. He taught at the University of San Marcos in Lima and in the Colegio de San Ildefonso, where he was rector, became prior of the Augustinians in Trujillo and Arequipa, and official chronicler of his order. The data in his *Crónica Moralizadora* are so gilded with optimism as to make it appear that he must have thought paradise on earth was indeed situated in America, as Vespucci and Columbus had declared. To him, Peru was swimming in abundance. "Here," he said, "the most worthless eat the year around food that only the rich eat in Spain, and a plebeian here eats more in a week than the most liberal man eats there in a month."

The Jesuit priest Alonso de Ovalle (1601–51) was born in Santiago, Chile, and educated in Córdoba, Argentina. He became rector of the Colegio de San Francisco Javier in Santiago, journeyed to Spain and Rome as solicitor of the order, and returned to die in Lima. He was the most brilliant of the Jesuits in Chile, where he took charge of instructing the Negroes while he longed for the life of a missionary. The Company of Jesus preferred to send him to Europe. When Ovalle was in Rome, he recognized the need for a written history of his country, including its customs and natural history. From that need came his *Histórica Relación*, which places Ovalle among the writers cited by the Spanish Academy in its dictionary of authorities. He is inscribed as a master of the language.

The wealth of Spanish Creole writers testifies eloquently to the general preoccupation with literature, both inside and outside the convents. The Spaniard born in America had the dual advantage of his inheritance from the Peninsula and of his knowledge of the languages and habits of the Indians. He had taken in with his mother's milk on-the-spot knowledge of the main actors in the Conquest and of the founders of the colony. In general, his point of view differed from that of the native Spaniard's in that he affirmed with greater vivacity what was American, often with such fervor that he showed in his work a flicker of independence. When a monk in Peru pointed out that Spain had never had an easy moment until the gold of America had been snatched from her, or when another monk from Chuquisaca noted that in Tucumán "a cow was worth a peso, in Paraguay half a peso, and about the same in Chile," they were using hyperbole to praise their own land, sowing the seeds of a national pride that would grow until its flag would be hoisted on the day when emancipation was proclaimed.

The most interesting product of this awakening is the literature written by Americans with Indian blood. Garcilaso de la Vega's work leads all the rest. This Inca, of whom we have spoken earlier, was more the universal man than the others. He translated *Diálogos sobre el Amor* (*Dialogues on Love*) by the Spanish-Jewish physician and poet Judah León Abrabanel (d. 1535), who is known in Spanish literary history as León Hebreo, i.e., Leo the Hebrew. In addition, he wrote about Florida, provided the world with a textbook on the history of the Incas which dealt generously and justly with the Spaniards, and by sheer patience made his way in Spain, where he wrote all his books. Other *mestizos* achieved success in America. Among them were some of the best historians of Mexico, New Granada, Peru, and Quito. Hernando Alvarado Tezozómoc (1519–99), the son of Diego Alvarado Huanitzin and a daughter of Moctezuma II, served the Royal Audiencia as interpreter and wrote the *Crónica Mexicáyotl*, and the *Crónica Mexicana*. Fernando de Alva Ixtlilxóchitl (1568–1648) came somewhat later. He was descended from the lords of Mexico and Texcoco. He, too, acted as interpreter to an Indian court of justice. He wrote the *Historia Chichimeca*. His *Reports* are rich in legends and songs taken directly from the old Mexicans and written down in Nahuatl. In New Granada, Lucas Fernández de Piedrahita (1624–88) was outstanding. Although his patronymic is Spanish, he was the son of a woman from the Chibcha nobility. He became an elegant Latinist and a very fine Castilian stylist. His *Historia General de las Conquistas del Nuevo Reino de Granada*, patterned after classical histories, placed cultivated speech, based on the testimony of their contemporaries, in the mouths of his characters. Jacinto Collahuasco, from Quito, wrote the *Guerras Civiles del Inca Atahualpa con su hermano Antoco, llamado comúnmente Huáscar Inca* (*Civil Wars between the Inca Atahualpa and his Brother Antoco, commonly called Huáscar Inca*) in 1708. This vanished work on the war between the two Incan brothers is often cited by other historians, among them Juan de Velasco. It drew a historic parallel between the fraternal civil war and the wars among the Spaniards. In Peru, Felipe Guamán Poma de Ayala (1526–c. 1614) wrote an independent history in his *Nueva Crónica y Buen Gobierno* (*New Chronicle and Good Government*), which extols the values of the Incas; he also transcribed Quechuan poems sung in religious ceremonies, which thus became a part of the written language for the first time.

¶ CREOLE POETS—THE GONGORISTS

The dominant literary theme of the first two centuries was history. Chronicles, poetry, even the rudimentary novel were naturally ruled by this genre, for history portrayed alternately the greatness and the sufferings of both Indians and Spaniards. History pervaded all forms of writing as political and natural history, the epic and sociology, customs and civics in treatises on good government, and, of course, poetry. Spanish America, or Hispano-Indian America, to be more accurate, was a land of poetry. Fernán González de Eslava (*c.* 1534–*c.* 1601) was a Spanish poet who had sent down roots in Mexico while very young and who left sixteen *Spiritual and Sacramental Conversations* (*Coloquios espirituales y sacramentales*) and more than a hundred and fifty *Canciones divinas* (Hymns). González combined plain speaking with crude irony. He said that the poets in Mexico "were more plentiful than manure," and wrote the *Entremés de dos rufianes* (*Interlude of the Two Ruffians*). The Spanish poets, of which he himself was one, were equally abundant and equally fertile.

One of the Mexican poets, Carlos de Sigüenza y Góngora (1645–1700), was a nephew of Luis de Góngora y Argote (1561–1627) the last great poet of the Golden Age, whose witty, elegant, and elliptical style made "Gongorism" the Spanish equivalent of the English style called "euphuism" because it was first exemplified in the novel *Euphues, or the Anatomy of Wit*, written in 1578 by the English poet and playwright John Lyly (1553?–1606). Góngora's nephew was a poet, mathematician, astronomer, cosmographer, historian, chronicler, and biographer; he was also a technical expert on fortification and a member of the Company of Jesus. He wrote *Belerofonte Matemático*, which kindled a raging controversy. When another Jesuit, Father Kino, tried to restrain him, Sigüenza replied: "Neither your Reverence nor any other mathematician, be he Ptolemy himself, may formulate dogmas in this science, for authority is of no use to it whatsoever; proof and demonstration alone will serve . . ." Here, then, was a rebel like his uncle. The Company of Jesus rejected Sigüenza, but he defended himself wonderfully well and finally sang his *Triunfo Parténico* (*Parthian Victory*). Alfonso Reyes calls it a "poetic showcase of that age." Sigüenza is considered another forerunner of the American novel because of his *Infortunios de Alonso Ramírez* (*Misfortunes of Alonso Ramírez*). He stressed everything American in vivid images. For example, he placed portraits of the Mexican emperors on the arches of triumph built to receive Viceroy Paredes. As a man half scientist, half poet, he willed his body to science.

Silvestre de Gamboa (1564–1644) made his literary debut in Cuba, though he was born in the Canary Islands. He narrated the sufferings of Bishop Altamirano in a hundred and forty-five *ottava rima* verses under the title *Espejo de Paciencia* (*Mirror of Patience*). He himself admitted that the verses were reminiscent of Italian poets. Bishop Altamirano, the hero of the story, was captured by the French pirate, Giron. A Negro killed the pirate and saved the bishop's life. The only casualty of the affray was an Indian. Anderson Imbert writes:

> When the bishop went back to Cuba a free man, the gods of mythology came out to hail him; they were carrying the flowers and fruits of America, many with Indian names that thus entered the Horatian literary phraseology. The religious and the heroic themes were interwoven. In the first canto, the bishop's sufferings revealed his piety; in the second they were avenged by the heroic punishment of the heretic. . . . This interweaving of Christian humility with the anger of a just man is very significant. Gamboa works with both traditions.

The most ambitious of the poets in Lima was a Sevillian, Fray Diego de Ojeda (*c*. 1571–1615). He donned the habit and composed *La Cristiada* (*The Christiad*) in Lima. His career was divided between Lima and Cuzco, where he taught theology, and he died in Huánuco. Hipólito Sancho calls him a poet "distinguished in Latin and Castilian." *The Christiad*, an epic of the life of Jesus, comprises twelve volumes of *ottava rima* stanzas. Except for his own evangelistic fervor, his American experience played no part in it. Each book carries on its opening page an *ottava* that sums up the content. The first one starts: "The Lord has supper with his devoted disciples; he washes their feet; ordains the sacrament—Judas reveals his sin to John . . ." The first of the poets to praise the work of Ojeda in verses introducing the epic was Lope de Vega. He was not sparing in his praise, which concludes:

> The Antarctic pole of the sphere
> And our part, too, is blest

With thine own evangelistic zest.
They call you an Apollo here,
The Fifth Apostle on the other shore,
A David reborn to sing once more.

The Limans were very fond of mystical poetry. Luis Antonio
de Oviedo, Count of La Granja (1636–1717), wrote his *Vida
de Santa Rosa de Lima* (*Life of Saint Rose of Lima*) in verse;
and Juan de Peralta (1663–1747) composed his *Tres Jornadas
al Cielo* (*Three Steps in the Journey to Heaven*) in verse also.
Juan Espinosa de Medrano (1632–88) composed *El Auto Sacramental del Hijo Pródigo* (*The Mystery Play of the Prodigal Son*)
in Quechuan verse and his Biblical drama *Amar su propia
muerte* (*To Love One's Own Death*) in Spanish verse. Mention of
Espinosa de Medrano introduces an obsessive theme running
through colonial poetry: Góngora. Espinosa de Medrano, commonly known as El Lunarejo (the Pied Poet), wrote an entire
treatise, the *Apologético en favor de Góngora* (*Apologia on Behalf of Góngora*), that was full of acute observations, passion,
and logic aimed against the Portuguese Manuel de Faria e
Sousa, who had dared to poke fun at the author of the *Soledades.*
"No one but those who envied him or could not understand him
ever spoke ill of Don Luis de Góngora," said the Pied Poet. "If the
latter [lack of understanding] be a fault, many blind men would
have reason to quarrel with the sun." The author of this defense
celebrated in *The Prodigal Son* the delights of the Peruvian
table, including potatoes from Laicacota, corn on the cob from
Potosí, and mushrooms from Cohdoroma.

Góngora's poetry sent an immediate echo through Mexico,
Santa Fe de Bogotá, Santiago (Chile), and Lima. The American
poets lined up for or against the Gongorists and Anti-Gongorists
because the subject was close to their hearts. Bernardo de Balbuena wrote in his *Grandeza Mexicana*: "Where in the world
have poets ever been as worthy of veneration as the very acute
Don Luis de Góngora?" In that same year, 1627, an allegorical
float in honor of Apollo was paraded in a carnival in Lima. The
figure presiding over the tableau wore the mask of Don Luis de
Góngora. He was as popular as Cervantes or Quevedo. What was
there about the poet that bewitched literary men and yet aroused
the enthusiasm of the common people? Possibly the explanation
lies in the two facets of his poetry. He showed one facet in his
short poems set to music and in his free burlesqued sonnets,

which constituted a direct, uninvolved kind of art within the grasp of everyone. His other facet was revealed in his solitary musings, the mazes of his thought, his recondite musicality, and his mystery. That ambivalence was American—both simple and complicated. The plain and the convoluted, the light and the dark, met in America.

Sor Juana Inés de la Cruz (1648–95) scaled the highest peaks ever reached either by Mexican poetry or by any other verse in the Spanish language written in her century. She has been called the tenth muse of Mexico. She was the mirror of the Gongorists. Like Góngora, she composed verse in an African idiom to describe scenes among Negroes, thus anticipating the West Indian poets of our day by several centuries. Like the Pied Poet, she wrote an allegorical religious drama in Quechua. Sor Juana employed the popular speech of Mexico to compose short poems to be set to music, religious songs for feast days, and a comedy that she wittily called *Los Empeños de una casa* (*Duties Around the House*), in an approximation of the Mexican vernacular. Alfonso Reyes writes:

> It is surprising to find in this woman an originality that transcends the garb she wore, and no less surprising such a world of religion and mundane art, learning and sentiment, feminine coquetry and maternal solicitude, boldness and tenderness, knowledge of the Court and the people, gaiety and gravity, and even a very clear consciousness of social realities: America before the world, the essence of the Mexican, the contrast between the Creole and the Spaniard, the rise of the Indian, the freedom of the Negro, the mission of woman, and reform in education.

Sor Juana was the most versatile writer of her time. She composed poems for such occasions as birthdays and weddings, salutes to the viceroy and his lady, and verses meant to flatter the bishop, and at the same time she engaged in theological argumentation with the Jesuit Father Antonio Vieira, then preaching with bellicose ardor in Brazil. Sor Juana's letters, signed Sor Filomena and containing her side of the argument, have been preserved. They show her knowledge of theology and the independence of her judgment. Sor Juana often felt a need to go into hiding, to seek a Gongoresque solitude. Out of this need she wrote her *Sueños* (*Dreams*), in which she seems to shut the mystery of her inner self behind lock and key. Those *Dreams* are the most famous Gongoresque poems in America.

With her overmastering talent, it was not easy for her to adjust to the humdrum life of the convent. Her differences with the other nuns and her superiors finally became so acute that she renounced poetry in a dramatic surrender to humility. But while the struggle was going on, she felt impelled to conceal herself behind enigmatic verses in images and symbols that endure in all their mysterious and poetical beauty. The opening of her "Primero Sueño" rings sonorously:

> *Pyramidal, baleful, born as a shadow*
> *Of earth, yet moving toward heaven,*
> *Obelisks fashioned to point upward*
> *In vain aspiration to light*
> *Shed by the shine of the stars*
> *Which, ever gleaming, ever free,*
> *Can mock the moving legions*
> *That menace in sable mists*
> *Whose darkling frown*
> *Never can reach the higher sphere*
> *Of night's sole queen, the moon*
> *Glowing still in triple beauty*
> *As she turns aloft in three fair faces,*
> *Forced to leave her undisputed mistress*
> *Of atmosphere that she has filmed*
> *With every vaporous exhalation,*
> *Serenely happy in the quiet*
> *Of her regency of silence,*
> *She permits no voices*
> *But those of the birds, who awaken at night*
> *Murmuring so gravely*
> *As to leave her silence undisturbed.*

Before the time of Sor Juana, but during the same century, Hernando Domínguez Camargo (1606–59) of Bogotá wrote the most extensive Gongoristic poem to come out of America. It comprises 1,116 ottava rima stanzas in praise of Ignatius Loyola. The work fills five volumes rich in magical poetic touches. Domínguez Camargo went to Spain from Bogotá to begin his studies in a Jesuit College, where he conceived his enthusiasm for the founder of the Company. After his return to New Granada, he spent the rest of his life as a parish priest in villages as insignificant then as now, but full of the enchantment of the cold and lonely regions of the Andes. Domínguez Camargo officiated as priest in Gachetá, Tocancipá, Paipa, and Turmequé, but his last years were crowned by a promotion to the parish of the largest church in Tunja. On the very spot where Juan de Castellanos had written the longest poem in Castilian literature in verses of scant lyricism, Domínguez Camargo composed his cultivated and refined poetry. Like Góngora's ballads, with a sparkling and lucid beauty that reached every ear, Domínguez Camargo's verses are on a par in quality with the following description of a leap across the brook of Chillo:

> *An arroyo running proud and free*
> *Through rugged cliffs and crags*
> *Is merry as a crystalline colt*
> *With a bridle made of pearls.*
> *Spray like dewdrops formed his coat*
> *So candid, clean, and clear*
> *That verdant myrtles curry him*
> *To catch each fallen hair.*

Domínguez Camargo was also influenced by Góngora's sonnets to the Manzanares River and the bridges of Madrid. One of the best and most ingenious examples of his light verse is a laughing picture of the village he served as priest. It gives the measure of the genius flowering in America during Sor Juana's century, and makes a perfect engraving of a village:

> *A mosque-like chapel of the Catholic creed,*
> *A lizard made of clods that leap and revel;*
> *Surfeited with the world, the flesh, the devil,*
> *Prolific herons reproduce their breed.*
> *And doctors fiddle while their patients bleed*
> *And ragged lawyers their rebuttals level*
> *Like bondsmen recently from bondage freed.*
> *Oh, it's a Barbary Coast of tittle-tattle:*
> *Sprinkling a drizzle of 'How-do-you-do's'*
> *Come frauds who love to gossip, loathe to battle,*
> *Like arrows shot at random, leaky shoes,*
> *People skilled with neither gloves nor spurs:*
> *This is our Guatavita, travelers.*

¶ THE THEATER

The theater was the ideal instrument for educating the Spanish and Portuguese people, most of whom were illiterate, and for amusing them, too. The missionaries in America quickly realized that they could do more to propagate religion through miracle plays and comedies than through their preaching. In Spanish and Portuguese America the theater was flourishing by the sixteenth century, presenting a great variety of plays—many more than those which have come down to us even by title—and they became popular as a kind of forerunner of radio. People learned more from the stage than from their primers, and many of the productions were in the native languages. In Mexico they were not only in Nahuatl, the most widespread language, but also in Zapotec, Mixtec, Tarascan, or Pirind; Peruvian shows were in Quechua and Aymará; the Brazilian and Paraguayan in Guaraní. A section just outside the monastery churches was reserved and enclosed like a plaza with open-air chapels. Except for their proportions these areas devoted to processions and sacramental performances might be compared with Saint Peter's Square in Rome, which serves as an open-air theater during great ceremonies. Processions often included ritual dances that accepted the native contribution without reservations. Religious songs, *posadas* (performances for visitors), interludes, dances, and balls were put on naturally and spontaneously by the Christian family, which met there ingenuously to rejoice. The Mexican playwright Rodolfo Usigli (1905–) has pointed out that the courtyard was a forerunner of the theater of the masses. All such functions were more ambitiously staged in the town or city with a main square planned partly for that purpose. The balconies of the principal houses were boxes overlooking the open-air theater. The stands and platforms in the square were ideal prosceniums.

The patios of some convents, monasteries, and secondary schools, town halls, and the viceroys' palaces also served as theaters, as did the street itself at times. The setting of some of the plays was the court or an Indian settlement. Some were dramas of social criticism, others satirical burlesques. Productions of such dramas as the *Conquest of Rhodes* and the *Destruction of Jerusalem* offered the public a chance to share in the acting, as in the Good Friday procession in Lima which became a spontaneous theatrical production, with the people hurling horrendous insults at the Jews or joining in praise of the Virgin and the Lord. The most singular and picturesque of the Peruvian traditions started there.

Espinosa de Medrano, the Gongoristic Pied Poet of Lima, whom we have mentioned as author of the *Prodigal Son* in

Quechua, is considered the possible author of *Ollantay*, a drama
of unknown origin which challenges scholars. It is of such importance that in the twentieth century the great Argentine dramatist Ricardo Rojas adopted it as the base of his own theatrical
work by the same title. Juan del Valle Caviedes (*c.* 1652–97),
an Andalusian who had moved to Lima as a child and became
known as the "Poet of La Ribera," the town where he conducted
his business, wrote plays not unlike Queveda's comedies. The
Entremés del Amor Alcalde (*Interlude of a Mayor in Love*) the
Baile del Amor Médico (*Dance of a Doctor in Love*), and *Baile
del Amor Tahur* (*Dance of a Cardsharp in Love*), are recorded
as being his work. In New Granada, Fernando Fernández de
Valenzuela (1616–?) wrote his interlude, *Laurea Crítica* (*Critical
Laurels*) in the same satrical vein. One of the characters, a disciple
of Góngora, is held up to ridicule. Rounding out the list of
Spaniards who influenced the American theater in its infancy,
Juan de Cueto y Mena (1602–*c.* 1669), who had settled in New
Granada and Cartagena, wrote many theatrical works, of which
the best known are the dialogue *La Competencia en los Nobles y
Discordia Concordada* (*Rivalry Among Nobles and Discord Con-
corded*) and *Paráfrasis Panegírica* (*Panegyrical Paraphrase*). He
also composed a *Canción describiendo el Cerro de la Popa*, a
long descriptive poem. One of the scholars who made a study
of Cueto y Mena in Colombia has traced *La Competencia* back
to the ecclesiastical drama of the great Spanish dramatist Pedro
Calderón de la Barca (1600–81) and holds that Calderón was
aware of Cueto y Mena when he wrote *La Vida es Sueño* (*Life
is a Dream*).

The theater made a greater impact on the people than any
other literary medium. Oftentimes the ending of a production
aroused the audience to enthusiasm or rage. The story is told
that a show in Mexico ended with the Moors, played by Indians,
being baptized after they had been conquered in mock battles with
the Christians. A great religious feast of conversion came as the
epilogue to that play. But elsewhere, as Alfonso Reyes observes:

> when the Inquisitor Moya de Contreras was appointed arch-
> bishop in 1574, his consecration was celebrated by public
> ceremonies. The priest, Juan Pérez Ramírez (who died about
> 1645) put on his *Desposorio Espiritual entre el Pastor Pedro
> y la Iglesia Mexicana (Spiritual Betrothal of Pastor Pedro to
> the Mexican Church*), and Hernán González de Eslava, a

dramatist who had become famous more than five years earlier, won the greatest success with his *Coloquio III*. Two farces were staged between the acts of the *Coloquio*: one made fun of a graybeard, and the other, *El Alcabalero (The Revenue Officer)*, a familiar Spanish work from the Lope de Rueda cycle, had, it seemed to the viceroy, been chosen intentionally and inopportunely to hold up to ridicule the excise tax recently levied in Mexico. The strained relations between the civil and ecclesiastical authorities which had existed since the time of Zumárraga snapped, and a public scandal ensued. To top it all, a lampoon of the viceroy came out. The priest Ramírez was called to account; the poet Terrazas was arrested, although, because he was the son of a Conquistador "a man of quality and the lord of villages," he was doubtless quickly released; but poor González de Eslava was held incommunicado for several days.

Sor Juana Inés de la Cruz wrote for the theater, as we have seen, but the most distinguished Mexican dramatist of the period was Juan Ruiz de Alarcón, born in Taxco about 1581. He spent his first twenty years in Mexico, then sailed for Spain, already known as one of the great figures in the Spanish theater. He collaborated with Tirso de Molina, himself identified with life in America, and with Lope and Calderón, the three great figures of the Spanish theater in the Golden Age. Alarcón's *La Verdad Sospechosa (Dubious Truth)* alone would be enough to establish the fame that his comedies *Los Favores del Mundo (The World's Favors)*, *No hay Mal que por Bien no venga (Every Cloud Has a Silver Lining)*, and *La Cueva de Salamanca (The Cave of Salamanca)* already had brought him. His carefully wrought dramas *El Tejedor de Segovia (The Weaver of Segovia)*, *Quien mal anda, mal acaba (He Who Does Evil Comes to a Bad End)*, and others further consolidated his literary greatness. *La Verdad Sospechosa* was the model for Corneille's *Le Menteur (The Liar)*.

Alarcón held a bachelor's degree from Salamanca, practiced law in Seville, returned to Mexico with Mateo Alemán, and later went back to Spain, where, in addition to his work for the theater, he collected information for the Council of the Indies. He had the misfortune to be deformed by a large hump on his back, which made him an object of ridicule. In the depths of his spirit lay a greatness that enabled him to rise above his misfortune. He kept himself under a self-contained discipline that distinguishes his dramas from the copious production that was *de rigueur* among lesser dramatists. Menéndez y Pelayo says: "His statue stands forever where Hartzenbusch placed it, in the temple of Menander and Terence, where he precedes Corneille and anticipates Molière."

X: *The Arts in the Spanish Colonies*

¶ MESTIZO ART

No temple was ever built in the Mayan, Aztec, or Incan style after the arrival of the Spaniards in America. Even the minor arts of weaving, goldwork, pottery, and featherwork were struck by a paralysis that only a few people were able to conquer by cunning and stealth. The Indian took care not to let his master see anything that would suggest that the ancient symbols still survived in his work. He had to lay aside or forget his original source of inspiration, to hold his tongue, to conceal, to sharpen his talent for shrewdness. In time, he might conceivably smuggle in something that would recall his native land, its gods, and its myths. The art of featherwork, mostly lost, survives today in small pictures: mere souvenirs.

But even if the Spaniard was interested in dethroning and exiling the American gods, he was nonetheless aware of the great value of the Indian's artistic talents, of his handicraft civilization. He needed them. Before long, Indians entered the locksmith's shop, the smithy, the tanner's, the cabinetmaker's and carpenter's, the workshops of the new goldsmiths and silversmiths with their new techniques, the stone quarries—wherever they could work side by side with Spaniards. Indeed, the arts and crafts became a sort of free port in which a tolerance of compromise had to prevail. In Mexico, people speak of a European plateresque style, a popular plateresque, and an Indian plateresque, referring to varieties of the achitectural style in which the rich ornamentation resembled that of silver plate. In Arequipa and Potosí, it is difficult to judge accurately where the mind and hand of the Spaniard left off and that of the Indian began—whether in stone, in woodcarving, or in the silverwork of the churches. On the altars in Tunja, New Granada, little heads of Indians peer out amid the gold of the Baroque retables. The priests who address the people from the pulpits in Quito seem to have stepped out of a frame built by masters of their craft. The fanatical Inquisitors rarely, if ever, scrutinized work in the plastic arts with as much suspicion as they did the books they expurgated. Indeed, the Inquisitors would have had to search with extreme care to find the fetishes that the Indians hid inside the crosses so that they might worship their ancient god while they appeared to be adoring Christ. If the devil lurked behind the cross, he must be cast out by exorcism. Even so, there were instances where the two religions came perilously close, and at such moments the priest might turn a blind eye, knowing that he could find no better way to insure the attendance of the Indians than to found a church where the memory of an indigenous deity would give surety to it.

No European nation was ever more kindly disposed to artistic miscegenation than Spain. The Arabic style is more prevalent there than in any other part of the Mediterranean. Indeed the Arabic style is often called Spanish. As a rule, Spanish Catholics worship in temples that show the flair and grace of the children of Mohammed. The Moors left their mark on Spain not only in the churches, but also in the palaces and mansions, and even in the houses of the common people. Brick, tile, carved wood, damascened copper, inlay in colored woods, mother-of-pearl, ivory, and tortoise shell; iron-lace locks, tooled Cordovan leather, carpets, cushions, divans, pools, and fountains, even the culinary art, particularly confectionery, showed an Oriental touch, which could be found everywhere in everyday life—in buildings, furniture, the trappings of horses, the interiors of houses, the table, and the bedrooms.

Spain brought a complete blend of styles and cultures to America. For example, when the Almagros and the Pizarros were at war in Peru, some two hundred converted Moslems stood shoulder to shoulder with the Spaniards. They proved to be invaluable auxiliaries trained to fight according to the excellent Arab school and skilled in melting down metal and forging fieldpieces in preparation for battle. One traveler remarked that it was like entering Damascus to visit the old city of Lima. Even today, Cartagena, on the shores of the Caribbean, resembles Damascus, for the city was built of kiln-baked or sun-dried brick that was later stuccoed and whitewashed or painted blue, pink, ochre, or red in the Arab style. Stone was also whitewashed. The jalousies or Venetian blinds at the balconies and windows give the Spanish cities in America an effect quite unlike that of cities in Central or Nordic Europe. In Mexico, the tiled cupolas of the churches are enameled in colors not of the Western world.

The patio of the old convent of Santa Mónica in Puebla, with its tile-covered walls, seems to have been flown directly from Seville to the heart of Mexico. The façade of the Church of San Francisco in Acatepec is dominated by an expanse of tile that not only serves as a background for the surface planes, but also adapts itself well to the curves of the baroque style. It looks like a beautiful monument done in porcelain, a china toy blown up to gigantic proportions. The sanctuary of the Virgin of Ocotlán, in Tlaxcala, has two lateral towers that are divided; the lower half of each is covered with terra cotta tile. Upon this base stands a sort of baroque stone box pierced by the window openings of the campanile and surrounded by elaborate floral decoration. Mexico opened joyous arms to the glazed tiles of Seville. Their designs were compatible with the spirit of the country, and within a short time after they were introduced, tiles were being made in Puebla. Manuel Toussaint has compiled a catalogue of the tile works of Puebla, many of them using Sevillian designs, which demonstrates that by the middle of the seventeenth century it was no longer necessary to import glazed tile from Spain. The work done in Puebla can scarcely be distinguished, even by experts, from what came from Seville, and a cupola of glazed tile in Mexico is enhanced by light, clear air similar to the transparent air of the Arab Mediterranean.

¶ A CHURCH FOR EVERY ORDER

When the first churches were built, the architectural skeleton might be Gothic or it might be Romanesque. The bearing beams of the old church buildings in the city of Santo Domingo were placed according to one or the other of the two styles, and the same was true of the Augustinian convents in Mexico, at Yecapixtla, Actopan, and Atotonilco. In Quito, only the plan of the vaulted ceiling of the choir in the church of San Agustín shows marked traces of the Gothic. There, says José Gabriel Navarro (1881–   ), "the type used by Herrera [architect to Philip II] is so firmly stamped on the first church, which dates from 1537, that it does not bear any trace of the Gothic, to which the environment around the city is definitely inimical." The tropical light, like the Mediterranean light, has but little tolerance for revamped medieval art. Italian models, especially those of the Renaissance, were better suited to the atmosphere of the New World. The courtyards of the convents and monasteries derived from Italy, owing to the odd chance that Flemings introduced the Renaissance style in Quito. Fray Jodoko Ricke de Marselaer, born in Ghent, who went to Quito with another Flemish monk, Fray Pedro Gosseal, designed the church of San Francisco. Germán the German and Jacome the Fleming also worked on it. Navarro tells us something about this building and the convent adjoining it:

> Work on the monastery building began in the years 1537 and 1538 and ended in 1560, a fact that makes it the most interesting architectonic work in the history of sixteenth-century architecture in South America—because there was no structure of an earlier date, because it adapted innovations from the most advanced European art, and finally because the Italian Renaissance entered the New World with it. It still poses the interesting problem of whether or not it antedates that style in Spain, for the first work on the Franciscan church in Quito was done in 1537, and the last toward the end of the sixteenth century, whereas the basilica of the Escorial was not even started in 1575 and was completed in 1582. Indeed, the first Italianate structure in the purest baroque style ever built in America is the Church of San Francisco in Quito and its adjoining convent with its two rows of superposed galleries: the lower one of vaulted arches and the upper one of segmented arches; its courtyard later became the pattern for all civil construction, not only in Quito, but also in Lima and Cuzco.

American architecture became more closely tied to that of Spain as the colony's development synchronized with the development of the plateresque and baroque styles in Spain. But as those styles became acclimated in the New World, they changed in obedience to the climatic conditions and environment to such a degree that special styles were finally originated. The Venezuelan churches are not like those of Peru. The great wealth of Ecuador and Bolivia, brought by the gold and silver overflowing from Peru and Potosí, is not to be found in the churches of New Granada or Venezuela, where the façades are plain, almost naked, and the interiors are less ostentatious. Two Jesuit structures, the Church of the Company of Jesus in Quito and that of San Ignacio in Bogotá, were created from the same Romanesque model, but seem only distantly related. In Mexico, the baroque style became so popular that it developed into a Mexican type in which Mayan and Aztec prototypes were embodied. In the California missions an architecture evolved which bears little resemblance to that of the mission buildings of Paraguay. The achitecture of Cartagena on the warm Caribbean is very different from that on the cold upland of Bogotá, though both were in the same viceroyalty. The style of church, palace, or house that came from Spain was rearranged in the New World, made individual by distance and environment. A Bogotan arriving in Arequipa or Potosí would be as dazzled by what he saw there as a Spaniard, even though there is a closer affinity between the Peruvian and the Mexican, however far apart they are, than between the Arequipan and the Colombian: the geography and history of Peru and Mexico more nearly match. When the characteristics of Californian Spanish architecture are adopted in South America today, the result looks exotic.

The Franciscans, the first order in Mexico, built monasteries and churches that are smaller than those built later by other orders. The Augustinians arrived after the colony was operating under a well-organized economy, and the Jesuits came a good while later. The Franciscan convent of Huejotzingo seems to preserve the root and flower of the Middle Ages in the Gothic ribs of its naves and columns, but the façade is done in Romanesque-Gothic reliefs, which lean toward the Renaissance and Moorish styles. There was a wide array of styles to choose from, but the natural tendency in America was toward the newer ones. In the Huejotzingo convent the frescoes, almost without design or color, demonstrate the complex fabric of art that came to be acclimated. But one feature from the past clung to convent design: those which were most exposed to the attacks of unconverted Indians looked like forts with a broad enclosure behind their battlemented walls. The church of the Franciscans in Tepeaca and that of the Augustinians in Acolman were built to that plan. The Church of San Agustín in Acolman dates back to the middle of the sixteenth century, and except for the fortress-like aspect, its façade is perhaps the most beautiful, best balanced, and finest example of the plateresque in America. Inside it, a row of portraits in fresco seems to show the influence of Michelangelo's protean style, which was then contemporary. The patios of the convent are beautiful examples of Renaissance art. The frescoes in the refectory are copies from drawings at the front of a book printed in Mexico City at about that time. Engravings were used often then as sketches for paintings. A third order, the Dominicans, showed in many buildings the monumental characteristic of solid construction inspired by Romanesque austerity, but the later buildings of the order flowered into elaborate baroque decoration, as on the doorway of the church in Tepozotlán (state of Mexico), which matches in stone the profusely gilded interior retables of wood. Manuel Toussaint indicates three successive phases of the baroque in Mexico: the austere, the rich, and the exuberant—milestones on the road of progress or, at any rate, of embellishment.

The colony undertook to build cathedrals and large churches even in second-class settlements. Two cathedrals in Mexico balance each other: the one in the capital city and the one in Puebla. Both departed from Herrera's spare style in the Escorial, and step by step, they approached the Churrigueresque, the extravagant style developed in Spain by José Churriguera (1650–1723) and later widely adopted in Mexico. The golden fronds of the American precursors of the Churrigueresque style were stirred, as it were, by the wealth of El Dorado, the measureless adventure of the Conquest, and the no less boundless power of the Spanish Empire in the New World. So much luck and so much adventure could throw men off their balance, but the admirable thing about the old Spaniard is a certain stern persistence that eventually brings order out of so much diversity. America's presence in Spain in the shape of the gold ingots from Peru inspired the exuberance of the Churrigueresque in Spain. When that style which in many ways echoed its American precursors came to America, it begot variants of itself in the New World: first, the famous Spanish-Mexican style, then the Quitan style, the Arequipan, and the Potosían, all in the fullness of their vigor when the Jesuits arrived to compete with the other orders, to make their vigorous thrust into America in a rapid and militant drive. The order was young then, younger than the New World, and it was blooded in America. The fathers were ardent from the firebrand that had moved the Company of Jesus to build the churches of Jesus and St. Ignatius in Rome in a true baroque that gave a fabulous appearance to the interiors, especially in the central nave, where the paintings seemed to soar to the ceiling.

The passion of the new order refused to bow before the prudent restraints of good taste. Only the Jesuit mission churches in Paraguay even approach the simple Franciscan style prevalent at the Company's dawning. The principal decorations in the simple old churches were wall paintings telling stories that even illiterates could read. In Paraguay the Jesuits were closer to the green hell of the jungle than to the silver coolness of Potosí.

If a Spanish church in America is a temple of some importance, it has twin towers and a broad atrium reached by stairways rising from the plaza. The campanile and the baptistery never are separate, as they were in the old Italian churches. The most distinguished church edifice in Latin America is the Cathedral of Mexico, almost two centuries in the building. Its five cupolas and twin towers, which seem like stone bells, called for a cathedral built to the most ambitious proportions. It still ranks as one of the half-dozen great churches in the Catholic world. It stands on the ruins of the most important of the Aztec temples, still visible as the bases of the pyramids that are broader than the cathedral's foundation. The Conquistadors could not let themselves be surpassed by the nations they were attempting to dominate. This competitive urge explains the vast number of huge, lonely churches scattered through the Valley of Anáhuac. They were built to remind the Aztecs of the power of the new church, the new government. The Indians accepted—how could they do otherwise?—the invitation of the Christians to join them in their artistic labors, and they accepted not as vassals alone, but as lovers of art driven by an inner need to use their skills as fine masters.

The Jesuits built their church of San Ignacio in Bogotá largely upon the pattern of the Church of Jesus in Rome. The architect was an Italian, Father Juan Bautista Coluccini, who was born in Lucca in 1569 and died in Bogotá in 1641. The most beautiful feature of the church is the cupola, which departs from the original model in obedience to local circumstances. The walls of the Roman cupola are of travertine; it is roofed with lead tiles. In the Colombian one the tambours is of brick, with graceful windows and roofed in glazed tiles. The anecdote concerning Michelangelo's comparison of his dome of St. Peter's with Brunelleschi's in Florence is appropriate. Michelangelo said: "I shall make a bigger one, but not a more beautiful one." Much of the beauty of the Florentine dome depends upon the facing of red tiles and the veined white marble, which give it a life lacking in the lead tiles roofing the great dome of St. Peter's.

An unusual material that gives color to a building is the native

Mexican stone called *tezontle*. This is a volcanic stone of a darker
red than brick and very light in weight. The walls of a palace
such as La Moneda—the seat of the Mexican government today
—on the capital's Plaza Mayor, look as if they were covered with
hangings for a festival. Another contribution to the outstanding
beauty of the Cathedral of Mexico is made by the architectural
jewel that stands like a candelabrum beside it, an elaborate filigree
of gray stone in the baroque style. This Chapel of the Ciborium,
commonly called the Sagrario, stands out against the background
of *tezontle* that forms the walls flanking it.

¶ SPANISH, ARAB, ORIENTAL, AND AMERICAN ELEMENTS
IN COLONIAL CHURCH DECORATION

Brick or adobe construction called for wooden furnishings inside the churches. Wood was used in panels, retables, altars, and
choir stalls. The vaulted ceilings, too, were decorated with wood
carvings polychromed and gilded against red or blue backgrounds.
At times, almost all the trimming was covered with gold leaf.
Whatever part of America's gold remained in the colonies was
devoted to the uses of religion. A church such as that of the
Jesuits in Quito, which was entirely covered with gold leaf—every
niche, every altar, every detail of a saint's image and of a little
cherub's polychromed head—was an item in a display of incomparable wealth. In other churches the altars were of massive
silver set with mirrors, Andalusian or Chinese ceramic ornaments,
and shells of mother-of-pearl. The Oriental influences that
began with the Arab style came to include Japanese and Chinese
elements when missionaries in the Philippines and the Far East
sent lacquers, porcelains, ivories, and gilded wood to their comrades in Mexico. Creole and Indian decorators found these a new
source of inspiration; Oriental elements soon showed up in the
glazed tiles and lacquers of Mexico and in the decoration of the
altars. The lamps, cruets, lecterns, candelabra, vases, pews,
frames, and trimming testified to the genius of the silversmiths,
cabinetmakers, and gilders. The chasubles and other vestments
embroidered in silk and gold and silver thread and beaded with
pearls were made by the nuns. The monstrances of gold were set
with emeralds, pearls, topazes, diamonds, and other precious
stones, some of them found in America. Many of the monstrances
are worth more than the most famous ones in European churches.

In the Church of St. Ignatius in Bogotá the monstrance alone weighs scores of pounds; no arm could lift it to give the benediction. It is displayed only on important occasions.

The Company's church in Quito, built on the plan of the churches of Jesus and St. Ignatius in Rome, is more resplendent than either. In Rome the church interiors are decorated in marble and bronze, but in Quito everything is gold, gold from the bases of the columns and the socles to the ribs of the arches. A balustrade runs along the tambour that supports the cupola; from it, a visitor may admire the portraits of nine cardinals, three archbishops, and three sculptured angels visible through a dozen window openings. The finial is a lantern with twelve lights. The decoration on the exterior and on the altars is all of a piece; it contains fruits, leaves, flowers, birds, angels, and seraphim. José Gabriel Navarro writes:

> The arches that form the ceiling of the tall naves of the church are splendidly decorated. Their elaboration, frankly Oriental, is a variant of the lacy intaglio of the Persians and Arabs, and between the ribs, held together by great keystone arches that describe huge bands reinforcing the central arch, the decoration is inspired by the Kufic script of the ancient Mohammedan classics. It might be said that those decorative tracings remind one of the poetry, *aleyas* [verses], and *suras* [chapters] of the Koran inscribed on the Moslem mosques, or of the eulogies to the sultans' magnificence in the palace of the Alhambra. Even the crescent-shaped decorations may well be considered a variant of the Arabic *ataurique* [carved gesso work].

The Mexican church of Santa María Tonantzintla near Puebla is considered the masterpiece of ultra-baroque style because of its interior decoration described by Fernando Gamboa (1909–   ):

> [From a most luxuriant vegetation] emerges a dizzying ballet of angels, cherubim, prophets, evangelists, saints, grotesques, and soldiers rising up the wall to the ceiling, which they illuminate with their own exophthalmic eyes. This is a popular native version of the Rosary chapel in Puebla, of pure Spanish inspiration. It might be termed a grotto with a pagan interpretation of Christianity; in fact corn, fruits, and so on, appear in it. It is the masterpiece of popular Mexican art, which goes even beyond the baroque.

The introduction of so many exotic elements still adds up to a completely Spanish total. Although Gothic, Romanesque, Arab, Chinese, Mexican, and Peruvian elements can be found by analyzing the decoration, though the cloisters are Renaissance and the cupolas Oriental, and though the setting is American, nevertheless the Spanish element binds this amalgam, for Spain herself contains a blend of European, African, and Asian elements, each ultimately adapted to her individual character. Throughout history the Spanish artists have kept an identity and way of thinking so distinctively their own that the very bells convoking the faithful in Toledo, Seville, and Salamanca, and in Mexico City, Lima, Córdoba, and Quito seem to summon them to unite as apostolic Spanish Catholics rather than as Roman Catholics. Hence the particular tone of the sermons. The influences that flow together in the Spanish American Church are more varied than the styles, with the result that the sum total seems a different and unique creation. The Cuzcans set mirrors in the frames around their images, as in the Venetian girandoles, which they may have copied. But they wear their mirrors with a difference. In Cuzco the mirrors are set in nests of gilded carving and silver repoussé, yet they retain much of the charm of magic which attracted the Indians from the moment when they first saw their own faces reflected in the looking glasses the Conquistadors offered them in exchange for gold, a trade they were more than happy to make. In the Rosary Chapel of Tunja, Colombia, the angels were born with Indian faces, like those of the *mestizos*, whose mothers had crossed their Indian blood with that of the white man. Those angels seem to be offering to carry the humble people's messages to heaven like the advocates of whom the Venezuelan poet Andrés Eloy Blanco was thinking when he asked God for little black angels.

Potosí has some famous churches, particularly San Lorenzo, with its magnificent entrance. According to Wenceslao Jaime Molina:

> Tradition assigns the execution of this profusely evocative structure to an Indian craftsman. What was his name? Kondori, a surname that could only come from Kuntur, the condor. . . . During the entire period of Spanish domination, the aborigine, trained by the Conquistador—and frequently by the friar—in the art of building, sought aesthetic expression in motifs familiar to him, in plastic materials identified

with the sun, in the resources of his rites, and in his autochthonous symbolism. . . . The sun, the moon, and the stars;
the condor, the llama, the puma, coca, the *kantuta* blossom,
and many other regional elements became the basic materials
for correlating his animistic feeling with elemental beauty in
carved stone.

¶ HUMBLE CHURCHES

Monumental church architecture rose like a Catholic affirmation both in the capitals and large cities and in the monasteries.
Until the eighteenth century the building of the great churches
that still stand as an expression of the power of the Church and
of Spain in the New World, was more or less continuous from the
north of Mexico to Potosí, Córdoba, and Santiago in the south.
In some of the abandoned cities, like Antigua, Guatemala, or
Monguí, Colombia, the church is almost larger than the rest of
the village, and such old houses of worship testify to a vanished
greatness.

But a minor art, a simple, intimate village art was developing
at the same time as those immense structures, in the little churches
with walls of brick or adobe, if not of hard-packed earth. They
were whitewashed and crowned by belfries or "candle campaniles,"
one or two snub-nosed towers (for tall spires might be knocked
down by earthquakes) which barely rose above the body of the
church. The broad roofs were tiled. Those were the "big houses"
of the villages as much as they were churches, standing in the
shade of a silk-cotton tree or a couple of palms that waved their
fans above them. They are expressions of the poor, austere, ingenuous America that was served by priests whose faith was as
elemental and simple as that of the charcoal-makers, and they
symbolized a rural life that prevailed through the four centuries
of the colonies and on into the century of the republics. Such
churches were built in the less prosperous hamlets or the missions,
and also on the big estates. The slaves, the farmworkers, the
owner's bastard children, and the owner and his family met to
worship in such chapels. There, amid the murmur of prayer,
the worries of the poor seemed to be softened, and there the
owner prayed for grace, pardon, and the salvation of his soul
through confession, while the humble hoped for a better life in
the next world. Scenes like that are common today. Brick floor,
grass mats. The images on the altar are the work of primitive,

anonymous artists. The devout women dress them in velvet and lace. The wealthy deck them with jewels. The poor cover the walls with votive offerings, which, together with the paintings of the miracles, would be worthy of a place in a museum collection of popular art. St. Joseph, St. Peter Claver, the patron of Negro slaves, Our Lady of Sorrows, Our Lady of Carmen, and St. Isidore, patron of farm workers, are the favorite subjects. Also St. Rose of Lima, shown rocking the Infant Jesus to sleep in a rose bower, and innumerable replicas of images of Our Lady of Guadalupe, or of Chiquinquira, or of Copacabana peer out from behind bunches of tissue-paper flowers. Everything testifies to a rural naïveté in these little whitewashed churches where a single big family meets in all its inequalities.

The architecture of the little churches scattered throughout Venezuela is admirably treated in *Templos Coloniales de Venezuela* (*Colonial Churches of Venezuela*) by Graziano Gasparini. What was true of Venezuela was also true of the villages in Peru, Ecuador, Colombia, the Caribbean islands, and Central America. This architecture has a charm as valid as the grandeur of the cathedrals. It is humble and authentic, and it unites the simplicity of rural Spain with a similar quality emerging in America. Even when some local artist tried his hand at the baroque or Churrigueresque style as he made a village retable, his version turned out as ingenuous as an old-fashioned gilded rose surrounded by such common and valueless objects as lanterns, candelabra, and tin wreaths and the candid atmosphere of a bare church.

¶ CIVIL ARCHITECTURE

Civil architecture in Colonial Latin America never attained as much distinction as did religious architecture. Of course, there was no reason why the governor's or the viceroy's palace should contain the lush ornamentation of a church. The house of the first viceroy, Diego Columbus, in Santo Domingo, was solid and plain, but the houses of Cortés in Cuernavaca and Mexico City ran the gamut of the history of art. The town corporation buildings were important only when the crier announced from the balcony the death of a king, the coming of a viceroy, or the levying of an excise tax. On the other hand, the Inquisition was housed in imposing palaces like the one in Mexico City later occupied by the School of Medicine, which is noteworthy for its "low door" and its great patio with angular arches unsupported by columns. Owing to some mechanically ingenious plan, the arches seem like hanging baskets with nothing to hold them up. The Palace of the Inquisition in Cartagena, Colombia, surpasses in size all the other colonial public buildings in Bogotá. Existing descriptions of the old viceroy's palace in Mexico seem to indicate that it was not of major importance, but as the viceroyalty gradually took on the air of a small court, its interior demanded a luxury appropriate to it. A suitable setting was needed for the viceroy in white wig and velvet coat trimmed with frogs, carrying a tortoise-shell cane or wearing a silver dress sword, and for the vicereine in lace and the lackeys dressed like knaves of hearts. The Treasury building, today a government house, is faced with stone and *tezontle*, very dignified in its simplicity and very Mexican in its red volcanic building material. This palace, at right angles to the cathedral and the Sagrario on the Zócalo in Mexico City, forms, with them, the most important aggregate that Spain left in her American colonies. Of course, nothing in the English colonies could compare with it. The original plaza was much smaller, however, and the façade we see today is a restoration completed in 1927.

In Lima, which was the seedbed of marquises and various other titles of nobility, civil architecture reached its peak at the beginning of the eighteenth century with the construction of the palace of the Marquis of Torre Tagle, the most beautiful mansion in the Peruvian capital. Its elaborately wrought wooden balconies, magnificent entrance, broad vestibule, and inner patios conformed to the basic plan of colonial houses, but its carvings, series of arcades, and glazed tiles all flaunted wealth as ostentatiously as an Oriental palace. The decoration is Andalusian-Arabic, but there are Chinese touches, too. The slightly pointed Romanesque arch, most commonly found in the convents, flowed into the Moorish horseshoe type, and even the belvederes on the roof, topped with little Moslem cupolas and railings, are as clearly reminiscent of the Orient as are the paneled ceilings.

The house of the man of importance in Spanish America was a miniature convent in a sense, for it was planned, at least in part, with the intention of keeping the woman apart, of shutting her away from the covetousness and temptations of the world. The patio in the rear was a second courtyard, like those of the Middle Ages, where all the work of the household was done. It was quite unlike the Andalusian patio filled with flowers and mur-

muring water. Mangers and granaries had their place in the
construction, for in the beginning the *encomenderos*, and later
the great landowners, ordered wagon loads of potatoes, corn, and
wheat from the city. This is evident in the old houses of Bogotá.
Enormous gateways framed in stone, sometimes with a carved
coat of arms above them, opened on the courtyard. The outer
door of the house was studded with bronze-headed nails. Inside
was the entrance hall—the waiting room of the poor—floored
with brick and small round pebbles in which monograms and
dates were inlaid in bone. At the far end of the entrance hall, a
second, inside door, used only by relatives and friends of the
family, led to the house itself. The women spent three quarters
of their lives in the first patio, watering the geraniums, sewing,
making pillow lace, and taking the air and sun that they were
obliged not to seek in the street. The windows were protected by
heavy wooden bars and lattices—the wrought iron grille was com-
moner in cities near the sea, such as Cartagena and Havana. The
windows themselves were designed more to let in air than to look
through. And always, without fail, the gates, the outer doors
and the inside doors were locked with bolts, padlocks, bars,
catches, and door-latches, and had small barred peepholes to reveal who was knocking at the door, keyholes with enormous and
complicated keys, and heavy knockers, all placed to guard the
fragile treasure of delicate women born into the world to bring
forth and rear a family and to live and die on their knees. The
great flying balconies beneath wide overhangs served as boxes
from which to watch passing parades and processions. The locksmiths had the opportunity to do beautiful work in iron, combining good craftsmanship with an art not entirely primitive, half
Arabic, half American. The beautiful keyholes and keys displayed in museums today were made with hammer, file, and
chisel.

Most of the American counts and marquises came from Mexico
City or Lima. Noblemen of their rank could hardly be expected
to refrain from displaying their escutcheons on the façades
of their houses or from creating an impression of wealth in the
interiors. When Humboldt visited Mexico City, he called it
"the city of palaces." The European was invariably surprised at the
sight of so many solid Spanish houses with noble doorways that
proclaimed them the property of the Count of Miravalles, say,
or the Marquis of Santa, or the Marquis of Ciria, marshal of
Castile, or the Count of Santiago de Calimaya. The dwellings of

the *nouveaux riches* like José de la Borda and Antonio Bascoco lacked coats of arms. The Count del Valle de Orizaba owned a most unusual house; its entire front was covered with glazed tile. Legend says that the father of the man who built the house —one of the descendants of Rodrigo Vivero—reproached his son for squandering his money with these words: "You will never own a house of glazed tile!" The young man felt the reprimand and later answered his father by building this palace, which would have looked less strange in Puebla, where there is a wedding-cake house of three stories, entirely faced with glazed tile. A house like the Casa del Alfeñique (House of Sugar-Icing) is an example of elaborate stonework. Its façade is sectioned by pilasters, with room between each pair for a large, iron-grilled window. Each pilaster has as its capital an elegant bracket-shelf holding fancy ornaments. Such elaboration, unusual in a residence, tickled the humor of the Mexicans who called it "The Figureheads," as if the pilasters were figureheads from ships.

Palace interiors were richer, as a rule, than they appeared from the outside. Pedro Rojas gives us a description of Count Bartolomé de Xala's house, which was built in the eighteenth century. On the ground floor were the porte-cochère and its elegant foot warmers, the porter's lodge, the wine vaults, the stables, and an open coach house where the covered carriages and six sedan chairs were kept. On the mezzanine floor were the guest rooms, the office or countinghouse, and quarters for the lackeys and for the manager of the estate to use whenever he came to the city. On the upper floor, the oratory, the dressing rooms, the pitcher room, where water was kept in cool jars, and the drawing room with its costly furniture and damask hangings. Beneath a damask canopy, an ivory and ebony crucifix with silver nails presided over the drawing room. The furniture in this room consisted of a mahogany settee with a caned back, four large mirrors in gilt frames, console tables, screens, chairs, and a grandfather clock. Two crystal chandeliers hung from the ceiling. A canopied room was kept closed except for the occasions when homage was paid to the monarch. A Nativity scene was set up in an anteroom for the December festivities. Pedro Rojas concludes his notes on the establishment with this paragraph:

The furniture included a good musical instrument, such as a monochord, screens, tables and chairs for their several uses, beds, commodes, writing desks, wardrobes, trunks, small

trunks, chests, sculptures in ivory, wax, and gilt relief, desk
clocks, large porcelain jars, writing cases, dishes, and glasses.
Religious paintings completed the décor of the living rooms,
and canvases of still lifes and trophies of war were hung in
the dining room. A large number of the items were of Chinese
origin; some were native, and the rest from Europe. Chinese
porcelain was valued for its various functions: the smallest
pieces as the most delicate tableware; the medium-sized as
flower vases placed in the hallways, and the largest and
heaviest as hiding places for gold. The work of the local
silversmiths had a thousand uses, one of which was as ordinary as dinnerware, for a service of silver was actually more
easily come by than one of porcelain. The polychrome pottery
of Puebla, called Talavera ware, was also made in Oaxaca,
Mexico City, San Miguel el Grande (Allende), and elsewhere. The kitchens, dining rooms, and drawing rooms contained any number of vessels of Talavera ware, and people
used and appreciated it so much that it was seen on every
side in solid chamberpots, barbers' shaving bowls, holy-water
fonts, and washbasins, to say nothing of the native glazed tiles
used prodigally on cupolas, walls, lambrequins, floors, fountains, and many, many other places. In time, the potters were
able to make such things as large, heavy bathtubs and huge
kitchen vessels or dishpans of pure clay. Some of the paintings and most of the clocks were of Dutch origin, others of
English provenance.

The *encomendero* or the important landowner was the real
master of the provincial cities and the villages, no less powerful,
sometimes even more powerful than the wealthy people in the
capital. This was true later of the rich bourgeoisie. The great
Spanish American colonial houses were scattered widely over the
vastnesses of the imperial dominions. Puebla, Mérida, Guadalajara, Morelia, and other provincial cities in Mexico, and
Trujillo in Peru, all had lordly mansions that testified to the
feudal grandeur based on the ownership of huge country estates.
The viceroyalty in Argentina was not established until the eve of
Independence, so that Buenos Aires, which had been a closed
port for more than two centuries, was only a large village when
the colonial period ended. Juan Agustín García (1862–1923)
made a study of Buenos Aires from 1600 to the middle of the
eighteenth century, and could find no more appropriate title for

his book than *La Ciudad Indiana* (*The Indian City*). Concolor-corvo (pseudonym of Alonso Carrión de la Vandera, *c.* 1715–78) described Buenos Aires in 1771 in his *Lazarillo de Ciegos Ca-minantes* (*Guide for Blind Travelers*) as rows of houses lacking all luxury lining streets that became impassable mudholes during the rains. Wagons loaded with meat sank to their hubs in the deep holes. The only building of any distinction was the Town Hall, which also served as the jail. Its arcades were the only ones in the city. As the city's loving historians have reconstructed it, Buenos Aires had the touching simplicity of the original build-ing that was thrown open on May 25, 1810, when the cry of independence rang through the streets. At that time a very com-monplace chapel served as the cathedral, but the citizens planned to rebuild it into a big, solid church. If it had ever been completed, Concolorcorvo wrote, it would have had no decorations, for the bishop was poor and the income insignificant. The other churches and monasteries maintained themselves in honorable mediocrity. The visitor to Córdoba, on the other hand, found an important cathedral; handsome, substantial, well-planned, and tastefully arranged one-story houses belonging to the rich; the university; and several convents of recognized importance. The cathedral of Santiago del Estero seems to have been even better than the one in Córdoba. All this may come as a surprise to anyone seeing Buenos Aires today—a very European city, embellished, in part, by the most famous sculptors and city planners of France. Indeed, Buenos Aires is a product of independence, a city created by the republic.

In New Granada, now Colombia, the Marquis de San Jorge's house in Bogotá is about on a par with the mansion of the Marquis de Valde Hoyos in Cartagena. Solid armorial houses are still standing in Antioquia, Rionegro, Popayán, Tunja, Socorro, and Villa de Leyva. There, as in most of the colonies, the grandeur of the aristocracy, and even of the religious missions, appeared widely scattered across the vast open countryside, in a wilderness broken only by the buildings of some huge estate, for the colonies were not mercantile and the bourgeoisie as such hardly existed. Hence the wealth was agricultural and mineral, based on the exploitation of the Indians and Negroes who did the work on the ranches and in the gold placers. The estate houses differed from those in the cities only in having open gardens and nearby corrals that brought the owner into more direct contact with his herds. The chapel on the estate contributed to the rancher's air of absolute overlordship in a small rural community. The novel *Gran Señor y Rajadiablos* (*Great Señor and Rakehell*), by the Chilean author Eduardo Barrios (1884–1963), indicates that this state of affairs lasted into the twentieth century.

¶ MILITARY ARCHITECTURE

Military architecture made its greatest strides in the cities on the Caribbean most directly exposed to attack by corsairs, pirates, filibusters, and buccaneers whose aim was to enter the colonies and sack them as a part of their larger campaign to diminish the Spanish Empire. Englishmen, Dutchmen, Frenchmen, and Danes attacked Santo Domingo, Veracruz, Havana, San Juan (Puerto Rico), San Juan de Ulúa, Puerto Cabello, Panama City, Cartagena, and even St. Augustine, Florida. Their repeated raids made it absolutely essential to build stout defenses, walled ports, castles, forts, and lookouts that still stand as documents in stone of the bitter struggles made famous by the Englishmen Hawkins, Drake, and Morgan, by the Frenchmen Ducasse and Baron de Pontins, and by the Dutchmen Roberto Baal and Adrian Juanes Pater, as well as such Spanish outlaws as Pedro Hernández de Avilés and Blas de Lezo.

The Caribbean fortress was built after sixteen-century European models of military engineering. In 1589, Philip II hired the Italian engineer Bautista Antonelli, his brother, and his nephew Juan Bautista the Younger. They carried in their memories the walls and castles of the Italian cities; from these, they drew their plans, began their work and, together with some Spanish engineers, supervised the building of the massive fortifications guarding the ports. Those works, completed after several generations of labor, show the great effort that Spain was making to keep in her hands, and hers alone, the power over most of the continent.

The largest of these constructions was in Cartagena, the gateway to South America. By 1632 "a wall seemingly impregnable, with three very important fortresses, sufficient to withstand the enemy" had been built there. The castle of San Felipe de Barajas was started in 1657; a century later it was still being expanded. As the bay has two entrances, Bocagrande and Bocachica, a castle was built at each. But in spite of them, Cartagena was sacked and humiliated several times. Not until 1741 was it finally in a condition to withstand the siege of the English admiral Vernon, who commanded the largest fleet ever seen until then in Caribbean waters. Vernon shelled the walls of the city with 28,000 cannonades and 800 bombs, but finally had to withdraw in defeat. The heroic organizer of the defense was the lame, one-eyed, one-armed Blas de Lezo, but success was won at the expense of the besieged, who suffered famine and thirst. This dark phase of the victory pinpointed the need for new water reservoirs, storehouses, living quarters, and underground passages that would enable the main castle of San Felipe de Barajas to keep open its communications with the other fortresses and thus help them to hold out against future siege.

Recently the underground passages of San Felipe de Barajas have begun to be cleaned and repaired, so that more than a kilometer of solidly constructed cylindrical arches can now be seen. The stone sides are broken at intervals by ingenious escape tunnels and hiding-places. The Spanish workmanship compares well with that of the Sangallos in Italy. Other castles in the defense network of Cartagena included San Fernando and San José, both at Bocachica, and those at Manzanillo, Santa Cruz, and San Sebastián del Pastelillo. The walls with their vaulted arches, the fortifications, and the bastions at Santo Domingo and Santiago, Cuba, are almost awe-inspiring, but no more so than the Dique Canal, built for defense and commerce, which connects Cartagena directly with the Magdalena River. This canal, still in regular service, was the work of thousands of slaves. Digging a "big ditch" like that in the eighteenth century called for daring as great as that required to build the Panama Canal in the twentieth.

¶ SCULPTURE

Pre-Columbian America expressed itself best in the art of monumental sculpture in stone. The anthropomorphic columns at Tula, Mexico, the gigantic heads of Las Ventas, and the Mayan reliefs at Palenque rank high among the masterpieces of world art. Those artifacts, like the ones in Guatemala, are thought to be descendants of the solitary, enigmatic statues on Easter Island or of the monoliths on the mainland of America at Tiahuanacu, Bolivia, or San Agustín, Colombia, all of which form a centuries-long chain of culture whose links challenge the archaeologists. This art died with the establishment of the colony.

It died at the very moment when the steel chisel and hammer might have made the sculptor's labor less arduous. Under the Spanish Empire, artists in stone helped to decorate the churches, both inside and out. Some of the best examples of their art are the crosses, elaborately decorated with representations of the instruments of Christ's passion, which still stand in front of some Mexican churches. They are the work of unknown artists, original creations with ornamental details of purely Mexican inspiration that are combined with features common to all Christian art. The center of the cross on the atrium of Tajimarca is set with an obsidian mirror in which a holy or divine face was usually centered. "The Indians mean to point out," Pedro Rojas says, "in their idolatrous terminology, that what was most precious to them, this mirror, was equivalent to the most precious symbol of the Cross." Moreno Villa compares these crosses to the ones placed as shrines along the roads of Spain in the Middle Ages, their decoration to the cross of St. James, its arms terminating in fleurs de lis. But there is a cross in Mexico on which the fleur de lis is worked into the design of the plumed serpent. Related carvings are not to be found elsewhere in America, oddly enough. Such crosses, standing in front of a church with a platteresque façade, like the one in Acolman, or the one in Atzacoalco, look neither Gothic, Romanesque, nor Renaissance, but only Mexican. Moreno Villa proposed to introduce the expression "Tequitqui Art" from an Indian word that means something like "unconverted" to designate Hispano-Indian works of that type, which also include certain well-known baptismal fonts.

In Ecuador, where wood sculpture flourished, examples of stone sculpture exist, but they are rare. One of the best is the statue of the Virgin of Mercy in Quito, sculptured at the behest of Charles V. In Bogotá there is the stone image of Our Lady of the Field in the little church of San Diego. In Peru, the soft Huamanga stone lends itself to carving pictures in relief of the Nativity, the Pietà, and scenes from the life of St. Rose. The image of the Virgin in the church of the Sisters of Mercy in Lima conveys the feeling of a painting, for it shows her sitting in a reed chair with a book in her hand.

Public fountains of stone are more common. They were of great practical use as the source of most communities' water and they stood like social monuments around which a certain section of the people, the water carriers, spent their lives. Many of the stone basins were built around a small monitory figure that represented order, prudence, and charity: the statue of silence, with the index finger over the closed mouth to remind the water carriers and the servants who met there not to pass on the trifling events and intimate details of their houses, scandalous stories, or the gossip of their quarter. A handsome fountain of that type is preserved in the main patio of the colonial museum in Bogotá.

The fountain on the main square of Lima is a famous baroque work of the seventeenth century, largely made of bronze. A French surgeon, Le Sieur Bachelier, visited Lima in 1709 while making a cruise on the ship *La Ville de Bourg*. He described the statue thus:

> In the center of the square there is a big fountain, but without a play of water; it is coated in bronze with some vases of flowers in relief here and there; in the center rises a fine pyramid composed of three basins one above the other, decreasing in size; upon the highest stands the statue of Fame, highly prized by connoisseurs, and around the rim are eight lions in combat with dragons; at the four corners are small fountains that would be convenient to draw water from, but no one ever does it, because it would be detrimental to a large number of slaves who have no other way to make their living than to carry water to private houses; they pour it into small casks transported upon the backs of donkeys. . . . All the ornaments on the fountain: the figure, the lions, and the small fountains, are of bronze, and they decorate the plaza handsomely and help to make it one of the most beautiful that can be found.

Bronze was one of the first of the new materials that the Spaniards introduced into America. Hernán Cortés was the first to build a foundry that succeeded in casting cannon similar to those cast by the Arabs who went to Peru with the Pizarros. "When the Conquest of Mexico was consummated," Manuel Toussaint says, "and everyone was more or less at peace, bronze was put to more pacific and charitable uses in the innumerable bells needed for the new churches." Toussaint wrote a brief history of bells with a description and enumeration of those cast from the sixteenth century on. The first bell bears the date 1578. Toussaint lists the names of the casters in his catalogue. In addition to the big bells in the campaniles, small ones for use during the Mass were made, some of them delicate works of art.

The most admirable work in bronze produced during the

colonial period is the equestrian statue of Charles V by Manuel Tolsa referred to earlier. It is one of the most interesting ornaments in Mexico City.

The stairways, the heraldic doorways, and the façades of the churches always demanded the best work of the sculptors for architectonic reasons. The façade of the church in Acolman is distinguished for its admirable statues of St. Peter and St. Paul and two beautiful caryatids. Even they, however, are surpassed by the Annunciation scene sculptured on two medallions, one on each side of the doorway, possibly gilded at one time, and still surprisingly beautiful. The medieval doorway with miraculous scenes of devils and mysteries grouped in the shadow of the Gothic ogive arches, so commonly seen in Spain, was never adopted in America. Colonial artists chose the Renaissance and baroque styles. The façades of some of the churches are translations into stone of the large wooden retables on the altars inside. Such structures as the Sagrario in Mexico City, the church of St. Gertrude in Orizaba, and the Sanctuary of the Virgin of Ocotlán belong to the colonial period.

¶ SCULPTURE IN WOOD

Wood sculpture flourished in a thousand forms and uses. Many schools and studios, such as those in Quito, were opened for training wood sculptors. So many people worked at the art that guilds of church sculptors were organized in the cities, with rules like those of the medieval trade societies and corporations of Europe. A man could not practice his craft as a master until he had passed the examinations. He then had to own his own workshop and all the tools needed for the work and for training apprentices. José Gabriel Navarro writes:

> The ability of the master sculptor was certified by a permit that the city corporation issued to him after he had offered sufficient theoretical and practical proof of his art. The theoretical proof was based upon the study of geometry, the knowledge of the proportions of the human body, and the rules and teachings of the art found in several books widely used at that time; the practical proof consisted in the execution of some work. When the sculptor had passed these examinations, he was recognized as a master, authorized to open a studio, and to admit other persons to it, in turn, as apprentices and workmen.

The master carved the wood until he had brought out the form of the image, which he then passed on to the embellisher, who stuccoed and painted it. The process of polishing it was done so perfectly that the face and figure came out as smooth as porcelain. Except for the Christs and the angels, nudes were never made, much less nude women. As a rule, glass eyes were set in the face, and natural hair, eyebrows, and even fingernails were glued onto the figure. The hands of the smaller images were made separately and fastened on with pegs. Their garments copied the richness and style of Italian paintings that the artists had seen or learned about through tradition. The final product, in all its color and gilt, was on a par with the best European images. The Spanish masters—Berruguete, Mena, Montañés, and Gregorio Fernández—were widely followed in major works, but the popular art triumphed in the innumerable statuettes or figurines, particularly those used in the Nativities. The artists made likenesses of all the local personages, who became a part of the scene as members of the retinue of the Three Magi or as shepherds kneeling before the Christ Child. Of course all the animals were there, too: the donkeys, horses, sheep, oxen, dogs, cats, and chickens. The village women with baskets on their heads went to do their washing in a rivulet of silver-coated paper or in a little lake of mirror. Or they were coming from the market with their bundles, or from the fountain with stone jars of water. The Indians came, carrying wood on their backs, and the slaves, as black as Balthasar. The blind, the halt, and the lame were there with their begging cups. Estate owners and lords, high on their horses. A crowd of pilgrims moving across a carpet of moss. All the *dramatis personae*, numbering as many as one or two hundred figurines representing actual people, filled the platform of the Nativity that was set up in every house. During Advent, the Biblical scene, translated into something domestic and American, came to life at night to the music of carols and local musicians.

Quito was the great workshop. Its famous Nativities entered the big estates and the principal houses in city and village, whether in Peru or New Granada. Where such delightful collections are still displayed—in some cases charmingly naïve, but not infrequently the work of a master like Caspicara, who was capable of caricaturing with sharp irony the boss arrogantly astride his horse or some personage on the supreme court—they do not look as theatrical as the Neapolitan or other Italian Nativities. The work of the school in Quito has not been lost, for there are still families of image-makers there: the tradition of Christ-mas that infuses the images, the settings and the music with the poetry and memories expressed in old Spanish carols has not died. The little verses about the Child, which might as easily be the work of Góngora as of some nameless author, are still being sung today. A magnificent example of this spirit is shown every year in Mexico in the Nativities composed by the great poet Carlos Pellicer. He may choose his figures from hundreds made by imaginative local image-makers. One year the scene of the Child's birth may be the Pedregal, the volcanic region not far from University City; another year it may be the shore of Lake Patzcuaro. The poet's art is so great that people from distant countries come to Mexico City in December to see his Nativity scenes.

The images on the retables of the churches were either brought from Spain or made at home. Those created in America show a great change in taste and inspiration. The sculptors in Seville liked to carve Christs streaming blood, *Ecce Homos* crowned with thorns, or the Lord tied to a column and terribly scourged. To some degree this is the type of the Catholic Re-form, which represents an escape from the insipidity of the Italian images. The preferred scenes in America were less dramatic, more Italianate. One of the favorites is the Flight into Egypt, with a smiling Virgin riding the donkey in the manner of the peasant women. The palm tree bends to offer the fugitives its fruit. Other favorites show St. Martín de Porres putting down food for the cat and the mice on the same plate or St. Isidore with his team of oxen.

Manuel Chili, generally known as Caspicara, was a great Indian sculptor of the eighteenth century. Well-known extant works of his include the statues of St. Francis and the Assump-tion of the Virgin in the Church of St. Francis in Quito, the statue of St. Francis receiving the stigmata, which is in the church of Cantuña, and the Descent of Christ from the Cross and the statues of Virtues, all of which are in the Cathedral of Quito. When the European influences evident in Caspicara's art are analyzed, the Italian seems to prevail, particularly the style of the Della Robbias. Caspicara's master hand modeled small images, frequently in collaboration with anonymous image-makers. Another Indian, Gaspar Zangurima, an architect and goldsmith as well as a sculptor, followed Caspicara. These are but two of the artists from the rich Quitan school that lasted for two or three centuries and trained such distinguished artists as Father Carlos, as well as other sculptors whose names are lost or known only to scholars. Among those whose names are known, Bernardo Legardo created a statue of St. Rose of Lima so delightful in its movement, as she rocks a baby to sleep, that it seems timed to music, and an Immaculate Conception that Gabriel Navarro—always enamored of Quitan work—ranks above the images by Cano and Montañés.

Mexico City's ordinances governing sculptors and carvers exemplify the theories that guided education in the field of the Fine Arts during the viceroyalty. The rules go back to the period of the Fleming Simon Pereyns, one of the most authoritative artists in the colony. The retable in Cuautinchán and the paintings at Huejotzingo are sometimes attributed to him. When the sculptors took their examinations, each was required to submit

> one nude and one draped figure, which must be acceptable as a drawing first. Then the candidate must make it in the round, well proportioned and with good grace, and if he knows how to do this, he is given a certificate of examination when he appears before the town corporation. [The carver] must know how to sculpture a capital, a column decorated with carving and foliage, a seraph, and a small bird, how to cut the wood well and follow the grain, and how to draw everything, and if he knows this he is given a certificate.

The Indians did not come under those ordinances; hence they were allowed to practice their crafts freely. But Toussaint says that no Spaniard, even though a certified master, was permitted to buy their work for resale in his shop.

While churches were being built all over Mexico, there was ample scope for sculptors and a ready market for their work. They came from many backgrounds. Adrián Suster, a Fleming born in Antwerp in 1564, went to Mexico as a young child, learned the art of sculpture, and left his work in Veracruz, Puebla, Michoacán, and the capital before he was indicted as a Lutheran in 1598. Juan Montaña, a Sevillian who supervised the sculptors' and carvers' guild in Mexico City in 1590, carved the choir stalls in the old cathedral. But there were many native-born sculptors in Mexico, Indians among them. The Franciscan monk and historian Fray Juan de Torquemada wrote:

> All told there are many sculptors, and I have an Indian in this village of Santiago, born here, whose name is Miguel Mauricio, one of the best of them, whose works are more

highly esteemed than those of some Spanish sculptors: and besides being such a good craftsman, he is not known to have any vice whatsoever.

One of the famous Indian sculptors, named Tito Yupanque, came from Potosí, now in Bolivia. In 1582–3, he chiseled the Virgin of Copacabana, still venerated in the sanctuary built in her name on the island of Copacabana in Lake Titicaca. The image acquired great prestige because it was the work of an Indian.

¶ EUROPEAN PAINTING IN AMERICA

The panorama of painting is wider than that of sculpture. Sacred images proliferated in that churchly environment. The convent cloisters were set aside as galleries to display paintings on the life of Jesus, the Virgin, and the founders of the respective orders, testifying to the active participation of the painters in matters of religion.

From the beginning of the colonial period, both churchmen and laity brought European art to America, and their devout faith played an important role in the founding of cities. When Doña Inés de Suárez, Pedro de Valdivia's companion, started with him on the conquest of Chile, she carried on her saddle a small image of the Virgin which she had brought from Spain. The figurine has survived and is venerated today in Santiago. Later it was copied in pigment. Murillo, the most indefatigable of artists, took his work to the fairs in Seville to be sold. His work was exported to all corners of America; four or five of his paintings have been found in Quito, among them a fine painting of St. Teresa of Jesús which hangs in the convent of the Carmelite nuns. Bogotá has, at the very least one of his paintings of St. Joseph and a sketch of Our Lady of the Rosary in the archepiscopal palace. One of Murillo's sons, a painter like his father, settled in Bogotá and worked there for the rest of his life. The number and location of works either painted by Murillo, attributed to him, or of his school, proves an interesting point, for together they show the environment then being shaped in the colony, and still visible in the churches today. Toussaint said of Mexico City:

We have a good collection of Murillos; those in the picture galleries, naturally: St. John the Baptist, St. John of God, and others attributed to his school. Don Diego Angulo Iñiguez recently reviewed the paintings and in some cases rejected their attribution to Murillo. In Guadalajara there are several paintings attributed to the Sevillian; a magnificent Immaculate Conception in the habitual style of the master, with [seemingly] unmistakable characteristics. A lengthy observation of these pictures reveals iconographic details such as the "petate" [Mexican] palms that cast a shadow over St. Francis as he scatters bread, and the portraits that appear in the composition, among them that of a bishop of New Galicia and of the donor, the latter erroneously thought to be a self-portrait. These details have made it impossible to attribute the work to him. But in any case the pictures were unquestionably the work of a pupil of the Sevillian who passed through Guadalajara toward the middle of the seventeenth century. In the museum of the cathedral in Mexico City there is a Virgin of Bethlehem that reveals the characteristic brushwork of the great Sevillian painter. A large number of paintings by this master are also in private collections, in one of which I saw a Virgin and Child much superior to the one in the St. James's Palace in London; also an Adoration of the Shepherds, done with great vigor; a St. John the Baptist as a Child, a St. Philip of Cantalicio that is equally interesting, and many other paintings that undoubtedly were either old copies or some of the latter-day imitations that flooded the world markets.

One of the Zurbaráns hanging in the British Museum was acquired in Quito. Toussaint says in commenting on the Zurbaráns in Mexico:

> Zurbarán is not a stranger to our collection; one of his most beautiful pictures hangs in our galleries: *Jesus at Emmaus,* signed by the master in 1639; other paintings by Zurbarán may be found in various spots throughout the Republic; in the collection of José Luis Bello in Puebla, there is a "St. Peter Hearing the Cock Crow," perhaps a copy of another, very similar, in the old church of the Carmelites in Atlixco. Two small saints, painted full length, in the old Franciscan church in Tlaxcala are reminiscent of the marvelous canvases in the Cádiz Museum.

A "Virgin at Prayer" by the Flemish painter Quentin Metsys (or Massys, 1466?–1530), is preserved in the Seminary Museum in Bogotá. In Mexico there are several canvases by another Flemish painter, Marten de Vos (1532–1603). Two of his most ambitious works are in the small Franciscan church at Cuautitlán: a St. Peter and a St. Paul; in addition, there are two lesser works: a St. Michael and a Conception. The museum of the cathedral in Mexico City owns his Saint John the Apostle, and one of the chapels has a "Tobias and the Angel" by him. Three paintings by Luca Giordano are hung in the Guadalajara Museum. In the Viceroy's Palace there is a portrait of Charles V by Titian.

In a sense, every church was a museum that collected the first American ventures into painting by the Spaniards themselves, the Flemings, and the Indians, all of them reflecting the lessons learned from Europe. Some of the Spaniards who came to live in America brought with them libraries and works of art. Antonio Caballero y Góngora emigrated as bishop of Mérida in Yucatán and later became archbishop of Bogotá, then viceroy-archbishop. On his way through Mexico, he had an inventory made of the personal possessions that came with him from Spain, this for the purpose of avoiding any confusion as to whether they belonged to him or to the Church. That listing, done in 1777, may be exceptional, but it shows what an ecclesiastic of the period of enlightened despotism might take with him as luggage. Aside from thirty-eight boxes of books, on which the experts confessed themselves unable to place a value—for who could set a price on such a rich and varied library, "the equal of which was never seen?"—aside from the wealth in vestments, chalices, silver vessels, and the collection of medals and coins (including 504 Roman coins from the beginning of the Roman Republic to the time of Julius Caesar, thousands of coins from the Empire, hundreds of old Spanish coins, coins of the Papacy and the monarchs of Castile, Arabic coins, and Gothic coins), he brought paintings, including six landscapes by Antolínez with figures by Murillo; a still life by Arellano; a Sleeping Christ Child and a Christ by Alonso Cano; a "Presentation in the Temple" by Carreño; four canvases by Antonio del Castillo; an Assumption by Mateo Cerezo; a St. Michael and a portrait by Pablo de Céspedes; a St. Peter by Francisco de Herrera; a St. Matthew and St. Anthony Abad by El Divino (Luis de Morales); four canvases by Murillo; a St. Peter by Ribera; and a portrait of a Dominican by Velázquez— all thus far the work of the Spanish school. The Italian school was represented by a panel in gilded bronze by Michelangelo and Rusconi; two panels by Giordano; a Denial of Christ by Guercino;

two works by Guido Reni; two by Giulio Romano; and two by Titian. From the Flemish school there were six works by Brueghel, a kitchen scene by Rubens, and three landscapes by Teniers.

¶ EUROPEAN ENGRAVINGS AND AMERICAN PAINTING

Fresco painting played an important and surprisingly large role in Mexico from the beginning. The Aztecs and Maya painted their murals on fresh plaster, thereby establishing a medium that came to be used extensively in the twentieth century by the Mexican painters Diego Rivera and José Clemente Orozco, and David Alfaro Siqueiros (1898–   ). Indeed, it might be called a technique natural to that country which the colony could not eradicate though it could change its course. In his *Historia de los Indios*, Fray Toribio de Benavente reports a happening in Tlaxcala in 1539 that would be inexplicable in any other colony so recently under the flag of a European nation:

> For Easter they had completed the chapel in the patio (where the religious festivities were to be celebrated by the Indians). It turned out to be a very solemn piece of work: they called it Bethlehem. They painted it outside in fresco within four days, because if it was done that way, the water colors would not bleed [run together]; in one of the spaces they painted the works of the first three days of the creation of the world; in another space they painted the works of the other three days; two other spaces contained, in one, Joseph's Rod, along with the conception of the Mother of God, which is tall and placed very beautifully, in the other, our Father St. Francis; in still another section they showed the Church, His Holiness the Pope, cardinals, bishops, et al; and in the other section the Emperor, kings, and knights. The Spaniards who have seen the chapel say it is as good as the most charming specimens of its kind in Spain.

Toussaint describes an even older mural in the Franciscan convent of Cholula, painted in 1530. Frescoes decorated other convents in many locations throughout Mexico for example, in Huejotzingo, Tlalmanalco, Cuernavaca, and Ocuituco. Toussaint also traces a similarity to European woodcuts of the sixteenth century, "even those which came from the incomparable hand of Dürer," in the Crucifixion made for the convent at Acolman.

The space beneath the upper choir in the church of Tecamachalco was painted on canvas in tempera by the Jewish artist Juan
Gersón. It shows scenes from Genesis and Ezekiel, some parts
of the Apocalypse, and the symbols of the four Evangelists. Pedro
Rojas has described these paintings as follows:

> The source of the strange and sometimes terrible iconog-
> raphy flung across that vaulted arch was supposed to have
> been woodcuts, but it has been possible to identify only
> those in two medallions which derive from the 1549 Spanish
> version of Holbein's *Icones historiarum veteris testamienti*,
> which he made in 1547. The two medallions depict the
> altar of Ariel and the temple of Solomon. Other medallions
> must have been taken from Dürer's woodcuts as reproduced
> by the illustrators of the Wittenberg Bible, which inspired
> later engravers, Holbein among them. A Renaissance Italian
> painting was used as a model for only one of the medallions,
> which shows the destruction of the temple mentioned in the
> Apocalypse.

An engraving by Schongauer has been identified as the model
used by Epazoyucan in his paintings for the cloister.

Among the Quitan painters of the earliest period was Miguel
de Belalcázar, son of the Conquistador Sebastián Belalcázar. In
1586 the Audiencia granted him permission to paint playing cards.
To the Spaniard, cards were a necessity for recreation and gam-
ing, and the use of cards was regulated by numerous ordinances.
Navarro reports:

> Miguel painted playing cards and sold them with the per-
> mission of the authorities . . . to earn the essentials of life;
> the authorities having later forbidden the said enterprise, he
> murmured against them, for which reason he was falsely ac-
> cused of sedition and was arrested. In prison he was tortured
> on the rack to force him to declare who the conspirators
> were; and as they could get nothing from him, they sen-
> tenced him to death. And he was hanged on the 27th of May.

Not everyone had such poor luck as the great Conquistador's
son. Card games were such a regular pastime during the Conquest that when the decks wore out from long use, they were
replaced with new ones made from the bark of trees. The figures
on the Spanish cards must have seemed to the Mexicans to resemble more closely than any other drawings the Aztec portraits

in their own pre-Conquest books, for during the colony the demand for decks of cards was so great that by 1582 nine thousand dozen playing cards had been printed in Mexico. Fray Pedro Simón says that Cartagena had a card-printing press in 1623.

Gabriel Giraldo Jaramillo lists in his *Historia del Grabado en Colombia* (*History of Engraving in Colombia*) the names of engravers other than those who made playing cards in Mexico, Guatemala, Quito, Lima, Paraguay, Cuzco, Potosí, and Buenos Aires. In addition to engravers of Spanish origin, others of French origin emerged—for example Juan Ortiz, the first name in the history of engraving in Mexico, and Fray Juan Nolasco, who worked in Lima in 1660. The Jesuit missions in Paraguay trained some Indians, among them Juan Yaparí and Tomás Tilcara, to be excellent engravers. They were reputed to be able finally to copy the illuminated letters of a missal printed in Antwerp with such perfection that it was difficult to distinguish the copy from the original.

Giraldo Jaramillo singles out the name of Dean Francisco Martínez, who published two scientific books in Santa Fe de Bogotá between 1791 and 1793: *Historia de las Ciencias Naturales* (*A History of the Natural Sciences*), translated from the French, and a treatise by Muratori on the power of human fantasy. With respect to engraving, Giraldo Jaramillo says:

> The influence of engravings is patent in the painting of the New Kingdom of Granada and its two basic schools, that of Tunja and that of Santa Fe. The development can be traced from the primitives—Medoro, Francisco del Pozo, Pedro Aguirre, and the enigmatic artist who painted a St. Bartholomew for the church of San Laureano in Tunja and M. Segundo Galberi, who copied a plate (Rome, 1560), showing the anatomy of the human body by Giovan Valverde di Hamusco, to the masters of the end of the eighteenth century, through Acero de la Cruz, the Figueroas, and Gregorio Vásquez Ceballos. A few examples will suffice to isolate such revelatory sources: The Flagellation by Gaspar de Figueroa (Colonial Museum in Bogotá) was directly inspired by a Flemish engraving of poor quality. . . . Baltasar de Figueroa copied the Adoration of the Shepherds (Colonial Museum) with minor variations, from an engraving, also a copy of the canvas by Gerard Seghers that is preserved in the Church of Our Lady in Bruges. Vásquez Ceballos made use

of engravings of widely different origin, for in his vast pictorial production we find traces of Raphael, Sassoferrato, and Guido Reni among the Italians; Murillo and Zurbarán among the Spaniards, to say nothing of out-and-out derivations from Flemish masters, plus a trace of the Germans.

One of the most obvious cases of copying from engravings was that of the rhinoceros and various symbols that appear in the fresco paintings adorning the house of Juan de Vargas in Tunja, Colombia. According to Giraldo Jaramillo:

The Tunja rhinoceros became the great-grandson in effigy of the flesh-and-blood beast that Sultan Muzafar of Cambay, in India, sent to Manuel I of Portugal, who, in turn, gave it to Pope Leo X in 1515, although it never reached Rome because it was drowned in the Gulf of Genoa. Dürer copied it from a drawing by a printer named Valentín Ferdinando de Moravia, which he inscribed with a picturesque descriptive caption. Juan de Arfe copied it from Dürer, and the Tunjan artist of *De Varia Conmensuración* from him. Elephants had a quite different provenance: they were copied from plates by the notable Flemish painter Giovanni Stradanus, also known as Johannes van der Straet, engraved by Johannes Collaert, and published in Antwerp in 1578 by the famous editor Philippus Galle in *Venationes ferrarum, avium, piscium*. The pagan deities Jupiter, Minerva, and Diana came from the Dutch painter Leonard Thiry, whose drawings were engraved by the French burinist René Boyvin in the second half of the XVI century. The other decorative details can be traced to the ornamentation devised by Jan Vredeman de Vries, published in Antwerp by Hieronymus Kock, and an engraving of Winter by Marc Duval.

Engraving also had its uses in sculpture. According to Pedro Rojas, the drama of the Last Judgment in one of the beautiful chapels of San Miguel in Calpán, Mexico, is "copied, in this case with very few changes,from the engraving inserted in the *Nuremberg Chronicles* of 1493, and published in other works such as the *Flos Sanctorum* by Pedro Vega and the *Gramática Burgalese* of 1498."

The influence of engraving on architecture was definitive: it was the only way by which to follow the lessons taught by Herrera and other Spanish architects, by the Italians, and by the

Gothic designers. Spanish architects brought their books to America, where they became the sole sources of inspiration for the Creoles. The favorite references were the treatises by Serlio and Vignola. Some startling discoveries have been made as a consequence. A doorway to a church in Pasto, Colombia, is a replica by Vignola of the one Michelangelo designed for the Grimani Villa on the outskirts of Rome. Bolívar's estate in Bogotá has a portico identical with Vignola's plan for the Caprarola Palace. The church of St. Ignatius in Tunja is modelled upon Serlio's work.

In his study of the circulation of books of engravings in Colombia during the seventeenth century, Santiago Sebastián writes:

> The major influence came through engravings and illustrations of treatises. The French traveler Mollien was correct in writing in 1826: "The art of architecture is the one that has made the most headway in Colombia; advancement in that field is all the more surprising because the only teachers they had to guide their steps were books and prints." Italian illustrations were not the only ones to be imported; prints of Spanish origin must have arrived, too, although like those reproduced in Juan de Herrera's work, they were full of Italian evocations. Philip II granted his architect the privilege of "printing and selling in the Indies, the islands, and the mainland of the Ocean Sea" the *Construction of the Escorial*. In 1558 an edition of it was printed with plates by the Fleming Pedro Perret. The following year, three hundred copies of this work were sent to Lima on the ship *Capitana*. There was nothing strange about the arrival of this work in New Granada, for it had already been reissued in 1619 "because it had been sold and very well received by foreigners and other curious persons who bought it."

The foregoing indicates that the printing press played a major role in the advancement of culture in the New World, not alone from the standpoint of literature, but also as a tool of visual education through engravings. This learning device set the seal of Europe on American interpretations of art. We can trace the last manifestations of work that records history in the Aztec style through the bound manuscripts describing the entrance of Cortés, his interview with Moctezuma, and so on. They follow the same style as the pre-Columbian manuscripts, but introduce, as the new members of the cast, the figures of the Conquistadors. But the native elements were already slipping away from the frescoes in the convents, easel painting, and sculpture. The general composition is identical with that of the models brought in by the official church. For example, an engraving by Dürer was developed into a fresco, and the result was a new version of the master's interpretation of scenes from the Old and New Testament. American painting became an adaptation or a mannerism on a very large scale. It would be hard at times to judge whether a work is by a Creole or by Murillo. The entire pictorial panorama of the colonial period must be viewed with this reservation in mind. If the Indian had a part in it, his was only one of the secondary elements. The artist was always aware that any deviations from the safe and the known might invite trial by the Inquisition.

Conversely, a great deal of the European information about America was imparted visually through engravings. Prints showing scenes of cannibalism and of Indians living in the Antilles or Brazil, engravings glorifying Columbus or Vespucci; others depicting Cortés and Pizarro leading their men on forced marches, portraits of the Conquistadors, and thumbnail sketches of filibusters, buccaneers, pirates, and corsairs were published in book form and loose leaf. They were based half on truth, half on fantasy. Thus America paid Europe in kind for its engravings of the Virgin and pictures of Christ's Passion.

A German engraving on file in the New York Public Library shows a scene of Brazil printed about 1505 which was probably an interpretation of one of Vespucci's letters. It depicts naked people, as dark and beautiful as legend described them, harmoniously made and prepossessing, with their private parts covered with feathers and their faces adorned with precious stones, people who owned everything in common and were given to roasting or smoking their enemies' arms and legs to provide the main course of a banquet. Giovanni Stradano of Florence created a lovely allegory picturing Vespucci in dialogue with a beautiful Indian girl, representing America, stretched out in a hammock. *Collectiones Peregrinationum in Indiam Orientalem et Indiam Occidentalem* (*Collections of Journeys to the East Indies and the West Indies*), by the Flemish engraver Théodore de Bry (1528–98), is a veritable museum of scenes from the most glorious moments of Columbus and Vespucci—the ships leaving Cádiz, the landing in Venezuela, cannibalism on the Brazilian coast, and so on. The iconography of the navigators was taken from maps with illuminations containing portraits of them, the iconography of the Conquistadors from frontispieces to books by the Spanish historians Antonio de Herrera y Tordesillas (1559–1625), Antonio de Solís y Ribadeneira (1610–86), and Francisco López de Gómara (1510–60?), printed in Antwerp. Engravings of that type later inspired Rabelais, Montaigne, and others concerned with the natural man and the noble savage.

In the *Voyages of L'Hermite*[1] some remarkable engravings illustrate the depredations of the Dutch pirates in Chile and the voyages of Drake, who sacked at will the cities of the Caribbean and of the Atlantic and Pacific coasts. The maps offered wonderful idealizations of the cities of Tenochtitlán and Cuzco. The America thus pictured was both barbaric and idyllic, free and savage, peopled by heroes both European and American, a version that was to prevail in Europe for three or four centuries and that would assume extraordinary importance during the period of the Enlightenment.

The history of American engraving begins with a son of one of the Conquistadors, a maker of playing cards. Toussaint gives us a long list of the engravers in Mexico, from Samuel Stradanus (1606–22) to such later artists as José Joaquin Fabregat, a Spaniard who came to America in 1788 to teach and died in 1807. Each played an important role in the school of fine arts that culminated at the time of the movement for independence. Among the first wood engravers was Juan Ortiz, the aforementioned playing-card artist of French origin, who was finally tried by the Inquisition. From such distant beginnings Mexico was to bring forth one of the greatest engraving geniuses in the history of art, José Guadalupe Posada (1851–1913).

¶ THE MASTERS

Oil painting, like sculpture, developed very rapidly to satisfy the demand for canvases to be hung in the churches. One of the first requirements that artists for the Church were obliged to meet was adherence to European norms in subject, composition, and technique. Essentially, painting was religious. But eventually it also included portraits of viceroys, justices, inquisitors, and monks.

[1] James the Hermit fitted out a fleet on the island of Juan Fernández, off Chile, to attack Chile and Peru. His rebellion was defeated by the Prince of Esquilache, but he left a diary of his voyage which is famous, in part because of its illustrations.

A Sevillian artist named Cristobal Quesada traveled with the expedition that set out to find the "Seven Cities of Cibola" in the sixteenth century. This search resulted in the discovery of the present states of Colorado and Arkansas, and as Quesada had gone along "to paint the things of the land," it is the first indication of an early desire to add graphic documentation to the reports of the Conquistadors, although no trace of such work is left, if indeed it ever actually existed. In 1566 a Flemish painter named Simon Pereyns went to Mexico with Viceroy Gastón de Peralta. Pereyns, who brought a hint of the baroque along with his Flemish tradition, is considered the greatest master of his time. His influence was reflected later by Diego Borgraf, another Flemish painter, who was established in Puebla. The Spanish painter Baltasar de Echave Orio went to Mexico in 1573 at the age of twenty-five and exerted a strong influence on painting through his own work and that of his sons, Baltasar and Manuel Echave Ibía. He introduced the school of Ribera, *El Españoleto*, markedly evident in the canvases of Cristobal de Vallalpando (1644–1714). Some of the paintings of José Juárez, a Mexican artist of the mid-seventeenth century, were inspired by Zurbarán, but others were obviously in the style of Raphael. Pedro Ramírez, also of the seventeenth century, was a follower of Zurbarán. Murillo influenced Francisco Antonio Vallejo, a prolific painter of the eighteenth century, and many others. Dozens of artists, some of them very productive, were working as though they were apprentices under the direct guidance of the masters who were the pride of Europe.

Much the same thing was true of Quito. The school of painting followed by the Spanish and Quitan artists was founded by the Flemish artist Fray Pedro Gosseal, a companion of Fray Jodoko Ricke. The school reached the peak of its development with Miguel de Santiago, who died in 1673, the most famous of the Ecuadorians whose large body of work was also inspired, according to the critics, partly by Murillo and Velázquez, and even by El Greco.

Painting in Colombia began as a sophisticated art with a famous composition, *Our Lady of Chiquinquirá*, by Alonso de Narváez (died 1583), a Spaniard who arrived in the colony as a youth, shortly after Bogotá was founded. He was followed by two artists who worked in the style of the Italian Renaissance of the sixteenth century. One, Francisco del Pozo, was born in Milan and in 1597 did paintings in the wilderness chapel of the Candelaria, near Tunja in New Granada. The other, Angelino Medoro, arrived in Santa Fe around 1587 and later painted in Quito and Lima. A national character began to emerge in the work of the Bogotan Antonio Acero de la Cruz, who was born in Bogotá early in the seventeenth century and died during its latter half. Giraldo Jaramillo calls him "the most authentic representative of what we have agreed to designate as primitivism in Colombian painting, although he also belongs among the leading lights who were to illuminate the later world of art." Then came the Bogotan painter Gaspar de Figueroa (died after 1658), through whom the Hispanic influence started to make itself felt. His son Baltasar, more important and moving as an artist and even more baroque, closely followed an engraving by Seghers in one of his paintings. The whole colonial movement reached its peak with Gregorio Vásquez Arce y Ceballos (1638–1711), a first-class draftsman and mature painter in whose work all the aesthetic currents of his time converge. He was a true Spanish American artist because of the dual character of his prolific production.

A more American type of painting might have been expected to come out of Cuzco, yet Italian masters were frequently chosen as the ideal there. The Divine Shepherd, for example, was a subject commonly treated everywhere in America. Here and there a certain leaning toward the primitive emerged after the Indians were converted. For example, the Trinity was often portrayed with three identical faces explaining to the Indian that the Father, the Son, and the Holy Ghost were one and the same god in three persons. This version of the mystery is seen in some of the early Italian paintings, although rarely. In the church of St. Francis in Mexico City, an imaginatively conceived painting of the Trinity represents the Three Divine Persons first by the sun shining in the sky, then as reflected in a mirror held by an angel on the edge of a pool, and finally as reflected back by the mirror of the water.

At the end of the seventeenth century, Melchor Pérez Holguín made his name as an artist in Potosí. His work is related both to the school of Murillo and to that of Zurbarán. He was the painter of the great silver city. The Indian enters the scene in his compositions, constantly appearing as a melancholy figure in the background. He looks like an inopportune guest who keeps reminding the white man how much he owes him for his labor, which might at least be repaid by works of mercy.

XI: *The Enlightenment*

¶ AMERICA BETWEEN THE RENAISSANCE
AND THE ENLIGHTENMENT

Spain's empire in America was poised between the Renaissance and the Enlightenment, two crucial moments in European thought which held the key to modern times. For obvious reasons, both the Renaissance and the Enlightenment had a great deal to do with America. As a New World, America was to be the proving ground and showcase that savants were seeking. But America was more than that, for not a few of the axial ideas behind the great forward steps in Western thought derived from its mere existence. Two centuries of tentative plans, of debate, of experimentation, of silence, and of academic daring (in which writers played an impassioned role) elapsed between the Renaissance and the Enlightenment. The colonies seemed to be on the sidelines, mere listeners. Then, like a second discovery, the Enlightenment aroused them and pointed the way to freedom. If the conquest of America was traceable to the Renaissance, the ending of the colonial period was a consequence of the Enlightenment. Those were the periods of greatest import to man and society in Spanish America, and each left a deep imprint not only on the history of America but also on the intellect of the West by clarifying the New World's symbolical role in the development of thought.

The humanistic phase of the Renaissance, with its scientific curiosity, its spirit of exploration and eagerness for discovery, and its uncontainable drive to broaden Europe's horizon, was satisfied when the Atlantic proved to be a seaway open to travel from shore to shore. Both the roundness of the earth and its size were demonstrated at one stroke by the discovery of the new continent.

The Renaissance and Humanism blossomed from Florence's innermost being, and her sons Toscanelli, Vespucci, and Verrazano took an active part in the exploits that marked the end of the fifteenth and the beginning of the sixteenth centuries. Toscanelli's teachings inspired Columbus, and Magellan validated them. The explorations that enlisted Vespucci enabled him to announce that a new continent had been found. Giovanni da Verrazano (1485?–1528?) landed on Manhattan Island in the course of his voyages of exploration along the coasts of North America.

Another Italian, a Genoese of humble birth and without a university education, was Columbus, who became the instrument for one of the greatest feats of the Renaissance, not as the fulfillment of the prophets' words, as he claimed half-distrustfully, half-cautiously, but as proof of a theory. His discovery of America provided the actual *terra firma* needed by science to verify the speculations and dreams of philosophers and poets. But that *terra firma* covered an expanse immensely greater than that of which the Conquistadors spoke.

Official Spain, in the person of Philip II, who lived a sequestered life in the cells of the Escorial, tried by political calculation and religious suspiciousness to keep to his exclusive use the unexpected gift that fate had handed him, for he feared the frivolities of the licentious Renaissance that was the source of his good fortune. Official Spain, wizened, shrinking, hampered by a church jealous even of Rome and distrusting even the Pope, rallied its spiritual militia to halt the new ideas issuing from the pen of Erasmus and to break its own traditional peaceful coexistence with the Jews. In America, the Counter Reformation became an evangelistic enterprise, a political program for missionaries and inquisitors under the iron central rule of Philip II. The pleasure that Americans have always found in smuggling dates from then. Those people in Spain who dreamed of greater freedom and were looking for a place to escape to, even the enlightened Erasmists, took to the New World ideas forbidden in the Peninsula. But as the inquisitors went there at about the same time, the scientific daring of Humanism in the fifteenth century was forced into hibernation in the colonies. That hibernation lasted more than two centuries, until the arrival of the second

Renaissance: the Enlightenment. Meanwhile, the Bourbons ascended the Spanish throne and, with their fondness for everything French, cut through blind alleys. And the *corpus Americanus* began to feed on red meat, developing an energy that finally led to independence.

¶ IDEAS WERE NOT MOVING IN THE COLONIES

The fulcrum that turned the lever of the Enlightenment was Descartes, a prime mover of the seventeenth century. His *Discourse on Method* was published in 1637, but neither its author nor his philosophy was known in America until a century later. When the acquaintance was finally made, the results were astounding. In the course of a few years, the ensuing struggle between the established Scholastics and the new Cartesians became a war of ideas raging through the Spanish capitals of the New World. The Scholastics defended themselves by summoning the powers of the Inquisition, the Cartesians fought back boldly. The debates between the two philosophies had changed the course of the colonies by the end of the eighteenth century. The curiosity of students awoke amid vacillation, victories, and tentative explorations. Even Spain stimulated their curiosity through the ministers of Charles III, who canceled the traditional courses of study. In 1771 the viceroy in Lima tried out a new plan that included the teachings of Leibnitz, Bacon, Gassendi, and Descartes. A few years later an actual battle was fought around the rectory of the University of San Marcos when the traditionalists' candidate was opposed by a distinguished Encyclopedist of the new era named José Baquijano y Carrillo. In Mexico in 1781, Juan Benito Díaz de Gamarra (1745–83) published his *Errores del Entendimiento Humano* (*Errors of the Human Mind*), criticizing Scholasticism in a kind of revolutionary prelude. Díaz de Gamarra interpreted Leibnitz and Descartes from his chair in the university and was denounced before the tribunal of the Inquisition. Professor Baltasar de los Reyes Marrero was suspended from his university position in 1788 merely for mentioning Descartes. And yet everything was moving. Ideas were traveling. Two years later, Dean Gregorio Funes (1749–1829) said in a public eulogy of Charles III in Argentina:

The wretched peripatetic school was making its final efforts to feed upon our Spain, keeping her behind bars, shunning the sublime meditations of Descartes, Galileo, Newton, Locke, and Leibnitz, but it recognized that it had reached old age, that its strength was waning, and that good taste, supported by the solid foundation of the throne, would inevitably spell its ruin.

Later, in 1795, José Agustín Caballero (1771–1835) emerged in Havana bearing Descartes's name on his standard. He declared:

> Galileo, Bacon, and the Spaniard Gómez Pereira were the first to throw off the yoke of a deep-set Scholastic tradition; they opened new roads by which many men notable for their culture would arrive at the reinstatement of the mechanistic philosophy already promulgated by Democritus and Epicurus in ancient times.

Felix Lizaso (died in 1891) picked up the thread of Caballero's historical exposition and wrote:

> Caballero marks the appearance of the two famous schools of the Gassendists and the Cartesians. The former, Caballero says, chose as its head a very learned man, the priest Pierre Gassendi, who reconciled the Epicurean philosophical system with religion. The latter followed René Descartes, who excelled in the study of mathematics. And going a step farther, he cited the school of Newton, whom he calls a distinguished mathematician and arrived at this synthesis: the truth is that the method of mechanistic reason has been accepted in Europe with such interest and adherence that no one considers those who follow another path to explain physical phenomena worthy of the name of philosophers.

Even the first Spanish American novelist, José Joaquín Fernández de Lizardi, noted these discussions in *El Periquillo Sarniento* (*The Itching Parrot*, 1816) wherein he made fun of the university of his youth, because only Scholasticism was taught there, and the names of Descartes, Leibnitz, and Newton were unknown. Yet he knew about them!

¶ COPERNICUS AND THE EIGHTEENTH CENTURY

The development of a new philosophy in Europe linked America into the chain of ideas. If America had not been discovered,

Copernicus could not have made his studies on the solar system, and without them, perhaps Descartes might not have been able to develop his philosophy or even his mathematics. (Voltaire thought Descartes was better as a mathematician than as a philosopher.) Descartes was able to develop his methodology, which divorced thought from the nebulous theorizing of Scholasticism, because Copernicus already had formulated the train of reasoning which marked the transition from astrology to astronomy.

A fragment from Descartes's life throws some light on his inner struggle. Convinced that the Copernican system was a demonstrated truth, and attracted by the work of Kepler and Galileo, he set out to write a new exposition of the system governing the world. He spent three years working on it; then in 1633 Galileo was sentenced to death and Descartes had no choice but to lay aside his book and give up any thought of publishing it. He went on to write his *Discours de la Méthode* (*Discourse on Method*, 1637), which ushered in the era of reason and gave a violent turn to ideas. With a clarity that reoriented European thought and style, Descartes condensed a revolutionary ingredient, the most explosive ever concocted by modern man, into the three famous words "*Cogito, ergo sum.*" With his "I think, therefore I am" he brought philosophy down to earth, made man responsible to himself in this world, sowed the seeds of doubt, and showed natural law to be a parallel of divine law. Henceforth physics stood in opposition to metaphysics, and that new stance aroused the enthusiasm of the first philosophers in America. From the time of Descartes on, they saw two clearly separate disciplines: physics and metaphysics. Physics came first, for the new thought quickly captured the new generations already alienated from the old seminary after a few sarcastic words of farewell. Actually, the gesture was a rather conventional one. Tradition had trodden two paths for speculation: one along which the divine wind of grace wafted the mystical call to religious faith, the other open to the building of a system that would supply the foundations of civil society.

The acceptance of Copernicus in Spanish America shows the extraordinary ascendancy the Enlightenment had won there. In Europe, the battle over Copernicus had been fought in the first half of the sixteenth century, but it was not engaged in Bogotá until more than two centuries later. *De revolutionibus orbium coelestium* (*Concerning the Revolutions of the Celestial Spheres*), his study of the solar system, appeared in 1540. Giordano Bruno, who defended him, was condemned to the stake in 1600. Galileo's trial by the Inquisition was held in 1633. From these dates, it is clear that from the moment when such new ideas were launched until Descartes came on the scene, every step had been perilous. A man could think only at the risk of forfeiting his life. *Cogito, ergo sum* might mean "I think, yet I am still alive." Copernicus himself, fully aware of the revolutionary scope of his system, knew that to affirm however softly that the sun was the center of the solar system and that the earth revolves around it was to offend the pride of the official schools of thought, even though it was obvious enough that the world is a sphere. In phrasing his idea for the first time, he therefore took pains to offer it as a "hypothesis" only, hoping by that note of caution to safeguard his book from the Inquisition's bonfires. But when he decided openly to defend his "system," the Lutheran Protestants turned on him as fiercely as the Catholics. These were questions of the 1500's and 1600's, however, questions for Europe.

The argument was stated in Bogotá at the end of the 1700's. Even in 1774, an eminent doctor, botanist, and mathematician, José Celestino Mutis (1732–1808), was denounced to the Inquisition for saying that the earth revolved around the sun. By great good luck, he was offered a chance to justify himself before the academic-inquisitorial tribunal instead of being clapped straightaway into prison. That act of leniency shows that the Enlightenment, triumphant in Spain, held out new possibilities to the colonies. During the hearing, the chapel of the Colegio del Rosario was filled to standing room, and justices, holders of degrees, canons, doctors, and students rubbed elbows with the general public. To the confusion of his accusers, Mutis demonstrated what he had been teaching as easily as two and two make four. From then on the name of Copernicus could be spoken openly in the capital of the New Kingdom of Granada. And on that day the earth began to revolve around the sun in Bogotá. Felix Varela (1788–1853) in Havana entered two novelties on the test papers for his bachelor's degree in 1806: the names and doctrines of Descartes, Feijoo, and Copernicus.

¶ THE STRUGGLE FOR ENLIGHTENMENT
IN SPAIN AND AMERICA

Debate raged through the Spanish territory of both hemispheres. The first skirmishes already had been fought in Spain;

the last battles in America, but the campaign was renewed in discussion again and again. As the debate was going on in America, certain hidden ambitions kept coming to the surface to lend it a touch of drama, to the confusion of the Americans themselves. The same themes were expounded at the same time, purely by coincidence, in Mexico, Buenos Aires, Chuquisaca, Córdoba, Bogotá, and Lima, as well as in Salamanca, Spain. In the final analysis, the difference between the dialogue in America and that in Spain was the degree of emotional involvement. The Creole in America who had entered the world of experiment and revelation was viewed as a chance participant. But he was awakening and affirming in himself the idea of freedom, of independence. Such ideas had seemed innocuous enough as they came from Spain. But they became explosive in America. The ships of the Enlightenment belonging to the Guipuzcoan Company were famous. Cacao from Venezuela was transported to Spain and books were brought back to Venezuela from Spain; books by the Encyclopedists. The ministers of Charles III thus offered a new primer, which they themselves did not know how to read. What they could have read in it—always assuming they knew how to read—was the end of the empire they loved so well.

In Spain, the Jesuits were venturing timidly, by the middle of the eighteenth century, to present the philosophy of Descartes and the Copernican system. Once in 1748 they chose the systems of Ptolemy, Copernicus, and Descartes as a subject for debate in a public competition. The boys were to elucidate, explain, and refute them. "They are to describe in detail the systems of Philo, Pythagoras, and Aristarchus of Samos as revised by Nicholas Copernicus; and at the same time they are to justify the censure that Galileo incurred from the Congress of Cardinals, the Roman Inquisitors, and wherefore it was permitted." That was a risky game. Twenty-two years later, Descartes's ideas were rebutted in the plan for study which the University of Salamanca sent to the government in Madrid: "In this author, propositions are found which are contrary to all natural reason and conforming but little to some Catholic feeling. . . ." The Cartesian writers were suppressed merely for being so.

In the same year that the Jesuits held their student contest, 1748, Jorge Juan and Antonio de Ulloa returned to Spain from Peru after going there to accompany some scholars from the Paris Academy of Sciences who were on a scientific mission to Quito. Jorge Juan published his astronomical findings, but was obliged to state that the earth did not rotate on its axis. The French translator Vaquette d'Hermilly offered the following clarification: "The author of this work does not speak as a mathematician in declaring that the feeling of those who declare that the earth rotates is false, but as a man writing in Spain, that is to say in a country where the Inquisition is active."[1]

For all that, the earth did move, and Spain was yielding ground. The same year that Mutis triumphed over the Inquisition in Bogotá, Jorge Juan was able to review the latest developments and to say that Spain had been in the rear guard of Europe's advance, with her eyes closed to Italy's repentance for condemning Galileo. He asked himself:

> Would it be suitable, perchance, to oblige our nation to explain the *Systems* and *Philosophy* of Newton, by following every phenomenon dependent upon the earth's motion with these words: "not to be believed: it goes counter to the Sacred Scriptures?" Is it not an insult to the Sacred Scriptures to claim that they are opposed to the stringent rules of geometry and mechanics? Could any enlightened Catholic listen to such things without being outraged? If there is not enough knowledge in the kingdom to understand these things, is not any nation that will uphold blindness like that open to ridicule?[2]

From the moment when debate began in Europe, scholars fixed their attention on America. Galileo considered moving to Spain, and from Spain to the New World to escape the storm that was about to break over his head in Rome. He got in touch with the Spanish ambassador in Florence, telling him that in the course of his studies he had come upon a system for marking the degrees of longitude which would be of great benefit to the ships that made the run to America. He would require accommodations for travel, and requested to be made a sort of master pilot to Spain who would train mariners in the use of telescopes of his own invention, which would enable them to see ten times as far. His petition was studied in Spain while the scholar was losing ground in Italy. If his petition was ever answered, the reply came too late. Raúl Porras Barrenechea (1897–1960) found the docu-

[1] Sarrailh, Jean: *L'Espagne éclairée de la second moitié du siècle XVIII*, pp. 188 and 494.
[2] Ibid.

ments relating to this plan in the Archives of the Indies in
Seville, and speculated on whether, if the Spanish government had
contracted with Galileo to make travel to America by ship safer,
he might not have had the opportunity to embark for the colonies.
One Florentine, Amerigo Vespucci, had already discharged the
office of master pilot in the preceding century and had held in
his hands, so to speak, the sphere of Spanish power on the high
seas.

¶ AMERICA'S ROLE IN EUROPE'S
INTELLECTUAL DEVELOPMENT

If, with such profound effect on European thought, America
offered concrete proof of the earth's size and spherical shape, man
in America, as a living problem in human liberty, became the
point of departure for a new philosophy that finally arrived, via
the Encyclopedists, at the Declaration of Human Rights. Never
before had such serious doubts concerning slavery been awakened
by the plight of men from Africa or Asia. Indeed, over the course
of two centuries, the hunting of Negroes had gone on uninterrupted in Africa and had increased. On the very eve of the Discovery, Ferdinand the Catholic had sent Pope Innocent VIII
a gift of a hundred Moorish slaves whom the pontiff distributed
among the cardinals and his friends. But a sudden change in
political thinking came after the voyage of Columbus.

On the arrival of the first American captives sent by Columbus
to be sold in Seville the king's conscience gave him such a twinge
that he forbade the sale. Later the preachings of Montesinos in
Santo Domingo laid on the Spaniards the responsibility for their
ill-treatment of the Indians and Fray Bartolomé de las Casas
began his impassioned campaign, which bore fruit in the Laws
of the Indies. Yet in the course of time a great shadow fell,
darkening European civilization for several centuries: the hunting
of Negroes in Africa for the purpose of enslaving them and selling
them in America. The Americans themselves were not to be
sold: the idea of the free man emerged with the American. A
fantastic and idealistic picture of the noble, free savage was built
on America. The European's attitude toward the American differed radically from his approach to the African. The cities of
Cuzco and Tenochtitlán, as described by the Pizarros and Cortés
demanded respect; added to that, the uncontaminated savage

seemed of a high moral quality. To Montaigne, the Indians were not the barbarians—the Conquistadors were. His concept of the noble savage was not presented as a fantasy, but as a study of reality. In a sense, he constructed his own "Discourse on Method" around America. He warned his readers not to let themselves be deceived by writers who, not content to present events as they were, must gloss them over and thus twist them, or must try to formulate general laws from fragmentary observation. The testimony of a plain, simple, ordinary observer interested him far more. And to inform himself about that world which had just been discovered, he made contact with a traveler who had spent twelve years in Brazil and with the Paraguayan Indians who arrived in France. He did not use as his literary documentation such passionate allegations as those of Las Casas; instead, he depended on a book considered favorable to the Spanish Conquest: Francisco López de Gómara's history. He quotes from the book throughout his *Essais* to draw moral comparisons between European ideas and American customs. What endows Montaigne's work with greater universality is his use of ancient authors to provide him with examples—texts from Greece, Babylonia, and Egypt, which he compares with American examples taken from the works of López de Gómara, from Bishop Jeronymo Osorio's Latin history of Portugal, and from Jean Léry's report on his voyages to Brazil. He said that no such works as the roads paved with stone which run through the craggy cordillera of the Andes from Peru to Quito can be found in Greece, Rome, or Egypt. He admired the Indians for using their gold for jewels, not for coins, and for dividing their parcels of land by nothing stronger than threads of cotton. Thanks to God there was no lying in America, nor treachery, nor dissimulation; greater human majesty than that shown by Cuauhtémoc or Atahualpa in their martyrdoms could be found nowhere else but on the roster of humanity's noblest heroes.

In 1562 a group of Guaranís were presented to the court of Charles IX at Rouen. Montaigne learned from them American songs that he compared with the music of Anacreon. He quotes one of the Indians:

> Someone asked him what, in his judgment, were the most remarkable things he had noticed in the Court; and he answered there were three, one of which he had forgotten, but two he remembered. He said that in the first place, he found it strange that so many large men, strong, armed, and

with beards, like those surrounding the king, should consent to obey a child instead of choosing one from among them to command them; the second that, having seen how half the people had enough comforts and more, while the other half were emaciated by hunger and poverty, he could not explain to himself how the needy half could bear such injustice, nor why they did not seize the others by the throat and burn down their houses.

The noble savage emerges from these pages, an arbitrary picture if you like, but one that was to bring a new concept to law, and restore to man, as man, a modicum of justice. Montaigne was not alone in his conclusions. The Indian communal plan in Paraguay, later followed by the Jesuit missions, made such a deep impression on Europeans that Montesquieu likened it to Plato's Republic. A prolific literature was born out of all that. The Italian antiquary and historian Ludovico Antonio Muratori (1672–1750) published a book, rich in data, entitled *Il cristianesimo felice nelle misioni dei Padri della Compagnia di Gesú nel Paraguai* (*Happy Christianity in the Missions of the Fathers of the Society of Jesus in Paraguay*), in 1743. The title gives his conclusions.

¶ CANDIDE TRAVELS FROM PARAGUAY TO GUIANA

America was once the land of Utopias. Columbus saw in Trinidad an earthly paradise, and Vespucci found his in the provinces of Brazil, charged with enchantment as lyrical as that which Politian breathed into Botticelli's *Primavera*. Las Casas longed to found a republic beyond good and evil. The Incas were pictured in the pages of the Inca Garcilaso de la Vega as a Utopian community. Might not Paraguay be the reality that would make such dreams come true? That was the belief for many years, but when it was discovered that the Jesuits' community was not as Muratori had glorified it, an abrupt change took place. A boundary dispute between Brazil and the Spanish colonies, which the Jesuits appeared to be escalating into a war, heightened the political jealousy already aroused by their activities and increased the ill will of the other orders toward them; finally it led to the expulsion of the Company. This precipitated a change of opinion that can be traced even through the articles of the *Encyclopédie*, some written before the event, some after. In the earlier articles, everything was

Utopian. In the later pages, the Company was painted in black. Though Voltaire published *Candide* at about the time Muratori's book appeared, Muratori still viewed the missions through rose-colored glasses, Voltaire through dark lenses. Voltaire returned to Montaigne's original idea: that barbarity was not in the Indians, but in the Europeans. The hope surrounding the noble savage remained untarnished.

In *Candide*, our hero leaves Portugal for the New World. First he goes to Buenos Aires, then to Paraguay. Some of his best adventures happen in Paraguay, the field of the missions. He finds the fathers in no way better than the rest of the world. Ambitious and domineering, they carry a load of sins on their backs and clever speech on their lips. Candide kills the father superior with one sword thrust and flees in the disguise of a Jesuit to the province of the Big Ears. The Indians, seeing him in his stolen garb, seize him and prepare to make him the main course of a big banquet. But when they learn that he is not a Jesuit, that he is the man who made an end to the father superior with a single slash, they set him free amid great rejoicing. The story would not be complete, however, without a picture of Voltaire's own conception of Utopia. Candide travels on to the Guianas, where, according to tradition, the last free Peruvians had taken refuge and had hidden El Dorado's gold. Candide walks through streets paved with gold and sees children playing with precious stones. This privileged republic had been established within a circle of inaccessible mountains. Candide inquires about the form of government, the customs, what the women are like, the public spectacles, and the art work. The first question that he asks as he converses with an old man while a servant who knows the Quechuan language interprets for him, is whether there is some form of religion.

> The old man flushed. "But how can you doubt it? Do you take us for ingrates?" "What is your religion?" Candide asked. The old man blushed again. "May there not be two religions? We have, I think, the religion of everyone: we adore God from night to dawn." "Do you adore a single God?" "Of course: there are neither two, nor three, nor four. I can't help being surprised at the questions the people from your world can think of." Candide asked how they address their god in their prayers and what they ask him for. "We don't ask him for anything; we have nothing to ask him for: he has given us all we need and we thank him for it un-

ceasingly." Candide inquired where the priests are. The old
man smiled. "We're all priests here; the king and all the
heads of family sing solemn canticles of thanksgiving every
morning, and five or six musicians accompany them." Then
Candide exclaimed: "What, you don't have monks who
teach, who argue, who rule, who make divinations, who send
to the stake those not in agreement with their dictates?"
"We'd have to be crazy to do that," said the old man. "We're
all of one mind here, and I don't understand what you mean
by your monks." Upon hearing this speech, Candide said
to himself: if only my friend Pangloss could have seen El
Dorado. . . .

¶ MME GRAFIGNY AND THE PERUVIAN QUIPUS

Decidedly, the simplicity of Utopia was inspiring everything.
A friend of Voltaire, Mme Françoise de Grafigny d'Issembourg
née d'Happoncourt (1695–1758), discovered while reading *Al-
zira* how much he admired the Incas. This moved her to read the
Comentarios Reales by Garcilaso de la Vega. Herself a writer,
she already had completed a novel about Spain, and now she wrote
Lettres Péruviennes (1747), which was uncommonly successful.
A copious literature grew up around it in France and Italy. Goldoni found material for his comedy *La Peruviana* there. Raúl Porras Barrenechea, a collector of books and pamphlets concerning
this dialogue, summarizes Mme de Grafigny's novel as follows:

> Zilia, a noblewoman of Cuzco and a sweetheart of the Inca
> Aza, is carried off by the Spaniards and put aboard a ship
> bound for Europe. On the way, she is captured by a French
> corsair, who takes her to Versailles. The presence at the
> French Court of the Indian woman from Cuzco gives the
> occasion for the innocent and virtuous savage to make the
> most ingenuous observations on court customs, by means of
> which the author slips in her own ironical criticisms of the
> court customs of France and of the style of Spanish life
> with its religious stereotypes, her remarks, of course, colored
> with ineradicable prejudice. From Versailles, Zilia commu-
> nicates with her Incan lover in Peru through the quipus, the
> knotted cords used by the Incas. Zilia longs, in her knotted
> letters, for the freedom of the forests and the rustic life;
> she compares the customs of the Incas with those of Euro-

peans. In her confused and ingenuous reflections, which are really frank ironies, she describes to her lover the religion, the monks, the convents, the etiquette, the houses (which she compares to prisons), the mirrors, the clothing, and the French theater, where, according to the innocent Peruvian, the actors shout and the women weep constantly, and nothing is shown except crimes and misfortunes.

Mme de Grafigny's novel moved Raimundo di Sangro to open a bulky correspondence with her on the language of the Peruvian knots. Their letters culminated in Di Sangro's *Lettera apologetica dell' Esecitato accademico della Crusca*, a beautiful book illustrated with colored plates. Its publication aroused some lively discussion. Porras Barrenechea wrote:

> The *Lettera* expounds all the historical and dialectical reasons that the imagination of the master of subtleties could offer his disciple in order to prove to him the excellence of the quipus as a medium for transmitting thought. He dissertates on sign language and turns to Plato to prove that script is harmful to the memory. The quipus, with their various kinds of knots, triangular, square, involved, the hanging objects and fringes, could express all the nuances of the word.

Oddly enough, Di Sangro's book was published in the year when Rousseau began to study the same subject, which became the theme of his *Essai sur l'origine des langues*, wherein he states his theory of the superiority of oral over written language. He cites the example of two great civilizations that never knew the alphabet: the Mexican and the Egyptian. Rousseau claimed that peasants speak better than city people, never stammering, in a voice audible over great distances, because their natural language is not a servile reflection of written language. He found the symbolical language of hieroglyphics superior to, or at any rate less harmful than, alphabetical writing. "The first form of writing does not consist in representing sounds, but objects themselves, taken directly as the Mexicans do now, or in allegorical figures, as the Egyptians did in ancient times."

¶ HOW AMERICA INFLUENCED ROUSSEAU

Of all the authors of that period, none stirred the Spanish world so vigorously as Rousseau. Owing to their centuries-old

popular tradition, Spain and Spanish America were better prepared than other regions to accept the philosophy of *Le Contrat Social*. The Spanish had known the power of a sovereign
people since the days when the Basques had met beneath the tree
of Guernica, since the formulation of the oath that they swore to
the monarchs of Aragon, and since the revolt of the commoners
against Charles V. Those traditions crossed to America with the
comrades of Balboa, Cortés, and Quesada. The authority wielded
by these great captains was a voluntary grant from their comrades-
in-arms, conferred upon their leaders by mutual agreement. It
could be revoked, as it was when Cabeza de Vaca's company rose
against him in Paraguay.

In 1762, at a time when *Le Contrat Social* was still far in
Rousseau's future, the *comuneros* of Paraguay revolted. Their
postulates of 1730 read almost like a rough draft of the Genevan's
basic pages. One of the *comunero* leaders, Fernando Mompox,
"talked about the power of the community in any republic, city,
town, or village and declared that it was more powerful than the
king himself. And that it lay in the hands of the commune to accept whatever law or governor it might wish, for even if that
law or governor is given by the prince, the commune may justly
resist and cease to obey him, if they do not like him." The doctrine
of Mompox sank so deep into the people's minds that Father
Lozano, historian of the Revolution, could report that it was:

> an amusing thing to hear and see a rustic who had chanced
> on a casual visit to the city to hear Mompox, and who, when
> he left, full of astonishment, would meet another like him in
> the country, and would say to him, raising his eyebrows and
> revealing in his face all the wonder in his mind: "My Lord,
> Brother, what great things I heard the learned man in the
> city say about what the common people can do; he says they're
> more powerful than the king, sometimes even more than the
> Pope. Just think, Brother, what we've had and we never knew
> it. They most certainly kept their mouths shut about this
> good thing before us, and they didn't want to teach us that
> the commune can quit obeying the viceroy." He would cross
> himself, and it was well he did, lest the devil enter his soul
> through this doctrine.

The voicing of the new philosophy, very communal and very
American, as we have seen, brought a train of consequences.
Shortly thereafter, the new governor designed by the viceroy

arrived in Asunción. The viceroy received a memorandum that pointed out the unsuitability of having a governor who was a friend of the Jesuits. Ensuing events in the town hall were more serious than the memorandum. Father Lozano describes them as follows:

> On the 28th of August, St. Augustine's day, the members of the town corporation attempted to go to the cathedral to pray for the public peace under the pretext of honoring the memory of the learned saint. They were carrying the royal standard. The common people seeing treachery in that act, or something equivocal at least, prevented the corporation from leaving the town hall, and to make sure they would stay there, they destroyed the staircase leading to the ground floor of the building, thus keeping the members imprisoned. The communal militia then entered the city amid cries of "Death to bad government!" The magistrate went out on the balcony to speak to them and to plead with them to withdraw to their houses in good order. A voice interrupted him: "Señor Purveyor: what does *vox populi vox dei* mean? You may answer any way you like, but you may be sure that this voice is the people's."

Thirteen years after this incident, which occurred in a far corner of America, Manuel Ignacio Altuna, a Basque, met Rousseau in Venice. Altuna was rich, noble, and generous, aflame with a desire to improve conditions in his country. Rousseau was then only a modest, luckless secretary to an arrogant French ambassador. A warm friendship sprang up between the Basque and the Genevan, a friendship that grew with the years and later resulted in providing entry for Rousseau's ideas into Spain. Rousseau became so interested in the picture of the Basque country drawn by Altuna, that of a region more jealous of its liberties than any other, that he considered going there to live. At least he arrived there in spirit, for when Altuna went home to Azcoitia, he initiated his friends into Rousseau's ideas and together they founded the Societies of Friends of the Country. Enlightened Spain, stimulated by the societies, became a boiling pot of contradictory feelings debated with intense heat. Deeply rooted tradition argued on the one side, and on the other *Encyclopédie* and the Francophiles. The customs houses were alternately opened and closed to Rousseau's works.

At the same moment, the gazettes in Madrid and France were

debating the ideas of Rousseau as expressed in his *Discours sur l'origine et les fondements de l'inegalité parmi les hommes;* in his *Discours sur les Arts et Sciences* (1750), a discourse on whether the re-establishment of the arts and sciences has contributed to the betterment of customs; in his romance *Julie, ou La Nouvelle Héloïse* (1761), in *Le Contrat Social, ou les Principes du Droit Politique* (1762), in *Émile, ou Traité de l'Éducation* (1762), in *Pygmalion,* and in *Les Pensées,* each of which had a distinct reception. In the comment or attacks on them, the entire politics of Spain was held up to judgment and the heritage of the Enlightenment from the past was argued. Rousseau's name was first mentioned in a Spanish newspaper when his *Discours sur les Arts et Sciences* was reviewed the year it was published. After reading the entire text, Feijoo attacked it violently. A news item appeared saying that the Paris Parlement had ordered the discourse on inequality among men burned by the public executioner, that every precaution had been taken in Brussels to make sure that the book would not enter the country, and that Switzerland had ordered Rousseau out of the country. A translation of *La Nouvelle Héloïse* into Spanish was published in Bayonne, and the *Le Contrat Social* was issued in London. Meanwhile, Rousseau's fame was on its way to America, and the Americans were following the fortunes of the author and his books with intense interest.

As Feijoo was denouncing the *Discours sur les Arts et Sciences* in Madrid, Christoval Mariano Coriche, a Dominican monk of Cuban birth who was rector of the secondary school of San Luis in Puebla de los Angeles and a great admirer of Feijoo, published an essay in 1763 supporting the Spaniard's stand. It was entitled *Oración vindicativa del honor de las Letras y de los Literatos.* The Cuban, like the Spaniard, evoked the name of progress to condemn Rousseau. The immediate effect of the dispute was to place Rousseau's name in a show-window. His *L'origine et les fondements de l'inégalité parmi les hommes (The Origin and Foundations of Inequality among Men)* was first published in Spanish translation not in Europe but in Charleston, in 1803, by an American. That edition contains a eulogy of the philosophers who laid the foundation for the independence of the United States.

Le Contrat Social contains the core of Rousseau's doctrine. After its publication in 1763, it spread all over America with such speed that even before 1780 both the literati and the general public were acquainted with it. In time it would provide the keynote for orations on independence. A Peruvian was largely responsible for the popular knowledge of Rousseau, even in Spain. This man, Pablo de Olavide (1725–1804), was a friend of Jovellanos, a translator of Voltaire and Racine, and the inspiration for Chateaubriand's *Le Génie du Christianisme* (*The Genius of Christianity*, 1802). Olavide applied Rousseau's philosophy to the great reforms he initiated. In 1769 he drew up the new plan of study for the University of Seville which served as the base of Salamanca's plan. The Society of Friends of the Country, which spread from the Basque country to other parts of Spain and later to America, came out in support of Olavide. In 1767 he organized and started a large settlement in the Sierra Morena. He influenced agrarian reform by sending implements and news to Cádiz, to Havana, and to the Carolinas. He became an important figure in Spain. And that meant his ruin, for the Inquisition accused him of heresy, atheism, materialism, reading forbidden books, and of friendship through correspondence with Voltaire and Rousseau. In 1778 he was sentenced to an indefinite term in prison; his property was confiscated; and he was forbidden ever to return to Lima. He escaped from prison, sought asylum in France, and was received in Paris as one of the great figures of his day, "a victim of the Inquisition."

By 1780 *Le Contrat Social* was so well known in Lima that when the Indians in Trujillo rebelled—in an extension of the Tupac Amaru movement—Bishop Martínez y Compañón attempted to pacify them by explaining the social contract in an adaptation that gave the king of Spain the right to delegate to the people their due powers. At the end of the pastoral letter, which was read from the pulpit of all churches, he said:

> By virtue of this contract the people merely intervene to the extent of binding themselves to transfer, and they do in fact transfer, in favor of their sovereigns, the rights that each one of them concurrently had received from God for the purpose of self-preservation, self-perfection, and self-defense, which transfer must yield two results, and did yield two results in the form in which they occur in private agreements, and these were: one, it is the obligation of each and every vassal to obey the sovereign and to permit him to reign and govern through his council; and the other, to extend to him [the king] the faculty and right to direct and govern, and to regulate the actions of the kingdom and of private persons.

This reply to the propositions formulated by Mompox in Paraguay during the war of the *comuneros* served the people fifty years later, inspiring the classical phrase of Latin American Independence: "Long live the king, and death to bad government," a phrase that toppled the secular edifice of the Spanish Empire in a matter of hours.

The flood was cresting, and *Le Contrat Social* was all too pleasing to the ears of the people and the most advanced leaders of the revolution, both for its ideas and for its revolutionary interpretation. Here and there scholars were rebelling against the thesis, either because they were prudent or conscientious or because they feared it might lead to such consequences as those brought by the French Revolution to France. Such reservations may explain why a man as deeply revolutionary and turbulent as the Mexican monk Servando Teresa de Mier (1765–1827) came out against Rousseau. To the underprivileged, however, the idea of the "sovereign people" came as a dazzling revelation. No sooner had the term "sovereign" been transferred from royal majesty to the man in the street than the juridical structure of the monarchy began to crumble. The day eventually came when in America the simple phrase "sovereign" began to mean the people, as it had meant when first used by the *comuneros* in Paraguay. The first use of the word in that sense marked the date of democratic independence. After the revolution of Descartes, who put reason in the place formerly occupied by Scholastic dogma, the second revolution was triggered by Rousseau's "sovereign people"—the revolution of the masses. The underdogs discovered how they could apply their own discourse on method. In Uruguay, the *gaucho* José Artigas organized and led the guerrillas of the pampas to achieve the independence necessary for a new Social Contract. Artigas talked to the ranch workers about the Contract and they knew what he meant. Rousseau's ideas were uppermost during the drawing-up of the Uruguayan constitution, which was declared to be a pact made by the common will of the "sovereign" (people).

That was the birth of constitutional law in South America. The *Semanario de Caracas* (*Caracas Weekly*) started publication in 1810, with Licentiate Miguel José Sanz as one of its sponsors. Humboldt once said that if he should wish to go Venezuela, it would be to meet Sanz. Seldom has the idea of the Social Contract been expounded with greater clarity than in Sanz's arguments:

To the People or Nation that is the proper, true, and essential sovereign, that is independent and absolute, that knows no superior on earth, belongs the authority, and it belongs to it alone and to no one else, to know and decide, for it is the medium through which the will of God to confer power is explicit; it is also the medium through which the power may be taken away from one and transferred to another, if the well-being, order, and tranquillity of the State so demand, for those are the aims of societies, and without them they cannot survive. Therefore no one may call himself Sovereign of a Nation without tyranny, nor may he attempt to govern in such a capacity without having obtained the consent of its general will from that Nation in lawful agreement, for that is what [sovereignty] contains in essence, what is, and what must be properly called sovereignty. He who seeks to reign without that concomitant attempts to reign without God's will, and he may not say that he reigns by the grace of God, nor may he force anyone to honor and obey him. In a word, he is a tyrant who usurps authority that has not lawfully been transferred to him, and if he uses force against the People, he may be met with force.

The proper study of Rousseau's philosophy called for centuries of experience, and that was lacking, especially in Spain and America. The ideas he developed should be traced before, during, and after Rousseau's lifetime. Although this may seem disingenuous and arbitrary now, it was perfectly clear in 1810, and Sanz in the *Semanario de Caracas* made a perfect connection between the Genevan's pact and the people's traditions. He analyzed that part of the political culture of the nation which evoked Rousseau's critique of the monarchs of Spain during the Conquest and corrected the thinking of those who spoke in terms such as those used by the bishop of Trujillo at the time of the Indian uprising in Peru. Sanz wrote:

> As the leaf on the tree moves through God, so are the executors of the sovereign will of the people permitted to rule through God whenever contracts are lacking, and the mutually obligatory Social Contract is nullified by procedures contrary to the fundamental laws of the State. It is fitting to recall to men's memories the formula used by the Aragonese in swearing fealty to their kings. "We," they said, "and each of us, who is worth as much as thee, and who together can do

more than thee, swear obedience to thee if thou keep our
laws and safeguard our privileges, and if not, not." Surely the
Aragonese, who were Christians, apostolic Roman Catholics,
understood to perfection the *Per me Reges Regnant* [Rulers
Rule through Me], and Authority would not yet undertake
to break it, or to extend itself beyond the periphery of the
circle in which the freedom and dignity of man were then
compressed. Many years went by before Philip II, in an
unjust and shameless act, arbitrarily ordered the Justice of
that kingdom, D. Juan Lanuza, to be beheaded, as he was the
only shadow of the bold Aragonese freedom still surviving.
Indeed a contract that would transfer to a sovereign the absolute power to do whatever he might wish without any responsibility to others would be impious, contrary to the laws of
nature and reason, and would besmirch divine justice. Only
ignorance, adulation, and superstition have been able to conceive and maintain such a political monstrosity to the in-
jurious oppression of humankind. There are those who say
that the authority of kings over men is the same as that which
man holds over the animals, apparently wishing thus to
justify the impious and extravagant argument of Caligula,
who believed himself to be of a higher, and divine, nature.

¶ AMERICA'S COURSE TOWARD ENLIGHTENMENT

These philosophical concepts provided the wheels on which
the American revolutions ran. The first constitutions were drawn
up in accordance with them—indeed some constitutions were
faithful transcripts of *Le Contrat Social*. The early drafts were
Utopian. In 1764, two years after Rousseau's book was published,
the ideal republic was sketched in Chile. It was meant to be the
herald of reform all over the world. The plan was to exchange
the monarchical regime for a republic and to place the government in the hands of a "sovereign Senate." Its authors were two
Frenchmen, Antoine Gramusset, a frustrated seminarian who had
invented a machine for raising water to a great height, and
Antoine Berney, a professor of Latin and Mathematics who was
reading the volumes of the *Encyclopédie* in Santiago almost as
soon as they were published in France. The two scholars were
joined by the Chilean José Antonio de Rojas and the Peruvian
pilot Manuel José de Orejuela. The *audiencia* in Lima got wind
of the plan. The two Frenchmen paid for their crime by being

deported. Rojas alone had a chance, later, to help his country achieve independence.

The ideas of the sovereignty of the people and of the social contract are tied in with independence by Rousseau himself. Fifty years before Bolívar, San Martín, O'Higgins, or Morelos had stepped onto the American stage, the Genevan had given the cry for freedom in *Le Contrat Social:*

> How can an individual or a people take possession of an immense territory and thus debar the human species from it, by any means other than a usurpation punishable by law, for such a usurpation robs the rest of mankind of their living and the food that nature offers to all alike? When Núñez de Balboa took possession of the Pacific Ocean from the beach and of all South America in the name of the Crown of Castile, was that sufficient reason to dispossess all the inhabitants thereof and at the same time to exclude all the princes in the world? Under those conditions a repetition of the ceremonies was in vain: the Catholic king did not stop short of taking possession of the entire universe with one stroke, without a qualm at suppressing immediately in his empire all that other princes had possessed.

Rousseau's argument against the colonial system was taken up by the other Encyclopedists, Diderot in particular. Diderot edited and annotated the third edition of the *Histoire Philosophique et politique des établissements et du commerce des Européens dans les Indes* (*Philosophical and Political History of European Settlements and Commerce in the Indies*), by Abbot Raynal, a book always at the bedside of many leaders of the American revolution, beginning with Bolívar. In Volume VIII Diderot inserted this paragraph referring to the Spanish settlements in Chile:

> The European nations justified themselves to themselves by those principles which seem to be eternal truth, and called their acts by whatever name they wished! Their navigators sailed to a region of the New World which was not occupied by any people from the Old World, and they placed on a plaque an inscription that read: "*This country belongs to us.*" Why? Is this not as unjust, as senseless, as if some savages were to land by chance on European shores and write on sand or on the bark of trees: "*This country is ours*"?

Diderot adopted Rousseau's words in this paragraph and applied them directly to Chile's case. But the same criterion pervades both this book and other works by the Encyclopedists. In 1771 a novel by Sebastián Mercier appeared under the title *L'an 2240* (*The Year 2240*). It drew an imaginary picture of the nations of the world if the Enlightenment were to triumph. In Chapter XXII, Mercier tackles the colonial problem, and Diderot borrowed from him the picture of a plaza somewhere in the New World with a statue erected on it to a Negro liberator. Yves Benot published a study of Diderot and Anti-Colonialism in the review *Europe* (January 1963). He takes the following lines from a work by Raynal, who quotes Diderot:

> I was going out of this plaza when I saw to my right on a magnificent pedestal the statue of a Negro in a noble and commanding pose, his head bare, his arm raised, his gaze intense. Twenty broken scepters were lying around him. At his feet this inscription: *To the Avenger of the New World.* I could not repress a cry of surprise and joy. Yes, I said to myself with a warmth equal to my surprise, Nature has finally created an admirable man, this immortal man who must have freed the world from the most atrocious tyranny, the oldest and the most ignominious. His genius, his audacity, his patience, his firmness, his avenging virtue have been repaid: he broke the chains of his compatriots. How many slaves, oppressed by the most odious servitude, must have awaited the signal to produce their hero. The flood has burst the dikes, the effect of lightning as it strikes is less rapid and violent. In an instant the blood of their tyrants was spilled. Frenchmen, Spaniards, Englishmen, Dutchmen, and Portuguese have all succumbed to fire, poison, and flames. The earth of America has thirstily drunk this blood it had long awaited, and the bones of his ancestors, miserably sacrificed, seem to rise from the tomb and dance with joy.

Diderot's eloquence became even more lyrical in his editing of Bougainville's voyage in the *Supplément*. During his trip around the world, Bougainville had witnessed the arbitrary rule of the Jesuits in Paraguay and the injustices of the Spanish Empire through all of South America. Diderot edited the later account of Bougainville's arrival in Tahiti and placed in the mouth of an old Polynesian a lengthy speech formulating the right of the sons of the earth to shake off the European yoke. He adopted

Montaigne's ideas, saying that if there is evil in the New World it arose from the vices imported by the Conquistadors. To Diderot, independence would mean that the noble savage would recover his old virtue and thus free himself from Western corruption. This was a scathing criticism of the entire European structure, which the Encyclopedists hoped to undermine, and this revolutionary program dropped as if by a miracle into the minds of the trail-blazers of independence, the men who were dreaming of a democratic republic.

¶ LE CONTRAT SOCIAL AND THE REVOLUTION

Those who did not read Diderot at first hand were already carrying the seeds sown by Rousseau. The Spaniards had established an enlightened despotism, but they were aroused by the tocsin of the French Revolution, which warned them that they were playing with fire. Spain was caught in the grip of fear, and ideas became contraband in America. We have already seen that Rousseau's discourse on the origin of inequality (*L'origine et les fondements de l'inégalité parmi les hommes*) had been published in Charleston. In 1803 an edict was published in the *Gazette of Mexico* to warn everyone, even those who had been granted permission to read forbidden books, that *Le Contrat Social* still was banned. In 1808 a circular announced that

> those ideas in Rousseau's *Contrat Social*, in *L'Esprit des Lois* (*The Spirit of the Laws*) by Montesquieu, and the works of other like-minded philosophers who hold that each private person with his own share of independence, which he may use at will, may concur in the election of the prince, are proscribed because they contribute to the freedom and independence with which they seek to destroy religion, the state, the throne, and all property, and to establish equality, which is an impracticable and chimerical system, as France herself has proved by her example to us.

Two Argentines, Manuel Belgrano (1770–1820) and Mariano Moreno (1729–1811), were far from home when they became acquainted with the French writers. Belgrano was studying in Spain when he read Montesquieu, Rousseau, and Fulganieri at Salamanca, where their books were in constant circulation. Belgrano, a devout Catholic, obtained permission from the Holy See to read them. Meanwhile, Mariano Moreno had found the same books and more in Chuquisaca, where Matías Terrazas offered him the use of a sort of super-encyclopedia: his library, which was full of proscribed books. Even though Chuquisaca was even deeper in the Andes than Córdoba, it drew students from Montevideo and Buenos Aires to its high-peaked recesses in Upper Peru, even though they had to travel for weeks by muleback. When they finally got there, they felt that they had entered the Salamanca of the New World. The literati enjoyed an almost godlike prestige. Concolorcorvo tells of a lady who left a substantial sum in her will for a doctoral robe to cover the image of the Most Holy Sacrament so that it would be rendered the same homage as the learned men of the *audiencia* whenever it appeared before the public.

Three remarkable documents were found in Mariano Moreno's student notebooks: a copy of Rousseau's discourse on the arts and sciences, an essay on religion, and a note on the French Revolution.[1] Like Bolívar as a mature man, Moreno as a student warned of the danger of the fantasies contained in literature:

> Rousseau has the courage to say to men: your arts and your sciences have corrupted you. After a long lamentation over the debasement and misery of the people, over public opinion that labels natural force brutal advantage, frankness rudeness, and sensitivity piety, he discloses that the arts have drawn us ever farther from nature. But in making clear to us the damage done by the arts and sciences, Rousseau stops short of a proposal to outlaw them from society, provided they will change their purpose and strive to serve human weakness, to make beautiful deeds immortal, and arouse us on behalf of virtue instead of turning us to selfishness and making us unhappy, hard, and cruel.

Moreno viewed *Le Contrat Social* as propounding a philosophy more for America than for Europe. After he had returned to Buenos Aires, where he held an important position, he published the *Memorial de los Hacendados*, the first point of departure for Argentine independence, in which he applied general theory to Argentine reality. Later, in 1810, he published a transla-

---

[1] Boleslao Lewin: "Rousseau en la raigambre ideológica argentina." In *Presencia de Rousseau*, University of Mexico, 1962.

tion of *Le Contrat Social.* It was one of the first books to come off the famous Argentine press of the Niños Expósitos. In the prologue he wrote:

> Americans do not consider themselves united with the Spanish monarchs through the social pact, which alone can support the legitimacy and decorum of a rule. If the peoples of Spain remain dependents of the prisoner king, waiting for their freedom and remission, all well and good. They established the monarchy, and the present prince, hewing to the line that he is in duty bound to reign over them by an express agreement with the Spanish nation, has a right to demand observance of the social contract at any moment when it is expedient for him to require that he be given what is due him. In no case can America consider herself bound by that obligation; she has not concurred in the celebration of the social pact from which the Spanish monarchs derive their empire's sole title to legitimacy. Force and violence are the only base of the Conquest that gave these regions to the Spanish throne; a conquest that has never been able, over three hundred years, to erase from the memory of man the atrocities and horrors with which it was carried out, and which, never having been ratified by the free and unanimous consent of these peoples, has added nothing to the primitiveness of the force and violence that produced it by its title of guaranty.

On this point there is a striking coincidence between the Americans' interpretation of the Social Contract and the old idea common among the rural masses of South America that a royal cedula that gave the people the right to choose their rulers had been concealed from them. The idea must have originated in the communes of Paraguay, for by 1780 it had spread among the Indians and Negroes of New Granada who fought their own *comunero* revolution.

Le Contrat Social was published in Buenos Aires in 1810 for adoption as a school text. Years later, Monsignor Muzi stated in a report to the Holy See that after its distribution to all school teachers for reading and assignment had been assured by decree, the Archbishop of Charcas and the Bishop of Salta opposed the decree so violently that it was rescinded.

In Chile, the "leading lights" were doing as much damage as the *Le Contrat Social* in Argentina. Monsignor Muzi was also reporting to the Holy See that the difficulties of the Church were not the result of the Masonic lodges, as had been believed, but of the theater, where anti-papist works were shown:

> . . . such as *Aristodemus*, brought here from Buenos Aires, or shadow plays injurious to the Pope. When the first one, concerning Bishop Rodríguez, was shown, the mob shouted: "Out, out of here!" At the second, about Muzi, someone cried, "Let him go back to his jungle!" whereas when silhouettes of Voltaire and Rousseau were cast, applause and huzzas resounded: "Forward! Forward! Enlighten the people!"[1]

In Mexico the priest José María Morelos y Pavón (1765–1815), the Liberator who marched during his revolutionary campaigns at the head of a group of pilgrims, was an arch-Rousseauan, the moving force behind the first constitution of the republic. For more than a year Morelos traveled from village to village, sometimes holding meetings under the trees, sometimes in the squares, from Chilpancingo to Las Ánimas, to the orchards of Huetano, then on to the country around Atijo, from Atijo to the Agua Dulce country, and so on until he reached Apatzingán. In Chilpancingo, Morelos said: "Buried though we are in stupidity and benumbed by servitude, we do not find the notions of the *Social Contract* strange, for they are not unknown to us." In Apatzingán, he approved Article V of the Constitution: "Sovereignty springs immediately from the People whose only wish is to deposit it with their representatives."

Rousseau himself might have created a character like Simón Bolívar (1783–1830). Born in Caracas, he was liberally taught by Simón Rodríguez (1771–1854) and Andrés Bello (1781–1865), though Rodríguez had him for twelve years, and Bello for only two. Rodríguez was of a Voltairean turn of mind, fully indoctrinated with the Encyclopedists' theories, and was such an *aficionado* of teaching that he invented a most extraordinary educational system and wrote a revolutionary book on his pedagogical ideas. Bello was his exact opposite: he seemed more mature, serene, erudite, and well-balanced, and was a very strong francophile. He taught himself foreign languages. Presbyter Montenegro reproached him bitterly for reading a book in one of the dangerous languages by saying: "It's a great pity, my friend, that you ever learned French!" Young Bello was one of those

---

[1] Pedro Leturia, S.J.: *Relaciones entre la Santa Sede e Hispanoamérica.*

closest to Humboldt during the great scientist's visit to Caracas. As Bello knew English, he was able to translate an article in the London *Times* carrying the news of Napoleon's invasion of Spain and the abdication of Charles IV. In that way the authorities were informed. Both teachers educated Bolívar, but Rodríguez stimulated him more, first in Caracas and later in Europe. Rodríguez always carried with him a book by his mentor in pedagogy, Rousseau. During his exile in Europe, he persuaded Bolívar to undertake with him the journey recommended by Rousseau, through central Europe to Rome on foot. In Rome he inspired Bolívar to make a vow on the Aventine Hill: "I swear that I will not die until I have driven the last Spaniard out of America."

As Bolívar was leaving Europe, he wrote a letter to Teresa Tristán in terms that could hardly be more Rousseauan:

> I am going to seek another way of life; I am tired of Europe and its old societies; I am returning to America. What shall I do there? . . . I don't know. You know that with me everything comes spontaneously and I never make plans. The life of a savage has many charms for me. Very likely I shall build a hut in the beautiful forests of Venezuela. There I shall be able to pull the branches off the trees to my heart's content, with no fear that anyone will grumble at me. . . . Ah, Teresa, happy are those who believe in a better world! To me, this one is quite sterile. If a man never has time enough to look at the clouds floating above his head, the leaves shaken by the wind, the water that runs in the brook, and the plants growing along its banks, life is sad for him, I should say, though I'd be taken for a madman. . . . The great Emperor has just invaded Spain and I should like to witness the way such an event will be received in America.

Bolívar was a revolutionary, an ideologist rather than a fighting man. His point of reference was the *Encyclopédie*—that is, France. He had followed Napoleon's rise closely. He called him the *caudillo*, but was indignant when the Little Corporal had himself crowned emperor. The possibility that Napoleon might make his escape to America was considered momentarily after the disaster of Waterloo. To Bolívar that would have been a calamity.

America adopted the best of the French philosophy, but did not follow it to the letter. Then suddenly a new star rose in the political firmament with the independence of the United States.

Would the new republic prove the best model for revolution in the South? Was the experiment in federation not a happy one, bearing better fruit than the French republic ever had borne? Bolívar was always very explicit on this point. The first document he ever wrote, his *Memorandum of Cartagena*, pointed to the clergy as the cause of the first defeat, which forced him into exile. He stigmatized them as royalists who used all the moral force at their command to combat both the republic and the theorists whom Jefferson inspired. "After the earthquake," he said, "the influence of the Church played a very considerable part in the uprising of the subordinate cities and villages and in the introduction into the country of enemies who sacrilegiously abused the sanctity of their ministry on behalf of the promoters of civil war." Of the revolutionaries, he said, "We had philosophers for leaders, philanthropy for legislation, dialectics for tactics, and sophists for soldiers." Then he added: "What most weakened the government of Venezuela was the federal form it adopted following the exaggerated maxims of the rights of man, which, by authorizing him to rule himself, break the social contract and plunge the nations into anarchy."

After the defeat at Cartagena, seven years went by in one of the fiercest, most heroic, and bloodiest wars in American history, indeed in world history, with a full accompaniment of victories and reverses. Bolívar convoked his famous congress in the wild solitudes of the Orinoco, to which most of the delgates came in rags. The Liberator proclaimed to the world the irrevocable determination of his armies not to accept any solution short of independence. He asked the assembly to assume the sovereign power to dictate the constitution, and offered them a plan, saying: "Representatives of the people! You are called together to consecrate or reject whatever may seem to you worthy of reform in our social contract, or of being rejected." But his advice echoed Montesquieu more than Rousseau:

> Would it not be very difficult to apply to Spain the code of political liberty, the civil and religious body of laws that are used by England? Well, then, how much more difficult it is to adapt the laws of North America to Venezuela. Does not the *Spirit of the Laws* say that they must be appropriate to the people who make them? That it would be a great coincidence if the laws of one nation were to suit another? That the laws must relate to the physical character of the country, the

quality of the terrain, its situation, its extent, its people's manner of life? Should they not conform to the degree of liberty the constitution can permit, the religion of the inhabitants, their inclinations, their wealth, their number, their commerce, their customs, their ways? That is the code of laws we must consult, not Washington's!

Bolívar marched from Venezuela to Peru, across mountains and swamps, carrying a traveling library in his luggage. He had translations of Homer read to him in French and quoted Homer as a poet who regarded freedom as the air a man should breathe. At night he read a copy of the *Le Contrat Social*, once the property of Napoleon, given to him by the British general Sir Robert Thomas Wilson. In a letter to Santander, Bolívar commented on an article by the French statesman Comte François Nicolas Mollien, which stated that the Liberator's education had been haphazard:

> Certainly I did not learn Aristotelean philosophy, nor the statutes of criminal law and misdemeanor, but it may be that M. de Mollien has not studied Locke, Condillac, Buffon, Helvetius, Montesquieu, Mably, Filangière, Llande, Rousseau, Voltaire, Rollin, and all the ancient classics as much as I have, nor the philosophers, historians, poets, and all the modern classics of Spain, France, and Italy, plus a good part of the English.

He harangued his soldiers on the eve of battle with words that echo the European romantics: "The freedom of America is the hope of the universe." Earlier he said in an address to the men at the congress of Angostura: "Here is the place to repeat to you, Legislators, what the eloquent Volney said in the dedication of his *Ruins of Palmyra:* 'To the nascent people of the Spanish Indies, to the generous leaders who are guiding them to freedom: may the errors and misfortunes of the ancient world teach the New World wisdom and happiness.' "

¶ CONTRABAND IDEAS

In France, the agitation of the Encyclopedists terminated at the guillotine that beheaded the king and queen. The next steps were the proclamation of the rights of man, the founding of the republic, and everything else that Charles III's ministers had failed to foresee while the king was writing copiously of his affection for the French. The royal councilors had felt only an occasional qualm as they permitted the ships of the Enlightenment to weigh anchor for America and let French savants go there on scientific missions. Now they were finding something more serious than the Jesuits' doctrine of regicide looming on the horizon—the guillotine. Charles III's foreign minister, the Count of Floridablanca, who was granted his title as payment for obtaining from the Pope the bull expelling the Jesuits, was the first to discover to his horror what was going on in France. Sarrailh reveals the Spanish state of mind of the moment in his work on the Enlightenment:

> The government in Madrid took a number of steps to protect itself from the revolutionary contagion. After the month of December 1789, officials were forbidden by royal decree to speak of France, and a short time later the same decree was applied to the newspapers. At the same time the Inquisition doubled its activity. The Spanish minister asked the directors of the mail to take charge of packages and confiscate those containing news of the French Revolution. The Foreign secretary was forbidden to hand on suspect letters coming through the diplomatic mail. Spaniards were forbidden to send their children to study in France. All those [Frenchmen] who held any but a well-defined position were expelled from Madrid.

Instructions were shot off to the colonies with impressive speed. On December 13, 1789, the *Declaration of the Rights of Man* was banned, and made subject to prosecution by the Inquisition tribunal in Cartagena—even though the text was not known in America, and though the recently ratified United States constitution had incorporated its principles as American doctrine. Ample news of the United States reached Mexico, owing to its nearness, and South America was able to read selections from the Constitution in *El Espíritu de los Mejores Diarios* (*The Spirit of the Best Dailies*), a digest published in Madrid.

In Bogotá, Antonio Nariño owned one of the best libraries of his time and was a faithful reader of *El Espíritu.* . . . Already prepared by his reading of the Encyclopedists for the removal of the veil from the French Revolution, he dedicated himself to a search for the text of the *Declaration of the Rights of Man.* He found it by chance in a book called the *History of the Constitu-*

tional Assembly by Galart de Montjoie—from the viceroy's library. He translated it in December 1793 and then, with the help of a typographer who knew nothing about it, printed the text in his own shop one Sunday in a leaflet that he distributed clandestinely the next day. Someone reported him and he was subjected to torture. The price of his crime was sixteen years in prison, part of that time in the dungeons of Cartagena, part in Spain; after serving his term, he was exiled to Africa.

Several years after Nariño's venture, a group of Spaniards met in Madrid, intent upon a conspiracy against the monarchy and upon proclaiming a republic. In 1797 they printed a translation of the *Rights of Man* and "a preliminary discourse addressed to the Americans." The author, Juan Bautista Picornell, was the director of the movement. Ironically enough, when Picornell called together his friends in Madrid, Antonio Nariño was in the dungeons there for starting the same enterprise in Bogotá. And by a greater irony, the ship that carried Nariño from Cartagena to Spain as a prisoner was named for the great minister of the Enlightenment who had arranged the expulsion of the Jesuits but had been terror-stricken by the French Revolution: Floridablanca.

The plot was discovered, and Picornell and his comrades were all sentenced to exile in America! The exiles succeeded in putting ashore on the island of Guadeloupe a number of copies of the book for circulation in America. In 1811 the work was reissued in Caracas. Of course Picornell and his friends organized a conspiracy in La Guaira and found active collaborators among the people, even among the Negroes, for the field had been fertilized by the new ideas.

All such matters already had permeated the minds of the commonest of the common people. This is illustrated by a curious episode in the history of Colombia's independence. A few days before the freedom cry rang out in Bogotá, a popular uprising took place in the town of Socorro, the cradle of the *comunero* movement. When the disturbance reached the point at which it seemed that blood was about to flow in torrents through the streets, the corregidor and his men surrendered and were taken as prisoners to the town hall. They were left in the patio while the people's representatives went into the assembly hall to deliberate. The following report was made to the viceroy:

> In the outbuildings of the town hall were found three chains for bringing in forty-four men. The people have not seen

them yet; and unless force of circumstance obliges us to take measures for safety, these dreadful instruments of despotism, this underhanded means of commanding some inhabitants worthy of better masters, these enormous chains, we repeat, and those owned by Don Joaquín Castro and others will be thrown by the hangman into a deep river. The prisoners will be taken to various ports to be sent to Philadelphia to take lessons in humanity.

When the wars of Independence were over, or as the last battles were being fought in Upper Peru, criticism of the French and North American ideas began to emerge in essays that demonstrated how carefully their authors had studied the writers and systems of France and the United States before arriving at their own American solution. One of the most felicitous expositors was a Cuban, Francisco Javier Yáñez, who emigrated to Venezuela, fought in the war, was exiled, and finally returned to Caracas, where he showed the quality of his jurist's mind in a booklet entitled *Manual Político del Venezolano* (*Political Manual for the Venezuelan*), published in Caracas in 1824. The "manual" is a study rooted in Rousseau's and Montesquieu's theories and concluding with those of the United States. Yáñez was well acquainted with *The Federalist* and its philosophy. He pointed out Rousseau's and Montesquieu's mistakes and attributed them to the fact that they had written before the experiments in the New World had begun. "Representation," Yáñez writes, "had its germ in the minds of the ancient societies, but it was perfected in the New World, and its progenitors are Washington, Franklin, Lafayette, Paine, Hamilton, Madison, Ustariz, Roscio, Lozano, Pombo, Torres, and others." Farther along he writes:

> The works of Montesquieu, Rousseau, and other great men must be read with caution and many reservations, for some of them wrote before the representative system had been perfected and others under governments whose main interest it was to destroy the republican regime or make it odious by confusing the times, the principles, and things.

Yáñez's task was to broadcast and give greater emphasis to the theories of the Encyclopedists and the authors of treatises on the world, and yet to adjust them with his scrupulous jurist's sense by a very clear analysis and with reservations. Less roundly critical than Bolívar of the Founding Fathers' philosophy—indeed he was their greatest admirer—he did not let himself be carried away by his own partiality; he pointed out the difference between the heirs of the English colonies and those of the Spanish as follows:

> The Republic of the North was founded originally not through conquest, but through Penn's peaceful negotiations. The legislators worked in an enlightened century, in a country where they had neither to fight and conquer a military power, nor to limit an absolute authority, nor to strip a dominant clergy of its powers or a nobility of its rights and privileges or a great number of families of their fortunes, nor to build their new edifice upon spoils drenched in blood. This is why they were able to found their institutions upon the principles of reason, liberty, political and civil equality, and universal justice. . . . Their laws, drawn with only the general welfare in mind, were traced, so to speak, upon a *tabula rasa*, untouched by class spirit, privilege, etc.

Thus the heritage of the European Enlightenment began to become a special element in the new republics. The same could be said of what the new republics were taking, with similar reservations, from the United States.

XII: *The Scientific Missions*

¶ FROM FATHER ACOSTA TO JORGE JUAN
AND ANTONIO DE ULLOA

Europe's interest in America was by no means confined to philosophic speculation. Scientists, navigators, botanists, and geographers wanted to rediscover that world still enveloped in mystery, distrust, and suspicion. As far back as the sixteenth century, natural histories had been written about it; its plants and animals had been studied; efforts had been made to rectify astronomical theories; maps had been drawn. But as science itself was in embryo, the studies were full of errors. By the eighteenth century, however, new elements for judgment were at hand, new tools, and greatly superior facilities for interpretation. Moreover, the period was ardent about scientific investigation, particularly in the natural sciences. As Copernicus, a Pole, had earlier divided the field of astronomy into two eras, now a Swede, Linnaeus (1707–78), was doing the same for botany. France assembled all these victories and issued the *Encyclopédie*. But science demands proof, and the ideal laboratory for experimentation lay in America.

Until just prior to the Enlightenment, the *Natural and Moral History of the Indies* by José de Acosta (1539–1600) was the final authority on America. The work of this Jesuit was not entirely original; he had copied in part from the Dominican Diego Durán (1537–88), whose still unpublished book the *History of the Indies of New Spain* is distinguished more for its literary beauty than for its scientific accuracy. Acosta dealt with "the remarkable things from heaven, the elements, metals, plants, and animals in the Indies, and the rites and ceremonies, laws and government, and wars of the Indians." His book was published in Spanish in 1591 at Seville and in Latin at Salamanca in 1595. It was translated and widely read in Italian (1596), Flemish (1598), French (1600), and English (1604). Acosta believed that the sun revolved around the earth.

> There is no doubt but that the opinion of Aristotle, the other Peripatetics, and the Stoics, that the sky has a round shape and is moving circularly and revolving, is true and correct. The sun, the moon, and the stars turn around the world. The earth is in the center, surrounded everywhere by heavenly bodies.

This did not imply that Acosta took everything exactly as Aristotle had left it. When he arrived in Panama, he said:

> I confess that I laughed and made sport of Aristotle's methods and philosophy, seeing that in the place and time when, according to his dicta, everything was to be on fire, I and all my companions were cold. . . . The ancients were so far from thinking that there might be people in this world that many of them did not wish to believe there was land in this part [of the earth]; and what is more wondrous, there were those who would deny there was even a sky here: for though it is true that most of the best philosophers felt that the sky was completely round, as indeed it is, and that thus it surrounds the earth everywhere and encloses it within itself, some, and no few, even those with the least authority among learned men of the Church, held a different opinion, imagining that the world was made like a house, with the roof over it surrounding it only at the top, not around it everywhere: giving as the reason for this that in every building the foundation is one part and the roof another; and thus by all the rules of good building, the whole sky must be an upper part of this great edifice of the world, and all the earth another separate part below.

Acosta's advance over Aristotle was about equal to Copernicus's advance over Acosta. But many problems still remained to be solved. The earth had to be measured, for its size was not known, and American nature had to be scrutinized through the eye of the man of that century. Under the first Bourbon kings, Spain favored these experiments. She granted entry to scholars from France, England, Germany, and Sweden—all of them well equipped with permits, to be sure. Her commerce spread more widely. When the port of Buenos Aires opened, the prospects of the South changed.

One of the first of the traveler-scientists was Father Louis Feuillée, a Frenchman who had visited half the Orient with Jacques Cassini by 1699. In 1702 he reconnoitered the coasts of Venezuela and Colombia, making a preliminary study of the botany and the general natural history of the region which was to place him at the head of the naturalists who later made their name in the Botanical Mission.[1] Feuillée traveled through Argentina, Chile, and Peru during 1711. Amédée François Frézier followed Feuillée's work in the south and wrote a most interesting description of Lima in 1713. Frézier speaks with enthusiasm of the Limans who, not content with the richness of the most beautiful fabrics, adorned themselves with prodigious falls of lace, and whose desire for pearls and gems in bracelets, earrings, and other jewels was insatiable. He describes the viceroy of Peru, "the viceroy of South America," framed in glittering wealth. He was shocked at the four thousand nuns in the city and the licentious life of the monks.

Other scholars followed Feuillée and Frézier. Their minds less tinged with fantasy, some of them captured the immediate interest of scholars in the European academies as they did what they were sent to do. One famous expedition was that organized by the Royal Academy of Science in Paris to ascertain the exact shape of the earth, whether spherical or ellipsoidal. If the earth was not a perfect sphere and the exact measurements of its circumference were unknown, someone would have to go over the whole surface of the earth to arrive at an accurate knowledge of it. The Cassinis —Jean-Dominique and his son Jacques—who were Italian astronomers and scholars, had posed the problem to the Academy in Paris, which appointed two commissions: one to go to Lapland and another to Peru. Charles-Marie de la Condamine (1701–74) was appointed head of the Peruvian expedition. Two other academicians traveled with him—the astronomer Louis Godin and the hydrographer and mathematician Pierre Bouguer—as

---

[1] Gabriel Giraldo Jaramillo, a student of his work, notes this in "Un precursor de las expediciones botánicas: El padre Luis Feuillée," *Cuadernos* (Paris, August 1964).

well as the botanist Joseph Jussieu, the surgeon Jean Seniergues, an engineer, a clock-maker, servants, and so on. Before agreeing to the trip, the Spanish Crown stipulated that two young Spanish engineers, Jorge Juan and Antonio de Ulloa, were to go with the Frenchmen. At that time they were only twenty-two and twenty-eight respectively, and their fame lay in the future. The expedition sailed in 1735. Never before had a commission of such importance visited Spanish America. It was well equipped with books, instruments, and assistants. The party arrived in Quito. The plan was to take the exact measure of a degree of circumference precisely on the line of the Equator. During the three years that the work went on, the scholars lived through the widest range of experience and accomplished a small revolution in Quitan society, which had always been averse to meeting outsiders.

Apart from its scientific content, La Condamine's memorandum to the Academy reads like a rough draft of a tragic novel of adventure. The surgeon Jean Seniergues was knifed to death in Cuenca during a quarrel that he himself had provoked over his love affair with Manuela Quesada. Jorge Juan fought with the presiding officer of the supreme court in Quito and had to flee to Lima. The academician Godin fell in love with a girl in Guayaquil, named Isabel Grandmaison—or Casamayor—and had so many adventures and mishaps and performed so many heroic deeds after their marriage that their story could hardly be squeezed into the framework of a thick novel. Godin went to explore the Amazon jungles, was captured by the Indians, and became so ill that it seemed he would not survive. Isabel found him in his desolation by following her sharp feminine intuitions, and she rescued him. La Condamine reported the most spectacular chapters of those adventures, presented his scientific data to the Academy, and brought back a sample of a gum that was to revolutionize modern life: raw rubber.

The fortunes of the two Spaniards accompanying La Condamine were more sedate. They recorded the important evidence of their scientific studies in a book containing the astronomical and physical observations they had made in the several regions of Peru, along with an historical account of their travels. Ulloa discovered platinum near Popayán, became superintendent of the mines at Huancavelica, and later governor of Louisiana and founder of the astronomical observatory in Cádiz. The scholarly Spaniards were scandalized at the abandon and abuses they saw and at the wretched colonial government. In the century of the Enlightenment, they found that native society had not risen above the most primitive level, that doctrinaire priests were exploiting the Indians, that the convents were licentious, and that the mines were not being exploited scientifically. They added a book of *Secret Memoirs* to their public reports. In time the revelations in the memoirs helped to breed another of the black legends about Spain, for they fell into the hands of the English and were published in London. The scandal never has completely died down. Indeed there is no better source from which to learn the abuses of colonial administration. The book is imbued with the spirit of renewal which motivated the ministers of Charles III. Many, if not all, of the damning revelations of the two travelers are confirmed in numerous documents and administrative memoranda. Apart from their freely painted picture of base behavior, their systematic presentation of their case was a novelty. The book made it easy to acquire some knowledge of the situation that led to independence. The two enthusiastic Spanish scholars actually wrote a prologue to the work of American emancipation.

¶ FROM LA CONDAMINE TO MALASPINA

La Condamine's expedition bore fruit in the growing interest shown in Spanish America by the scientific centers of Europe. Francis I of Austria lent his patronage to the Dutch botanist Nikolaus Joseph von Jacquin (1727–1817), a naturalized Austrian who was able to go to the Caribbean to study the plants of that region as director of the Imperial Botanical Gardens of Vienna. Jacquin's *Selectarum Stirpium Americanum Historia*, published in 1736, records his trip. Spain later engaged a Swede, Pieter Loefling, to carry on Jacquin's work, but Loefling died on the banks of the Orinoco of a pernicious fever at the age of twenty-seven. Linnaeus published his posthumous work, *Iter Hispanicum*. Jacquin and Loefling were the first to christen the plants of the Caribbean islands, Colombia, and Venezuela with Latin names in conformity with the practice of Linnaeus.

The man who was to become a second La Condamine through his influence on Diderot and the Encyclopedists and through his information on America, was Baron Louis-Antoine de Bougainville (1729–1811). Bougainville's curiosity about Spanish America was awakened by a trip to Canada. He was dreaming then of founding a colony under the French flag on the Malvinas Islands, which he named after St. Malo, where his expedition started. A Benedictine monk, Dom Pernaty, accompanied him on the voyage. As the islands actually belonged to Spain already, Bougainville was forced to abandon his plan and decided to sail around the world. He touched at Montevideo in 1767, and visited Paraguay. He rounded Cape Horn through the Straits of Magellan. He made a stop in Tahiti. When he returned home, he displayed in Paris the things he had collected on his travels, and introduced a beautiful flower that he had found in America, which brought him two rewards: one, the flower was named for him, and the other, its beauty aroused in another scholar—Baron von Humboldt—the desire to know America. Bougainville and La Condamine were the two travelers from whom Diderot took most of his information on America.

Jean-François de Galaup, Count de La Pérouse (1741–88), followed Bougainville's itinerary in 1786. Through him, Europe learned of Easter Island, isolated in the lonely wastes of the Pacific. The first known drawings of the gigantic monoliths representing fantastic human figures date from then, and their style and presence still offer archaeologists one of their greatest enigmas. Among the English travelers were the poet Byron's grandfather, John Byron (1723–86), who visited Patagonia in 1764, Samuel Wallis (1728–95), who discovered Tahiti and Wallis Island, and Philip Carteret (died in 1796), to whom the world owes one of the charts of the Straits of Magellan.

An Italian, Alessandro Malaspina (1745–1810), undertook the most ambitious exploration project. Educated in Palermo, he entered the Spanish maritime service and, after an eighteen-month voyage around the world, suggested a great scientific expedition that would not merely compete with the French and English expeditions at the time when James Cook's famous voyages recently had been completed, but also would make the most comprehensive scientific survey of the Spanish Empire. Malaspina proposed that botanists, draftsmen, surveyors, cartographers, and mineralogists should accompany him. They would make new maps, measure the heights of mountains, bring back samples of minerals, sketch plant life, and study and make drawings of the inhabitants and their customs. The expedition was Spanish, but it included colleagues from other countries: the French botanist Louis Nees, the Polish naturalist and cartographer Thaddeus de Haenke, and the Italian draftsman Brambilla.

The group sailed from Cádiz in July 1789, the month and year of the French Revolution. Enlightened Spain seemed to be approaching progress by another road with Malaspina. The two copper-hulled corvettes, *La Descubierta* (*The Reconnaisance*) and *La Atrevida* (*The Bold*), were veritable floating laboratories. They first stopped at the mouth of the Río de la Plata to make a topographical plan of Buenos Aires and Montevideo, as well as of the surrounding countryside. In Patagonia, they made maps and studied the manners, customs, and religion of the Tierra del Fuegans. They rounded the Cape, reached Chile, and, after completing a study of the island of Chiloé and Valparaíso, went on to Callao. They stayed four months in Peru. While they were in Callao, the cartographers were at work and the botanists were journeying with the draftsmen to the interior to explore such items of archaeological interest as the ruins of Pachacámac. They made a long stop in Guayaquil which permitted a trip to the interior to determine the altitude of Mount Chimborazo. On the way back from Panama they studied the Galápagos Islands. In Panama they spent a month making observations on the levels of the two oceans and their tides and investigating the possibilities of a canal to link them. In Mexico they collected data while the ships were being fitted out for Alaska, a voyage of exploration that would place Malaspina at the head of those who followed Cook to study little-known regions. Back in Mexico City, Malaspina persuaded Viceroy Revillagigedo to build the corvettes *Sútil* and *Mexicana* to explore Vancouver Bay. No one before Malaspina had ever assembled such a mass of samples, drawings, maps, and the like. But for all that he was never able to enjoy the glory of his achievements or to write his memoirs. For political reasons he fell into disfavor with Manuel de Godoy, the powerful favorite of Queen María Luisa and Carlos IV, and was sentenced to ten years in prison. That was the moment when the Enlightenment lost all its impetus, under a regime in which Spain's previous glories entered a total eclipse.

¶ THE BOTANICAL EXPEDITION LED BY MUTIS

In 1761 a young physician in Seville, José Celestino Mutis (1732–1804), was called upon to accompany the recently appointed viceroy to New Granada. Mutis was already an outstanding and dedicated student of the natural sciences. He suggested either the establishment of a new academy of science or the renovation of the academies in Madrid and Seville, which were lying stagnant, or the compilation of a critical history of all the Spanish authors. The authorities decided it would be best to ship him off to America. Loefling had just died in the Orinoco, and Mutis saw an opportunity to carry on his work. But before long he came up with a more ambitious proposal. Once he had settled in Bogotá and had scanned the field offered him for work or investigation, he conceived the idea of a mission that would begin as a botanical survey but would eventually study the fauna, the topography, and the customs of the inhabitants, as well as the flora of the region. This would provide work for many scholars, investigators, physicians, and painters. He would lay before Linnaeus a picture of the New Granadine flora and a sample of the riches of the New World. America is rich not only in its gold, silver and precious stones, he said; it yields plant dyes that would soon be discovered by industry, raw rubber and many other gums that could be put to good use in the arts, and an infinite variety of woods. He added, "It is foolish to persuade one's self that quinine, cascarilla—another very varied plant—*guamoco* bark, ipecac, bramble, lignum-vitae, Tolu or Zaragoza balsam, mangrove resin, caraña gum, Peru balsam, copaiba balsam, and many other familiar simples are the only medicinal plants produced by America."

Yet—and that was the apogee of the Enlightened Despotism— the bureaucratic lethargy of the court was legendary. Twenty years went by before the letter in which Mutis offered his plan was granted a reply. Those were twenty years during which Europe kept moving forward. Mutis was using them as best he could by carrying on a profitable correspondence with the scholars of the continent, particularly with Linnaeus, and by training a new generation of scholars. Finally, on the eve of Humboldt's arrival in America, the king accepted the Mutis plan and created the Botanical Mission. Everything was then ready to start one of the most significant scientific undertakings of the period. The disciples had been waiting only for the moment when they could explore New Granada. Some were already engaged in exploration, eagerly collecting plants, minerals, and insects and listening to the Indians' stories that explained their medicinal uses. Not strangely, some of the investigators risked their lives in experiments they considered essential to the advance of science. One of them let himself be bitten by a viper in order to try out the effects of an antidote on his own body. The observatory of Bogotá was built. New maps were made correcting the errors of the old ones.

Mutis ultimately entered the priesthood, but his mind was always so closely attuned to the scientific world that he willingly opened the doors of New Granada to a mission of German Protestant engineers who accompanied the Spanish scholar Juan José de Elhuyar. We have already seen that Mutis had the courage to stand up to the Inquisition in order to teach the Copernican and Newtonian systems. He introduced vaccination. But his most ambitious work was to collect the flora of the Kingdom of New Granada with the help of botanists and draftsmen who contributed their herbaria and plates in order to create one of the richest collections in the world. The perfection of the colored drawings on the large plates is a marvel. They equal if they do not surpass the best English and German drawings. Humboldt said that Francisco Javier Matiz was "the best flower painter in the world." The artists of Quito, who until then had worked only on images for altars, were drawn into the scientific field not only in New Granada but also in Mexico, Peru, and Chile. The Bishop of Trujillo in Peru, Martínez y Compañón, lent a hand to the task of reproducing the types of people, costumes, customs, and dances of his diocese.

Forty painters were employed in the Mutis Mission. They came from Quito, Bogotá, Cartagena, Lima, Popayán, Havana, and Guaduas. Only two of the draftsmen were from Madrid, one of whom worked for only a day, the other for a year with but poor success. Mutis actually created a corps of American scholars and artists. When Humboldt arrived in Santa Fe and saw the work done by the Mission, he was astounded. The collection that has survived in the Botanical Gardens of Madrid alone contains 5,393 plates of plants; 2,495 of them are in full color and 2,488 in pen and ink. They show 2,696 separate species. According to the prudent estimate made during the past few years, the herbaria include from 20,000 to 24,000 specimens representing some 5,000 distinct species. As for the botanical library founded by Mutis in Bogotá, Humboldt considered it better than the best in Europe.

Francisco José de Caldas (1770–1816), a Colombian scholar born in Popayán, collected, by his own account, books, a telescope, and surveyor's instruments, and whenever he was unable to obtain from commercial sources any other instruments he needed, invented his own. He became a fast friend of Mutis, his teacher, and corresponded with him for years. His letters began with such words as: "I received your first letter, and what a letter! Two good barometric tubes, and Linnaeus's masterworks!" A long letter of his from Quito ended: "I will conclude by saying that a big box with my skeletons, sketches, and descriptions of plants and birds will follow this. Among them is the Chinchona de Intac, with its bark, and seeds of Polymnia. I am sending also some skeletons of a Valea, which differs from yours only in the absence of stipules. Mejía is putting in for you four skeletons of plants that I possess." In the large box of plants which he sent to Mutis he listed: "twenty of my drawings of plants, five of Mejía's, mine of birds, 30 sheets of my descriptions of plants, descriptions by Mejía," and also roots, barks, and skeletons of plants. This was at the very time that the students of Linnaeus at Upsala went out to the open country and came back by night singing hymns and carrying torches, thus surprising the citizens with their triumphal parade, their pride in the botanical treasure they were bringing back in their saddle bags, and their joy in their discovery of Scandinavian natural history.

On the day when Caldas joined forces with Mutis, he arrived with what looked like a traveling museum loaded in cases on a string of mules. Caldas called it the summary of his work:

> It amounts to a respectable herbarium of five or six thousand skeletons dried in the midst of the anxieties and speed of travel; two volumes of descriptions; many sketches of the most noteworthy plants done by my own hand; seeds, useful barks; some minerals; the materials needed to draw the geographical map of the viceroyalty; what is needed for botany, for zoology; the profiles of the Andes; the geometric altitude of the most famous peaks; more than 1,500 altitudes of various towns and mountains based on barometric deductions; a prodigious number of meteorological observations; two volumes of astronomical and metrical observations; some animals and birds. With this material, contained in sixteen loads, I presented myself to Mutis.

Such men as the Spaniard Mutis and the American Caldas became world famous through their heroic labors, carried forward in the scientific field with a passion that far surpassed the effort the Conquistadors had put into mastering the land of America. They created a body of work unequaled before or since their time. Some of the work was done amid extreme hardship. America was a new jungle, where man was often the wildest of the beasts, and the vicissitudes of politics and revolution might engulf those new discoverers, but could never cow them. Mutis had to wait twenty years for authorization of his botanical mission; then, owing to the machinations of the court bureaucracy, the news of his discoveries was held back until after another famous pair of botanists, Hipólito Ruiz and José Antonio Pavón, who had accompanied the Frenchman Dombey, had completed their study of chinchona in Peru. The work by Pavón and Ruiz was published in 1787, but the one by Mutis was lost in the storehouses of the Botanical Garden in Madrid until José Cuatrocasas, a Spanish botanist of this century, discovered and rescued it during the Civil War and took the heroic step of having the first prints from it published during that bloody upheaval. Years later, in 1954, publication was continued, now in monumental form, under the direction of a Colombian botanist, Enrique Pérez Arbeláez.

Caldas met an even worse fate. He was caught up in the War of Independence while directing the observatory in Bogotá. Of course he joined the armies of the revolution, became an engineer in the artillery and a founder of field pieces. During what was known as the Reconquest or Pacification, the Royalists captured him and shot him in Bogotá. The Spanish general Pablo Morillo, Count of Cartagena (1777–1838), made peace by killing.

¶ FÉLIX DE AZARA

Félix de Azara (1746–1821), a military engineer and naturalist, came to America in 1781 to fix the boundaries between the Portuguese and Spanish possessions along the Río de la Plata. He transformed his mission into a study plan that covered twenty years spent absorbing the history, geography, plant life, and animal life of the Plata and Paraguay rivers. Two books came out of this, *Viaje a través de la América Meridional desde 1781 a 1801* and *Apuntamientos para la historia natural de los cuadrúpedos y pájaros del Paraguay y Río de la Plata*. Azara's descriptions are marked by great precision and are accompanied by beguiling accounts of animal life. He could make natural history come alive; indeed he might be called a forerunner of other literary naturalists of the same region, such as William Henry Hudson (1841–1922), author of the classic *Green Mansions*, and Horacio Quiroga (1878–1922), who wrote *Anaconda* and *Cuentos de la Selva*. Azara's stories about snakes are famous; they end with this thought:

Perhaps no creature has so many enemies as the serpents and vipers, for the eagles, hawks, and falcons, all the herons and cranes hunt them to death, as do the iguanas, man, frequent fires in the open country and even they themselves, for they eat one another. They have almost no means of self-defense other than to bite and to hide in already existing holes, in the water, or among the matted straw of the fields. The herons and cranes waste no time in catching them, owing to the advantage of a long neck and beak. They catch them near the head, chew them a bit until they are stunned, and then swallow them whole. Birds of prey approach them from the side, using a dragging wing as a shield, and try to peck the viper or serpent in the head until it is dead, after which they eat it piece by piece.

The description of the Mboi Chumbe recalls the picture of the serpent that bit Rima in Hudson's novel: "a yard long, round and beautifully banded, one band a yellowish white and the other very bright; and so they run along the entire body and head."

Azara is a master at describing and telling stories about birds. He tells this yarn about the *rasón* (razorbill) or *ypaca'a* which was tamed and allowed to run free in the yard.

He ate squash, bread, and all kinds of meat, although he preferred worms. When he was fully grown, he fought with the hens and roosters; and when the roosters would brace themselves for the *ypaca'a*'s attack, he, incomparably quicker, would bend his head and run between the rooster's legs, and upset him, then without a moment's loss, he would peck him on the breast and tail before he could get up again. He knew when the hens were about to lay and would station himself not far from them, and when the egg emerged, the *ypaca'a* would seize it in his beak and carry it a long way off, where he would carefully pierce it and suck it without breaking it. If the hens were slow to lay, he would grow impatient and would peck them on the part where they laid and would run after them and peck them angrily. He would do the same thing at the neighbors' houses, for he went about everywhere, and would climb to the roof tiles, so that he had to be killed because the neighbors complained.

¶ SOCIETIES OF FRIENDS OF THE COUNTRY

The Crown's main interest in America was, of course, the mines. Gold and silver were the chief incentives to the Conquest,

and legends played an important part. Yet in spite of the tremendous wealth that the Spaniards took out soon after their arrival, the mines became less important than playing cards, rum,
or tobacco, as a source of income during the three centuries after
the discovery. The dismal fact was that the El Dorados seen in
dreams had dwindled away in time. Potosí, the great mineral
center of Upper Peru, once a larger city than the capital of Mexico,
became only a ghost of its past greatness by the end of the
eighteenth century, when the mines were worked out.

The value of platinum was unknown until the end of the
eighteenth century. The rich mines of the Choco were not worked
because the mineral could not be extracted. It was despised as a
kind of intractable gold, and the miners threw it into the river.
But during the Enlightenment, the members of the Societies of
Friends of the Country in Spain, particularly the Basques from
Vergara, showed a great interest in mineralogy. In 1753 a Spanish
minister commissioned the Englishman Bowles to study platinum.
Bowles reported: "Platinum is a metallic sand *sui-generis* that
may prove harmful to the world because it can be mixed easily
with gold . . . so that fraud is within hand's reach if platinum is
permitted to circulate in commerce."[1] Valentín Foronda, of Vergara, later proclaimed a "citizen of the world," was proud of his
village, because, although it contained only some two hundred
houses, it had eleven subscribers to the *Encyclopédie*. He joyfully
announced that the Vergara school, which he had promoted
with enthusiasm, had achieved glory "one morning in May 1786
when a famous chemist, a learned physicist and mathematician, an
alert observer of nature, a wise and reflective genius, in short,
M. Chabaneau, had the honor of purifying platinum completely
by a very simple process and at a very low cost."

That same Society of Friends of the Country in Vergara trained
two brothers, Juan José and Fausto Elhuyar, whose names are
associated with another famous discovery: the isolation of tungsten or wolfram. The Elhuyar brothers studied in Paris, Frei-
berg, Bohemia, and Sweden. Although they traveled apparently
as students of the Basque society, they were actually carrying
out a secret mission for the Spanish government to obtain data
on the casting of cannon in Sweden and England. The interests
of the brothers were very broad. Anything to do with mining

---

[1] Sarrailh: *L'Espagne Eclairée dans la second moitié du XVIII siècle,*
pp. 450 ff., on the investigation of platinum.

attracted them; Juan José spent some time in Upsala. Upon his return to Spain, the government was cool toward him, perhaps because it did not share his ideas on the subject of cannon, or because he had spent more time than expected and had used funds for purposes other than those which interested the government. The two brothers had isolated tungsten, but as they were interested in the work of extracting silver, they decided to go to America after learning of the advancing exhaustion of the mines in Potosí and Mexico.

Juan José went to New Granada. Mutis welcomed him, and under his patronage, Elhuyar worked in the silver mines of Mariquita and the emerald mines of Muzo. Meanwhile Fausto Elhuyar succeeded in obtaining for Baron Furchtegott Leberecht Nordenflycht an invitation to come to Potosí to resume the working of the mines.

Fausto Elhuyar went on to Mexico, where he founded the School of Mines that is famous all over America. Among the graduates of the school were the Mexican astronomer Antonio de León y Gama (1735–1802), and Andrés del Rio, a learned Spaniard who discovered vanadium. After the founding of the School of Mines, the Botanical Gardens, and the Academy of Fine Arts in Mexico City, Humboldt wrote: "No city in the New World, not excepting those in the United States, has scientific establishments as large and solid as those in the Mexican capital."

This flowering of Mexico was nothing new. The Enlightenment found there a fertile field for germination, as Humboldt himself demonstrated. José Antonio Alzate Ramírez (1729–90) founded the *Literary Gazette* and wrote such valuable scientific essays as his *Observaciones meteorológicas* and *La Noticia sobre las minas de azogue [mercury] que hay en la Nueva España*. A poet of the Encylopedist type, Joaquín Velásquez de Cárdenas, who was initiated into the science of astronomy by an Indian named Manuel Asentzio, blended the science of the Aztecs and that of Newton in his store of knowledge. He made for himself the instruments he needed for his observatory at Santa Ana, and when the Frenchman Abbot Cheppe arrived in Mexico City, he noted with surprise that the "astronomer" Velásquez had predicted eclipses accurately, fixed their points on the map, and made most precise observations of the passage of Venus between the earth and the sun.

¶ HUMBOLDT

No scientific mission was more important to America and Europe than that of Baron Alexander von Humboldt (1769–1859). This German scholar was not privileged to travel during the full bloom of the Enlightenment under Charles III. Instead his work was done in the reign of Charles IV, of unhappy memory, when the Spanish Empire was in eclipse and moribund. Alexander von Humboldt and his brother Karl Wilhelm, the philologist-diplomat (1767–1835), raised German science to new heights by their work. Alexander became a naturalist, geographer, and historian whose work on America is still one of the greatest monuments ever built by European scholarship. He began his career by studying philosophy, sociology and literature; later he made a start in medicine, took a degree in mining, and worked with geological expeditions in Prussia. His interests were universal. After his plans to go to Africa had been frustrated by Napoleon's unexpected Egyptian campaign, he fixed his sights on America. He had already been attracted by reports of the experiences of La Condamine and Bougainville, and finally decided on his trip when he met the French naturalist Aimé-Jacques-Alexandre Bonpland (1773–1858) in Marseilles. The two men set out together on foot for Barcelona. In 1799 Charles IV gave them free entry to the colonies even though Spain was still in the grip of fear. Some officious functionaries considered this *carte blanche* from the king so reckless that they set spies on the naturalists. Such acts were inevitable in the last days of the Enlightenment. But that did not keep Humboldt and Bonpland from visiting Venezuela, Colombia, Ecuador, Peru, Mexico, and Cuba during the next five years. They collected a herbarium of 60,000 plants, made all sorts of geographical observations, and took samples of minerals. But best of all, they made the acquaintance of a large number of Creole scholars, studious men thirsting for contact with such savants. The colonies had never felt a stimulus to compare with this visit.

An epidemic aboard ship forced the scholars to stop in the first port they came to in Venezuela. The dazzling sight of the tropical world lured them to take a trip up the Orinoco. They went on from there to explore first the entire captaincy of Venezuela, then to New Granada, Ecuador, and Peru. The observations they made on this first voyage are most interesting from the point of view of natural history, for they gave Humboldt the material for his first lengthy work: *Voyage to the Southern Regions of the New Continent*, five volumes published in French in Paris in 1807. On their second voyage they headed for Mexico, where they stayed for a year. Another work, still cited as one of the most comprehensive and best-documented studies on Mexico ever made, came out of this voyage. Entitled *Political Essay on the Kingdom of New Spain*, it also was published in French in Paris, in 1811. From Mexico they went on to Cuba, where they stayed seven weeks, a visit reported by Humboldt in another book. From Cuba they entered the United States. At the end of 1804, Humboldt and Bonpland arrived in Paris, where they were given a triumphal reception such as few scholars have ever received. For weeks the academies and high society revolved around them.

Humboldt dedicated the best years of his long life to publishing excellent accounts of his trips through America and to visiting distant lands. Bonpland went to Buenos Aires and inadvertently entered Paraguay, where, though he was not swallowed up by the jungle, he was held prisoner by the dictator, Dr. Francia, who refused to permit Paraguay to have any relations with neighboring countries. He never let Bonpland cross the border again. Not even the efforts of the most influential men, including Bolívar himself, could change the dictator's mind.

Humboldt's interest in America never flagged. He made the acquaintance of Bolívar in Paris, where they discussed the subject of independence as a solution for America in conversations that, except for some minor references, have been lost. Humboldt considered the step ineluctible, but could see no one capable of leading it. The German scholar's very extensive body of work revolved about American themes, as the following titles, selected from many, indicate: *On the New Conditions in the States of Central America and Guatemala; On the Province of Antioquia and the Recently Discovered Deposits of Platinum; Observations on Some Little-Known Phenomena: Goiter in the Tropics, on the Plains, and on the High Mesas of the Andes;* and *The Possibility of Connecting the Two Oceans Through America*, which last awakened the curiosity of Humboldt's great friend Goethe.

Humboldt's interest in American history was no less keen. He gives ample proof of his alert and penetrating mind and his abilities as a discoverer in his *Critical Examination of the History and Geography of the New Continent* (Paris, 1814–34). In it, he makes an exhaustive review of the problems of Columbus and Vespucci and provides a key to the solution of an old historical

debate by naming the basic document that has helped to vitiate
the "black legend" of Vespucci created by Fray Bartolomé de las
Casas—the booklet by the canons of Saint-Dié that indicates they
were the inventors of the name "America."

Humboldt's mark is plainly visible on the work of such scholars
as Caldas, who finally took up arms, and on such grammarians
as Bello, who later codified the American body of law and founded
universities. Thanks to him, many European scholars turned their
eyes toward America—hence Darwin's trip to the new continent.
Humboldt always harked back to America in his academic ad-
dresses and his scientific publications. Once, as he was reading a
memoir in the academy at St. Petersburg after the Czar had
awarded him the highest Russian medal, he said:

> I could never have dreamed, when I returned to my country
> after traveling across the snowy crest of the cordillera and
> the forests of the regions below the Equator, when I found
> myself once more in restless Europe after enjoying for a long
> time the calm that springs from nature and from the impres-
> sive sight of her wild fecundity . . . that I would be brought
> into your presence, my Lord, only after visiting the banks
> of the Irtysh, the confines of Sangaria China, and the shores
> of the Caspian Sea. By a happy interlocking of events in the
> course of a restless and sometimes laborious life, I have been
> permitted to compare the gold-bearing lands of the Urals
> with those in New Granada, and the porphyritic and tra-
> chytic outcroppings of Mexico and Altai and the plains of
> Venezuela with the steppes of southern Siberia, which offer
> a vast field for the conquests of agriculture.

¶ BOUSSINGAULT

The scientific missions forged strong links of communication
between the Americas and western Europe. The resurgence of
the regions colonized by the Spaniards moved to a more rapid
tempo owing to the interchange with Spain and the copious flow
of European thought. The visits of scholars and the sympathy
shown by the Encyclopedists for American emancipation left a
deep impression on the liberators and the civilian founders of the
new republics. After independence, the Americans themselves
would open the road to scholars and sponsor new scientific
missions.

When Bolívar was right in the thick of the military campaigns fought from Colombia to the South and while General Francisco de Paula Santander (1792–1840) was carrying the burden of the presidency of Colombia, a great project in education was beginning. Santander opened the campaign for elementary schools by decree, founded grade and high schools in Colombia, Venezuela, and Ecuador, girls' schools and normal schools and universities in the provinces, established the national museum, the library, and the academy. But he needed the contribution of Europe. Santander found help there through a Colombian named Francisco Antonio Zea (1766–1822). Zea was a former member of the Botanical Mission and a poet who had directed the Botanical Gardens in Madrid. He was in Paris when he was asked to assume the task of founding in Bogotá a school of mines similar to the one in Mexico. Zea appealed to the French naturalist Baron Georges Cuvier, chancellor of the University of Paris, who had founded the schools of Paleontology and Comparative Anatomy, and to other eminent scholars. They chose the members of a mission to New Granada organized by Jean-Baptiste Boussingault (1802–87), a very young man who in later life was to found the world's first experimental station in agronomy at Bachelbronn. Other scholars joined the expedition, among them François Désiré Roulin, a physician and zoologist (later librarian of the Institute of France); Justin Goudot, a botanist and preparer of specimens; the Peruvian chemist Mariano de Rivero, who had made studies in Paris, and the entomologist James Bourdon.

Humboldt was delighted by this interest in science shown by the new republic. He rated the members of the mission on the same level as such great men of the period as Gay-Lussac, Laplace, and Arago. He wrote to his old friend Simón Bolívar:

> I flatter myself that the amiable character that distinguishes Messrs. Rivero and Boussingault will make them worthy of receiving the generous hospitality I was so generously and affectionately shown during my stay in Caracas, Santa Fe, and Quito. Such things as the exploitation of the mineral deposits and the conversion plants of Pamplona, the environs of Santa Fe, the prairie of Tupia, Antioquia, the Chaco, and the regions to the south of Quito; investigations of platinum, in particular, and the leveling of the Isthmus of Panama at Cupica are matters connected with the country's industrial and commercial interests worthy of these scholars' concern.

That was the first letter from Humboldt that Bolívar had received in fifteen years. They had been together in Paris and Rome, and had climbed Vesuvius with Gay-Lussac. Humboldt reminded the famous American liberator of those times, and Bolívar returned the compliment by saying that the name of the great German scholar was engraved on the hearts of Americans. Behind these interchanges lies an important fact: the community of ideals which united the learned men of Europe and the creators of the American republics.

Boussingault stayed ten years in America and established chairs of chemistry and mineralogy. According to Carlos A. Chardon, his scientific production embraced 213 works, of which sixty-one are devoted to American subjects. His book on the rural economy, published in 1851, "marks the beginning of agricultural chemistry as an independent science." Goudot put together rich zoological collections. Roulin left a marvelous profile of Bolívar among his beautiful drawings.

In England, Joseph Lancaster (1778–1838) had invented a new system of pedagogy which specified that students in training would automatically become tutors of newcomers. In this way, his schools were able to provide a body of teachers to speed up the campaign against illiteracy. Lancaster had achieved marked results in England. Bolívar, who had visited the Lancasterian school in London with Francisco Miranda, could testify to that. Later Andrés Bello recommended the system to the Guatemalan Antonio José de Irisarri, then living in Chile. The Scotsman James Thompson introduced it to Argentina during the regime of Rivadavia. When San Martín entered Peru and took charge of the government in 1821, he arranged that all teachers were to attend the normal school which he had founded in Lima. They were expected to be accompanied everywhere by two pupils with whom they would acquire practice in and familiarity with the Lancastrian system. He decreed that any school that had not adopted the method within six months would be closed. Later, after Bolívar had entered Lima in 1824, he expanded San Martín's orders by extending the system over the entire republic.

About the year 1818, the Church of England, seconded by the Royal Society, unleashed a campaign against Lancaster. He hastened to accept Bolívar's invitation to Venezuela and worked there for a time. The Liberator turned over to Lancaster's schools half of the pension of a million *soles* granted him by

Peru. All over America, the enthusiasm for Lancaster was so great and so durable that even in the time of Benito Juárez (1806–72) it was considered in Mexico the best scheme for learning. Don Justo Sierra says:

> Juárez proved his deep love for his native country, his faith in the future of the republic, and his adherence to the principles constituting his political religion by the zeal he always showed for public education.

During his government, new primary schools were established, and an attempt was made to bring rudimentary instruction to every corner of the Oaxacan Mountains, where the race to which the great governor belonged was languishing in ignorance. Normal schools were founded to prepare teachers in the Lancastrian method, which, today abandoned, meant at that time a pedagogical advance, bringing free education to a large part of society.

¶ CODAZZI

As Lancaster was on his way to America, a young Italian artilleryman from Napoleon's armies named Agostino Codazzi (1793–1859) was also heading westward eager to offer Bolívar his services as a soldier. He sailed on a ship in the fleet commanded by the corsair Louis Aury which flew the flag of Buenos Aires and Chile, and landed at the mouth of the Orinoco. The fleet went on to Panama, but Codazzi started out to find Bolívar in Bogotá and deliver to him a message from Aury. He traveled through the jungles and mountains of the roughest and wildest sections of Colombia. By the time he met the Liberator, the war was almost over. That ended Codazzi's chances of fighting with the republican troops, and he went back to Italy, only to return to America, not as a soldier, but as a geographer. In 1830 he arrived in Venezuela, where he was appointed Chief of Staff so that he might map the country. The creators of the new republics believed firmly that the war for independence must culminate in schools. If the armies later turned out to be fighting armies, that was only because the states had a fatal inclination toward war. As for Codazzi, his principal interest as he offered himself to Venezuela's service was in geography. But for ten years he covered the country inch by inch as an artilleryman using topographical instruments. His explorations bore fruit in the first great atlas of an American country. He offered it for study to the Academy of

Science in Paris. Berthelot, Élie de Beaumont, Arago, and Boussingault all studied it. They praised the atlas, published in a
handsome edition, in the highest terms. It contained historical,
physical, and political maps accompanied by a summary of the
geography of Venezuela written by Rafael María Baralt and
Ramón Díaz. The Venezuelan draftsman Carmelo Fernández collaborated in its ornamentation. Codazzi was called to the academies
of science and geography. Humboldt often visited him for the
mutual enjoyment of long discussions on scientific projects for
the new republics. The German scientist recommended the establishment of the Observatory of Caracas. Meanwhile, Codazzi was
planning to go back to Venezuela, but he did not wish to go until
he had completed preparations for the founding of a colony of
Germans which finally started with three hundred and fifty immigrants who settled there as the Tobar Colony. This early experiment survives today. The Venezuelan coffee plantations began
with the Tobar Colony. Its first hundred trees yielded the best
Venezuelan coffee.

By that time, Codazzi had become a citizen of Venezuela. After
he had been working in the country for twenty years, the Monagas
dictatorship came into power and suspended the Venezuelan congress. Codazzi was persecuted until he decided to leave the country. He moved to Colombia. There he planned to do on a larger
scale what he had done in Venezuela. He suggested an atlas of
fifty maps to cover the geology, hydrography, history, agriculture,
climate, and economics of the country. His plan was accepted and
he worked on it during the twenty years when Mutis and his
botanical mission were completing their work. Codazzi was still
laboring on his Atlas of Colombia when he died, and it was published posthumously in Paris, a worthy successor to his Atlas of
Venezuela. A *History of Colombia*, by the soldier-historian
Joaquín Acosta (1795?–1852), written along the same lines, was
issued at the same time as the atlas. One of Codazzi's companions
on his tour of the republic was an excellent writer, Manuel Ancizar
(1812–82), who wrote a masterly travel book under the title,
Peregrinación de Alpha. Artists, draftsmen, and naturalists also
worked with Codazzi. They compiled the *Album of the Chorographic Commission*, the first work of its kind done under the
republic, a great human document of inestimable value which recalls the labors of the botanical mission.

Codazzi was a many-sided man. Through his scientific work
he became interested in archeology. Except for a brief note left

by the scholar Francisco José de Caldas, Codazzi was the first to mention the archeological region of San Agustín, later the subject of many famous studies. When Humboldt saw the extent of Codazzi's work in Venezuela, he wrote to him:

How glad I am that I have lived long enough to see such a vast undertaking completed. . . . What I tried to do on a quick trip by fixing a network of astronomical and hypsometric positions in Venezuela and Colombia has resulted in a confirmation and expansion through your noble investigations which surpass anything I could have hoped for.

Thus the scientific missions in the colony during the eighteenth century were linked to those of the republic in the nineteenth century.

XIII: *Independence*

¶ REVOLUTION ON THE LAND AND IN THE UNIVERSITY

The independence of the Spanish colonies in America did not begin with an overt military uprising and it was not decided by war. The process was much deeper and went far back into a long and complicated past. God knows when it began, and it still goes on, for the ideal has not been attained. The freedom cry, uttered in 1810, when the main city councils in Spanish America issued a formal declaration of separation from Spain, came after forty years of popular protest, always echoed by the new generations in the universities and their teachers, imbued with the spirit of the Enlightenment and driven by their romantic fervor. War was only a part of the liberating process. The actual fighting lasted some fifteen years, an episode of physical violence essential for driving the representatives of the Spanish government from American soil. When the war was over, the new states had to face the problem of how to make themselves truly independent. As the years passed, the new republics realized with increasing clarity how much of their independence was illusory and relative and just how effective had been that rending apart—so necessary, so heroic, so joyously proclaimed, but so fatally limited. The new Spanish America has never had that feeling of independence so evident in the United States. Circumstances in the South ruled out a result as radical as that in the North.

The revolutionary development of Spanish America began to shape up to reality with the cry of "Death to bad government!" Those words echoed from Paraguay to Mexico in the second half of the eighteenth century and re-echoed in 1810. In 1780, José Gabriel Condorcanqui (1742–81), a direct descendant of the Incas, who had assumed the name Tupac Amaru in 1771, led an abortive Indian rebellion in Peru after proclaiming himself emperor of his part of America. After a brief success, he was captured and put to death with great brutality, but on the plains of Venezuela people still speak of him as king, and people on the pampas remember that he died to bring about some of the reforms that actually came later. Independence was a heroic moral attitude when the break was made with Scholasticism, which came to be replaced by philosophies that rejected traditional authorities in the intellectual field. Independence was the stubborn determination to read the forbidden Encyclopedists. Independence was the huge trade in smuggled reading matter active all over America. Eventually the philosophical attitude stated in such documents as the *Representation of the Landowners*, edited by Mariano Moreno in Buenos Aires, or the *Memorandum of Grievances*, by Camilo Torres of Bogotá, was reinforced by obvious economic and political considerations. The charges against the Spanish government were made in Europe by Francisco Miranda and by the delegates from America to the Cortes of Cádiz. These were all maneuvers of the mind rather than of war; yet they succeeded in throwing very little light on the problem. In the United States, the period preceding the revolution was much shorter, and the war was decisive. The dramatic tone that marked the creation of the Hispano-Indian political culture and its lack of stability arose from circumstances that accompanied the formulation of its independence.

General San Martín was almost the only Liberator who had had previous military education. The "generals" of the War of Independence were students, farmers, even village priests who stepped forward to lead the rebellious masses of Creoles, Indians, and Negroes. They received their rank by popular acclaim and started campaigning without weapons or uniforms. All they had in the beginning was sticks, stones, and lances made in the village smithy. Once on their way, eager for battle, the "troops" acquired arms little by little and responded to some degree of impromptu discipline. The two first generals of the Mexican war of independence were rebel priests from the provinces: Miguel Hidalgo y Costilla (1753–1811) and José María Morelos y Pavón (1765–

1815). José Gervasio Artigas (1774–1850), the leader of the Uruguayan struggle for independence, was a gaucho. Whether priest or gaucho, the fighting man needed only to be a good horseman, a man on horseback. Some of the decisive battles of the war were fought by troops wearing no uniform but rags. The name "*farrapos*" (ragtag) was applied later, certainly in Brazil, to the rabble that made up the armies in the war of Rio Grande do Sul. Some showily uniformed British officers arrived at the *llanos* of Venezuela to fight beside the republicans, but before long they sold the uniforms they had brought from England to the Negroes, who were delighted with the bright-colored cloth and gold braid. Even the leaders often were without uniforms or wore them only at moments when it was tactically important to cut a good figure.

One time when Bolívar, already the hero of great battles and the Liberator, was spending some weeks resting in Bucaramanga, he went on a trip to the village of Girón. Two of his aides-de-camp, one British and one French, went with him. Halfway there, they stopped at a hut. The little woman who lived alone there could offer them only two chairs. She presented them to the two uniformed officers, and gave Bolívar, the Creole dressed in cotton trousers and a linen shirt, a hide and the floor to sit on. The Liberator sat down on the hide to spare her the embarrassment of discovering what she had done. As he said good-bye to her, he chatted with her about her personal problems. The woman told him how poor she was and how hard it was for her to take care of her children. As Bolívar pressed her hand in farewell, he put a gold Spanish doubloon in her palm. She stared at him in astonishment, then guessed that "that one" was Bolívar.

José Manuel Restrepo (1781–1863), the historian, was a minister in Bolívar's government. He wrote the history of the period, entitled *History of the Revolution in the Republic of Colombia*. The operative word was not war, but revolution—that is, the struggle to bring about a change in institutions by creating a republic. The war was nothing more than an accident of that undertaking. Military campaigns were a section of the road to be covered. The fight was for a common cause carried on in common by the people of all the countries. San Martín took his Argentine troops to battlefields in Chile and pacified Peru with them. Bolívar united Venezuelans, Colombians, and Ecuadorians in his march to Peru and Upper Peru. When Mexico's independence was in danger, Santander, the Colombian who was Bolívar's companion in the Colombian campaign, offered his sword to the

GUATEMALA. *Antigua: Palace of the Captains General*

GUATEMALA.
Guatemala City:
Mayan Bas-relief

MEXICO. *Teotihuacán: Pyramid of the Sun and Roadway of the Dead*

MEXICO. *Uxmal: Quadrangle of the Nuns*

MEXICO. *Tepotzotlán: Façade of the Convent*

PERU. *Arequipa: Façade of the Church of Yanahuara*

PERU. *Machu Picchu: The "Torreón"*

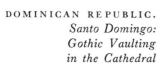

DOMINICAN REPUBLIC.
Santo Domingo:
Porch of the Cathedral

DOMINICAN REPUBLIC.
Santo Domingo:
Gothic Vaulting
in the Cathedral

ECUADOR. *Quito: Façade of the Church of the Compañia (Jesuit)*

BRAZIL. *Congonhas do Campo: Prophets by Aleijadinho*

BRAZIL. Opposite top. *A Prophet by Aleijadinho*

BRAZIL. Opposite bottom. *Rio de Janeiro: Copacabana*

VENEZUELA. *The Church of Santa Ana de Paraguaná (1681)*

VENEZUELA. Opposite top. *The Church of Clarines (restored, 1963)*

VENEZUELA. Opposite bottom. *Carora: The Calvary Chapel (1787)*

PUERTO RICO. *San Juan: The Fortress of El Morro*

BOLIVIA. *Church in the Highlands*

COLOMBIA. *Mompox: Church of Santa Bárbara*

COLOMBIA. *Bogotá: Detail of a Tabernacle in a Colonial Church*

COLOMBIA. *Popayán: Pulpit Stairs, Church of San Francisco*

PANAMA. *Old Panamá: Ruins of the Cathedral Tower*

Mexican republicans. This spirit lasted as late as the Cuban war for independence (1895-8), almost a hundred years later, when Americans from the entire Caribbean zone appeared on the island's battlefields. The first governors of Peru were an Argentine, San Martín (the Protector), and a Venezuelan, Bolívar (the President). Antonio José de Sucre (1795-1830) and Juan José Flores (1800-64), both Venezuelans, became presidents of Bolivia and Ecuador, respectively.

In spite of this remarkable cooperation, the leaders of the armies, victorious generals on foreign soil, never thought of taking possession of an inch of land to enlarge the boundaries of their own countries. They never followed Napoleon's example; they did not adopt European tradition. Their ambition was not to change the frontiers or to be crowned emperor, but to serve as liberators. This phase of political culture, original in America, has never been sufficiently stressed. The word "liberty" rang with magic in America. No hymn to any republic is without its salute to liberty. Liberty meaning the independence of the country; liberty meaning opposition to slavery; liberty meaning a natural extension of the dignity of man; liberty meaning the road to the recovery of democratic social justice.

¶ NEW STUDY PLANS

The new courses of study in the universities favored independence and opened the way to revolution. The expulsion of the Jesuits was of no small consequence to university reform. After the Company had vacated the secondary schools under their control, the classrooms had to be put to new and better use. Both in Spain and America the protests against Scholasticism, the criticism of the old philosophy, and the clamor for mathematics and the natural sciences had been listened to. But they had to be translated into concrete reforms. The scientific missions had pointed the way, one which would tend to diminish the importance of the ancient tradition of the universities, which is the pride of Spanish America even today.

Although the universities in the Spanish colonies were founded more than a century before the oldest in the English colonies, they clung to the idea of educating priests and preserving the Catholic doctrine, even though they were not and would never be centers of higher theological learning. Their by-laws were full of regulations on fasting and abstinence, on the celebration of religious feast days, on the kind of soutanes to be worn, on the color of the hose, and on the mutual vigilance that students were to maintain over one another lest one of them succumb to temptation, which amounted to a system of mutual espionage.

A model of these minutely detailed regulations is contained in the by-laws of the University of Córdoba, Argentina. Ceremonies were the most important events in the lives of many students, who conversed in a mixture of Latin and the vernacular. Even in Mexico, which had many outstanding teachers in the sixteenth century, the decadence was visible. Almost all that was left of the academic life was the spectacle of the ceremonies. For two centuries the by-laws of the sixteenth century ruled the universities. A typical excerpt from them follows:

> The promenades are to be held on the afternoon of the examination. The escort from the graduate's house. The Beadles on horseback, their gowns of damask, tawny-colored with red facings, caps to match, silver maces; the Proctors of the University, the Master of Ceremonies, the Secretary, the four Modern Doctors, the Rector, the Dean, on horseback with sumpter-cloths, bareheaded, and if a priest, with biretta; it will proceed to the Chancellor's house, whence he will accompany the Procession, presiding at the right side of the Rector. On this day they go without insignia; at the front, walking, the University's flageolets, playing their instruments as far as the Cathedral church, all of this to be done in time to arrive near the time of the night prayer. . . . If the examinee is approved, he is so notified; on the following day the Dean, the Rector, and the four Modern Doctors go to his house at ten o'clock in the morning; the Secretary, the Master of Ceremonies, and the Beadles escort him in the afternoon to the Holy Church Cathedral.

During the Enlightenment two centuries later, the by-laws were modified "with the absolute and perpetual prohibition that at no time may the Pomp and the Procession on horseback be practiced, under any pretext whatsoever, for the degrees of Master and Doctor." The day had come to think of other things. The reform was passed in the year 1767, the very year when the Jesuits were expelled—a reform that called for fewer flageolets and more mathematics and natural science.

In Bogotá, the distinguished author of a *History of the New Kingdom of Granada*, Francisco Antonio Moreno y Escandón (1736–92), held the office of justice of the supreme court. As such it fell to him to carry out the order for the expulsion of the Jesuits. As soon as the governor had taken possession of the Society's old college, the justice issued a new course of study. Algebra pitched camp in the halls where the Jesuits had discussed theology. A new generation was enrolled for training in the mathematical sciences. The viceroy, who was also the archbishop, Antonio Caballero y Góngora (1723–90), a child of the Enlightenment, witnessed and encouraged these changes. In his report on his office, he wrote:

> The whole object of the plan for study is aimed at substituting the useful, exact sciences for those merely speculative, on which so much time has regrettably been wasted up to now; for certainly a kingdom full of most beautiful products to be put to use, with mountains to level, roads to open, swamps and mines to drain, water to control, and metals to smelt needs more subjects who know how to acquaint themselves with and to observe nature, to manage the calculus, the compass, and the rule, than it needs persons who understand and believe in such entities as reason, prime matter, and substantial form.

In Lima, Hipólito Unanue (1755–1833), a royal physician, proposed to rid Peru of its medicine men. To that end, he put into effect his plan to found the School of Medicine of San Fernando. An official of the viceroy wrote:

> I do not care to repeat the lively and penetrating expressions which Unanue uses to describe the calamitous state of Peru and the great ills it is suffering for the lack of good doctors. But who does not know that with the exception of a qualified physician here and there in one of the capitals, all the rest of South America is fair game for ignoramuses, adventurers, charlatans, and rascals who make themselves out to be doctors and surgeons so that they can spend their lives without working and pursue the phenomena of their vices? It is painful to listen to the reports made concerning their blunders by people of judgment who have lived in the provinces. All the way from Panama to Lima the royal expedition for vaccination almost never found even a mediocre surgeon who

stocked the salubrious serum. Theology and jurisprudence
have a multitude of colleges, but there is not a single one for
medicine in the whole viceroyalty. The chairs established in
the University of San Marcos for this purpose were vacant
for several reasons.

Unanue's School was founded for the study of mathematics,
astronomy, clinical medicine, botany, chemistry, and mineralogy.
It was located not far from the big hospitals then being built or
from the site upon which the Botanical Garden had been established. "The actual work of the college began with income derived
from private donations, from the box office receipts of four bull
fights, and from six thousand pesos donated by the Archbishop."

Unanue wrote a remarkable essay, *The Climate of Lima*, in
which he anticipated the thinkers who created the science of
human geography. He was also one of the founders of the *Mercurio
de Lima*, published from 1791 on, and an assiduous contributor
to it. The *Mercurio*, one of the great gazettes of the America of
that day, disseminated the theories of Newton, Kepler, Leibnitz,
and Locke.

The introduction of vaccine was one of the basic moves by the
Enlightenment in America, where smallpox was killing off the
native population. The efficacy of vaccination was announced in
England in 1798, and the Societies of Friends of the Country in
Spain welcomed the life-saving campaign with fervor, particularly
for the colonies. In 1803 the corvette *María de Pita* sailed from
La Coruña with ten doctors and twenty-two children exposed to
smallpox, along with their mothers and nurses, who were to keep
the virus alive by successive inoculations during the crossing.
Those children were declared special children of the country;
they were adopted by the government, which would take charge
of their education. Chile already had the serum, sent from Brazil
by way of Buenos Aires. In Bogotá, Mutis of the Botanical Mission was in charge of distributing it. In Caracas, Andrés Bello
composed an ode to the introduction of vaccination. The present-
day reader is astonished to read a poem like that, written with
all the lyrical passion of Romanticism to celebrate an event so
much a part of the field of medicine. But there is no cause for
surprise. The republics were born of such enthusiasms. Vaccination was the first important thing that had been done for the
Indians since the laws of Charles V. With enthusiasm such as he
had never before put into a salute to a prince, Bello saluted the

king of Spain in song because he had sent the smallpox mission. The heroic quality of the venture also evoked in Spain such lyrical outpourings as the ode written by the poet-statesman Manuel José Quintana, which credits the physician Francis Xavier Balmis with these words:

> *Deep in infected America*
> *I shall plant the tree of life.*

This was another thread in the interweaving of a new pattern. University reform was synchronous with the approach to the people, the Indians. One of the professors of San Marcos, José Baquíjano y Carrillo (1757–1817), was entrusted with the address of welcome to the new viceroy at the very moment when Tupac Amaru was leading his Indians in a revolt against the Spanish authorities. The customary way to salute a new ruler was to compose a dithyramb for him which passed over his merits and shortcomings. Baquíjano simply said:

> Glory and immortality are not wedded to or dependent upon eulogies and public inscriptions, by which dependence and fear are consecrated and paid tribute: the happiness and the unburdening of the vassal are the specifics needed, the soothing balm that alleviates, that insures and eases the harsh mechanism of the Empire.

From that opening paragraph, Baquíjano moved on to such unheard of criticisms that he became suspect from then on and his academic horizons shrank. But he had given a turn to the wheel of revolution. Behind his words lay an explanation of the Indian revolt. The day was not far off when the Liberator San Martín would propose a republication of the *Comentarios Reales* by Garcilaso de la Vega, which had been banned as reading matter for the colonies by Spain, because it acted as a stimulus to emancipation. As Miranda wrote his utopian constitution for American self-rule, he was dreaming of a state that would be headed by two Inca consuls. (His purpose in writing was to win the English to his cause.)

Spain considered Lima her stoutest bulwark. It was the capital of the oldest viceroyalty in South America and of the nobility, the cradle of the greatest privilege. Last to fall to the revolutionaries, Peru became independent in 1821, as the armies brought from Argentina and led by San Martín and the troops from Venezuela led by Bolívar converged on Lima for the final effort to achieve complete liberty for South America. Neither of the liberators entered Lima with the intention of seizing the vacated viceroy's palace; instead they visited the university. San Marcos is the only university in America whose classrooms were honored by the two men. Both went there to affirm the authentic ideal of the revolution. San Martín founded the national library and the Patriotic Society of Lima. After the first stage of the war in Peru, he established the normal school. At the ceremonies inaugurating the library, he said: "As the Spanish Government is convinced that ignorance is despotism's doughtiest column, it has placed the strongest fetters on American enlightenment and kept thought in chains to prevent [Americans] from becoming aware of their dignity."

Bolívar, in turn, founded the university at Trujillo after he had gained control of all of Peru. He decided that every province should have its normal school, decreed the establishment of elementary schools in the convents—the monks and nuns to be paid by the state—established a college for the study of jurisprudence, philosophy and mathematics in Ica, and one for science in Cuzco, where he also founded the first woman's college in Peru.

¶ THE PRINTING PRESS AND THE GAZETTE

Less than a hundred years after Gutenberg invented his press and fourteen years after Cortés completed the conquest of Mexico, America had a printing shop, opened by Johann Gromberg in Mexico City, in 1535. Several books in the American languages, Latin, and Spanish were printed there. The first press runs were mainly of prayers, grammars, and books on disputed theological matters. Later the gazettes were founded and they opened another of the roads leading to independence.

In 1580 the governor of Nicaragua authorized Antonio Ricardo to take a printing press with him to Lima. "I understand that this press will render service to God and to the conversion of the natives of that land." The press was not received with gratitude by the authorities. Although Ricardo had worked in the Jesuits' printing shop in Mexico City, the Peruvian Jesuits would not help him. Indeed, they tried to stop him by invoking the royal decree that prohibited the use of a printing press in the country. But Ricardo was stubborn, and he won over the members of the town corporation, who appealed to the King, saying:

To these, your kingdoms of Peru, came a printing press for books, and wishing to make use of it, there was no place for it, for Your Majesty has forbidden the printing of books in these kingdoms. Your Majesty issued the said prohibition at a time when there was no need for the said press in this kingdom, and now there is, for there is a university in this city.

Authorization was granted. But before that, Father Ludovico had already edited and published a vocabulary in Aymará in the town of Juli. "In that isolated spot," Luis Antonio Aguiguren reported, "near Lake Titicaca, a clandestine press was in operation, under the inspiration of Francisco de Canto from Lima."

In the seventeenth century, printing shops were opened in Puebla, Bogotá, Guatemala, and the missions of Paraguay; in the eighteenth century, in Santo Domingo, Havana, Oaxaca, Ambato, Quito, Córdoba, Buenos Aires, Cartagena, Santiago (Chile), Guadalajara, and Veracruz; in Montevideo and Caracas by 1807, San Juan by 1808, and Guayaquil by 1810.

The style and format of the first gazettes were the same as those of Spain, such as the famous *El Espíritu de los Mejores Diarios*, remote ancestor of the *Reader's Digest*, containing abridgments from articles on science, history, geography, politics, and so on. This journal became a most effective voice for American independence as literary, philosophic, and political essays kept appearing in addition to the news notes. The Societies of Friends of the Country planted their propaganda in Spain and America alike in this way. The *Gazette of Mexico* was founded in 1667 and the *Mercury of Mexico* in 1740. The very Mexican tone of their pages and the amount of space they gave to reviving the memory of Aztec heroes and myths were striking features of the first Mexican news organs. In 1784 the Viceroy served notice that he was sensitive to the danger of such articles:

I hold the *Gazette* to be very useful, always provided that it confines itself to general news notes; arrivals, departures, ships' cargoes, and the products of nature; the election of prelates, or ordinary mayors; installation of canons and other appreciable items that occur in such a wide open country. All this is soon forgotten, and among so much that is useless and trifling, always to be found in this class of writing, it would be a means of preserving those public events which

are forgotten after a certain time, though they might well
be perpetuated. . . . Furthermore, it is important to offer
innocent matter that will satisfy the curiosity of the public.

José Antonio Alzate Ramírez (1729–90) established several
gazettes in Mexico and left in their pages an accumulation of
meteorological observations, news of the mercury mines, and
so on. His mind had been shaped by the authors of the Enlightenment; consequently, his papers were suspended several times.
Alzate was a physicist and astronomer, while José Ignacio
Bartolache (1739–90), who founded the *Mercurio Volante* (*Flying Mercury*), was a physician. Bartolache wrote: "As for supernatural science or sacred theology, suffice it to say that it is for
the saints and that our intention is to revere it but not to con-
fuse it with the rest of the human sciences." These human sciences
as recorded in the gazettes provided a key to the door of revolution.

No colony had as many printing presses as Mexico, yet the
revolution there immediately engendered fifteen newspapers. Between 1810 and 1821 there were forty in the territory. The revolu-
tionist-priest Miguel Hidalgo y Costilla published *El Despertador
Americano* (*The American Clarion*) in Guadalajara in 1810
and 1811. Its editor was the priest Severo Maldonado (*c.* 1770–
1832), a kind of socialist of the period. Another priest, José
María Cos (1774–1819), published the *Ilustrador Nacional* (*National Enlightener*) in an improvised printing shop where he
himself carved the fonts out of wood. When Morelos went on a
tour with the congress that was to write the first national constitution, he launched the *Avispa de Chilpancingo* (*The Chilpancingo
Wasp*). The "clarion," the "enlightener," the "wasp" all indicate the course being followed by the press. The first newspaper
in Central America was the *Guatemala Gazette*, which began publication in 1729.

The Bogotá *Papel Periódico* (literally *The Daily Paper*) was
started by Manuel del Socorro Rodríguez (1758–1818), a Cuban
born in Bayamo, the son of a carpenter. Early in the nineteenth
century, the viceroy of New Granada invited him to direct the
public library in Bogotá. This simple intellectual laborer, who
wanted above all else to be useful to the Society of Friends of the
Country, established a conversation group called the "Moderate
Society" which met in the library reading room. This informal
organization was similar to the societies spreading through Spain

and almost all of the colonies' capital cities. The Patriotic and Literary Society of Buenos Aires became famous. Rodríguez himself was not aware that he was contributing to the revolution through the library, the gazette, the conversation group, and the Society of Friends of the Country. A weekly called *El Semanario del Nuevo Reino de Granada* emerged at about the same time as the *Papel Periódico*, to become one of the gazettes of real importance to culture. Published in 1808 and 1809, it was encouraged by Francisco José de Caldas of the Botanical Mission. The best studies on commerce, botany, medicine, and astronomy written by a new generation of scientists appeared in the *Semanario*. One of these was "El Influjo del Clima" ("The Influence of Climate") by Caldas, his famous essay that marks a notable advance over Unanue's on the geography of Lima. Humboldt's essay "The Geography of Plants" first appeared in the *Semanario*. Publications of this kind were very similar to much more advanced European literary and scientific reviews. The *Semanario* suspended publication in 1809, but Caldas continued to publish his *Memorias Científicas*. And properly so, for the passage from the sciences to revolution was normal. More than normal, inevitable. Caldas moved from astronomy into the army. But for five months of 1810 he still managed to edit his *Diario Político*, which gave information on the progress of the revolution all over America. He wrote in the Observatory Hall, where he was director, and where he had done the last few years of his scientific work. When Caldas heard the call to military service, he went into the army as an engineer. He explored the iron, coal, and mercury mines of the country, hoping they would supply raw materials for the manufacturing of cannon and guns for the armies of the revolution. First in Medellín and later in Bogotá he set up two academies to train army engineers. Later they became the schools of mines of the universities in those two cities. At the appropriate time he asked the United States for a printing press. But he was shot.

At that time Colombia had a peripatetic gazette, the *American Argus*. Between 1810 and 1812 it was published in Cartagena, from 1813 to 1815 in Tunja, and from 1815 to 1816 in Bogotá. The year 1816 was when the lights went out—the year of the executions, the year the gazettes were suspended. That was the year when Morillo, the "Pacifier," believed that he had succeeded in stopping the revolution.

The ephemeral career of the *Primicias de la Cultura de Quito* (*The First Fruits of the Culture of Quito*), a newspaper that published only seven numbers (January–March 1792), is a curious venture by a famous and original figure of the revolution: Francisco Javier de Santa Cruz y Espejo. Despite the impressive length of his names and patronymics, Espejo was the son of a Peruvian Indian and a mulatto woman from Quito. On both sides he typified the *mestizo* who was struggling to emerge. Augusto Arias said in speaking of Espejo's grandfather: "The father of Luis Espejo was no barefoot Indian in a chamois jacket, sombrero, and short trousers, but a native who wore shoes and covered himself usually with the typical cape worn by the less enslaved natives." Espejo studied medicine when it was somewhat rudimentary, but his imaginative genius and the acuity of his judgment led him to make the most sarcastic criticisms of the science of his day. He was a forerunner of the learned men of the nineteenth and twentieth centuries in the war against microbes, in hygienic methods, and in combating the prejudices of healers and false doctors: he was unrepentantly polemical. Under the pseudonym Marco Porcio Catón (Marcus Portius Cato), he wrote such essays as *La Ciencia Blancardiana* (*Blancardian Science*, Moisés Blancardo being a fictitious character invented by Espejo), and *El Nuevo Luciano* (*The New Lucian*): richly inventive satires against the flowery grandiloquent literature of the preachers and teachers of his time. Espejo inveighed against the lack of hygiene in the convents, against the custom of burying the dead in the churches, thus turning them into foci of infection, and against the filth of the cities. His paper—the first to use the word "culture" in its title—served as the organ of the Society of Friends of the Country and worked actively to spread the use of vaccination against smallpox. *The New Lucian* was a direct attack on the preachings of Father Sancho de Escobar, consequently guaranteed to win Espejo a host of enemies. He was denounced as the author of lampoons that were actually calls to revolution. The presiding officer of the *audiencia* sent him to Bogotá as a prisoner, writing to the viceroy: "Liberal ideas are boiling, not only in Espejo's head, but in the many literati and persons of great influence, which is why I am sending him to Bogotá, without stating any charges against him, lest I might implicate the most outstanding and distinguished subjects."

In Bogotá, Espejo met Antonio Nariño, the translator of *The Rights of Man* and then went back to Quito even more highly charged with the new ideas that so alarmed the *audiencia*. The publishers of the Peruvian *Mercurio* invited him to Lima. Espejo considered a visit to that capital and to Buenos Aires, Mexico City, and Caracas. He moved about like a restless spirit, but did not leave his country. Enrique Garcés, who has studied the most abstruse episodes in the secret life of this imagined conspirator, reached the following conclusions:

> Espejo thought of the possibility of sending some scholarship students to France to learn just what the French Revolution and the Rights of Man were like. . . . What Espejo would have wished was to bring the French Revolution over intact, guillotine and all, and put it to work in the main square of Quito. When the French beheaded their king, Espejo, who was taken to be a sorcerer fully informed of everything in Quito, said that the French people had done well and that they had a right to rebel, a comment that caused him to be accused of heresy and impiety.

The imprisonment that he subsequently endured prepared him for death. On the day of the Holy Innocents, December 28, 1795, he died without ever seeing the uprisings he had longed for so ardently.

A printing press in Buenos Aires started work in 1780, brought from Córdoba after it had been used in the Paraguay missions. The first gazette was founded by a Spaniard, Francisco Antonio Cabello y Mesa, who had started the *Diario Curioso* in Lima in 1790. On reaching Buenos Aires (1801), he established the oddly named *El Telégrafo Mercantil, Rural, Político, Económico, e Historiográfico del Río de la Plata* (*The Mercantile, Rural, Political, Economic, and Historiographic Telegraph of the Plata River*). As the electric telegraph had not been invented at that date and messages were sent over distances mainly by flag signals, the name *Telégrafo* really signifies semaphore. The paper was suspended a year after it was founded, and Cabello was charged with disloyalty to his country and overfriendliness toward the English. He was put into prison on his return to Spain and later shot in Seville. The sequel in Buenos Aires is complicated. The story of the first steps to independence there is unlike anything that happened in any other country in America.

The Spaniards themselves were among the first to think of independence for the Río de la Plata colony. One of the most distinguished of them was Martín de Alzaga (died 1812), who was born in the Basque country. Two parties formed: one of Spaniards, the other of Creoles. They agreed in despising the Spanish government. Already in 1804 the royal favorite Godoy had been burned in effigy, and in 1806 Alzaga was making plans for independence and a republic. People would run through the streets shouting, "Death to the viceroy and the justices! Out with the *audiencia!* Let's plant the Republican flag!" But Alzaga was dreaming of a republic in the hands of the Spaniards, only the Spaniards. Mariano Moreno (1779–1811), a much more enlightened man and a Creole, wanted Spaniards and Creoles to have an equal share in it. Later he requested that the men in government be Americans only. The power of the city council, held by Alzaga in 1806, passed to Moreno in 1810. Alzaga was finally shot in 1812.

Mariano Moreno was the great apostle of the Argentine Revolution of May 1810. In June 1810, a month after the freedom cry rang out from the town hall, he founded the *Gaceta de Buenos Aires*. It was published by the Niños Expósitos (Foundlings) Press, which became the republic's official printing shop after much travel and many changes of hands. In a letter to Madrid, a Spanish official expressed the opinion earned by Moreno's *Gazette*:

I am enclosing for Your Excellency the *Gazette of Buenos Aires* for the 13th and 15th of November, for they are more convincing than any speeches or demonstrations, not only of the fact that the revolutionaries are aspiring to independence, for no balanced mind has doubted that since its first number or circular was published inviting the people to send their deputations to the Congress, but also that their doctrine is the basest and most infernal that could be conceived and that if it is not attacked promptly and with force, all the Americas will be lost; there is scarcely a line in the said gazette which does not contain a Jacobin principle, a blasphemy; to them it is not merely a question of not recognizing the Supreme Council of the Regency or any other legitimate authority which governs us, but of manifesting that the monarchs of Spain have no right whatsoever in the Americas, and consequently even our beloved monarch, the most sacred vows, the most solemn oath sworn by the people in token of their vassalage, everything is false on the lips of these vile revolutionaries who hold nothing sacred but what flatters their ambition to command, and I could go on at great length listing the many defamatory libels against the indisputable rights of our unfortunate monarch.

The Jesuits introduced the printing press into Chile in 1748, but not much came off it other than prayers and thin books in Latin. When the Jesuits were expelled, the press went to the university. It was put to use as an instrument of revolution only in 1811. The press that truly served the cause was taken to Valparaiso by a Swedish trader. The *Aurora de Chile* was printed on it. The editor of the newspaper was a monk of the order of Buena Muerte named Camilo Henríquez (1769–1825), an Encyclopedist educated at the University of Lima, a utopian who believed that "men would be happy if the philosophers ruled, or if the emperors were philosophers." His colleague and editorial partner was Manuel de Salas (1754–1841), who had studied at San Marcos in Lima and who was in Spain during the apogee of the Enlightenment. Salas returned to America as an ardent propagandist for the ideas held by Jovellanos. He was an enemy of violence, an enthusiast for progress. After the establishment of the republic, he directed the National Library, founded the Agricultural Society, and then spent his old age cultivating silkworms. The two idealists were joined by a third, a restless, bold man from Guatemala named Antonio José de Irisarri (1786–1868), who performed brilliantly, with varying degrees of luck, in many spots all over America. When the *Aurora* expired a year after its founding, Irisarri replaced it with the *Monitor Araucano*, and later founded the *Semanario Repúblicano;* both papers fought openly for independence. As a young man of twenty-eight Irisarri, in the Chilean revolution heart and soul, presided over the government of his adopted country for a week. He was its seven-day dictator, as he put it.

Later he traveled to Europe where he presented a memorandum on Chile to the British Foreign Minister, Lord Castlereagh. Then he returned to Chile, where he himself became Minister of Foreign Relations. He founded another gazette, *El Duende de Santiago*, went to Buenos Aires on a diplomatic mission, then on to Europe, and finally to his own country, where he founded *El Guatemalteco* in 1827. Still later, he became a friend of the dictator of Chile, Diego Portales (died 1837), and of Marshal Andrés Santa Cruz (1792?–1865), who headed the Confederation of Peru and Bolivia (1863–9). He was the right-hand man of General Juan José Flores (1800–64), president of Ecuador; counsellor of the great General Tomás Cipriano de Mosquera (1798–1878), president of Colombia, and of General José Antonio Páez (1790–1873), president of Venezuela. In Bogotá, he pub-

lished the novel *El Cristiano Errante*, which includes a large
amount of history. His *Historia del Perínclito Epaminondas de
Cauca*, a picaresque novel making fun of American anarchism,
was printed in New York. In 1861, his book *Cuestiones Filológicas* appeared. Irisarri was a mobile, daring indefatigable,
and difficult man. At the end of his life he said with regard to
Chile: "I gave her my fortune; I gave her my first printing press;
I influenced her revolution; I wrote in defense of her cause; I
established her credit abroad; I saved her honor and her army;
and now, you see, my children, how I have been repaid. A
cursed country!" He had similar things to say about other countries.

All the newspapermen of Chile who were Irisarri's contemporaries and colleagues on the *Aurora* were eccentric. The editor-in-
chief, Camilo Henríquez, was full of philosophical enthusiasms; he
was a satirical poet and dramatist, author of the plays *Camila, o
la Patriota Sudamericana, La Procesión de los tontos* (*The Parade
of the Dunces*), and *La inocencia en el asilo de las virtudes* (*Innocence in the Asylum of the Virtues*), none of which was ever
staged.

¶ THE JESUITS IN EXILE

The first Americans who took with them to Europe an irrevocable determination to be independent began to arrive on the
continent at the end of the eighteenth century. As children of
the Enlightenment, they found the atmosphere of the century of
revolution congenial to them. They kept appearing in Paris, London, and Bologna as eager students or frank adventurers seeking
contact with the French liberals, the English who were interested
in the overthrow of the Spanish Empire, the disgruntled Jesuits
who had turned into eloquent defenders of America under the
yoke of the Spaniards, the Masons who helped them to become
acquainted with politicians, statesmen, and philosophers. Of all
these groups, the Jesuits were the vanguard.

An old Mexican Jesuit, a native of Veracruz, Father Francisco
Javier Clavijero (1731–87), settled in Bologna and opened the
House of Wisdom, a kind of academy that might well have been
named the House of America. An elegant and outspoken writer,
with the boldness that marked the Jesuits who had fallen into
disfavor under Charles III, he published *Physica Particularis*,
attacking the Scholastic philosophy; the *Historia Eclesiástica de*

México, a history of the Tlaxcaltec Colonies, and his famous *Historia Antigua de México*, in its way a declaration of independence, which vigorously highlighted the historic character of America, of the American aborigine as opposed to the Spanish American colonial.

Alfonso Reyes sums up his judgment of Clavijero as follows:

> He stands out among historians, for he was the first to organize a methodical exposition of the indigenous history and of the Spanish landing. A theologian, a scholar, a humanist, and master of many languages, as were almost all the men of this brief Mexican Renaissance in the eighteenth century, his book *par excellence* is the *Historia Antigua de México*, which he rounded out with his *Disertaciones*, in which he refutes the errors concerning Mexico spread by de Pauw, Buffon, Raynal, and Robertson. [He was] a consummate ethnographer who already understood history as the description of the character of a people; his work is fundamental and indispensable; it still retains its value in spite of [the need for] partial rectifications. His exactitude and precision do not debar elegance. His method is correct, his style clear.

What Clavijero did for Mexico, Abbot Molina did for Chile. José Ignacio Molina y González (1740–1829) was born in Huaraculén, a product of six generations of Creoles. He began his education with the Jesuits in Talca, and moved on, still with the Company, to Concepción and Santiago. After the expulsion, he settled in Bologna, like many others. He spoke Greek and Latin, learned French, and wrote in correct Italian. His famous *Saggio della Storia Natural de Cile* (*Essay on the Natural History of Chile*), written in Italian, was translated into German, Spanish, French, and English. "All nations," the Abbot said, "be they American, European, or Asiatic, have been much alike in their savage state, a state that none has had the privilege of escaping." The Abbot was a genius at uncovering natural history. Francisco A. Encina writes of him:

> . . . in confronting prehistory, with neither excavations nor documents to testify to it in irrevocable form, he saw with the clarity of noonday that a people with a culture superior to what the Spaniards found had settled there, and that that people had developed the language. He divined what neither

Barros Arana nor any of the other nineteenth-century historians managed to grasp, even though they had before their
eyes Molina's inspired observations and the arguments proving them with decisive force. Not until the twentieth century
were his remarkable intuitions confirmed by anthropological
observations, after he had been an object of mockery to those
who lacked the brain power to realize the strength of his
groundwork.

Humboldt visited both the Abbot and Clavijero in Bologna. The
Abbot's natural love for birds is revealed by an anecdote that he
himself told. It concerned a linnet that was always at his side as
he worked in Chile. It would fly around him and caress him, and
when he gave it a signal it would sing.

Among the Ecuadorians in the Company of Jesus who were
forced into exile was Father Juan de Velasco (1727–1819), born
in Riobamba. He wrote a *History of Quito*. Velasco's character
was not as resolute as Clavijero's, but other Ecuadorians with him
carried their campaign from Bologna to London. Fathers Manuel
de Salas and José del Pozo came under the influence of Miranda
there and signed the agreement of the Spanish American conspirators. Others who stayed in Italy intervened on behalf of the
Indian Tomás Catari, who led an abortive movement to secure
the power of the natives in Quito under his adopted name of
Francis I, the Powerful.

José Domingo Coleti (1727–98), a Venetian who went to the
missions of Ecuador as a Jesuit priest, also was expelled. Later
he published a number of studies in Italy. Among those that dealt
with America was his *Dizionario Storico-Geografico dell 'America
Meridionale* (1771), which preceded the notable *Diccionario
Histórica Geográfico de las Indias Occidentales o América* by
Antonio de Alcedo y Herrera (1735–1812), written between 1786
and 1789. Gabriel Giraldo Jaramillo considered Coleti "one of
the precursors of geographical science in America." The Paraguayan Jesuit Domingo Muriel wrote the history of Paraguay
from 1747 to 1767 in Latin. Father Antonio Julián recorded
his admiration for Santa Marta in *La Perla de América* (*The
Pearl of America*), and said, "In both Americas there is no more
estimable and beautiful province than the province of Santa
Marta." Enthusiasm for the New World still burned among the
exiles in Italy.

One of the distinguished Jesuits in exile was the Peruvian Juan

Bautista Vizcardo y Guzmán (died 1798), who shed his clerical garb in London. Although he left no historical work as famous as those of his Mexican, Chilean, and Ecuadorian comrades, he played a most important role in the history of the political uprising with his *Letter to the American Spaniards*. This letter, printed in Philadelphia, was one of the papers most widely read during the struggle immediately preceding the war for independence. In it Vizcardo wrote:

> The Motherland separates us from the world and shuts us off from all communication with the rest of the human race, and does something else no less vexatious and harmful, in addition to this usurpation of our personal liberty, which is the usurpation of our property. From the time when men first joined together in a society for the purpose of mutual benefit, we are the only ones in the world whom the government forces to pay so dearly for the satisfaction of our needs and to sell so cheaply the products of our labor. And in order to suppress all the effects of this violence, it has locked us into a city under siege, as it were. We are forced to recapture possession of the natural rights we owe to our Creator, precious rights that we do not have the power to transfer, and of which we may not be deprived without the concomitant commission of a crime. Can man renounce his reason? Well, then, his personal liberty belongs to him no less inalienably.

No wonder Vizcardo became one of the most active propagandists in the American lodges while Miranda was working with those in London.

¶ MIRANDA

Among the trail-blazers to rebellion, the truly universal man was the Venezuelan, Francisco de Miranda (1750–1816), born in Caracas. No other Spaniard in a century had operated directly in Europe with so resounding an effect or attained such important positions as did this brilliant agitator. His name is engraved on the Arc de Triomphe in Paris as one the great French generals of his day. With Dumouriez he carried on the campaign in the North during the French Revolutionary Wars; as a lieutenant general, he conquered Valmy and laid victorious siege to Antwerp. A loyal friend of the Girondists, he was on the verge of losing

his head to the guillotine when Robespierre rose to power with
the Jacobins. Only his prestige saved him from persecution by
the Inquisition and the Spanish despot. He became the incarnation of the fabled American rebel, a myth that he himself set out
to create. The host of his men and women friends who moved in
the most influential circles of European political society awarded
him the rare privilege of escaping with his life during the Reign
of Terror brought about by the chaotic Parisian Assemblies. His
escape was a victory won by eloquence, by the pamphleteers, and
by public opinion. Catherine of Russia, whose amorous friendship
he cultivated with gallant success in St. Petersburg, granted him
the title of general of her armies, and on his departure from
Russia she gave him warm letters of introduction to monarchs and
statesmen which opened doors to him in the Scandanavian countries and Prussia.

Miranda was a friend of Alexander Hamilton, and if the brilliant
American Secretary of the Treasury had not died in a duel, he
might have obtained for Miranda the effective help of the United
States for the revolution. Moreover, Miranda carried on a long
and intricate series of conferences in an attempt to define England's prospective role in the plan for independence that was
bubbling in his head. Pitt has been considered the black bird—
that is, the cold calculator—who froze much of the Venezuelan's
initiative. But in the long run the doors opened by Miranda stayed
open, and in one way and another the revolutionaries relied upon
England to advance their cause in war and politics. That an
American persecuted by Spain without truce or rest was able to
take his place as one of the key men of his day was a marvel.
Through Miranda, James Monroe (1758–1831) first became interested in Spanish American affairs just after the future formu-
lator of the Monroe Doctrine was appointed ambassador from
the United States to the French government. Napoleon, who then
was only beginning his rise to power, recognized something un-
common in Miranda. He said—and this the Duchesse of Abrantès
set down in her notes: "He is like a Don Quixote, without being
mad."

As a product of his time, Miranda read with equal interest
Julius Caesar's *Commentaries* and Vitruvius's *On Architecture*.
He collected antiques and works of art and assembled a remark-
able library. He stopped over in Switzerland to talk with Edward
Gibbon at the moment when *The Decline and Fall of the Roman
Empire* was beginning to be widely read. Of course he spent

hours talking with the rebel Jesuits in Verona. In London he made friends with the philosopher Jeremy Bentham (1748–1832) and the educator Joseph Lancaster, who was to have a strong influence on the new courses of study instituted by republican governments. He was intimate with Madame de Staël. Madame Roland, whom he met in prison, left important reminiscences about him. His amorous adventures, comparable to Casanova's, were recorded in his detailed diaries, which have provided material for emotion-charged biographies. As the focal point of the Americans in London, he met Bernardo O'Higgins (1778–1842), the future liberator of Chile, and together they founded the first Masonic lodges in Spanish America. Simón Bolívar and Andrés Bello joined him in taking the first steps toward the independence of Venezuela.

With the old Peruvian Pablo de Olavide, Miranda sketched on paper the powers of the American people which enabled them to treat with the European powers on the problems of the war being plotted. In 1806 he financed in Boston the first revolutionary expedition that landed on the coast of Venezuela. He planted the tricolor flag there—a yellow, blue, and red standard that he had designed and that still flies over Venezuela, Colombia, and Ecuador. He named the land Colombia, a name chosen by him to give back to Columbus all the glory due him. Miranda carried a printing press on his ship, and many copies of the Jesuit Vizcardo's *Letter to the Americans* were run off in leaflet form. After the defeat of that first expedition, Miranda went back to London, but then returned to America to join Bolívar and begin the war. Finally he was taken prisoner and died, years later, in a dungeon in Cádiz.

Some idea of the regard the French felt for Miranda may be gathered from the words of the Girondist Brissot, spoken when he was considering sending Miranda to govern Santo Domingo at a difficult time:

Miranda will soon settle the miserable quarrels of the colonies; he will make the white men see reason, turbulent though they are; he will become the idol of the colored peoples. And with what ease and speed he will rouse to rebellion the Spanish islands, or the [areas on the] American continent that have been in the power of Spain! At the head of twelve thousand troops of the line who are now in Santo Domingo, ten to fifteen thousand fierce mulattoes whom our colony will supply, and with the use of a fleet as a second arm, of course, it will be possible to invade the Spanish colonies, and the Spaniards will have nothing with which to oppose him. The name of Miranda will be worth an entire army, and his talents, courage, and genius all spell success.

¶ SIMÓN RODRÍGUEZ AND
FRAY SERVANDO TERESA DE MIER

Two most unusual agitators met in Bayonne in 1800. One was from North America, the other from South America. The first was a Dominican monk born in Monterrey, Fray Servando Teresa de Mier (1765–1827), the other a superhuman pedagogue born in Caracas, Simón Rodríguez (1771–1854). Their eccentricities and reasonings explain their discovery of each other in Europe.

By his own statement, Fray Servando had entered the preaching orders "under an imprudent vow taken in my childhood, and certainly I did not practice my calling except by deceit." At the age of twenty-seven he was a doctor of theology holding the chair of philosophy in the Dominican convent of Mexico City where he was known as one of the most eloquent orators in the country. One year he was entrusted with delivering the customary sermon for the festivities of the Virgin of Guadalupe. The words he spoke landed him in the prison of the Inquisition. He said that his country did not owe the coming of the Gospel to the Spaniards, because St. Thomas had preached it before Columbus, and that the image of the Virgin, which the little Indian Juan Diego allegedly had found, actually had been painted before the time of the Spanish colony, as the canvas, of a type made only in very ancient times, would prove. Indeed it was the very canvas that St. Thomas had worn as a cape. Jesus had bidden his disciples: "Go forth into the whole world and preach the Gospel unto every creature under heaven." Would it be likely then that such a strong, general, and peremptory command had failed to include half the globe? What excuse could the apostles give for not obeying it after their Master had communicated to them expressly the powers of his omnipotence to remove obstacles? The Gospel was not implanted through the strength of miracles alone; and if, according to St. Luke, the Apostle St. Philip was borne through the air to bring word of the Gospel to a single city of the Philistines called Azote, where could his feet not have taken him? Could there be more difficulty for St. Thomas, or Santo Tomé as the Indians say, or would he be less interested in carrying the Gospel to nearly half the world? By calling upon the most unlikely witnesses, Fray Servando offered proof that St. Thomas had preached in Mexico.

These seemingly innocent disquisitions implied a calculatedly daring act of independence. Fray Servando redeemed the patroness of Guadalupe, who had been to the Mexicans the constant symbol of their nationality, and attacked the Spaniards with weapons as improbable as a piece of canvas, a painting, and a tradition based on legend. A week after Fray Servando's sermon, he was hotly contradicted from all the pulpits by order of the archbishop. The convent had to barricade itself lest the faithful attack Fray Servando with cudgels. "The archbishop," Fray Servando declared, "the enemy of our country and its glories, was shouting that I had attempted to deny that his countrymen had brought the Gospel."

Fray Servando was seized by the Inquisition and packed off to Spain to be tried there. He escaped from one prison after another until he arrived disguised in France, and as he crossed the frontier he sang the word "liberty." He and Simón Rodríguez met in France. Don Simón had been a precocious student of Rousseau and Montesquieu in Caracas and a teacher of Simón Bolívar, whom he tried to educate in accordance with the standards of the Genevan philosopher. Well known for his strange ideas—some of which were similar to those of certain modern Communists—he was blamed, without conclusive proof, for fathering intellectually a plot against the government, uncovered in Caracas. Thanks entirely to the influence of Simón Bolívar's family, he was merely exiled.

After those two restless characters met in Bayonne, they traveled together to Paris. Fray Servando managed to obtain a parish. That was in the days when France was anticlerical and revolutionary, and as the income from the parish was not enough to keep the two philosophers, they opened a school that taught the Spanish language. Thinking to make their instruction more attractive, they translated Chateaubriand's *Atala* into Spanish the year after it was published. Romanticism reached its pinnacle in this novel, for it was set in America, which was one of the constants of the new literary school, full of enthusiasm for the exotic. Just as the philosophers of the Enlightenment took the ingredients for their noble savage from the Paraguayan Indians, the Romanticists turned their eyes toward America in search of strange landscapes.

Fray Servando and Simón Rodríguez separated. Fray Servando wanted to go to Rome to request the Pope personally to let him leave the Dominican order to become a secular priest free to move about the world. Rodríguez longed to know the world and to shed the Enlightenment everywhere on earth. Fray Servando kept watching his own country, seeing the spread of the desire for independence which he had helped to ignite. Released from the Dominican rule, he went back to Spain and fought against the French. He was imprisoned, but true to his tradition and his genius, he escaped. He fled to London, where he began his great work as a publicist. As such he wrote a series of important books: *Las Cartas de un americano a un español* (*Letters of an American to a Spaniard*), *La Historia de la Revolución de la Nueva España, El Manifiesto apologético* (*Justificatory Manifesto*), and the delightful *Memorias*, which recalls with an art bordering on the picaresque his escapes from prison and his persecution by the Archbishop of Mexico. He paints a wonderful picture of the European cities and villages he visited. He later went back to Mexico, took part in the revolution, and was thrown into prison again. He was deported to Havana. Finally he returned to Mexico, and died there in the governmental palace.

Simón Rodríguez taught in France, England, and Austria and directed an elementary school in Russia. He and Bolívar met again in Vienna and, in keeping with the precepts of Rousseau, traveled together on foot to Rome. There Rodríguez took Bolívar on a romantic climb up the Aventine Hill and swore him to a vow that he would dedicate his life to driving the Spaniards out of America. Bolívar went back to America to become the Liberator, and at the peak of his triumph, he helped his former teacher after Rodríguez had entered America again. In Chuquisaca, Rodríguez founded a trade school run according to a new theory of pedagogy. He wrote three works: *Sociedades americanas en 1828; El Libertador del Mediodía de América y sus compañeros de armas defendidos por un amigo de la causa social* (*The Liberator of South America and his Companions in Arms Defended by a Friend of the Social Cause*), and especially *Educación Popular*, a highly original work on pedagogical ideas and systems which, in spite of his eccentric presentation, must be rated as one of the most curious and intelligent works ever written on its subject in America.

❡ ANTONIO NARIÑO AND CAMILO TORRES

Very few of the writers and agitators who fathered independence managed to enjoy in repose the new republics that emerged victorious from the battlefields. Almost all the Jesuits in Bologna had died before the final battle of Ayacucho, which in 1824 insured victory over the Spanish armies in South America. Mariano Moreno died in 1811, Espejo in 1795, fourteen years before the proclamation of Quito, Miranda in 1816, precisely when the troops of the Reconquest seemed to have quashed the movement. But Fray Servando died in the palace of the Republic of Mexico, and Antonio Nariño (1765–1823), the Colombian patriot, lived four years after the last battle had been won. The fate of his comrade Camilo Torres was very different.

After Antonio Nariño was released from the Spanish prison where he served time for publishing the *Rights of Man* in Bogotá, he issued a gazette called *The Bagatelle* which in 1811 became the mouthpiece for independence. He took part in the republican campaign in the southern part of Colombia and rose to the rank of general. He was as daring as he was unlucky. In another of the pendulum-like swings that marked his life, he became president of Cundinamarca and one of the outstanding figures at Colombia's birth. Before he died, he was actively engaged in the struggle between parties which broke out after the coming of the republic. Nariño and Camilo Torres (1786–1816) played a leading part in the first of the splits that were to become common in politics all over nineteenth-century Spanish America. Nariño came out for centralism, Torres for federalism. Both men had been trail blazers in Colombia even before the freedom cry was shouted. Nariño began his subversive work in 1794, when he translated the *Rights of Man*, Torres when he signed the *Memorandum of Grievances* in 1809.

The *Memorandum of Grievances* ranks with the Jesuit Vizcardo's letter. Presented in Bogotá, it is an allegation that poses the problem of America against Spain. A juridical document, with virile energy it proclaims the rights of the Creoles, and declares that their rights are equal to those of the Spaniards:

> The Americas are not made up of people foreign to the Spanish nation. We are the sons, we are the descendents of those who shed their blood to acquire these new dominions for the Crown of Spain, of those who have extended her

boundaries and given her the political balance in Europe, a status she could not have obtained by herself alone. . . . We are Spaniards as much as the descendents of Don Pelayo, and therefore as deserving of the distinctions, privileges, and prerogatives of the rest of the nation as those who came forth from the mountains to expel the Moors and who subsequently peopled the Peninsula; with this difference, if any there be, that our forefathers, as aforesaid, discovered, conquered, and peopled this New World for Spain by dint of indescribable labors and hardships. Surely those men would not leave their children the heritage of an odious distinction between Spaniards and Americans; they would rather believe that they had acquired by their blood an eternal right to recognition, or at the very least, eternal equality with their compatriots.

Torres built his theory of a federal Spanish American world on the assumption that America's share in it would equal Europe's and that the men of America would have an access to power equal to that of the Europeans. The *Memorandum* was a timely warning to the Spaniards: "Beyond a doubt, the seven millions who constituted Great Britain in Europe carried more weight than the three millions who had only just created the England in America; yet for all that, justice was weighted on their side and tipped the balance." Torres aimed for unity in the Hispanic world through equality between Europe and America. His paper was called the *Memorandum of Grievances* because it offered the firmest and best reasoned criticism of colonial administration. These lines testify to his defense of man's freedom:

On the ground of enlightenment, America is not vain enough to consider herself superior, or even equal, to the provinces of Spain. Thanks to a despotic government, the foe of enlightenment, she could not hope to make rapid progress in human knowledge as long as the one consideration was to hobble the mind. The printing press, the vehicle of enlightenment, and the surest medium for spreading it, has been more sternly forbidden in America than anywhere else. Our studies of philosophy have been reduced to metaphysical gibberish written by the most obscure and despicable authors. Hence our shameful ignorance in the midst of the rich treasure surrounding us and its application to the most common usages of life. Not very many years ago, to the horror of reason, this kingdom saw the chairs of natural and human law suppressed because a study of those subjects was held to be harmful. Studying the first moral rules that God engraved on man's heart harmful! Harmful to study that which teaches him his obligations to that Prime Cause as the Author of his being, for his own sake, for his country's sake, and for the sake of the king himself! The barbarous cruelty of despotism, the enemy of God and man!

To assess correctly the boldness of this memorandum, we must remember that it was presented while the colonial regime held full sway, the viceroy was in plain sight, and the *audiencia* all-powerful. And we must bring to mind the history of the *comuneros*, whose leaders were shot for treason after their memoranda had been accepted and peace had been restored to the country. Torres declared:

The Spaniard's table is heaped with the finest delicacies that the soil offers, but he does not know the exploitations that the Indian suffers, condemned to never-ending slavery and an ignominious tribute imposed on him without justice or reason. Neither does he know what tears it costs the laborer to see a swarm of the satellites of monopoly uprooting him from his fields and forbidding him to cultivate the plants that nature spontaneously produces, which would bring happiness both to him and his family and to the state itself, if a barbarous statute had not forbidden trade in them.

Torres died in the same year as Miranda, the year the Spanish Reconquest seemed victorious. But Miranda died a natural death at the age of sixty-six, after a long, active, and glorious life, whereas Camilo Torres was shot just after he had turned thirty. He was shot, like the leaders of the *comuneros*, after mounting the scaffold in the Plaza Mayor, and his head was cut off and set up for exhibit in a cage at the entrance to Bogotá.

XIV: *Romanticism and Liberalism*

¶ CHATEAUBRIAND'S IMPACT ON AMERICA

In Europe, Romanticism exalted the idea of man's freedom, his personality. It made a passionate attempt to redeem the dignity of the human being, crushed beneath the weight of secular privilege and fanaticism. It turned for inspiration and example either to the medieval past or to distant, wild, and unknown regions. When the English invented the word that was to be written on the standard of the new school, they coined it from the sixteenth-century "romance," a ballad form adopted for relating legendary deeds. The fascination of the romances ensnared the Germans, too, as they were searching their Gothic roots for a single, national force that would oppose the classic, the Roman. Their idealistic fervor took them into the spheres of metaphysics.

All the romantic elements were being precipitated by society as the Americans in the Spanish colonies were awakening to a consciousness of themselves as a people. But America found little inspiration in exotic countries or the distant past: she turned back into herself to rediscover herself. This process of introspection went on for years. It goes back at least to 1780, the year of the Indian rebellions and the scientific missions whose work became a rediscovery of America.

Chronologically, the Romantic school proper began in Germany in the year 1797, when the literary journal *Athenäum* was founded by the brothers August Wilhelm and Friedrich von Schlegel. In England it dates from 1798, when Wordsworth wrote his famous preface to the *Lyrical Ballads*, which he and Coleridge composed. The translation of the Schlegels' works introduced Romanticism to France in 1813. These dates parallel those of the Spanish American Revolutions that exploded in 1810, after forty years of preparation, as the freedom cry rang and was echoed from bell tower to bell tower, in all the town halls, from the village of Dolores in Mexico to Buenos Aires, the capital of the viceroyalty on the Río de la Plata.

The Spanish Americans who traveled in Europe during the second half of the eighteenth century and on into the nineteenth— Miranda, Fray Servando Teresa de Mier, Simón Rodríguez, Bolívar, Andrés Bello, Nariño, Irisarri, and O'Higgins—were there at the very moment of Romanticism's awakening. As the movement unfolded and embraced every phase of art and politics, as music found in it new inspiration and revolution a new content, its consequences became more positive and radical in America than in Europe. The Romanticists in Europe were given to languishing fashionably of consumption, like Camille in her long decline through the pages of *La Dame aux Camélias*. It was equally modish to blow one's brains out like Werther or to be defeated like Napoleon on St. Helena. But in America, the Romanticists won the revolution for independence. The republics that were born romantically in the New World constitute the greatest work, the masterwork of the Romantic Spirit. The revolutionary soldiers of Spanish America ended their careers as liberators not long after Beethoven removed his dedication to Napoleon from the "Eroica" when he realized that the formidable Corsican, who had transformed Europe's institutions, was besotted with ambitions for empire as he dragged Europe down into the quagmire of his wars. In the end, however, no romantic undertaking could surpass the freeing of a continent, regardless of the consequences.

Added to that, America was dynamic and exotic, and the European Romanticists inevitably turned to it as the source of their ideal of the free man. Montaigne and Rousseau, Montesquieu and Diderot hailed the "Noble Savage" of the New World as the archetype of those seekers after liberty who would dethrone monarchs through their affirmation of the natural right to independence. To find in European history anything resembling events in America, writers had to turn back to the Gothic centuries, as

Sir Walter Scott did in *Ivanhoe*. But there in Mexico, in the time of Montaigne, was a Cuauhtémoc, dauntless unto death, the embodiment of the romantic hero of all time. Amidst all his sarcasms, Voltaire invented his own Utopia, but set it in the Guianas among emigrants from Peru.

To the Americans, such a link across the Atlantic with the free men on the other side was quite unexpected. But it was not by sheer coincidence that Simón Rodríguez and Fray Servando were the first to translate Chateaubriand's *Atala* into a foreign language. That the setting of this charming idyll should be the New World was bound to arouse the sympathetic interest of the Americans. José María Heredia (1803–39), the great Cuban writer of the period, was inspired by Chateaubriand to make an almost religious pilgrimage to the regions near Niagara Falls where the Frenchman had set his novel. The outcome was his "Ode to Niagara," a poem as beloved as *Atala*, which evokes with nostalgia his greatest love, the land of Cuba:

> *But what do my eager eyes seek in thee*
> *With vain desire? Why can I not see*
> *All around thine immense cavern*
> *The palms, ah! the delightful palms,*
> *That are born and grown in the smile of the sun*
> *On the plains of my warm country*
> *And wave to the breath of the breeze off the sea*
> *Under a cloudless sky?*

Both the originality of American Romanticism and its difference from the European variety are embodied in that poem. Its source of inspiration and its references are to the landscape of the fatherland, the setting of the theater where the struggle for freedom is being played. That kind of romantic understands and evokes freedom in his native land, not with simple nostalgia, but with a warlike affirmation that leads to war. Heredia, who had learned in childhood to express himself in Latin, who grew up with the writers of the Enlightenment, matured with Chateaubriand, Byron, Foscolo, and Lamartine. Almost all his work was written in the exile to which his love of liberty condemned him. His caress touches even the most remote history of America as he exalts the fundamental themes of the struggle in which he was involved. In his poem "En el Teocali de Cholula," he brings back to life, as he faces the sacred pyramid, the great ceremonies of the kings of Anáhuac, but he does not deal with the time between the Aztecs and the Americans of the nineteenth century.

He is concerned with time as it moves from slavery to liberty. "This immense structure bears witness to the most inhuman superstition enthroned upon it. . . . Yet better the superstition you served than the weeks of centuries you have wasted as you lay sleeping in the abyss of hell!"

Instead of going to Europe to find Chateaubriand's poetic spirit, the Americans transferred it to America. A Colombian poet, José Fernández Madrid (1789–1830), staged two plays in Havana in 1823: *Atala*, a tragedy in three acts; and *Guatimoc* (*Cuauhtémoc*), a tragedy in five acts. Romanticism was still the medium for the unburdening of the American soul. The last happy tryst with Chateaubriand came years later. A Colombian of English-Jewish origin, Jorge Isaacs (1837–95), wrote the best of the romantic novels, *María*, in 1867. He turned back to the idyll in its purest, most translucent form. The music and mastery of his landscapes recall *Atala*. He began by evoking Chateaubriand: "On an evening, like most of those in my country, veiled with violet-colored clouds and pale gold lamps, beautiful as María, beautiful and transitory as she was to me, we were sitting on the broad stones of the slope from which we could see at our right the turbulent rush of the river crossing the deep plain, while at our feet lay the majestic and silent valley. I was reading an episode from *Atala*, and the two girls, María and my sister, admirable in their motionlessness and abandonment, heard all the melancholy that fills the poet as it blossomed from my lips 'to make the world weep.' "

Atala and *María* seemed to be twin works, but the procedures of the authors were antithetical. Chateaubriand moved far from France; Isaacs entered the land of Colombia. With a poetry that was Biblical as much as French, Isaacs pictured *his* valley of the Cauca. He made its geography a sensitive mirror. The moon, the rivers, the Negroes, the stags, and the dogs are all reflected in a small drama. The drama ends in tears, of course, but it shows the inner world of the Americans in relation to their native landscape. Apart from this, Isaacs shouldered his standard and his rifle when the hour of combat struck.

Chateaubriand's influence lost some of its power with the revolution, but did not end. Isaacs used the Frenchman as an excuse for painting a picture that still has force. Some of his pages anticipated *Modernismo;* others, which revealed the poetry and stories of the Negroes, were outcroppings of the mine of Afro-American literature which others were to develop.

In 1879, a dozen years after the publication of *María*, the

Ecuadorian novelist Juan León Mera (1832–94) published *Cumandá*, which was patently derived from Chateaubriand. The
Indian characters are exotic and imaginary beings in a conventional poetic drama. It contains genuine poetry, but a poetry more
pleasing to Europeans than to Americans. Chateaubriand may
be said to have died in America, with *Cumandá* as his winding-
sheet. Everything that had made him an effective prime mover
at the beginning of the nineteenth century had flickered out.
Nothing was left of his school but the mannerisms. *Cumandá*
as a novel would have corresponded to the Spanish Romanticism of Zorrilla, Núñez de Arce, Martínez de la Rosa, and especially Bécquer, if Mera had been more nearly contemporaneous
with them. Their names appear in the epic poem *Tabaré*, written
at about the same time as *Cumandá* by the Uruguayan Juan
Zorrilla de San Martín (1855–1931). His romantic picture is
one of the purest of its kind in American letters, but the author
cannot be considered a late-blooming Chateaubriand; rather, he
is a link between the Romanticists and the new poetry that fore-
shadowed Modernism. The great American poets of the late
nineteenth century were Romanticists not because they belonged
to that school, but because the drama of the struggle for freedom
was still going on in their homelands.

¶ AMERICAN ROMANTICISM IN EUROPE

From the beginning, the Romanticists of Europe were sensitive to the awakening of America. If any one person could be
said to lead that vanguard, it was Mme de Staël. Her book *De
l'Allemagne* was the bell that aroused the Romanticists of France.
One of her letters, hotly discussed, contributed to the start of the
movement in Italy. Mme de Staël was one of Miranda's *grandes
amies*. Their warm friendship began just as she was assuming
leadership with her salon in Paris, soon after she had come from
Germany and Italy where she had been the recipient of Goethe's
most obsequious gallantry and had talked with Wilhelm von
Humboldt, Schlegel, and Sismondi. Her book on Germany was
still incubating at that time. In her salon Miranda talked with
Alexander von Humboldt, recently back from America, and
picked up the thread of his earlier chats with the Abbé Raynal in
Marseilles. The abbé was then about to complete his massive
*Histoire Philosophique et politique des établissements et du
commerce des Européens dans les deux Indes*, which invited his
contemporaries to take a closer look at the almost unknown world

of America. The book won a prize from the Academy of Sciences, Arts, and Letters of Lyon, as the best piece of work ever done on the consequences of the discovery of America.

Diderot, Chateaubriand, and Jacques Henri Bernardin de St. Pierre (1737–1817) were equally faithful members of Mme de Staël's salon. So, too, was Benjamin Constant (1767–1830), then at work on his novel *Adolphe* and deeply involved in his love affair with Mme de Staël, as recorded in his *Journal Intime*. America was often discussed in that parlor where Romanticism was being forged as a movement. Miranda was in his element. He was seeing before him new roads to be opened for literature and politics.

At a later date, Lord Byron shone among the enthusiasts of Mme de Staël. But he was no less attracted by the achievements of Bolívar. To Byron, Bolívar was the hero who best embodied his ideal of heroic independence. Indeed, Byron might well have fought in America instead of in Greece. In August 1809, when Bolívar's campaign to free Colombia seemed to be having its worst difficulties, Byron wrote from Bologna to his friend John Hobhouse: "I have two plans: one to visit England in the spring; the other to go to South America. Europe's decrepitude is increasing; everything here is the same, everything repeats itself. There the people are as fresh as their New World, and as violent as their earthquakes." A few days later, Byron named the country he definitely intended to visit: Venezuela. He wrote to Hobhouse:

> My South American plan is this: I have seen in the papers, which I am enclosing for you, the advantages open to whoever goes to settle in Venezuelan territory. . . . The Anglo-Americans seem overly crude to me, and their climate too cold. I prefer the others. I shall make rapid progress in the Spanish language. Ellice, or somebody else, will be able to give me letters to Bolívar and his government. . . . I assure you I am thinking about this very seriously, and have cherished the idea for some time.

Byron failed to go to America because the nearer and more immediate adventure of Greece attracted him more strongly. But his enthusiasm for Bolívar was so great that he called him "the model of political virtues and moral enlightenment" and named his yacht the *Bolívar*. That was the yacht he sailed to rescue the body of Shelley who had drowned in the waters of the Italian Mediterranean.

As Byron went to Italy, he left a London that was, to some

degree, a Spanish and American city. Émigrés from Spain had set up their headquarters there, and they had been joined by distinguished Spanish Americans who shared with them a common repudiation of the absolutism of Ferdinand VII, the unfortunate successor to Charles IV. The English capital became their salon, their coffee house, their conference hall, the printing press for their gazettes. In one section of the city, the accents of all the provinces of Spain and Spanish America were heard on all sides. It looked like the Puerta del Sol wrapped in a fog. That was the best period of English Romanticism, the subject of many sketches of manners and customs composed by Mariano José de Larra (Figaro), writing in Spain, and by Spanish American writers in all the republics.

A common English style eventually developed among the Spanish *émigrés*. Many of them wrote in English, satirizing the Francophilic Romanticists of the Peninsula. They published gazettes and reviews, the most distinguished of which were the *Museo Universal de Ciencias y Artes* (*The World Museum of Science and Art*) and the *Correo Literario y Político de Londres* (*The London Literary and Political Mail.*) Joseph Blanco White (1775–1841) and José Joaquín Mora were perhaps the most distinguished of these Hispanic writers of English.

The best-known among the Spanish Americans in London, and the man who lived there longest was Andrés Bello (1781–1865). He edited the first *Biblioteca Americana* (1823) and later the *Repertorio Americano* (1826), two basic publications in the history of Spanish American letters. Bello translated Byron and steeped himself in the work of the Scottish philosophers Reid, Stewart, Brown, and Hume, as well as that of Berkeley and Hobbes. He became interested in Lancaster's educational system and personality, but was more intimately associated with the philosophy of Jeremy Bentham, the father of Utilitarianism. Bello's friendship with James Mill (1773–1836), father of John Stuart Mill, who founded the system of philosophic radicalism, facilitated his completion of a singular task: the orderly arrangement of Bentham's manuscripts. Through this work, he acquired his store of ideas and his philosophy and served his apprenticeship in the English method of working which was to become so much a part of his personality.

In the *Biblioteca Americana*, Bello published his "Alocución a la Poesía" ("Apostrophe to Poetry"), a fragment of a projected canticle to America which never was completed. His ode "A la

Agricultura de la Zona Torrida" apeared in *El Repertorio*. This ode is an enduring lesson in beauty which lyrically poses the Americans against their landscape and the labor in their fields. Romanticism is present in his passionate eulogy to tropical plant life, which he recalls as vividly in London as if he were enjoying it directly through his senses:

> *You gave us the stalk of the emerald cane*
> *From which such sweetness is distilled*
> *As puts to scorn the comb of the bee.*
> *You set the crystal drop that's spilled*
> *From the foaming chocolate cup like rain.*
> *Bright scarlet moves in your cochineal tree,*
> *More vivid than the hues of Tyre.*
> *The generous indigo seems to drain*
> *Its blue from the heavenly star sapphire.*
> *Yours is the heady wine that runs*
> *From the wounded agave's carapace*
> *To the thirsty mouth of Anáhuac's son.*
> *You gave us the dried leaf's spiral grace*
> *That rises as smoke from dreams new spun.*

He goes on to speak of coffee, pineapple, yucca, sweet potatoes, cotton, corn, bananas . . . All his poetry was drawn from the forgotten depths of natural history, but he gave it a romantic life of its own. A few years before Bello wrote his poem, Rafael Landivar (1731–93), a Guatemalan Jesuit, one of the exiles who met in Bologna, wrote a Virgilian eulogy of work in the fields entitled *Rusticatio Mexicana*, which frequently employed realistic imagery. This extraordinary man wrote his poem in Latin. And though his stanzas, charged with the homesickness of the exile, are moving, one may ask with Mariano Picón-Salas:

> Why was such a delightful panorama of landscape and customs, where the song of the quetzal alternates with the cries of the Indian oarsmen on Xochimilco, or the excited shouting of a cock fight—why was this world in which so much may be found that is novelistic, where there is such a lyrical wealth of genre scenes, ever written in Latin, thereby restricting itself to a circle of learned men?

Landivar's poem is remembered by few, though the name of its author is not forgotten. On the other hand, Bello's work fathered a generation of singers of the tropics stretching from Heredia, his contemporary, to Leopoldo Lugones of our century.

The Romanticists in Germany grew interested in America through Humboldt. The great naturalist set up his working head-quarters in Paris in the years following his visit to the New World, and traveled through Europe later, taking with him the voice of the Americas and extolling the wondrous vision of its landscapes. Goethe's interest in American affairs was sparked by his friendship with Humboldt. The great poet's astute assessment of the problem of the Panama Canal was stated in his remark that the United States would not let the opportunity to build it slip from its hands.

Heinrich von Kleist (1777–1811) was one of the most eccentric of the German Romanticists. "Tense to the point of pathological crisis," Maxime Alexandre said, "Kleist is a romantic in his dissatisfaction with reality. Before he took refuge in mysticism or mythology, he confronted the element of revolt which was an ingredient in his struggle against destiny. In this sense he is a precursor of Kafka and generally of the literature of our day." Kleist was the son of a Prussian officer, but he left the army at twenty-two to go to Paris because he was fascinated by the Republic. His beautiful sister Ulrika, who was loved by Byron and Chateaubriand, went with him disguised as a laborer. Kleist went from Paris to Switzerland, intending to put Rousseau's ideas into practice. When he and Goethe met in Germany, Goethe listened to him with a blend of interest and horror, as if he found in him a man who was prey to the most recondite and incurable torments. Kleist committed suicide at the age of thirty-four, and Henriette Vogel, a married woman joined to Kleist by the same dark destiny, killed herself with him.

Kleist's very meager body of work, which was published in part, in French translations, in the *Revue de Paris*, includes two long stories set in Chile and Santo Domingo respectively. The Chilean one, entitled "The Earthquakes of Chile," was later given the more accurate title of "The Nun of Santiago in Paris." The other story was entitled "The Sweethearts of Santo Domingo." They are works of pure imagination, full of high romantic drama. Oddly enough, Kleist fancied that America was the right place to set his drama—America, with earthquakes in Chile, the Mapocho River in flood, and the Negroes of Santo Domingo engaged in an all-out struggle for freedom:

Toni asked how it was that the whites had made themselves so hated on the island. The foreigner who was asked this replied: "Because of the relations they have had with the Negroes as masters of the island, which, to be frank, I should not venture to defend, even though they go back centuries. The mad thirst for freedom which has seized all those who work on the plantations has impelled the Negroes and Creoles to break the chains that bind them and to avenge themselves on all the white people by inflicting on them the same manifold and damnable excesses that they have suffered at the hands of certain evil white men."

In Germany the dialogue concerning the colonies came at the same time as the awakening of the Romanticists, indirectly sponsored by Humboldt, the second discoverer of the New World. The popular translation of Jorge Juan and Antonio de Ulloa's letters, copiously annotated by the lexicographer and Greek scholar Johann Gottlob Schneider (1750–1822), testifies to that interest. This work served, appropriately, as the basis of a later translation made in France.

¶ ESTEBAN ECHEVERRÍA AND VICTOR HUGO

In 1825, Esteban Echeverría (1805–51) sailed from Buenos Aires to Bordeaux.

With canvas taut, the barque all aquiver
As slim-keeled she moves through the swift Plata River
At daybreak's first gleam.
And over the bright and undulant plain
She carries the wanderer down to the main
As the breeze from the South speeds her on like a dream.

In no other way could he express himself—this twenty-year-old romantic poet who played Argentine *cielitos* on his guitar like the best of the *payadores*, the wandering *gaucho* minstrels who performed at trading posts and ranches.

Echeverría was in Paris during the battles over Victor Hugo's play *Hernani* and the ban that suspended the presentations of *Marion de Lorme*, also by Hugo. The Socialist philosopher Saint-Simon died at about the time of the poet's arrival in Paris, leaving his disciples this prophecy: "We are conquered, but the future is ours." When Echeverría left Paris five years later, he took with him one of the first copies of *I Promessi Sposi* (*The Betrothed Couple*) by the Italian writer Alessandro Manzoni. A German friend introduced him to the daughter of the poet Schiller whose work he had already read, along with the works of Goethe. He translated Byron. By night and by day he was making the most of his European experience, improving each hour. Freedom was a constant stimulant to his romantic imagination, and he was revolted when Bolívar, "having been asked by the Bolivians for a constitution, sent them one that established the presidency for life and gave [to the president] the power to name his successor: thus the very name of president is prostituted, and is turned into that of a monarch." When the poet returned to Buenos Aires, the despot Juan Manuel de Rosas (1793–1877) was in power. From then on, Echeverría lived on the firing line; he started his battle with the weapon of literature. He was one of the Romanticists who met in the social group that frequented Marcos Sastre's bookshop in Buenos Aires. Juan Bautista Alberdi (1810–84) recalled that Echeverría there "first heard of Lerminier,[1] Victor Hugo, Alexander Dumas, Lamartine, Byron, and everything then labeled Romanticism, as opposed to the old Classical school." Alberdi was so enthusiastic over Larra, who wrote under the pseudonym of Figaro, that he signed his chronicles "Figarillo," and it was he who finally cemented together the country's constitution with his *Bases y Puntos de Partida para la organización política de la República Argentina* (*Foundations and Points of Departure for the Political Organization of the Argentine Republic*).

Another of Echeverría's initiates was Vicente Fidel López (1815–1903). Like Sarmiento, López gave education strong support. He established the Normal School. His father was the author of the patriotic anthem that perpetuated the sacred freedom cry. López wrote a historical novel as romantic as its title: *La Novia del Hereje, o La Inquisición de Lima* (*The Heretic's Sweetheart, or the Inquisition in Lima*). He reports in his auto-

---

[1] Eugène Lerminier was a professor of philosophy who had little importance in France but considerable in Argentina. He wrote *De l'influence de la philosophie du XVIII siècle*, *Introduction à l'histoire du droit*, and *Lettres à un berlinois*. Canal-Feijoo said that he was "a brilliant and superficial expositor, with intentions of combining Kantian ethics, Savignyan historicism, and Hegelian idealism, but in the effort did not succeed in showing any originality."

biography that the French Revolution of 1830 inspired a flood of books which in turn stimulated debate on letters, politics, and fashion.

We were carried away by the work of Victor Hugo, Sainte-Beuve, Casimir Delavigne's tragedies, Dumas's and Victor Ducange's dramas, George Sand, et al. . . . We would read by day, converse and argue by night. The famous preface to Victor Hugo's *Cromwell*, then known as the "New Poetic Art," or the new literary dogma, dominated ideas like a constitution.

The theater was used as a rostrum for literature and ideas. In 1831, Schiller's *William Tell* and *Mary Stuart* and Ducange's *Thirty Years, or The Life of a Gambler* were presented in Buenos Aires. In 1834, Dumas's *Antonino* was presented. But by 1835, Victor Hugo's *Hernani* was banned by the Rosas authorities. A battle was fought over *Hernani* in Buenos Aires and eventually it was won in Montevideo. An enthusiast wrote to the director of the company: "Give us *Hernani*, Señor González. Don't be afraid of anything, and do believe that a drama that has been the delight of Paris cannot cause scandal in Buenos Aires." That enthusiast was mistaken. Before long the Argentine Romanticists had to cross the river, or the mountains, to Montevideo or Santiago, Chile, with their traveling French theater.

The Romanticism of Victor Hugo burned with a bright flame in America, a flame quite unlike the glow that was kindled by Chateaubriand or Lamartine. A thick volume of Victor Hugo's works was published in America and his poetry was translated by the best poets in every country, all of whom were either liberals or socialists. The Romanticists were bound to attack the classical patterns, but the nineteenth century added a new ingredient to the struggle: progress, plus a pinch of anticlericalism. The result was a blend of romanticism and enlightenment guided by liberal principles. As this synthesis was evolving, Echeverría noted: "Mme de Staël, who imported Romanticism from Germany, was the first to attack Classicism face to face, and the famous Victor Hugo gave it the death blow when he said in his preface to *Cromwell:* 'The literary reform of France is consummated and classicism is totally annihilated.' " In *Victor Hugo y los Románticos argentinos*,[1] a study from which I have taken much of the

---

[1] *Cuadernos* (Paris, August, 1963).

data in these paragraphs, José Luis Lanuza states Alberdi's position in these words: "Alberdi published a 'monthly gazette' at about that time called *La Moda*, in which he glories in being up to the minute on literary matters, and asserts: 'We are not nor do we wish to be Romanticists.'" To the editors of *La Moda*, Romanticism was already falling behind, it was a movement

> of feudal origin, with an anti-social instinct, absurdly sentimental, lunatic, misanthropic, eccentric, eternally cherished by the men in the ministry, rejected by those in the opposition, appearing in Germany at a murky time, at a worse period in France, in no way entitled to the adherence of those who want a true, not a coterie art . . . for the new art must be an art that sets matter above form, rational without being classical, free without being romantic, philosophical, moralistic, progressive; it must express the public feeling, not individual caprice; it must discuss the fatherland, humanity, equality, progress, liberty, glory, victory, passions, desires, the national hopes, and not the pearl, the tear, the angel, the moon, the tomb, the dagger, poison, crime, death, hell, the devil, the witch, the hobgoblin, the owl, or any of that hodgepodge vocabulary that constitutes the esthetics of Romanticism.[1]

Echeverría, a Romanticist to his dying day, is famous for *El Dogma Socialista* rather than for *Elvira, o la Novia del Plata* (*Elvira, or the Sweetheart of the Plata*), a poem that antedates by a year the first Romanticist poetry written in Spain. *El Dogma Socialista* is a political program that develops around the fifteen words that symbolized the new doctrine: association, progress, fraternity, equality, and so on. *Jóven Argentina* (*Young Argentina*) was patterned after Mazzini's recently found *Giovine Italia* (*Young Italy*), but it was soon outshone by the *Asociación de Mayo*, which became the boiling pot of the struggle against the Rosas dictatorship. The most vigorous of Echeverría's works is *El Matadero* (*The Slaughterhouse*), a brief picture of the worst political practices. *El Matadero* is the period's small masterpiece of realism because Echeverría wrote it to expose the bloody dictator and his devices in all their rawness.

Meanwhile, a theatrical impresario planned to present productions by Victor Hugo, Dumas, and Ducange in Montevideo in

[1] Ibid.

answer to the public's clamor for them. A whole team of translators was put to work on Spanish versions of their plays, which then were performed in Montevideo at the same time as the original works were premiered in Paris. The translators were Ventura de la Vega, Colonel César Díaz, Sergeant-Major Adriano Díaz, Captain Bartolomé Mitre, and Santiago Viola. In those days of the struggle for freedom, a man was often a dramatist or poet as well as a sergeant. Between 1838 and 1839, Hugo's *Ruy Blas*, *Lucrèce Borgia*, *Angelo*, *Le Roi s'amuse*, and *Marion de Lorme* were produced in Montevideo. Bartolomé Mitre (1821–1906), the captain who translated *Ruy Blas*, later became president of the Argentine Republic (1862–8) and the founder of *La Nación* of Buenos Aires. While he was in Montevideo, he translated Longfellow, Thomas Gray, Byron, and Dante. He rendered the *Divine Comedy* in Castilian tercets before anyone else had done it. Mitre embodied the restlessness of the progressive Romanticists. In Bolivia, he wrote a novella, *Memorias de un Botón de Rosa* (*Memoirs of a Rosebud*), *Las Ruinas de Tiahuanacu* (an archeological study), and *Ollantay*, a study of the Quechuan drama. His monumental *Historia de Belgrano y de la Independencia Argentina* was written later.

From Montevideo, Echeverría was watching the slow, the desperately slow, decline and fall of Rosas. In that period, in order to please Rosas, a Neapolitan intellectual in the tyrant's service whose name was De Angelis echoed Chenier's attacks on Chateaubriand, which discredited Romanticism. Echeverría seared De Angelis: "Good God! A poor worm, crawling around in putrefaction, wanting to spit on the sun!" Romantically enough, at the time of Echeverría's death he was so poor that he had had to sell books from his library in order to eat.

Montevideo was like a free Argentina, readying its weapons for battle against Rosas while its pens, more deadly than the sword, were fattening the newspapers. José Marmol (1817–71) published as a newspaper serial the novel *Amalia*, which was to make him famous. To us it is a historical novel, a realistic picture of the Rosas dictatorship. To the *émigrés*, the story was true, and they were living it as a chapter in history. *Amalia* was the normal product of a Romanticism being forged as a tool for undermining the foundations of despotism. Marmol had been imprisoned by Rosas. In his novel he records the day when he wrote with charred yerba maté stems on the walls of the dungeon under the prison in Buenos Aires: "Show dreadful death before my eyes. Put all my limbs in chains. Barbarian, you will never kill my soul. Nor place bars before my mind, no!" On the other side of the Andes, Sarmiento wrote something similar: "Barbarians: ideas are not killed!"

They all made drama, but they wanted to write it, too. Echeverría died regretting that he had not been able to complete a play he had sketched to immortalize the heroic Colombian woman Policarpa Salavarrieta as a symbol of embattled womanhood shot by the Spaniards. Mitre treated the subject in a play staged with great success in Montevideo. Marmol composed *El Poeta*, a five-act drama in verse. But one of the Romanticists' greatest achievements was to help mold the character of one who was to carry the flambeau of freedom to Europe—Giuseppe Garibaldi (1807–82), soon to become the romantic leader of the Italian Risorgimento. Garibaldi found a refuge in Montevideo after campaigning in the south of Brazil. He brought with him, as his companion and wife, the Brazilian woman Anita. Like the other romanticists, he fought in the armed struggle against Rosas. The Italians already had begun to notice him and Anita—so American, so daring—and they asked them to come to the fields of Italy. As a consequence, the "gaucho" Garibaldi's sculptured figure stands on the square of almost every Italian city, large or small, and Anita's is honored in a fine heroic monument on the peak of the Janiculum Hill. They constitute a memorial in bronze to American Romanticism, which, like the Mazzini-Echeverría link, binds America and Italy in perpetuity.

¶ SARMIENTO AND BELLO IN SANTIAGO

Many Argentines and Spaniards who represented the Romanticist left, José Joaquín Mora among the latter, emigrated to Chile as well as to Montevideo. In Chile they were opposed by the right wing of their own school, some of whom were Chilean whereas others, like Andrés Bello, had come from elsewhere in South America.

Among the great Argentines who moved to Chile—Mitre, Vicente López, Alberdi, and others—the most distinguished was Domingo Faustino Sarmiento (1811–88). He was the most vigorous figure in the mid-century from the Plata region. Born in the interior, he established a vehement newspaper, *El Zonda*, in his native village of San Juan. When the paper was suspended, he took refuge in Chile, where he wrote his *Recuerdos de Pro-*

vincia, a polemic book filled with sketches so exact and evocations so felicitous that the Argentines know many of its pages by heart from anthologies. Almost everyone in Spanish America can recognize them. Sarmiento arrived in Santiago resolved to double his fight against Rosas. His immortal book, *Facundo*, originally published as a serial, came out of his work as a journalist.

The gazettes convey the ardent tone of the argument over Romanticism and reflect the literary battles. The Argentines in Valparaíso founded their own newspaper, the *Revista de Valparaíso*, edited by Vicente Fidel López (1815?–1903); Juan Bautista Alberdi and Juan María Gutiérrez (1809–78) collaborated on it. Gutiérrez was a poet and humanist, who was evaluated by the Spanish critic Marcelino Menéndez y Pelayo, in his *Antología de la Poesía Hispanoamericana*, as the most finished man of letters born in South America. The *Revista de Valparaíso* was founded in February 1842. In April of that year the famous *Museo de Ambas Américas* appeared, edited by the Spaniard Manuel Rivadeneira and published by the Colombian Juan García del Río (1794–1856). García del Río already had established two newspapers in Chile and was one of the publishers of the *Argos Americano* of Cartagena, Colombia. His Chilean papers were *El Sol de Chile* and *El Telégrafo*. He wrote a biography of San Martín, whom he had accompanied in the Andean campaign, and *Meditaciones Colombianas*. His biographical sketches demonstrate the mobility of the men who had only one country: their American world. Rivadeneira was one of the greatest editors of the Enlightenment in Spain and America. He issued Larra's complete works in Chile. After his return to Spain, he edited the most important nineteenth-century collection of Spanish classics. *El Semanario de Santiago* was more or less the counterpart of the *Revista de Valparaíso*.

With the arrival of José Joaquín Mora (1783–1864) and later that of Bello, Santiago was like another London for the Spanish-speaking world, a London *in parvum*. Mora assumed the leadership of the liberal Chileans. In England he had translated Scott's *Ivanhoe* and *The Talisman*. He moved to Buenos Aires, and thence to Chile, where he headed *El Mercurio Chileno*. The Lyceum of Chile deferred to him: he occupied its first chair in political law. Through his newspaper, he attacked the laws of primogeniture and entail as a relic of the middle ages, one of the privileges of oligarchy. Mora was a passionate champion of freedom of the press. Eventually he made himself a nuisance to Diego Portales, the strong man, shrewd, domineering, Voltairean, and cold, who dominated the political scene in Chile from 1830 until his assassination in 1837. Both as poet and journalist, Mora was sarcastic and formidable. He drew up the constitution that governed Chile in the early period; he was declared by Congress a citizen of the country. When the differences between him and Portales arose, Mora emigrated to Peru, leaving the literary field to Andrés Bello.

Bello was Chile's greatest acquisition in the realm of culture. As he spoke from his rostrum, he was heard all over the continent. He drew up the Civil Code, an American version of the Code Napoléon which shaped the law into a systematic structure. This work satisfied a great need, for under the Spanish Empire the royal cedulas had piled up into a shapeless mountain of voluminous papers which embodied a residue of medieval ideas. The Civil Code of Chile was adopted by other republics. Bello drew it up in the university and infused it with an American spirit all its own. Another of his great contributions was the systematizing of grammar. He laid out guidelines for the language based on its common rules instead of following the custom of applying Latin rules to Spanish. His grammar, worked out "for the use of Americans," eventually was adopted by the Spaniards. Bello also was a moving force in the sciences and arts.

Although Bello would seem to be more closely affiliated with the conservatives, and although as a successor to Mora he took the side that opposed his old comrades in letters, he played a positive role in the revolution for independence by giving the new republic a juridical foundation, a university, and an organized language. He never came out either for or against Romanticism, but in accepting the new literary school of Victor Hugo, the eulogy of the revolution implicit in *Hernani*, in translating Dumas's *Thérèse* and publicizing his work, Bello almost seems a counterpart of Sarmiento. His version of Victor Hugo's *Prayer for Everyone* is better than the original. Any kind of disturbance irritated him. Yet disturbance and uproar are specialties—perhaps fatally so—of the Latin American character. That quality irritated Bello and haunted Miranda and Bolívar in their most melancholic hours. Sarmiento brought tumult into polemics, and Bello left the last word in that contest to Jotabeche (José Joaquín Vallejo, 1811–58), one of his disciples, who was fired by an article on Classicism and Romanticism, the work of Vicente Fidel

López that opened the struggle between the literary right and left.

Jotabeche was a sharp, lively chronicler, famous among the Chilean writers on manners and customs. He attacked Romanticism in a mocking and aggressive letter addressed to a friend in Santiago. The battle over *Ruy Blas* was joined. Jotabeche wrote:

> Make yourself over into a Romanticist, for God's sake! Find out that all it takes is to open your mouth, to slap and slash at the aristocracy, raise democracy to the stars, talk about literary independence, and write so that only the devil can understand you, steep yourself in arrogance, show how self-sufficient you are, address Hugo, Dumas, and Larra familiarly, and talk about them as so many highbrows whom we can come to terms with, *sans compliments*.

Salvador de Sanfuentes (1817-60), a poet-politician more mildly of that opinion, wrote:

> However many beauties of a high order we may find in Victor Hugo's works, we can't help rebelling against him when he portrays for us in *Ruy Blas* a lackey who was never more than a lackey madly enamored of a queen, a lackey with a heart full of thoughts and aspirations that would scarcely befit one of the proudest grandees of Spain.

Sarmiento replied:

> In *Ruy Blas*, we see a principle developed, a product of equality. The lackey is a man of the people, his beloved is an aristocratic queen, yet they love each other, for the ignorant have their passions and the queen scorns rank, despises the nobility, and raises up the lackey she loves. Well, there may be exaggeration in this play, but there is poetry, too, and it says to the commoner: "You, too, may love a queen or become president of Chile." The war for American independence has familiarized us with these Ruy Blas who have seized the occasion of a social upheaval to come forth, shoulder a gun, and end their campaigning as generals, governors, representatives of the people; and there is no Republic in America to this time which has not had generals and diplomats who were actually lackeys in the beginning. . . . This writer [Sanfuentes] has taken the lackey as the lackey and nothing more. He has not realized that the lackey is the

peon, the craftsman, the seaman, the butler, the ragamuffin, in short, the man ill-situated in society who nevertheless may be an extraordinary man.

The battle over *Ruy Blas* was only a skirmish. Sarmiento rejected a truce and began to search for a definition that would cover the entire question:

> The Romanticist school of Europe was buried and entombed alongside its literary ancestor, Classicism, because ten years ago, in 1842, both of them became spirits from the other world, God bless them. . . . The socialist and progressive schools have taken their stand upon the solid and sound pedestal of society's needs, liberal tendencies, and the working out of the world's future.

What about Bello? These are his conclusions:

> In literature, the Classicists and Romanticists resemble not so distantly what the legitimists and liberals stand for in politics. While to the former, the authority of the doctrines and practices bearing the seal of antiquity is beyond appeal and any deviation from those well-trodden paths constitutes rebellion against sound principles, to the latter, in their endeavor to emancipate the mind from useless and pernicious hobbles, liberty may sometimes become confused with the most untrammeled license. The Classical school divides and separates the two types as carefully as the legitimist sect disjoins the various social hierarchies: the aristocratic gravity of the Classical tragedy and ode will not permit the slightest taint of the plebeian, the familiar, or the domestic. The Romanticist school, on the other hand, prides itself on approaching and intermingling conditions: the comic and the tragic rub elbows, or to put it better, blend their heterogeneous dramas with such intimacy that the interest of the spectators is divided between the clown and the monarch, between the prostitute and the princess; and the splendor of the court contrasts with the sordid egoism of the sentiments it cloaks, indeed studiedly highlights the contrast in brighter colors. This parallel could be carried much further; perhaps it would show us some curious affinities and analogies. But what is most noteworthy is the natural alliance between literary and political licitness. Romantic poetry, like representative government and trial by jury, is of English lineage.

The eruption of such matters among the peoples of southern Europe came simultaneously with democracy. And not infrequently the writers who have jousted against progress in affairs of legislation and government have carried on the struggle against the new literary revolution and have defended the antiquated authorities at all costs through a superstitious respect for our elders: the poetic rules of Athens and Rome and the France of Louis XIV.

¶ VICTOR HUGO IN COLOMBIA

The whole question of Romanticism was debated for a century and is still discussed. Victor Hugo's hold on America is in direct relation to his long lifetime. Twenty years after the battle in Santiago over *Ruy Blas*, which corresponded to the battles in Paris, *Les Misérables* appeared, in 1862, and both Paris and America were moved. Hugo was still the mentor of the radicals in Chile, Argentina, Colombia, Mexico, and Paris. In that same year, Sarmiento wrote to a friend from his village of San Juan: "Have you read *Les Misérables* yet?" In Ecuador, the black, theocratic dictatorship of Gabriel García Moreno (1821–75), who handed the spiritual direction of the country over to the Jesuits, was just beginning. Victor Hugo was one of the weapons with which the opposition attacked the dictator. Raúl Andrade wrote:

> For the first time in literature, the sun began to shine on the miserable, and it set fire to the fighting spirit of his contemporaries and channeled them toward the social struggle. *Les Misérables* is the first valid attempt to seek out the humiliated, the persecuted, the despoiled, and to draw them out of their melancholy solitude and isolation. After Hugo, Tolstoy was to descend to that world with tear-filled eyes, and Dostoievski with the illumination of the epileptic.

In 1863 a constitutional convention met in Colombia. The abolition of capital punishment, identified with Victor Hugo's preachings, was high on the agenda. Fidel Cano, founder of *El Espectador* (*The Spectator*) and one of the great Colombian journalists, was working on his masterpiece, the *Pastoral Laica*, which pursues the theme of the right to live. Every picture of Cano writing in his workroom, shows a large portrait of Victor Hugo in the background. The scene has been hung in many American parlors. As soon as the constitution was ratified, Colombia commissioned a special ambassador to place a de luxe copy of it in Victor Hugo's hands because the document was considered a faithful translation of his ideas. The aging Frenchman wrote to the ambassador:

> I can never express to you how deep an impression your letter has made on me. I have dedicated my life to progress, and the inviolability of human life is the point of departure for progress on earth. The end to war and the abolition of the scaffold emanate from this principle. The end to war and the abolition of the scaffold would mean the suppression of the sword. Once the sword is suppressed, despotism must vanish, for it no longer has a reason for being or a means of existing. This constitution finally abolishes capital punishment, and you have deigned to attribute to me a part of that magnificent step forward. . . . The main highway lies open. May America travel it, and Europe will follow her.

After twenty more years had gone by, Victor Hugo was still moving ahead. To the Americans who visited Europe, a call on Victor Hugo was a required item of the itinerary. He was still keeping up a fruitful and high-minded correspondence with the poets of America who had been translating him for forty years. When the old man died, America put on mourning.

¶ . . . AND IN ECUADOR

Everything was immersed in the romantic spirit—poetry, the novel, politics. The Ecuadorian Juan Montalvo (1853–89) was one of the most distinguished stylists in the Spanish language, smiting the tyrants of his country hip and thigh. When he learned the news that an obscure fanatic had done García Moreno to death (on August 5, 1875), he exclaimed, "My pen killed him." His *Mercurial Eclesiástica* and his *Catilinarias* are models of political pamphleteering. The pages in *The Spectator* which reflected his life in Paris were reprinted in anthologies. He made great play of his quixotry and his mastery of language in

Capítulos que se le olvidaron a Cervantes (*Chapters that Cervantes Forgot*). His eulogy of Bolívar is on a par with Rodó's. During the period of his greatest literary fertility, as much of his life was spent in exile as in his own country. While he was in Paris as minister from Ecuador, he found out that Lamartine was living in dire poverty and obscurity. And as Lamartine, like Hugo, was required reading for every American, Montalvo proposed in an article to invite him to America. Even though the trip was never taken, Lamartine could not read the invitation without emotion. Montalvo had written:

> How happy it would make me to be his guide on the long trip! How happy to take him with me! He would see so many things worthy of him there! I would invite him on a mythological sail up the Duale: the tall tamarinds and the pineapples would bow to his passing. We would climb Chimborazo. From the peak of the Andes, he would cast his eyes over that immense America. We would descend the other slope to find ourselves in the midst of those plains where the green shoots of wheat quiver. There, where the old willows bend their heads, I have flowers and laurels. I would bring my guest to my father's house; we would wander together through the forest of Ticoa, and as we moved along our road, he would suddenly feel inspired by the divine fire to rest his eyes on the poetic lakes of Imbabura.

The journey that Montalvo proposed for the aged Lamartine would have killed him, but an unrepentant Romanticist could say no less.

¶ POLITICS AND LITERATURE

Politics was Spanish America's principal theme during the nineteenth century. It had to be. The nations had ceased to be colonies and were trying to work out a republican society. The ideas, the literary currents, the debates necessarily moved always in that direction. But if independence was the goal that the revolutionaries reached, revolution was not everyone's wish. A huge sector of conservative opinion still held the belief that the conservatives were the elect, even though they were being forced to resign themselves to the unleashed forces that proclaimed emanci-

pation. Within the republics, the conservatives thought of themselves as the heirs of the Crown. They took pride in maintaining
their religious tradition; they cherished monarchist sympathies
and kept before their eyes the picture of a central authority not
unlike the one that had been displaced. Independence without
revolution was the formula of these oligarchies, and they still
had some viability in Latin America. The collision between the
two bodies of opinion started a struggle that lasted through an
entire century.

The revolutionaries began as children of the Enlightenment,
then were converted to Romanticism, and finally to Positivism.
Those were the three stages of liberal thought. Each of the new
schools became in its turn an ideological tool for adapting the new
European philosophies to American reality. How each European
or North American country made its contribution can be seen as
though in a motion picture sequence. When Spain became a
Francophilic country, Jovellanos, Campomanes, Floridablanca,
and Feijoo all helped to make it so. They were Monarchists, but
they were also Voltaireans; they read Rousseau without realizing
that by so doing they were importing ideas that were to undermine the empire. When José Antonio de Rojas, a Chilean, went to
Spain, he was able to buy, with few restrictions, and to send
back to Chile a number of books that would be read in Santiago
as the last word: Diderot's *Encyclopédie;* the works of d'Alembert, Montesquieu, Helvétius, and the Scottish historian William
Robertson (1721–93); and the *Système de la Nature* by Baron
Paul Henri Dietrich d'Holbach (1723–89). Cities both large and
small received books more or less in the same way, and they were
read in Mexico City, Morelia, Lima, Chuquisaca, Buenos Aires,
Córdoba, Bogotá, Popayán, Caracas, and Guatemala City. The
literature of the English Industrial Revolution arrived later—
Hobbes, Locke, Hume, side by side with James Mill, John Stuart
Mill, John Austin and Jeremy Bentham. And from the United
States, the works of the Founding Fathers: Jefferson, Franklin,
Hamilton, Adams. . . . All those names held great political
significance during a period of crisis. From the beginning, the
republican culture of Spanish America adopted a political tone
that lasted through Romanticism and went on into Positivism.
The novel, the theater, and poetry all had an ideological base.
The contribution of the United States was immense. Sarmiento
introduced the theories of Horace Mann (1796–1859) into his
educational revolution. The struggle against slavery found a

romantic ally in *Uncle Tom's Cabin* by Harriet Beecher Stowe (1811–96). The heroism of the Indian nations was the theme of such novels as James Fenimore Cooper's *The Last of the Mohicans*. Henry David Thoreau (1817–62) set an example as a great writer who chose to go to jail rather than countenance slavery. Eventually federalism's divergence of aim and the suspicions aroused by the imperialistic posture of the Americans with the Big Stick forced the Latin Americans to maintain a critical attitude, but they balanced that against their devotion to Lincoln and their respect for the work of such great students of the southern continent as William H. Prescott (1796–1859), who penetrated the life of the Aztecs and Incas as few writers have and left imperishable works concerning them.

The first great Latin-American novel, *El Periquillo Sarniento* (*The Itching Parrot*), by José Joaquín Fernández de Lizardi (1776–1827), was an anti-Romantic work published in 1816. The author, a spiritual child of the French Revolution, was able to stand up to the Inquisition on behalf of freedom of the press. He adapted the picaresque style of Quevedo's *El Buscón* to depict the miseries of Mexico. *Don Catrín de la Fachenda,* another of his novels, presents a series of genre paintings like Goya's. Lizardi was a journalist with a sharp tongue as well as a liberal in the vanguard of the struggle for independence. He was sent to prison because his gazettes had created a great scandal. He was as much interested in social criticism as in libraries, freedom of the press, and Rousseauan pedagogy. The literature of manners and customs which he initiated was to become one of the popular forms in America. His divertisements were not gladdened by good humor; they were etched in acid to show the vices of the colony and the misery of the people. Fernández de Lizardi was writing at the time when Fray Servando Teresa de Mier was composing his travelogues of Spain and Europe. All that Fernández de Lizardi was saying freely, sarcastically, and mockingly about Mexico City, Fray Servando was saying about Rome and Madrid.

Romanticism and Realism were two different ways of expressing the same political attitude in the same period. Realism portrayed the vices of society; Romanticism spun the ideals for reform. Mexico will always oscillate between its romantic, poetic dreams and its ironic sense of reality. The Indian and Spanish elements fuse in the two attitudes, and the result is dualism, a chiaroscuro of internal struggle.

¶ MONARCHY OR REPUBLIC

The democratic, liberal type of republic which was to prevail in Hispano-Indian America was not in the beginning the obvious and natural solution it seems today. Until 1810—the year of independence—just two examples of the modern republic as a system of government existed: the United States and France. The United States came first, and it must be recognized as the first great invention of the New World. Although it had not yet stood the test of time, its success seemed assured. All the leaders of the other Americas admired that happy solution found by the Anglo-Saxons in becoming united, federated, free, and imbued with a broad feeling for progress. The French Republic, on the other hand, had been a failure. It had not withstood the heavy assaults of monarchical tradition, the longtime European yearnings for empire. Apart from the American example, monarchy was visible everywhere. Indeed some Americans were thinking of monarchy because it was a world-wide tradition; others hoped for a Utopian republic.

Bolívar made fun of the ancient Incan emperors evoked and extolled by José Joaquín Olmedo (1780–1847), the Ecuadorian who composed the "Oda a la Victoria de Junín," one of America's great lyric poems. Yet Bolívar set up the presidency for life in Bolivia's constitution. The "Incanate" form of government proposed by Miranda would have been a hybrid of the English Parliamentary monarchy and the past traditions of Peru, with a nobility composed partly of Indian chiefs. The plan was seriously considered.

Over almost all of America, when rebellion broke out, the cry was raised, "Long live Ferdinand VII and death to bad government!" An adroit tactic, because a sudden call to reject the monarchs who reigned by divine right and were supported by centuries of tradition could not rally full agreement. But the picture painted of the "beloved monarch" was that of a legitimate ruler being trampled on by Napoleon's boots. The Congress of 1822 in Mexico City petitioned Ferdinand to come to reign over America. The idea was not entirely extravagant, for the King of Portugal had already had to flee to Rio de Janeiro to escape the tempest raised by Napoleon. The difference was that Mexico would have liked Ferdinand simply as king of Mexico. Then along came Augustín de Iturbide (1783–1824), a vain and naïve man, fatuous and opportunistic, who had entered the Mexican capital in triumph in 1821, more by good luck than good management. Iturbide modeled himself on Napoleon and seized the moment to proclaim himself Emperor Agustín I. He was crowned amid great pomp and with a *Te Deum*. The most timorous Mexicans gave sincere thanks to God that a king had fallen to them from heaven, as it were. Iturbide created the Order of Guadalupe, gathered a court around him, and began to reign—without a peso. Fray Servando initiated the literature that made Iturbide an object of ridicule. And though he and many others were thrown into prison for *lèse majesté*, Agustín I was overthrown. His reign had lasted ten months.

All in all, paving the way to a republic in independent Mexico was turning out to be arduous work. The revolution was no longer against Spain; it was against monarchist, conservative, reactionary Mexico. The civil wars that broke out in Iturbide's time extended well into the twentieth century. Benito Juárez followed Iturbide to become the leader of the republic. A united front of reaction, conservatism, oligarchy, and the hierarchy of the Church harrassed him. They were all crying out in chorus for a king, and they sent a commission to Europe to find one; its headquarters was in Paris. Eugenia de Montijo, the beautiful and provocative Spanish wife of Napoleon III, encouraged and abetted it. The commission finally chose the Austrian archduke Maximilian and his Belgian-born wife Carlota, and the young couple accepted the invitation. Pope Pius IX gave them his blessing and encouragement to go to Mexico. When the ready-made emperor and empress entered the capital, the Church received them as no other ruler had ever been received there. Yet Maximilian was not precisely what the official church of Mexico would have wanted. His style collided with tradition: in a way, he was a final product of the Enlightenment, perhaps the herald of a false dawn of liberal thinking. To the nation, he seemed an intruder whose sovereignty was propped up by the French Army. Popular, democratic Mexico rejected him, and although a three-year struggle ensued, Maximilian was shot on the hill of Las Campanas near Querétaro. The republic recuperated through the efforts of Juárez.

Bolívar rejected the solicitations of some of his comrades in arms who insisted he ought to be crowned. In their opinion, no one but an emperor in the style of Napoleon would be able to control the nascent anarchy. The monarchical party was formed in Caracas, with José Antonio Páez, (1790–1873), Bolívar's chief of staff, at its head. Páez wrote a fervent letter to Bolívar, urging him to accept the crown. Briceño Méndez also favored the plan and wrote to the Liberator: "Believe me, this had hardly been mentioned in Caracas and other departments before each man had rushed up to offer his support. It is astonishing to see how the first Jacobins and the most fanatical demagogues have run to enlist under the new flags." Bolívar had to write a letter to Páez, checking their movements in these terms:

> I am not Napoleon nor do I wish to be; neither do I wish to imitate Caesar, much less Iturbide. Such examples seem to me beneath my dignity. The title of Liberator is superior to any that human pride can offer. Therefore, it is impossible to degrade it. Furthermore, our people are not French— at all, at all, at all. The republic has raised the country to glory and prosperity, given it laws and freedom. The magistrates in Colombia are neither Robespierre nor Marat. . . . Colombia is surrounded by republics, and Colombia has never been a kingdom. A throne would be appalling for its height as much as for its brilliance. Equality would be destroyed, and the colored [people] would see all their rights lost to a new aristocracy.

Long before independence, there had been monarchists in Argentina. General Manuel Belgrano (1770–1820), the designer of the national flag, was one of them. In a dialogue between a Spaniard and a Spanish American, he said: "We lack the main foundations, that is, the knowledge and the royal and real wealth on which to cement the republic." In 1808 a strong faction led by Belgrano asked for a constitutional monarchy to oppose the republican faction headed by Martín de Alzaga. The monarchists opened a correspondence with Princess Carlota (1775–1830), the sister of Ferdinand VII, then in Brazil, with the purpose of inviting the Spanish king to reign from Buenos Aires. Concerning this situation, Enrique Williams Alzaga wrote:

> At the close of the year 1808, the situation was alarming. Napoleon had fixed his eyes on the New World: Liniers, the viceroy of Río de la Plata was under suspicion owing to his national origin. Nothing good could be expected from the court of Brazil, either, known to be avid for territorial expansion into the Plata basin; Princess Carlota, in her turn, supported by the Creole party, insisted upon making a triumphal entry into Buenos Aires.

A confidential agent of the Prince Regent wrote him:

> A private letter from Buenos Aires, which I have before me, contains this phrase: "Yesterday the oath to our lord, Ferdinand VII, was taken in spite of the great Napoleon's orders, and there are as many opinions concerning our luck as there are heads." Another letter from the Inca Manco Capac, a descendant of the ancient kings of Peru, reveals that his pretensions are being put into play; so far the republicans have not raised their heads.

The final cry for freedom rose in Buenos Aires in 1810, and the Congress of Tucumán met and proclaimed the united provinces independent of Spain. General Belgrano declared that "even though the republican spirit ruled in former years, today it is a question of making everything a monarchy." He proposed the adoption of a constitutional monarchy and the offer of the throne to the Incas of Peru. Others favored continuing the negotiations started in Europe by Manuel José García and Bernardino Rivadavia before Charles IV, the queen mother, María Luisa, the minister Godoy, the cabinet of Brazil, and Ferdinand VII. On this occasion the man who came out for the republic and against the monarchy was a monk: Fray Justo Santa María de Oro. In 1819 special consideration was given to a proposal made by the French minister of foreign affairs through the Argentine envoy extraordinary, José Valentín Gómez, to place the Prince of Lucca on the throne of the constitutional monarchy thenceforth to be known as the United Provinces of the Río de la Plata. The French government offered to smoothe out whatever difficulties might be raised by the foreign powers. The secret record of the proceedings contained the following clauses:

> That these provinces must recognize as their Monarch the Duke of Lucca, under the political constitution to which they have sworn, with the exception of those articles that may not be adaptable to a form of government with a hereditary monarchy. . . . That the agreement enacted between the Minister of Foreign Relations of France and our envoy in Paris must be ratified within the period set by His Most Christian Majesty, and by the Supreme Director of this state. . . .

But Luis V. Varela says in his *Historia Constitucional de la República Argentina* that by then "the only thing that was wanted

was the independence of the United Provinces, recognized and
guaranteed by the European powers; the only thing not accepted
was the coronation of a prince of the ruling house of Spain."
Yet in 1823, as a consequence of agreements with the Holy Alliance, France planned a combined action against Spanish America
for the purpose of salvaging the monarchical ideal by setting up
a string of petty kinglets.

Two late-blooming cases of monarchical leanings appeared in
Ecuador. The first was that of General Juan José Flores, who
became the first president of the country and even though he was
a Venezuelan, was twice re-elected. When he was finally obliged
to step down from power, he went to Europe to interest Queen
María Cristina in an expedition of reconquest, which the Queen's
friends took up. Troops were recruited and their assignment to
quarters was authorized. But it came to naught. Later, the reactionary dictator Gabriel García Moreno entered into correspondence with the French chargé d'affaires to offer Ecuador to
France as a protectorate under Napoleon III. That was in 1859,
just fifty years after the freedom cry in Quito. García Moreno
wrote to the chargé d'affaires:

> I do not propose an honorary protectorate which would be
> a burden to France, as she would be mistress of these beau-
> tiful regions, and they would be of no use to her. . . . Here
> is what I am thinking of doing, and I shall certainly do
> it as soon as you give me confidential assurance of the pro-
> tection of His Imperial Majesty's government. The pro-
> visional government of Quito will inquire of the people
> whether they wish to be united with the French empire
> under whatever name you might well indicate to me before-
> hand.

France heeded the solicitation. If the project was left dangling,
it was only because the Emperor was considering a more tempting proposition from Mexico. In that case Napoleon III com-
promised himself to the extent of sending his troops to invade the
country.

The history of such monarchical glimmerings is long and sustained. It triumphed nowhere but in Brazil, and that was for very
special reasons. In Spanish America, which lacked an aristocracy
or a nobility, where a population alien to the traditional hierarchies
of Europe had matured, everything was conducive to a search for
a democratic system within which to order political life. Officially

the Church in Rome took the opposition, but that attitude merely served to create problems in the bosom of a Catholic society without halting the inevitable advance of the republic. In the end, the liberal intellectuals carried the field. The role of initiating the republican-democratic system in the world was given to America. Europe is moving slowly and with difficulty along the same route. France, the first country to become a republic there, the country that contributed as none other to laying the foundations for the democratic republic through the works of its philosophers and theorizers, is into its fifth republic. In Spanish America, where republican government—except in Mexico, with its two shaky monarchies—was in uninterrupted operation, the nineteenth century proved turbulent and difficult. But the new governments were always on the lookout for the best road toward true democracy. Independence for Haiti, however, started with a king.

¶ THE CHURCH AND THE REVOLUTION

The war for independence was the work of people who for four centuries had no religion other than Roman Catholicism. The revolutionaries did not abjure it. They started their war by invoking the name of God. In Caracas, at the moment when they vowed their independence, they also swore to defend the Immaculate Conception. In Mexico, Argentina, and Colombia, the troops carried pictures of the Virgin of Guadalupe, or Luján, or Chiquinquirá on their flags. Belgrano and San Martín held Rosary services with their troops at night. But practically and ideologically the revolution depended on liberal France, Protestant England, and the non-Catholic United States. The Masonic lodges and the French *Encyclopédie*, which served the cause of independence so well, were hotbeds of Protestants, freethinkers, and atheists. To the minds of the Liberators, the mere thought of being Protestants or atheists was altogether alien. Spanish America was carrying a heavy enough load on its back in fighting for independence from Spain without adding the burden of independence from Rome. On the other hand, anticlericalism was rife.

The Church had been too closely bound up with the fortunes of the Spanish state. It had shared the task of government. Education, hygiene, hospital services, control of immigration, and the defense of sovereign principles were all in its hands. Its wealth in America had increased disproportionately in the sun of privilege. Not only were immense tracts of land and extremely wealthy estates owned by the Church but it also held a good share of the urban property as well. Nothing could impel it to give up its share of responsibility. This was true particularly of the upper hierarchies and the innermost recesses of the religious orders.

On the other hand, the new philosophers had been introduced into universities run by the friars themselves—and not without effect. The village priests were more sympathetic than the hierarchy to the miseries of the faithful. And so the rebel priest and the revolutionary monk emerged beside the other partisans of independence. A Royalist Church and a Republican Church confronted each other face to face. A great many of the old Jesuits, the monks, and the parish priests did their share in organizing the new agitational groups. The official Church and the Inquisition moved against them. In Mexico the whole struggle was religious to some degree. Fray Servando Teresa de Mier, the forerunner, was persecuted and spent years imprisoned in monasteries. War began to the pealing of the church bells. The revolutionary priests Hidalgo and Morelos raised the standard of the Virgin of Guadalupe, and were tried by the Inquisition and shot after their defeat. Nevertheless, Catholicism was proclaimed the state religion in the Constitution of Chilpancingo. In Venezuela the insurgents were led by a Chilean canon, José Cortés de Madariaga. Another priest declared from the pulpit during an earthquake that God had sent it as a punishment for rebellion against the king. Bolívar quieted him by saying: "If Nature is aligned against us, we must fight against Nature." In Bogotá, Canon Rosillo was the hero of the day when independence was declared. In Chile, an Argentine canon, Juan Pablo Fretes, fought in the war.

The revolutionaries had to fight their hardest to gain control of the capitals of the viceroyalties, where the interests of the ruling class, the Crown, and the Church were most deeply rooted. The war itself was fought in the provinces, which accounts for its popular tone. All of America from Venezuela to Argentina had to mobilize before Lima would surrender. The resistance of the city of Mexico lasted until the second half of the nineteenth century. Opposition to the republican cause on the part of the Mexican ecclesiastical hierarchy lasted so long that the anticlericalism which it aroused has persisted into our own day: the frescoes by Diego Rivera on the walls of the National Palace and the portrait of Juárez by José Clemente Orozco testify to that feeling. Benito Juárez adopted a Protestant term for his campaign to re-establish the republic. He called it the "Reforma," a name given as a symbol to the main avenue of Mexico City. The laws of the Reform aimed to clip the wings of the Church's economic power, to undermine the foundations of its national influence. A philosopher of the period of the "Scientists," Ignacio Ramírez, "the Necromancer," poet and founder of the National Library, entitled the academic thesis that he presented to the university "God Does not Exist," and Diego Rivera painted that statement on his fresco for the Hotel del Prado.

❡ IN PARTIBUS INFIDELIBUS

The new republics were obliged to go ahead with their plans for civil reorganization, but the Church proved indecisive—when it was not openly hostile. Rome yielded to the pressure of the Spanish ambassadors, as Spain, in turn, played a protestant role by threatening to break with the Holy See unless the Pope refused to receive the ambassador whom Bolívar sent from Colombia. By that time there was not a single Spanish batallion in America. All the great powers had granted recognition to the Spanish American republics. Yet the ambassador from Spain to the Vatican was insistently claiming that the Spanish Crown must choose the bishops for America, and was citing the right of patronage. If upheld, Spain would be able to place her monarchist bishops in free democratic republics, which, in turn would mean a renewal of the war on the spiritual front. The ambassador managed to persuade the Pope to expel from the Papal States the representative of Bolívar, Ignacio Sánchez de Tejada, whóse mission it was to open relations with the Holy See and to plead that the sees falling vacant be left without appointed bishops. The ambassador also urged a policy of adherence to the Spanish monarch.

The first move made by Pope Pius VII on behalf of King Ferdinand came in 1816. That year was the worst republican America had to go through, as Spain made her strongest and most brutal effort to break it during the so-called Reconquest and Pacification. General Pablo Morillo (1777-1838) had the great scientists and thinkers who had embraced the republican cause shot in the Plaza Mayor of Bogotá. At the same time, the Pope promulgated the encyclical that stated:

> Whatever we do in this world through the power of Him who is a God of peace, and Who, in being born to redeem the human race from the tyranny of the Devil, announced

Himself to man through the medium of the angels, we have
believed to be proper to the apostolic functions that fall,
even though we may not merit them, within our competence,
which means we must arouse you further through this letter
to spare no effort to uproot and destroy completely the
pernicious discord and sedition that the enemy has sown
in these countries. . . . Such a holy purpose may be achieved
easily if each one of you will demonstrate to his flock with
all the zeal at his command the terrible and most serious
harm done by rebellion, and if you show forth the illustrious
and unique virtues of our dearest son in Jesus Christ,
Ferdinand, your Catholic King, to whom there is nothing
more precious than his subjects' religion and happiness;
and finally, if you fix your eyes on the sublime and immortal
examples which the Spaniards have shown Europe in scorn-
ing their lives and property in order to demonstrate their
invincible adherence to the faith, and their loyalty to their
sovereign.

Father Pedro de Leturia, S.J., has listed the pontifical stipulations that followed this encyclical: the faithful of America had to
confirm the new Order of Isabel the Catholic; grant the King
of Spain a third of the episcopal income and certain revenues from
the sale of cathedral and convent chapters in order to help equip
the squadron being fitted out in Cádiz to sail against Buenos
Aires; thank the metropolitan chapter of Mexico City for a gold
chalice and some money contributed to Ferdinand VII by promising them "to say the holy and pontifical Mass not once but many
times to obtain the perpetuity of Catholic unity, obedience to the
eminent prince Ferdinand VII, mutual concord, and a lasting
peace." Between 1815 and 1818, the Pope also distributed several
sees that fell vacant in the viceroyalties to persons loyal to the king,
mainly those native to America.

In 1821 the Congress of Chile sent one of its members to the
Holy See to establish and regularize relations between the republic and the Papacy. The result was the dispatch of the first
apostolic mission to America since independence. Giovanni Muzi
headed the group, which included two eminent figures in the
Church. One of them was Canon Gian Maria Mastai-Ferretti, of
the Italian aristocracy, a young man full of evangelistic fervor,
who "dreamed somewhat romantically of emulating St. Francis
Xavier in the missions to Arauca or Paraguay" (years later he

was to be crowned Pope Pius IX). The other distinguished missionary was a learned abbot, Giuseppi Sallusti, who wrote a picturesque, whimsical record of his trip. Father Leturia called him a "voluble and intriguing spirit, the dislocated joint in the mission."

The missionaries made their first stop in Montevideo. A year before the arrival of the Muzi mission, an English philanthropist had visited the city to peddle the Bible and proselytize on behalf of the Lancaster system, which had spread all over America, even though it was Protestant in origin. Montevideo was the first city in South America into which the Protestants had moved; they had held their own services there since 1807. With Protestantism came Freemasonry. That same year the Masons celebrated the feast of St. John by parading through the streets in full regalia. The lodge, which took in all the great Uruguayans of the period, was called The Brotherhood of Charity. In line with the Uruguayan practice, Canon Mastai-Ferretti was received in the lodge, and his signature was kept on the rolls. The Jesuit Guillermo Furlog based the following statement on Sallusti's report of the Canon's admission to the lodge:

> The chronicler says nothing as to whether the same honor was conferred on Sallusti and Mastai, but we suspect it was. . . . The truth is that shortly after Canon Mastai ascended the throne of St. Peter, the Italian and even the French press stated that he had been received in a lodge of the sect in America.

The mission moved on from Uruguay to Buenos Aires.

The situation in Argentina was so difficult that the mission failed completely. Bernardino Rivadavia, the man of the hour, was staunchly in favor of a liberal government. He had arranged for the suppression of some religious orders and for controlling the others by amending their by-laws; for confiscation of the property of the orders that were dissolved; for secularization of the cemeteries; for establishment of state primary schools; and for an official university in Buenos Aires with foreign lay professors. He was called "The Reformer." An Argentine patriot declared that Rivadavia's Buenos Aires should be dubbed "the new Geneva." But Buenos Aires was not the only liberal city. In San Juan (Argentina), the Basic Law, or the Charter of May was decreed, establishing freedom of religion. Muzi and his colleagues were not officially received, and although many people escorted them to their lodging in a parade from the port, with lanterns and singing children, they continued their tour a few days later without accomplishing a thing. Canon Mastai-Ferretti described Rivadavia as "hell's prime minister in South America."

The mission had a right to expect something better of Chile. After all, its government had invited the Roman envoys. But differences had arisen within the Church itself, and at what should have been the mission's finest hour, a liberal *"pipiolo"* [member of the liberal, anticlerical party] named Francisco Antonio Pinto was given the portfolio of Minister of the Interior. The dictatorship of General Ramón Freire (1787–1851) was proclaimed, freedom of the press was restored, and violently liberal newspapers were issued. The lodges and the anticlerical theater stepped up their activities. The bishop was removed from his diocese by decree as an enemy of independence, and the property of the churches was confiscated. Monsignor Muzi had no choice but to ask for their passports. He sent a final letter from Montevideo in which he tried to establish a bridge of understanding with the new republics. He said that the Holy See should adopt some appropriate means of fulfilling their spiritual needs even though the states had not been recognized politically. Father Leturia wrote:

> In honorably making this last acute observation, Monsignor Muzi could never have imagined that the readers of his letter in America would soon hear two news items that seemed designed to negate it: Pope Leo XII had expelled Tejada, the ambassador sent to Rome by Great Colombia, and had written an encyclical that upheld the rights of the King of Spain against the Spanish American revolution.

Pope Leo's encyclical stated:

> We have hoped for peace, but tranquillity has not ensued; we have waited for the time of healing, and terror has supervened; we have trusted in a time of health, and disturbances have occurred. But truly we have been pleased to think that a matter of such a serious nature will, through your influence and with the help of God, yield the prompt and happy result that we promise ourself, if you dedicate yourselves to making clear to your flock the august and distinguished qualities that characterize our dearly beloved son Ferdinand, the Catholic King of the Spains, whose solid and sublime virtue leads him to place the luster of religion

and the happiness of his subjects above the splendor of his greatness, and if you expound with due fervor for the consideration of everyone the great and inaccessible merits of those Spaniards resident in Europe who have given earnest of their always constant loyalty, together with the sacrifice of their own interests and their lives in homage to and defense of religion and the legitimate power.

Leo XII's encyclical was signed near the end of September 1824. Two months later, on December 9, the final battle of the war for independence was fought at Ayacucho. The armies of Ferdinand VII were defeated conclusively, and the last viceroy was expelled. The priests in America who had kept an eye on events as they developed sought some face-saving formula. The liberal minister of Santiago sent a copy of the encyclical to the bishop and asked him: "What have the Americans done that the universal shepherd of the Church should despise them?" The bishop wrote a pastoral letter labeling the apostolic brief an apocryphal document, a spurious substitute drawn up to disturb the people and turn them against the head of the Church. Opinion in Mexico was divided: the bishop of Puebla explained the encyclical as an abuse of the Holy Father's good faith, based on false and sinister information. The cathedral chapter of Chiapas declared it apocryphal.

The Pope seized his first opportunity to wipe a sponge across his encyclical, sending a letter to Guadalupe Victoria (1789-1843), the first president of Mexico which hailed him as the *"inclito duce"* (rightful leader) and congratulated him on the peace he had brought to the Mexican nation. He wrote affectionate missives to the acting president of Colombia, General Francisco de Paula Santander (1792-1840), and cleared the way for Tejada, the once-expelled ambassador, to return to Rome. But as the representative of the Spanish government still rejected Tejada's credentials and refused to abandon his own claims, the Pope received the Colombian ambassador clandestinely at night and then took steps toward recognizing him publicly. Spain had been routed more easily at Ayacucho than in Rome.

The encyclicals on behalf of Ferdinand VII brought Spanish America to the brink of schism. The Protestants and Masons were agitating for separation from Rome or, at the very least, for the appointment of bishops from the national clergy. The Abbot Pradt interceded from Paris as the combined Spanish-speaking republics continued to resist the efforts of the Holy See to subdue them through its proconsuls. An out-and-out schism split Guatemala. The Congress established an episcopal see in El Salvador and named José Matías Delgado, the father of his country, as bishop. The archbishop of Guatemala rebelled and declared the creation of the new diocese null and void. Fiercely polemical parties sprang up. The Pope was forced to fulminate against the Delgado "parish," really a creature of the republic's Congress, before the bishop would leave. Leo XII wrote to Delgado: "We are giving you a period of fifty days, which will be counted from the day when you receive these lines, which command you with our authority and exhort you with fatherly charity and the intimate affection of the heart to withdraw yourself from the illegitimately usurped ministry and return from the road to perdition onto which you have precipitated yourself, and to make amends that will fully satisfy us for the scandal you have given the faithful."

Bolívar was preparing to withdraw his mission from Rome and to protest to the Pope, with due moderation, the manner of his treatment of three million Catholics, with the warning that he could not be responsible for the consequences that might arise from agreement among the other states met in the Congress of Panama. That statement nearly amounted to a declaration of schism. But the letter instructing his ambassador to that effect was never delivered. It crossed the dispatches of Ambassador Sánchez de Tejada informing Bolívar of the Pope's new attitude and announcing that the bishops suggested by Bolívar had been appointed. The Pope's actual appointment of them gave the republic *de facto* recognition. The bishops were not like their predecessors who had been appointed *in partibus infidelibus* (to the territories of the infidel).

That was the end of the dramatic struggle and of the equivocal and unfortunate role played by Rome as the liberal republics were trying to get on their feet.

XV: *Civilization and Barbarism*

In Europe, the struggle for democracy was marked by bloody collisions between the nascent third estate and the nobility and clergy, some of whom were of the secular branch. In Spanish America, the new philosophy dashed itself against the tradition of three centuries. In Europe, the next hundred years were to be known as the "dull century." In America, it was the century of the *caudillos*. Blood was shed copiously on both continents. In the Old World, the dethronement of monarchs resulted in ephemeral republics, in efforts to found new empires, in the incorporation of principalities, duchies, and old aristocratic republics into larger nations, in supporting nationalism by a profit-seeking soldiery. Those political maneuvers cost the Old World infinitely more bloodshed than the civil wars in the Latin American republics. The methods of fighting were equally brutal everywhere, and the guillotine and the lash prevailed with apalling ease. In adopting democracy, the newer America had an advantage over Europe: it lacked a nobility. But the absence of a large, enlightened middle class made its situation manifestly inferior. The rise of its middle class took more than a century. Meanwhile the minority graduated by the universities had to perform many varied tasks. The highest political offices were held by a succession of physicians, engineers, and lawyers who left the professions they had mastered in the universities to enter politics. Otherwise, the military would have taken power. The educated leaders had been born into nations that were not only illiterate but also rawly inexperienced in the functions of representative government. They had to invent everything, to violate a tradition of three hundred years. The copious intermingling of blood strains could be considered conducive to a humble recognition of equality; nevertheless, Hispanic America was virginal in self-government.

In the United States, each town had a measure of self-government in the town meetings held by the citizens from the beginning. As a republic, it had only the one social problem of the Negroes as a stumbling block to normal political evolution. We remember the bloody war that problem gave birth to, and the consequences it left. In Spanish America, however, everything was a problem, everything an experiment. As for the Negroes there, although there was prejudice favoring purity of family blood, evident in genealogical pride and exclusive legislation, even though the slave was as much a slave there as in the colonies to the North—the problem was eventually solved in blessed peace. The laws abolishing slavery were approved with relative ease. But the sum total of the problems of that civilization, of its political and material progress, of training citizens and creating a civil society, was much more difficult to solve, more difficult than in Europe, more difficult than in the United States, because of the customs inherited from the monarchy and the obstacles created by an aggressive geography and a society of mixed blood. Neither the Indians nor the Negroes were an obstacle in themselves; the real stumbling block was history and a variety of circumstances. Few dictatorships have ever been as brutal as that of Rosas in Argentina, yet Rosas was a white man with blue eyes. Few men proved as effective in the liberation as Bolívar, who had a few drops of Negro blood. The leader who contributed most to the formation of Mexico as a nation, Juárez, was a full-blooded Indian who did not know a word of Spanish until he was eleven years old.

Everyone wanted justice. But how were they to kill the roots of colonial injustice? How discover the roads that would lead to the triumph of human dignity? They believed, and rightly, and they still believe, that the choice that corresponds to the expectations of the people can be achieved only through the democratic process. They saw in this process every kind of opportunity within the reach of everyone. All the lackeys—like Ruy Blas, as Sarmiento said—could aspire to the love of the high-born and to the presidency of the republic. But, for all that the Faustian sociologists of that new world always opened their drama by saying: in the beginning was chaos. Then came the sorting-out.

The viceroyalty of New Spain—Mexico—stretched its protective shadow across Central America and over vast regions held by the United States today. Finally it was bounded on the north by the Rio Grande, while in the South it gave birth to five new republics as each governorship or captaincy declared itself a sovereign and separate state. The viceroyalty of New Granada was divided into three republics: Colombia, Venezuela, and Ecuador. Later the United States arranged for its own advantage the emergence of a fourth, Panama. The viceroyalty of Peru left Peru, Bolivia, and Chile as its heirs. Argentina, Uruguay, and Paraguay were created from the viceroyalty of the Plata. Each division engendered in each new republic, large or small, a feeling of the touchiest kind of sovereignty. Each wanted to enjoy an independence as radical as it was sensitive. If there were not more wars among the nations, that was only because the frontiers were jungles, the peaks of the cordilleras, deserts. Then the national and nationalist *caudillos* emerged. The disunion of the republics was an emotional reaction against the blind, implacable centralism that Spain had exercised. For three hundred years even the remotest corner of America had been under the thumb of the officials, cedulas, and decisions of a distant court. Now the provinces that had suffered that kind of civic death were being reborn. People who had never known how to express themselves or to solve their own problems had now become "citizens" of "free states." The isolation of one from another was not completely arbitrary, however. The distances were enormous, the regions varied, and the economies different.

While the war for independence was going on, a common cause made all men brothers. Peru was governed successively by an Argentine, San Martín; a Venezuelan, Bolívar; a Bolivian, Santa Cruz; and an Ecuadorian, La Mar. Generals from Venezuela held office in five of the republics—Bolívar and Urdaneta in Colombia; Flores in Ecuador; Sucre in Bolivia; Bolívar in Peru; Páez in Venezuela. Chile granted a Spaniard, Mora, legal citizenship as a reward for drawing up its first constitution. Chile appointed a Venezuelan, Bello, rector of the University and named a Guatemalan, Irisarri, an ambassador. We could go on giving examples indefinitely. But as the century moved on, the *caudillos* dug themselves in behind the national boundaries. The word "foreigner" became more and more widely used as suspicion of neighbors increased.

Some of the republics never fought a battle against Spain. Uruguay and Paraguay did not win their independence from Spain, but from Argentina. And so the divisions went: Bolivia separated from Peru; Venezuela and Ecuador from Great Colombia. El Salvador petitioned the United States to back its withdrawal from the Central American Federation in order to be free of the Iturbide monarchy. Rafael Carrera took the government of Guatemala by assault to the cry of "Long live religion and death to the foreigners!" Francisco Morazán, the hero of Honduras, who then was governing El Salvador, represented the foreigners.

All over Spanish America the process of development was the exact reverse of that in the United States. The dialectical method ruled in Spanish America, obstinately, relentlessly, reiteratedly denying the old Spanish centralism and all its works—to such a degree that bullfights were forbidden and Castilian calligraphy was abandoned. The English derby and frock coat were adopted, Jockey Clubs were established, horse racing was encouraged, English furniture introduced. Each item was a "no" to everything Spanish. Anything English was liked because it was most expressively anti-Spanish. What was the point of the oft-repeated dialectic? Was it a fruitful source of progress? The truth is that the Spanish Americans, for all their negations, which grew into a destructive vice, could never succeed in accomplishing what the United States had accomplished by its accumulation of affirmations. There was civilization in the federalism of the United States, barbarity in the disparate Latin American states that walled themselves in behind their boundaries. Dialectic was not the formula for progress in the history of America during the nineteenth century. The Protestant God favored the northerners because they were more liberal, less exclusive. And whether the Anglo-Saxon did not have it in him to go from negation to negation, or whether he was encouraged by an empirical philosophy to be constructive, at the time when the hour of independence struck, he was more preoccupied in affirming himself as an entity than in deploring the past.

The final outcome of the negative Spanish American attitude, a mind-set so anarchical that it would not consider the confederation that Bolívar had dreamed of, was that it finally arrived at the theory of permanent revolution. When revolution as such had ceased and become government, the guerrilla fighters felt that they had been defrauded, wasted in the desolation of peace, "peace with all its horrors." A case in point is that of a man who had fought beside Juárez, a most distinguished and loyal general who vanished when Juárez became president. Juárez asked about him, and was told by his secretary: "I'm sorry to have to tell you this, Citizen President; the general has just come out against you because you're in the government now."

Yet in spite of everything, there were admirers of the federal system everywhere. And there were federal constitutions. Today most of the territory of America is ruled by federal constitutions: Brazil, Argentina, Mexico, and Venezuela. But not infrequently the rule of the *caudillos* was imposed over the federal law. Although Rosas maintained the most centralized of all the despotisms, his rallying cry was "Long live the Holy Federation!" Juan Vicente Gómez (1857–1935), once a member of the "liberal" party, ruled "federal" Venezuela so tyrannically (1908–35) that no leaf on a rain tree could move unless he said it should.

The organizers who did the most for Latin American progress bowed to the Anglo-Saxon formulas. Andrés Bello's good sense, English common sense, caused him to be labeled a conservative in Chile. Sarmiento, who stated the dilemma in *Facundo, o civilización y barbarie en la república argentina* (*Facundo, or Civilization and Barbarism in the Argentine Republic*), based his theory and practice of progress on the experience of North America and took Horace Mann as his guide when he laid out his school campaign. Rivadavia, Bolívar, Juárez, and Morazán opted for the Lancastrian system as a positive formula with which to start their campaigns for schools. University philosophy was reformed according to Bentham's tenets. But these aids to the spirit which the Anglo-Saxon lent were lost in the hereditary strife among the white, the Negro, the Indian, the mulatto, and the Latin American *mestizo*, a contradictory and difficult character.

¶ THE LIBERATORS IN EXILE

The contention between civilians and the military seemed to personify the clash between civilization and barbarity that Sarmiento had analyzed. In the beginning, the military were the liberators. All afire with the ideal of a civil republic, they headed the revolution, often without titles of rank, and in the course of time graduated into fighting generals. Many of the men who came after them had not fought in the war for independence or had served as minor officers, yet they believed they had an absolute right to govern with borrowed laurels as their crown. The war, so long and bloody, left the memory of heroism and victories. And as the republics were being born, they were stunned by the blare of brass and drums. The men in uniform absconded with the flags of freedom. That was a colorful war. But the liberators died in exile.

San Martín spent the very long twilight of his old age in Europe, forgotten by his own people. He had done more for Argentina by his example in retiring than by his martial triumphs, and for that reason it might be said that his exploits were acted on a stage twice the size of his country's territory. His retirement set an incomparable example in detachment as he bowed out to let democracy play its part. He could have claimed the presidency of his country with a better right than any man; he could have been the Washington or the Bolívar of Argentina. But he refused. By his exemplary gesture, he fixed the limits beyond which a general should not go by force of arms. He died in exile.

José Gervasio Artigas (1774–1850), the *caudillo* who created the republic of Uruguay, spent the last thirty years of his life as a simple farmer in Paraguay, his only companions a Negro and a dog. And that is how he died. Having set the republic of Chile on the right path, Bernardo O'Higgins retired to Peru and died in Lima like any ordinary citizen. Bolívar died an exile from Venezuela, on whose earth he could no longer rest his tired feet, and where his mines were in danger of confiscation. As he was on his way to Europe, where he and San Martín might have met in a melancholy exchange of views totally unlike their meeting in Guayaquil, death overtook the Liberator, but not by surprise. Sucre left Bolivia, the daughter born of his victory, after his troops had rebelled against him, shot at him, wounded him in the arm, and otherwise harmed him more than the Spaniards had been able to. Finally he was murdered from ambush. In Mexico, Hidalgo and Morelos were shot, as was Morazán in Costa Rica.

As the Liberators were dying in these various and tragic ways, the republics they had created were going to the devil, the devil who possesses those born in the shadow of heroes. In the end, the civilian had to be the hero who faced up to the devil. The nineteenth-century drama of Latin America was begotten by the conflict between devil and civilian.

¶ LIBERALISM IN ACTION

Bernardino Rivadavia (1780–1845) was a man of the Enlightenment and Liberalism in Argentina. Passionately eager to civilize, he brought into the university "the impious teachings of Locke, Condillac, Bentham, and the others, which the gaucho-colonial forces of reaction, incarnate in the tyranny of Rosas and equivalent to that of Ferdinand VII in Spain, had proscribed as nefarious and Europeanizing." The propitiatory agrarian reform already had been proposed as a sop. Belgrano said he would force the landowners to grant land, not by lease, but by emphyteusis [perpetual right], to those who were actually farm workers . . . in order to keep them on the estates, which they were to work as if they were their own. Rivadavia issued the decree forbidding the sale of land owned by the nation, but permitting it to be granted in emphyteusis. Andrés Lamas commented:

> Through this arrangement, one of the most essential foundations of the social order was changed. Individual ownership of public land came to an end. That land was to remain the property of the state in perpetuity—that is, it would be the property of the community by social law as well as by natural law. . . . But according to Article Two, the lands would be turned over to human labor under a perfected contract of emphyteusis. Such a contract would grant the land freely as an implement of work because the law would substitute for the fixed rule of ancient legislation another more flexible rule which, by reserving to the individual the capital and labor that were his, would absorb only that portion of the income derived from social work and social progress.

Thus, the agrarian problem that was stirred up and precipitated as if it were a new thing in the twentieth century had been stated a century and a half earlier with complete lucidity.

Reaction found its instrument in Rosas. Juan Manuel Rosas (1793–1877) was born of a rich family in the capital. As a young man, he decided to go native, to live the life of the gaucho, to be the first among the gauchos. He possessed both a strong will and decisiveness. Whenever he made a mistake, he himself would ask for punishment by the lash. In that fashion he learned, through his own flesh, to speak and to listen by means of the lash. The other gauchos were devoted to him. They followed him faithfully wherever he led them. As a soldier, he took no part in the war for independence. As an officer of the militia from 1813 on, he fought only the *caudillos* of the interior and the Indians whenever he had to put down sudden attacks. He did not have a drop of Indian blood.

His first step toward supreme power was the governorship of Buenos Aires. He would dash into the city at the gallop, surrounded by a retinue of gauchos also on horseback. He intended to set up against Rivadavia's liberal Argentina another Argentina as raw and wild as the pampas. He hauled down the blue-and-white flag of May and hoisted the red one as he pronounced himself the restorer of religion and law. By law he meant his will. He who was not for *him* and for *them*—i.e., religion and his law—was an enemy of his country, a *"vende patria"* (man who sells out his country), as Perón phrased it a hundred-odd years later. Rosas set up a police state that was always busy "cleaning up," with its own squad of "cleaners." These were the *"mazorcas"* (*más-horcas* or gallows-plus), a forerunner of the Gestapo and the Black Shirts, who used enemas of red pepper instead of the castor oil later administered by the Fascists of Italy. When, after surrendering his office, Rosas retired to the pampas in 1832, his wife, Doña Encarnación Azcurra, from one of the best families in Argentina, stayed in Buenos Aires to start a movement called the Popular Restorative Society, which would prepare for the *caudillo*'s return. Doña Encarnación doubled the resources of the police by enlisting Negro women in domestic service for her formidable espionage system.

Rosas let himself be called back once, twice, three times, before he finally yielded to the pleas of his followers. He entered the city in a wagon drawn by hundreds of men loyal to the red flag. He announced that he had come to wield "the entire sum of the province's public power for as long a time as should, in his judgment, be necessary." That mandate was given him. He would defend the Catholic, apostolic, Roman religion, and the cause of federation. The motto printed at the top of public papers and painted in red letters on the government buildings, the phrase that echoed and re-echoed during the night in the loud and monotonous voices of the nightwatchmen was: "Down with the savage, loathesome unitarians, long live the holy federation!" The women wore bows of red ribbon in their hair; the gentlemen donned red waistcoats. Finally the façades of the houses were painted red. Anyone who dissented from the motto fell into the hands of the *mazorcas*, who were rapidly degenerating into a band of assassins. The portrait of Rosas was mounted on the altars of the churches.

The Rosas dictatorship inspired the most brilliant period in Argentine literature, written in exile. The masterpieces of the nineteenth century were sometimes published in Montevideo, other

times in Santiago, Chile. The formula that Rosas offered for peace
was federation or death. Those who were not for *his* federation
were forced to flee and encamp in some other country. Of course
the federation perished because Rosas wanted to exercise absolute
power over the entire nation. Facundo Quiroga represented him in
the interior, Estanislao López along the coast. The two men were
equally zealous, but Rosas suspected that Facundo might be thinking of supplanting him. He therefore invited Facundo to visit him
in the capital, where he heaped him with honors and attentions.
They said good-bye as the best of friends and parted with an
embrace. When Facundo reached Barranco Yaco, Rosas's men
riddled him with bullets, a scene masterfully described by
Sarmiento in his book *Facundo* and by Jorge Luis Borges in a
poem. Rosas ordered a splendid funeral for him.

Rivadavia opened Argentina's doors to the world and laid the
foundations for the future of his country through immigration.
Argentina could not have kept her tryst with destiny without trans-
fusions of European blood into territory only thinly populated by
the Spaniards. Rosas, however, never thought along those lines.
He closed the doors to immigrants and antagonized England and
France by his conduct of foreign affairs until they blockaded the
port with their squadrons of ships. He involved Argentina in a
dispute with the United States and Great Britain over the Falkland
Islands, then picked up the gauntlet and kindled the national pride
by declaring himself the defender of the fatherland.

The fatherland that Rosas claimed was a country of small
farmers. He put through an agrarian reform, like Rivadavia, but
in reverse, giving everything to the landowners, "his" landowners.
So ran the Rosas dictatorship from 1835 to 1852. Meanwhile, a
constant succession of rebellions had been organized against him
by secret revolutionary groups, and at last the country was able to
rebel successfully. The gospel of the exiles echoed throughout
Argentina. Even the landowners finally ranged themselves alongside the "unitarian savages," and Rosas was defeated by Justo José
de Urquiza (1800–70), a former Rosas general, at the Battle of
Monte Caseros. The dictator escaped to Europe and died in England of old age. An abundant literature was written about him. His
biography can be drawn indirectly from the books of Sarmiento,
Alberdi, and Echeverría. News notes by travelers contain a wealth
of information about the Rosas regime. Among the visitors was a
great English scholar who stopped off in Argentina during his trip
around the world—Charles Darwin.

Men like Domingo Faustino Sarmiento (1811–88) and Bartolomé Mitre (1821–1906), who were to build a new republic, fought beside Urquiza to overthrow Rosas. But Urquiza's triumph did not immediately tip the scales on the side of Buenos Aires, for after all, he was a mere *caudillo* from the interior. But it opened the way for the new progressive constitution inspired by Juan Bautista Alberdi (1810–1884). Alberdi's formula can be stated simply: to govern is to settle. Soon Buenos Aires became the Mecca of immigrants from Europe. "America must become coastal and maritime, instead of mediterranean and internal," he said. Mitre, imbued with that idea, returned the capital to Buenos Aires as governor of the province and later president from 1862 to 1868. Sarmiento succeeded him. Always an extremist, Sarmiento prescribed a white civilization. He said: "South America will lag behind and will lose its holy mission and become a subsidiary of modern civilization unless we follow the United States." He considered white immigrants by far the most desirable—Anglo-Saxons if possible, but not Spaniards. He organized the magistracy, multiplied the number of primary and secondary schools, encouraged technical instruction, established the library, museums, and the observatory. He was the initiator of railroads and the telegraph. The anarchy of the early years of independence had abated to some degree by then. After all, Rosas had taught both his enemies and his friends to obey. This involuntary service performed by despotism was to prove useful in the future because it helped a patriot government to move ahead, although it had been sterile under the government that had created it in the interests of its own selfishness.

¶ A PRELUDE TO DESPOTISM

Rosas seized power as a restorer of religion. All over America, others followed his example. They sought support for their ambition from the clergy and the old families who were suspicious of liberal reforms like those made by Rivadavia. Any ambitious man could fly the standard of the Virgin, ring the bells, and rise to the presidency. In Ecuador, the Virgin of Quinche was publicly denounced for permitting the defeat at Valdivieso. Rafael Carrera in Guatemala and García Moreno in Ecuador rose to power as soldiers of Christ.

Guatemala then included all of Central America, which formed a bloc initially called the United Provinces of Central America. If this union (which lasted from 1821 to 1823) had continued, the provinces would have acted as a strong state between Mexico and Colombia. The actors in the conflict in the United Provinces were Francisco Morazán (1792–1842), the "father of his country," who favored federation, and the *caudillo* Rafael Carrera (1814–1865), who brought about the fragmentation. Morazán, a Honduran, was the son of a French Creole from the West Indies. His ideas came from his reading of books by the Encyclopedists, which caused him to fall in love with liberal principles. Carrera lived and died illiterate. He was born in Guatemala and fought in the name of religion.

Once Central America became independent of Spain and Mexico, the federation was proclaimed and a charter inspired by the United States Constitution was ratified. But it was not at all easy to centralize in Guatemala City, the capital, a power that the other provinces would not accept on the basis of the oldest history. Morazán, president of the federation, had to travel with his government from one city to another and face the fire of his enemies. He was sustained by his faith in progress and in enlightened revolution, by his courage and military genius. One of his first statements as syndic of the peasants was:

Not silver nor any of the precious metals is the wealth of a realm; it is agriculture. The metals are nothing more than the price of everything and the prime movers of dissension whenever they are the source of abundance and of all virtue. . . . There is no village, however poor and miserable it be, that does not have a schoolmaster to educate the youth. And yet, who could believe that wealthy Tegucigalpa, with so many patriotic citizens, does not have one? . . . Without a school there can be no enlightenment; there can never be good customs; there will never be equality either of persons or of interest, or of property; and without education we shall expose our necks to a yoke that we shall never be able to shake off.

When Morazán came to power, he implanted the Lancaster system. It is touching to read today the reports on the examinations held at that time in Guatemala to test the value of the system. The tone is anticlerical. Capital punishment, employed previously by the conservatives, was abolished, but anyone who appeared to be an enemy of liberal thinking was exiled. Among the exiles were Archbishop Casaus and the monks of the Dominican and Franciscan orders who were "believed to be responsible for the assassination of Vice-President Cirillo Flores by a mob of Indians incited by some priests." A penal code copied from the code of the United States was drawn up, inspired by the ideas of Edward Livingston (1764–1836). The civil code was reformed, and the residue of Spanish legislation was set aside. Civil marriage was made legal, and legitimate and illegitimate children were given an equal right to petition for a pension in case they did not inherit. Natural children shared equally in the estate if they were recognized by their fathers. "The clergy, the nobility, and the servant class called upon heaven, declaring that the skies would rain fire on a country that had provoked the divine and celestial wrath in such a way."[1]

Carrera, at the head of the clerical party, rebelled against Morazán and forced him to leave the country. Morazán went to Peru but returned with a fleet of five ships. Costa Rica received him with acclaim. His triumph was ephemeral, for the opposition regrouped its forces, took him prisoner, and, after a summary trial, shot him. Today he is remembered as "the father of his country."

Carrera then took over the government to the cry of "Long live religion and death to the foreigners!" What he killed was the federation. A proclamation distributed in Matequescuintla reveals the tone of reaction:

> Let us turn our eyes to God and His Most Blessed Mother. . . . We have met with many and various people to make an end to the foreigners, the heretics of Guatemala. We shall do away with them by bloodshed and fire. . . . We have patron saints and divine patronesses who shall lead us.

As soon as Guatemala, where Carrera remained in charge, broke away from the other provinces, each one took its own path. He governed from 1838 until 1865, the year of his death. As *caudillo* he kept a hard, despotic peace. He blazed trails. He annulled the anticlerical laws. He opened the country to the Jesuits and placed the schools in the hands of the clergy, as in the time of the Spaniards. He signed a concordat with the Holy See, the first of its kind in America. The Pope decorated him for his services to the faith. Justo Rufino Barrios (1835–1885) succeeded Carrera. Barrios, a progressive, introduced electric lighting and the first rail-

---

[1] Dueñas: *Biografía del General Morazán.*

way. He was the "scientific man" of Central America, who confiscated church property, expelled the Jesuits, and did away with tithing. He proclaimed freedom of religion, re-established civil marriage, which had been initiated by Morazán but abolished by Carrera, and multiplied the number of public schools. He even exiled the archbishop. Immigration and coffee-growing were encouraged. In an attempt to restore Central American unity, Barrios invaded El Salvador, but he was killed at the battle of Chalehuapa, leaving a "liberalized" Guatemala . . . for a short time. Reaction came back into power under Manuel Estrada Cabrera (1857–1924), who restored the barbaric cycle, although with some touches of progress. The Cabrera dictatorship lasted twenty-two years after its beginning in 1898. The men who succeeded him played roles that did little to diminish the turbulence of Guatemala's political history.

In the other Central American republics the swings of the pendulum were similar. Dictatorships have lasted into our day. Tiburcio Carías Andino (born 1876) ruled Honduras for sixteen years, from 1932 to 1948; Maximiliano Hernández Martínez (born 1882), "the sorcerer," headed the government of El Salvador for fourteen years, from 1930 to 1944. Nicaragua has been a dictatorship ruled by Anastasio Somoza (1896–1956) and his family since 1933. Guatemala brought forth Castillo Armas and Miguel Ydigoras Fuentes in the second half of the twentieth century. The break-up of the United Provinces prolonged into our day the rule of the barbarian *caudillos* of the nineteenth century.

¶ GARCÍA MORENO, THE JESUIT DESPOT

The most remarkable of the dictatorships in Spanish America was that of Gabriel García Moreno (1821–75), founded beneath the shelter of religion in Ecuador. That republic, born of the separation from Great Colombia, was the ancient kingdom of Quito. For a while after the split, the country was in a state of almost total anarchy. The boundaries were uncertain and its leaders came from everywhere. Three times the Venezuelan general Juan José Flores (1801–64), a *mestizo* from Bolívar's armies, was president. Another general rose against him: General Luis Urdaneta, a white man. The mulatto Colombian general Juan Otamendi smothered the uprising by primitive methods; on one occasion he shot three hundred veterans. Foreign names abounded, too: Colonel Hall, Colonel Wright, Colonel Klinger, Captain Illingsworth. . . . Flores fiercely defended the borders of his adopted country, but in adversity his patriotism waned, and he opened negotiations with Spain for the reconquest of Ecuador. Finally a man who embodied the principles of enlightened revolution, Vicente Rocafuerte (1783–1847), emerged out of the chaos. He had been the envoy from Quito to the Cortes of Cádiz in 1812 and was affiliated with the Spanish liberal party, so loyal to it that when the Peruvian delegates invited him to Ferdinand VII's levée, he returned a haughty refusal. He was expelled from Spain. After that, he dedicated himself to the struggle for independence and became a friend of Bolívar. Rocafuerte traveled in the United States, and went on to Mexico, where he became a true Mexican. He published a pamphlet on the representative system. The Mexican republicans sent him to Washington to negotiate for the non-recognition of Emperor Iturbide. When Iturbide fell, the republicans sent Rocafuerte to England as secretary to the legation empowered to negotiate for the recognition of the republic. There he was known as "the principal instigator of the anti-Díaz and anti-Catholic campaign then being plotted from the Thames, [at White-hall] in such alarming proportions as to cover almost all the Spanish American continent."[1]

Rocafuerte later was sent to Denmark and Hanover to conduct negotiations with their governments. He traveled through Holland, Prussia, and France. He arranged a loan from England. When he was informed that Bolívar was planning to accept the crown as emperor, he wrote a fiery pamphlet attacking the Liberator before he had paused to verify the news. Rocafuerte and Bolívar already had had differences. "He opposed the Liberator," O'Leary tells us, "because the latter would not permit the Methodist missions to preach in Colombia and Peru and because he did not wish to appoint a patriarch independent of the Pope or to establish a Church of Colombia." Rocafuerte went back to Ecuador to preside over an enlightened government. He closed the convents and opened schools. He initiated education for women, established chairs of philosophy, law, and medicine, founded the national museum, created a school of agriculture, and established a naval training school. Like Jovellanos, he sponsored agriculture: "The number of lawyers," he said, "is rising to infinity, and they are a veritable plague in a country as ill-civilized as ours . . . yet we have no agronomists." He devoted a good deal of thought to

[1] Leturia: *Relaciones entre la Santa Sede e Hispanoamerica.*

public works. "We are surrounded by high mountains that shut off our access to the sea, and we are not engineers." He saw that textbooks were published for distribution in the schools. Like Olavide in Spain, he hoped to colonize the Esmeraldas River basin regardless of whether or not the immigrants were Protestants. He wrote:

> I know very well that deluded men unversed in the field of colonization, government, and moral sciences, characterize freedom of religion as heresy, impiety, a direct attack on Christianity, and a horrendous crime against religion; nevertheless, patriotism demands this new effort on behalf of the principle of tolerance, upon which, I am convinced, the future prosperity of the republic depends in great part.

But rejection of reaction provided only the flimsiest base for hope. Rocafuerte was president of Ecuador only four years, whereas García Moreno was its dictator for fifteen. And García Moreno was no mere illiterate like Carrera; he was a well-grounded fanatic who had studied science in France and was as much in favor of material progress as he was an avowed enemy of liberal advancement. He wrote verse in the neo-classical style. His will was of cold steel. García Moreno's political career began when, as a leader of the conservatives, he forced the entry of the Jesuits into Ecuador after their expulsion from Colombia. The matter was brought before the national assembly, which instantly expelled them. As he watched the priests leave, surrounded by people who had gathered to say good-bye to them, García Moreno shouted: "We shall sing a *Te Deum* when you come back before another ten years have passed." He was as good as his word after he came into power. Some people considered this a miracle and the fulfillment of a prophecy. García Moreno turned the schools back to the priests and consecrated the republic to the Sacred Heart. Even before he had taken over the government, he wrote to the General of the Company of Jesus: "I am addressing Your Reverence to beg him to send without delay forty or fifty Jesuits to Guayaquil, the main port of this republic." He applauded the delivery of Mexico to Emperor Maximilian and inveighed against Italian unity. Nevertheless he encouraged public works, opened technical schools and academies, the library, and the conservatory of music. He brought technical missions in under contract. But he punished his enemies with unspeakable cruelty. He executed mercilessly, torturing his victims in order to wring the hearts of mothers, wives, and daughters. Whenever anyone tried to intervene on behalf of the victim, he defied the public's charity with arrogance. He named his first newspaper *El Zurriago* (*The Scourge*), the term that best fits his character. When it seemed to him that the Church was not as strict as he would like it to be, he rounded even on it. He was more Papist than the Pope. When a priest was caught *in flagrante* with a woman, García Moreno forced him to appear before the Senate drunk and in his smallclothes. The papal nuncio protested and asked that the priest be released from jail, but the inflexible dictator turned a deaf ear. "His" congress approved a new constitution that was called the "Black Charter."

Emotional and emotion-evoking biographies have been written about García Moreno by Ecuadorians and non-Ecuadorians. The Jesuit Father Pedro Severo Gómez Jurado said in his *Vida de García Moreno* that to many Catholics in America and Europe the greatest man the continent ever brought forth was not Bolívar but García Moreno. Benjamin Carrión subtitled his book about the dictator *El Santo del Patíbulo* (*The Saint of the Gibbet*). The Argentine Manuel Gálvez (1882–   ) eulogized both Rosas and García Moreno in separate books with the same point of view. But Juan Montalvo wrote: "García Moreno divided the people of Ecuador into three equal parts: one he dedicated to death, another to exile, and the third to slavery." The Pope thanked García Moreno for his devotion to the Church and sent him the relics of a saint for the cathedral in Quito. Leo XIII said after the dictator's assassination that he had died for the Church at the hands of the impious. The archbishop of Quito began the required maneuvers for his canonization.

Later events were the fruit of the passions the dictator had aroused. Ignacio de Veintemilla (1830–1909) was at the opposite pole from García Moreno as a person, but even worse as a dictator. After balancing one against the other, Montalvo preferred García Moreno and wrote the goriest of his books to attack Veintemilla, whom he called "Ignatius the Knife." Montalvo entitled his book *Las Catilinarias* (*Orations against Catiline*). He also wrote a book fiercely opposing the archbishop entitled *Mercurial eclesiástica* (*The Mercurial Ecclesiastic*). The archbishop fumed. "We condemn *The Seven Treatises* because they contain heretical proposals, scandalous maxims, principles contrary to the revealed dogma."

The struggle in Ecuador lasted more than a century. Eloy Alfaro (1864–1912), the spiritual opposite of García Moreno, fought him and Veintemilla with equal passion. As a liberal, he supported the free public school, confiscated the properties of the convents or the "dead hands." Yet he was tolerant and always ready to conciliate. Far more Christian than García Moreno, he even fought for the canonization of Mariana, the Lily of Quito, the flower of mysticism. During his progressive administration, he was responsible for the construction of the railroad that joined Quito to Guayaquil, the American railway most difficult to build. But the religious struggle had penetrated his country so deeply that he had to fight a running verbal battle and suffer a rain of stones because the engineers who built the railroads were English and Protestant. The reactionaries believed they were doing religion a great service by hindering the work of the Englishmen in Ecuador. Alfaro's embattled opposition had the air of a barbarian crusade as Bishop Schumacher, of German birth, led an army of ragamuffins across a jungle to the capital. The Bishop encouraged them with speeches that sound like a pastoral letter:

Choose between God and Satan, for that is the question! Christian Soldiers! He who falls in the battle against impious radicalism will win the palm of martyrdom. Rescue the Lord from the spirits of Hell. We ask this in the name of the Father, the Son, and the Holy Ghost!

Alfaro was overthrown in 1911. In 1912 he was captured, taken to the panoptican, a circular prison in Quito, and turned over to the aroused mob, which murdered him and dragged his naked body through the streets.

¶ DOCTOR FRANCIA

Dr. José Gaspar Rodríguez Francia (1776–1840), the taciturn despot of Paraguay, set up a dictatorship that might be characterized as black in comparison to the red dictatorship of the Argentine Rosas. Francia was elected dictator in 1814, perpetual dictator in 1816, a position that he held until death. But whereas Argentina wanted access to the sea in order to navigate and establish contact with the world, Paraguay wanted to draw into itself and hide within its own seclusion, an impulse inherited from the Jesuits. Dr. Francia, true to that heritage, would have no relations with any country in liberated America. In his view, such friendships corrupted. He believed that his neighbors were sowing the seeds of anarchy, which he did not intend to let germinate in his land. That turn of mind suited the nascent national consciousness. Independence had hardly been proclaimed in 1812 before Paraguay established the *albinagio*, "that is, the inability of Europeans to transmit their property by will or inheritance, to any relative or foreigner resident abroad: it must of necessity pass to kinsmen in Paraguay, or in default of them, into the control of the exchequer."[1] This point of view prevailed for a long time. Natalicio González states that as a result of the rout of the Paraguayan forces in 1870, which ended the War of the Triple Alliance,

> a foreign citizen was named head of the Paraguayan Church. The people, depressed by their terrible defeat, rose from their prostrate position to reject this affront to them. Such a schism resulted that there was no way to restore religious peace until a son of the Paraguayan earth was anointed bishop of the offended nation.

In contrast to the Rosas dictatorship, with its gauchos rioting through Buenos Aires, Francia's was dark and silent. The despot had been educated in Córdoba, Argentina, had started a career in the Church, and then had changed over to law. He had read the Encyclopedists. He interpreted the Social Contract as an accord between himself and the people by which the people delegated all their power to him. Rousseau himself had foreseen such a contingency. Even the archbishop of Córdoba was refused permission to cross the border when he tried to enter Paraguay as he fled from Argentina. The future Pope Pius IX, who dreamed in his youth of living in the old missions, once wrote in Rome:

> At the time of our stay in America, Paraguay was inaccessible to such a point that not even news could be sent out of it because of Dr. Francia's rules. Suffice it to say that the bishop of Asunción, who is still living, was confined to the convent of his Franciscan order two years ago by order of that very same Francia.

As we learned in Chapter XII, the great naturalist Bonpland, a companion of Humboldt, crossed the border inadvertently, and Francia never let him leave. Bolívar petitioned Francia in vain to release him, but Francia was content to give him the keys to

---

[1] Natalicio González: *El Estado Servidor del Hombre Libre.*

the country in prison, and provide him with a good country woman as a companion.

The dictator was responsible for the shooting of the towering figures of the May revolution: Yegros, Iturbe, and Montiel. He was capable of blood-curdling refinements in cruelty. When it was his whim to make a concession to a condemned man, he would let him choose the bullet that was to be loaded in the gun that would kill him. Francia broke with the Vatican and appointed his own bishops. He shunned women. He had no friends. He was a spare eater, a more than moderate drinker, and he always dressed in black. Even his mind was somber; his punishments were implacable, utterly cold. Comte dedicated one day of the year on his calendar to Dr. Francia, an act consistent with the sociologist's way of drawing up the almanacs of his religious creed.

Francia's regime could not be called barbarism: it was silence. Barbarism began after Francia, as Paraguay made contact with other peoples. "El Supremo," the name by which Francia passed into Paraguayan history, had forewarned the country of that danger. Six months after El Supremo's death, his nephew Carlos Antonio López (1790–1862) took over the power and opened relations with Argentina and the Vatican. After Carlos Antonio's dictatorship came that of his presumed son, Francisco Solano López (1827–70), who had been educated in France. When he returned to Paraguay, he brought with him his Irish mistress, Eliza Lynch, whom he had been keeping at Quatrefages in France, and their son. After he succeeded his father, Solano López promoted the priest who married them in Paraguay to a higher place in the hierarchy. Mme Lynch was a formidable lady; he was arrogant and vain. He fancied that he resembled Napoleon. As he dreamed of an industrialized Paraguay, he introduced railroads, built ships, manufactured paper—and fieldpieces and rifles, too, for he aimed to keep a big army in the European style in the green heart of his country. He got into difficulties with Brazil, and before long his small country was fighting hand to hand against its united neighbors: Argentina, Brazil, and Uruguay. Everyone fought, even the old men, the children, and, of course, the women. Looking like a fiery Amazon, Mme Lynch rode her horse among the troops as they moved through the jungle. Half the population was sacrificed. Of the 525,000 inhabitants of Paraguay before the war, only 221,000 were alive when it was over. Most of them were children, old men, and women, although the women had been killed off like the men. Toward the end of the war, when the men ran out of cartridges, the women would come boiling out of the trenches and drive back the Brazilians by breaking bottles over their heads. Solano López himself died in 1870 on the field of battle.

The epic of Paraguay is one of the fabulous true stories of America. The country fell back into its silence. Talking was but a murmur in Guaraní among the women who wove a cloth like cobwebs, called *ñanduti*. Those Paraguayans who were in good enough condition to beget and conceive slowly brought life back to the hearths, hands back to labor. The heroic style of the struggle was revived and re-enacted in the Chaco War with Bolivia between 1932 and 1935. H. G. Warren noted that from it Paraguay gained twenty thousand square miles of territory at the cost of two Paraguayans and three Bolivians for every square mile.

The latest dictator, Major Alfredo Stroessner, born in 1912, seized power in 1954. He still rules by the sword and the prison. Four hundred thousand Paraguayans are now living in exile by choice, mainly in Buenos Aires. Father Ramón Talavera ventured to denounce from the pulpit the tortures to which political prisoners were subjected. The vicar general and the archbishop of Asunción supported his speech. Father Talavera was exiled. His expulsion marks the extent to which the country has evolved. In Francia's day, everyone, alive or dead, stayed inside the country. Today, it is possible to escape, owing to the development of communications. Stroessner is a product of the German race. He comes from one of the families that established a small anti-Semitic colony in Paraguay at the beginning of the century. Nietzsche's sister helped to select its members. Stroessner typifies a phase of the German's philosophy—the will to dominate. He is a Zarathustra who has had his will of a people who like to play country dances on the harp. He rules with a German fist from a city in which the streets are perfumed with orange blossoms.

¶ THE BARBARIAN CAUDILLOS

The expression "barbarian *caudillos*" became current after Alcides Argüedas (1879–1946) chose the phrase as the title of his *History of Bolivia*, in which Mariano Melgarejo (1818–71) stands out as the most dramatic figure. This bold and irresponsible despot came from a background stranger than that of any other *caudillo*. Sensual, alcoholic, and almost illiterate, he dismayed everyone by the brutality of his actions, and by his success in having his own way by stunning boldness and self-assurance. This Bolivia of the barbarian caudillos was born as a republic bearing the Liberator's name as its lodestone, out of a background of great culture focused around the amassing of the traditions of an indigenous civilization that culminated in the Incan Empire. It was the first to send forth the freedom cry in 1809. The University at Chuquisaca (now called Sucre) and the Academia Carolina had educated a generation whose members were to shine brightly in Upper Peru and illuminate Buenos Aires, Santiago, and Lima. One of the most distinguished men in Spanish colonial culture, whose name is remembered today, was the archbishop Benito María Moxo (1763–1816). This great cleric fought in the Indian and *mestizo* uprisings of 1809 and was expelled by General Rondeau, the rebel leader of the country. Moxo carried the philosophy of the Enlightenment first to Mexico and later to Upper Peru. He belonged to the monarchist school, and was one of the company of advocates of enlightened despotism, like Archbishop Caballero Góngora of New Granada. Moxo traveled with a museum and library, was an enthusiastic student of botany, and left a work of high literary quality in his *Cartas Mexicanas*.

One of the most brilliant Bolivian writers of the past century, Gabriel René-Moreno (1836–1908), drew a magnificent picture of Chuquisaca in *Los últimos días coloniales del Alto Peru* (*The Last Colonial Days in Upper Peru*). Justices, professors of theology, intriguers, embryo politicos, and syllogists file through its pages against the background figure of Archbishop Moxo. "A peripatetic republic of pompous doctors, competitive lawyers, lecturing schoolmasters, and assiduous students . . ." It was a drawing and a satire, with some resemblance to Concolorcorvo's earlier *Lazarillo de Ciegos Caminantes*, but with a knowledge of the outstanding figures of Chuquisaca who, like Mariano Moreno, went forth to breathe the spirit of May into Argentina, or like the restless Bernardo Monteagudo (1785–1825), born in Tucumán, Argentina, a comrade of San Martín and O'Higgins and later a friend of Bolívar, a revolutionary who took part in the uprising at La Paz in 1809, a journalist who organized the Patriotic Society of Buenos Aires and founded the newspaper *Martir o Libre*, and a politician who helped to establish the Peruvian republic. Bolivia produced great minds worthy to rank alongside the best of the Argentines. For example, there was Vicente Pazos Khanti (1779–1845), a pure-blooded Indian on his mother's side, who was born in the village of Ilabaya. He traveled through

Europe, where he concerned himself with a great variety of things. He was one of the trail blazers of independence. In London, he published his translation of the Gospels into Aymará and addressed a number of letters to the Earl of Aberdeen on the political problems of Spain and America. Diez de Medina wrote of him:

> Historian, sociologist, a journalist of quick insights, he was accustomed to soar among the splendors of the authentic man of letters. In describing the landscape of Upper Peru in evocative images, he remarks on the natural grandeur of the Andes, 'where only man is small,' in a masterly sketch that shows for the first time the dramatic antinomy of our republican reality: a stage too big for such a diminutive settler.

After Bolivia had been established, generals from every country met there. Venezuelans, Colombians, Peruvians, and Argentines. Many of the great officers—Santa Cruz, Blanco, Ballivían—had been trained in the royalist armies. As the war progressed, they moved over to the republican cause, and in the end they superseded the men with a university tradition. Then came the moment when the frail lamp of science was put out as the campfire was lighted.

Antonio José de Sucre (1795–1830), a great, disinterested, and courageous man, opened the history of Bolivia. He was a Venezuelan, victor in the battle of Junín, marshal at Ayacucho, and liberator of Bolivia. He became president of the country, was dragged from office and forced to resign at gun point, with barely time to turn over the command to another marshal: Andrés Santa Cruz. Santa Cruz convened the congress, which elected General Pedro Blanco president. Blanco was nominated in Chuquisaca and entered La Paz on December 25, 1828. Within five days, he was a prisoner. They gave him the palace as his prison and murdered him. His body was dragged through filth. General José Miguel Velasco succeeded him. Velasco, a more prudent man, summoned Marshal Santa Cruz to take over the command. Another kind of story begins with Santa Cruz.

The presidency for life which Bolívar had proposed was changed to a two-year term. The Bolivian Constitution of 1826 was nullified in 1831; that year's, in turn, was nullified in 1836; that of 1836 was replaced by another in 1939; and that was exchanged for still another in 1943. . . . By 1961, the country had had twenty constitutions. The earlier ones were annulled by decree of the generals. Sucre and Blanco were both murdered. Troops from Peru under Gamarra invaded Bolivia and withdrew only after the expenses of the expedition and all their other expenses had been paid. When Santa Cruz finally appeared, a priest said that his rise to power had come through the designs of Divine Providence. Anyone who reads the Bolivian documents of the ninteenth century might gather that Divine Providence has played a leading role in its history.

Marshal Andrés Santa Cruz (1792–1865) was born in the small settlement of Huarina, on the shore of Lake Titicaca. His mother, Juana Basilia Calaumana, was descended from Chief Calaumana of the Incan dynasty. The marshal's ambition was to rebuild the Incan empire. He was not alone in that. Many had dreamed of an Incan empire and planned it to the last detail. When the Constitution of 1831 was being debated, one of the deputies who presided over the convention said: "In Bolivia, the Indian villages, such as Ayoayo and Tapacari would be able to elect their chiefs or *ilacates* to the Senate; the greatest evil would be for a certain type of man, such as the lawyers, who abound in Bolivia, to be in the Senate." But the Incanate republic never was born; nor did the *ilacates* become senators. But the son of a chief's daughter, Marshal Santa Cruz, was able to set Bolivia's house in order.

For ten years Santa Cruz served as a progressive governor and a good administrator, though he was a vain man, proud of the scroll given him by the French Legion of Honor. He loved titles. During his term, weaving, glassmaking, gunpowder, and shoe industries were started. The gunpowder enterprise fared better than the shoemakers'. Santa Cruz used to say that everything for the army was manufactured in Bolivia except the rifles. The Army was his cradle and his destiny. He planned a Peruvian-Bolivian confederation, created it, and then unmade it. Bolivia and Peru preferred to stay apart. Someone in Chile said, "The plan to unite the republics of Peru and Bolivia, whether as a confederation or in any form whatsoever, has spread alarm through every mind." Chile sent her minister to Peru with the following instructions:

> The great objective with which you are entrusted may be expressed in this brief phrase: independence of Bolivia. The incorporation of the two republics into one would place the

security of their neighbors in obvious jeopardy. . . . It matters not to us whether General Santa Cruz commands in Peru or in Bolivia; what matters to us is the separation of the two nations.

They remained separate.

The dream of the rebirth of the Incas was expressed in literature as well as in politics. Emeterio Villamil de Rada (1800–76), a philologist and scientist, was an extraordinary man with some very curious ideas, which he expressed in *La Lengua de Adán* (*Adam's Language*). He traveled through California, Alaska, and half of Europe, sometimes in the company of Lord Behring, a British explorer who was studying indigenous languages. Villamil de Rada develops in *Adam's Language* the theory that America is the oldest continent, and Sorata—the village where he was born—the seat of the earthly paradise. He based this on a study of the Aymará language, which he related to Sanskrit, although he gave his own first place. However fantastic such theories may seem, the author's fertility of invention and ingenuity made his book noteworthy in American bibliography. Such overvaluations of the Inca drew Santa Cruz out of his political orbit and changed the focus of Villamil de Rada's linguistic studies. Villamil de Rada ended his life by suicide in Brazil.

Peculiarities like his were to be preferred to what came later in Bolivia's agony during the rebellion of the masses under Belzú, and in the unleashed barbarity of Melgarejo. The circumstances of the country fostered such events. The university glittered on the heights, but the darkness of rank ignorance reigned down below. At the end of 1842 there was not a single school in Bolivia granting the bachelor's degree. When José Ballivián (1804–52), who followed Santa Cruz, left the government in 1847, there were only fifty-four elementary schools in all Bolivia. That was the aftermath of wars and dictatorships, for Bolívar's first concern in founding the republic had been to establish schools, and Simón Rodríguez, Bolívar's unusual teacher, had experimented with trade schools in Chuquisaca. Military uprisings, the adventure of confederation with Peru, and the ambitions of the *caudillos* made the raising of armies a necessity and did great harm to everything else. Barbarism was the camp follower of the armed forces.

The first man to rise against Ballivián at the head of the rabble was Manuel Isidro Belzú (1808–65). He talked like a present-day revolutionary, saying:

Cholos (half-breeds): while you are living in hunger and misery, your oppressors, who call themselves gentlemen and exploit your labor, are living in opulence. You must learn that everything before your eyes belongs to you because it is the fruit of your hard work. The wealth of those who call themselves nobles is a rape committed on you.

The interesting thing about that philosophy as he stated it was its consequences. When Belzú made his first appearance on the balcony of the presidential palace, he declared, as Argüedas reports:

"The cause of the miseries of the people is the titles of nobility and the aristocrats." And the people, enraged by his wild accusations, or incited by the rain of new silver coins that the *caudillo* spilled over its monster head, assaulted the houses of the leading citizens, plundered the stores of foreign merchants, and from that night on, gangs of *cholos* could be seen running through the streets, drunk and in tatters, to the sound of hoarse guitars insolently and provocatively acclaiming their new Messiah: Long live Papa Belzú!

The dictatorship that rose on such foundations began to create rivalry and to fear rebellion. Belzú established a *mazorca* in the Rosas manner for espionage, information, and brutal punishment. One day some seminary students dragged a black effigy of Belzú through the courtyard of the palace. It was only a prank, but the dictator sent soldiers to the school, and forty students were arrested and flogged. One of those who were punished resolved then to kill Belzú. He surprised him, shot him in the face, and twice more in the head after the dictator had fallen. The student left him for dead, but the wounded man survived by a seeming miracle attributed by his adherents to the direct intervention of Divine Providence. The attempt was used as an excuse to shoot a number of politicians. One of them was the president of the Congress, whose crime was to have said good morning to the man who made his attempt on the president's life hours afterward.

Nevertheless, Belzú was no illiterate. He was a forerunner of socialism in Bolivia. José María Linares (1810–61), a more cultivated man, succeeded him and brought about some liberal reforms. He also encouraged education. In part, that was the cause of his downfall, in 1861, after which Dr. José M. de Achá became president. In 1865, Belzú and Melgarejo rebelled against him. Melgarejo attacked the president's palace and proclaimed himself president. Belzú raised a faction against Melgarejo and took over the presidency in La Paz. Melgarejo then decided to march on La Paz and overthrow Belzú. The troops were unwilling to follow him, for Belzú still had some popular prestige. Melgarejo attacked Belzú's army and was defeated. Melgarejo tried to kill himself, but a friend wrested the weapon from his hand and said to him: "Let's try again."

Belzú was celebrating his victory in the palace. Below, in the public square, the people were applauding him. Suddenly a hush of astonishment fell. Melgarejo had appeared at the mouth of one of the streets, accompanied by six lancers. He moved forward and a path opened to let him pass. The hoofbeats of the horses were the only sound. He rode to the entrance of the palace and went in alone. Was he going to embrace Belzú in a gesture of reconciliation? Belzú came to meet him, and as Melgarejo climbed the staircase, Belzú was waiting for him in the entrance hall. One of Belzú's officers tried to stop Melgarejo by pointing a pistol at him. With one hand Melgarejo shoved it aside and fired at the officer with the other hand. The officer fell. Melgarejo went up to Belzú. A single shot rang out. Belzú fell dead. With utter disdain, Melgarejo stepped over him, crossed the hall, went out on the balcony and shouted, "Belzú is dead. Who lives now?" A shout of acclaim filled the square. "Long live Melgarejo!"

Melgarejo was a strong man who had spent most of his life in barracks, moving from garrison to garrison. "Devoid of any notion of history," Argüedas wrote, "he maintained that Napoleon was superior to Bonaparte, and that Cicero was a very second-rate general of antiquity. . . . As soon as he was notified of the Franco-Prussian war, he agreed in the council of ministers to remain neutral in the conflict." During his stay in office, one of his ministers came to report to him on the problems of public land. Melgarejo received him in a parlor which he had made his bedroom by tossing a mattress on the floor, without any sheets. Seated on this bed, he invited the minister to speak. He neither understood nor cared for what the official had to say. He knew only that there was no money and that his ministers were not able to raise any. He despised them. "If money is needed," he said, "there's no problem. I'll make war on Peru, and that will solve everything." He consigned his minister to the devil and started to prepare for war.

Argüedas concluded that during the first century of Bolivia's independence more than forty presidents, almost all of them tyrants, governed the country. Six were assassinated while in office. The armed rebellions numbered one hundred and eighty-seven. The only law was the law of bullet and bayonet.

XVI: *From Utilitarianism to Positivism*

¶ THE EXAMPLE OF THE UNITED STATES

In America, the downfall of Scholasticism, which coincided with the second stage in the historical evolution envisaged by Comte, implied the adoption of a philosophy that would lay a strong ideological foundation for the new republics. Although the Enlightenment and Romanticism favored liberal ideas and progress, they lacked a philosophy that would define their terms. Several schools appeared in succession and various names emerged to fill this vacuum: first Saint-Simon, the precursor of modern Socialism; then Bentham, the preacher of Utilitarianism; Comte, the apostle of Positivism; and Spencer, the great individualistic exponent of evolution.

To Spanish America, those names and schools formed a chain that marked the way of the pathfinders of new thought. Their systems of philosophy were politically oriented and therefore useful in defining parties, combating anarchy, and guiding legislation. Two influences, French and English, balanced each other. Ideologically, Hispano-Indian America seemed as much Anglo-Saxon as Latin at the beginning of the nineteenth century. Paris, Manchester, and Philadelphia were points of reference to which all eyes turned. France had demonstrated how to dethrone a monarchy. The optimism of the English Industrial Revolution offered concrete formulas for progress and a more experimental, less lyrical search for freedom. The example of the United States served to point up by contrast the vices of the Spanish heritage.

Alberdi said: "My conviction is that without England and the United States freedom would vanish in this century." Sarmiento: "Let us not detain the United States in its march, as some are definitely proposing. Let us emulate the United States. Let us be America, as the sea is the ocean. Let us be the United States." In Chile, Francisco Bilbao stated:

> Spain conquered America; the English colonized the North. With Spain came Catholicism, monarchy, feudalism, the Inquisition, isolation, deprivation, the exterminative genius, intolerance, sociability of blind obedience. With the English came the liberal currents of Reform: the law of the sovereign individual, of the thinker and worker with complete freedom. What has been the result? In the North, the United States, the foremost of nations, both ancient and modern; in the South, the Dis-United States, whose progress depends upon de-Hispanicizing itself.

In spite of such words, all was not complete trust. Bolívar already had written: "The United States, so enamored of its own liberties, is already much less fond of the liberties of others. Quite the contrary: it has made of this liberty an instrument for causing other people misery." Bello entered an objection to the impassioned anti-Spanish testimony. He pointed out that there were Spanish values, beginning with the language, worth conserving, within the sound assets of an emancipated America. In short, the new philosophy was not accepted unanimously. It was formulated through debate. But it was moving ahead.

¶ THE HEYDAY OF UTILITARIANISM

Bentham's utilitarian philosophy—which replaces the idea of natural law with the principle of utility—materializes, "realizes"—that is, converts into reality—the dream of the men who freed America in order to bring happiness to the people. Bentham's principle "the greatest good for the greatest number" is written into the preamble of the constitutions. Utilitarianism was translated to mean reforming the laws. Philosophically, Bentham was the antithesis of the concept of the "vale of tears" which the sons of Spain worked into their orations. To Bentham whatever would bring enjoyment was useful; that is, he set up pleasure against sorrow. Not unbridled pleasure, to be sure, for this was a philosophy formulated amid the fogs and coal smoke of England, not on

a Mediterranean island. In this world, law must aim for usefulness and well-being.

It happened that Bentham made a tour very like Miranda's during the same years. He traveled through Italy, visited Constantinople and Russia. Like Miranda, he was a friend of Catherine the
Great, and also like Miranda, he was concerned with prison reform. He invented a prison in the round, which could be watched
over from a central spot. That was the panopticon, which was
promptly introduced into republican America. Miranda and Bentham met in London and became friends. Their friendship lasted
and grew over the years. Miranda introduced Andrés Bello to
Bentham, and when Bello was looking for a job that would enable him to survive in London, Bentham turned over to him the
task of arranging his files. This work left a deep impression on
the Venezuelan. His lessons in philosophy, written in Santiago,
show his utilitarian, orderly, natural background, as well as the
breadth of his learning.

Bentham had much in common with the Americans. He had
been a friend of the French Encyclopedists and was on friendly
terms with D'Alembert. He knew French, Italian, and Spanish.
He belonged to the circle of James Mill, John Stuart Mill, and
John Austin, whose names kept dropping off the pens of the intellectuals in Spanish America. In 1789, France handed down to
the New World the ten commandments of revolution, and Bentham followed with his *Introduction to the Principles of Morals
and Legislation*. Rivadavia, who became a friend of Bentham in
London, took Bentham's ideas back to Buenos Aires as the basis
for his country's new legislation. José María Luis Mora (1794–
1850), one of the most influential Mexicans of the time, a liberal
and a Mason, who wrote the *Catecismo Político de la Revolución
Mexicana*, was another of Bentham's disciples, as was José Cecilio
del Valle (1780–1834), a Honduran who drew up the act of independence for Central America and was one of the great intellectuals of his day. Bentham always kept as a precious relic the
Guatemalan coins that Valle gave him.

In Colombia, the struggle between the partisans and opponents
of Bentham became quite dramatic. Antonio Nariño had already
called attention to Bentham in 1811 through his newspaper *La
Bagatela*. In 1825, Santander decreed that all the secondary
schools must teach Bentham's law. In 1827, Bolívar wrote an
answer to a letter from Bentham saying:

I had the honor to receive the catechism on economy which you were kind enough to send me with a letter most flattering to me, for I have always viewed your authority and learning with deep veneration. Later, when I looked through this elementary work, it seemed to me that it was of such exquisite merit as to make it worthy of being placed in the hands of the people for their instruction, and consequently, I have ordered it to be published in Spanish. Doubtless that will be done, for the minister of the interior, Señor Pando, a well-educated man, was quite interested in your work. But what has pleased me most in this event is to have received the assurance that you remember me in the midst of your far-flung meditations. The name of a happy soldier enters the philosophical world. . . . My distance from Europe and the splendor of the cause I have served have shed their rays on me and made me seem what I had not hoped to be. You yourself have just proved to me how indulgently the first geniuses of the Universe regard me.

Enthusiasm for Bentham and for everything English reached such a pitch in Bogotá that a newspaper filled with eulogies of the father of Utilitarianism was published there in English.

For a time, the Church was fully preoccupied with keeping the new generations off this trail. The fiery orator Father Margallo preached from the pulpit a famous sermon against Vicente Azuero on the question of Utilitarianism. There were violent exchanges between pulpit and press. Santander was exiled under the pretext that he was weaving a plot to assassinate Bolívar. The Liberator, like the astute politician he was, seized upon the first gestures toward reconciliation offered by Rome to make numerous concessions to the Church and thus to range it on his side. For those reasons he issued decrees against impious teachings—Bentham was impious—and against the Masons. "My plan," Bolívar wrote to Páez, "is to support my reforms with the solid base of religion. In my speeches and rebuttals I have mentioned that to the clergy and laity, and they have been delighted." Nevertheless, English philosophy had its foot in the door, and the struggle over it lasted half a century. A bigoted Catholic writer, Marco Fidel Suárez (1855–1927), famous for his studies on grammar, a student in depth of Bello's work, and above all else a conservative, wrote in his study on the Colombian author and politician Miguel Antonio Caro:

During fifty years of the past century, it can be said that the republic was kept in a state of agitation over a moral thesis which, while it did not properly constitute a political principle, nevertheless came to be a cause of differences among our parties and a summons of the mind to a very stubborn battle that recalls the politico-religious controversies of the Eastern Empire. That thesis was the Utilitarianism expounded in Bentham's books and transplanted to Colombia's official instruction during the early years of the republic. A system like that is not only contrary to science, but also alarming to patriots, and it rightly scandalized the Christian conscience of the nation. It had its opponents, men who were distinguished for their wisdom and their exalted political and social standing: Señor Don Joaquin Mosquera, father of his country and president of Gran Colombia; the presbyter José María Botero, a kind of Antioquian Savonarola, as wise as he was vehement; Señor Don José Eusebio Caro; Doctor Ospina, learned in the various branches of science and politics; Señor Don Mario Valenzuela, today a luminary and a glory to the Company of Jesus. . . . But the most formal and conclusive refutation of the principle of utility was the book wherein Señor Caro analyzed that doctrine with such vigor and method that he never evoked an answer.

Santander, a better Catholic than Bolívar, remained faithful to Bentham during his exile and visited him in London. He recalled his first interview in an intimate portrait that included these lines:

I dined with Jeremy Bentham today. He is an old man of more than eighty years, gay, short, fat, robust, with completely white hair that falls to his shoulders, and dressed in old, plain clothes without a cravat, or any adornment. Patriarchal manners, a frank and pleasant manner, with a clear mind, although nowadays he forgets people's names, tremendous talents, and a touch of vanity. Before dining, we walked in his little garden, and he showed me the house where the famous poet Milton lived, which is his now, and the small one where Mill, General Miranda's friend, used to live. He showed me the bust of him that was the gift of the Parisian sculptor David, and the portrait of General Miller in the service of Peru. He talked to me favorably about Rivadavia and with great respect about General Lafayette. At the table, two youths who correspond with him were seated with us; with me facing him; the dinner was quite ample and excellent; not much wine because he is not used to it. During the meal we talked about Colombia and Bolívar, and his opinions are eminently liberal. He said there was no tyrant who did not have his Timoleon, and he hoped that Bolívar might not be the exception to this rule, which is the consolation of liberty.

On another occasion they talked for four hours concerning politics and jurisprudence. Santander was "a man of law." Colonel Francis Hall arrived in Ecuador bearing a letter from Bentham to Bolívar. Hall accomplished more in Quito as a philosopher than as a colonel, and after aligning himself with the adversaries of Flores, contributed to the foundation of the liberal party in Ecuador. He brought the teachings of utilitarianism, which he fervently supported, into the party during its formative days.

With another Englishman, Colonel Wright, Hall helped to found *El Quiteño Libre* (*The Free Quitan*), a newspaper that brought together the most distinguished liberals in Ecuador. In 1833 an uprising against Flores occurred. The rebels stormed the barracks to the cry of "Long live *The Free Quitan!*" The troops fell on the ingenuous attackers and a slaughter ensued. At dawn on October 20, the bodies of the philosophers were swinging naked from the plaza lampposts. Among them was that of Colonel Hall. The Carmelite nuns provided him with a shroud.

¶ SAINT-SIMON

Claude-Henri de Rouvroy, Comte de Saint-Simon, stood in the front rank of political literature—in America; more than that, his philosophy was a part of the background of many of the builders of the new republics. Saint-Simon knew America firsthand because he fought in the war for the independence of the United States as a volunteer in Washington's armies before he was twenty years old. Later, in Mexico, he drew up for the viceroy a plan for building a canal to connect the two oceans. His subsequent trip to Spain gave him a new chance to become acquainted with the Hispanic world during the period of the Enlightenment. As a consequence, his socialist philosophy came from a background of sympathy with the Americans emancipated from Spain which gave it easy access to the New World. The mystical trend in his new

Christianity fitted in very well with the spirit of people who remained loyal, often without confessing it, to the Spanish home tradition. The philosophies of Esteban Echeverría, Bernardino Rivadavia, and José Victorino Lastarria all derived from Saint-Simon. Those who were to find their final refuge in Positivism took their first step with Saint-Simon.

The word "Socialism" was introduced into the political parlance of the new republics through the influence of Saint-Simon, and Echeverría properly entitled his book *Dogma Socialista* (*Socialist Dogma*). Sarmiento proclaimed himself a Socialist in his tirade against Romanticism. The men who needed some anti-metaphysical basis for the new anti-Spanish republics, found their keynote in Saint-Simon's words: "The base of liberty is industry; liberty cannot grow except through it, cannot fortify itself except with it." Saint-Simon found in his follower Pierre Leroux, one of the new thinkers made known by Echeverría in Buenos Aires, an excellent popularizer for America.

Positivism was to guide the next step, for as Zum Felde said: "Saint-Simon as a replacement for Bentham gives no guaranty of a greater awareness of and control over the American politico-social phenomenon; all that it means is that the actors are the same men in a change of clothes." Auguste Comte became Saint-Simon's logical heir in formulating the new philosophy.

¶ COMTE

Auguste Comte summed up in his motto of Order and Progress the ideal of the struggle against anarchy and barbarism which had engaged the liberals of America, who might even be said to have anticipated him. José Victorino Lastarria (1817–88), one of the great national figures of Chile through his influence on politics and the cultural life of the nation, wrote a memoir in 1844 entitled *Investigaciones sobre la influencia social de la conquista y del sistema colonial de los españoles en Chile* (*Investigations of the Social Influence of the Conquest and Colonial System of the Spanish in Chile*). He thought that he had anticipated Comte's ideas in Chile, but doubted that they had been understood. That was his tragedy. He believed, too, that he had discovered Kant's ideas, but that he had not been able to recognize them at the time. In his memoirs he says:

The calamity of 1844 took us by surprise, we must confess. In fact we did not know of any writer who thought as we did; and even though at that very moment, Auguste Comte was completing the editing of his *Cours de Philosophie Positiviste*, we had not had the remotest knowledge of the name of that great philosopher, nor of his book, nor of his system of history, *which was ours*; we do not believe that anyone in Chile did have, however often the editor of the *Mercury* may point out to us today that he gave us a piece of advice at the end of his criticism in which, by a kind of presentiment, he placed us in the future positivistic school by bidding us: "Follow the positive turn that you have begun to give your studies; don't let yourselves be distracted by trouble."

Lastarria could have been right in regard to his personal case, but it is naïve to think that he alone was able to anticipate. In fact, all those working on the same subject in America were anticipating. Alberdi already had mentioned social science in 1837 when he said: "The science that seeks a general law for the harmonious development of human beings is *social science*." Saint-Simon used the term "Positive policy" in 1820.

In fact, Comte's theory of the three stages of history was to the Spanish Americans an exact picture of their own experience. They saw the first, or theological stage, reflected in the history of Spain, when every happening was attributed to supernatural beings or causes. America had lived through the second, or metaphysical stage, which holds that the law derives from abstract principles apart from experience. In Mexico, Gabino Barreda interpreted Comte's theological stage as the colony, the metaphysical stage as the independence, and the third stage as the appearance of Positivism under the Juárez government. All the literature of the period of independence aimed to contradict the metaphysical stage dialectically and to arrive, through science as diffused by the Enlightenment, at that Positivist philosophy which affirms progress in the new society as an immediate reality. Reason was the new goddess that was worshipped while a French Revolution occurred in the world of ideas. Comte, a democratizer of philosophy, as it were, had made Positivism more than a philosophy. It became a policy, even a religion, when he founded the Positivist Club in Paris with two doctors of medicine, a bill broker, a literary man, a machinist, and a cabinet-maker. He dedicated the twelfth month of his revolutionary calendar to politics, under the aegis of Frederick the Great, and chose three American "saints' days" to honor the very unlike contemporaries:

Bolívar, Toussaint L'Ouverture, and Dr. Francia.

In Chile, one of the most vehement theoreticians of the new society was Francisco Bilbao (1823–1865). He was aroused by the book *Paroles d'un croyant* (*Words of a Believer*) by the liberal priest-philosopher Lamennais, and translated that author's *De l'esclavage moderne* (*Modern Slavery*) in 1843. The following year he published his first work, *Sociabilidad chilena* (*The Civics of Chilean Society*), which aroused the greatest scandal of the day. The book was a judgment on the Spanish past, summed up in these words: "Slavery, degradation: that is the past. . . . Our past is Spain. Spain is the Middle Ages. The Middle Ages are composed, body and soul, of Catholicism and feudalism." The *Catholic Review* entered a fiery protest, and Bilbao was tried for abuse of the press. He was his own counsel for the defense. He looked the prosecutor in the eye and said: "Who are you? Philosophy assigns you the name of reactionary. An innovator, that is what I am; reactionaries, that is what you are." The youths who heard him applauded. But he was sentenced to a fine of twelve hundred pesos. Within a few minutes the public had taken up a collection and paid it. Bilbao was carried out on the shoulders of his admirers and acclaimed through the streets. Nevertheless, he was ousted from his chair at the university and his doctrines were condemned from the pulpit. His book was officially burned by the hangman in a public bonfire. Bilbao went to France, where Lamennais welcomed him like a son. He became a friend of Quinet and Michelet. He returned to Chile with great prestige and founded the Society of Equality. All those who frequented the Society of Equality were called Saint-Simonians, men without god or law in the eyes of the common people. The profession of faith required of initiates to the society was contained in these three questions: "Do you recognize the sovereignty of reason as the authority of authorities? Do you recognize the sovereignty of the people as the basis of all policy? Do you recognize love and universal brotherhood as the moral way of life?" Eusebio Lillo, a romantic poet who used the name Rouget de L'Isle in the secret meetings, edited *El Amigo del Pueblo* (*The People's Friend*) "to pull the people out of their abyss of backwardness and darkness." Santiago Arcos based his social program on the following formula: "To take away the land from the rich and distribute it among the poor; to take the tools of labor from the rich and distribute them among the poor." Like Lillo, they all adopted names of Girondists: Lastarria called himself Brissot; Bilbao, Verginiaud;

the future president of Chile Domingo Santa María (1825–89) took the name Louvet, and so on.

Bilbao, bent upon changing his words into deeds, organized an abortive revolution after Bishop Valdivieso had already officially excommunicated him. The people, shocked and convinced that he was a dangerous heretic, united under the wing of the clergy. The Society of Equality's last peaceful demonstration was a parade of four hundred members, Bilbao leading them. He had "a nosegay of scented and showy flowers in the buttonhole of his blue frock coat, gracefully fitted at the waist, and spotless white trousers." He was carrying the tree of liberty. After the revolution that he had sponsored was smothered in its cradle, he was forced to sail for France again. There he found his old friends in hiding or exiled. He visited the revolutionary writer Edgar Quinet in Belgium, then returned to America, not to Chile but to Buenos Aires, where he published his last works and died at forty-two.

In Chile, other men were keeping alive a flame less troublesome than Bilbao's. Lastarria, the most loyal of the Positivists, followed the battle, but eventually parted company with Comte because the philosopher had supported the republican dictatorship, applauded Napoleon III's *coup d'état*, and listed Dr. Francia among his saints. What really revolted Lastarria, however, was the religious turn that Comte's Positivism had taken. Lastarria said: "After studying human progress and linking its laws with all truth, he has failed in his attempt to formulate the new synthesis between an absurd religion and a political system that repels good sense." When Lastarria opened the Academy of Fine Arts, he substituted the motto "Liberty and Order" for Comte's "Love, Order, and Progress." "Liberty and Order" became the motto on Colombia's coat of arms. In Brazil, a great center of Positivism, "Order and Progress" was inscribed on her flag. Gabino Barreda in Mexico chose "Liberty, Order, and Progress."

Jorge Lagarrigue maintained such an adherence to Comtism that he became a French citizen. Lagarrigue followed the philosophy to its farthest extreme by supporting the religious cult to which it turned and asking his friends in Chile to contribute money for the purchase of the house of Clotilde de Vaux, with whom Comte was united in 1845, a year before her death. Comte idolized his mistress and, after her death, built around her name a cult that bordered on mystical veneration among the small group of his faithful followers.

¶ PORTALES IN CHILE

The period of Comtism in Chile overlapped the period of Diego Portales (1793–1837), who emerged as head of the anti-liberal reaction, which began with a newspaper that attracted the masses: *El Hambriento* (*The Hungry*). Portales gave Victorino Lastarria's liberal career a start by pointing him out to the Bello regime as a kind of counselor. Portales was a leader but never a president. The struggles in which he engaged were always inflammatory, but there was no Rosas in the seat of power. In literature, Lastarria had an equal, if not a better, in the great historian of Chile, Benjamín Vicuña Mackenna (1831–86), whose large production included such books as the *Historia Crítica y Social de la ciudad de Santiago* (*Critical and Social History of the City of Santiago*). Lastarria indignantly attacked Vicuña Mackenna because Mackenna did not assail Portales in his monumental history of the presidency (1851–61) of Manuel Montt (1809–80). The field was wide open to polemics. The great Argentines had come to Chile in order to be able to speak their minds.

Portales believed that republican government was the only possible solution for America, but he also thought that it needed very strong governors to educate the people before a liberal system could be implanted. He was never strongly attracted by power; he was a gay man with a gift for mockery. He could play the guitar. He had many love affairs, but he wrote: "The holy state of matrimony is the holy state of fools." With a Voltairean gesture, he said to Mariano Egaña: "Don Mariano, you believe in God. I believe in priests." Portales dominated the political scene for twelve years. But the day came when he was taken prisoner and shot in an uprising led by Colonel Vidaurre. That was all. In Chile, one talked, wrote, argued passionately, made history, adopted codes of law, created a university, went to jail, and was shot. But liberty always found someone new to sponsor it. Philosophy always found someone who would inject doubt at the opportune moment and open the way for other ideas. There, as everywhere else in America, the rigor of Comte followed Spencer's evolution. Positivism lingered into the twentieth century in Chile.

¶ THE "SCIENTIST" IN MEXICO

Comte penetrated Mexico more deeply than elsewhere, but also more rationally. Mexico and Brazil represent the two great examples of Comte's influence on the political world. The history of his phase in Mexico began with Gabino Barreda (1820–81), a physician who studied in Paris, taking the courses which Comte gave. He was one of the few Latin Americans with that sort of background. Barreda arrived in Mexico burning with positivistic fervor at the moment when Juárez had seized the government and was trying to lay the foundations for educational reform. Alfonso Reyes described those events:

> At the beginning of the second half of the nineteenth century, when the republic was still tender, resentful of its nervous infancy, two great parties already had matured: the Liberal, which leaned toward a new concept of the State which blended the philosophy of the *Rights of Man* with American presidentialism and federalism; and the Conservative, in which steadfastness to hereditary norms and the zeal to preserve the framework of already created interests exerted a strong pull toward a headlong fall into anti-national aberrations. The French invasion stretched out its blood-stained hands while that hereditary surplus product of the Houses of Europe arrived without a valid claim. In the imperial rip-tide, the republic was brought down to the proportions of the stage coach that carried Benito Juárez into exile. But the tide ebbed and the republic triumphed forever. The country was left in ruins; everything had to be done over. Political measures offered emergency remedies. Only culture, only schools, could offer remedies of long duration. Juárez, with the standards of a liberal and a layman, undertook the reorganization of public instruction and entrusted that arduous task to the Mexican philosopher, Gabino Barreda.

Barreda founded the National Preparatory School, an original institution that was an improvement over the French Lycée; there a student could earn an encyclopedic baccalaureate based on the tenets of Comte's philosophy. A new generation of Mexicans was trained in its classrooms and the greatest teachers of the period did some brilliant work. The "scientists," who were eventually to open the way for the dictatorship of Porfirio Díaz (1830–1915), came out of that preparatory school. Although Barreda died before the advent of Díaz, his adherence to Comte implied the possibility of an enlightened absolutism in America which al-

ready had a working model in Charles III. The great name among
the Mexican scientists is Justo Sierra (1848–1912), a modernistic
poet and essayist who left an enduring work in his *Evolución
Política del Pueblo Mexicano* (*Political Evolution of the Mexican
People*) and wrote *Juárez, su obra y su tiempo* (*Juárez, His Work
and His Times*). Sierra represented the Enlightenment within the
regime of Díaz—the so-called Porfiriate (1877–1911). As minister of education, he established the new university and doubled
the number of schools.

The Porfiriate was a regime of great vigor, like that of the
older Enlightenment—rich in railroads, telegraphs, academies,
and urban elegance. But the ground was being laid for revolution,
the second revolution for independence, with Francisco I. Madero
as its apostle. Thus Comte's Positivism helped to accomplish a
labor of basic revision in Spanish America which brought hos-
tility to it along with its own triumph. Today the National Preparatory School contains a monumental fresco to the Revolution
and the historic memoirs of the teachers of the Reform. Diego
Rivera (1886–1957) and José Clemente Orozco (1883–1949)
painted on its walls a record of the new Mexico that emerged from
the revolution. A Mexico that remembered Saint-Simon and the
Physiocrats and forecast the Russian Revolution. Madero's and
Zapata's guerrilla fighters march in a parade like a motion picture
sequence, carrying as their banners new ballads that united
the people. Their skill in positive revolution wins with the
bayonets. That was the revolution of *The Eagle and the Serpent*,
described by Martín Luis Guzmán (1887–   ) in the novel bearing that title and in his memoirs as a journalist and, for a time,
secretary to Pancho Villa. It was the revolution of *Los de Abajo*
(*The Underdogs*), as revealed by Mariano Azuela, the first novelist of the period.

Sierra won the pre-revolutionary skirmishes in the schoolroom
while Ignacio Ramírez (1818–79), poet-collaborator of Juárez
and Minister of Justice in the first administration of Porfirio Díaz,
preached the policies of the land and the Mexican people. (Ramírez was the author of the statement "God does not Exist," the
journalist who signed himself "the Necromancer.") Ramírez, who
was part Indian, debated the theme of America and Spain with
the Spanish statesman-historian Emilio Castelar. He had no fear of
revolution; indeed, he was a poet of revolution and a daring man.
Speaking of social enlightenment, he said: "We congratulate
ourselves that it has been granted us to contemplate this sublime

spectacle, even though we may be its victims. Silence and confusion to cowards!"

¶ SPENCER IN COLOMBIA

Comte's philosophy and dictatorship could not last long on
a continent as hungry for liberty as the America that emerged
with independence. The religious aspect, incarnate in Clotilde de
Vaux as the Goddess of Reason, was not convincing. That gave
the Anglo-Saxon with his more judicious and sensible standards
an entrée into the game through the English philosopher Herbert
Spencer (1820–1903). Spencer was not seeking order enforced
by despotism. He believed in peaceful evolution and abhorred the
violent contradictions of revolutionary dialectics. His sociology
offered a point of view on people and societies which was opposite
to the political struggles and the cult of the hero that have filled
the history of nations. In his new picture, based on the theory
of progress, the new peoples had a social value in terms of human
experience which Spencer analyzed by the rules of science. He
was as much interested in a community of Indians as in English
society. To him, evolution from the simple to the complex, from
the homogeneous to the heterogeneous, must begin with observation of people already evolved and of those on the path of evolution. Darwin's travels, which included America, yielded him data
that he used in developing his theory of evolution and his views
on progress as a sociologist. Americans, whose independence
began at the same time as his studies of "society," caught some
glimmerings of them. The theory of the Social Contract implied
that kind of study as an adaptation of Montesquieu's theories.

The Colombian Rafael Núñez (1823–94), a poet like all the
others, an essayist and sociologist who became president of his
republic, anticipated several of Spencer's theories, as Lastarria's
speeches matched Comte's lessons, to his surprise. Núñez broadcast Spencer's philosophy in Colombia, where the English brand
of Positivism awakened an immediate echo. Indeed, Salvador
Camacho Roldán (1827–1900), a student of the United States,
which he described conscientiously on his travels, established a
chair of sociology at the University of Bogotá in 1862. At that
time there was no such department in most of the European
universities. Soon afterward, Nicolás Pinzón W. in Bogotá set
up a private university in law and political and social science.

Colombia's venture into positivism was strange. During the

years of radicalism, of the "Olympian radical" who drew up the constitution of 1863 called the Río Negro charter, faith in progress was so strong that under that very free constitution each of the nine states in the republic apparently held more power than the republic itself—each having its own army, customhouses, and laws. In spite of so loose a concept of federalism, the university attained a brilliant stature, normal schools proliferated, a pedagogical mission was invited from Europe, steamboat navigation was introduced on the Magdalena River, telegraph wires were strung, rails were laid for the first railway, and a great variety of industries was established. Laws were passed to recover property held in "dead hands," civil registration was initiated, the economic power of the Church was reduced, and the Jesuits were expelled—in short, a kind of Mexican reform was carried out. The enthusiasm for all things Mexican was so great that Colombia conferred on Juárez the title *"Benemérito* (well-deserving) of the Americas," which has come down in history. Such enthusiasms were checked by Rafael Núñez himself, despite the fact that he was the author of certain of the measures that had lopped off some of the economic power of the church. The formerly radical Núñez veered suddenly to the side of suppression and joined the reactionary forces, won power, and decreed the death of the constitution of 1863 and the birth of the charter of 1886, which had just been drawn up in haste. This was an echo in the conservative style of Melgarejo's course in dealing a barbaric death to Belzú and proclaiming it from the palace balcony.

Under the new charter, a concordat was signed giving the Church a hand in the schools on terms that Garciá Moreno himself would have approved. The Jesuits were called back; the power of the states was annulled, and a closed political centralism was established, with political centralization and administrative decentralization. An article giving the intimate reasons for the changes proposed by Núñez was inserted in the civil code: "Catholic marriage *ipso jure* annuls any civil marriage previously contracted." Núñez himself benefitted by this article when during a state dinner the papal nuncio led Doña Soledad Román, the *soi-disant* first lady, to the table on his arm in an ecclesiastical gesture of ostensible moral solidarity.

That was the end of Spencer's sociology. Miguel Antonio Caro (1843–1909), the son of one of Colombia's greatest poets and himself a poet, was, with Núñez, the architect of Conservative Colombia. Caro could write poetry with equal ease in Latin or Castilian. He was a grammarian whose name ranks beside Bello's, and a distinguished essayist and orator. Caro drew up the new constitution and became president of the republic. He rested from his executive labors by translating the *Aeneid*. According to experts, no better translation of Virgil exists in Castilian. To some degree Caro followed in García Moreno's footsteps. Marco Fidel Suárez absolves him with these words:

> Caro has been criticized for the convention on ecclesiastical judicial power concluded with the Holy See; but his critics have failed to see that it was not his government that proposed or carried out that arrangement; and they have forgotten that today conventions of that kind are accepted all over the Catholic world. Furthermore, if that criticism had been just, it would have included the pontiff with whom the pact was made, and the Catholic García Moreno, the author of an arrangement that served as a model for the one that was agreed to by Colombia.

Actually that was a period during which García Moreno could have been fitted very neatly into official Colombia. Suárez himself ranked García among the first of the "martyrs in Christ" in his prayer to Jesus Christ which mentioned the faithful who had followed him among the defenders of freedom, among the great legislators, and even among those who seemed to have been guided by the hand of God to transform nations. As for Spencer, Suárez expressed the sum of conservative thought by calling him the new Machiavelli.

> The evolutionary morality of some contemporary philosophers must yield in practice fruits both pagan and Machiavellian. In Spencer's system, as well as in those of Bentham and Epicurus, the intrinsic morality of man's acts is confused with the sensations they yield, and good deeds will harmonize with wretched results in time with the fatal forward movement of human evolution. . . . Moral Positivism is nothing but Machiavellianism disguised under a new terminology and a modern apparatus.

Núñez's inverted Positivism brought Colombia a conservative dictatorship that lasted about half a century.

¶ THE ARGENTINE SCHOLARS

Argentina moved from Echeverría's Saint-Simonism to the Spencerian Positivism advocated by Alberdi. Canal Feijoo summarizes Alberdi's remarks on the civil code of Dalmacio Vélez Sarsfield: "The Civil Code is nothing more than the social code of a country. The main base of legislation is sociology. Its principles can be no other than those upon which society itself rests. Legislation can only be the expression of the natural constitution of society. It must be a product, not a program . . . it must be understood as a natural product of social evolution or of the history of societies, as it were, which is always a natural history. . . . All this is literally Spencerianism. Spencer also transposes to or superposes the concept of society upon that of the nation in order to sustain, in strict Alberdian terms, that the forms of government and organization 'have no value except insofar as they are products of the natural character,' and they emerge as adaptable rules acquired along the road of evolution 'during the course of social progress.' (Alberdi himself arranges this very convenient quotation.)" Such distinguished men as José Ingenieros, Juan B. Justo, and Carlos Octavio Bunge, all of whom enjoyed continent-wide prestige, went beyond Spencer, but even into the twentieth century they remained inside the lines of Positivism in the evolution of Argentine ideas.

Like Gabino Barreda, José Ingenieros (1877–1925) was a physician. In his youth he enlisted in the ranks of the socialists. For years he published the *Archivos de Psiquiatría y Criminología* (*Archives of Psychiatry and Criminology*). His work as a publicist made him influential throughout America, principally in the field of penal law. He opened a window to Positivism, which revolutionized the old ideas on criminology. All the universities of America began to study the pioneer criminologists Garofalo, Lombroso, and Ferri. Never before had the Italians been read with such diligence. The new generation went to Rome to study under Ferri. Ingenieros wrote the *Evolución de las Ideas Argentinas*, which is still a basic book, and *El Hombre Mediocre*, a great popular success. In his *Evolución sociológica argentina: de la barbarie al imperialismo* (1910), he wrote:

> Biological sociology permits a genetic explanation of the evolution of human societies; economic history, far from being a concept antagonistic to it, is a particular way of facing up to its general problems. . . . The natural development of human societies may be understood if the classic Spencerian 'organism' is replaced with a biological interpretation of social evolution. Societies are simple 'colonies

organized by the division of the social functions,' and not 'superorganisms.' Biological sociology raises the problem to its general, biological phase. On the other hand, the orthodox organistic sociologists restrict themselves to explanation by analogy.

Ingenieros parted company with Spencer, immersed himself in the Italian Positivists, and became one of the teachers to whom the youth of the university revolution of 1918 would listen. At that time he wrote a brief essay called *La Universidad del Porvenir.* His sympathies were with the Russian Revolution. He said that "the most complete moral solidarity with the Russian Revolution" must be maintained. As he died in 1925, he could not know what occurred thereafter.

The son of an Italian socialist immigrant, Ingenieros viewed Argentina's progress as dependent strictly on "a white Argentine race" that would erase "the stigma of inferiority with which the Europeans have always branded the South Americans." To that degree, his racist position is like Sarmiento's. Sarmiento traced the superiority of the Americans of the United States to the Anglo-Saxon's freedom from "any mingling with races inferior in energy." Alberdi, too, had dreamed of a white Argentina. He had conceived of its being made up largely of immigrants who would push back the frontier and thus exclude the Indians, as General Roca had done. Apparently he was following the example of the Americans in the North. One of the most original of Spanish America's scholars was the naturalist Florentino Ameghino (1854–1911). He made his name by his thesis of the antiquity of American man, but he left the prehistoric bones for his erudite colleagues to gnaw on and came out for the white man in modern times. "The white race is superior among all humans: the future dominion over the terrestrial globe is reserved for it." Ameghino was an atheist and a materialist.

The thesis of European immigration was a specialty of Carlos Octavio Bunge (1875–1918), whose book *Nuestra América* is considered the first systematic essay on the racial types in America. Bunge came to the same conclusion as the others, that the recipe for national progress is immigration. In addition to his studies in social biology, he concerned himself with education. The theses he formulates on the subject are not new, but his work is full of information. The Latin American reader can find there a sort of master plan to use in orienting himself on educational ideas through the centuries. In dealing with the period contemporary to him and with the case of Argentina, Bunge showed his admiration for what had been done in the United States. In this respect, his theories were in harmony with those of Sarmiento, and he started from the latter's *Conflicto y armonías de las razas de América* when he wrote *Nuestra América*.

Juan B. Justo (1865–1928), a professor and physician, moved from Spencer's Positivism to Marxism, translated the first part of *Das Kapital*, founded the Argentine Socialist Party and wrote several books, including *Teoría y Práctica de la Historia*.

¶ VENEZUELA FROM GUZMÁN BLANCO TO VALLENILLA LANZ

As Argentina was evolving under the momentum of brilliant progress, all these debates were conducted in a forum unrestricted by dictatorship. The country may have had political lapses and more or less despotic governments, but an annual increment of a hundred or two hundred thousand immigrants, the fabulous wealth of the pampas, divided by barbed wire and crossed by railroads, the rural society, culminating in the Jockey Club, the growth of Buenos Aires, which was the wonder of Europeans— all this helped to keep academic debate on a lofty plane and to carry progressive Spencerian Positivism down to very recent times. To try to do the same thing in the same century in a country like Venezuela while the wealth later found in petroleum was still far in the future was something else again.

Positivism's advocate in Venezuela was Antonio Guzmán Blanco (1829–99), known as the "enlightened American," who opted for the Comtian formula for dictatorship during the eighteen years he controlled the country's government. He had been trained in France, and tried to make Caracas a little Paris. Until the time when Caracas took the sudden, radical turn that gave it the appearance it wears today of a gigantic city, everything admirable that met the eye, notably, all the public works, was the work of Guzmán Blanco: the opera house, the presidential palace, the Pantheon. Guzmán Blanco was anticlerical, progressive, and a Mason. He gave ample encouragement to the coffee plantations, confiscated the Church's property, founded the national bank, established civil marriage, built aqueducts, considered establishing a national church, and decreed obligatory public instruction. He fell short of achieving some of his objectives, but he made a beginning. As "The Regenerator" he wanted to bring a new birth to Venezuela through the Masonic lodges. But his megalomania, his thirst for personal glory and prestige, his desire to dictate from Paris through his surrogates all came first. One day while he was in a clinic in Germany, he was informed that his surrogate had declared himself president by squatter's rights, as it were.

After Guzmán Blanco, men who fancied themselves little Caesars began to emerge. One of them was José Gil-Fortoul (1852–1943), novelist, historian, essayist, who joined the company of Juan Vicente Gómez. He was the author of two novels, *Julián* and *Pasiones*, and expounded Positivism in Venezuela in a book of sociological essays entitled *El Hombre y su Historia*. His *Historia Constitucional de Venezuela* was a cynical defense of dictatorship. Gil-Fortoul typifies a Venezuelan state of mind shared by Juan Vicente Gómez, to cite the most conspicuous example, who called himself a liberal. "If the two antagonistic and irreconciable tendencies had never existed in Venezuela, the words 'Conservative' and 'Liberal' did exist to distinguish at given moments the personalist or accidental parties." Antonio Leocadio Guzmán, the father of Guzmán Blanco, who had also been president of Venezuela, once said in the National Congress:

> I don't know where the idea arose that the Venezuelan people love federation when they do not know what the word means. The idea came from me and a few others; we talked the question over and said to one another: granted that every revolution needs a flag, and seeing that the Convention of Valencia did not care to christen the constitution with the name "federal," let us invoke that idea; otherwise, gentlemen, if our opponents had said 'Federation,' we would have said "Centralism."

Positivism to Gil-Fortoul meant recording the events of Venezuelan life as positive fact, like snapshots by Machiavelli, and using them according to circumstances. This was also what Laureano Vallenilla Lanz (1870–1936) did in his book *Cesarismo Democrático*, written in 1919 to defend the system and all its consequences: the system of Juan Vicente Gómez (1864–1935), the rustic despot who between 1908 and his death transformed the country into a big ranch and ruled it as if men and livestock belonged to the same herd. Mussolini's government ordered the translation of *Cesarismo Democrático* into Italian and praised it loudly. It was recommended to the European reader as a felicitous harbinger of the Fascist regime.

Both Gil-Fortoul and Vallenilla Lanz were educated men and distinguished historians. They met with Rubén Darío, Amado Nervo, Louis Bonafoux, Enrique Gómez Carrillo, Santiago Pérez Triana, and José María Vargas Vila in the Paris café Le Criterion. The men who gathered there were the flower of American literature in *modernismo*'s heyday. The Venezuelans studied sociology at the Sorbonne. When Vallenilla Lanz returned to Caracas, he was all the better equipped, like Gil-Fortoul, to serve the cause of dictatorship. His son said that it was necessary for him "to break with Romanticism and become analytical, cold, like Hippolyte Taine, whose work *Les Origines de la France Contemporanée* exerted a great influence over him." To be sure, serving the dictatorship of Guzmán Blanco was not the same as serving that of Gómez, but the "scientific" principle of Gil-Fortoul and Vallenilla Lanz provided the protocol for both. Laureano Vallenilla Lanz, Junior, was the brain and ghost writer of the more recent dictator, Colonel Pérez Jiménez, thus following in *his* father's footsteps. Vallenilla Lanz, Junior, published a book entitled *Escrito de Memoria* (*Written from Memory*), which served as a guide to his deplorable course.

Against that sociology which accepted from "science" the Comtian dictatorship and made it Creole, other writers emerged, such as Juan Vicente González (1811–66), author of *Historia del poder civil en Venezuela*, and Cecilio Acosta (1811-81), a poet and teacher to whom José Martí dedicated an unforgettable eulogy. Acosta wrote five volumes of essays, including, notably, a study called "Estado político y moral de las repúblicas hispanoamericanas."

¶ THE CUBAN ENLIGHTENMENT

A unique chapter in the Romantic, Liberal, and Positivistic development in America was written in the West Indies. The entire continent was able to free itself, but the armies of freedom could not undertake a war to include the islands. The Battle of Ayacucho in 1824 sealed the independence of the other colonies, but Cuba, Santo Domingo, and Puerto Rico, from which the Spanish Conquest had started, remained under the aegis of Spain. And there they stayed until the nineteenth century was nearly over. Cuba was freed in 1898 and became an American protectorate until 1902. Puerto Rico, freed at the same time, remains under the flag of the United States. Santo Domingo suffered the dictatorship of Haiti from 1822 to 1844, existed in chaos from 1844 to 1916, was occupied by United States troops from 1916 to 1930, and began that same year a dramatic struggle to achieve internal freedom during the lugubrious days of Trujillo's long dictatorship: thirty-one years! How ideas were mobilized under such circumstances is a matter for a separate history, which would have its moments of extreme tension.

The first American university was founded in Santo Domingo; the first colonial palaces and churches were built there; the first viceroyalty had a brief life there; historians and poets were born there; some of the basic books in American culture were written there. The printing press was introduced into Cuba in 1723 and the university was founded there in 1728. Puerto Rico shared many of those firsts as the other island in the trinity of the Greater Antilles. But the principal school that shaped the personality of the islands was the college of struggle with the corsairs, the pirates, the buccaneers, and the filibusters in the international cockpit of the Caribbean, which turned to smuggling and became the market for Negroes. The neighboring French were there for a time, then the Negro nation of Haiti, which led all Latin America in achieving independence and then succumbed to despotism. The English took Cuba by assault and held it from 1762 to 1763. That experience left a residue of new ideas in the island, among them the feeling that to trade is to live, and introduced Masonic lodges that were very active for a century thereafter.

The Enlightenment was not strange to Cuba, for the lodges certainly respected it. The Count of Aranda, an extremely influential minister in Spain during the reign of Charles III, was himself at the head of Hispanic Freemasonry. The *Papel Periódico*, the Patriotic Society of Friends of the Country, and the Consulate of Agriculture and Commerce were initiated in Cuba and a public library was opened there. Bishop Espada favored the Enlightenment and exerted a strong influence on the priest José Agustín Caballero (1771–1835), who was the first to come out against Scholasticism, to spread the word of Descartes, and to awaken opinion through his gazette. Caballero, in turn, smoothed the way for the fighter and philosopher, Félix Varela (1788–1853), also a member of the clergy, who took holy orders at the age of twenty-four, and, like Caballero, entered the Enlightenment movement. Caballero wrote: "What recourse has a teacher, however enlightened he may be, when he is ordered to teach Latinism by a

writer of the iron age, to swear blindly to Aristotle's words, and
when the same holds true of every other course?" Varela, his
pupil, wrote:

> There is a *Graeco-Latin-barbarian-arbitrary* idiom, which
> they call "Scholastic" and some formulas and ceremonies,
> which, they say, must be taught in the philosophy classes.
> I shall teach nothing of this, for I am not a teacher of idioms
> or of stupid formulas. Instead I am a comrade who smoothes
> the way for beginners in the study of nature, which has
> no idiom and admits of no rules.

Varela disseminated the philosophies of Locke and Condillac.
"The Holy Fathers," he wrote, "have no authority whatsoever
in matters of philosophy. . . . The Holy Scriptures, as St. Augustine observes, do not aim at training philosophers or mathematicians, but, rather, believers. . . ." Father Varela was heading
straight for politics along this road. In 1820, when the empire
under the Constitution of 1812 was being re-established in Spain
—and this was immediately proclaimed in Cuba—Bishop Espada
decided to create the chair of Constitutional Law and handed
it over to Father Varela.

> The accompanying exercises were considered the most bril-
> liant ever presented in Havana up to that time, and the
> chair was occupied constantly after January 18, 1821, when
> Varela delivered his opening oration to ninety-three students,
> and called it *the chair of liberty and the rights of man.* An
> unusual crowd kept the great hall of the College filled; every-
> one wanted to audit the lessons in politics.[1]

Elections for deputies to the Cortes in Spain were held in Cuba.
Naturally, Varela was among those chosen. The plans he had to
offer were radical: abolition of slavery, autonomy for the island,
and recognition of American independence. As if that were not
enough, he voted for the creation of a regency council that would
declare Ferdinand VII incompetent. He was tried for *lèse majesté*
and sentenced to death. By some miracle he escaped and fled to the
United States. The last thirty years of his life were spent there.
He founded *El Habanero*, a short-lived gazette, collaborated on
El Mensajero Semanal (*The Weekly Messenger*) of Philadelphia,
and translated Jefferson's works and a book on chemistry. Varela

---

[1] Felix Lizaso: *Panorama de la Cultura Cubana.*

died in exile, the first of the wandering Cubans whose lot seemed to be linked to the fate of the island, where the search for independence has gone on for centuries.

The question of slavery, raised by Varela in Spain, was to increase markedly in Cuba thanks to the man who took Varela's place in the university and eventually followed him into exile: José Antonio Saco (1797–1879). Saco was truly liberal. "Every enlightened young man of our time is necessarily a liberal." He declared for independence, whereupon the reactionary government presided over by Governor Tacón ordered him exiled to Trinidad. Saco refused to leave for Trinidad; instead he found sanctuary in the United States. Later he traveled extensively through Europe. After fifty-three years spent outside Cuba, he died in Barcelona at the age of eighty-two. He wrote his great work, which never has been surpassed, in Paris: *Historia de la esclavitud desde los tiempos más remotos hasta nuestros días* (*History of Slavery from the Most Remote Times to Our Day*), a comprehensive history of slavery published in four languages.

José de la Luz y Caballero (1800–62) continued Saco's work. He was called "the Cuban Master." His position vis-à-vis the Negroes was the same as his teachers': "On the question of the Negroes, the least black is the Negro." His vocation was teaching. He initiated the new generations into the most advanced thought of the century. He was acquainted with the United States and Europe and was a friend of Longfellow and Prescott, of Gay-Lussac, Cuvier, Champollion, and Humboldt. He conducted a famous interview with Sir Walter Scott, and translated *Voyage en Égypte et en Syrie* by Count de Volney.

During Luz y Caballero's stay in Paris, efforts were made to draw him into the "staircase plot." This conspiracy was the work of Negroes who planned to assassinate all the whites. It resulted in a great loss to literature in the death of the mulatto poet Gabriel de la Concepción Valdés, known as Plácido (1809–44), one of the great lyricists of his time. Plácido earned his living by doing the fretwork on tortoise-shell combs and writing verse for *La Aurora de Matanzas*. As he mounted the scaffold with ten other colored men, he was reciting the "Plea to God" which he had composed while he was waiting for the hour of his execution. Luz y Caballero returned to Havana to defend himself and never left the country again. He dedicated himself to teaching the coming generation. Thousands of students marched in his funeral cortège. He was the herald of independence.

Enrique José Varona (1849–1933), the man who bridged the
gap between the colony and the republic, followed Luz y Caballero.
He was a child when Luz y Caballero died; he became a
friend of Martí, whom he survived. He fought first against
colonial ideas and later against the dictatorships that gripped
the republic. During the 1933 student rebellion against the dictatorship of Gerardo Machado (1871–1939), he became the revered
symbol of an ideal; as a Positivist, he originally had followed
Comte, but had rejected him later because he could not accept
his creed. This brought him over to the side of Spencer and John
Stuart Mill, "leaving behind Comte's Positivism like a lighthouse
illuminating shores to which I will never return." Varona was
a skeptic and a man of faith. He knew doubt and summed up his
thoughts in aphorisms. *Con el Eslabón* (*The Link*) is a work of
exemplary thought: "How is a tyrant made? Out of the vileness
of many and the cowardice of all. . . ." " 'I feel Spanish,' exclaims
a new-baked Creole. Well, what matters is not to feel that you
are Spanish or English or Patagonian or Lucumi; what matters
is to be a man." "Our pedagogues are chasing a chimera; teaching
what they do not know.—How can that be? Don't they know
mathematics, physics, chemistry? . . . What they do not know is
the science of life."

One of Varona's contemporaries was a Puerto Rican who holds
an eminent place in the history of Latin American culture: Eugenio
María de Hostos (1839–1903). His work belongs in common to
the three islands. In New York he joined the Junta Revolucionaria
to fight for Cuba's independence; in 1898, when Puerto Rico
was occupied by American troops, he argued that his country
should be considered a state of the Union. He became rector of
the normal school in Santo Domingo, and in 1884 delivered a
speech that is judged to be a masterpiece of Spanish American
moral thinking. His immense output includes poetry, essays,
novels, and history. *La Peregrinación de Bayoán* is a novel, but it
is also the most fervent and poetic summons to a West Indian
federation which would unite Cuba, Santo Domingo, Puerto Rico,
and Haiti. Drawing the theme from an indigenous evocation,
he reconstructed from it the epic of the Indians. He wrote like
a Romanticist, using techniques that were new and surprising in
the Spanish novel. But his stature is not based on literary creation alone; it is the result of his teaching. His name is mentioned
along with those of Bello, Rodó, Sarmiento, and Martí. His
activities took him to both continents. In Spain he was a compan-

ion of Pi y Margall, Castelar, and Giner de los Ríos. In Chile, where he taught for nine years, he left an imprint almost as deep as Bello's. In Caracas, Lima, Buenos Aires, and New York he worked tirelessly and completed writings that fill two dozen volumes. His philosophy was Spencerian. His political doctrine is synthesized in his most comprehensive study, *Moral Social*. Hostos had the fighting spirit that Bello lacked, plus a poet's feeling for the struggle which moved beyond Positivism and the dogmatism inherited from Comte. Azcárate said of *Moral Social* what could be said of few other texts: "The work is steeped in a scent and taste so pure and delicate that it is a pleasure to read it." Unfortunately, Hostos built his dream for his continent upon an archipelago.

XVII: *Brazil from Colony to Empire to Republic*

¶ EXPULSION OF THE JESUITS

The earthquake of 1755 left Lisbon in ruins. The temblors that reduced it to rubble lasted only eight minutes, but left no stone standing on another. Local moralists who looked askance at the Enlightenment said that it was a punishment sent by God. Voltaire gives a detailed description of the calamity in *Candide*, after placing his hero *in medias res*. The Marquis de Pombal, who was the actual ruler of Portugal by virtue of his position as secretary of foreign affairs and war, said: "Let us bury the dead and take care of the living." He called in the leading architects and city planners, who mapped out a splendid city of broad avenues and beautiful buildings. From the ruins a new capital and an iron government arose. Pombal was no admirer of Voltaire, but he was allergic to the Jesuits, and his antagonism to them increased when an attempt was made on the life of the king which would have succeeded but for a seeming miracle and the courage of a coachman. Pombal made a secret and scrupulous investigation of the attempt. Extorted confessions revealed that the plot had involved four Jesuits and had originated with the noble Tavora family. The Tavoras were wiped out without mercy. The marchioness was beheaded and the marquis and the Duke of Aveira were cut to pieces on the wheel by blows from a machete. Count Atouquia, a relative of the Tavoras, his children, and four of his servants were decapitated. Gibbets were erected in the square and unspeakable cruelty was publicly flaunted. The Jesuits were punished less cruelly, but effectively, in a manner that embraced the entire order in the kingdom and the colony.

A brief memorandum was published on the Company of Jesus in the Spanish Colonies and Brazil. It was couched in words so virulent that the hangman in Madrid burned it in an official bonfire; however, it was circulated in Portugal as a state paper from Lisbon. Pombal sent a special ambassador to Rome to request the reform of the order, which, according to him, had violated the rules of St. Ignatius by delivering itself over to commerce and to the by-no-means spiritual exercise of the temporal power. The Indians in Brazil were set free—that is, made independent of the missionaries—by proclamation. The decree of expulsion was issued at the end of 1759. In January 1760 all the Jesuits in Brazil were put aboard a ship in Rio de Janeiro. But that was not the end of the matter. Pombal said: "This court considers the extermination of the Company of Jesus more useful than the discovery of India." Yet the cradle of the order had been rocked by the monarch of Portugal himself. Four years later, the Jesuits were expelled from France, and in 1767, from Spain, Naples, and Parma. Pombal went so far as to propose an invasion of the Papal States by France, Spain, and Portugal unless Rome would agree to suspend the order. He spared no money, influence, or threats until he had seen his wishes carried out.

Brazil paid both for the earthquake and the expulsion of the Jesuits. Lisbon called upon all the extraordinary resources of the colony for the reconstruction. Since the discovery of gold and diamond mines, Brazil looked very rich. The exile of the Jesuits left a great vacuum in Bahia, Belém, Rio de Janeiro, São Paulo, in Recife, and Misiones. The Company had owned houses, ranches, churches, colleges, and schools. In the state of Maranhão alone, they could count as theirs fifty-one villages and fifty-six ranches. Nowhere else in America had they dug in so deeply. But the after effects of their expulsion were handled very differently by Portugal than by Spain. In Spanish America, the Crown hastened to keep the schools going after the departure of the priests. Pombal was interested in Portugal alone. He stimulated the reform of the University of Coimbra, but only of Coimbra, where departments of physics and astronomy were inaugurated, a chair of chemistry and a theater of anatomy were established, and botanical gardens were created. It happened that two illustrious sons of Brazil, the magistrate Juan Pereira Ramos and Francisco de Lemos de Faria, were among those who encouraged those reforms and helped to make them possible. Lemos de Faria, who had never been granted the office of dean in Rio de Janeiro, was appointed rector of Coimbra. Another distinguished Brazilian, José Correia Picanço, who held a chair in Coimbra, was the first man to teach anatomy by dissecting cadavers. But Brazil had to wait until the Portuguese monarch moved across the Atlantic to the colony before such innovations could be introduced in America. José Correia Picanço left Coimbra to accompany the king. He opened a school of surgery in Bahia, which was soon augmented by other facilities for the teaching of medicine.

On Pombal's initiative, a glass works was founded in Portugal, and a duplicate of it was set up in Brazil after the arrival of the king. Before that time, industry had been forbidden in Brazil on the theory that it would be an incentive to independence. Queen Maria had decreed that all the shops or mills for making cotton cloth, other textiles, or embroidery then operating in Brazil were to be closed. Also, as soon as Lisbon learned in 1747 that a printing press had been taken to Rio de Janeiro by Antônio Isidoro da Fonseca, an order was sent out forbidding its work. Printing was not restored in Brazil until 1808.

In 1759, Pombal delegated the preliminary moves for expelling the Jesuits to the magistrate José Mascarenhas in Brazil. This gentleman, who favored the Enlightenment, was not entirely successful in accomplishing the mission entrusted to him. But he created an academy of forty distinguished men, the *Brasílica dos Renascidos* (*The Brazilian Renaissance*). The members were Benedictine, Carmelite, and Franciscan monks, canons, hidalgos, magistrates, and military officers, in short, anyone who counted in Bahia except the Jesuits, whom Pombal took good care to exclude. The academy held its meetings in the school of the Barefoot Carmelites. On its opening day the ceremonies started at three in the afternoon and continued until four in the morning. Sonnets were recited in Latin, Portuguese, Spanish, Italian, and French. According to Calmón:

Native themes were introduced, full of a sentimental novelty: the Indians (who rejoiced in the king's good health), historical problems surrounding the founding of Bahia, Brazilian bibliography, and the case of the grant of Bahian land

to the king by Paranguança in the light of the history of law.
. . . A member of the academy presented a list of the Indians
worthy of fame, like a roll call honoring the race. This glorifi-
cation of the men of Indian origin and its accompanying
exaltation of Brazil might have been considered inimical to
the Portuguese and indicative of a moral separation. The
insistence on speeches with a Brazilian flavor would confirm
that literary policy.[1]

The policy was in fact both Brazilian and French, for Mascarenhas
was a Francophile, and as such could hardly be pleasing to the
Crown. He was exiled to Santa Catalina and imprisoned there.
The academy was suspended.

¶ THE ROMANTICISTS

From Montaigne to Voltaire, the philosophers who expounded
the ideal of the noble savage in Europe for the most part based
their conception of him on the accounts of life among the Guaraní
Indians, natives of Paraguay and Brazil. Not surprisingly, the
Europeans' ideas made the return trip and revived the Brazilians'
picture of them. In the eighteenth century, before Romanticism
emerged, nature and the country were looked upon with romantic
affection. The seal of love was placed on the landscape by a
Franciscan monk, Manuel de Santa Maria Itaparica (1704–68?),
who wrote a description of the Island of Itaparica in seventy-two
stanzas of ottava rima. Claudio Manuel da Costa (1729–89),
one of the members of Mascarenhas's Academy, who signed
himself Glauceste Satúrnio in line with the vogue for adopting
pen names prevalent in the group, composed a number of sonnets
in the manner of Camões and wrote the *Canto to the Vila Rica*,
Vila Rica being the early name of Ouro Prêto (a gold-rush town
in the seventeenth century, later capital of Minas Gerais). Da
Costa also wrote the poem *Ribeirão do Carmo*, a precursor of *O
Uruguai*, the most important poem written by José Basílio da
Gama (1741?–95). José Basílio was educated in a Jesuit school,
visited Rome, where he became a member of the Arcadia, a sort
of academy of the Jesuits, and later moved to Coimbra. There
he was denounced as an ex-Jesuit and sentenced to exile in Angola,
but he saved himself by composing an epithalamium for Pombal's
daughter. He further ingratiated himself with the regime by

[1] Calmón: *História do Brasil*.

introducing malicious references to the Jesuits into *O Uruguai*. Machado de Assis believed that José Basílio inspired Voltaire to write *Candide*. But Afranio Peixoto claimed that it was the other way round. Actually, each influenced the other. No one can deny that *Candide* had a root in America. José de Santa Rita Durão (1722–84), an Augustinian monk, was graduated from Coimbra at about the time when José Basílio was there. Durão recognized that the atmosphere was hostile to him and emigrated to Rome, where Pope Clement made him a librarian. Durão, who considered that Brazil deserved a poem as much as India, wrote *Caramuru*, the Indian patriarch of which has the stature of a classical hero.

> Durão believed in man's goodness in his natural state, like the Humanists of the sixteenth century (Montaigne) and certain philosophers of the eighteenth (Rousseau). In the preface to his poem, he says he is writing it to unveil to the eyes of libertines what Nature can inspire in men who are far away from what are known as the preoccupations of sick minds.[1]

Tomaz Antônio Gonzaga (1744–1810) surpassed the aforementioned authors. Born in Portugal of a Brazilian mother, he went to live in Brazil. There he fell madly in love with Maria Dorotea Joaquina de Seixas. The love affair was thwarted, for Gonzaga was charged with being the rebel leader of the *Inconfidencia*, a freedom movement inspired by liberal ideas and the emancipation of the English colonies in the north. He was exiled to Mozambique, where he told the story of his love in a series of poems entitled *Marilia de Dirceu* ("Dirceu" was Gonzaga's pen name). His verses were welcomed with great acclaim in his day and stand as a pure outpouring of that Portuguese Romanticism which was inspired by Brazil.

In 1789, Brazil had its own miniature French revolution in secret. The conspirators all swore a vow to the republic and to a flag bearing the picture of an Indian breaking his chains. The leader of the group was Joaquím José da Silva Xavier (1748–92), nicknamed *Tiradentes* (Tooth-Puller). The plot was laid in Minas Gerais in the year that the Bastille fell. This identity of dates was a coincidence, for the real inspiration of the plotters was the example of the United States, not the Encyclopedists. The

[1] Bandeira: *Noções de Historia*.

only French book in evidence was one about United States constitutional law. Tiradentes wanted to have it translated. Actually the conspiracy was organized months before July 14, and it never moved beyond the stage of secret preparations. But someone informed on Tiradentes and the authorities captured him with the other conspirators. The first victim was the poet Claudio Manuel da Costa, who committed suicide in the dungeon where he was being held to await trial. The real martyr was Tiradentes himself, who assumed full responsibility for the plot and was hanged in Rio de Janeiro three years after the movement was discovered, the trial having moved at snail's pace. Tiradentes has passed into history as the first martyr of Brazilian freedom.

While Tiradentes was in prison and during the next few years the spirit of the French Revolution was spreading. In 1794 the members of the Literary Society met in Bahia at the house of the poet Manuel Inácio da Silva. Those present included a professor of Greek, a physician, and a professor of Latin grammar. When the authorities learned that the subject of their discussions was the French Revolution, they closed the society, threw the members into prison, and confiscated their books.

¶ THE NATURALISTS

An important scientific and naturalist movement began in Brazil on a scale smaller than in Spanish America. Fray José Mariano da Conceição Veloso (1742–1811) compiled an eleven-volume work entitled *Flora Fluminense* (*Plant Life of Rio de Janeiro*). We have already seen that Picanço, a Brazilian, introduced dissection to his anatomy classes in Coimbra. Another doctor, Professor Francisco de Melo Franco, was a very early predecessor of the twentieth-century U. S. pediatrician Dr. Benjamin Spock (1903–   ). He was also a sarcastic poet; his poem *Reino da Estupidez* (*Kingdom of Stupidity*) was composed in 1787.

Culture in Brazil made a place for itself mainly in the convents or the big houses of the estates. Antônio de Moraes Silva (1757?–1825), an owner of a sugar mill, humanist, and philologist, who compiled a *Diccionario da Lingua Portugueza* (*Dictionary of the Portuguese Language*, 2 vols., 1789), told a friend of his about the first translation of Adam Smith's *Wealth of Nations*, and before long it was being passed around among the groups of intellectuals. The Bishop of Olinda, Azeredo Coutinho, introduced the Encyclopedists into the seminary that he had founded. He wrote on problems of the greatest importance to the economic development of Brazil: the cultivation of coffee and cotton, the manufacture of porcelain, and tariffs. The Bishop attacked the old-style teaching that stopped with grammar, rhetoric, and Latin, and favored the teaching of the sciences. One of the Carmelite monks educated in that atmosphere later became Emperor Dom Pedro II's tutor and introduced the future emperor to the work of Rousseau, Helvetius, Condillac, and others. The Bishop of Olinda defended agriculture against the pipe dream of wealth from the mines. According to Calmón: "His fantasies culminated in the conviction that some day balloons with wings would be guided by a rudder ('the bird of Brazil'), for his philosopher's temperament also included an interest in physics. The bishop was not satisfied with the slow pace of earthly transportation; he was ambitious for space."[1]

¶ THE THEATER AND MUSIC; "O ALEIJADINHO"

During his trip around the world, Bougainville discovered that Rio de Janeiro had a theater. He noted in his book:

The viceroy was attentive to us for several days; he announced to us that he was giving a luncheon for us on the beach in the shade of orange and jasmine trees, and he reserved a box for us at the opera. We were able to see the master works of Metastasio played by a cast of mulattoes in a very beautiful hall and to listen to divine excerpts from the Italian masters performed by a poor orchestra that a hunchbacked priest in clerical garb was directing at that time.

At the beginning of the eighteenth century, Antônio José da Silva (1705–39) was the most important writer of comedies. He put on with great success the *Historia do Grande don Quichote de la Mancha e do Gordo Sancho Pança*, an early opera based on *Don Quixote*, and other works. However, he was tried as a Judaizer and sent to the stake in Lisbon. He continued to be known as "the Jew." But though his life came to an early and tragic end, his plays survived. He was put to a second, posthumous ordeal by fire when one of the two opera houses in Rio de Janeiro

[1] Calmón: *Historia do Brasil.*

burned to the ground during a performance of his comedy *Encantos de Medeia* in 1776.

Music always was, and still is, important in Brazil. The rhythms of Africa spread from the big houses to the court. Religious music was composed. Musicians from Minas Gerais wrote scores for da Silva's plays.

The most enduring art was created by the sculptors. True, the Lusitanian Baroque of the churches and altars never rose to such heights as the elaborate architecture in Mexico City, Quito, and Arequipa; and the style of the missions, though original, is modest. But the name of one sculptor stands out and will not be forgotten: Antônio Francisco Lisboa, known as "O Aleijadinho" ("The Little Cripple"—1730–1814), the son of a Portuguese carpenter and a slave. Fantastic legends were spun around him, but his true story is that of a heroic will. From leprosy or deforming rheumatism, his hands became almost useless, but his genius refused to be restrained. He painfully continued to carve stone and to create great works for posterity. He carved his most famous sculptures in soapstone, though he also made compositions in gilded wood and designed architectural work. His best-known statues, which adorn the massive staircase to the atrium of the Good Jesus of Matosinhos, portray twelve of the Hebrew prophets, men of the Old Testament whose characters most nearly approached his own mystical genius: Obadiah, Jeremiah, Isaiah, Habakkuk, Amos, Baruch, Ezekiel, Nahum, Jonah, Daniel, Hosea, and Joel. They constitute the most famous example of the Brazilian Baroque. In a study of "O Aleijadinho"[1] Romualdo Brughetti points out a juxtaposition of styles in his work: a Christ that adheres loyally to the German Baroque but does not reject the naturalism of the Italian, angels that seem to be copies from the eighteenth-century French, and reliefs from the French Gothic. The same multiplicity of schools was present in his sketches and engravings, but the deformed but vigorous hands of the son of the carpenter and the slave blended them into a sum of genius. "O Aleijadinho" made a synthesis with all his ability by absorbing the cultures of his cosmopolitan race.

¶ THE MONARCHS MOVE FROM PORTUGAL

On November 28, 1807, a fleet of eight English ships set sail from Portugal carrying ten thousand tightly packed

[1] *Cuadernos* (Paris, February, 1964).

fugitives bound for Brazil. The fugitives were the monarchs of Portugal, their court, and their servants. If their departure had been delayed by even twenty-four hours, they would have been captured by Napoleon's troops commanded by General Junot. Queen Maria and her son, the regent Don John, would have fallen like Charles IV of Spain. Queen Maria I, "an apathetic idiot," had lost her mind soon after mounting the throne. Her son Don John ruled as regent in the shadow of her melancholy. He spent fifteen years watching his mother attend ceremonies like the ghost of a queen. France and Spain had resolved to take over the kingdom of Portugal; consequently the escape of the court was a setback for Napoleon. But England rejoiced:

> This great Prince, the wealthiest in the world, preferred to leave the country in which he was born and his treasures and property in order to elude the French alliance and unite with us. He was the first sovereign of that land to cross the tropical seas to a nation that will be one of the richest in the world, and to unite himself with us. The King of England and Parliament swear in the name of the nation that they will defend this Prince against his enemies; they will avenge him; and will sacrifice their normal power and their industry to defend his heroism.[1]

The fleet touched at Bahia on its way to Rio de Janeiro. Beautiful landscapes, warm lands, a raw but promising world, though lacking the splendor of the courts of Europe, which had acquired the polish of centuries. The leading families lived in mansions on the plantations. The cities could not display such luxury as the viceregal courts of Mexico or Lima, but the mere presence of its sovereign was to work a magical change in the realm and eventuate in its independence. Local men of ambition reasoned that a monarch *in* Brazil was monarch *of* Brazil. And so he was, more or less. From the first moment, the regent promoted industry. He opened the country to trade with other nations, meaning England. The traffic that had come and gone between Brazil and Lisbon until the eve of the royal departure shifted now to the run between Brazil and England. A marine insurance company was founded. Business houses in London and Liverpool opened branches in Bahia and Rio de Janeiro where they started at once to export coffee and other tropical products and to receive foreign merchandise.

[1] Calmón: *Historia do Brasil.*

The ten thousand fugitives—queen, regent, royal family, nobility, ministers, ladies-in-waiting, and pages—all had to settle down, maintain their protocol, and show their breeding. The ten thousand *émigrés* brought their furniture, china, linen, clothing, jewels, books, and *objets d'art*. Industry was forced to step up its pace to provide the new seat of government with pleasures and luxuries. The bourgeoisie, who acted as the dynamic and positive element in the period, had to be granted privileges in order to operate. A bank was established, the mint started to coin money, a new theater was built, a school of music opened, botanical gardens were planted, and an academy of science and another for training the armed forces were founded. The military academy brought together mathematicians, physicists, and botanists who, with the philosophers, later would make of it an institution intimately bound up with the historical and cultural evolution of the country.

The printing press made its debut with the publication of such works as the translated *Statement by the Landowners of Buenos Aires*, Mariano Moreno's document that rang in Argentina's independence, and a compendium of Adam Smith's *Wealth of Nations*. The *Gazeta do Rio de Janeiro* began publication. There was much talk of freedom for industry; the Masonic lodges expanded; the exploitation of iron was initiated; a mission of artists was imported to promote a school of painting and help the museum. Distinguished travelers came and recorded in their journals the marvels of Brazilian nature and the bounty of the country's natural resources. Calmón writes:

> Aside from the foreigners under contract for public service, Eschwege, Varnhagen, Freyress, Feldner, and the artists of the Lebreton mission, which included Debret, who left us an excellent book of engravings in addition to his designs, we must list the learned men who came with Archduchess Leopoldina: Martius, Spix, Pohl, Nattere, Raddi, Mickan, Buchberger, and the artist Thomas Ender, whose watercolors constitute a beautiful documentary picture. . . . The *Historia Natural das Palmeiras* by Martius, beautiful in its learning and art, alone would be enough to grant the mission sent by the Austrian government an outstanding place in modern culture. The naturalist Swaison met traveling scholars from the courts of Austria, France, Russia, and Tuscany in Rio.

Queen Maria died in 1816 after twenty-five years of insanity. The regent was proclaimed King: John VI, just as he would have been in Lisbon. By that time Brazil had become a chapter in the history of monarchy in Europe. But new ideas were gaining ground. In the years between 1789 and 1816, the world had seen kings fall, the bourgeoisie rise, and the people come into government. Philosophers were reigning in the monarchs' stead. The republic of the United States was born and the war for Spanish American independence had started. In Spain, the Cortes of Cádiz were welcoming liberal ideas and Lisbon was following suit. The downfall of Napoleon was similar to the toppling of many thrones. In 1817 a revolt broke out in Pernambuco. The native Brazilians rose against the Portuguese. People poured into the streets shouting, "Long live our country! Death to the *marinheiro!*" A *marinheiro* was anyone from across the sea. Nationalism and the philosophy of the Enlightenment were playing background parts, but the preponderant role was the Masons'. The mulatto Cabuga was delegated to carry a communication from the lodge in Brazil to the "brother president of the United States." The republican flag was blessed and the lodge members hailed one another as patriots and citizens, as titles were done away with. Yet nothing happened. The revolution was smothered, leaving the red residue of the dead that always is the remnant of popular effusions. The reaction came; the king issued a decree against the Masons. But the memory of rebellion still floated in the air. Three years later another revolution broke out in Pará and Bahia. People said that as the Estates General had met in Portugal under pressure from the lodges, the monarchy in Brazil must be constitutional and the king must swear allegiance to the constitution. The troops rebelled, shouting "Long live the Constitution!" The clergy, who had not stood aside during the revolution in Pernambuco, now sided with the military. King John VI finally swore by the constitution—a constitution unknown to anyone.

The liaison agent between the constitutionalists and the king was Prince Pedro (1798–1834), already adept at such employment. King John was acclaimed by the people and knew his moment of glory. When he went out in his state carriage, he was greeted with unanimous enthusiasm. The people unhitched his horses and pulled his carriage all the way to the palace. The new circumstances released many feelings hitherto repressed. Liberals and conservatives alike delivered themselves of ardent polemics. Later, the Congress, irritated by the tumult, met in closed sessions and appointed a conservative cabinet. The people paraded in front of the palace shouting, "Down with the aristocrats! We want a People's Parliament!" The king tried to speak, but could not make himself heard. At about that time he was being called back to Lisbon; the mother country, rid of Napoleon, wanted its king. John was preparing to return. One day he said to the crown prince: "Pedro, if Brazil separates from Portugal, it will remain in your hands because you are bound to respect me. Don't let it fall into the hands of any of these adventurers." Thus he turned the government over to Prince Pedro, packed the silver from the public coffers into his trunks, and left the country. That was in April 1821. Masonry took a deep breath. In June the brothers of the great Eastern lodge and the members of the lodge of Commerce and Letters paraded publicly through the streets.

¶ INDEPENDENCE WITHOUT BLOODSHED

The idea of independence was spreading, especially encouraged by José Bonifácio de Andrada e Silva (1763–1838), a poet, naturalist, translator of Virgil, and one-time professor at Coimbra. He adopted the pen name "Americo Elysio" when he published his *Poesias avulsas* (*Sundry Poems*). After his return to São Paulo, he founded the Economic Society, patterned after the Spanish Enlightenment. Moreover he became the patriarch of independence. He favored a constitutional monarchy ruled by Prince Pedro. He also cherished a romantic notion of government by tribes and proconsuls. In São Paulo he founded a society that laid the foundations of the new state and he proposed to start the regime with a junta presided over by the governor. His ground rules were approved, and the other provinces were invited to adopt the plan.

Meanwhile, the rulers were beginning to fear that the presence of Prince Pedro in Brazil would lend wings to the movement for independence. They therefore called him back to Portugal for "a journey of study." Prince Pedro received the summons with indignation, knowing that it would take from him a country in which he felt himself rooted. The Brazilians also rebelled; the summons to Prince Pedro would mean returning to the absolutist colonial system. The Club of the Resistance was formed in Rio de Janeiro. It sent manifestos all over the country rejecting Lisbon's decrees. José Bonifácio echoed the resistance in São Paulo. The whole nation was in agreement. The Senate moved for a demonstration before Prince Pedro, who acceded, saying that none of the decrees from Lisbon would be complied with as long as he refused to give them his "order to comply." The Masons granted Prince Pedro the title of "Perpetual Defender of Brazil," and the Chamber and Senate approved it. Some months later, as the prince was fording the Iparanga River, near Santos, on horseback, he received a bundle of mail containing letters from Lisbon which treated him as a rebel and a letter from José Bonifácio urging him to declare independence. Prince Pedro rose in his stirrups and gave his famous battle cry: "Independence or Death!" He had crossed the Rubicon. Brazil was independent. Prince Pedro entered São Paulo to clamorous acclaim. That night the audience in the São Paulo opera house gave the new sovereign a standing ovation. "Long live the first king of Brazil!" On his return to Rio he was proclaimed emperor.

The doctrinal struggle between democrats and monarchists provided a natural cockpit for debate among the champions of independence. The lodges of Buenos Aires, Montevideo, Bahia, and Rio de Janeiro were stirring up public opinion. But nothing could mar the magnificence of the coronation. As a token of honor to the land, the king was wearing "a splendid cape of toucan feathers, which made him look like an Indian chief" instead of the ermine worn by European monarchs. Dom Pedro had not been aware of the art of featherwork as it was practiced by the Indians until 1824, when he was visited by Kamehameha II, King of Hawaii, who gave him a beautiful feather mantle that is preserved in the national museum.

Brazil had won independence bloodlessly, but the struggle among monarchists and republicans, federalists and centralists, clergy and anticlericals, slaves and abolitionists still raged in parliament and in the newspapers, streets, and offices. The press was more active than ever. In 1825 the *Diario de Pernambuco* was established, and in 1827 the *Jornal do Comercio*, which still is published in Rio de Janeiro. Only the United States has dailies older than these in Brazil, although in Spanish America a daily had been published in Lima between 1790 and 1793, and the *Diario de Mexico* had been published in Mexico City between about 1790 and 1817. Brazil, the last colony to make the acquaintance of the printing press, turned it into a weapon almost before anyone could enjoy it, and never has ceased to use it as such.

Brazil's liberal principles derived from France, the organization of her law courts from England. The Consul General of São Paulo proposed in the Chamber the abolition of a celibate clergy. Some priests supported the plan with fervor. The would-be reformers of the state also desired reform of the clergy. The Emperor was not enthusiastic. By 1830 he tried to elude such battles because he believed that his presence would only make the situation more difficult. True to his slogan "Independence or Death," he felt that he was not capable of keeping order in the independent country, and he abdicated—of his own free will. Five years earlier he had renounced the crown of Portugal, relinquishing it to his daughter Maria da Gloria, who became Queen Maria II. Now he left the throne of Brazil to his son Pedro, a child of six. José Bonifácio was to stay with the prince as his tutor. At three o'clock in the morning of April 7, Dom Pedro handed his renunciation to his chief clerk, Frías. It was dated "the tenth year of independence." He said to Frías: "Here is my abdication. I believe they will be the happier for my leaving. I am going to Europe, away from a country I have always loved, and shall go on loving."

❡ DOM PEDRO II (1825–91)

The nine years that followed, while the young prince was being educated, saw no truce in the arguments between the Masonic lodges and the Church. A separate republic was proclaimed in the South. One of the leaders of the rebels was Garibaldi, an almost unknown guerrilla fighter who had come to Brazil bringing messages from Young Italy. Garibaldi who was destined for glory as the Gran Condottiere of Italian Unity, fought at the head of the "*descamisados*" ("shirtless ones"), the rag-tag and bobtail known as the "*farrapos*." This experience on American soil did so much to increase his stature that he became the hope of Italian patriots. The war in the South ended with a victory for the government.

Bishop Romualdo issued a pastoral letter attacking the Masons. Canon Batista de Campos used it to arouse the people not only against the Masons but also against the regency. The governor of Rio Grande province mobilized a flotilla that defeated the rebels. Canon Campos died while trying to escape. The governor and the commandant of the army were murdered to avenge him. The French in Guiana made a bid to extend their possessions by invading from the north. The republic of the *piratini*—members of a local movement to make part of Rio Grande do Sul independent of Brazil—was proclaimed.

In 1841 it was decided to declare Dom Pedro of age, though he was barely fourteen, and to place him on the throne in order to prevent anarchy. One of the deputies put forth a simple legal statement: "Senhor Dom Pedro II is declared of age from now on." To avoid a vote on the question, the regent suspended the Chamber. The deputies refuse to yield and appealed to the Senate. The people were singing in the streets:

> *We want Dom Pedro the Second,*
> *For now he has come of age.*
> *He was born to dispense our laws,*
> *Long live His Majesty.*

The senators and deputies united in a single bloc and sent a commission to Dom Pedro. The commissioners asked him: "Will Your Majesty wait until the second of December, when he reaches the age of fifteen to assume the government, or does he wish it now?" Dom Pedro said, "*Quero ja*" ("I want it now"). And that was the end of the matter. On the morning of July 23, the Chamber and Senate met and proclaimed the prince of age. Dom Pedro took the oath in the afternoon: "I swear to uphold the Catholic, Apostolic, Roman religion, the integrity and indivisibility of the Empire, to observe and have observed the political constitution of the Brazilian nation and the laws of the Empire, and to oversee the general welfare of Brazil insofar as it lies within my power."

¶ THE ENLIGHTENED EMPEROR

The man who first undertook to educate Dom Pedro was José Bonifácio. He introduced the prince to the natural sciences, poetry, and languages. Dom Pedro was a model of enlightenment without despotism. He used to say that he would rather have been a schoolteacher than an emperor. He felt that the duties of his position as prince and sovereign kept him from devoting himself to a career of scholarship. He was a friend of the learned men of his time. He loved the study of languages, and said at one time:

I can translate at sight Latin and English, which are languages I also speak fluently, and Greek and German, too, which, however, I speak poorly. I have expressed myself in French since I began to talk. Italian and Spanish I have spoken from childhood. As for the other languages, I have studied them only in relation to philology, although I have translated them.

He studied Tupi and Guaraní, Arabic, Provençal, Hebrew, and Sanskrit. He had always been interested in the history of the Jews and was seen in the synagogues of London and San Francisco, California, translating at sight from the Talmud. Longfellow considered that the emperor's translation of his "Story of King Robert of Sicily" gave new charm to the tale because it had a more musical ring in Portuguese. Dom Pedro was enthusiastic over Thucydides. He wrote to his close friend the diplomat, Orientalist, and sociologist Count Gobineau: "In my leisure moments, I translate Thucydides. How I should like to have read his funeral oration again in front of the ruins of the Acropolis!" His enthusiasm for history and geography made him a patron of the Brazilian Institute from childhood. When he was barely fourteen years old, he had it installed in one of the rooms of the palace, and through the years he made it one of the richest institutions of its kind by endowing it with the finest collections, buying up libraries, maps, medals, and documents, and he was able to take a discreet part in its debates. He also had an observatory built on the palace terrace where he participated in astronomical studies. The Botanical Gardens were enlarged by his contributions.

The Emperor's patronage of the arts was famous. He wrote to Gobineau, asking for news of a Brazilian of Italian parentage who was then studying sculpture with the Italian naturalist Giulio Monteverde. Gobineau sent a good report on Rodolfo Bernardelli (1852–1931), and Dom Pedro became his patron. Bernardelli, one of the outstanding sculptors of Brazil, composed such famous groups as *Christ and the Woman Taken in Adultery* and *The Mourning of the Tribe*, and helped to decorate the Municipal Theater of Rio de Janeiro. The musician Antônio Carlos Gomes (1839–96), at the age of twenty-three, asked the help of the Emperor in order to study at the conservatory. Dom Pedro granted it, and within two years Gomes had completed his first opera, *O Noite no Castelo* (*Night in the Castle*). When this work and another had been staged with great success, the Emperor, a Wagner enthusiast, planned to send Gomes to Germany, but the Empress decided on Italy. Gomes studied in Milan and composed several outstanding works, among them *O Guaraní*. This was the only opera by a South American composer sung in La Scala; it is still occasionally heard in Italy. In 1870 it was presented in Rio de Janeiro to wild applause.

Dom Pedro's patronage also extended to writers. The first of these was Brazil's greatest romantic poet, Antônio Gonçalves Dias (1823–64), whom he sent on a mission to Europe to collect documents pertaining to the history of Brazil. Dias came back with forty volumes. The Emperor was mainly interested in having the poet's work published in Europe. This protégé of the Emperor was the bastard son of a Portuguese immigrant and an Indian or mulatto woman. His father took him to Portugal, where he studied at Coimbra and learned French, English, German, Spanish, and Italian. Dias made his mark as a poet with his *Primeiros Cantos*. After his return to Brazil, he worked in the Ministry of Foreign Relations until Dom Pedro sent him back to Europe. The poet showed the breadth of his romantic interests in his translation of Schiller's *Die Braut von Messina* (*The Bride of Messina*) and two theatrical works: *Patkull*, taken from a Swedish legend, and *Beatriz Cenci*, based on Italian history. But his heart was in all things Brazilian, which he treated both scientifically and lyrically. He collected a *Vocabulario da Lingua Geral Usada no Alto Amazonas* (*Vocabulary of the Lingua Geral Used in the Upper Amazon*), and later a *Dicionário da Lingua Tupi* (*Dictionary of the Tupi Language*). His volume of *Cantos* begins with an Indian theme, treated in the epic poem *Os Timbiras*, and subjects of that nature appear throughout his work. He has been called "the first authentic voice of Brazilian poetry."

Dom Pedro helped the poet Domingo José Gonçalves de Magalhães (1811–82) and paid for the publication of his *Confederação dos Tamoios* and two translations from the Italian. Magalhães was a poet of lesser stature than Gonçalves Dias, but he holds an important place in Brazil's literary history as author of the Manifesto of the Romanticists, published in Paris in the review *Niterói*, a magazine that brought together a group of Brazilians representative of the period. The Manifesto, which is written like an essay on the history of Brazilian literature, was a bugle call to enroll Lamartine, Victor Hugo, and Schiller among the major gods on the poetic Olympus of Brazil. Another of the Emperor's protégés was the poet Manuel de Araujo Porto-Alegre (1806–79), who was also a painter and architect, as well as one of the editors of *Niterói*. A man of broad interests, he published in the review an essay on Brazilian music. After returning to his own country, he founded the Conservatory of Dramatic Art and the Imperial Academy of Opera. Although not an outstanding poet, he ventured boldly into the field of archaeology in his comedy *A Estátua Amazônica*. Such ventures were characteristic of the Romanticists. Dom Pedro maintained an unbroken correspondence on history with Francisco Adolfo de Varnhagen (1816–78), the great Brazilian scholar whose *Historia Geral do Brasil* crowns the historiography of the empire.

¶ THE REPUBLIC BEGINS WITH THE FREEING OF THE SLAVES

The dissemination of liberal ideas prospered under the emperor. The first objective of the liberals was the abolition of slavery. In the time of Dom Pedro I, a treaty with England was signed in 1826, by the terms of which Brazil agreed to end the importation of slaves. The treaty was not kept because the slavers found ways to smuggle in such saleable merchandise. An attempt was made to renew the treaty in 1845. As England was far from sure of the attitude of the traders, she approved the Aberdeen Law, which enabled the Crown to pursue slave ships on the high seas. The next step taken by Great Britain was to exercise direct control over the ports in Brazil. The only chance Brazil had to avoid such humiliation was to adopt a policy of her own and attack the smugglers. In 1850 a law was approved which Dom Pedro put into effect immediately. The number of imports fell abruptly. In 1851, 3,287 slaves were landed; in the following year 700, and in the next, 56. Twenty years later, José Maria da Silva Paranhos, Viscount of Rio Branco (1819–80), succeeded in steering through parliament the law of *Liberdade do Ventre* (Free Birth, literally, "Freedom from the Womb," i.e., the granting of freedom from slavery to the children of slaves). The galleries of the Senate were packed. When the voting ended, a rain of flowers fell upon the members of Parliament in the midst of a tremendous ovation. The minister of the United States, who had attended the historic debate, asked one of the ushers to pick up some of the flowers for him so that he could send them to his own country to show how Brazil had done with flowers what had cost his country rivers of blood. Antislavery literature then reached its romantic apogee. Antônio de Castro Alves (1847–71), a dramatist and poet, came to be known as the "poet of the slaves." His work *Os Escravos* (*The Slaves*) has been rated superior to *Uncle Tom's Cabin* owing to the force of its style and the warmth of its feeling. The famous poem "A Cachoeira de Paulo Afonso" (Paulo Afonso Falls), a small but intense melodrama of the interior of Brazil is in *Os Escravos*; also the "Navio Negreiro" (Slave Ship), which pictures the horrors of the vessels loaded in Africa to satisfy the slavers' unbridled greed.

The liberals fought on all fronts for the advanced ideas of their time. Their leader was the Viscount of Rio Branco, who sponsored free examinations, laicism, and Masonry. He boldly raised the burning question of the power of the bishops, posed by the decree of suspension issued in 1870 by the Bishop of Rio de Janeiro against Father Almeida Matins, the orator of the Masonic temple of the Great Eastern Lodge of Lavradio, because the latter offered homage to Rio Branco, the Grand Master. The presence of a priest in a lodge during such an affair was condemned by the Pope. The struggle between Church and State continued for two years more and created some major difficulties with Rome. No accommodation could be reached until the Viscount of Rio Branco became head of the government.

The question of the slaves had not been settled yet. Abolition was not to come until 1888, while the emperor was in Europe traveling for his health. The man who gave his name to the liberation party was Joaquím Nabuco (1849–1910), the poet and historian who wrote *O Abolicionismo* (*Abolition*) and one of the orators who helped put the law through the congress. The measure was contained in a single article which said: "Slavery is declared extinct in Brazil." This has been called "the Golden Law." The birth of the republic is identified with this happy ending. The remarkable feature of the whole process is that it began amid flowers and ended in a kind of carnival. Another wonder is that it all happened within a monarchy which, more than any other, had been wedded to slavery, a monarchy in which the last slave ships to leave Africa made port. The law of Free Birth, approved in Rio de Janeiro in 1871, had been ratified by Colombia in 1821. Slavery was declared extinct in Brazil seventeen years later. The Chilean constitution of 1833 stated: "There shall be no slaves in Chile: he who walks its land is a free man by virtue of that fact alone." In 1850, Dom Pedro passed the decree forbidding the trade in slaves which was the same law passed in 1812 by Rivadavia in Argentina. Only in Cuba did slavery last almost as long as in Brazil, but Cuba was a colony still under the Spanish flag. Slavery was abolished in Mexico in 1828. In 1856 the adventurer William Walker conceived the idea of seizing the government of Nicaragua and making it one of the slave territories of the United States. He was able to maintain his "presidency" for a year but was captured by the British in 1860, turned over to Honduras, and shot.

In 1889, precisely a hundred years after the French Revolution began, a republic was proclaimed in Brazil as a sort of gesture by America in honor of the fall of the Bastille. Dom Pedro had just returned from Europe to find himself with a slaveless empire. On July 14, the republic was born to a song as the students poured into the streets singing *La Marseillaise*. The army heard them with joy. Benjamin Constant was then lecturing on the Positivist and republican philosophies to the cadets and officers in the Military Academy. Manuel Deodoro da Fonseca (1827–92), commander of the army, bowed to the republic. He was Constant's closest friend. On November 14, the rumor spread that Constant and Manuel Deodoro were about to be arrested. On the fifteenth the republic was born. Everything happened with seeming naturalness. When Ouro Prêto, the president of the Council, learned that an insurrection was getting under way, he fortified himself in the Palace of Justice. But there he could count only on his fire brigade, which could not fight bullets with water. Floriano, the commandant, reminded him that the Paraguayans had attacked the artillery by throwing their arms around the cannon. In Brazil, however, the artillery was so persuaded by Benjamin Constant's theories that no gunner could bring himself to fire on the republic that was being proclaimed. Deodoro rode forth on his beautiful horse at the head of his army and the troops followed him as if parading in peace time. Floriano saw Deodoro, held out his hand, and said to him: "Now we are all Brazilians!" The republicans marched through the streets amid fanfare and flags, as the anniversary of a battle would be marked in another country.

"We are all Brazilians!"—starting with Dom Pedro. When the Emperor was notified that the republic had been proclaimed, he said: "So be it." He composed a short letter of farewell and sailed for Europe a few hours later. Many of his former subjects escorted him to his stateroom; later he was granted a pension. If he had been deposed in earlier times, Dom Pedro would have had to live his years of exile with all the decorum of a former emperor of Brazil. He would not have liked that. He went back to Europe to pick up the threads of his conversations with other scholars, which sufficed to fill his life and soothe his vanity.

¶ DISCIPLES OF COMTE AND CLOTILDE

The new philosophy of Positivism, which had been propagated during the empire, was to turn out to be the fairy godmother of the republic. The Military Academy was first and foremost a polytechnic school for engineers, but it had some philosophical embellishments. By 1850 some candidates for the doctorate were submitting dissertations inspired by Comte. When Benjamin Constant Botelho de Magalhães (1830–91) joined the military training school in 1852, the environment was ready for him. From his chair of mathematics he taught the Positivist philosophy to his future republican squadrons. The military historians who have since studied the process from the strictly professional point of view, never cease to be astounded. Captain Severino Sombra has said:

> In Brazil, Comte's ideas relative to the end of the military spirit exerted a regrettable influence on the armed forces by bringing to the troops the idea of themselves as natives of the country, which resulted in a spirit of revolt against our military traditions. Within a short time the inspiring moral position of the army was destroyed. The "secret incompatibility between the scientific spirit and the military spirit," indicated by Comte, vitiated deplorably the teaching in our military schools, uprooting from the centers of military education their essential character, which entails a moral and intellectual training for war. An influence so harmful has been able to make headway only in Brazil.

After quoting these words by Captain Sombra, Jaçinto Camilo Oliveira de Torres, the historian of Positivism, comments: "I have little to add to what this patriot philosopher says. But that such an influence should be recorded only in Brazil reduces any cause for alarm. Especially as Brazil was the Canaan of Positivism. And owing also to the transformation of our officers into professors of mathematics."

Perhaps these comments have an unduly tragic ring. In brief, what happened was that the army, instead of fighting for the monarchy, turned to fighting for the republic. Something similar was noted earlier at the Seminary of Olinda, established by a bishop of the Enlightenment, where the seminarians enrolled to serve the Church, read the *Encyclopédie*, and graduated enthusiasts of Rousseau. Such things made the period swing like a flying trapeze. Benjamin Constant's students discussed war only to criticize what had been done against Paraguay. They were more interested in the abolition of slavery than in remaining under the yoke of the mother country. The Military Club became a Positivist club. A flag was designed for Brazil soon after its independence was won. In the center of the banner, the motto of Positivism was inscribed: "Order and Progress," which is still Brazil's slogan.

What was the Emperor's attitude toward Positivism? Something more than benevolent. Dom Pedro was pleased to attend the graduation exercises at which Comte's thesis was defended. He appointed Benjamin Constant tutor to the imperial family. He kept Miguel Lemos in the position he had won in a competition, ignoring the opposition of the conservatives who objected to his work in the National Library.

Some of the most distinguished Positivists in Brazil were possessed by Comtian zeal to such an extent that they were not content to follow their master's philosophy, but also became converts to his religion. This creed was a by-product of an ideological development in Comte's mind after he had lost the freshness of his best days. Benjamin Constant himself adhered at first to the Positivist religion but later rejected it. Miguel Lemos and Texeira Mendes remained devout converts to it until the end of their lives.

Miguel Lemos (1854–1916) was the son of an army officer. In his youth he became a republican, even though his family was Catholic. He studied at the polytechnic school. At the age of twenty-five he went to Paris as a student all aglow with Positivistic zeal. By the time he reached France, Comte had been dead for twenty years, and his disciples had split into two branches: one, headed by Littré remained on the strictly scientific plane; the other, led by Lafitte, followed Comte's mystical religion and paid homage to the memory of Clotilde de Vaux. The Religion of Humanity was postulated during that twilight. To Lemos, who clung fervently to Lafitte, Littré was a traitor. Lemos wrote a description of his first visit to Clotilde's house, which had been made into a

church: "I came out tasting in anticipation a universal regenera-
tion. One sensed there a new world and a religion consecrated by
its adepts to self-sacrifice and to the martyrdom of its founder.
I suspected that the new redeemer might have his Judas as well
as his Cross."

Lemos revived Comte's "prophecies," which chose America
as the continent of Positivism:

> The nations of South America, born of the same Western
> civilization but without the retarding obstacles that hamper
> the victory of the new faith in the Old World, without a
> powerful clergy or dominant scientific corporations, without
> parliamentary traditions, without an oppressive and lawless
> industrialism, are nations that lend themselves to an accept-
> ance of the regenerative doctrine in both the temporal and the
> spiritual field. Children of the hidalgos who were the Cid's
> compatriots—Nuño Álvarez, Cervantes, Camões—they re-
> tain all the puissance of southern enthusiasm which leads
> them to sympathize spontaneously with a religion conceived
> to revivify the feeling deadened by revolutionary doubt and
> to exalt the vivid enlightenment of science. The progeny of
> the founders, devoted to the ideal of Mary, must perforce
> grasp with sympathy the religion that has been founded on
> the worship of woman and proclaims the supremacy of love.

By these statements of principle Lemos managed to convert his
fiancée to the religion inspired by the angelic mysticism of Clotilde
de Vaux. Lemos went back to Brazil as a priest consecrated to
Positivisim and erected the temple to Humanity where his body
would lie in state twenty years later after his brothers carried
it down from the mountains. He was buried to music by Beethoven
and a long speech by Texeira Mendes.

Raimundo Texeira Mendes (1855–1927), the intimate friend
and successor of Lemos, wrote the *Life of Benjamin Constant.*
Mendes was the noblest and most mystical of the Positivists in
his country. Like Lemos, he started his studies in the polytechnical
school. He and Lemos went together to Paris, where Mendes
studied medicine. He wanted an Encyclopedic training. After
returning to Brazil, he consecrated himself to the evangelical
type of Postivism. In 1884 he celebrated the feast of the Virgin
Mother, whom he worshipped as an idealization of the Great
Being, Humanity, and an embodiment of the Positivist religion.
He instituted a semi-idolatry of woman in the abstract, which

began on the date that Catholicism has set aside for glorifying the Virgin Mary, the goddess of the Middle Ages. Oliveira Torres states:

> In 1882, Texeira Mendes contracted marriage with Senhorita Ernestina Torres de Carvalho. This was the first time that a wedding ceremony was performed according to the Positivistic rites anywhere in America, perhaps in the world. The man who officiated was Miguel Lemos, Lafitte's delegate. . . . At the time, Positivism was not a legally recognized religion. This created a serious problem, which Texeira Mendes finally solved by having a minister stand by to officiate. The wedding took place three months after the couple began to live together. Those three months of keeping house proved that the young people were well suited to each other and would be able to get along well. We are reminded of the experiences of Comte and his wife. Hence their prudence in demanding a three-month experiment before contracting marriage.

Texeira Mendes, influenced, like Comte, by Catholic memories, was an apostle of the new religion. He went to Paris to make a pilgrimage to the "holy places," that is, the spots where Clotilde and Comte had spent their brief life together, and later wrote the "holy life" of the two founders. Clotilde had to be made to seem as positivistically inspiring to Comte, as St. Clare had been to St. Francis.

Texeira Mendes introduced two courses in philosophy in the normal school. He and Lemos wrote the outlines of a "dictatorial federative" constitution "for the republic." One notable feature of their plan was that it provided for the protection of the Indians. José Bonifácio had agitated for that idea ever since the days of independence, but many people were still discussing it in Brazil, particularly the Germans who clung to the old belief that "the only good Indian is a dead Indian." Cruz Costa recalls in *O Positivismo na República* (*Positivism in the Republic*) the debate between Texeira Mendes and the director of the São Paulo museum, Dr. Hermann Ihering, a German naturalist, who maintained that because the Indians were not an element for progress, but a nuisance to colonization instead, there was nothing to do but to exterminate them. At any rate, the "*wild*" Indians.

¶ THE BACKLANDS

Until far into the twentieth century, Brazil had to juggle two
different and simultaneous processes. One was that of the cities
and estates, where civilization became stabilized. The other was
that of the frontier, which the *bandeirantes* had gradually pushed
inland toward the backlands—*o sertão*.

In Brazil the concept of the frontier is as old as the nation.
It was born at the time of the captaincies in the sixteenth century.
Nuclei of violent adventurers kept forming around the outposts.
In 1692, the governor general wrote: "The city of São Paulo
has much about it of a republic, observing no law, either divine
or human." The will-o'-the-wisp that beckoned the *bandeirantes*
onward was not gold, but emeralds. The hero of the time was
Fernão Dias Pais, the protagonist of the first epic poem written
in Brazil: *A Relação Panegírica em Oitava Rima . . . do Gov-
ernador Fernão Dias Pais, Descobridor das Esmeraldas* (*The
Panegyric Account in Ottava Rima . . . of Governor Fernão Dias
Pais, the Discoverer of Emeralds*). Its author was Diogo Grasson
Tinoco, whose character is surrounded by mystery. The *bandeirante* in the poem

> *Departs now at last for the boundless frontiers*
> *To open new paths never trod, never known*
> *Leaving his home and his country in tears*
> *To slash through the underbrush, scale ramparts of stone*
> *Ford turbulent rivers, build canoes, rafts, or bridges*
> *Pushing on despite obstacles through every zone*
> *Now defying the jungle, now heedless of cold*
> *Conquering summit or valley, a man strong and bold.*

Olavo Bilac, whose full name was Olavo Bras Martins dos
Guimarães Bilac (1865–1918), returned to the same subject
two hundred years later, in the period of Brazil's Parnassus, using
it in one of the most beautiful poems of his time: *O Caçador de
Esmeraldas* (*The Emerald-Seeker*).

The frontier was no more an exclusively Brazilian phenomenon
than were the international brigades that moved inland. The
frontier of the United States was an unstable line that the English and other colonists kept pushing westward. As they did so,
the Europeans, chiefly Anglo-Saxons, kept despoiling the Indians
of their land. Spain herself had known a frontier on the Iberian
Peninsula which receded southward in the course of the eight

centuries of warfare against the Moors and ended when the last of them were driven from Granada. In the middle of Chile, South America had a conventional frontier that kept retreating for three centuries from Valdivia's time until the entire country came under the flag of the white men. The same kind of mobile frontier existed in Argentina from the time of Rosas to that of General Roca, pressing the surviving Indians back until they made their last stand in Patagonia. But the frontier in Brazil was of unparalleled immensity and diversity. Its background was the hot green tropics, the Amazonian jungles, and the northeastern deserts, all of which provided a stage for a spectacle unique in history. The *bandeirantes* kept forcing their way through jungle Siberias, green hells, lured on by the dream of an earthly paradise, the *Canaan* depicted by José Pereira da Graça Aranha (1868–1931) in his novel of that title, which was translated into every language and read all over the world. One of the oddest notes in *Canaan* is the fact that Germans played the role of conquerors in some of the new lands. Those Germans who keep moving through the jungle in the novel were the ones who later, increased to thousands, established one of the richest colonies in twentieth-century Brazil.

As the moving frontier subdued the land to plantations, it brought a sense of hope, or rural repose containing an element of conservatism. Wherever the driving force was mining, it unleashed turbulent men driven by the thirst for precious stones and metals. All the races mingled in the stew of the tropical hells. Slavery was the miners' chief capital. In the heat of struggle and weather and in the alternation of work and idleness, sexuality overflowed. Beautiful mulatto girls triumphed over family ties. Smuggling was everyone's sport. The air was filled with the music of Portugal and Africa, and the instruments evoked the echo of the jungle. This life made its own laws according to the degree of success and circumstances.

João Fernandes de Oliveira, a diamond dealer, the richest and most powerful man in the kingdom during the decade between 1760 and 1770, had as his mistress Xica da Silva, a capricious mulatto woman who may be singled out as an example of the elasticity of the social conventions. Xica was the one person bold enough to share Fernandes de Oliveira's empire. An historian of the diamond region tells us in his memoirs: "Xica was obeyed blindly; her slightest and most frivolous whim was satisfied on the spot. Through the influence and power of her lover, the mistress of Tijuco could boast of luxury and grandeur that dazzled the great families." When she went to church, elegant and covered with jewels like an empress, a suite of twelve splendidly dressed mulatto women accompanied her, and the best spot was reserved for her. On the slopes of São Francisco Mountain she had an imposing palace built, with a rich and beautiful chapel and a broad salon for her private theater and all the necessary machinery, a luxury inconceivable even in our time. The palace was surrounded by exotic European gardens with artificial fountains and waterfalls. One day, Xica, who never left Tijuco, fancied she would like to have a sea of her own with a real ship on it for her outings on the water. The magistrate João Fernandes built a dam to fill the great lake and ordered a sailing ship built and fitted out with the most complete naval equipment. That legendary bark, where the demon-ridden mulatto woman went for a sail with a half-dozen of her most intimate cronies, was seen wandering over the waters of that sea, so expensive and so exclusive. The couple entertained frequently and gave huge parties where the best families of Tijuco gathered, plus all the riffraff of adventurers in the kingdom, the "*marotinhos*" [rascals] whom Xica saw fit to summon. Splendid banquets were put on, ending in walks through the gardens or fishing parties in gilded launches on the lake. At night, concerts or theatrical productions were given. *Medea's Enchantments*, *Amphitryon*, *Porfiar Amando*, *Xiquinha*, *For the Love of God*, and other plays in the repertory of the day were staged. The egregious Xica, queen of festivals and hearts, swimming in wealth, power, and ostentation, permitted herself the pleasure of educating her daughters in the austere boarding school of the Macaubas, and provided them with a private residence.[1]

On Brazil's other outpost, the wild and desert region of the Northeast, the outlook for the *sertanistas* (backwoodsmen) was otherwise. Even today, the contrast between their poverty and the wealth of the South, concentrated in São Paulo, constitutes one of the most serious problems that Brazil has to face. About

[1] José Ferreira Xarrato: *A Crise dos Costumes nas Minas Gerais do Seculo XVIII.*

1877 there appeared in Canudos, in that region, one of the most fantastic figures in Brazilian history and literature: Antônio Vicente Mendes Maciel, commonly called Antônio o Conselheiro (Anthony the Adviser). He called himself "The Prophet." Dressed in a blue linen garment like a pilgrim, he walked leaning on a staff, his beard blowing, his hair falling to his shoulders like the Nazarene's, fixing his fiery gaze on everyone, his eyes charged with a magnetism born of a furious fanaticism. He preached constantly against the republic, collecting followers as if he were a reincarnation of Sebastián, the last knightly king of Portugal, whose image moves like a phantom through the chronicles of the sixteenth century and who was expected for three centuries to return as the Portuguese messiah.

The ragged people of the Northeast trooped after "The Prophet," fascinated by his eloquence, and he led them into lands that they hoped to make their own. He settled on an old estate and in the country surrounding it and started the construction of a village for his followers. The church, rising above the ruins of the estate chapel, began to look like an old and mysterious fortress, and indeed it was an inspired architectural labor on the part of "The Prophet," who planned the building as a bastion in which to defend himself from government troops. The Capuchins asked permission to preach there. "The Prophet" let them. The people gathered around them and listened to them for an hour, then dragged them away, shouting: Why should they listen to the poor Capuchins when they had a prophet right there in Canudos?

The government organized a well-equipped military expedition to crush the people at Canudos. Once, twice, three times, four times, "The Prophet" and his ragged followers drove the troops back. Finally a big national expedition was organized, with artillery battalions and several thousand infantrymen. Only an operation on that scale could overthrow him. The fanatical defenders met the attack pressed together in a single mass, ready to die to the last man. "The Prophet" went up to the altar of the Good Jesus. His large domain was covered with the bodies of the faithful. Finally, at the command of the Blessed Antônio, the last six hundred men left alive in the village surrendered. They were beheaded. "The Prophet" was found dead of starvation in front of the altar. Brazil, which enjoyed unquestioned independence and had proclaimed itself a republic, paid with thousands of lives for the adventure of "The Prophet" of Canudos.

Euclides da Cunha (1866–1909) based *Os Sertões*, one of the

masterpieces of Brazilian literature, on this incident. José Verissimo calls the account the work of "a man of science—a geographer, geologist, and ethnologist; a man of thought, a philosopher,
sociologist, and historian with a sensitive spirit, a poet, novelist,
and artist, who knows how to observe as well as to describe and
who reacts with sympathy to the phenomena of nature as well as to
man." Circumstances have made this book, like its opposite number, Sarmiento's *Facundo*, difficult to classify. Da Cunha traveled
with the last contingent of the expedition against "The Prophet"
as correspondent for a São Paulo newspaper. He had been
trained in the military academy and had specialized in mathematics and science. Soon after the book was written, he was
killed in Rio de Janeiro. He was the last victim of the story
he himself tells in his book.

¶ FROM PARANASSUS TO MODERNISMO

Ever since Portugal installed her court in Brazil, the people
in the cities have kept contact with Europe. All the French
movements have aroused a constant echo in Brazilian letters. But
basically, the jungle, the backlands, the wilderness still to be conquered, were, and still are, a challenge to the life forces of the
nation, a theme of struggle, creation, and meditation. The Amazon
constitutes an immense and mysterious redoubt that has yet to
surrender to the forces of civilization. At a time when a great part
of Argentine and Uruguayan literature was totally bound to the
European, the theme of the Negroes and Indians, of the jungle
and the desert, dominated in Brazil. That literature preserves the
tone of the sixteenth-century accounts written by the Spaniards
in the Conquest, a tone that has persisted into the twentieth century. In Brazil the conquest has not yet completed its cycle.
Nowhere else in the New World has the struggle lasted so long,
nowhere have literature and art been so greatly influenced by the
fusion of the races, the heat of the tropics, contact with virgin
land. The new city of Brasilia is a *bandeirante* capital, an urban
symbol of the present day marking the conquest of the backlands.

In the middle of the nineteenth century, when Romanticism
as a school of literature was in full sway, José Martiniano de
Alencar (1829–77) won fame with a strictly indigenous novel:
O Guarani. The novelist whose name resounded most loudly inside and outside the country came later. This was Alfredo
d'Escragnolle de Taunay (1843–99), a grandson of the painter

Taunay, who had gone to Brazil with a commission of artists. The younger Taunay fought in the war with Paraguay and wrote an account of it in *The Retreat from Laguna*. But his most famous book is *Inocência*, which describes the interior of Brazil in the manner of Chateaubriand. *Inocência* came as a belated echo of that school, which the younger generations were already rejecting. It was published in 1872 after the so-called Battle of Parnassus had been fought in the *Diário do Rio de Janeiro* in 1870. The Parnassians won out over the Romanticists, for that was the period when the French poets Heredia, Gautier, Banville, Baudelaire, Leconte de Lisle, Sully Prudhomme, and Coppée were being read widely. The head of the new school was Artur de Oliveira, who had lived side by side with those poets in Paris. The slogan of the new men was "Fewer tears and more art." They were searching for a change in style. The principal Parnassians in Brazil were Antônio Mariano Alberto de Oliveira (1857–1937), Raymundo da Mota Azevedo Correia (1859–1911), Vicente Augusto de Carvalho (1866–1924), and, of course, Olavo Bilac. That generation in Brazil paralleled the contemporary generation in Spanish America, led by Gutiérrez Nájera, Guillermo Valencia, Julián del Casal, Rubén Darío, and others. The Symbolists, who followed the Parnassians took their inspiration from the Belgians and the French—from Mallarmé and Samain, from Maeterlinck and Verhaeren, from Verlaine and Rimbaud. Alphonsus de Guimarães (1870–1921) belonged to that same school. He translated Heine and wrote a book of poetry in French entitled *Pauvre Lyre*; as a Catholic he gave testament of his faith in *Setenario das Dores de Nossa Senhora*. João da Cruz e Sousa (1861–98), a pure-blooded Negro, drew more attention and criticism than the other Symbolists. He was a rebel who broke some of the traditional rules of grammar, but the magic of his poetry assures him a place on Parnassus. Both Parnassians and Symbolists chose form as their goal, as Olavo Bilac said in his *Profissão de Fé*. To the end they were

> *Ready to fall and to shatter the lance*
> *While fighting the battle for Style!*

That generation came closest to art for art's sake. And yet, Olavo Bilac sang of the first *bandeirante*, and the Negro João created his symbolism out of the element of magic in his blood. But first and last, the reaction against Romanticism was formal. And form eventually shared the field with Naturalism, as exemplified by the novels of Zola and those of the Portuguese novelist José Maria Eça de Queiros (1843–1900). The spirit of social reform was accentuated in Zola. Queiros was a fountain bubbling over with irony and sarcasm, but with a national feeling that prompted him to declare that foreign languages ought to be pronounced proudly with a Portuguese accent. Queiros was very close to the Brazilians. He collaborated constantly on the *Gazeta de Noticias* of Rio de Janeiro, which he said he preferred to other newspapers because it paid better than those in Portugal, gave him more freedom, and brought him more readers. He was anti-clerical enough to satisfy the Brazilian liberals. Queiros echoed all things Brazilian. Jacinto, the protagonist of his novel *A Cidade e as Serras* (*The City and the Mountains*), was also very Brazilian and identifiable as a well-known personage of the time.

The Naturalists wrote such works as *O Mulato*, a novel by Aluizo de Azevedo (1857–1913) which gave the racial problem a penetrating scrutiny. The backlands (*sertão*) provide the theme of *Fruta do Mato*, a novel by Afrânio Peixoto (1876–1947). João Simões Lopes Neto (1865–1916) wrote a collection called *Contos Gauchescos*. The varied production of Joaquim Maria Machado de Assis (1839–1908) is granted a separate chapter in literary histories. The son of an incompetent mulatto painter, he started work as a typographer, but eventually he became a poet, a journalist, and a writer of comedy. His stories are famous. The influence of Queiros, Flaubert, Pascal, Renan, and the English humorists can be traced in his work. "He did not seem Brazilian," Calmón writes. His sensitivity was universal. *Dom Casmurro*, a novel of his that was translated into almost all modern languages, was read with enjoyment in France. His novels *Ressureição*, *Memórias Póstumas de Braz Cubas*, and *Quincas Borba* fill an entire period in Brazilian literature. Machado de Assis was a man of the academy who believed that there should be literary unity in an atmosphere of political federation. He could never have imagined that from the rostrum of his own academy, Graça Aranha would say a few years after his death: "Either the academy must change or it must disappear; we cannot go on being Portugal's mortuary chamber." Machado lived in a period ruled by French influences. His ideal world was balanced and serene. Art seemed to him to be moving always toward Parnassus. But before long, *modernismo* shook that illusion to its very foundations.

¶ THE MODERNISTS

Until the death of Machado de Assis, which also marked the demise of Parnassus, Spanish Americans and Brazilians were working within the same schools. But fundamental differences between them arose with the emergence of "*modernismo*." In Spanish America, the Modernist movement that buried both Parnassians and Symbolists was never for a moment a school with nationalistic overtones; its general headquarters was Paris. Brazilian *modernismo* was born in Brazil, however, and Brazil supported it. It emerged as a consequence of internal affairs. National economic problems were projected into the world of literature. Brazilian *modernismo* came later than the Spanish American movement and was different. In Spanish America it came to the fore near the close of the nineteenth century through Martí and Darío. Darío took it to Spain and the rest of the world twenty-five years before the Modernist Manifesto of São Paulo. The year of the Manifesto, 1922, marked the peak of coffee production in Brazil—four-fifths of the world's coffee was then of Brazilian origin—and the same year saw the beginning of social agitation as seventy thousand workers went on strike.

"A week of modern art" was shown in the Municipal Theater of São Paulo. Graça Aranha, author of *Canaan*, presided over it. The atmosphere was highly charged. Apollinaire and Marinetti were creating as much of a furor in São Paulo and Rio de Janeiro as in France and Italy. José Bento de Monteiro Lobato (1886–1948), author of *Urupês*, *Cidades Mortas*, and *O Choque das raças*, opened a violent attack on Anita Malfatti's show, where her famous painting *The Yellow Man* was exhibited. She not only introduced her own art but also showed the work of contemporary Cubists. Monteiro Lobato's criticism was a call to battle, and his opponents hoisted the flag of *modernismo*. The painters, sculptors, poets, sociologists, and musicians whom history records as the "Generation of 1922" formed the new group. The São Paulo movement spread to Rio, and before long every city in the country had its Modernist groups and newspapers. The new school leaned toward nationalism. José Oswald de Sousa Andrade (1890–1954) sent his first message through *Pau Brasil* and later through his review *Antropofagia*. The group that opposed both publications hoisted the colors of the national banner, the yellow and green flag, and called itself *verde-amarelismo*. Plínio Salgado (1901–   ), Paulo Menotti del Picchia

(1892–   ), and Cassiano Ricardo Leite (1895–   ) were all active in it.

Mario de Morais Andrade (1893–1945), who taught philosophy at the university and the history of music in the Conservatory of Music and Dramatic Art in São Paulo, carried the new tendencies to all fronts as a poet, novelist, and short-story writer. His idea was to make the Brazilians a hundred per cent Brazilian and "to nationalize a nation that lacks national characteristics." Menotti del Picchia published the poem *Juca Mulato*, "one of the first in the phase of nationalist recuperation, which might be characterized as the swan song of the agrarian era of an essentially agricultural Brazil at the moment when industrialization began to shake the rural foundations of the state." At the opposite pole, Raul Bopp (1898–   ) became the poet of the Amazon jungle, of the primitive world. He fixed his eyes on Africa and caught its rhythms in:

> *There once was a tree that said*
> *"I wish I were an elephant."*
> *So it wandered around through the silent night.*
> *Aratabá-becúm*
> *Aratabá-necúm.*
> *Oh, but that night was long, so long,*
> *So long that it turned men black.*
> *Aratabá-becúm. . . .*

Until 1922 the cities, and especially Rio de Janeiro, had grown along European lines. But Rio is a city with a setting not reminiscent of any other in the world. Whatever was built in Rio was bound to be different, largely because Brazil, as a country, imposes a new style. That explains how Brasília could be created as a city unlike any ever built before. Erico Verissimo (1905–   ), a writer full of the charm and sharpness of "Brazilianism," has revived the history of the South in a series of novels. He gives the following watercolor sketch of Rio:

> The waters of the bay are bottle green, sprinkled with islands, ships, lighthouses, buoys, and sails. . . . Overhead, the sea gulls and airplanes trace ellipses, and at times flocks of green parrots with strident voices cut across the sky. The prodigal sun throws handfuls of coins on the water. On certain days a luminous blue mist, faintly tinged with pink, rises through the air, giving the city the look of a toy

wrapped in cellophane. Who can remember the names of the innumerable mountains or recall their outlines? The light deceives the eye, changes the shape and color of the peaks. We go to bed certain that we know the names of those ramparts of rock, only to rise the next day and descry a new peak, a new chain of mountains, and to discover that during the night an invisible and mocking sculptor was at work, bent solely upon changing the landscape for us or on inventing some new wonder. There are days when the clouds hide the summits, or invent feathers, wigs, veils to place on their heads. The air smells of sun, sea, and jungle. The visitor who comes to Rio is instantly imbued with its festival spirit, with an almost pagan attitude toward life, as if his internal melancholy were swept suddenly away under the influence of this ardent sun, of those fragrant scents. For there is magic and music in the air, and the wind is caressing, and there is a dazzling mystery in the luminous city of São Sebastião do Rio de Janeiro.

The Modernists decided to look for new lines along which to orient in some new sense the fabulous development going on in the cities. São Paulo was growing faster than the other cities in this century. And Rio, the country's most beautiful city, was following her own bent instead of observing the world norms of urban growth. In the fine arts, Lucio Costa, has supported the French modern movement from the beginning. Shortly after Le Corbusier published his *Vers une Architecture* in 1927, he was called to Brazil to plan the Ministry of Public Education, a palace that is one of his claims to fame. The Brazilian architect Oscar Niemeyer (1907–   ), who worked with him, later became famous, as did a painter destined to shine in international art: Cándido Portinari (1903–1962). Both were of the "generation of 1922." Niemeyer had the good fortune to plan and supervise the building of the city of Brasília. His chapel of St. Francis of Assisi in Pampulha, Belo Horizonte, completed in 1941, is a fine, graceful structure that is one of the best, as well as one of the first churches built anywhere in the new style. Its façade is decorated with a superb mural by Portinari. Earlier, Portinari painted the murals in the Ministry of Public Education and contributed to the decoration of the United Nations Building in New York and the Library of Congress in Washington, where he painted a vigorous picture of South American life.

Music also reached its peak in the generation of 1922. Heitor Villa-Lobos (1887–1959), noted for his versatility and fecundity, composed hundreds of pieces in a bewildering variety of forms, conducted, and educated. Villa-Lobos built his music around folkloric elements of Brazil and other American nations: his musical comedy *Magdalena* was based on Colombian themes.

¶ THE GEOGRAPHY OF HUNGER AND OTHER MATTERS

The awakening in arts and letters came simultaneously with a less felicitous phase of political revision. Brazil found modalities with more assurance in artistic culture than in politics. In 1922 and the years immediately following, the philosophy of Karl Marx, the totalitarian principles of Mussolini and Hitler, the themes of the Russian Revolution, and the Portuguese corporatism of Antônio de Oliveira Salazar were spreading all over the world. In 1924 a former Brazilian army captain, Luiz Carlos Prestes, bent upon a Communist revolution, organized an expedition to the interior. Although it was defeated, it marked the beginning of the Brazilian Communist Party. In 1930 a revolution headed by Osvaldo Aranha (1894–1960) and Flores da Cunha broke out in Porto Alegre. It started with fifty men, but ended with Getulio Vargas (1883–1954) seizing the government. Vargas was a charismatic figure in Brazil's political history. He represented a pre-Fascist ideology, but he leaned more toward Portugal's corporatism in the Brazilian manner, which meant that he gave it a paternal air, bonhomie, and the smile of a shrewd and patriarchal *gaucho*. The Communist movement grew under Vargas. Elections were suspended in 1938 and a dictatorship was declared; "his" constitution was decreed, and the struggle against Communism began. For fourteen years Vargas ruled with an iron fist in a velvet glove. He would have none of Hitlerian violence. A second republic was inaugurated in 1945. Then Vargas could no longer put off elections, and General Dutra rose to power. Vargas went back to his ranch like a rich and astute landowner. Five years later, another election was held and Vargas won as "the candidate of the shirtless, the father of the people" (*"O pai do povo"*). Less lucky this time, he let the government slip out of his hands and finally committed suicide. He had unleashed administrative disorder; there was corruption, and Rio was a turbulent river indeed. The men and the politicians who were quarreling then are the same men who have been making the contradictory and adventurous policies of the past few years.

Two background problems preoccupied the intellectuals of the generation of 1922: that of man and that of the land. Studies on Brazilian man have yielded one of the largest collections of books ever published in America. The evaluation of the Negro found a virtuoso exponent in Gilberto Freyre (1900–   ). His book *Casa Grande e Senzala* (*The Masters and the Slaves*) keeps growing with every new edition. It is a classic study of social life in America. According to Arthur Ramos (1903–49), the number of slaves imported into Brazil amounted to about five million. On this broad base a world of unbelievable human commingling has grown. "If a Negro in the United States is a man who has one drop of Negro blood, in Brazil a white man is a man with one drop of white blood." Ramos was a professor of anthropology and ethnology at the University of São Paulo. He made a basic study of Negro cultures in Brazil in *Introdução a Antropologia Brasileira,* and produced a huge body of scientific work on the same subject. Francisco José de Oliveira Viana (1883–1951) showed the other face of Brazil's population in his *Evolução do Povo Brasileira* (*Evolution of the Brazilian People*). Sergio Buarque de Hollanda (1902–   ) dealt with the same subject in *Raízes do Brazil* (*Origins of Brazil*).

As for the problem of the land, Josué de Castro (1908–   ), a doctor, tackled it in his studies of diet and race. His famous *Geografia da Fome* (*Geography of Hunger*) aroused world-wide interest from the date of its first French edition. The book opened the world campaign against hunger which has transformed the work of the Food and Agriculture Organization (the FAO), a branch of the United Nations. Castro started his studies on hunger with Brazil and later broadened them to include the rest of the world. He studied the backlands of northeastern Brazil in the *Geography of Hunger,* not as in the time of Antônio O Conselheiro, but in all its raw, present-day reality. The most pressing problems that emerge from his study are political instability and social revolt rising out of a situation that Castro has summed up dramatically and scientifically in a single word: hunger.

The impact on the world made by Castro's book demonstrates plainly the force that scientific studies have acquired in Brazil. Oswaldo Cruz (1872–1917), educated in Pasteur's school in Paris, initiated a broad campaign against tropical epidemics, particularly yellow fever. He is honored as the man who made Rio de

Janeiro a place fit for human habitation. Additional studies in
São Paulo on tropical medicine have attained considerable stature,
and the Butantan Institute for the study of reptiles is famous. In
Brazil, there are twenty-five hundred known species of serpents,
a number of which are venomous. Thirty thousand persons die
every year of snake bite. In Butantan, the snake garden of the
world, a reptile nursery adopts specimens sent to the institute from
all over the country. Anti-venom sera are made there and the
venom is used also for thousands of studies having to do with the
treatment of diseases. César Lattes (1924–   ) is another of
the scientists who exemplify progress in Brazil. Lattes discovered at Bristol in 1947 that mesons are present in cosmic radia-
tions. A year later he produced artificial mesons, then went on to
direct the Brazilian center for physical investigation.

Culture in Brazil is associated with a great variety of activities.
A former professor, Francisco de Assis Chateaubriand (1891–   ),
became the most powerful newspaper impresario in the country
and also controls a large broadcasting system. He gave São
Paulo a museum containing many treasures of world art ranging from Greek, Egyptian, and Byzantine artifacts to paintings by Goya, Rembrandt, Delacroix, and Picasso. When a part
of the Chateaubriand collection was shown at the Metropolitan
Museum in New York, American and European critics were
astonished at the riches this man had assembled to provide Brazil
with a center of artistic culture.

Politics and literature usually go hand in hand in Brazil. In the
days of Getulio Vargas, the Communist Luiz Carlos Prestes was
in prison with Jorge Amado (1912–   ), the novelist of fishermen,
laborers, and abandoned children and of divertissements in
a much lighter vein. Graciliano Ramos (1892–1953) was
jailed during the police roundups of 1937 and later deported to
the penal colony of Ilha Grande. His masterpiece was appropriately titled *Memórias do Cárcere* (*Prison Memoirs*). Jorge de
Lima (1895–1953), a physician and poet, wrote under the influence of the Parnassians until 1922, but crossed the lines of
literary warfare when the Modernist movement began. His later
poems portray the life, sufferings, and hopes of people in the
Northeast. He is the author of one of the most refined and sensuous
poems in Brazilian art, *Essa Negra Fulo* (*This Negro Woman,
Jane Doe*), written between times as he was composing such
essays as *Medicina e Humanismo*, and the novels *Calunga* and
A Mulher Obscura (*The Dark Woman*). Manuel Bandeira

(1886–   ), poet and patriarch of Brazilian letters, is a towering figure. He was among the pre-Modernists in the days when Verlaine and Baudelaire were their models; he took part in the revolt of 1922, and spent his life in dedication to literature at the university, writing his history of literature and various essays and compiling anthologies. Bandeira sums up his vision of his country's literature by accentuating its continuity, its constant evolution, and its vigorous life. Few countries have a man of letters like him, who has faithfully followed the country's destiny step by step, and who has penetrated deeply into its innermost vacillations, struggles, and hopes.

XVIII: *Haiti in Black and White*

¶ FILIBUSTERS, NEGROES, AND FRENCH

On the day of St. Nicholas, December 6, 1492, Columbus discovered the island of Hispaniola. Fate could not have chosen a better time. St. Nicholas, the great wonder-worker, had calmed a great storm as he was on his way to the Holy Places, so he was chosen the patron saint of navigators. Like Columbus, St. Nicholas bridged the gap between the Orient and the Occident. His image is venerated by Greeks and by Oriental slaves, as well as in the western Mediterranean. The merchants of Bari, Italy, stole his relics, which had been left in the Orient, but ultimately gave them back to the saint's birthplace, Myra, in Asia Minor. In the west, St. Nicholas is revered not only as the patron of sailors, but also as the gift-giving saint—Santa Claus—who brings toys to children and fills their stockings on Christmas Eve. In the old days, the feast of St. Nicholas extended from December 6, his day, to the day of the Holy Innocents, December 28.

To stretch the long arm of coincidence farther, Columbus founded the first city in America on December 24 and gave it the Spanish name for Christmas, La Navidad. This settlement was Exhibit A in Spanish colonization. A handful of Spaniards stayed there, protected by a "fort" of logs and trampled earth, while Columbus went back to Spain with word that he had reached the Orient. La Navidad was founded near what became the French city of Cap-Haïtien centuries later. When Columbus returned from Spain and went to visit La Navidad, he found nothing there but the bones of the Spaniards—unless the Indians ate bones and all. Where the fort had stood there was a pile of ashes, not a trace of the gold that his comrades had dreamed they would find during his months of absence. The aftermath is the terrible story of the destruction of the Indians. Their case histories fill pages in the charges laid against the Spaniards by the fiery Father Las Casas. When the number of Indians was hopelessly depleted, Negroes were brought in on the advice of Las Casas. And in the fullness of time, a Negro king, like a character set up in a Nativity scene, ruled where Columbus had founded La Navidad. The king in Cap-Haïtien was the first Negro ruler in America.

In the beginning were sugar and rum. As both prospered, the number of Negroes multiplied. Once cane had come, it ruled the island through the labor of the slaves. Slavery made a modest beginning in the sixteenth century. By about 1730 the slave trade had grown to be one of the largest industries of the century. Manhunts were big business in Africa. By about 1780, nearly half a million Africans were working in Haiti. The shipowners, capitalists, and impresarios had never been so active in transporting any other kind of merchandise. At about the same time, the French established themselves on the island, and the fleur-de-lis flew over a part of the West Indies. The story of that event is tied to the history of the buccaneers and freebooters. Until the eve of the Treaty of Ryswick (1697), the island, called Hispaniola first, Santo Domingo later, was as Spanish as New Spain or New Granada. But by the end of the reign of the House of Austria, Spain had lost all that she had won in Naples and Portugal, and was embroiled in the harassing revolt of Barcelona, which cost her twelve years of strife and lost her half the island of Santo Domingo.

The English, Dutch, and French buccaneers and filibusters maintained their general headquarters on the island of Tortuga, to which they returned from their adventures. With their wide-ranging marauding, they gave an English accent to Jamaica, a Dutch accent to Curaçao, and a French accent to Haiti. The island was cut in two by the Treaty of Ryswick: Santo Domingo remained under Spain's aegis, Haiti came under that of France. Of the island's 30,000 square miles, Haiti occupies 11,000. The rest belongs to the Dominican Republic. Haiti is smaller than Belgium, one-eighteenth the size of France. After Haiti became a

French colony, French buccaneers and filibusters settled down to living there as honest colonials. Their work would be done by the Negroes. The densest concentration of Negroes in the New World was gathered there. Ships brought cargoes of Congolese, Mandingos, and Dahomeyans and scattered slaves all over the continent. Brazil, Buenos Aires, Cartagena, Havana, New Orleans, and Haiti all had their slave markets. But whereas elsewhere this section of the population was small and was being absorbed, whether in the houses of the masters or in the fields, as the colored portion of future nations, the Negroes were so closely packed in Haiti that they were able to establish in time the first Negro republic in the world.

The Spanish city of Santo Domingo was founded in 1496; the French capital of Haiti, Port-au-Prince, in 1749. The two and a half centuries that lay between the founding of the two cities may be commensurate with the distance between the spirit of the two colonies. In spite of the destruction of most of the Indians, the Spanish colony contained three distinct races: white, Indian, and Negro, plus all their blends. In Haiti the distribution of the population, likened to a white band on a black field, was ruled by the stipulations of the Negro Code, sanctioned by law in 1685 and by custom. The code provided that if children were born of the union between a Negro woman and a white man, the mother and child would be free. Although the clauses of the code were flouted often, there were always some free mulattoes and manumitted Negroes who acquired wealth. But the majority of the mulattoes suffered brutal punishments, labored under onerous conditions, and were debarred from public office, for discrimination was implacable in colonial Haiti. Nevertheless, there were always a few who were given an education, who were able to go to France and to become champions of freedom.

¶ THE CATHOLIC CHURCH

The Church never penetrated Haiti as deeply as it did the Spanish and Portuguese colonies. It never established any missions. The first buccaneers and filibusters were without god, king, or law. Of the religious orders that came to the new colony, the Jesuits were able to spend only a few years there before being expelled in 1769. They were replaced by a secular clergy that left no deep impression and by the Capuchins, Carmelites, and Dominicans. The Negro Code obligated masters to indoctrinate slaves in the Catholic faith and to see that the sacraments were administered to them. That was one of the provisions of the law that the masters quickly forgot. James G. Leyburn wrote:

> Some priests were in any case not too zealous. It was much more agreeable to attend only to external forms, and so participate in the charming life of high society, than to stand firm against laxity. If a priest showed enthusiasm for his duties to his African charges he was almost certain to be accused by the planters of stirring up the slaves and undermining the foundations of colonial society. This was, in fact, the very accusation leveled at the Jesuits to bring about their expulsion from the colony in 1764. The example was not lost upon other priests.

Father Cabon quotes a report sent to Rome in 1794 which read: "Since the expulsion of the Jesuits, the majority of the priests have led such indecent lives . . . that the citizens and the Negroes have lost all the religious feeling that the Jesuits had inculcated."

¶ THE CITIES

Baron de Wimpffen, who visited Port-au-Prince in 1770, compared the city to a "Tartar camp." The streets, like cowpaths, were lined with huts ranged side by side; in the rainy season, they became quagmires. Two tasteful public fountains had been built, but owing to the great number of water carriers and the trampling of the donkeys, they were impossible of access. Twenty years later, the white people on the island numbered thirty-six thousand. They moved about through the city in carriages and displayed a luxury worthy of Paris. The commandant lived in a palace. The esplanade was a promenade that resembled a rustic or village version of Mexico City's Alameda. There were two large ponds, one for public bathing, the other for watering the stock. And a theater. The theater was fashionable. To quote Scharon:

> Quite close to La Place de la Vallière, in the little street that bears the name Saint-Philippe, the theater of M. Acquaire was built in 1777 and was usually filled with eight hundred spectators. All of Molière was shown, all of Corneille, all of Racine, and all of Voltaire, besides modern works such as *The Barber of Seville* and *The Marriage of Figaro*.

The city of Cap-Haïtien competed with Port-au-Prince. Cap-Haïtien had a population of 15,000, 3,600 of them white; 1,400 freed Negroes, and 10,000 slaves. Its church was richly decorated inside. Carriages rolled through all the central streets. There were public fountains and baths. Everyone bathed, to the wonder of Europeans. Again to quote Scharon:

> Visitors never fail to stare at an imposing building rising on Montarcher Place: it was the Government Palace. Surrounding this magnificent building was a beautiful garden, the meeting place of elegant society. The colonists reveled in ostentation, showing off their beautiful horses and mastiffs, going about in coaches and giving receptions. Suppers and dances occupied a good part of their lives, and during carnival time, masked balls were given. During those gala days, the ladies, behind their masks, provoked intrigues reminiscent on a small scale of those that went on at the Paris Opéra. A showing of *Le Misanthrope*, which opened the season in 1764, was a great success. An intellectual center came with opera. Gastonnet des Fosses reports in *La Revolution de St. Domingue* that several periodicals were published in the city: *Les Affiches Américaines*, *La Gazette de Médicine* and *L'Almanach de St. Domingue*. A Society of Arts and Sciences was established, and it endowed the city with a museum and botanical gardens. After some private interests had obtained permits to set up printing presses in Cap-Haïtien and Port-au-Prince, the number of periodicals multiplied. The circumstances of the period gave rise to new organs: *Le Courrier Politique et Littéraire du Cap Française; Le Courrier de St. Domingue, La Gazette de St. Domingue; Le Citoyen Véridique, Le Moniteur Colonial;* and the official organ of the colony, *Le Moniteur Général.* Newspapers from Paris were distilling drop by drop the idea of the Revolution. Groups gathered in Cap-Haïtien to comment on the articles in the *Mercure de France* and, after 1789, on those in *Les Revolutions de Paris*, Le Brissot's *Patriote Français*, and *Le Courrier de Provence.* This wealth of information encouraged gatherings to discuss the news of the day in supper clubs in the metropolis of the North. Clubs called Sociétés des Amis de la Constitution, which operated in Cap-Haïtien, Port-au-Prince, and Cayes, resembled the Jacobin clubs in Paris.[1]

[1] Faine Scharon: *Toussaint L'Ouverture et la Revolution de St. Domingue.*

This intellectual awakening was exclusively for the white people. On one occasion, the governor of Martinique wrote to the Minister of the Navy: "The well-being of the white people demands that the Negroes be kept in the most absolute ignorance, and I am so firmly convinced of this because the Negroes must be treated as domestic animals are treated." But these "animals" finally heard about what men were writing in Paris.

¶ DISCRIMINATION

The slave quarters where the Negroes lived were somewhat like open corrals containing huts with walls of wattle and daub and thatched roofs. They contained little, if any, furniture. The table service was of straw. Adults and children gathered around the fire to escape the mosquitoes. Although the law required that slaves be provided with two cotton garments each year, they were often seen going about naked. The law set minimum food rations for the slaves, but there was no control over this. The masters saw fit to dole out a certain amount of rice or oatmeal, herring, crackers, and molasses. Some landowners turned over a piece of ground for the slaves to cultivate, but thereby forced the Negroes to spend the days that were supposed to be holidays working in order to eat.

Many of the slaves carried on their backs scars left by an overseer's lash. The masters were irritated whenever the slaves were ill, and as relations between white man and Negro breed strange complexes, the white man showed his slave less consideration than his livestock, even though the Negro was the colonist's greatest source of wealth. The men were treated more harshly than the women. Some of the mulatto girls were very beautiful, and Negro women attracted their masters, too. According to Scharon:

> The white women rivaled the men in cruelty. They did not hesitate to have the more elegant and beautiful Negro woman servants killed if they suspected that they might be having relations with their husbands. The slave cook who had the bad luck to ruin a dessert might be thrown alive into the oven, as may be seen from the account written by Baron de Wimpffen of his trip to Santo Domingo.

¶ CREOLE AND VOODOO

In 1804, after Haiti's independence had been declared, Toussaint L'Ouverture stated that during the time of the colony not one public school had been established. The lower classes did not know how to read or write, and the language itself was becoming a blend of African tongues, Spanish, and French, out of which the Haitian Creole patois emerged. Unlike the Spanish or Portuguese colonies, Haiti had no literature in a European language except for the gazettes. Dantès Bellegarde writes: "The proclamation of the rupture with France was published in French, and this act, written by Boironde-Tonnerre, the son of a French colonist and an African Negro woman, is our 'Strassbourg Oath,' and, properly speaking, constitutes the first monument in Haitian literature."

The songs that summoned the Negroes to voodoo meetings where the cry of independence was shouted, are taken from the linguistic background of Dahomey:

> *Eh! Eh! Bamba! Heu! Heu!*
> *Canga, bafia té.*
> *Canga, moune de lé*
> *Canga, do ki la!*
> *Canga li!*

"Without a grammar, or a system of spelling, or a literature, Creole cannot be the material for methodical teaching, because it is unstable, subject to constant variations in its vocabulary, its pronunciation, and its syntax."[1] The phenomenon of Creole extends throughout the Antilles and into such cities as New Orleans in the United States. It is a linguistic case not unique in the Caribbean region. Papiamento, spoken in Curaçao, has similar characteristics. What is noteworthy in the Haitian Creole is the African element, dominant in poetry. Creole is a language equidistant between the French the white people knew and the pure African predominant in the Voodoo ceremonies. Fédéric Doret tried to compile a grammar that would reduce the Creole usage to rules. He retained the French spelling for the written language and allowed complete freedom in pronunciation. Those who speak Creole use the phonetics that their tradition imposes in each case. Below is a double column written by Doret, which tells the history of the language. The text in Creole is on the left; the French on the right.

---

[1] Dantès Bellegarde: *Haiti et son Peuple.*

Chaque pays gagner langue-li. N'en Partie de l'Est, Dominicains parlé espagnol. C'est pour ça nous hélé-yo Pagnols. C'est espagnol yo parlé n'en Amérique du Sud tou,[1] et anglais n'en Amérique du Nord. Nous-mêmes Haitiens, nous parlé Créole ac français.

Mais créole pas tout-à-fait ioun langue, bien que li composé presque ac mots français seulement. Français, c'est langue yo parlé en France. Gagner d'autres pays qui parlé créole tou. Yo pas loin nous: la Martinique, la Guadeloupe, la Guyane, la Lóuisiane. Créole, c'est ioun patois français. N'en point livres ni journal qui écrits en créole. Si ou vlé apprendre quèque chose n'en livres, il faut que c'est n'en livres-francais.

N'en temps longtemps, Haiti té ioun pays indien, mais quand blancs espagnols rivés n'en pays-là, yo détruit toute race indienne-là. Comme yo té besoin moune pour travailler la terre, yo ramassé nègres en Afrique pour faire yo servir comme esclaves. Toutes nègres-là, yo pas té parlé même langue, parce que Afrique c'est ioun pays qui grand enpile, et yo toutes pas

Chaque pays a sa langue. Dans la Partie de l'Est, les Dominicains parlent l'espagnol. C'est pourquoi nous les appelons Espagnols. C'est l'espagnol qu'on parle dans l'Amérique du Sud aussi, et l'Anglais dans l'Amérique du Nord. Nous-mêmes, Haitiens, nous parlons le créole et le français.

Mais le créole nest pas exactement une langue, bien qu'il ne soit composé à peu près que de mots français. Le français, c'est la langue qu'on parle en France. Il y a d'autres pays où l'on parle aussi le créole. Ils ne sont pas loin de nous: la Martinique, la Guadeloupe, la Guyane, la Louisiane. Le créole, c'est un patois français. Il n'y a pas de livres ni de journaux écrits en créole. Si vous voulez apprendre quelque chose par la lecture, il faut que ce soit dans des livres écrits en français.

Il y a longtemps, Haiti était un pays indien; mais quand les blancs Espagnols arrivèrent dans le pays, ils détruisirent toute cette race indienne. Comme ils avaient besoin de monde pour travailler le terre, ils allèrent prendre de nègres en Afrique pour les faire servir comme

[1] *Tou* means "also," from the English *too*, or perhaps from the colloquial French *itou*.

té sortis même côté. Ioun
partie, c'était Congo; ioun
l'autre, Sénégal; ioun l'autre,
Dahomey. Lorss yo va montré-
nous géographie, n'a connain
pays çà-yo plus bien.

Mais blancs Français metté
Espagnols dehors, prend place
yo. Comme nègres-yo té besoin
communiquer ensemble et que
yo pas té sottes, yo couté qui
genre blancs français a pé
parler. Yo essayé parler tant
cou blancs yo. C'est comme
çà créole trouvé li faite. Faut
pas croué c'est nègre seulement qui te parlé créole.
Blancs français metté parlé-li
tou pour yo capable com-
prendre ca nègres-là a pé dire.

esclaves. Tous ces nègres ne
parlaient pas la même langue,
parce que l'Afrique est un très
grand pays, et ils ne sortaient
pas tous des mêmes endroits.
Les uns venaient du Congo,
d'autres du Sénégal, d'autres
du Dahomey. Lorsque vous
apprendrez la géographie,
vous connaîtrez mieux ces
pays-là.

Mais les blancs français
mirent dehors les Espagnols
et prirent leur place. Comme
les nègres avaient besoin de
communiquer les uns avec les
autres et qu'ils n'étaient pas
des sots, ils écoutèrent les
Français et essayèrent de
parler comme ces blancs.
C'est comme ça qu'est né le
créole. Il ne faut pas croire
que c'étaient les nègres seulement qui parlaient le créole.
Les blancs français se mirent
aussi à le parler pour être
capables de comprendre ce
que disaient les nègres.

Language was also a barrier to religion. The priests preached
in French, to the double mystification of the Negroes who knew
neither French nor Latin. The voodoo religion was more accessible
and familiar to them. Although some wealthy mulattoes and Negroes—a very small minority—were able to go to France to be
educated, the practice of medicine was closed to them. The whites
feared the use of such scientific knowledge to poison them. Today,
three quarters of the people in Haiti express themselves in Creole.

Even though the Catholic religion never reached the people intimately and though segregation in the churches was strictly observed—indeed sometimes there was no room for the Negroes to
hear Mass—Christianity came to Haiti only through Catholicism.
And although the rebellious slaves were estranged from the church
that served the whites first, there were exceptions. Scharon writes:

What was the situation of the priests during the revolt of the slaves? A large number of the ministers of the faith were not molested in their parishes and continued to live as before. They were true counsellors to the Negroes. Were not Father Bienvenu, the priest of Mermelade; Father Sulpicio, a Capuchin, the priest of Trou; the parish priest Father Boucher in Terrier-Rouge; and the Abbé Delahaye in Dondon the men who first drew up their manifestos? Father Delahaye was arrested in Saint-Raphael. He and his company were imprisoned in the dungeon of Cap-Haïtien in January, 1793.

In the beginning the revolutionaries would have liked to move hand in hand with the Church. Toussaint L'Ouverture said, when he proclaimed independence in 1801: "The Catholic Apostolic, Roman religion is the only one that will be practiced publicly." But after all, the word "publicly" was a loophole that left the people free to worship otherwise in the dark. Voodoo was practiced at night.

The word "voodoo" comes from Dahomey; it means "god" or "spirit." The music and dances of the voodoo religion, its songs and magic ceremonies, can be traced back to Africa. The European element derives from hybridization with Catholicism. Voodoo is an American creation. It grew strongest and developed most rapidly during the period of independence, in part as a consequence of the schism that kept the official Catholic Church out of Haiti for fifty-five years. During this period, the Holy See refused to recognize the island's independence. In retaliation, Haiti would not permit Catholic priests to enter. King Henri-Christophe appointed the archbishop and made the clergy autonomous. Priesthood became a business. Adventurers who knew a smattering of the Catholic ritual took over the office of priests. They baptized the houses, the doors, and the pots and pans; they blessed fetishes and amulets and charged for their services whatever the traffic would bear. In 1805, Dessalines undid what Toussaint L'Ouverture had done by declaring: "The law admits no dominant religion; marriage is a purely civil act, authorized by the government; divorce is permitted by the state." In 1847, Faustin-Élie Soulouque seized power. Leyburn wrote:

The Negro general, raised to the highest office by a whim of fortune, was a man of the people in his religious attitudes. All the people's beliefs in magic, in the mystical power of certain rites, in enchantments and spells—all their "super-stitions," as the Catholics put it—were shared by Soulouque. For the first time in Haitian history, it was clear that the people's beliefs, brought from Africa, had been welded into recognizable shape under the name of voodooism. . . . Men who held high positions revealed their belief in the native dogmas. For twelve years, voodooism prospered with official approval.

As in the case of the Brazilian *macumba* cult, the powers of black magic were fused in voodoo with those which the Negroes granted to the saints of the Catholic Church. Anything that might possess some power was appropriated for invocations. The Cross holds an important place among the cabalistic signs. Leyburn has attempted to reduce what is essential in voodoo to a "Credo." It starts:

> I believe in many gods and spirits, guardians of the earth and heaven, and of all things visible and invisible; I believe that all these voodoos, acts, or mysteries are powerful, although less majestic than "*le bon Dieu*" of the Christians; that some of them come from our ancestors, from our old home in Africa, while we have met others in our homeland of Haiti. . . . I believe in the efficacy of curses and spells, and in the Holy Catholic Church.

Apart from the mixture so common in the development of Spanish American religious worship, which was a fusion of certain Indian traditions and Christian ceremonies, there are three cases of completely articulated religions that are New World inventions: Mormonism, the *macumba* of Brazil, and the voodoo of Haiti. English, Portuguese, and French. The Europeans gave voodoo a force both active and passive. Independent Haiti's break with the Holy See left a vacuum that the natives hastened to fill. In doing so, they made use of Christian invocations. Dr. Pierre Mabille writes:

> The European influence is important in voodoo. The names of Jesus and the Virgin Mary are invoked and venerated, and Christian prayers are mingled with the others. The Catholic saints are on the list of the powers that are wor-shipped, and public worship of the saints becomes a short religious ceremony the attributes of which more or less coincide with the popular image of the saint. . . . European

magic has left a deep impress not only on voodoo but also on all Haitian witchcraft. Books like those of "Albertus Magnus" and "Albertus Parvus" have found an echo in the Antilles. All the heterodox tendencies of the eighteenth century in France, including Mesmerism, have left their traces. The freed slaves have faithfully preserved the superstitions of their masters and blended them with their own. In *The Haitian Voodoo*, Dr. Maximilian insists that this intermingling of European and African magic has been possible thanks to common fundamental concepts. Freemasonry has helped to shape present-day voodoo. We know that the lodges flourished in Santo Domingo at the end of the eighteenth century and that freedmen were admitted to them; the ceremonies that took place during the meetings aroused their curiosity. The influence of Masonry is evident in the drawings of certain "Vêvers," in the initiations, in certain passages of the ritual.

The stranger and more mysterious the Catholic religion appeared to the Negroes, the more they respected it. In accepting baptism they believed that if the officiating priest was a Negro, the baptism "wouldn't take." The priests had to be white. The slaves used to stone Negro priests. One of the attractions of the Mass was that it was performed in one language and the sermon was preached in another, neither of which the Negroes understood. The greater the mystery, the more potent the magic.

¶ VOODOO, WAR, A MONARCHY, AND A REPUBLIC

Dancing, music, and song are all indispensable parts of voodoo, as they are of all primitive religions.

The wild dance, performed to the beat of drums, fire, and the invocation of spirits worked together to unleash the forces enchained by slavery during the struggle for independence. Over long distances, the drums summoned the sorcerers. The frequent assemblages so convoked finished off France's power in the island. Chronologically, first England was deposed in the North; then France was driven from Haiti; immediately afterward Spain lost South America; and finally Portugal relinquished Brazil. That is the order in which the four European empires in America fell: the Negroes freed themselves soon after the English colonists. But what was accomplished in Britain's possessions by the

454   LATIN AMERICA: *A Cultural History*

speeches of Jefferson and Adams was the work of voodoo in Haiti, magically convoked by Boukman, who, with his comrades Baissou and Jean Français, lighted the torch of revolution.

The forehandedness of the Haitians was remarkable. Even before they had challenged France in their own country, eight hundred Negroes and mulattoes from Haiti had fought for the freedom of the thirteen colonies in 1779 under the command of Count Jean Baptiste Charles Henri Hector d'Estaing (1729–94). Most of them lost their lives at the Battle of Savannah. Among the survivors was Henri-Christophe, Haiti's future king.

The debate in the National Assembly was heard as news and was circulated in Haiti. Some of the free Negroes and mulattoes who were educated in France listened in Paris to the speeches delivered against slavery and for the rights of man. A longing for emancipation was engendered in the wealthy Creoles who wanted Haiti to be independent of France, with themselves as its rulers: the paradox of a free Haiti, with slaves. The colonists sent thirty-seven delegates to the National Assembly of 1788. They brought with them a list of grievances, and demanded that the colony be given the right to rule itself. The Assembly would admit only six of the delegates. The Negroes, for their part, heard and rejoiced over the news of the founding of a society called Les Amis des Noirs (The Friends of the Blacks). Vincent Ogé (1750–91), a mulatto educated in France who had attended the National Assembly, returned to Santo Domingo with a plan that would open the campaign on behalf of the Negroes' political rights. Ogé and his friend Jean-Batiste Chavannes (1749–91) headed a revolt in Cap-Haïtien which cost both of them their lives. They were hunted beyond the borders of the country, and after a trial that lasted six months, were sentenced to death. Discrimination lasted unto death. The execution took place on the opposite side of the square from that used when whites were punished. The condemned men were turned over to the executioner at the door of the cathedral. They were in their shirtsleeves, each with a rope around his neck and holding a candle. They were obliged to kneel and confess their crimes and ask for forgiveness. Then they were exposed on the scaffold. Their arms, legs, and elbows were broken on a platform. They were tied to a wheel facing the sun, to wait for death and for the buzzards to eat them. The Spanish authorities of Santo Domingo and the French officials of Haiti had worked together to achieve this happy ending. Ogé and Chavanne had fled to Santo Domingo seeking sanctuary, but the governor, Don

García, had turned them over to Haitian justice. As compensation, he was awarded the Cross of St. Louis at his own request. The slaves knew then that their freedom would cost them dear, but they decided to win it by fighting.

An open slave rebellion followed the Ogé uprising on August 14, 1791. "The foremost Negro in the world," as Pierre-Dominique Toussaint L'Ouverture (1746?–1803) was called, made his name then. Toussaint had been a slave, but he had been able to get an education owing to the tolerance of a good master. He had read the lives of Alexander the Great and Julius Caesar. The first thing he used to spur his people on to rebellion was a false rumor that France had passed a law allowing the Negroes three days of leisure a week and abolishing punishment by the lash. But, he said, the white men were keeping this law a secret. A bogus gazette reporting the alleged dispensation was printed, and the gazette was read in a secret meeting. Boukman, who was there, announced that troops were to be sent from France to guarantee compliance with the law. A voodoo meeting was called in Boi-Caiman. It was raining hard, but the magical ceremony was performed against thunder and lightning. A priestess slit a pig's throat and the congregation drank its warm blood. The song of freedom was sung:

Eh! Eh! Bamba! Heu! Heu! . . .

Soon all the North was aflame. The sugar mills and the white people's houses were burned. Then the slaughter of the French began. Negroes with torches, machetes, sticks, and knives flowed like an outpouring of black lava over the countryside, proclaiming liberty amid flames. The news sped on. The whites in Port-au-Prince, Cap-Haïtien, and Cayes were in desperate straits. France had no way to check the violence. She begged her neighbors for help, but the invading English and Spanish troops created new problems for the colony. As a last desperate resort, the French general who was governing Haiti made a pact with the Devil by obtaining the help of the two most influential Negroes. One of them was General André Rigaud (1761–1811), an educated dark mulatto who had fought under D'Estaing in Georgia. The other was Pierre-Dominique Toussaint L'Ouverture. By 1797, Toussaint had won control, had got rid of the French commissioners one by one, had driven the whites from the island, and had overthrown the mulatto Rigaud, who fled to France.

Napoleon felt that Toussaint had won a victory over him. He

observed angrily that Toussaint was on friendly terms with the United States and that President John Adams admired and supported him. This, he feared, would interfere with his plans for expanding the French colonies in North America. To regain control of the situation, he sent deceitful messages and turned the job of pacifying the island over to his brother-in-law, General Charles Leclerc, Pauline Bonaparte's husband. Leclerc and Pauline sailed from France with a brilliant army. Napoleon wrote to Toussaint: "Help General Leclerc with your advice, your talents, and your influence. What is it you wish? The freedom of the Negroes? You know that in every country where we have been, we have granted it to the people who did not have it." But his secret instructions to Leclerc were: "The moment you have got rid of Toussaint, Christophe, Dessalines, and the leading bandits, as soon as the mass of the Negroes have been disarmed, send all the Negroes and mulattoes who have taken part in the civil struggles to the continent. . . . Get rid of those enlightened Africans for us." Leclerc arrived with full authority. Toussaint fell into his trap, was taken prisoner by a trick, and was sent to France, where he died years later in the prison of the fort of Joux, near Besançon. General Leclerc was halted on his road to glory by the burning finger of yellow fever, which ended his life and killed many of his troops. Only Pauline escaped the scourge. And Haiti escaped servitude, for Napoleon was defeated in Haiti as decisively as in Russia. Snow had rescued the Russians; mosquitoes helped the Negroes. Toussaint was granted so high a position in history that he became one of the saints on Comte's calendar and Wordsworth wrote a sonnet to his memory.

After Toussaint came Jean-Jacques Dessalines (1758–1806), who defeated General Donatien Rochambeau (1750–1813), Leclerc's successor. Rochambeau, more ruthless than the others, believed he could stamp out the rebellion by hanging, shooting, and burning the Negroes whom he captured, and by hunting the fugitives with five hundred dogs bought in Jamaica. He followed that plan, but he failed. Dessalines adopted the name of Haiti for the new state, replacing the French name *Saint-Domingue* with an Indian word. He headed his decrees with his motto, "Liberty or death." Instead of paying a hundred dollars for a dog to hunt the Negroes, as Rochambeau had done, he offered to pay American shipowners forty piastres for the passage of each Negro who wished to return to the island. He proclaimed himself Emperor Jacques I, and laid the foundations of a new city, which he named Dessalinesville and made the capital of his empire.

Within a few weeks the streets had been laid out in straight lines, and small villas had been built as if by a miracle.

Dessalines founded the first socialist state in independent America. He confiscated white people's property, forced those who owned large estates to turn them over to the state, debarred free Negroes and mulattoes from becoming powerful landowners, and imposed a regime of labor backed by force. On one occasion he exclaimed: "Take care, Negroes and mulattoes! We have all fought against the whites; the property we have won by shedding our own blood belongs to all of us. I demand that it be shared equally!"

Dessalines was frank enough in stating his ideology. To have spoken of a republic would have been a euphemism, a farce. He declared himself emperor, but he was assassinated, possibly by the mulattoes. Henri-Christophe (1767–1820) succeeded him, appointed by the Assembly which had met for that purpose. Once in control, he proclaimed himself King Henri I. He reigned for thirteen years either from Sans Souci, the Versailles of Haiti, or from the Citadel, his stone shield, both of which he had built. The Citadel is one of the most daring and grandiose structures in the New World. It stands at the top of a high mountain and contains a huge network of storerooms, reservoirs, and defenses that made it impregnable. According to Henri-Christophe, the Haitians could withstand a siege of months. All the people worked like a single slave on the construction of the fortress. Their ruler reasoned that they had become the slaves of their own independence, slaves to their own liberty. Henri-Christophe punished laziness with a club of jaguey wood wielded by the foreman. He ordered decency in dress. By implacable punishments he did away with thievery and made honest people of the Haitians. In 1820 a rebellion broke out against Henri-Christophe and he was deposed. The conquered emperor leaped to death from his Citadel.

During the kingdom, vestiges of the republic lingered. In the southern part of the island, Alexandre Sabiès Pétion (1770–1818) became president and governed in Port-au-Prince while King Henri-Christophe reigned over the North in Cap-Haïtien. Pétion, an educated Negro who had played a part in Dessalines's downfall, felt that he was pledged to liberty in the form of a republic. During the days when Bolívar's struggle as Liberator of South America looked almost hopeless, when he could see no way of returning to Venezuela from Jamaica, Pétion helped him to reach the Orinoco and begin his campaign again.

At Henri-Christophe's death, a republic was proclaimed

458 LATIN AMERICA: *A Cultural History*

throughout Haiti. But it was to change to an empire again under Faustin-Élie Soulouque (1785–1867), who proclaimed himself Emperor Faustin I in 1847. Soulouque intended to run his country in the style of Napoleon. The crown that was placed on his head cost a hundred thousand dollars. He promoted an invasion of Santo Domingo, but the attempted conquest failed. The illiterate and bloodthirsty emperor was dethroned in 1859 and fled the country. All told, Haiti had managed to produce three kings or emperors. Because the country was deeply impressed by European monarchy, it was the one spot in America where so many reversals of that kind came out of independence. On the other hand, the African past was always in the blood. President François Duvalier (1907–   ) a physician elected president in 1957, embodies the entire Negro tradition of the state. He is an enemy of the mulatto and Grand Master of voodoo. Alfredo Pareja Diez Canseco says in his biography of Duvalier:

> In the nocturnal ceremonies, at the dark hour of apparitions, the devil's magistracy comes at the invocation of the *houngan*, the priest who speaks in rhythmic, metallic Creole: "Au nom Baron du Cimetière, guardián de tous les morts, Messié Candelú, vous, vous, vous seul qui traverzes le purgatoire, nègre guedevi, nègre ceclay, nègre rouse, nègre trois auous, trois pince, trois picais, trois gamelles, nègre lenvére, nègre cordon noir, nègre roidu, Ago-Acocy Agola. . . .[1]

Diez Canseco points out the similarity between Dessalines and President Duvalier in the words of Duvalier which accompanied the announcement of the danger of a North American invasion: "Blood will flow. The island will be aflame from the North to the South, from the east to the west, and there will be mountains of the dead, of those who would like to enslave us to foreigners. It will be the greatest slaughter in history. A Himalaya of cadavers will pile up." In 1959 Duvalier expelled the Catholic priests who refused to be his tools and was excommunicated by the Vatican. He took advantage of his rejection by Rome to affirm his own religion: voodooism.

Since the time of Napoleon, literary men all over the world have found material for fabulous stories in all this Negro history. Victor Hugo used the slave rebellion as the subject of his first

[1] *Cuadernos*, Paris, August, 1963.

novel, *Buj-Jargal*. Lamartine wrote a dramatic poem in honor of Toussaint. Chateaubriand compared Toussaint with Napoleon in his *Mémoires d'Outre-tombe* (*Memoirs from Beyond the Tomb*). Christophe inspired Eugene O'Neill to write *The Emperor Jones* (1921).

The stir made all over the world by Haiti's saga, with its link to France, began when free Haiti started to write. The early newspapers conveyed a romantic air that rings in their titles. They were christened *L'Abeille Haytienne*, *L'Éclaireur*, *L'Union*, *Le Télégraph*. Haiti's first poet, Corolian Ardouin (1812–35), died very young. Some of his stanzas were written on the walls of a dungeon. His complete work was not published until 1881, half a century after his death. Another poet, Alibée Féry (1819–96), was influenced by Voltaire and André Chénier. Pierre Faubert (1803–68), was a follower of Lamartine. He wrote *Ogé et le Préjugé de Couleur*, a drama that was staged in 1841.

The theater is one of the country's favorite forms of expression. Because so many of them are illiterate, it serves the Haitians better than their newspapers. One of the native Romanticists, Charles-Seguy Villavaleix (1835–1923), was inspired by Lamartine. Almost all Haitian novels are historical, the work of men who continue to record the past as they adopt the medium of fiction. Éméric Bergeaud (1818–58), in his novel, *Stella*, tells the story of the martyred pre-revolutionaries Ogé and Chavanne and of Henri-Christophe's campaigns. By the end of the century, the poets of the patriotic school, the national novelists, and the writers who made an approach to the uncompromising art of the French Symbolists had struck a balance. Some of them were introduced to the French world. Oswald Durand (1840–1906) was a poet whom François Coppée took to the Paris Société des Gens de Lettres. Emmanuel Édouard (1858–95) wrote in Paris *La République d'Haiti à l'Apothéose de Victor Hugo*. In 1927 the *Revue Indigène* was founded and a native school formed around it. Philippe-Thoby Marcelin (1904–) won a prize in a Latin American novel competition offered by a New York publisher in 1943 with his *Canapé Vert* (Ciro Alegría won the first prize with *El Mundo es Ancho y Ajeno*). Little by little other non-French influences were coming to bear on Haiti, particularly through the U.S. Negro poet Langston Hughes (1902–) and Nicolás Guillén of Cuba.

In the field of education, the Lancastrian school was the first to be adopted in Haiti soon after Toussaint L'Ouverture pointed out the need for instruction. Today, school attendance is obligatory. Haiti has three million inhabitants, of whom 238,000 are enrolled in the schools. Its university has schools of medicine, arts and sciences, law, and so on. Six daily papers were being published in 1960; together they had a press run of thirty-eight thousand. That means that eleven out of every thousand Haitians were then taking a daily paper. In the Dominican Republic, twenty-seven out of every thousand read a paper; in Cuba eighty-eight; in Puerto Rico sixty-one; in Panama one hundred and four; in Costa Rica ninety-four; in El Salvador forty-nine; in Guatemala thirty-one.

Even though President Duvalier, who dissolved parliament in 1963, loves voodoo, not everything in Haiti is black.

...

XIX: From *Modernismo* to *Anti-Modernismo*

¶ THE POETIC CONTINENT

The nineteenth century was the least dull of all centuries to Latin America. It was a time of high intelligence and deep feeling. At its beginning, the rationality of modern times stood face to face with the unreason of the Spanish Empire; at its end, the young republics were searching for a vista broad enough to encompass the panorama of the world. The evolution entailed was not the work of the intelligence alone; it was also a flight of imagination. But as reason is a limiting force, whereas revolution must overflow rationality and rise to heroism, America reacted romantically, refused to be constricted by reason. Instead the continent took the death-defying leap for freedom. "In the beginning was action." Later, the century caught the contagion of its early temerity. A poet sleeps in every man, but he is awake in the Latin American. It is always just as possible to make a poetic history as to make a political or an economic history. The history of literature is not itself poetic. Nor is the history of poetry. What is poetic is the development of people as seen through their poetic impulses or images. Latin America revolves around her fate as a poetic area that cannot be fitted into the rigid confines of reason. In the course of the normal processes of the intelligence, it always perceives a reality and another magical ingredient that transforms it. The history of culture cannot be written without taking these elements into account. Oftentimes the magical element soars above sense, and paradoxically this very lack of sense has been the greater stimulus to progress. Magic uplifts, unbinds things, raises them to a height at which they can be seen better. Romanticism was fertile in Latin America because it contained a dream element, an irrational magic. It made people shed resignation and moved them to recapture a historical personality that then seemed to have little viability.

Reason and magic either complement each other or contradict each other. Antiromanticism in Spanish America was always paired with romanticism. Genre paintings were instruments of social criticism: they portrayed the Cartesian doubt. In America, humor, that recourse of the English, that genial instrument of Larra in Spain, helped better than anything else both to put the new citizen on his guard against committing himself blindly to the new and to sweep away the last vestiges of the colonial system. Poetry served the same purpose. In Argentina, a school of *gaucho* poets developed. They delved antiromantically and ironically into the strange world of the man on the pampas. Estanislao del Campo (1834–80) poses the gaucho against the city man in *Fausto*. There the element of magic is not so much in the dialogues between Mephistopheles and Faust as in the revelation of the possible reactions of a man bred on the pampas to a presentation of Gounod's opera. *Gaucho* poetry reached its peak in one of the greatest works of Argentine literature: *Martín Fierro*, by José Hernández (1834–86). Martín Fierro, the *gaucho*, tells in the first person the story of his life in the open, his conflicts with authority, his hunger for freedom. "After God, nothing." He speaks in the popular idiom; he reasons as men reason on the pampas. Himself, his horse, and his knife form an invincible trinity. This is the theme of Hernández's 7,218 verses; his 1,203 stanzas, which are like a commentary in ballad form on Sarmiento's *Facundo*. Many Argentines know whole sections of the poem by heart.

When Romanticism was in full flower there were poets of impassioned, sometimes grandiloquent, lyricism, to be sure. The hidden forces of nature in America seemed to be unleashed in them, and they seemed to balance life against death. Manuel Acuña (1849–73) in Mexico, Julio Flórez (1867–1917) in Colombia, and Juan Zorrilla de San Martín (1855–1931) in Uruguay were typical of that school, which retained its vigor into the twentieth century. The later exponents of it were Almafuerte

(Pedro B. Palacios, 1854–1927), who wrote in Argentina, Salvador Diaz Mirón (1853–1928) in Mexico, José Santos Chocano (1875–1934) in Peru, and Andrés Mata (1870–1913) in Venezuela.

Modernismo captured the last echoes of Romanticism. It also conveyed to America the aesthetic preoccupations of Europe, especially French Symbolism, a movement that was a parenthesis, a pause for reflection, a participation in the life of the Occident which had a profound effect on the culture of the New World. A moment, brief but decisive, came while Verlaine was the "master mechanic" under whose influence another kind of writing made its start.

¶ MODERNISMO

Modernismo was revolutionary. It erupted in new forms. It attacked every tenet of Castilian literature, which had been dozing for centuries. To America, it meant independence from Spanish literary tradition. And though it is true that ultimately it became a projection of the new French spirit over the Spanish, *modernismo* cannot be dismissed with that, nor can it be considered in general as merely a new form of Francophilia. Originally, the new literary generation longed to embrace all of European culture and to go on from there. The Modernists looked to Poe and Whitman in the United States; to D'Annunzio and Leopardi in Italy; to Schopenhauer, Nietzsche, Schiller, and Hegel in Germany; to Tolstoy, Marie Bashkirtsev, and Gorki among the Russians. Bécquer gave a Spanish ingredient and some memories of the Golden Age to the school. Nevertheless, American *modernismo* was the sum that came out of all those influences. As in the time of Ruíz de Alarcón or Bello, the Spaniards picked up the American import, and it became a vital part of the renewal of their own cultural background. The *modernismo* of the Spanish-speaking republics was an inspirational element in the poetry of Valle Inclán, the Machados, Juan Ramón Jiménez, and others. This American presence has continued as a part of the development of Spanish literature. "They talk about the mania for seeking European roots in American poetry," Guillermo de Torre once said, "but it is all the other way round."

Modernismo was by no means Latin America's first contact with France; indeed, though it seems paradoxical, *modernismo* finally freed Latin America from French influence. It opened the way to greater originality. The Americans already had attained a certain maturity in style, and Gallicisms were less frequent among the Modernists than among older writers of the nineteenth century. Rubén Darío, the leader of the new movement displayed a surprising poetic mastery that transcended the Spanish tradition and French Symbolism alike. The new poet absorbed all cultures and gave them his own accent.

It is significant that Darío should have chosen the label of "Modernist" at a moment when the word carried so strong a revolutionary connotation in the Catholic world that the Pope finally condemned it. Catholic Modernism came out of France, from the Catholic Institute of Paris, founded by Father Duquesne in 1880. Abbé Loisy applied the new critical method to the study of the Bible and tried to bring Catholicism closer to modern culture, hence farther from the old tradition that had been knitted together by St. Paul, Origen, St. Augustine, and St. Thomas Aquinas. Such books by Catholic Modernists as *La Vie Catholique* by Pierre Dabry and Paul Naudet's *Justice Sociale* anticipated the Christian democratic formulas of the second half of the twentieth century. The Christian modernists entered the field of the novel with *Il Santo* by the Italian Antonio Fogazzaro, which was widely read in America. The Roman Curia followed the movement with keen interest as it leaned toward liberal formulas, and Pope Pius X issued the first alarm in his encyclical *Pieni d'animo* (*Full of Courage*). The following year the Holy Office signed the document *Lamentabili*, and immediately afterward the Holy Father openly condemned Modernism as heretical in the new encyclical *Pascendi Dominici Gregis*. It also condemned "Americanism" as the liberal movement for the reform of the Church which originated in the United States was called. If the Modernists in literature had nothing to do with such religious questions, neither did most of their leaders feel any great concern over censure from Rome. Whenever the readers of Nietzsche and Schopenhauer turned their eyes toward Jesus, they did so only to see Renan's Jesus better.

Rubén Darío was almost the first and the last of the Modernists. The movement reached its zenith with him. When he died, new changes were beginning to appear in America and to give life to new points of view. Darío's *modernismo* was primarily literary, with no marked philosophical overtones. What followed was the prelude to social protest. At the apogee of *modernismo*, democracy was in crisis all over America, under the satrapies of the last of

the barbarian *caudillos*. This mattered little to Darío. He gave
them a passing blow in verse worthy of his talent:

> *Christ walks, thin and feeble through the streets.*
> *Barabbas keeps his slaves, his toadies lick his shoes,*
> *And the land of the Chibcha, Cuzco and Palenque,*
> *Have seen the panthers sleek and in their prime.*

But Darío was never an aggressive man. His approach to Spain
was without republican reservations. He paid court to the court
with the severe demeanor of a taciturn Indian, with no trace of
servility, as a simple lover of beauty. The early Modernists were
another breed of man, particularly Martí.

¶ JOSÉ MARTÍ

José Martí (1835–95) fused his poetry and his patriotism
into a single weapon. He was a sleepless fighter for the cause
of freedom and represented the life blood and the whole of Cuban-
ism. He is known not as "The Teacher," but as "The Apostle."
"He writes more brilliantly than anyone in Spain or America,"
Darío averred. Martí revolutionized poetry free of the sin of
outside influences. His was original sin. He visited Paris only
twice, and then briefly. On the other hand, he lived for a time
in Spain and much longer in New York. He knew French poetry
well, but English poetry better, though he preferred the French.
He wrote about Walt Whitman with greater understanding than
others have. He praised Oscar Wilde, though with reservations.
His *modernismo* is evident more in his prose than in his verse,
which recalls the work of the Spanish poets Campoamor and
Echegaray to some degree, and that of Bécquer more; he never
denied his Spanish blood. But he did not take from that blood the
worship of the mother country, for he was not a Hispanophile.
It gave him a love for liberty, for the rebellion of the common man.
His first immortal pages, those of his book *El Presidio Político
en Cuba* (*The Political Prison in Cuba*), written in 1871, hold
a beauty that flowers from the most brutal scenes in political
despotism. As a child he sprinkled with his blood the stones of
the quarries where he and the other prisoners broke rock under
a fiery sun. His finest speech in *Los Pinos Verdes* (*The Green
Pines*) is an address to the exiles who earned their living rolling
tobacco leaves in Tampa. In it, he reminds them of the official
slaughter of the medical students in Havana. His final pages,

perhaps his most beautiful, were written as he was on his way to death in the revolution that he had unleashed to free Cuba from Spanish domination.

Martí found the pure source of his magical lyricism not in the Symbolists or the Parnassians, but in his vision of America, which he mined from the deepest Castilian lodes. He was in revolt against the dictatorships of Mexico, Guatemala, and Venezuela. Paradoxically, he could find freedom only in Brooklyn, where he was able to establish a paper called *Patria*. While a student in Havana, he had been imprisoned for bringing out a leaflet entitled *Patria Libre*. In the United States, he set up the machinery for Cuban independence. His work brought him face to face with harsh alternatives, disillusionment, and disappointment. One time the ships carrying his sacred contraband cargo were seized almost at the moment of sailing. But for all that, he found the most efficient tools for his fight for freedom on United States soil. Did this bind him beyond the limits of noble gratitude? Never. He protested angrily that the aid given him could not possibly be construed as surrender to the United States. But he paid heartfelt homage to Lincoln and told in pure verse the epic story of the descendants of the *Mayflower* passengers who founded the English colonies. Yet he analyzed the differences that separate the two Americas, saying:

> However great this America may be, and however consecrated it may be to the free men of the America in which Lincoln was born, to us in the depths of our hearts, the America in which Juárez was born is greater, and no one can blame us for it, nor think ill of us for it, because it is ours, and because it has been more unfortunate.

❡ GUTIÉRREZ, NÁJERA, CASAL, SILVA

The Mexican Manuel Gutiérrez Nájera (1859–95) and the Cuban Julián del Casal (1863–93) were Modernists contemporary with Martí. They never struck a note so American as "The Apostle" did. Like Darío they had a strong predilection for all things French. Gutiérrez Nájera, an elegant and aristocratic poet, wrote *Cuentos Frágiles* and *Cuentos de Color de Humo* in a highly refined style. He was the high priest of art, neither Spanish nor Mexican. "French thoughts in Spanish verses," Justo Sierra pronounced them. And Nájera himself wrote:

> *France, France, the transparent vitrine*
> *Wherein the human soul must waken*
> *an echo answered with a cry of pain.*
> *Immense, eternal heart that beats*
> *so strongly that the universe is shaken.*

Julián del Casal moved away from Bécquer, Zorrilla, and Campo-amor and closer to the French, particularly Baudelaire. His choice brought him the melancholy of escapism in search of the exotic. To him France was a golden door to Asiatic dreams, an attitude common to the Modernists who came later. Casal took his inspiration from such French painters as Moreau and Delacroix. In *Nostalgias*, he sighs, "Ah, if only I could go to Algiers some day, with what joy I would depart; I would travel to the Yellow River, in the glow of the full moon." In *Neurosis*, he composed such verses as: "A silken red screen from China unfolds its leaves in a nook unseen." And "White fan and blue parasol . . ." or "In a porcelain cup that blends the tints of morning, the tea's green soul winds upward like smoke."

One of the greatest poetic talents was discovered in the haunting music of *Nocturne* by the Colombian José Asunción Silva (1865–96). Unamuno said: "Silva was the first to bring Spanish America into poetry, and with it certain tones and airs from the Spanish." Luis de Zulueta stated: "His poetry, which Spain accepted immediately, gave the first impulse to the new Spanish poetry in turn." Juan Ramón Jiménez might dispute the worth of many poets and even express reservations about certain aspects of Silva's poetry, but he bowed before *Nocturne* with ever-increasing admiration; it enchanted him. *Nocturne*'s poetic intimacy contrasts with Darío's cosmopolitan touch. Its music is muted, with a magic born of the Bogotan countryside. The poem was written out of a universal experience. Bécquer and, more particularly, Bartrina were trying to lure Silva to Spain. Verlaine was calling seductively from France, but, as Rufino Blanco Fombona reminds us, Silva's poems were written before Jules Laforgue sealed the triumph of Symbolism in France with his verse. If there is some outside influence in the intimate structure of *Nocturne*, it is the faint echo of Poe's or Schiller's music. Silva "knew Poe by heart." But Baldomero Sanín Cano has recorded in an explanatory note in the margin of Alberto Miramón's book on Silva that the poet was responsive to other, more abstruse influences. Sanín Cano wrote:

When I noted that Silva had been reminiscent of Schiller in *Día de Difuntos* [*Day of the Dead*], I did not mean to imply that his intention had been to imitate him in idea. I was referring to the rhythm. The German verse is not metered by syllables, but by feet, which makes its metric scheme a more demanding entity. The accents are strictly stressed, according to whether they are iambs, troches, and so on, which give the verse a less monotonous sonorousness than is usually found in the Romance languages when concise measures are used. Silva noted this. I read to him some excerpts in German from the *Song of the Bell*, and he beat with his hands the rhythm that manifestly attempts to imitate the sound of bells.

Silva's friendship with Sanín Cano, which started the poet on his study of the inner structure of German verse, led him to learn something of the other aspects of German culture. Sanín Cano read Nietzsche to his conversation groups, and the Colombians of the day listened with pleasure to the resonance of *Also Sprach Zarathustra* (*Thus Spake Zarathustra*). The German writers provided an approach to Spain in the work of Bécquer and Hartzenbusch. Sanín recalls that Bécquer's rhyme ending "As long as there is a mystery for man—there will be poetry!" derives from the German poetry of Anakasius Grur. Silva was interested in the Russians, too. He wrote a short essay on Tolstoi as the prologue to a small book published in Bogotá containing some of the master's best pages. *De Sobremesa* (*After Dining*), an autobiographical novel by Silva, a work basic to an understanding of the life of a Modernist lived in the Parisian style in Latin America, is an elegiac song to the memory of Marie Bashkirtsev. Silva writes: "There are pages in the diary of the Russian woman that translate my emotions, my ambitions, my dreams, my whole life so sincerely that I could not have found more accurate formulations for annotating my own impressions." He felt equally close to Leopardi and D'Annunzio. When he says in one poem, "He read Leopardi and Schopenhauer," he seems to be speaking of himself and suggesting his later suicide. D'Annunzio's work was with him at his final hour, for *Il Trionfo della Morte* (*The Triumph of Death*) was found on the night table in the bedroom where he ended his days by his own hand. Silva applied all his enormous curiosity, all that world of reading to a small body of work into which he delicately decanted the environment, the landscape, and the humanity closest to him. No trace of exoticism marks his masterpieces: *Nocturne, Día de Difuntos, El Recluta* (*The Recruit*), and *Vejeces* (*Old Age*).

José Martí and Silva, the forerunners of *modernismo*, were also the last of the Romanticists. The mystery and the resonance of their poetry lie in that duality of style. What Luis de Zulueta said of Silva may be said of both men: "He was born and he died Romantic."

¶ RUBÉN DARÍO

Rubén Darío (1867–1916) was born in the village of Metapa, Nicaragua, in the year that Baudelaire died in Paris. He was christened Félix Rubén García Sarmiento, but his first move toward literature was to cast aside most of his names and simply call himself Rubén Darío. The school he attended was the best one for a future career in letters: provincial life. He found the first books he ever handled in a bookcase belonging to an aunt of his. The reading matter was the kind always kept in the old houses of Spanish America: a volume of comedies of the Golden Age, the Bible, *Don Quixote, The Thousand and One Nights*, Cicero's Letters, and Mme de Staël's *Corinne*. Darío was precocious enough to find in those books the key to his destiny. Later the child went to the capital and devoured all the books he could lay hands on. He wrote verse. At the inauguration of the national library, he read a poem in ten *décimas* (Spanish stanzas each consisting of ten octosyllabic lines) which was "explosive and red with radicalism." Even before he was nineteen years old, he was deeply in debt and leading a Bohemian life. With the help of his friends, he sailed for Chile. At twenty-one he published a small volume, half prose stories, half verse, entitled *Azul* (*Blue*), which established his name as the very model of *modernismo*. The first story is set in a café somewhere in France; another was inspired by a passage in *Romeo and Juliet;* another derived from the fiction of Daudet; another from that of Rémy de Gourmont. The Spanish writer and statesman Juan Valera, ever alert to what was going on in America, wrote to Darío from Spain:

> None of the men in the Peninsula seem to me ever to have been so imbued as you are with the spirit of France. . . . No Castilian author is more French than you, and I say this without praise or censure, merely to affirm a fact. . . . In the prose stories and the poetry, everything is chiseled, burn-

ished, made to last, with beauty and nicety, as Flaubert or the most finished Parnassian might have done it. And yet the effort does not show, nor the work of polishing, nor the labor of gleaning; everything appears spontaneous and easy as if written at full speed of the pen, without any want of conciseness, precision, or extreme elegance. . . . I do not know which I prefer in this book, the prose or the verse. I am almost inclined to see equal merit in both means of expressing your thought. In the prose there is a greater wealth of ideas; but the form is more in the French style. In the verses, the form is more chastely Spanish.

Eight years later, Darío published *Los Raros* (*The Strange People*) and *Prosas Profanas* (*Profane Prose*), in Buenos Aires. By that time he was a master of his art. José Enrique Rodó began an essay on Dario with these words:

"He is not the poet of America," I once heard someone say as the course of an animated literary conversation paused at the name of the author of *Prosas Profanas* and *Azul*. The remark conveyed a sense of reproach; but though the opinions that might be deduced regarding this judgment were different, the negative consensus was almost unanimous. Of course Rubén Darío is not the poet of America. . . . Need I say that an inferior literary status is not to be inferred from that fact, as I merely set down the remarks from memory in my own words? . . . It seems to me quite right to deplore the conditions of a period of formation which does not have the poetic quality of the refined ages and therefore tends to postpone indefinitely the possibility of a truly free and autonomous art in America. But just as it seems to me senseless to try to fill the gap with paltry originality attained at the price of intolerance and lack of communication, I think it puerile of us to persist in pretending to a rich content where one can live intellectually only by borrowing. Let us confess it: our present America is not a very rich soil for Art.

When Darío made his first visit to Paris, a poverty-stricken old rake was drinking himself to death on absinthe and had only three years left to him. That man was Paul Verlaine. Enrique Gómez Carrillo (1837–1927), a Guatemalan who, possibly more than any other Latin American, had established and maintained friendships with the great of France, was able to introduce Darío to the literary circles of Paris. That was in 1893, when Gómez Carrillo was only twenty years old. Verlaine wrote to him from the hospital: "I am now installed in my Winter Palace; come and see me so we can talk about Calderón and Góngora—that Symbolist! My day for receiving is Sunday." A real intimacy existed between Verlaine and the young Guatemalan, to whom Darío had given an overcoat as he was leaving his country to sail for Europe. Gómez Carrillo, in turn, gave the overcoat to Verlaine. Gómez Carrillo was a literary journalist, a chronicler who raised that type of writing to new levels. Darío was a chronicler, too, but of another type. Above all, he was a poet. When Verlaine died, Darío wrote *Responso* (*Responsary*) which begins:

> *Father and magic master, celestial lyrist,*
> *Who, to Olympic instrument and oaten flute*
> *Gavest thine own rapt note.*

This poem holds an enduring place among the treasures of Castilian lyricism.

Darío was the most felicitous vessel for the new art of France, the last of the great Symbolists. But his Spanish background set him apart from the French writers. He derived as much from Góngora, whom the "father and magic master" had thought about in the hospital, as he did from Verlaine himself. But above and beyond all influences, Darío's work is highly personal. It cast a sorcerer's spell over Spain which captured all the poets of the time. Salvador Rueda, Valle Inclán, Antonio Machado, Villaespesa, and Juan Ramón Jiménez all recognized unreservedly that the Nicaraguan had given Castilian letters a new direction. The generations that came later wrote the book that Darío failed to write and Rodó did not believe in—the book of America. Darío barely scratched the theme somewhat gingerly in his magnificent *Canto a la Argentina* and the "Ode to Roosevelt" in which he drew a line between the North and the South. He preached Hispanism in his *Letanías a Don Quijote* (*Litanies to Don Quixote*). But his proper environment was Paris. He returned to his own country only to die. As he closed his eyes, he pressed to his breast a figure of Christ given him by Amado Nervo. He was the greatest Spanish-speaking poet of his time, and will dominate the panorama of Castilian letters for centuries.

¶ THE EXOTICS

Gómez Carrillo, Verlaine's friend, was also a member of the same set as Moréas, Theodore de Banville, Oscar Wilde, Charles Maurras, Jean Lorrain, and Huysmans, all of whom were also his personal friends. He was a singular figure in literature. No one in Spain or America had as many readers as he. It is doubtful that his novels will survive, but he influenced an entire generation as he revealed new horizons through his newspaper work. His book *Literatura Extranjera* (*Foreign Literature*) covers much more than the French. His chapters on Pushkin and Marie Bashkirtsev, Heyse, and Hauptmann; Ibsen, and Björnson, D'Annunzio, Whitman, and Swinburne were very popular. He visited Russia and wrote a very comprehensive political and social report on the country, sketching the problems that later would cause the Russian Revolution: the poverty of the peasants, the purges that spattered the streets of St. Petersburg with the blood of students, the preachings of the Socialists. The book appeared in 1905. Gómez Carrillo made a trip to Japan with the books of Pierre Loti as his Baedeker. He toured the Holy Land, Turkey, Greece, and Egypt, for one of the elements that fertilized the New World was exoticism.

The cradle of the exotics was Paris. Delacroix started the style by introducing Oriental subjects into his painting; music, poetry, and the novel picked up the theme. Paris was full of *chinoiserie*. The Spanish American Modernists were meeting in Paris when Henri Matisse was painting *Odalisque, Lady in the Turban*, and *Window on Tangier*. Gauguin, who was part Peruvian, had gone to Tahiti; Ravel was writing his *Rhapsodie Espagnol* and *Schehérazade*, Debussy his symphonic poem *Iberia*. Rimsky-Korsakov was composing the *Capricio Espagnol*, his fantasies on Russian themes, and his symphonic poem *Schehérazade*. The Bolivian Ricardo Jaimes Freyre (1868–1933), who with Rubén Darío founded the *Revista de America* in Buenos Aires, dealt with the Scandinavian themes in Wagner's operas in his *Castalia Bárbara*. In his poem *Russia*, written the year after the publication of Gómez Carrillo's book, Freyre said: "The bonfire to consume the residue from the past will come out of the viscera of the land of snow."

The Colombian Guillermo Valencia (1873–1943) published *Ritos* (*Rites*) in 1898. He brings the Egyptian desert into *Ritos* in the poem "Los Camellos," ("The Camels"), alongside translations of poems by Hugo von Hofmannsthal, Stefan George, and D'Annunzio. "Los Camellos," one of the most felicitous of Symbolist poems begins:

> *Two languorous camels with weaving heads,*
> *Limpid green eyes, fur like silk to the hand,*
> *Their necks boldly arched and wide nostrils flaring,*
> *as long-legged they measure off Nubia's sand.*

Valencia lived long enough to be able to re-enter the intimate life of his country and to devote many of his best pages in prose and verse to the men of Colombia and to Popayán, his cradle. But he never outgrew his curiosity concerning the exotic. In *Cigüeñas Blancas* (*White Storks*) he seems to abandon himself to the fate of those birds, which

> *Are soaring out of the frozen mists*
> *in search of a shelter in golden Greece;*
> *now they are clapping their snow-white wings*
> *on the reed-covered banks of the river Nile.*

He discovered the Austrian poet Peter Altenberg at the end of the nineteenth century, and in 1928 he published an entire book of his own translations of ancient Chinese poetry, which he entitled *Cathay.*

José Juan Tablada (1871–1945) introduced the *haiku*, a Japanese poem of seventeen syllables, to Spanish literature and published books of verse with such titles as *Li-Po* and *Hiroshige* and a prose work called *En el País del Sol* (*In the Land of the Sun*). A poet with Chinese blood emerged in Cuba: Regino Pedroso (1896–   ), the author of a number of beautiful works, including *El Ciruelo de Yan-Pen-Fon* (*Yan-Pen-Fon's Plum Tree*).

To a Spanish American, exoticism began beyond the Rhine. Greece was already but a distant outpost of the Occident, so the erotic pages of Pierre Louÿs, inspired by Greek motifs, and Lafcadio Hearn's books on Japan made a great impression on Spanish American writers.

Other poets of the day followed an escape route into an ivory tower or a mystical seclusion. Julio Herrera y Reissing (1875–1910) started a conversation group, which he called Tertulia Lunática (Moonstruck Talkers), in Montevideo. Out of that group came *La Torre de las Esfinges* (*The Sphinxes' Tower*) rather than an ivory tower. A poet of refined symbolism, Herrera restrained in himself the restlessness that impelled others to travel. He wrote *Los Peregrinos de Piedra* (*The Stone Pil-grims*). Amado Nervo (1875–1919), a Mexican who earned continent-wide prestige with his prolific work, was starting to write *Poemas Interiores*. In later years he laid aside his love poetry and his personal mysticism to move to the higher ground of the Oriental philosophies, spiritualism, and Christian Fran-ciscanism—from which derived "Plenitude" and "Elevation," two of his best poems. A deluge of poets joins the already impres-sive multitude of the nineteenth century. The same may be said of prose: novel, short story, essay, drama. . . . Their biblio-graphic list can only be compiled in the histories of literature. The examples in this chapter are only meant to be illustrations.

¶ ANTI-MODERNISMO

The Spanish Modernists, Juan Ramón Jiménez in particular, had signaled a significant return to regional themes. Jiménez struck a note of childlike beauty in creating Platero, the little donkey hero of *Platero y Yo* (*Platero and I*). Unamuno raised his voice in *¡Adentro!* (*Within!*) which helped to close the spillways opened by Darío. In 1915 the Mexican poet Enrique González Martínez (1881–1952) wrote the famous sonnet that was adopted as a revolutionary manifesto:

> *Wring the neck of the swan that's illusively plumed*
> *To contrast with its whiteness the blue fountain's flow,*
> *Gracefully drifting, content not to know*
> *The voice of the land or the soul's constant quest.*
> *Put all form aside and let language go*
> *If they're not in accord with the rhythm compressed*
> *In the depths of reality . . . clasp life to your breast,*
> *And may life then receive all the gifts you bestow.*
> *Look to the owl, quitting Pallas's knees,*
> *Escaping Olympus, floating down through the trees*
> *Till in silence it settles from taciturn flight. . . .*
> *He lacks the swan's grace, but his vigilant eyes*
> *With inscrutable gaze scan the nocturnal skies*
> *There to read the mysterious book of the night.*

The first line of the sonnet made an impression on everyone. The man who wrote it was to become the companion, the brother, of the Modernists. But if the change from swan to owl marked a shift in philosophy, a change in aesthetic norms, it was not as

radical as the sweep toward American Realism, a movement
that became entrenched on Mexican soil with the Revolution. The
first and most daring attack on *modernismo* came from Luis
Carlos López (1881–1951), a Colombian with a talent for sarcasm. López issued his first book, *De Mi Villorrio* (*From My
Hamlet*), in 1908, when *modernismo* was at its zenith. Barely
three years earlier, Darío had written his *Cantos de Vida y
Esperanza* (*Songs of Life and Hope*), but his *Canto a la Argentina* (1914) was still in the far-off future. *De Mi Villorrio* deals
with matters more serious than the wringing of a swan's neck.
In contrast with Darío's wistful princess, Watteau-like landscapes, princes of Golconda and China, and pearls of Ormuz,
López sketched in cold print the mayor in a dirty top hat bound
with tricolor silk; the village barber who worked gossip into his
lather; the priest, "absolute lord of the ignorant, the asinine
people." A man with a saturnine humor not unlike Goya's, López
compressed into the traditional structure of the sonnet a talent for
caricature appropriate to America. He was a born poet, tinged
with a Chaplinesque wistfulness that shows up in the sonnet to
his native city, heroic Cartagena, already sung by José María
de Heredia in a classic sonnet included in *Les Trophées* (*Trophies*).
The sonnet by López, which flouts Heredia's noble sentiments,
is worth all the other manifestoes:

Seignorial home of my forbears: alone
I walk your mean alleys, and in fancy catch
An echo of yesterday's cross and the throne,
The vanquishing blade, sooty lamp, and twisted straw match.
It's all over, walled city. Your glory has gone:
Your adventurous age, when the galleon's patch
On the harbor's blue water at anchor oft shone.
Gone, too, is the oil in the earthenware flask!
Your epoch of gold was the colony's day.
Like imperial eagles your sons soared away,
For heroes could never do else but refuse
The chimney swift's life, with its petulant cry.
Now your sadness and squalor evoke but a sigh
And the smile of affection one gives to old shoes.

The poets' itinerary was clear. Their adventures had taken
them to France, over all the European world, to Eurasian Russia,
Japan, Egypt—and back to America. Leopoldo Lugones (1874–

1938) made the grand tour. Like Darío, he reached the summit
of *modernismo* only to return to his own country to write his
Odas Seculares—a sustained song to the herds of cattle and the
wheatfields—and, in prose, *La Guerra Gaucha* (*The Gaucho
War*), which treats the episodes of the war for independence and
Sarmiento's life. After joining the choir of the Symbolists, always
in good voice, he turned to the Argentina of the pampas and the
gauchos rather than to the cosmopolis of Buenos Aires. Gabriela
Mistral (1889–1957), a Chilean, could hardly bear to read the
Modernists. She carried the human substance of America, at
once magical and Biblical, in her spirit and her very bones. She
moved through Europe like a somnambulist, possessed by the
spirit of her native land. Her work, which won a Nobel Prize,
demonstrates, in comparison with Darío's, how great was the
change of theme in the American lyric.

¶ ULTRAISM

The Martín Fierro group was formed in Buenos Aires in 1924.
Oliverio Girondo (1891–   ) and Jorge Luis Borges (1899–   )
headed it. It came to life at the moment when Futurism, Ultraism,
and Dadaism were making their bows in Europe. In Madrid,
Ramón Gómez de la Serna and Guillermo de Torre became the
opposite numbers of the new group in Buenos Aires. In France
and England, the leading lights of that moment were André
Breton, Louis Aragon, Paul Morand, T. S. Eliot, and Ezra
Pound. The Chilean poet Vicente Huidobro (1893–1949), with
Apollinaire, were the moving spirits in Creationism; thus Huidobro provided the link to Europe. In the manifesto of the Martín
Fierro group, Girondo said: "Martín Fierro believes in the importance of America's intellectual contribution, in an early severing of
the umbilical cord." Jorge Luis Borges added: "I believe that our
poets must not vitiate the essence of the longing in their souls
and of the suffering, yet most pleasant, Creole earth on which
they have spent their days. I believe that our verse must contain
the savor of our country." Borges became the Hispano-American
poet most widely read in Europe; he was awarded the Prix International des Editeurs in 1961, along with the Irish novelist and
dramatist Samuel Beckett. The road to fame for Borges started
with *Fervor de Buenos Aires* in 1923. His influence finally
extended throughout the entire Western world. His great culture,
which included a knowledge of the esoterica of the East and the

West, makes him universal. In Europe he is considered a European. But is he? Does he not resemble closely his country's epic hero, Martín Fierro? Does not the Ultraism of Buenos Aires, if analyzed, contain "the savor of the country," without provincialism? "Dead Ultraism," Borges says, "whose ghost always haunts me, enjoys these games." Being so Argentine, yet so universal, has made Borges a man of mystery. Some critics do not agree that he is Argentine; they argue, with some heat, that he is a Western author. Others, refusing to let Europe steal him, extol him as an American. All this amuses and stimulates Borges. He explains himself in words that might serve as the metaphor of the new generation:

> To deny temporal success, to deny the I, to deny the astronomical universe, are acts of apparent desperation, but they are also secret consolations. Our destiny . . . is not frightening because of being unreal; it is frightening because it is irreversible, ironclad. Time is the substance of which I am made. Time is the river that carries me along, but I am the river; it is a tiger that destroys me, but I am the tiger; it is a fire that consumes me, but I am the fire. The word, alas, is real; I, alas, am Borges.

Thus a complicated, multifaceted America stares at *modernismo* and *anti-modernismo* alike across a distance that cannot be closed, and, according to Borges, moves forward toward a dispersion of contemporary America's poetic ingredients. Dadaism, Ultraism, Futurism, Stridentism all sent up brief and rampant offshoots in Mexico, Chile, and Peru. But little by little each poet was fitting himself into his own being. In Colombia, an earlier movement had preceded the Martín Fierro, and had been no less rebellious: it was the *Panidas* movement, which emerged in 1914 under the leadership of León de Greiff (1895–). De Greiff, destined to become one of the richest and most complex of American poets, was an iconoclast. He stood apart from any group until he was made head of the Panidas.

All over America, short-lived reviews appeared, each casually bringing together a half dozen of the "new men," who separated shortly afterward. The Spanish Civil War caused a group of poets to migrate, including Juan Ramón Jiménez, Rafael Alberti, Pedro Salinas, Jorge Guillén, León Felipe, and Casona, to America where they became a part of the intellectual life of the New World. They kept the memory of Federico García Lorca and Antonio Machado green with a devotion that they could not show so spontaneously and enthusiastically in Spain. Poetry has continued its advance. To single out all the poets, one by one, would be a task difficult to perform even in a history of literature.

¶ FROM MODERNISM TO THE AMERICAN NOVEL

The Modernist interlude was much less fruitful in the novel. The last novels written in the nineteenth century, which closed the Romanticist ring, approached the men, the land, and the history of the American nations and revealed a social consciousness absent in such idyllic tales as *Paul et Virginie, Atala* and *René.* In 1878, *Enriquillo,* by Manuel de Jesús Galván (1834–1910), was published. It extolled the nobility of an Indian chief who was vilely betrayed by the Spaniards. This story derives from the pages of Oviedo and Fray Bartolomé de Las Casas and takes its place beside their already legendary defense of the natives of America. The merits of Galván's work are doubled by the fact that Santo Domingo was still a Spanish colony when he wrote it. Such Cuban novelists, as Cirilo Villaverde (1812–94), who wrote *Cecilia Valdés,* an attack on slavery, and Gertrudis Gómez de Avellaneda (1814–73), author of *Sab,* labored under the same handicap. But Doña Gertrudis achieved a distinguished place in Spanish letters. In Bolivia, Nataniel Aguirre (1854–79) wrote, in *Juan de la Rosa,* an account of the war for independence from the liberal point of view. Clorinda Matto de Turner (1854–79) opened the cycle of the novel on Indian life in Peru with her *Aves sin Nido (Birds Without Nests),* which indicts the oligarchical and clerical society that kept to itself more closely in America than elsewhere. Of course the book aroused the anger of that class. *Aves sin Nido* is noteworthy also because it was published a year before Rubén Darío's *Azul,* and when *modernismo*'s day was over, novelists again picked up the theme of social consciousness which Clorinda Matto de Turner had treated in *Aves sin Nido.*

All of these novels contain to some degree the romantic theme of America. But the novel of the nineteenth century grew up and put aside what it had absorbed from Victor Hugo. One of the best novelists on the continent, Alberto Blest Gana (1830–1920), turned to the Naturalism of Zola and applied it to reality in Chile. He started to publish in 1858; then nothing more was heard from him for more than thirty years. He spent his silent period, between 1863 and 1897, in Europe, mainly in Paris, while the Symbolists and the writers of all the related schools were emerging. How much did they influence the Chilean novelist? They did not touch him. After his long silence, Blest Gana produced his masterpiece, *Durante la Reconquista*, the great tapestry of Chile's history.

> The number of human beings that appear before our eyes and the lack of a unified action work together, so that upon completing the reading of these thousand tightly packed pages a curious thing happens in the reader's mind, which, in a sense, is the highest praise that can be paid to a work, and which is what Blest Gana possibly aspired to: that is, we feel that John Doe or Richard Roe was not the protagonist or protagonists, for our impression is that the individuals who fill the novel move down to a secondary plane as the republic of Chile moves up to occupy the primary plane. Chile, the Chilean soul in its struggle for independence, is the real protagonist of *Durante la Reconquista*.[1]

The Modernist novel has the unreal beauty of the parasite. Its artifice in itself has a beauty that the novelists on the continent had never achieved before. But like parasites, these novels existed on air. Their scenes were laid in exotic lands—in a greenhouse, as it were. There was always something false in novels of that type, something that misfired and injured itself. Not because the people who wrote them lacked the requisites for writers. Novelists of less skill came after the revolution in the novel, but they gave it a vigorous American stamp, and they were successful. Their triumph emphasizes the weakness of the Modernist novel.

The most felicitous of the Modernists was Enrique Larreta (1873–1961), author of *La Gloria de Don Ramiro*. This loving and labored reconstruction of Spain during the reign of Philip II is set in the city of Ávila. The author ends his story in Lima, sweet with the legend of St. Rose, yet he seems to have chosen his ending in order to testify to Spanish America's loyalty to the Mother Country. For five years Larreta worked in the Spanish archives, documenting his work. He was indeed the standard-bearer of Hispanism. Darío was the first to praise him. Later the book circulated through Spanish America and in France, where

---

[1] Eliodoro Astorquiza, as quoted by Alone in *Historia Personal de la Literatura Chilena*.

the translation bore the prestigious signature of Rémy de Gourmont. Larreta was deeply influenced by the painting being done
in France. The Impressionists stimulated and guided his poetic
sensibilities, as Amado Alonso sagely remarked in his study
on Larreta. That was an apt observation, for at that moment
in the cultural development of Spanish America, the discovery
of the new painting was as important as that of Symbolist poetry.
Few other novelists followed the school of *modernismo*, and none
of them made as much of a stir as Larreta. The Venezuelan
Manuel Díaz Rodríguez (1871–1927) followed the esthetic
of D'Annunzio in the refined pages of *Sangre Patricia* (*Patrician
Blood*). Pedro César Dominici (1872–1954), another Venezuelan,
an erotic writer, in his novel *Dyonysos*, dealt with Greek subject
matter in a manner reminiscent of that of Pierre Louÿs. José
Asunción Silva's novel *De Sobremesa* provided a valuable document on Latin American circles in Paris.

When the novel turned back to the American scene, it began
to grow. American originality gave a hitherto unknown vigor to
literary creation. The Modernists who could manage the return
trip home perceived this themselves. Ricardo Güiraldes (1886–
1927), for example, started his career with a book of verse
derivative from Verlaine and Laforgue which he entitled *El
Cencerro de Cristal* (*The Crystal Lead Bell*), and ended it
with the masterpiece, *Don Segundo Sombra*. *Don Segundo* is the
story of a flesh-and-blood *gaucho* who made a deep impression
on Güiraldes, then a child living in San Antonio de Areco.
Güiraldes created his *gaucho* character as a symbol; indeed *Don
Segundo* was the incarnation of the symbolic *gaucho* of the pampas. Carlos Reyles (1868–1938) proclaimed a "new novel" in
Uruguay and Rodó hailed it effusively, rejoicing that the wandering expert of the interior world had appeared to offer us "in
the exquisite chalice of his stories, the subtle extract of his intellectual tortures" to place beside that of the regional novelist
with an ear for the word of the plebeian muse. But *El Embrujo
de Sevilla*, the "new novel" by Reyles was not nearly so successful
as his *Gaucho Florido*, which he wrote as a result of his life in
Uruguay. Eduardo Barrios (1884–1963), a Chilean, began his
novels such as *El Niño que enloqueció de amor* (*The Child Who
Went Mad with Love*), *El Hermano Asno* (*Brother Donkey*),
with the sum of his psychological gleanings, but he crowned his
career with a picture of the feudal landowner in *Gran Señor y
Rajadiablos* (*Great Señor and Rakehell*). Enrique Larreta also

came to a recognition of the signs of the times, for he used an estate not far from Buenos Aires as the stage for his characters in Zogoibi, which he wrote after *La Gloria de Don Ramiro*. But his conversion came late, and the product was an unsuccessful *gaucho* novel.

The fiction coming out of America today is brutal, violent, at times subhuman. It is the novel of the *páramos* (cold desert or mountain regions) and the jungles, the poor Negroes and starving dogs, of violence, of revolution. The new books chide the Modernists for aping France; if they discuss the movement at all, they stigmatize it as escapism. But in general the authors do not argue; instead, they marshal facts. They are militant, not meditative; denunciatory, not rhetorical. Life in America predominates as subject matter—more strongly than in the Realism of other times or in Naturalism. Whether in the desolate landscape of the *puna* (high, cold mountain region) or in the green hell of the jungle, the story goes straight to the most intimate recesses of the taciturn and inscrutable Indian, the jesting *roto* or the rebellious *cholo*. Nothing that is in any way European could serve as a model for such case histories. A literature that is brother to it emanates from the United States, but the social and racial denunciations of Erskine Caldwell, Richard Wright, and John Steinbeck, as well as the socially realistic fictions of Ernest Hemingway and William Faulkner, were written after those by the Latin Americans. Some of the northern authors in that group have gone either to Mexico or Cuba to look for atmosphere and character and have stayed to write their novels—as if they were brothers.

The Uruguayan writer Horacio Quiroga (1878–1937) published his *Cuentos de la Selva* (*Jungle Tales*) in 1918; in 1920 came *El Roto* (*The Ragged*) by Joaquín Edwards Bello (1888–   ), a Chilean; José Eustacio Rivera (1888–1928), a Colombian, published *La Vorágine* (*The Vortex*) in 1924; the Argentine writer Benito Lynch (1885–1952) published *El Inglés de los güesos* [*huesos*], also in 1924; the Ecuadorian writer Jorge Icaza (1906–   ) published his novel *Huasipungo* in 1934; the Mexican writer Gregorio López y Fuentes (1897–   ) published *El Indio* (*The Indian*) in 1935; the Peruvian Ciro Alegría (1909–   ) published *Los Perros Hambrientos* (*The Starving Dogs*) in 1939; and the Guatemalan writer Miguel Ángel Asturias (1899–   ) *El Señor Presidente* in 1941. Nature moves as in a motion picture through these novels and is endowed with the value of a character that enslaves man. Quiroga's vipers, the fauna of his stories, and the utter misery of his characters raise the curtain on the great drama of Rivera's jungle, where flesh-eating fish, trees that imprison men, and the black magic of the Amazon basin are even crueler and more inexorable than the men who exploit the rubber workers. Lynch became a *gaucho* to learn the speech of the "cowboys of the pampas," and Icaza lived with the Indians to give his style all the inflections of the lament, the weeping, the muted anger of desolate misery. López y Fuentes portrays the Indian before the long-awaited revolution, and Ciro Alegría places him in a broad and alien world without hope, where the barking of the starving dogs is heeded more than the voice of a poor human being abandoned in the solitude of the *puna*. Edwards Bello brings the broken-down ragged man out of the uttermost depths of picaresque depravity. Asturias gives a nauseating description of the sores that eat away the flesh of the destitute people under the despotism of "Señor Presidente." This literature gives no quarter, and it is all the more pitiless when it comes from the Pacific side of America rather than the Atlantic side, which is refreshed by frequent winds from Europe.

Rómulo Gallegos (1884–) first became known in 1920, when his novel *Reinaldo Solar* was published. His work reached its peak with *Doña Bárbara*, published in 1929. One of the most prolific and comprehensive novelists in America, he wrote about the Venezuelan landscape and its human inhabitants with the sure hand of a master; all types of people file through his pages: the plainsmen, the mountaineers, the Negroes, the foremen, the *gringos*, and the humble poor. They are shown in action on the plains, on the coffee plantations, and in the jungles. He wrote most of his work when Venezuela was in the grip of dictators, and his portrayal of conditions was a strong message that reached everyone. Juan Vicente Gómez eventually died, and it became possible for the first time to consider republican government as something more than a figment of the imagination. One day the people were able to vote, and they voted for Gallegos. Gallegos, president of the republic! Though it may seem absurd that a novelist should be chosen to preside over a republic, the explanation lies in his novels, in which he painted a unique picture of his country and presented the everyday life of the people in a balance that weighed their miseries and their hopes with a humane nicety.

The Mexican Revolution, a great revolution that preceded Russia's, a revolution that fought the last battle of the secular struggle for independence, confronted the heirs of the Crown with the republicans, that is, the people who demanded land from the owner who monopolized it; the Church that kept a tight grip on privileges it had enjoyed during four centuries with the State that was determined to vindicate his rights. The civil war, unleashed by the "apostle" Francisco I. Madero, was accompanied by barbarous acts. The troops of Pancho Villa, who sang *La Cucaracha* (*The Cockroach*) and *Si Adelita se fuera con otro* (*If Adelita Should Go with Another*) as they marched, resembled the Russian revolutionaries only in their cartridge belts and bandoliers. The Mexican fighters knew no shelter other than that of their huge sombreros. They walked arm in arm with death, like a sister, as the genius of the engraver Guadalupe Posada has pictured them. Distinguished men of letters fought shoulder to shoulder with illiterates. One friend of Pancho Villa was José Vasconcelos (1882–1959), teacher, philosopher, and lover of wisdom and of Oriental curiosa, who wrote *Estudios Indostánicos* (*Hindustani Studies*), the autobiographical *Ulises Criollo* (in four volumes), and a *History of Mexico*. He emerged from his experiences in the revolution to become the greatest promotor of culture of his day. Martín Luis Guzmán (1887–   ) was secretary to Pancho Villa for a while. This close contact enabled him to write his later *Memorias de un guerrillero*, in reality the memoirs of Villa, and in 1928 *El Águila y la Serpiente* (*The Eagle and the Serpent*), which gives a vivid account of the revolution and is considered a classic.

The initiator of this type of literature was Mariano Azuela (1873-1952), with his novel *Los de Abajo* (*The Underdogs*), published in 1916. Interestingly enough, that was the year that Henri Barbusse published *Le Feu* (*Under Fire*) in France. Except that each book covered a war and that their interpretations of the wars were spontaneous, the books are totally unlike. After all, the ingredients of the Mexican revolution were all too human; it contained no part of the gamble of the international struggle, with its monstrous, repellent calculation. "Let's go with Pancho Villa!" was the war cry of the Mexican people, who were truly plebeian. When the great adventure was over, the Mexicans even were able to ridicule it a little, as José Rubén Romero (1890–1952) did in *La Vida inútil de Pito Pérez* (*The Futile Life of Pito Pérez*), a novel of 1938 that gives the great adventure a counterweight of humor not unlike that of *Don Catrín de la Fachenda* (*Don Catrín's Vanity*) by José Joaquín Fernández de Lizardi, the Mexican novelist of the preceding century.

¶ ON THE FRINGE OF MODERNISMO

Modernismo cannot be granted an achievement beyond that of bringing together a very select group of writers, mainly poets, who provoked the reaction against it called *anti-modernismo*. The great novelists of the first half of the twentieth century were the reactors. Neither of the two groups or schools ever was able to see the whole literary panorama. Meanwhile, some great writers were working apart from either the action or reaction, feeling no obligation to throw themselves into any current of the great debate. Two men who exemplified this kind of detachment were Ricardo Palma in Peru and Tomás Carrasquilla in Colombia.

Ricardo Palma (1833–1919) chose for his own amusement to recreate history in a humorous vein, sometimes ironical, sometimes so scandalous that one of his works, *Tradiciones en salsa verde* (*Traditions in Green Sauce*), could not be published. His *Tradiciones Peruanas* are Peruvian to the bone, not only in their theme, but in their slant, in the mocking smile with which he disposes of the matters discussed by the conversation groups. Palma delighted in reliving colonial days; he undressed and dressed it; placed it in a state carriage with La Perricholi, and put the viceroy's wig on it. At times he did the same for the republic. Haya de la Torre wrote: "No institution or man in the colony or even in the republic escaped the mordancy—so often hitting its mark—of the irony and ridicule of Palma's critiques." Manners and customs form a genre apart, and Palma gives a recipe for writing about them: "A little, and yet a little more, of lies, a pinch of truth, however infinitesimal and homeopathic it may be, a generous dash of nicety and politeness and language; then taste the flavor of the recipe for writing about traditions." He made fun of Romanticism in much the same terms, and at the time when the Modernists were echoing French Symbolism, he published his *Ropa Vieja* (*Old Clothes*). As a liberal, he enjoyed rummaging into the past of the Church as recorded in the Annals of the Inquisition in Lima. And as an American, he demanded, in *Papeletas Lexicográficas* (*Leaves from a Dictionary*), that many words not from Spain but from all over the world, be granted a certificate of legitimacy.

Tomás Carrasquilla (1858–1941), probably the greatest Colombian novelist, might be taken for an anti-Modernist on the basis of his *Homilías* (*Homilies*), in which he attacks with greater vigor than any of his contemporaries the feebleness of Rubén

Darío's imitators. He read with the closest attention the authors who interested the Colombian Modernists and applied to them a corrosive that eventually consumed them. But such critical commentaries were only the choppy surface of the water; in his basic work he penetrated the innermost life of the Colombian provinces, sometimes with a humor approaching Palma's. His fiction was stubbornly rooted in his land and his people. The first chapter of his last great novel, *La Marquesa de Yolombó*, stands out as the most purposeful and accurate essay on the dregs of colonial economy, but it is a by-product of the story. His succeeding work allowed his genius to expand. It was the re-creation of popular legends done with a subtle art that records and shows the color of the life led by the pious ladies and the *señoritas* of the village, the life of miners and muleteers, in his *Frutos de mi Tierra* (*Fruits of My Land*). Carrasquilla was a liberal of no school but his own.

¶ AMERICANS WHO BECAME EUROPEANS

All these developments place the writer who will come later more firmly in the American scene, but with greater participation in the European, in the Occidental. In the long run, relations between the hemispheres became more natural, less subject to outside influences, less subservient to them. This brief review would be incomplete without some cases of Americans whose influence was the reverse of the norm. Two of the great artificers of the French schools were born in Uruguay. Count de Lautréamont, whose real name was Isidore Lucien Ducasse (1846–70), left Montevideo to study at the École Polytechnique in Paris. Coming under the spell of literature, he wrote the *Chants de Maldoror* (1868–1870), which foreshadow Surrealism. His compatriot Jules Laforgue also was born in Montevideo. He went to Paris as a child, and later played an important part in the emergence of Creationism. Naturally his South American origin made for closer relations with the Modernists of the Río de la Plata with whom he kept in touch. Similar cases have existed since the days of the Cuban writers José María de Heredia and Gertrudis Gómez de Avellaneda and the Mexican writer Juan Ruíz de Alarcón, whose names resound through poetry, the theater, and the novel. Among the novelists of *modernismo*'s heyday were the Argentine, William Henry Hudson (1841–1922), whose parents were from the United States and who made his name in England. The themes of most of the works that made him famous, such as *Tales of the Pampas*, *The Purple Land*, and *The Naturalist in La Plata*, came directly from the Argentine or neighboring countries. *Green Mansions*, which left its mark on English literature, is set in the Venezuelan jungle, in the region of the Orinoco.

On the other hand, a number of Europeans and North Americans went to Latin America to write. Valle Inclán's *Tirano Banderas* (*The Tyrant Banderas*) takes place in a Latin American republic. Hemingway was awarded the Nobel Prize after publication of *The Old Man and the Sea*, set in Cuba. John Steinbeck, another Nobel Prize winner, wrote some of his novels in Mexico. Thornton Wilder found the subject for *The Bridge of San Luis Rey* in Peru. Salvador de Madariaga chose Mexico as his theme in *El Corazón de Piedra Verde* (*The Heart of Green Stone*), and wrote his trilogy on Columbus, Cortés, and Bolívar with his eyes fixed on America. The influence of America, an occasional crumb at the beginning of the twentieth century, became the daily bread of its second half.

XX: *Between Ariel and Caliban*

¶ RODÓ

Ariel, by José Enrique Rodó (1872–1917), published in February 1900, seemed to be the last message from the nineteenth century. The tone of the book was unusual. For the first time since independence, a master was addressing all of "Our America," a term proposed by Martí and adopted by Rodó. At that moment a literary current was joining the scattered islands of the Latin American republics, previously separated by the turbulent seas of anarchy, civil wars, and dictatorship. *Modernismo* was at least uniting the poets, and the poets were playing important roles in the political life of that part of the world. The standard-bearer was Darío, a Nicaraguan who made his name in Chile and became sanctified in Argentina. The Peruvians, Bolivians, Venezuelans, Uruguayans, and Ecuadorians met at the café tables in Paris, and clasped hands. Some new force was preparing to rebuild the lost continent. And the image of Ariel came forth.

As a salute to the newborn century, Rodó pointed to several ideal routes leading to a new orientation. If our America, he said, makes itself a repository of spirit, of beauty, of fruitful leisure, of a democracy with an aristocracy to direct it, it will be the pedestal on which the figure of Ariel may be mounted. A true Statue of Liberty in contrast with the one in New York, which was a gift to a people without a soul. The United States is utilitarian; it lacks kindness; it believes that it can rewrite Genesis to the formula of "Washington plus Edison" and so occupy the first page itself. Thus, there was no lack of caricature in the musical, Gallic, harmonious prose of *Ariel*.

So as not to deny his origins, Rodó professed the Positivist faith. He accentuated Comte's idea that "in questions of the intellect, of morality, of sentiment, it would be mad to pretend that numbers could substitute for quality in any case." He recalled a speech given by Spencer in New York in which he preached the gospel of rest to the Americans, the virtue of fruitful leisure. In an access of enthusiasm for Renan, his teacher, the Uruguayan said, "Read Renan and you will be bound to love him as I do; no one seems to me as great a master of that art of teaching with grace, which Anatole France considers divine."

In Rodó's portrayal of the ugly American, he fancied that as Positivism had crossed from England to the United States, it suffered a sea change that robbed it of all its idealistic elements. He made a cult of contrasting the United States with Shakespeare's England, and paid tribute to the author of *The Tempest*, from which he took the characters in his study. In his opinion, Utilitarianism in England held a hidden poetic force that it lost when it crossed the Atlantic. He never stopped to think that Great Britain had consolidated her Empire with little regard for sentiment and had thrust her implacable power deep into South Africa and the heart of India.

After drawing his line of demarcation, Rodó assigned the role of Ariel to "our Latin America," that of Caliban to the United States. He believed, paradoxically, that North American Positivism would serve the cause of Ariel and that South America would dignify what northern people, "that very shallow monster," as he called Caliban, would conquer for the sake of its material well-being:

> Thus, the most precious and fundamental of the acquisitions of the spirit—the alphabet that lends the wings of immortality to the word—will arise from the heart of the factories of Canaan and become the treasure trove of a mercantile civilization which, serving exclusively mercenary ends, is unaware that the genius of the superior races would transfigure it by converting it into the medium for propagating the purest and most luminous essence.

Having finished his discourse, which was received in Latin America and Spain with delight, Rodó retired to cultivate beauty. He died in Sicily as he was planning to see Renan's Greece with his own eyes.

¶ THE CÓRDOBAN REVOLUTION OF 1918

Rodó's message was delivered during Theodore Roosevelt's most aggressive phase. The great hunter who preached the gospel of "Manifest Destiny" and carried "a big stick" cast a shadow over the Statue of Liberty as he struck his brutal blows in the Caribbean and walked off with Panama. Indignation in Latin America was boundless. Rodó supplied the tinder to light the blaze. Roosevelt's raw aggression revealed a gross sensuality in the domineering power of Washington. A year after the rape of Panama, Darío wrote his "Ode to Roosevelt," in the last verse of which he says:

And though you count on everything, you lack one thing:
God!

After Rodó's pages, shimmering with Latin music, came the sizzling phrases and resonant oratory of the Argentine Manuel Ugarte (1878–1951); those of the Mexican Isidro Fabela (1882–), the diplomat and historian who wrote *Los Estados Unidos contra la Libertad;* and the calm and magisterial words of the Peruvian Francisco García Calderón (1883–1953) in his book *La Creación de un Continente.* Latin America rebounded from the blow with a feeling that it was less disunited. Aggression had brought the countries together. When the centenary of independence was celebrated throughout Spanish America in 1910, a new continental consciousness was born, and passion and optimism were rife. The desire for renewal inspired Justo Sierra to remodel the University of Mexico and encouraged Joaquín V. González to found the University of La Plata, which opened a new era in Argentina. These acts were a testament of faith in another kind of Manifest Destiny—in freedom. The whole world defended it, proclaimed it. When the First World War broke out, "Latin America" ranged herself beside France. Hipólito Irigoyen (1850–1933), president of Argentina, proclaimed the country's neutrality, but only to affirm its sovereignty, expressed in the crusade to recover the petroleum of Argentina for the Argentines.

There, as in the rest of South America, public sentiment was mainly Francophile. No capital in the hemisphere failed to celebrate the Allied victory. On Armistice Day even the question of the United States was put in abeyance; the Stars and Stripes flew beside the other flags.

The war had been a shock to Latin America. The old Germany, once the refuge of liberals and freethinkers and the center of a culture that the Latin Americans had learned to love, had trampled over Belgium. France escaped conquest only by a miracle; demonstrably she had been unprepared in 1914, and the joy of victory in 1918 was mingled with bitterness. The lines of communication between Latin America and Europe had been broken, and the Latin countries had achieved closer relations with the United States during those four years. North American reviews were beginning to be read in the universities. The breaks in trade had to be repaired; production started in the first Latin American factories as the war gave industrialization its initial stimulus. In the new generations a desire was born for revision, for a re-examination of the past and present, for a new continental consciousness. That feeling led eventually to a revolution in the universities.

The university revolution began in Córdoba, Argentina, in 1918, a few months before the end of the war in Europe. To the new generation, civilization in Europe was in crisis, and America, hurt by its backlash, had to prepare to master its own destiny. The separate countries began to think of themselves as a continent. The Córdoba manifesto was addressed "to the free men of South America." The document declared: "Until now, the universities have been the secular refuge of the mediocre, the income of the ignorant, safe hospitals for invalids, and—worse still—the place where every means of tyrannizing over and dulling the mind had chairs from which to manipulate it." The ideas thus expressed were clarified further by a demand for a statute for the universities which would provide more elasticity and security, would allow for renewing the faculty, would give the students a voice, and would aim to inculcate a broader knowledge of contemporary ideas. A plan was anounced for a study of current national conditions, to forge the tools for investigation, to project changes in the social, economic, and political structure with the university as their base. The new Latin American generation posed early the problem of the university, which the Spanish philosopher José

Ortega y Gasset dealt with much later in *La Misión de la Universidad* published in 1930.

The Argentine University Federation was established in 1918. Similar federations followed in the other republics. International congresses of students were fostered. One of them, which met in Montevideo, adopted the words of the Peruvian poet José Gálvez, set to music by the Chilean composer Enrique Soro, as a youth anthem, thus joining in song Chile and Peru, which had fought a war by no means forgotten. Colombia, Venezuela, and Ecuador had held the first students' congress in Caracas in 1910, before the one in Córdoba; a second was held in Quito. The congress that was most important, because it was continental, met in Mexico City in 1921. José Vasconcelos was then Secretary of Public Education and a teacher of youth.

All these events opened the way for agitation that was projected into politics instantly. The graduates of the student federations became leaders who did away with dictatorships. The classroom revolt had begun; in time it became a customary feature, occasionally a vicious one, of Latin American life. An attempt was made to bring the university to the people as an experimental phase of the student's approach to his country and his countrymen. In 1925, José Ingenieros and Alfredo L. Palacios founded the Latin-American Union to group the intellectual element around the teachers of revolution.

¶ GONZÁLEZ PRADA AND HIS HEIRS

Those years also saw the birth of APRA (The American Popular and Revolutionary Alliance), which aspired to become the first international American political party. Its immediate origin was in the González Prada Popular Universities, established in 1920 by Victor Raúl Haya de la Torre (1895–   ), which offered extension courses. Students of medicine, law, engineering, and the humanities went out from them to teach laborers and farm workers, thus making the university an institution of the people. González Prada's name was chosen as its symbol.

Manuel González Prada (1844–1918) was a poet who experimented with felicitous innovations in verse and became a leader of the Modernists. A man of ideas, he listened religiously to Renan's teachings in Paris. Renan's preoccupation with the fundamental problems of human nature influenced the Peruvian to become an anarchist and an atheist. He attacked the old colonial structure violently, and though he came from an aristocratic family, he was converted to defense of the Indians. As a writer he was brilliant, incisive, implacable. He was known simply as "Don Manuel," the title that Luis Alberto Sánchez (1900–   ) gave to his best biography. Sánchez, a historian of Peruvian literature, also wrote a biography of Haya de la Torre. "Peru," Don Manuel said, "is a sick organism; wherever a finger touches it, it shoots out pus." He also said:

> If the Indian spent on rifles and bullets all the money he squanders on alcohol and fiestas, if he were to conceal a weapon in a corner of his hut or on the top of a cliff, he would change his condition; he would make his property and his life respected. Violence would be answered with violence, and the boss who fleeces him, the soldier who drafts him in the name of the government, the rustler who steals his cattle and his beasts of burden, would be taught a lesson.

On the evening of July 28, 1888, Don Manuel delivered a speech in the Politeama Theater in Lima which ended with the provocative sentence that became the motto of the new men and was echoed and re-echoed: "Old men to the tomb; young men to work." Don Manuel was not of the generation of 1918, for he was born in 1844, but he happened to die in 1918.

The first of Don Manuel's disciples to distinguish himself was José Carlos Mariátegui (1895–1930). He instigated a radical change with his *Siete Ensayos sobre la Realidad Peruana* (*Seven Essays on Peruvian Reality*), and introduced Marxism as a method for studying economic and social life, literature, and education. He exposed the seven cardinal virtues of Peruvian life alongside its seven deadly sins. He edited the review *Amauta*, a word that means "teacher" in Quechua. A paralytic confined to a wheel chair and wearing the halo of a fighting invalid, he assisted at the awakening of the new generations like a spectator always eager to play midwife to the movement in which he had invested all his hopes.

Haya de la Torre did not operate from a wheel chair. He was a strapping, athletic youth who picked up the torch when it fell from Mariátegui's hand. He was fired with the ambition to create an independent entity. "The doctrine of APRA signifies a new and methodical confrontation of Indian-American economic reality within Marxism, on the foundations that Marx postulated for Europe as an outgrowth of the reality of Europe in the middle of the past century." Haya made more use of his voice than of his pen. He was a great orator, with a touch of the pedagogue. He liked to teach as he talked. He formulated the program of the "three eights" for his popular campaign: eight hours of work, eight of study, eight of rest. Practical medicine and natural science were taught to the workers enrolled in the popular universities he founded—and they sang. Fifty thousand students from all over Peru enrolled in the first year. Students and workers together constituted a dominant force.

The dictator Leguía soon decided to nip the movement in the bud. The first great popular demonstration in Lima was greeted with shots and several people were killed. Shortly afterward, Haya de la Torre was exiled. He established APRA in Mexico. Its platform was to fight: 1. against imperialism; 2. for the political unity of Latin America; 3. for the nationalization of land and industry; 4. for the inter-Americanization of the Panama Canal; 5. for solidarity with all oppressed people and classes all over the world. After thirty years of constant preaching, APRA has not become the international movement that Haya de la Torre hoped it would become, but it has won the allegiance of the majority in Peru even though it has been nullified by the stubborn opposition of reactionary governments and has never been recognized. If the illiterate as well as the literate had voted in the elections, the *aprista* majority would have climbed to overwhelming numbers. But Haya de la Torre was working not only against the unshakeable refusal of the old oligarchy to yield up its power, but also against all-out opposition to Communism. Added to that, he was primarily a preacher of idealism rather than a politician trained for internal struggle. The last contest was won by Belaúnde Terry, a man who came out of *aprismo* but turned aganist Haya de la Torre. The "González Prada–Mariátegui–Haya de la Torre line" was a signpost on the road to a new policy that would give the Indians and *cholos* some voice in the government. The first republic, which had lasted more than a hundred years, had been a closed corporation, hostile to the underdogs. The second, truly democratic republic was yet to come.

¶ THE MEXICAN REVOLUTION

A century after Mexico won her independence, Francisco I. Madero (1873–1913) sparked the revolution of 1910, which aimed to depose General Porfirio Díaz (1830–1915). Díaz had ruled the country since 1887. In February 1911, Madero, called "the Apostle," crossed the border from the United States, and in June he entered the capital. Díaz fled to Paris. Two years later, President Madero was assassinated, but the road to revolution stayed open. A popular *caudillo*, Emiliano Zapata (1883–1919), and Pancho Villa (nickname of Doroteo Arango, 1887–1923), most famous of the guerrilla generals, came forth to lead the rural masses and reclaim the land for the people. Huerta, who had brought about Madero's death and who followed him as president, was forced to resign, and General Venustiano Carranza (1859–1920) replaced him. Then Zapata was murdered. But the revolution still marched on. In 1917, Mexico was given a new constitution that marked a daring step in political culture and produced the greatest changes of the century. The charter decreed that land and water were the property of the nation. Property could not be transferred to individuals except under restrictions imposed by the public interest. This was the basis of the agrarian reforms. The nation was declared the owner of all minerals, of the subsoil, and of petroleum. The workers' charter established an eight-hour day, controlled wages, equal pay for equal work, the right to organize freely, and the right to strike. The Church was debarred from public education. Civil marriage was established. Members of the clergy lost the right to vote and to hold public office. This revolutionary charter incorporated the 1810 principles of independence and those of the Juárez reform, modified to meet the conditions of the twentieth century. Mexico fought her revolution between 1910 and 1917 before Lenin rose to power and crowned her revolution in the year that Lenin began his.

During the presidency (1921–24) of General Álvaro Obregón (1880–1928), José Vasconcelos, as Secretary of Education, obtained the biggest budget ever granted to the schools of Mexico. Vasconcelos founded the House of the People and called in Rivera, Orozco, and Siqueiros to decorate government palaces and public buildings. From then on, even the illiterate could read the history of Mexico, in a revolutionary interpretation, on the public walls. Diego Rivera (1886–1957) began his career as a child through his contact with the greatly talented engraver José Guadalupe Posada (1851–1913) instead of in a school of fine arts. Posada made 15,000 engravings in Goyesque style which Mexico can be proud of. He illustrated ballads and songs, made drawings of the Mexican Revolution up to the date of Madero's triumph, and showed political and popular life as a theater of skulls, a representation of life as a dance of death. Rivera traveled in Europe, joined the Cubist movement, became a friend of Picasso ("I have never believed in God," he said, "but in Picasso, yes."), fraternized with Apollinaire, quarreled with and made up with Modigliani, and witnessed the First World War. He stayed a long time in Italy studying the frescoes of the Renaissance. He glowed with enthusiasm for the new Russia that was emerging from the revolution. An indefatigable worker to the very end, he painted miles of frescoes. When Rivera went back to Mexico, Vasconcelos turned over to him the walls that became the back-drop to his glory. In 1923 he signed a contract to paint the hundred and twenty-three frescoes that now adorn the Preparatoria in Mexico City. Vicente Lombardo Toledano (1894–   ) then director of the school, later headed the Communist Party in Mexico. By 1922, Rivera was enrolled in the Party, holding card #992, which signified that the Communist Party had at least 992 members in 1922. Hence Rivera was a charter member. Later he was expelled from the party, but he continued to be a Russophile. (He painted Stalin feeding doves.) Rivera was litigious, argumentative, always bold. He handled his publicity like a genius, but he was indisputably the captain of a renaissance as valuable to art in America as the Renaissance to Italian art. Rivera did not so much introduce innovations as reveal a world with secular roots. When the Mayan frescoes were discovered in the ruins of Bonampak and Rivera realized that people of the seventh century had been painting walls as he was painting them, he wept at the sight of the ancient frescoes. José Clemente Orozco (1883–1949) and David Alfaro Siqueiros (1898–   ) worked with him. Orozco sometimes surpassed him as a painter, and Siqueiros usually outdid him in creating scandals.

The revolution aroused people and all their passions in every phase of Mexican life. For ten years, General Plutarco Elías Calles (1877–1945) was in charge of government, acting either for himself or through a person he had sponsored. That was the time when the struggle with the Church was fiercest. On July 31, 1926, masses in the churches ceased. This suspension lasted three years. Mexico was on the verge of war with the United States. But some seventy-five million acres of land had been apportioned among the farm workers, and three years later that figure was almost doubled by General Lázaro Cárdenas (1895–   ). Cárdenas was a different type of man. He rose to power in 1934. During his term, the revolution was consolidated when on March 18, 1938, he signed the decree expropriating the oil fields, which meant carrying out a replevin of the greatest and most basic resources. The English companies, who owned sixty per cent of the oil fields, and the Americans, who owned forty per cent, had to turn their workings over to the state. This was the first time in history that companies with holdings of such a size had been confronted with a measure so drastic. The President had only the full backing of his nation with which to defy the mighty. The people were behind him without reservation, with unanimous fervor. Cárdenas was friendly to the Spanish Republic and welcomed a huge number of Republican refugees, most of whom were able to fit themselves into cultural positions. He established the Casa de España, which later became the College of Mexico, similar to the Collège de France.

Mexico had undergone experiences that were not shared by the rest of America. Her sense of nationalism and her combativeness first had been sharpened by the French invasion that placed the Austrian archduke Maximilian on the throne of Mexico with the support of the Roman Catholic hierarchy. (The boundless economic power of the Church was with her always.) Then came her troubles with the United States: the Mexican War (1846–8), which cost her vast territories that were annexed by the United States, and later, the invasion by United States capital. The intent of the Revolution was to put a period to all such ventures, but eventually there came a day when the Mexicans considered that it was time to regard the revolution as a *fait accompli* and to strike a balance. The balance was not necessarily favorable. In 1949 the essayist Daniel Cosío Villegas (1900–   ) wrote:

All the revolutionaries turned out to be unequal to the work that the revolution had made necessary: Madero destroyed Porfirism, but did not create a democracy in Mexico; Calles and Cárdenas did away with the *latifundio*, but did not create a new Mexican agriculture. . . . The men of the revolution may now be judged with safety: they were magnificent destroyers, but nothing they created to replace what was destroyed has turned out to be indisputably better. That does not mean, of course, that the revolution accomplished *nothing:* in its course new institutions were born, an important network of roads, impressive and daring public works, and thousands of schools were built; a large number of public services, industries, and important agricultural zones were created; but none of these things has managed to transform the country tangibly, to make it happier, despite their great importance.

The tone of this criticism marks an important divergence between the Russian and the Mexican Revolutions: the latter allowed for the possibility of wide differences of opinion. One did not necessarily have to join the chorus of applause, and if he did not, he ran no risk.

In any case, Mexico has now entered the "conservative" phase of her revolution. She is trying to keep the gains represented by the Constitution of 1917 and to follow the process of evolution so as to correct the failings noted by Cosío Villegas. Cultural advances, no less important, were made on every front, apart from the political evolution. The plastic arts, principally painting, adopted new values, moved in new directions. A new renaissance took place in poetry, the novel, the essay, and music. The Fondo de Cultura Económica, a new enterprise for non-commercial and far-reaching objectives, was created as a tool for the furtherance of literature, art, and the sciences. The review *Cuadernos Americanos* was founded to be a guidepost for America's culture. In the volcanic wastes of the Pedregal, a spot fit only for thistles, a new university was built. It is a uniquely Mexican showpiece architecturally. President Miguel Alemán (1902–   ) inaugurated it. During the presidency of Adolfo López Mateos (1910–   ), three billion pesos out of an estimated national budget of 13,800,000,000 were set aside for schools. One Secretary of Public Education was Jaime Torres Bodet (1902–   ), a poet and former director of the United Nations Educational, Scientific, and Cultural Organization. Under his administrative guidance, a new classroom was opened every two hours. After 1946 the presidents of Mexico were men with university degrees; they were not generals.

From 1950 to 1963 the exposition of Mexican art mentioned at the beginning of this book was shown in all the great capitals of Europe: Brussels, Zurich, Cologne, The Hague, Berlin, Vienna, Moscow, Leningrad, Warsaw, Paris, and Rome. The show was a maximum expression of the country's culture, organized by the painter, musicologist, and art critic Fernando Gamboa (1909–   ). It came as more than a revelation to Europe; it was a new discovery of a fabulous America. It included artifacts ranging from the lower pre-Classical civilization (1500–1100 B.C.) to the latest

work by Rufino Tamayo (1899–   ) and other outstanding
painters of the past thirty years. The art treasures moved from
place to place in a train of a hundred cars. Never before had a
single train traveled over European railways carrying such artistic
wealth. It included unique works such as the Heads of *Las Ventas*
in basalt three meters high and weighing eighteen tons each, which
were sculptured twenty centuries ago. The most ancient European
art has nothing like them or like the very delicate pieces of pre-
Columbian pottery. The palaces of fine arts in the European
capitals were transformed to present the two thousand-odd items.
During the same period the Mexican ballet was a great success in
the theaters of Paris and other capital cities. Its folkloric spectacles
were as rich as those staged by the Russians.

Mexico has attracted many foreigners working in the field of
experimental art, beginning with Eisenstein. After making films
in Russia which had a great influence on the world art of motion-
picture making, Eisenstein went to Mexico to look for a more
propitious environment. The film he worked on but never completed was *Que Viva Mexico!* Even unfinished, it left its mark.
Later Luis Buñuel went to Mexico from Spain for the same purpose and had better luck. Some of his masterpieces were produced
in Mexico. The country has a cinema tradition of its own, too.
Salvador Toscano, who died in 1947, gave motion-picture makers
the world over something to think about with his documentary
film on the revolution from the days of Zapata to the presidency
of Calles. No other country has so complete a document of those
years. In Europe, the picture ran for two hours and was judged a
masterpiece of the period by the critics. Toscano opened the first
motion picture theater in Mexico in 1896. A year after the first
French films were shown in Paris, they could be seen in Mexico
City. Mexico's own productions came later. Among the most
original of her native actor-artists is Cantinflas. Mexican motion
pictures have won world-wide recognition, as have those of Argentina and Brazil.

¶ AN INSTITUTIONAL REVOLUTION

The Mexican Revolution aroused an interest in the life of the
laborer and farm worker which found its complement in art. Thirty
years after Madero and Zapata, the Mexican novel turned back
to elemental themes and developed them in a topical and convincing
manner. The Latin-American novel is of the left, a novel that

denounces misery and lays it before the reader's eyes. Because the Revolution took its stand between Cuauhtémoc and his descendants of the twentieth century, Agustín Yáñez (1904–   ) was inspired by Fray Bartolomé de las Casas in his search for Indian myths. Consequently he turned to the peons who had taken part in the Revolution and made them the protagonists of *Al filo del Agua* (*The Edge of the Storm*) and *Las Tierras Flacas* (*The Exhausted Lands*). Carlos Fuentes (1929–   ) is primarily concerned with the people of Mexico City, no longer "the most transparent region," as Alfonso Reyes once called the Valley of Anahuac. Juan Rulfo has used the poor soldier of the Revolution as his anti-hero; his novel *Pedro Páramo* plunges into the muddied waters where the peon walks hand in hand with death. Rosario Castellanos (1925–   ), a young poet, made her bow as a novelist with *Balún Canán*, which brought her fame, and in her *Oficio de Tinieblas* (*Ceremony of Tenebrae*) she enters the shadowy and magical realms of the country people, relics of the old days which revolution was not able to wipe out, for it was not a sponge that could erase the past or cover it with a colored print.

Daniel Cosío Villegas (1900–   ), undertook a monumental task in the cultural field with his *Historia Moderna de México*. Cosío spent many years as director of the College of Mexico, where he trained a school of historians. In his study he recreates the past with ample documentation, impeccable scholarship, minute detail, and irony. Jesús Silva Herzog (1896–   ), editor of *Cuadernos Americanos*, wrote *Un Ensayo sobre la Revolución Mexicana* (An *Essay on the Mexican Revolution*), which maintains that the Revolution struggled and is still struggling for social justice: food, shelter, clothing, culture, and the enjoyment of all the goods within the reach of everyone, not as free gifts, but as the fruits of labor. He inveighs against the corruption of unscrupulous employees and officeholders and speaks of the friendship between Mexico and the United States that "must be based on justice, equality, esteem, mutual respect; it must be a friendship between gentlemen with identical obligations and the same rights." The poet, Octavio Paz (1914–   ) considers in *El Laberinto de la Soledad* (*The Labyrinth of Loneliness*) that the limitations which have hampered the Revolution spring from circumstances imposed by contemporary world history, but affirms that the results have been a

... discovery of our selves. ... Chronologically, the Mexican Revolution is the first one in the twentieth century. To be understood fully, it must be viewed as a part of a great process that has not yet reached its end. Like all modern revolutions, ours proposed, as its point of departure, to liquidate the feudal regime and to transform the country with the aid of technology and industry in order to obtain, at the end of the revolution, economic and political independence and, finally, to institute a true social democracy. In other words, it took the leap of which the most lucid liberals dreamed in order to make independence and reform effective realities and to turn Mexico into a modern nation. All this without self-betrayal. On the contrary, change revealed in time our true self, a visage alternately known and unknown, a new, and yet at the same time an old, face. The revolution invented a Mexico true to herself.

Leopoldo Zea (1912–   ) wrote the history of Mexican thought with emphasis on Positivism, linking her to the movement of contemporary world history. History was an invention of the Occident. The West views as exotic, colonial, subsidiary, whatever is not of the West. America, which has tried to be original, sees herself as outside history. But the concept is beginning to slip away from the West. One of Toynbee's virtues, which has won him great esteem in America, is that he includes America in the general picture of the new history. Zea points out in *América en la Historia* the variations in that process and its development and departs from the old individualism.

This individualism will prove to be that which opposes the incorporation of other peoples in any other form than subordinate, into the history that they [the peoples of the West] constructed. Asia, Africa, and Latin America must be excluded from the environment of modernity under several pretexts. This exclusion will assume a touching guise in America, for the people excluded from the new history know full well that they are a part of it, owing to their European origin. They are not the only people of European origin excluded. Spain, even though she exemplified one of the most brilliant stages of European culture, of world history, could not do so now; her work belonged to the past, a past that would not be re-enacted. The Spanish and Portuguese colonies in America were a part of that past. The peoples who emerged from them were maculate with the sin of belonging to a bygone stage of history.

Silvio Zavala (1909–   ), who succeeded Cosío Villegas at the College of Mexico, reinterprets ancient history and picks out the original experiences that, from the sixteenth century on, indicated a leaning toward humanitarianism among the Spaniards to whom Fray Bartolomé de las Casas and Motolinía did not appeal in vain on behalf of the Indians. Zavala wrote *La Utopia de Tomás Moro en la Nueva España* (*Thomas More's Utopia in New Spain*), and compiled the *Ideario de Vasco de Quiroga*. Edmundo O'-Gorman (1906–   ), gave a new dimension to the role of men like Amerigo Vespucci in his historical interpretation *Invención de América* (*Invention of America*). The poet Carlos Pellicer (1899–   ) used his imaginative genius to revolutionize the museums. In Mexico City he assembled Diego Rivera's collections of pre-Columbian pottery and arranged them in one of the most beautiful museums of the country; in Tabasco he collected the pottery of Palenque and Las Ventas. Alfonso Caso (1896–   ), the archaeologist who explored Monte Albán, added a touch of magic to the new museums with a display of the jewelry he had found. The archaeological work in Mexico has given this region of America a high place in world culture alongside Assyria and Egypt. In the last years monumental editions have been devoted to the Mayan and Aztec ruins, to the fresco paintings of the Revolution, and the work of José Guadalupe Posada. Other studies slated to become classics are those by Manuel Toussaint (1890–1956) and the three volumes on Mexican art compiled by the director of the Institute for Esthetic Investigations and a group of students.

Mexico shares with certain cities of America a common characteristic in her hospitality toward free men, many of them exiles —writers, artists, and intellectuals to whom Mexico City has become home. Since the time of José María de Heredia and José Martí people have gone there from everywhere in South America. Gabriela Mistral wrote some of her best work there in response to an invitation from Vasconcelos. Pedro Henríquez Ureña (1884–1946), a Dominican who lived in Argentina and Mexico, spent his last years there as mentor to the continent. The Honduran Rafael Heliodoro Valle (1891–1959), like many other Central Americans, did almost all his scholarly work in Mexico. The Colombian poet Porfirio Barba Jacob (1883–1942) worked there as an ultra-Modernist, and Germán Pardo García (1902–   ), also from Colombia, published twenty volumes of poetry in Mexico. Both are listed in anthologies, sometimes as Colombians, sometimes as

Mexicans, for they spent most of their mature lives as intellectuals in Mexico. Two other Colombians, the sculptors Rómulo Rozo (1899–1964) and José Arenas Betancourt, made contributions to their art there. Among the Venezuelans, Rómulo Gallegos spent his years of exile there, and the poet Andrés Eloy Blanco (1897–1955), a star of the first magnitude in Latin American poetry, died there in exile.

¶ THE SICK CONTINENT

Every time there is a war in Europe, Latin America loses, regardless of who wins. The First World War brought confusion to Western philosophy and sowed the seeds of totalitarian government. As a kind of by-product, for the first time in a century, a generation of essayists appeared in America, distrustful of their own people and their own country and dubious of the value of liberty. They turned against representative democracy. Violent acts that tended to reverse the traditional line of history followed upon these literary exercises. The theorists were only a minority and their attempts at subversion never yielded results, but that new ingredient in the field of political culture is still active. Such men, nostalgic conservatives who favored a prepotent authority, a hard line, a strict oligarchical order, found that the time was ripe for a revelation of their feeling. The Catholic element was sympathetic to Hitler's scheme of things. In the hierarchy of the Church, his racial theories and his anti-Semitism were received with expressions of sympathy and not infrequently were applauded. The philosophical presentations by the intellectuals in the Spanish Falange of their objections to freedom were picked up and adopted by the Left as Communism spread. Calls for revision of the democratic systems became ever louder, more embattled, more dialectical.

Aníbal Ponce (1898–1938), a disciple of José Ingenieros, of Marxist tendencies, went into voluntary exile in Mexico, where he became one of the most seductive sympathizers with Russian Communism. Leopoldo Lugones, once the Modernist poet of Argentina, turned to realism and satire to interpret the existing doubt of democracy in *La Grande Argentina* (1930). Manuel Gálvez (1882–   ) adopted the Naturalistic style of Zola in his successful novels on Argentine life. He was also a bigoted Catholic who wrote a dithyrambic biography of García Moreno and became an anti-Semitic Argentine Naziphile.

With the triumph of Franco in Spain, the word "movement" was substituted for the word "party" in America. The "movements," whether of Left or Right, always were calculated to sow confusion in the traditional parties. The movement headed by Franco has served to draw political dividing lines and is used as a basis for judging political convictions in Latin America more than in any other part of the world. The most conservative elements have rallied around the flag of the "*Caudillo* of Spain by the Grace of God." They extol Hispanism, a return to the mother country, and the philosophy of dictatorship.

Ideas have stepped down from the purely intellectual level and gone into cells for political action, thereby arousing the sleeping ambitions of military *caudillos* in embryo. In the war colleges, cadres of general staff personnel have been formed, composed of fanatical admirers of the Prussian system. Germany's defeat in 1918 merely fed a reflective desire for a comeback which found its tool in Nazism. It might almost be said that Nazism was born in Germany and Bolivia at the same hour. The Nazis Colonel Kundt and Captain Röhm were invited to Bolivia to instruct the army. They founded the military lodge whose purpose was to spread the Nazi ideal in Bolivia and to radiate from there all over South America. When Röhm returned to Germany, he became one of Hitler's closest cronies until the Führer "purged" him in 1934. But Röhm had not wasted his time in Bolivia. The planks in the platform of the National Revolutionary Movement of 1941 were copied from the basic points in the program approved by the German National Socialist Party.

The first step in the conquest of Argentine power was taken by Juan Domingo Perón (1895–), who had studied somewhat more than the art of war in Mussolini's Italy and who later traveled through Germany and Spain. Perón set up an officers' lodge in Argentina with General Edelmiro Farrell. "Turn your eyes to the triumphant Germany of Hitler," he preached. At that time the greatest Nazi organization in America was functioning in Argentina, with its general headquarters in the German embassy. As the civil element kept yielding step by step before pressure from the military, Perón came into power. The Nazis and Fascists, meanwhile, had lost the war in Europe. Perón said: "Mussolini was the greatest man of our century, but he made some disastrous mistakes. I, who have had the advantage of witnessing what he did, shall follow in his footsteps, without falling into his errors."

Chile, the country that had made the greatest progress in social legislation and which had laid a very solid groundwork as a nation, witnessed a parade of twenty thousand Nazis goose-stepping and giving the Nazi salute through the streets of Santiago. In Colombia, a group of fanatical Catholic youths were holding meetings in the editorial rooms of *El Siglo* (The Century), a conservative daily owned by Laureano Gómez (1889–1965). The young "Black Shirts" swore by Hitler. Although the Führer was not the perfect model that Gómez was looking for, his adherence to Franco's Spain was complete. Nowhere else in America have eulogies of the *caudillo* been uttered as fulsomely as in the conservative assemblies of Colombia.

Given such circumstances, a pessimistic literature was bound to appear, full of doubt of the American man, of the tropics as territory fit for humanity, and of the *páramos* of Bolivia as terrain capable of sustaining any civilization. The writers of that persuasion chose to describe life in the deserts, the swamps, the jungles. The doubts they expressed came from far in the past, but they grew more insistent, and were dressed up in the trappings of science. In Bolivia, Gabriel René-Moreno (1836–1908) wrote:

> This copper race has already given a demonstration of its secularity. Its power and its civilization during the Peruvian Empire could not stand up to the first contact with a group of adventurous white men. Today its heritage is nothing to us. Not one new factor, not a single one, has this race brought to culture or to the sum total of human activity.

Alcides Argüedas (1870–1946) wrote his books on history with such brilliance, and his analysis in *Pueblo Enfermo* (*Sick People*) is so implacable, that the term *argüedismo* was coined to express the idea of an illness in Bolivian thought. To Argüedas, the *cholo* represented the greatest evil: "A career in the military, as in journalism, jurisprudence, teaching, politics, or anything else has become progressively tainted with the *cholo*, making it all plebian, ordinary, as everything in Bolivia has been so colored and made ordinary for many years." *Pueblo Enfermo* was published in 1909. In 1936, Argüedas issued a third, corrected edition. "To his initial mistake," Zum Felde commented, "he now adds still another and grosser one. The author and some other intellectuals of the period, of less prestige than he, have let themselves be seduced and upset by the aberrations of the Nazi-Facist doctrine that was spreading at the time and was addling many brains." Argüedas did not spare the Indian in his analysis.

At the mercy of various contradictory beliefs, entirely subjugated by the material and moral influence of his *yatiris*, the priests, the bosses, and public officials, his soul has been a depository of resentment ever since the time when the flower of his race was locked, against its will, in the depths of the mines, where it came to a rapid end, with no mercy from anyone. And that hatred has kept accumulating as the race lost its dominant characteristics and traits; this in turn increased the dominant man's confidence in his ability to dominate. . . . The Indian race has borne without complaint the hateful servitude that was pressed down upon it most heavily by the very people whose duty it is to redeem it, that is, the monks, the public officials, and the bosses.

Long before that, Bolívar in Venezuela had had his doubts about the human material that he had to deal with, but in spite of everything, he accomplished a giant's labor, which implied that he had sufficient faith to struggle with nature and conquer it. The pessimism of the twentieth century has an effect that can only be described as liquefying. César Zumeta (1860–1955) published a pamphlet in 1899 which is better known for its title than for its content. This was *El Continente Enfermo* (*The Sick Continent*), containing charges that had nothing to do with the land or man. To Zumeta, the continent was sick because it was not armed. His cure, that it must arm itself, was worse than the disease, which other people also recognized. Zumeta eventually became a minister and agent of the dictatorship of Juan Vicente Gómez, whom he considered "a man with a heart." From Zumeta it was but a short step to Vallenilla Lanz's championship of the virtues of Democratic Caesarism.

In Colombia, some conjuring tricks were performed with human geography, the science founded by the German geographer Ratzel and with the racial theories of Gobineau so that Laureano Gómez could reach the conclusion in his book, *Interrogantes sobre el Porvenir de Colombia* (*Questions on the Future of Colombia*), that the country had been founded on the most inclement soil in the world and populated by the offscourings of the human race. Gómez became head of the Conservative party, which enabled him to wield great political power. (He was president of Colombia from 1950 to 1953.) At a certain phase of his struggle upward, his creed, frankly stated, was:

Spain, which is marching forward as the lone defender of Christian culture, has headed the vanguard of the Western nations in the reconstruction of the Empire and of Hispanism, and we inscribe our names on the roster of her phalanxes with indescribable pleasure. We thank God that He has permitted us to live in this period of unforseeable transformations, and that we can cry out from the very depths of our feelings: "Arise, Catholic and Imperial Spain!"

Miguel Jiménez López, a distinguished professor in the School of Medicine and a statistician as well as an educator, ranked Colombia at the very bottom of the list in human qualities in an essay entitled *¿Nuestras razas decaen?* (*Are Our Races Becoming Decadent?*), which became the basis of an ephemeral school of literature on the so-called degeneration of the race. Paradoxically, the school accomplished something positive by awakening a preoccupation with geographical and anthropological studies, so that the alarm bell was not rung in vain.

In Mexico, José Vasconcelos sketched an idealistic vision of America's future in his books *La Raza Cósmica* and *Indología*. But after his ambitions to be president were thwarted, he became a bitter and belligerent pessimist, and though it was he who had raised the standard of the Indians, he changed his beliefs and held that Catholic Spain and her heirs knew the formula that could save America, honeycombed with Freemasonry, Protestantism, and capitalism, which, according to him were the three demon sons of the Yankees.

¶ THE MILITARY GO INTO BATTLE FOR POWER

The depression of the 1930's struck Latin America a hard blow. Previously, the solutions sought for had tended to invigorate representative democracy and to place the blame for bad administration on the old politics. Later, the weaknesses and the failures of the traditional system, which had hampered any progress great enough to confront successfully the surprises of a world in crisis, were pointed out. Social agitation spread. The military men, who never had had anything to do with economic crises, and who never had studied anything that would equip them to solve such problems, decided that Providence had singled them out to undertake the mission of straightening with an iron hand what had become twisted through the fault of regimes born of representative democracy. As they went about the task of imposing their own rule, their "raids" soon became routine events. Their vanity bubbled up like foam, along with their flashy uniforms and their salaries. Mussolini, Hitler, and Franco were in the ascendency.

To be sure, the majority of the people did not share those totalitarian sentiments, and when the Second World War broke out, Latin America again lined up on the side of the democracies. The warm voice of Franklin D. Roosevelt helped to hold this alliance together, for his popularity in Latin America was greater than that of the local strong men. The outcome of the war seemed to affirm democratic principles, and the overthrow of Hitler and Mussolini were taken as salutary warnings. But two parallel developments supervened: the United States concentrated its greatest effort on the rehabilitation of Western Europe and the Russian socialist empire evolved beyond all expectation. A series of miracles —German, Italian, and French—added up to only one: the miracle of Europe's recovery. With American aid, the Western world surged upward from its old, solid, secular bases—while Latin America lost the war for the second time. Germany and Italy won it, and were promptly forgiven because their people had been the first victims of the diabolical dictators. Meanwhile, the republics of South America, which, to say the very least, had made it impossible for Hitler and Mussolini to open a new front in the Western hemisphere by their refusal to let Hitler have any spot where he could establish a base, and the bulk of whose production had gone to serve the Allies, were forced to watch the prices of their goods drop precipitously. Nobody offered to save them or to help them perform a miracle of their own. All their hopes were crushed; as Europe was on the rise, Latin America was on the decline. Their governments went into crisis. The military men emerged. Thus the breakdown of representative government was caused from the outside. To Latin America, it was as if the war were just beginning.

Perón in Argentina, Trujillo in the Dominican Republic, Pérez Jiménez in Venezuela, Odría in Peru, Stroessner in Paraguay, Rojas Pinilla in Colombia, Remón in Panama, Batista in Cuba, Busch in Bolivia—soldiers of every rank from sergeant to generalissimo became a single fresco across the wall of Latin America. Some of the dictatorships showed a touch of progress; some of them created bogus paradises. But all of them were darkly tinged with despotism by terror. The Spanish general Millán

Astray, who shouted "Down with intelligence!" in the presence of Unamuno at the University of Salamanca, had his doubles in Argentina as Perón's fanatics paraded in front of the university shouting, "Rope sandals, yes; books, no!" Perón was shrewd enough to pose as a popular leader asking for nothing but what the people deserved, needs that the civil officials had forgotten about. But Perón was not alone; the armed forces grew monstrously everywhere on the continent.

All this occurred in the one region of the world that seems really safe against international wars because the mechanism of the Organization of American States presumably can stop any conflict automatically. Nevertheless, the continental armies totaled 541,000 men by 1955. No doubt this number has increased as dictatorship became a natural thing and since Fidel Castro has been trying, with Russian aid, to build the most powerful army in Latin America. National budgets are now war budgets— on the continent where there is no war. Twenty-five, thirty, and thirty-five per cent of the budget in the various Latin-American countries is spent in the armed forces; to this is added the American military aid. Paraguay's draft has passed the sixty-per-cent mark.

The change in orientation brought about by military *coups d'état* cannot be explained solely by the sympathy some generals feel toward totalitarianism. The new direction constitutes a denial of an entire historical process and cultural vocation.

Whenever Latin American culture is discussed, politics must be one of the major topics. Politically, the continent has always striven for the best: independence, initiative versus the colonial system, the struggle for the freedoms, obligatory arbitration. In human terms, Latin America's "civil disturbances" have been justified because they have arisen from the search for formulas embodying the highest aspirations of the modern civilized world. They have never cost anything comparable with what Europe has sacrificed to its international wars. Yet all of America's efforts suddenly vanish at the shout of the "Halt and about face!" that issues from the barracks. The original army, the army of the war for independence, kept in view its objective of bringing representative democracy to the people and of implanting the civil freedoms. The army of today wants only to seize power. How has this change come about?

The Second World War left as its heritage the idea fostered in the Pentagon at Washington that Latin America ought to be an armed continent. To this end, the widest credit was granted and the most generous donations made. This is still going on. Between 1951 and 1957, the United States handed out 284 million dollars worth of arms as a part of the program of "mutual security." Old arms, new arms, air, land, and sea arms were distributed in profusion. The general staffs of the beneficiary armies became the owners of powerful armaments that they were free to use internally. Maneuvers have become raids from the barracks. The initial stimulus provided by the United States was followed by that of the dealers in armaments. The buyer was cajoled doubly by the thought of owning the most modern materiel, and by being paid a commission. During the presidency of General Dwight D. Eisenhower, the White House demonstrated the most extravagant friendship for Pérez Jiménez, Trujillo, and Somoza. Such manifestations aroused a resentment among civilians which it will be difficult to cauterize. Decorations were handed out from Washington worth as much on a military man's chest as the crosses of war. In addition, various Latin-American dictators and other generals have received from Franco the Cross of Isabel the Catholic and some even have been given the Vatican's Piana Order and the French Cross of the Legion of Honor.

The Colombian Eduardo Santos (1888–   ), expressed the Latin American civilian point of view in the speech he delivered in New York during the ceremonies marking Columbia University's centenary. Santos said:

Against whom are we Latin Americans arming ourselves? What is the reason that our countries are ruining themselves with very costly armaments that we shall never use? For the crime of an American international war would be one of those crimes that the Holy Ghost does not pardon—a crime that nothing could explain, that nothing could justify except the personal interest of certain individuals, except the monstrous self-interest of the arms salesmen. We have no reason to fight one another; we have reasons only for drawing closer together and living in brotherhood. . . . Have we any military roles to play in the great international conflicts perchance? Never. That would be an act of foolish braggadocio that could not be sustained for five minutes. In this period of the atomic bomb, with these new and fabulously expensive weapons, with these technical systems based on thousands of millions, what would we poor countries be thinking   to ruin ourselves with armaments that would be worth absolutely nothing at a moment of international conflict? What then? We are building armies that are meaningless in international terms but devastating to the internal lives of our countries. Every country is being occupied by its own army.

From the moment of Perón's downfall, the struggle for the recuperation of civilian life has succeeded in dislodging other military men. One by one, Rojas Pinilla, Pérez Jiménez, Odría, Batista, Trujillo, and Somoza have fallen or have died. But their influence has not been eradicated entirely. They have all left behind them the interests they created, and new circumstances have supervened. Communism is growing and has taken over Cuba. The revolution there began with the just demands of the people, which could be formulated everywhere else as well as in Cuba. But the traditional wealthy class and the *nouveaux riches* who have emerged with industrialization, with the fly-by-night businesses linked with political corruption, have not surrendered. They are fighting any reduction of their ample profits. The middle class is more hard pressed than ever. A situation of conflict, or contention, is shaping up. Budgetary deficits are growing as the result of the limitless increases that the armed forces clamor for, the growth of bureaucracy, and the unprecedented expansion of the public needs for roads, hygiene, and schools. These demands have synchronized with the drop in the prices of Latin American products and the rising costs of everything that the industrialized countries sell to Latin America. Ernesto (Ché) Guevara (1928–   ) the Argentinian who was formerly second only to Castro among the revolutionary leaders of Cuba, reeled off these figures in Geneva like a man recounting a fable: to buy a certain type of tractor, Brazil had to pay 2.38 tons of coffee in 1955, 4.79 tons in 1962; Venezuela paid 938 barrels of petroleum in 1955, 1,118 barrels in 1962. Those increased costs mean that Latin America must work harder and produce more, but is receiving less and falling deeper into debt. It is becoming an explosive continent.

¶ THE LITERATURE OF VIOLENCE

The dictatorships have dragged Latin America back onto a plane of violence reminiscent of the crudest days of the nineteenth century, aggravated by methods imported from totalitarian

Europe. When man suddenly sinks into the darkest realms of his being, he behaves basely whether in a society as civilized as Germany's or one on the most primitive level. Correspondingly, the novel that has developed during these years and that reflects the new situations, is generally raw, even macabre. The stimulus needed for writing such exposés is not unique to Latin America, as Caldwell, Wright, and Faulkner have demonstrated in the United States. In any case, the literature is American. French fiction has little to do with it; such Italian novelists as Silone may have influenced it; but nothing like it can be found in the Russian novel of the present day, for contemporary Russian writers must limit their criticism to past history.

Some first-class artists have worked during the dictatorship in Venezuela: Miguel Otero Silva, Antonio Arraiz, José Rafael Pocaterra. Otero Silva (1908–), a poet who languished in prison under Juan Vicente Gómez, described the students' struggles against the dictatorship in *Fiebre* (*Fever*), and revealed the drama of political prisoners, and poverty existing in the midst of the profitable exploitation of petroleum in *Casas Muertas* (*Dead Houses*) and *Oficina número 7*. In *Muerte de Honorio* (*Death of Honorio*) he goes to the farthest extremes of realism in reporting the tortures practiced under the Pérez Jiménez dictatorship. Arraiz (1903–) describes the lot of the prisoners under Juan Vicente Gómez in *Puros Hombres*. Pocaterra (1889– 1955) laid aside the short story, his real medium, to write *Memorias de un Venezolano de la Decadencia*, an extensive record of the tortures and sufferings of the Venezuelans under the dictatorships of Cipriano Castro and Gómez.

Violence in Colombia has provided matter for many works of fiction, of reportage, and of sociological study. The most widely read of the novels is *El Cristo de Espaldas* (*Christ Turns His Back*) by Eduardo Caballero Calderón (1910–), which enters the intimate moral conflicts of violence in a parlance and method similar to that of the great Spanish novelists. A good priest and a bad bishop share the stage. *Tío Pancho* tells the story of a man who carries death on his back, as in a plot by Faulkner. Jorge Zalamea (1905–) wrote *El Gran Brundum Burundá ha Muerto* (*The Great Panjandrum Is Dead*), which describes with ironic humor the future funeral of Laureano Gómez. It is almost a new genre, containing a mixture of great folly, bestiality, and fabulous caricature in the manner of Goya or Hieronymus Bosch. Behind the bier march the hierarchies of the Church, the academies, and the military. Gómez comes back to life in the cemetery in the form of a parrot. Hernando Téllez (1908–   ), an essayist with a fine French lucidity, approaches violence through the reports collected in his *Cenizas para el Viento* (*Ashes for the Wind*). But violence played on a muted trumpet with an art that makes it appear less repugnant is not much of a rallying cry. The art may fail to reach the heart of the matter, which is particularly true of *La Exterminación* by Téllez, not yet in publication as a volume. Manuel Mejía Vallejo (1923–   ) places the theater of violence in a provincial village in *El Día Señalado* (*The Appointed Day*), which won the Nadal Prize. His story rings true, but the touches of poetry in it mitigate the brutality of the picture. These fictional accounts are arranged with academic discipline, as in *La Violencia en Colombia: estudio de un proceso social*, by Monsignor Germán Guzmán, Orlando Fals Bord, and Eduardo Umaña Luna, which was published by the School of Sociology of the National University.

Many books have been written on the Trujillo dictatorship in the Dominican Republic. Quite a few of them were not the work of Dominicans. One book by a Spaniard, *La Era de Trujillo*, stands out in bold relief owing to the circumstances surrounding its author, Jesús de Galíndez (1915–56). Galíndez knew his subject intimately after living in Ciudad Trujillo as a Spanish refugee. He paid a heavy penalty for his study: he was kidnapped by Trujillo's agents in New York, taken back to Santo Domingo by ship, even though he was employed at the time as a professor at Columbia University, and executed before Trujillo's eyes on one of the dictator's estates. In the ten years after this event, the detective-story plots inspired by this dramatic case contributed decisively to he dictator's decline and fall.

The Peruvian dictatorship was more openly revealed in the anti-Modernist novels that took up the fate of the Indians. The same is true of Ecuador. The novel on Bolivia is colored by a particular circumstance: the Chaco War (1932–35) a war between Paraguay and Bolivia over the northern part of a region known as the Gran Chaco, of which the southern and central parts lie in Argentina. This war was the culmination of an eighty-six-year dispute between Bolivia and Paraguay which erupted into armed clashes in 1928 and developed into a full-scale war by 1932. After the cease-fire in 1935, a peace treaty, signed in 1938, awarded a larger part of the Northern Chaco to Paraguay, a smaller part to Bolivia. The war involved international petroleum interests and drew the Indians into hostile territory where their first enemy was thirst. Augusto Céspedes (1904–   ) mined this history in *Sangre de Mestizos* (*Mestizo Blood*), a collection of stories, one of which is a small masterpiece entitled "El Pozo" ("The Well"). Later Céspedes completed the cycle of the luckless Bolivians with *El Metal del Diablo*, a novel aimed directly at Simón Ituri Patiño (1862–1947), the tin magnate who became one of the wealthiest men in the world by exploiting the Bolivian mines. The workers in the story are devoured by greed. The novel, though not a work of art, is a document of the Bolivian revolution.

No great work of fiction has covered the Argentine dictatorship, but it evoked a wealth of essays and newspaper reports. Most of the intellectuals resisted it. Jorge Luis Borges resigned from the National Library so that he could live as a free man. Victoria Ocampo (1891–   ) whose review *Sur*, founded in 1943, has been an open forum for world thought, did more than anyone else to spread the best of Western and Far Eastern literature and was herself an original writer. She was arrested and was forced to spend a couple of months among prostitutes in a woman's prison, not for her writing but because she had sung the national anthem in the street. Bernardo Houssay (1887–   ), a physician who was awarded the Nobel Prize, was ousted from his chair at the university with three hundred and eighty-five of his colleagues for refusing to march with the Peronists. Six hundred other members of the faculty were dismissed for supporting the rebels. A study by Risieri Frondizi, who later became rector of the university, throws light on the case in *Las Universidades bajo el Régimen de Perón*. After the seizure of the newspaper *La Prensa*, its editor, Alberto Gainza Paz (1899–   ), wrote a book on the suppressions imposed by the dictator.

¶ FIDEL CASTRO AND COMMUNIST CUBA

The Cuban revolution brought a completely new ingredient into America's political stew. In the beginning, the struggle to pull down Batista showed the traits normal to similar undertakings that summon all of America to unite for the sake of a sister country's freedom. Fidel Castro (1927–   ) organized his expedition against Batista in Mexico and led his group into the Sierra Maestra mountain range in Southeastern Cuba, where the rebels dug in and were joined by others until the hideout overflowed. Aid and comfort came from Venezuela, from Costa Rica, from the entire

Gulf of Mexico region. A great number of sympathizers lived in the United States awaiting the call to action. They were led by several well-known Cubans, among them Manuel Urrutia (1901–   ), the first president to succeed Bastista. Castro was then proclaiming the objectives traditional to such movements: the abolition of political imprisonments, the restoration of popular elections, a congress, and a free press. What actually came later was a change-over to Marxist Communism, withdrawal from the society of American nations, repudiation of the Rio de Janeiro Pact, and increasingly intimate contact with Russia and China. All these moves signified a radical break, not merely with the original principles of the revolution but also with the concepts current among the democrats of America. The three-party coalition supporting Castro, (which was later replaced by a single revolutionary party) took over all power. Counterrevolutionaries were lined up against a wall and shot. The press, the university, the theater, the motion picture, the radio, books, and pamphlets all became the tools of the government; free elections and the congress were done away with. The system of submitting the programs of the "maximum leader" as (Castro was called) to plebiscites was inaugurated; a squadron of political technicians, military men, and administrators from the Communist countries set up a new state, strategically situated in the Caribbean, face to face with the United States. Cuba then aligned herself not with the history of the West, but with the Communist East. Fidelism seduced a portion of the Latin American people because it is an anti-Yankee movement. A book by Castro's comrade Ernesto Guevara was circulated all over America as a manual for waging guerrilla warfare. A brushfire war flared up in Venezuela, then ruled by an old friend of Castro, Rómulo Betancourt (1908–   ), and Castro fanned it. The Cuban revolution began to affect the internal affairs of the rest of Latin America, with the result that almost all the other countries broke with Cuba, to the great satisfaction of the United States.

From the standpoint of the development of political culture in Latin America, the Cuban revolution posed this dilemma: either an authentic and independent development of Latin-American thought must come or the countries will enter the Communist orbit, whether Russian, Chinese, or Russo-Chinese. Speculation on these matters has yielded an enormous literature all over the world. For several years now, a new book on Cuba has come off the European press almost every day. Such intellectuals as Sartre have led the debate. The discussion touched off in the United

States by Herbert Matthews, a veteran correspondent of *The New York Times*, is still raging. Matthews, sent to cover Cuba, learned one day that Castro was still alive, though everyone believed him dead. Certain aspects of the revolution, particularly agrarian reform, have been taken up and exploited by agitators. To say the least, the whole panorama of relations between Anglo-Saxon and Spanish America has had to be reconsidered, and some notable variations have been proposed and tried.

Although the subject of the Cuban revolution has not crystallized in a work of literature, Communism has won exponents as distinguished as the Chilean poet Pablo Neruda (1904–   ). Neruda outdid the Russians in his poem "Canto a Stalingrado," which sent his Chilean voice around the world and earned him the Stalin Peace Prize (which counts for little today). Like Darío, like Nervo, Neruda wrote under a pseudonym. His real name, Neftalí Ricardo Reyes, would have gotten him nowhere. His choice of a pen name reveals his bent, for he chose the surname of the Czech lyricist Jan Neruda (1834–91). The image of Chile keeps appearing in his poetry as a romantic background.

José Martí, Cuba's most distinguished literary figure, is still revered in his homeland, but his work has been made to fit into party interpretations like those put forth by the Communist leader Juan Marinello (born in 1898), in his essays. But the biography written by Martí's disciple Jorge Mañach (1896–1961) has never been surpassed. Nicolás Guillén (1904–   ), the poet of the Cuban Negroes, is still remembered for his *Songoro Cosongo*, published in 1931. Since the revolution, Guillén has dedicated all his time to propaganda and public relations. The novelist Alejo Carpentier (1904–   ) has never written anything to surpass his *Los Pasos Perdidos* (*The Lost Steps*) and *El Reino de Este Mundo* (*The Kingdom of This World*), both of which are novels published in 1949. The Cuban government is now devoting itself to issuing a formidable number of edited editions; a new type of cultural extension is being introduced in Cuba. Party activity expresses itself in the publication of bulky reviews and of mass editions tailored to the revolutionary cycle that summons everyone to public service for the new regime, and in Cuba's theaters.

¶ CHRISTIAN DEMOCRACY

A new international political force opposed to Communism has come to the fore in Christian Democracy. The movement was welcomed by conservative and mildly liberal youth inspired by the encyclical *Rerum Novarum*, to which the humanitarian teachings of Pope John XXIII added luster. The Christian-Democratic parties are beginning to sponsor radical reforms that have more to offer, in many instances, than Communism, but which affirm their Christian basis. In Chile, Eduardo Frei (1911–   ) won the election of 1964, thus becoming the first Christian-Democratic president in America. The new party was organized in 1925 and held its first national congress in 1939. The world conference of Christian Democracy was held in 1961. Argentina, Cuba, and Venezuela sent delegates to it. The party in Venezuela, headed by Rafael Caldera (1916–   ), took second place in the presidential elections of 1964. No other political force has developed so swiftly in Latin America. In Chile the party numbered 300,000 members in 1925, 1,800,000 in 1961. When Frei won the presidency in 1961, the Christian Democrats outnumbered the old Socialist Party, with which the Communists were united, by half a million votes. "Christian Democracy," Frei said, "is nourished on the philosophy of Integral Humanism. The Christian-Democratic Party wants to implement this philosophy, which means that it is fighting for a society in which man can develop fully and integrally."

¶ GREAT CAPITALS AND SHANTYTOWNS

The most far-reaching change in Latin America has been effected by the sudden growth of the cities. At the beginning of the twentieth century, no city there had a population of a million; in 1960 many cities had between one and six million people. As the industrialization of the nations has not kept pace with the growth of the cities, these metropolises contain widely varying conglomerations of the enlightened and the illiterate, of workers and unemployed, of sections with dazzling wealth and "shantytowns," or *"villamiserias,"* a name given to the quarters into which the poor people from the country have poured in answer to the attractions and temptations of the city. Latin America was rural; now it is urban to a great degree. Even those who cannot read know what is going on. They know what is happening in the rest of the world and have become individuals with new ambitions, new diseases, new miseries, new perspectives, and new leaders. The ex-rustic feels no nostalgia for the country. Agrarian reform can neither keep the rural population on the land nor solve the problems of excess population which, either landless or unemployed, goes to meet adventure offered them for the first time by the highway that the trucks of the poor can roll along. Whoever reaches the city stays there.

Someone once called Buenos Aires the "Big Village." Today it is a city, designed in part by Le Corbusier and embellished with monuments by Rodin and Bourdelle. Its population exceeds that of many European capitals, and a European feels quite at home. On the Atlantic side of the Americas, from New York to Buenos Aires, a strong European accent comes from Italian, English, Polish, German, Spanish, and French immigrants and their off-spring—and there is a paucity of anything to do with Indians. On the Pacific side, growth has come from Spanish and Indian roots. On the Atlantic side, communication with Europe is easy and the migratory flow of men, ideas, and fashions is uninterrupted. On the Pacific side, the flow is from within, nourished by tradition. The sea before it is that Pacific whose opposite shore is unknown. This explains why Buenos Aires and Mexico City, Montevideo and Lima are so unlike. Suddenly, however, all cities, on both oceans, have become giants eager for improvisation, with a contagious anxiety and a new poverty. There are the new rich and the new poor. Civilization has become exacerbated.

Wherever the growth of the cities is monstrous as compared with that of the rest of the country, as in Buenos Aires, some striking features appear. Eduardo Mallea (1903–   ) has probed them in his work, particularly in *Historia de una Pasión argentina*. He searches through what is hidden in the city for the authentic Argentine. To the true Argentine, this search is drama. Ezequiel Martínez Estrada (1895–   ) sees Buenos Aires as *La Cabeza de Goliath* (*Goliath's Head*) and continues to analyze it relentlessly in *Radiografía de la Pampa* (*X Ray of the Pampas*). Perturbed by the new circumstances, he studies the pampas, stretching to infinity, and finds there things that Sarmiento never dreamed of. Buenos Aires and Montevideo have produced from the European element in Argentine and Uruguayan literature some brilliant writers who achieved places in English or French literature, for their authors are always closest to the Western world. The literature of the great cities on the Pacific keeps to their more abstruse, often more predominantly Indian background, which places them at a farther remove from world literature. All in all, the life of the new cities is being discussed everywhere, for cities that fifty years ago were comparable in size to the provincial centers of Europe now are larger than Rome or Madrid.

¶ THE END OF THE MONROE DOCTRINE

Pan-Americanism has changed radically in response to the new circumstances. The old Pan American Union, created in Washington, functioned as an agency more or less mindful of the shy interests of Latin America. Now it has become the Organization of American States. This new dispensation is the subject of lively debate. Actually, if its efforts to unify Latin America are not vigorous at the present time, that is largely the fault of the Latin Americans. Indeed, the new charter approved by the Ninth Pan-American Conference in Bogotá, marked the end of the Monroe Doctrine and the beginning of a system freely chosen by all America. In great part, the new constitution was the work of the Colombian Alberto Lleras Camargo (1906–   ) and its range may be summed up in the following words he spoke before the Congress of Colombia:

> That system was not born, as some claim, out of an evolution of the Monroe Doctrine, but out of the need to replace and repeal it; to retain of it, under the control, the vigilance, and the decision of the twenty-one nations that constitute the system, only a defense against any act of intervention, threat, or extracontinental act against its autonomy. To be sure, the Monroe Doctrine preserved the independence of the young American republics when it was proclaimed by one of them which had the capability of implementing it through its already remarkable physical power. Attempts to restore or establish colonies on American soil, which were pursued persistently until the Monroe Doctrine was proclaimed, were not repeated. But another grave danger replaced them. The Latin American republics lay at the mercy of the protector state, which appeared to demonstrate an interest in the creation of an empire no smaller than that of the European monarchies. Successive acts of force on the part of the United States, some of which gave it its present geographical conformation, demonstrated the tremendous possibilities of a new imperialism and the difficulty of confronting it. Nevertheless, and mainly during the past thirty years, there has

come forth in America, not a defensive alliance in the old style, but, on the contrary, a rational effort to place the hemisphere under international law, to proscribe war, to condemn any form of imperialism, to invigorate the association of the States, to eliminate intervention, and to preserve unity and solidarity for collective defense against external threats.

The new organization was a door opened by President Kennedy to usher in a new political front for Latin America, a vigorous rectification of the policy of Manifest Destiny. But the Organization of American States lacked economic means to stimulate a more rapid progress among the Latin American nations. Kennedy broke his country's prejudices against making that possible. The Punta del Este charter, drawn up at a special meeting, at the ministerial level, of the Inter-American Economic and Social Council, held at Punta del Este, Uruguay, August 5–17, 1961, was the first step toward implementation of his policy. But with or without economic aid, the Bogotá charter was still a document that went beyond the charter of the United Nations. It contains the most important body of principles which the New World has brought to the juridical evolution of the world. It has made war among the twenty countries impossible, and thus also has made America the first place that has practically freed itself of this scourge wielded by Western tradition itself.

¶ IT WILL SPEAK ITS MIND

Anyone who takes a backward look in order to view Latin-American life in perspective is certain to recognize some obvious facts; the persistence of intellectual curiosity, the desire to find a philosophical route to follow, and an esteem for literary values. Even though the rawest kind of illiteracy still exists, even the illiterates grant a magical power to literature. They are fascinated by an educated man, a man with a doctorate.

The Spanish conquest, with its weapons, its dogs, its sweat and dust, often was brutal; the colonies, with their slavery, were harsh; the hierarchies, the barbarian *caudillos*, and the Indian chiefs bore down hard on the people. In more recent times, despotism, firing squads, guerrilla wars, and every other kind of violence have done nothing to soften the picture. For all that, teachers have kept their prestige and have made themselves heard, for their voices recognize no boundary line. The inclination to think, the habit of listening, the latent curiosity always have been present. Some literary names top those of the strong men in politics. One is that of Alfonso Reyes (1899–1959), whose thread of wit no one and nothing could break. In his Mexico, where the air was most transparent, he taught all literatures, from the Greek to those of present-day America. He subtly drew the Humanistic lines of demarcation. He is not so well remembered as a poet as he is as a writer of prose that fills nearly twenty volumes and will pass thirty volumes before it is all published. Reyes was always considered a possible candidate for a Nobel Prize, which his American friends would have granted him, though Sweden did not. The Colombian Baldomero Sanín Cano (1861–1957) would have lived a century if he had been granted four more years. Restless and versatile like Reyes, he taught several generations in Argentina and Colombia, studied Scandinavian, English, German, and Spanish literature, and plumbed the depths of political problems. As a Humanist, Cano kept his distance in order to avoid entanglement in party struggles—though he was awarded the Stalin Prize in his old age —and was disturbed by the persistently Anglo-Saxon shading in Humanism. He was born in Río Negro, a small town in the Antioquia district of Colombia; he became a professor in Edinburgh, lived in London for years, and died in Bogotá.

Like Rodó, Carlos Vaz Ferreira (1873–1958) carried on a long teaching career in Uruguay. He rejected Positivism as his views broadened, and he became the representative of Uruguayan philosophy. Later, Alberto Zum Felde (1890–   ), considered Uruguayan although he was born in Argentina, summed up his studies on the history and sociology of Uruguay in his monumental work *Índice Crítico de la Literatura Hispano-americana*. One of Argentina's teachers who exerted a great influence on the country was Alejandro Korn (1861–1936). His *La Libertad Creadora*, a sourcebook for a new generation, was published in 1920. Francisco Romero (1891–1962) followed Korn in philosophy both as an outstanding creative writer and as a disseminator of ideas. He occupied a chair at the university, directed the publications of the philosophical library, and greatly stimulated philosophical studies in Latin America.

The consciousness of America as a continent led to collaborations among the intellectuals of several countries. The Cuban Roberto Agramonte (1904–   ) published *Sociología Latina Americana*. Enrique Anderson Imbert (1910–   ), an Argentine, and Luis Alberto Sánchez (1900–   ), a Peruvian, wrote histories of Spanish American literature. Pedro Henríquez Ureña composed a history of culture. The Mexican Fondo de Cultura Económica brought out the collection *Tierra Firme*, one of Latin America's most ambitious works. The language academies held international conferences. The Commission on Pan-American History and Geography has sponsored an immense body of co-ordinated work. First-class research work is beginning to be published by all the universities. Puerto Rico has added her contribution as a part of Spanish America in spirit. Reviews have let in fresh air and light. Joaquín García Monge (1881–1958) published over a period of years the *Repertorio Americano*, of historical value to both continents.

In this general picture, the work of new masters keeps emerging, within the confines of their particular subject, yet stimulating even so. Mariano Picón-Salas (1901–1965) in Venezuela, wrote *De la Conquista a la Independencia*, a model book. Arturo Uslar Pietri (1905–), also a Venezuelan, added a new touch to what he had learned from his predecessors in his *Las Lanzas Coloradas* (*The Red Lances*). The mordant work of the deep pessimists in Colombia who portrayed the degeneration of their people has evoked sage, learned, and well-grounded answers from such men as Luis López de Mesa (1884–), Fernando Diez de Medina (1908–) and Guillermo Francovich (1901–) in Bolivia have contested the theories of Argüedas, while Franz Tamayo (1879–1956) championed his Indians with a more than democratic enthusiasm. And so they keep coming. For the names of all the new masters, one must turn to specialized histories. But one thing is evident: the university has overflowed its boundaries; books and reviews have proliferated; the agitation—there is no other word for it—of the intellectual currents has hastened a kind of university extension outside the campus. Radio, television, and the theater have expanded in every large city. A city that leaps within fifty years from a hundred thousand inhabitants to more than a million—and in Latin America many cities have done so— is an effervescent place in which the danger to culture is not that it may lag behind, but that it will go ahead in leaps and bounds, that it will overwhelm. That very exuberance demands a decantation which is now evident. If Latin America has not created a culture, it has developed a style that has made itself felt, the style that circumstances has imposed. A culture does not achieve a personality of its own through a deliberate desire to be unique, but because forces unlike those in other countries are at work within it.

All America has as much European blood today as Europe itself.
But that blood has mingled with other blood and its children have
seen other lands and have had other experiences. All this has made
for a unique destiny. It is not necessary to go as far as José Vasconcelos, who said that the spirit would speak through this race
—Rodó's new formula. But what speaks will be its own spirit.

To say that Puerto Rico, of all that was Spanish in America, is
the only territory that has remained under the control of the
United States would be inexact. During the natural expansion of
the colonies that signed the Declaration of Independence at Philadelphia, and then under the pressure of manifest destiny, Texas,
New Mexico, California, Florida, and—by way of the French
transfer—Louisiana were incorporated into the United States.
Then the Panama Canal Zone. But certain circumstances make
Puerto Rico unique. The island, invaded by American troops in
1898, passed directly from Spanish to American hands. Thereafter, it did not, as Cuba did, succeed in freeing itself. Only in
1952 did it become a freely associated state and lose its colonial
status. To be sure, its flag is that of the United States, but the
island's traditions have been superior to literal facts. Its language
remains Spanish, the language of the people, a language of high
value now in literature and culture. Education maintains that
spirit. Some of the foremost Spanish émigrés preferred Puerto
Rico as a refuge: Juan Ramón Jiménez, Casals, Pedro Salinas.
Exiles from the republics of Latin America have taught in its
university. Its university publications—*Asomante*, *La Torre*—
have reached the highest level among Spanish periodicals. Election of the island's governor is freer than that of the president in
many Latin American republics. Administrative control excludes
corruption, the cancer of the Caribbean area. There are no soldiers! Puerto Rico is a bridgehead of Latin America in the United
States. Luis Muñoz Marín, creator of the juridical formula in
which the state has evolved, is a poet and writer, one of the most
alert political figures of the Latin American world. The university, with Jaime Benítez as rector, stands among the first in Latin
America. Thus the tradition of Eugenio María de Hostos, precursor of the formulas of liberty in the Antilles, has achieved an
ingenious adjustment that gives the Puerto Rican indisputable opportunities within the areas that Hostos's thought illuminated.

XXI: *Appointment with Necromancy*

¶ THE HORIZONS OF MAGIC

The magic of three worlds meets in Latin America: what Spain brought; what the Indians had developed; and what the Negroes introduced. But that was only the beginning. The Chinese came later to Panama, Cuba, and Peru, bringing opium and a big lottery of dreams and illusions. The Italians carried some of the sorcery of Sicily and Naples to Buenos Aires. And so on. These elements rooted themselves wherever the sap was rising from a distant past and from all the continents. The mystery, the mazes, the poetry, the complexities and bold deeds, were nourished on such juices. There is something in Latin America which can be explained only by the inexplicable. For centuries it has not been possible to make a rational response to the everyday problems of medicine, for example. Artificial boundaries have confined reason; it has been pruned, compressed, threatened. And as always whenever no reason worthy of the name exists, the urge to move forward still remains. Whenever an impulse makes the soul rebel against a feeling of confinement, escapes are found through flights of divination, heroism, or daring, and such flights may determine the forward course of history.

Poetry owes its eminence partly to those very circumstances. It reached a point of lyrical excess in Gongorism, for poetry is a creative art that the imagination uses to probe recesses that reason

cannot reach. The Latins call their poets *vates*, that is, sorcerers.
Vaticinio is an act of sorcery. Fray Bartolomé de las Casas reminds us that in Exodus, Pharaoh called his magicians and sorcerers together to work their "incantations," in other words to chant.
"The Arcana," he commented, "are secret words that no one may
hear, and that is why they are called incantations, chants, even
though they are uttered silently in the grammatical figure they
call antiphrasis, which means talking backward." The chanting
was secret, for people have always chanted inwardly to advance
their hopes.

The history of Latin America shows a special predisposition
toward the black arts. Discussing idolatry, Voltaire said: "History
cannot be read without a feeling of horror for the human race."
In America the people who made up their minds to rebel set the
bells of their hopes to ringing and were accustomed to hearing
incomprehensible voices that fascinated them. Their great leaders
knew this and acted on it. To tell the ignorant and credulous person (sometimes even the educated and sophisticated person)
something he does not understand is like addressing him in a
tantalizing tongue. It is easy to convince him, for the arcane words
tap that lode of confused desires which he himself cannot explain
and he already has been trained to accept the supernatural and
the illogical. Credulous people always have been shown a picture
in which the divine and the diabolical, grace and temptation, occupy most of the space; natural reality is merely a dark border
beneath this chiaroscuro. The man who sets himself up as a
liberator knows that the best road he can choose for his adventure
is the magical one. His own experience has shown him that
reason is the strait and narrow way, narrower in America than in
Europe, although Europe is not excluded from the circle of magic.

The very year that the revolution began, 1812, an earthquake
struck Caracas. A priest declared from the pulpit that it was obviously a punishment from God. Bolívar, who was listening to
him, seized the speaker by the nape of his neck, pulled him down
from the lectern, and grasped the argument by the horns. He
turned to the people and gave them his magic formula: "If
Nature opposes our plans, we shall fight Nature." That was just
what the people needed to be told. Later, Bolívar spoke to his
soldiers in terms that they could not understand but that charmed
them: "You have won the palm of victory and have raised this
privileged country, which has been capable of inspiring heroism
in your dauntless souls, to the highest pitch of glory!" What could

those rustics from the wilderness know about palms of victory or the highest pitch of glory? "Fly above the tracks of the fugitives, above those bands of Tartars. . . ." Who were the Tartars? "Victory is moving on before us. . . . We are moving in the shade of a forest of laurels. . . ." Mystery! That was what lured them to follow him.

To be sure, many of Bolívar's words had already been spoken from the pulpits: "sacred rights," "sacred soil," "altars of liberty," "sublime courage," "the blessings of peace and liberty," "the angel of victory is moving on before us. . . . We are moving in the shade of victory," "heaven is watching over us," "long live the God of Colombia!" Each phrase contains a religious meaning that could be applied to liberty and was so applied for the first time as the initial shots were fired against an oppressive government, against servitude, and even against the Church. The Negroes in particular heard all this with wonder and infinite gladness. It seemed to them incredible, and they were carried away by the unbelievable. Without so much as a glimmering of comprehension, the masses rushed forward, filled the armies, followed their leader through strange, harsh, wild, hostile territory . . . to do away with the Tartars! One of the boldest and most widespread of all the wars in history was carried on by such means. All of it was magical.

¶ FRAY BARTOLOMÉ DE LAS CASAS, THE SORCERER'S APPRENTICE

From the moment of America's birth, magic has presided over it. Columbus finally had to turn his back on reason in order to begin his Operation America. At the University of Salamanca, he left the road of reason for the supernatural. He went there with the little or the much that he had learned from Toscanelli, that is, with his store of science. The learned men tried to explain to him that what he said was unacceptable, citing the Holy Bible in their hands and the Holy Fathers in their minds. Columbus warily crossed the line to meet them. He talked no more of science and much later went so far as to say: "In this matter of the discovery, maps of the world have been of no use to me; the prophecies have been fulfilled in me." He picked up the globe on the cosmographers' desk and put it on his shoulder, thus becoming St. Christopher. Toscanelli's statement that anyone who kept sailing westward would come to the Orient fell from Columbus's lips like a sorcerer's incantation. He signed himself with a cabalistic monogram that has not been deciphered yet. Always he was a man of mystery who hid his reason behind a mask. He wrote his book of prophecy and found the true site of the Earthly Paradise. His biographers always have been fascinated by his alleged Jewish background, in which they thought they had found a partial explanation for his dual personality. Bartolomé de las Casas was so taken with Columbus that he was able to persuade himself that the myth making Vespucci a thief was true. Las Casas loved mystery, and Vespucci seemed to him the embodiment of the Renaissance rational mind. The only scholar equipped to argue with Columbus in Salamanca was Abraham ben Samuel Zacuto, author of famous astronomical tables for navigating, who was a professor of astronomy until the expulsion of the Jews forced him to leave Spain and find a refuge in Portugal.

The fabulous adventurers who set out to look for the kingdom of California, the realm of the Amazon women, the Fountain of Eternal Youth, the land of the men without heads or without ears, all sailed in the wake of Columbus. Later, as the cauldron of the Conquest came to a boil, men began to travel at will from one place to another in the New World. Díaz del Castillo ruled out every rational element of their adventure when he said that after God, the horse could be thanked for the Conquest. Either men wandered clinging to the tail of the supernatural or they moved on horseback with their dogs and other men, all of them from the same zoo. A moment came when the Emperor grew alarmed at such impulsiveness, when he feared the wings lent to the mind by the novels of chivalry, and banned them. After the colony finally had calmed down, the witches set up shop. Magic sailed from the ports of Spain to the New World, sometimes by sea, sometimes through the air.

The power of the black arts is obvious even in the name America, a poetical invention of some canons. They discovered that voice, which carries some mysterious power to conquer. All the literature of the Conquest contains a wealth of apparitions, wonders, marvelous prophecies, and devils. During the colonial period, Sor Juana Inés de la Cruz asked:

> *What magical infusions*
> *from the Indian herbarium*
> *of my country can sprinkle*
> *my writing with sorcery?*

The first novel on America, by Fernández de Lizardi, pictures the normal situation of his contemporaries:

> For eight or ten years now I could not hear a small noise at midnight without being frightened, nor see a strange package or a funeral, nor enter a dark room because my whole being was filled with terror; and even though I did not believe then in ghosts, I was persuaded that the dead did appear quite often to the living, that demons would come to claw us and wrap their tails around our necks any time they took a notion to; that there were bundles that would jump on us; that souls walked in torment begging for our help; and I believed other nonsense of the same kind more firmly than the articles of faith.

Bartolomé de las Casas included Greek and Latin among the sources of magic. "Virgil," he said, "was no less a great magician, sorcerer, or necromancer than he was a distinguished poet, and in the Eighth Eclogue he introduces the magical and diabolical means by which men's hearts were darkened, obfuscated, and perverted." Fray Bartolomé was particularly impressed by Ovid's examples, for he found confirmation of some of the points made in *The Metamorphoses* in St. Augustine's texts. Such poetic magic, the eternal magic, convinces the ignorant and the educated alike. In his *Responso a Verlaine*, Rubén Darío says: "May youthful canephoras offer you acanthus." Someone has said that many people would not know what this meant word by word, but no one could resist the charm of the verse. Alfonso Reyes rated charm first in his speech on method and he invented the word *jitanjafora* to describe a kind of nonsense rhyme. He coined the word after reading the poem "Verdehalago" by Mariano Brull (1891–1956), which goes:

> *Por el verde, verde*
> *verdería de verde mar*
> *erre con erre*
> *Viernes, virgula, virgén*
> *enano verde*
> *verdularia cantárida*
> *erre con erre.*[1]

The word *jitanjafora* itself came from another of Mariano Brull's poems that his daughter loved to recite:

[1] See footnote on p. 528.

Filiflama alaba cundre
ala alalunea alifera
alveoles jitanjafora
liris salumba salifera. . . .[1]

The annotators of Reyes said: "In every current of air there are angels and *jitanjaforas.*" From primitive magic to *jitanjaforas* stretches a series of signposts marking the road that mystery has followed through the centuries of Latin America.

¶ THE WITCHES FLY FROM GERMANY TO AMERICA

In the matter of black magic, Spain was a patchwork quilt or, to change the metaphor, a mulligan stew containing Moorish enchanters, the cabala of the Jews, gypsy lore, Christian superstitions, witches' sabbaths, and various residues from medieval sorcery. Love philters, amulets, talismans, public prayers, exorcisms, blasphemies, secret ceremonies, hidden synagogues, all together formed an intricate labyrinth that led to trouble with the Inquisition. A sort of competition or rivalry grew up between the Church and magic, each of them attempting to prove itself the more powerful. The rival actors were the witches who worked with the Devil and the ministers of the faith who performed their exorcisms. The contest raged at the very borderline between the orthodox and the heretical, where the good angels wrestled with the Prince of Darkness and his cohorts. The breath of magic blows through all the literature. Cervantes introduced Merlin into the pages of *Don Quixote. La Celestina* followed the popular line by introducing magic formulas which would bring the lovers Calixto and Melibea together. Indeed not only literary, but actual procuresses also turned to the devil because their normal field of action was sin. As late as the eighteenth century, witches flew across the sky above Spain, as Goya showed in his etchings, and they still cluster on Zuloaga's twentieth-century canvases.

During the period of colonization in America, witches were on the wing not only in Spain but all over Europe. About 1510, Prague was the center of magic to which Johann Faust—the future Dr. Faustus—Paracelsus, and Cornelius Agrippa went to be initiated. Dr. Faustus later worked in the courts and universities

---

[1] Neither this poem, nor the Brull, being composed of nonsense words, can be translated.

of Central Europe. After Charles V signed his famous imperial decree condemning witches during a meeting of the Diet of Regensburg, Germany reeked more strongly of scorched flesh than Spain did. Fifty thousand people were burned at the stake in Germany, Belgium, and France. But that holocaust did not keep sorcery out of the courts. Henry VIII had to accuse Anne Boleyn of witchcraft before he could banish her to prison.

Charles V was said to have held an interview with Dr. Faustus during the Diet of Innsbruck. By that time, Faustus had made friends with Martin Luther and had also won widespread fame as an alchemist. As he and the Emperor were seated at the same table, Charles V expressed to Dr. Faustus his wish to see Alexander the Great and his wife, the Empress Roxana, in flesh and blood. "If you promise not to speak to them," Faustus replied, "I will make them walk through the room." He opened the door, and Alexander and the Empress walked in. Charles hoped to see a mole on the back of the Empress's neck, often mentioned in stories. Empress Roxana made such a deep obeisance in front of Charles that he could see the mole. Then the two specters vanished, and Charles gave Dr. Faustus a handsome gift.

Luther learned many things through his friendship with Faustus, but he never cared to go as far into the occult as the doctor, who allegedly had made a pact with the Devil. Luther said later: "These are not stories pulled out of the air or invented to inspire fear; they are real, truly frightening, and not childish tales, as some who wish to pass for learned pretend." On that point, Luther and Fray Bartolomé de las Casas were in complete accord. Fray Bartolomé made a study entitled *Pruébase que la creencia en las operaciones mágicas no está condenada por la iglesia* (*Proof that the Belief in Magical Operations Is not Condemned by the Church*). Charles V believed that the Devil was Martin Luther, and if Luther could make it possible for his disciples to enter the Catholic churches and make bonfires of their images, Charles V could order Luther's books cast into the flames. That was the war of the bonfires.

In this renaissance of the diabolical, new winds of witchcraft blew over Spain from Germany. Enter the Devil dressed as a doctor. The Inquisition undertook to censor books. Las Casas cites the most astounding case histories in the references to German witchcraft included in the lengthy study of magic which forms a part of his *History of the Indies*. To him, there could be no doubt

that the Devil had the power to transport people from one region
to another through the air, as Jesus Himself had proved, or that
the Devil could change men into beasts.

The witches had the power to make rain, lightning, and hail.
They could call up storms, unite and separate lovers, commit
infanticide, and foster temptation. Fray Bartolomé's work provides an important background to magic in America. Some of
his most noteworthy chapters are headed: "Of the things that
can be done by magical art"; "Of how men may be carried from
one place to another by demons"; "Of other prodigies and fascina-
tions that the demons and sorcerers perform"; "Of the infanticides
the sorcerers commit, and of the vice of eating human flesh"; and
"Of how men can be transformed into beasts through the art of
magic."

¶ SPANISH MAGIC

This glimpse into history makes it easy to guess what magic
the caravels from Spain brought to the Indies. The literature on
the cannibals in Brazil and the Antilles is directly related to what
Las Casas had to say about the people in Calahorra (Logroño
Province, Spain) who killed their wives and children and ate
them to avoid having to surrender to Pompey. The Roman Army
had surrounded the town and threatened it with starvation "and
in order to make their flesh last longer, they put it into a salt
bath, as if they were hams or shoulders of pork or other animals."
The first illustrations of the New World made by German engravers showed human haunches being smoked, as described in
the stories then current. All the chronicles of the Conquest are
peppered with references to "the abominable sin," the great European sin. Fray Bartolomé took his information from Albertus
Magnus, the "Doctor Universalis" who (supposedly) had deciphered Aristotle's secrets and the sciences of the Arabs and the
Rabbis. Fray Bartolomé wrote: "This vice of bestiality, i.e., homo-
sexuality, is the opposite of heroic virtue, which is almost a divine
virtue, for whereas heroic virtue is the most excellent of human
virtues, the vice of bestiality is to the same degree the worst and
most detestable, according to the Philosopher. And because the
good and favorable situation of these lands in the Indies, the clem-
ency and softness of their air, the noble influence of the stars, and
the healthfulness of the greater part of them . . ." make the New

World a paradise, the fact that men had fallen into the vice of eating human flesh, as well as committing "the abominable sin," can be explained as "beginning with some particular persons and on some particular occasion, rather than through a corruption of Nature."

The subsequent trials for witchcraft, which can be followed through the archives of the Inquisition in Mexico City, Lima, and Cartagena, seem like appendices to the reports written by Fray Bartolomé on the German witches. In *El Carnero* (*The Sheep*) by Juan Rodríguez Freile (1566–1640), inspired in part by *La Celestina*, the case of the witch Juana García, who plied her trade in the capital city, is cited. As the story goes, a certain woman whose husband had sailed to Jamaica on business, became pregnant while he was away. Juana García learned by the witches' grapevine that the husband was returning, and she gazed into the water in a washbowl where she saw and told the lady all that her husband was up to in Jamaica. The story is told in great detail and ends with Juana being sentenced for witchcraft. She was exhibited on a dais in the church holding a green candle in her hand and with a penitent's gown draped over her shoulders. "Everyone does it," Juana cried, "but I alone must pay for it." After her chastisement, Juana mounted her broomstick one night and flew to Jamaica, where she could go on practicing her calling.

The Spanish gypsies sent America the art of reading palms, the curse, the dance, and a particular kind of playing cards, the Tarot deck, for telling fortunes. Beginning in the 1300's or possibly earlier, the gypsies had spread across Europe from the lands formerly included in the ancient Byzantine Empire, whither they had migrated from northern India some time before A.D. 900. Their way of life was an invitation to "Bohemianism" (they were thought to have come from Bohemia) and to vagabondage. Their very name was surrounded by tales of stolen children. They knew all the thieves' arts and how to disguise stolen horses. They brought with them the tambourine and castanets. Charles V, who dealt more harshly with German than with Spanish witches, who preferred Dr. Faustus to Martin Luther, who made possible the sack of Rome, then later retired to pray and ask forgiveness when he knew the full extent of what had happened as a result of his act, always was ruled by a secret system of checks and balances. He kept in effect King Ferdinand's edict expelling the gypsies, whom he lumped with the Moors and Jews, but he never enforced it very strictly. As time went by, the Spanish gypsies withdrew to caves in Granada, and eventually some of them went to America. They are still coming, looking like pictures out of García Lorca's poems.

Converted Jews spread out all over America, where they never were called *marranos*—the Spanish word meaning swine —as they were in Spain. The Inquisition labored hard to expose them, but the converts, as they went about their business, were almost indistinguishable from the other Spanish colonists. They brought neither their cabala nor their science with them. The Inquisition was able to ferret out more Lutherans than Jews. A few of the new converts who went to Brazil and later to the Dutch colonies brought the Torah with them. The trial in Mexico City of Luis de Carvajal, "the Enlightened," and his family was an exceptional case. Whole regions, such as Monterrey in Mexico, and Antioquia in Colombia, are believed to have been settled in great part by converted Jews who had nothing to do with the cabala. A bishop of Tucumán turned out to be the son of a Jew who was burned at the stake in Granada. Whether or not St. Teresa, Fray Luis de León, Fernando de Rojas, and Juan Luis Vives actually had Jewish blood, which is thought to be an ingredient contributing to their writing, there is no doubt that the mysticism of the *Mansions*, the lyricism of the *Song of Songs*, the tricks of Celestina, and the passionate defense of peace all resounded throughout America. Their books were basic. The work of Jorge Isaacs shows no trace of the cabala, but his *María* carries a half-hidden echo of Biblical poetry, also found in Gabriela Mistral's verses. But those descendants of the Jews were converted, rather than converts; they were Christians rather than *marranos*, Christians believing in both Testaments. Displaced Jews came to America in the twentieth century, able to say where they came from without arousing much adverse reaction. Among hundreds of others must be mentioned Alberto Gerchunoff (1883–1950), the author of *Los Gauchos Judíos (The Jewish Gauchos)*, and the remarkable Argentine diseuse Berta Singerman, who has done more than most others for the appreciation of poetry in America.

Authentic Spanish witchcraft as practiced at the Biscayan witches' sabbaths figured later in the trials by the Inquisition on the peninsula. During the century of discovery, the Biscayan adepts prayed to the Santa Camisa (Holy Shirt), to San Juan Trastornador (St. John the Troublemaker), and to the Seven African Powers. Those same prayers may be found in print today, for sale like fruit in the markets of Santo Domingo, and even in New York. The poor Puerto Ricans in Harlem, appalled at the harshness of the Yankee world, go to the *botánicas* ("herb stores," literally) to buy colored candles, lucky stones, *amansaguapos*— potions to tame rebellious beaux—and every kind of herb, not to mention prayers. The Prayer to San Juan Trastornador reads:

> Thou who hast the power to overcome thy wife, I conjure thee now to disturb the five senses and seven thoughts of So-and-So [here the foot is stamped three times to summon So-and-So]. By the omnipotent power of Beelzebub Artaclán . . . three infernal spirits higher than the other spirits. They must be those who will read, who will interpret the mind, the heart, and the thoughts of So-and-So, that thou wilt not let him sit down in a chair, nor sleep in a bed, nor talk with woman, married, widow, or single, until he comes to me, not fierce nor mad like a dog, but meek as a sheep at my feet. I Thus-and-So.

In Santo Domingo a prayer is said to St. Martha the Negro and the Spell of the Baron of the Cemetery is recited. Father Enrique Pérez Arbeláez in Magdalena, Colombia, has made a collection of many prayers. Among them is the Credo said backward in the church of San Juan Bautista and one addressed to St. James the Apostle, to be safe from the mayor's staff or heavier penalties, a prayer like that of the epic hero Martín Fíerro, who prayed to escape justice.

To return to Charles V: when he was informed that witch-hunts were starting in America, he dispatched Bishop Juan de Zumárraga (1468–1548) to Mexico, according to Fray Servando Teresa de Mier. The Royal Chronicler Gil González de Ávila (*c.* 1578–1658) stated that the Bishop and the Emperor had met in the convent of Abrojo near Valladolid. He sent the Bishop to Mexico because he had played a strong role in ousting the witches from Biscay. On this side of the water, Zumárraga kept seeing them everywhere; he made autos-da-fé of all the Indians' manu-scripts, such as enchantments and magic figures, and Torquemada says that he imprisoned several Indians as sorcerers in the dun-geon of San Francisco.

The defense against witchcraft was to unbind the spells, a countermagic permitted by the Church. Fray Bartolomé de las Casas gives many examples of it. On the island of Santo Domingo, rosaries made of ten of the fresh-water crabs called *yabas* were hung at the entrances of houses to frighten away moles. Mercury, "which contains within it great and marvelous forces and virtues," was effective against demons and the evil spells of necromancers. Men's urine would undo the spells of sorcerers. This was attested to by something that happened to the Blessed Aparicio, who lived in Mexico, and whose life is illustrated in a book of extraordinary engravings that can be seen in the library of the Mexican scholar Joaquín García Icazbalceta (1825–94), preserved in Austin, Texas. Each scene is a steel engraving. One night the Devil persisted in appearing so often before the holy man, tempting him, that the Blessed Aparicio rose from his bed, picked up the night jar, and emptied it over the Devil, who took himself off for good.

Fray Bartolomé lists as the first line of defense: the Cross, holy water, and naming the Holy Trinity. But he adds that there are also "things . . . found in the gamut of items created by Nature which are said to have the virtue of driving away demons and undoing the magic tricks and spells cast by sorcerers, magicians, and enchanters." Guillermo Parisiense mentions "a snake or serpent that ties or binds the hands of magicians or sorcerers in such a way that in its presence all the wonders they perform must cease." It was thought that animals could be born without the intervention of male or female, merely by virtue of a movement by Nature at the impulse of the divine powers: toads and serpents were thought to be born that way. "The heavenly bodies can, by their influences, virtues, and help, make an inextinguishable light, and this is done with art and the aid of the heavens and the stars; thus can be made a candle that cannot be snuffed out naturally either by water or wind, as St. Isidore made two candles, naturally, which stood, one at his head and the other at his feet, for two hundred years after his death." The first historian of Spanish America believed this.

¶ AMERICA'S MAGIC

The Indians had their magic, too. When Spain extended her conquests, she planted crosses and hung bells wherever she went, taught the Credo, and baptized the people en masse. Faith was like a light blanket over everything, sometimes smothering what went before, sometimes clothing it. In any case, it served to dissimulate. But what lay under the covering?

The native religions practiced throughout any large region were few. Those of the Aztecs in the center of Mexico and the

Maya in the south; that of the Incas in Peru. But in every fold
of the Andes, in every island of the West Indies, in every corner
of the jungle, there were gods. Some of the people adored the
sun, others water, others fire, always in their own way. The
Ticunas made long journeys by canoe on the Amazon, carrying
live coals, until they reached the spot where the fire festival was
being held every year. The Chibchas venerated frogs, lizards,
and serpents, which carried messages to the goddess of rain, the
mother of agriculture, as they moved from land to water and back
again. The astronomers of Peru and Mexico studied the movements of the heavenly bodies and worshipped the sun and the
moon. The Mexicans adored the plumed serpent, the eagle, the
jaguar-knight, and the god of corn. Pumas were the sacred symbols on the Sun Gate in Tiahuanacu. In the most primitive tribes,
totems that would fill a huge zoo were scattered over a continent,
a landmass several times the size of Europe.

Religious ceremonies among the Maya, the Aztecs, and the
Incas developed great elaboration and sumptuousness. The dances
and rites performed to celebrate victory were painted at Bonampak during the eighth century. They showed the headgear worn
by the devout in the form of fabulous animals and such musical
instruments as *maracas*, trumpets, and drums. The written accounts of the Conquistadors and Indians record the tragic festival
at Toxcatle with detailed accuracy that spells out how Alvarado's
soldiers treacherously put to death the priests who were perform-
ing their rites before the altar of Huitzilopochtli. The pyramids
at Teotihuacán and Palenque, the temples of Tula, Tikal, and
Petén, testify to the power of the religions that the Christians
destroyed. But the conquered gods would not stay dead. The
Indians still invoke them confusedly in a nostalgia centuries old.
They have not been happy under the rule of the whites, and they
dream of a lost paradise, the paradise in which they were free.
If despotisms existed in the old days, as they did, the tribes either
have forgotten them or would prefer them because they were
their own. Nostalgia sends the music of the Indian flute through
the air of the Incan *puna*. Magical elements live on in the minds
of the Indians, who have been humiliated and exploited in colony
and republic alike. They tell their troubles to their own gods,
mingling their own prayers with the Christians' in a kind of contraband plea that circulates clandestinely. The Indians' lie is the
custodian of their truth.

In Spain magic was a fabric woven of many strands. In

America, it existed in lonely islands. The tremendous size of the continent, which lacked any means of communication, isolated it. In the Amazon Basin there is an infinity of separate tribes, many of which still do not know one another, who have their own languages and their own gods. Some regions still do not know of the existence of the Maya, Guaraní, Aymará, or Quechua languages. Tribes remain faithful to their own totems. And to their deserts. And to the unpeopled pampas. What might be in Mexico a potent memory means nothing in Argentina or Uruguay. The Incan, Aymaran, Aztec, and Mayan dances have been reborn where they were first performed; they persist, they are performed today before the Virgin in religious processions. On the other hand, the tango, the Argentine *pericón*, and the Chilean *cueca* carry traces of Europe which were transformed in Buenos Aires, Mendoza, and Santiago, where the Indian had no share in the culture. The people of Mexico dream their dreams on pulque; those in Peru, Colombia, and Ecuador on *chicha* (corn liquor); those in Paraguay, Buenos Aires, and Montevideo on mate: those in the Antilles on tobacco. The people who drink or inhale as an unconscious ritual do not even know what was sacred about those beverages or that smoke.

The Indians had their book of Genesis: it is preserved in the pages of the *Popol Vuh* of the Maya and in other codices. The books of *Chilám Balám* contain dark prophecies that foretell the Conquest:

> *Eat, eat, you have bread;*
> *Drink, drink, you have water;*
> *On that day, dust will cover the earth;*
> *On that day, plague will cover the face of the land;*
> *On that day, a cloud will arise;*
> *On that day, a strong man will seize the country;*
> *On that day, the houses will fall in ruins;*
> *On that day, the tender leaf will be destroyed;*
> *On that day, there will be three signs on the tree;*
> *On that day, three generations will hang there;*
> *On that day, the flag of battle will be hoisted;*
> *And they [men] will be scattered afar, through the forests.*

Poems like those collected by Fray Bernardino de Sahagún still survive from Aztec poetry. *Ollantay*, a tragedy by Ricardo Rojas which recreates the Incan theater, has been staged in Europe. Even the *Yurupary*, from the unknown lands of the Vaupés in

Colombia, has been preserved. According to Javier Arango Ferrer:

> The *Yurupary* is less terse than the *Popol Vuh* of the Maya, but, in my judgment, it is no less lyrical and profound in the magical significance of its myths. Yurupary was a civilizing hero embattled against the primitive matriarchy. No one can imagine the symbolic beauty of this poem of the Vaupés jungle, which the Amazon Indian José Roberto wrote in the Ñengatú language and in Latin script at the end of the past century. Count Stradelli, an explorer of the Putumayo who was versed in the native languages, translated it into Italian and published it in the *Geographic Bulletin* of his country about 1890.

The Spaniards who saw the West Indies for the first time were amazed to discover two novelties: tobacco and the dance. The first man to write about tobacco was Columbus. The first to write about American dance was Gonzalo Fernández de Oviedo, who described the dancing of the Areyto. They sang as they danced the Areyto during the fiesta that the chronicler watched. It was presided over by Queen Anacaona, "charming and queenly in her speech and arts and movement." The dancers, some holding hands, others with arms extended, formed a line or a chorus and did whatever the one who was leading them did as she stepped forward or back, all in good order, singing, now loudly, now softly to the beat of the drums. The songs relate the events and the legends of the tribe. The Spaniards said that the things they did reminded "us of the songs and dances performed by our people in some parts of Spain to while away their working hours in the summer sun, as men and women amuse themselves with their tambourines." Four and a half centuries have gone by. Tobacco has spread all over the world from the West Indies. The Areyto is still being danced. The magic lives on.

The similarities that the Spaniards found between the dances on the island and those in Spain seem like the magical coincidences that occur in star-crossed love affairs common among the primitives of America and the peasants of Spain—or Germany. Guamán Poma de Ayala wrote a small treatise on American sorcery, the first to appear in South America. His accounts reveal little difference between the witches' sabbaths of the Indians and those of the Spanish adepts: "They are accustomed to giving one another poisons and venoms to kill with, which they call *hanpicoc*: some of them kill quickly, others slowly. . . . Some take a toad, remove the venom from its tail, and they say that they can then talk and give venom to men. Others, talking with the Devil, take the toad and sew up its mouth and eyes with thorns, and tie its feet and hands, then bury it in a hole near where their enemy lives or the one they wish evil to, so that he may suffer and die. The toad does not die there, but he suffers, and they keep and breed toads and serpents for this purpose." On higher levels, the Indians' version of the great scourges afflicting humanity correspond to passages in the Bible. There are widespread versions of the Flood, of the worship of the virgin mother, and of the coming of a bearded prophet who foretells the future fate of the people.

Some hallucinatory drugs are native to America. Marijuana (hemp, *Cannabis Sativa*) has bridged the distance between Asia and the New World; it probably came from southwest China or Tibet via India, and its present-day use as a drug in the Americas is thought to have begun in Mexico, although hemp, as a fiber plant, was introduced into Chile in about 1545. The coca leaf, as cocaine, has traveled all over the world from Peru. The medicine of the Guaranís and Incas was first described by the botanical study missions of the eighteenth century. Medicine men always have practiced on every level: to cure disease or lovesickness, or to cause death. They cast their spells to rid cattle of worms or to treat other domestic animals. The Augustinian monk Antonio de la Calancha discovered a university for sorcerers in Upper Peru: such universities were the medical schools in the days of magic. The Negroes had one in Tolú, where the air was filled with the aroma that now pervades pharmacies.

¶ AFRICAN MAGIC

The Negro arrived in America after the Indian and the white man. The white man became the master; the Indian the ward of the white man, the Negro his slave. Fray Bartolomé de las Casas pleaded for the importation of Negroes from Africa to spare the Indians from slavery. The market he opened by his words surpassed all expectations. Europeans hunted or bought Negroes in Dahomey, the Congo, the Sudan, and elsewhere in Africa, loaded their captives on slave ships, and set sail for America. Europe enslaved Africa; America later gave her back her freedom. Africa suffered the greatest hemorrhage in history, it has been said. Some people believe that sixty million Negroes were taken away; others say a hundred and fifty million. Halwachs (as quoted by René Dumont) states that a fifth of the human race was living in Africa in the seventeenth century. In fifty years, two million two hundred thousand Negroes were taken to the island of Santo Domingo (Hispaniola) alone, of whom only six hundred thousand were left in 1764. Dumont comments:

> In exchange for the slaves, the raw rubber, the ivory, the gold, and other "sundry riches," Europe introduced into Africa glass beads, breechclouts, trinkets, and tobacco, gunpowder and fire arms, and—the crime of all crimes—alcohol. "From the first contact of the Europeans with the African coast," Captain Meyner says, "alcohol held a special place in the merchandise for trade. When the king of Abyssinia ceded his territory to Louis Philippe in 1843, he received in exchange, among other things, six shipments of rum of two hundred liters each, and four cases of Liqueurs."

Melville J. Herskovits (1895–) wrote: "Africa's contribution to the population of the New World is much more important than is generally thought. Those who carry African blood in their veins add up to some forty million. A tenth part of the population of the United States falls within this category." The history that carries the Negroes on its back casts a great shadow over the continent. They have tried to safeguard themselves with magic, music, and dancing. When the Negro population of a certain region reached a certain density, the people formed their own nations. They reproduced the map of their Africa in miniature. Some were Mandingos, others Congolese, and so on. The "nations" survived in Buenos Aires in 1870. In Cuba they still survive. The Cuban Fernando Ortiz (1881–), who fathered Afro-Cuban studies, has traced the history of Negro secret societies, nation by nation, and he documents the persistence of their rites, initiations, and dances; he has followed the legends of the drums and all other musical instruments. Negro music has spread widely. The *candombé* was danced in the parlors of Buenos Aires during the past century. In our own time, dances such as the rumba, the samba, the conga, the merecumbé, cumbia, and mambo are danced everywhere—to the beat of Negro jazz.

St. Peter Claver (1580–1654), the "Apostle of the Negroes," said: "Witchcraft seems to be the oppressed slave's irrational defense against those who subjugate him." In the background of the work done by the "Apostle," who wished to be, and was, a slave to slaves, were the witches of Tolú. Dr. Gaspar Navarro's well-documented book arrived in Cartagena with the Inquistor Juan de Mañozca. It was a summation of Spanish witchcraft which Mariano Picón-Salas regarded as authentic. It was called *A Tribunal of Crafty Superstition, Explorer of the Knowledge, Shrewdness, and Power of the Demon, Condemning What Is Generally Considered Good in Spells, Auguries, Vain Quacks, Curses, Conjures, the Notorious, Cabalistic, and Pauline Arts.* Mañozca filled the prisons of the Inquisitions with witches, but the Devil managed to get in, too. Before long, the witches were pregnant. Picón-Salas wrote:

> The witches came from Tolú, a sort of Devil's capital in New Granada. From the balsam trees that waft their marvelous scent through the tropical forests, they take off for their aerial wanderings over seas, valleys, and cordilleras. As the testimony substantiated by Mañozca reveals, they dance around a goat, kiss its rump, and fly around bleating like kids, with torches in their hands. . . . Whenever people meet near the forests of Tolú, they recall the evil that must have been done there, such as crippling or maiming grown men, strangling babies, cutting down and destroying the fruits of the earth, and hindering the mining of gold. [The witches] anoint themselves with an unguent made from a toad and certain herbs; they fly high above the sky; they foretell future events and divine occult things; they constrict or impede men in the act of generation, and make them and the women fertile by sorcery.

Witchcraft may rise above such baseness, however, and enter the sphere of the heroic. In all Latin America, Haiti was the first colony to gain its independence. The scenes accompanying the rebellion of the slaves often were barbarous. Mackandal, who allegedly could talk with the Devil and knew where and when drums were being beaten, was a cripple, which made him all the more eloquent as an agitator. He planned to end the power of the whites before the English colonies dreamed of independence. Forty years before the French Revolution, he tried to transfer power to the Negroes—that is, to the people. The Negroes gathered for voodoo at the sound of the drum, and Mackandal would then intone a fierce hymn in Creole which brought forth an hysterical howl of joy:

> *Bon Dieu, qui fait le soleil,*
> *qui claire nous en hau,*
> *qui soulève la mer,*
> *qui fait l'orage gronder . . .*
> *Jetez portraits Dieu Blanc*
> *qui soif d'l'eau dans yeux nous*
> *coutez la liberté qui nan coeu a nous tous! . . .*[1]

Mackandal's plan was to poison the wells and carve up the white people as a means of doing away with the lash and slavery, and to burn the houses on the estates. The blaze never amounted to much: the authorities burned Mackandal first. Then came the French Revolution and the island trembled to the rites of voodoo. On the night of the August 14, 1791, the most fabulous operation in magic took place. All the Negroes from leagues roundabout answered the summons of the big drum and their song was a radical shout of rebellion:

> *Eh! Eh! Bomba, ben! Hen!*
> *Canga cafio te*
> *Canga Moune dele*
> *Canga doki la*
> *Canga li. . . .*

"Canga, canga, canga" ("Kill, kill, kill") . . . and the mob hurtled into the night swinging machetes that gleamed red from the flames of the night fire and immediately became redder with blood. As we learned in Chapter XVIII, Pierre Dominique Toussaint, later known as "L'Ouverture"—"the Opener," the former coachman of M. Bayon de Libertat, led the revolution. He made Haiti independent of France and became president for life. Negro monarchs came after him, and a nation inwardly maddened by voodoo emerged. When Bolívar was defeated early in the war for independence and wandered through the West Indies in search of some means to invade Venezuela via the Orinoco, Alexandre Sabès Pétion (1770–1818), then ruling in Port-au-Prince, lent

---

[1] Dear God, who makes the sun
  To shine on us from above
  Who makes the sea to rage,
  Who makes the storm to moan,
  Show us Thy face, white God,
  Who thirsts for the tears from our eyes
  Grant us the freedom we all carry in our hearts! . . .

him support, and with that magical aid the Venezuelan liberator was able to begin his war again.

Negro witchcraft was a power in Cuba while it was a colony and after it became a republic. The art of the *mayomberos*—graduate magicians—has been employed both to kill snakes and to wish death to the Yankees. The Feast of the Magi was the great holiday in Havana because one of the three Magi was the Negro Melchior. The masters gave the slaves Christmas and New Year gifts of money, which they spent on rum and masquerades. A Frenchman who visited Havana during the past century wrote:

> The Day of the Magi is the Negroes' day. Besides the Christmas and New Year's gifts from their masters, they collect more by begging at the doors of the leading houses. From one end of the city to the other, craftsmen, laborers, and servants gather in separate groups around a Negro who represents the chief of the tribe. The African population comes from different races, all living under the same yoke, but keeping their distinct racial characteristics and customs. Here are the Negroes from the Congo, generally lazy, bad, fond of rum, mad about music and dancing; the Lucumis, haughty and proud; the Macuas from the Mozambique Coast, indolent, sweet, and peaceful by nature; the Carabalis from the West Coast of Africa, niggardly, industrious, and often turbulent; the Minas, with stupid faces; the Araras, without character or energy; the Mandingos, docile and honest. On the Day of the Magi, each tribe appears in Havana in its native dress and with its own musical instruments. . . . The chiefs are splendid. Some move along on tall stilts. . . . Some wear castles of feathers on their heads, a whole forest of artificial fronds. . . Some paint their faces like birds of prey.

Dancing followed the parade, ending with the cobra dance. The Negroes made an artificial boa constrictor that moved in the parade like the dragon in Chinese processions, and burned it later in the palace courtyard during a frenetic dance that ended with the chant:

> *The serpent is dead,*
> *Sángala muleque.*

According to Fernando Ortiz, this rite comes from a celebration held annually in Dahomey, where the serpent is paraded through the streets of Whydah. The magical connotations of the serpent are worldwide. If charmed, it helps to divine; if offended, it bites. The Havana boa, so closely associated with the Negroes, is brother to Python, the sacred serpent of Delphi, the shrine presided over by the Pythia, a seeress, because of whom familiar spirits were named pythonesses. America has its benevolent serpents kept as domestic animals to cleanse the house and its deadly reptiles such as the rattlesnake. The Ecuadorian Adalberto Ortiz (1914–   ) tells in his novel *Juyungo*, how the *rabo e'queso* (rattlesnake) is charmed:

> They did not dance the conga, nor the samba, nor the bomba, caramba! The Negro woman and the *zamba* [daughter of a Chinese and an Indian] raised their arms and strutted up to the bench with a supple roll of their hips, hot to the fruitful touch. They twisted from their waist and hips, turning, running, calling to the men. They sweated to the beat of the big drum, to the rocking rolling of the *cununos*. And the Devil came forth, it's the truth. And the beat of the palm-wood marimba went on and on and was lost in the jungle. Marimba upon marimba. Drums, and more drums, and more drums; beat, beat, beat, beat, beat, beat, beat.

Evidently a prose-writer does not easily escape the rhythmic beat of the dance as he describes it, as frequently happens in all the literature written for the ear. Nicolás Guillén (1904–   ) has been particularly successful in catching these sounds. He takes the serpent as a subject from what the Negroes of Cuba and Venezuela say, and shapes it into a poem. They are trying to kill the snake:

> *Mayombe-bombe-mayombé!*
> *Mayombe-bombe-mayombé!*
> *Mayombe-bombe-mayombé!*
> *The serpent has eyes of glass*
> *The serpent comes; he twines around a tree*
> *With his eyes of glass on a tree,*
> *With his eyes of glass*
> *The serpent moves along without feet;*
> *The serpent hides his color in the grass.*

> *Moving, he hides in the grass,*
> *Moving without feet!*
> *Mayombe-bombe-mayombé!*
> *You hit him with the ax and he dies;*
> *Hit him now!*
> *Don't stamp him with your foot or he'll bite,*
> *Don't hit him with your foot or he'll move away!*

To follow the penetration of black magic throughout Latin America is a job for specialists. Since the time of Sor Juana Inés de la Cruz, poetry has profited from it. The poetry based on speech and sound culminated with Candelario Obeso (1840–86), a Colombian Negro of the past century who composed verses of great delicacy from the sounds made by oarsmen on the Magdalena River. His poetry is better than that of the famous Cuban mulatto Gabriel de la Concepción Valdés (1809–44), known as "Plácido," to whom the Negro theme is quite incidental. In our century, the Afro-American ingredient in poetry, the novel, the short story, and the theater has acquired extraordinary importance. The idea of bewitchment by the magical words of the *mayomberos*, as expressed by Nicolás Guillén, was first introduced into Spanish poetry by the Puerto Rican poet Luis Pales Matos (1898–1959). His book *Tuntún de pasa y grifería* (*Boomdelay of the Nappy and Kinky-Haired*) was acclaimed in 1937. The Negro dance it contains begins thus:

> *Calabó and Bambú*
> *Bambú and calabó*
> *The Big Cocoroco[1] says: tu-cu-tú.*
> *The Big Cocoroco says: to-co-tó.*
> *It's the iron sun that burns in Timbuctu.*
> *It's the Negro Dance of Fernando Po.*
> *The pig in his wallow grunts: pru-pru-prú.*
> *The toad in the puddle dreams: cro-cro-cró.*
> *Calabó and Bambú*
> *Calabó and Bambú.*

Black magic has the virtue of tying together the literatures of the Caribbean, in which French, English, Dutch, Papiamento, and Creole voices blend with Castilian and African, always lamenting the lack of freedom, uttering revolutionary intentions and rallying cries, and nostalgically sighing for Africa or accusing

---

[1] The Gran Cocoroco or Big Crocodile, sometimes a totemistic African demigod like Mumbo Jumbo; a grotesque, punishing deity.

the Yankees. Afro-West Indian revues and plays have been fostered. Research studies, such as those begun by Fernando Ortiz, were carried on by hard-working successors such as Lydia Cabrera (1900–   ). Through a series of interviews with sorcerers and *mayomberos*, she has been able to establish that they are seeking intimate relations with spiritualism or the Catholic religion. She asserts:

> The sub-religion, or extra-official religion of Cuba, on the fringe of the Catholic and on good terms with it, is the Lucumí or Yoruba religion solidly established in the provinces of Pinar del Río, Havana, Matanzas, and Santa Clara; it includes in its group the followers of the Arará Dahomey Rule, which, in its turn, must not be confused with the Mayombé, the everyday magic of the Congo.

Let us quote this fragment from Lydia Cabrera's experiences:

> I shall record here the first time that I saw, with stupefaction—even, I confess with fear—a mulatto woman who must have weighed more than two hundred pounds fall to the ground, stiff, at the beating of the drums for *chango*. She hit the base of her head a blow that seemed to me mortal. In the throes of a seizure, she kept pounding her head violently. Later she got up and gambolled like a lamb! Frankly, I could not understand how that corpulent woman, who seemed so impeded by excessive fat, so quiet or indifferent until that moment, had not killed herself by fracturing her skull. "That's nothing," people said. "She's just got a very fierce *chango*." On that occasion I had the feeling that I was indeed seeing *chango* danced.

Such things can be seen on a much larger scale in the *macumbas* of Rio de Janeiro and Bahia. The *macumberos* hold their ceremonies regularly on the hills inside the city limits of Rio de Janeiro, and they consummate their nuptials with the sea on the beaches of Copacabana. José Madeiros of the review *O Cruzeiro* was able to make a complete photographic documentation of the initiation ceremonies, from the first preparatory operations performed on the initiate to the consecration, when the blood of a duck was poured over his shaved head and a great ceremony and ritual banquet were held. I myself have seen a collection of images taken from Catholic churches in a cellar under the yard where the *macumba* is celebrated in Rio. In Brazil the *macumba* is more open than the African ceremonies in Cuba. Tourists may attend the ceremonies in Rio de Janeiro. Both the officiators and the faithful have some white blood. Sometimes most of them are at least partially white, for the *macumba* has sunk deep into the nation's life.

Sociological and anthropological studies on Brazil are very advanced. A school of Afro-Brazilian research has grown up, with Arthur Ramos as its former leader. His *Introdução a Antropología Brasileira* is basic to the study of the non-European cultures of Brazil and of the contacts between European cultures and the indigenous races and cultures of Brazil.

¶ THE SUMMA MAGIC

The magic elements of Negro, Indian, Sicilian, Gypsy, and Chinese, of spiritualism, theosophy, and the remnants of the Spanish witches' sabbaths, keep moving constantly; they crisscross like the races, and even penetrate the Catholic religion. They make a potent cocktail, a blend, a linkage that pervades everyday life, appears surprisingly in folk lore, infects political life, fills the pages of novels, gives poetry its meter and music its beat. During carnival time in Montevideo, the Lubola masquerade, created by the Society of Lubola Negroes, retains its original vigor in the second half of the twentieth century, although the colored population of the city now is sparse. Those who join in the masquerade have taken part in the dances and burlesques with names that mark the roads followed by folk lore: The Liberators of Africa; the Humble Congolese, the Cubans, the Sons of Cuba, the Liberators of Havana, the Cuban Race. The *candombé* danced in Buenos Aires during the past century is still performed in Montevideo.

In the Pentecostal Churches of New York, there are paintings of the life of the Virgin taken from the Catholic creed, psalms are read as in the Protestant services, and the congregation sings to the accompaniment of guitars and drums with a conga or samba beat. Suddenly everyone will begin to sing a psalm at the top of his voice, an excerpt from the Book of David set to the Brazilian Carnival music of *Mama, eu Quero* (*Mama, I Want*). The whole group works itself up to a collective hysteria, and the congregation begins to leap and dance as frenetically as in a voodoo meeting. The congregation that does those things is composed of Puerto Ricans brought up in the Catholic faith and living in the monstrous hell that they encounter in New York. In the novel *Canaima*, Rómulo Gallegos explains through the character Marcos Vargas the need felt by the people of America at certain moments of their lives to rid themselves of everything they can find within them of conventionality, of civilization, and to plunge into the jungle, fling themselves head first into the world of magic. Count Giaffaro, an Italian living in the jungles of Guarumpín, formulates the urge in a conversation with Marcos Vargas:

> Believe me, you have to watch out for periodical cures effected through human intimacy; be careful about opening the escape valves to the indecencies that keep accumulating in your soul, and make sure they don't end by intoxicating us completely. For this purpose, boy, there's nothing like the jungle. . . . You treat your soul like a boiler full of steam, keep your eye on the gauges that register the pressure, and when you notice that the boiler is in danger of bursting, turn off the pressure without any false scruples, and open the safety valve to the shout of *Canaima*. And let who will get lost in conjecture as to what the warning whistles mean, and so be done with it.

In the world that sustains the debate between wealth and poverty, between God and the Devil, the unhappy mortal must live with his anxieties trembling in the balance. Tomás Carrasquilla paints the most finished picture of Negro witchcraft practiced in the heart of the most Catholic country of America; in the Antioquia Mountains of Colombia, the crossroads of the witches:

> Their articles of faith do not begin with a breakaway from Catholic beliefs; they enclose them in their own religion. Was there not a dogma on the existence of the Devil? Well, then, all those wicked adepts of the black arts, whether from the country or the city, were Satan's special agents, sent to disturb souls and see to it that they were lost completely. And if to make pacts with Satan and to negotiate with him was a sin, it might be wrong to believe in his agents and their snares, to. . . . Doña Bárbara, more superstitious than they, for she was young and a woman, offset those fears of demoniacal things and persons merely by her trust in the divine.

548 LATIN AMERICA: *A Cultural History*

Doña Bárbara, so named by necessity and coincidence, as in the Gallegos novel, was a real woman in Carrasquilla's work. She placed the Devil in front of her on the one side and the Virgin of Pilar, St. Justa, and St. Rufina on the other side. In the background, the Illusions move through the jungle, on their way to whisper ugly and sinful secrets into the ears of innocents; One-Leg, too, who came out of the wilderness in three strides, broke through barricades, knocked down roofs with his single hoof enlarged like that of the Gadarene swine; Cloven Hoof, a giant who had only one flesh and blood leg and who fitted a piece of bamboo to the stump of his other thigh and filled it with pestilential liquids. . . .

The Abakuá African Society of Havana has identified the Christian divinities with the African. The patron saint of Cuba is Oshun, the Virgin of Copper, and the patroness of Havana harbor is Yemaya, the Virgin of the Courses. The great warlock of the Abakuás was the son of a Frenchman. His name was Andrés Facundo Cristo de los Dolores Petit. He knew Latin and Greek, lived in the convent of St. Francis, and gave away images of Christ that had been charged with magic. Petit went to Rome, according to legend, talked with the Pope and the cardinals, sat at their table, and traveled on to the Mount of Olives. There he cut an olive branch to signify a pledge. A Kimbisa Negro told Lydia Cabrera this story of the mystical beginnings of the Rule of Santo Cristo del Buen Viaje (Holy Christ of the Good Voyage), which Petit founded. He said: "All religions are good, and the more they are practiced, the better they are." Petit belonged to them all, and that was the basis of the Institución de Santo Cristo del Buen Viaje. A fusion of all faiths and cults. Of the material with the spiritual. Nganga, nkisi, orisha, Catholicism, spiritualism, etc.

¶ MAGIC, DREAM, AND POETRY

Communism has made its way among the common people of Latin America not by its materialistic interpretation of history but by its mystique, its secrecy, by its plans covering many years, by its magical numbers. *Caudillismo* depends upon the "prestigious," as Fray Bartolomé de las Casas explained. He cites St. Isidore's *Etymologies* when he says:

Prestidigitation is a deception or tricking of the senses, according to St. Isidore and according to Alexander of Allis, sleight-of-hand is a diabolical art that deceives men, so that they may not see what is true but believe true what is not; or, according to others, sleight-of-hand is a trick of the Devil for no other purpose than to transmute the object, as it does not lose its shape or its entity except to the person who is tricked; when they are perturbed, they trick themselves, and consequently cause their mental judgment and reason to be deceived; it is called prestidigitation because it binds and compresses the senses so they may not feel or see or hear or taste or touch things as they are except as though they were other things, and thus it is a deception of the senses.

Before Raúl Roa (1907–   ) started to work for Fidel Castro's prestige, he commented enthusiastically on the work of the famous Cuban historian and politician Manuel Sanguily (1848–1925) and was an implacable foe of the magical concept of the *caudillo*. Later he accepted it. The *caudillo* is an American phenomenon, whether in the barbarian phase of the nineteenth century or in the better-calculated despotism of the twentieth century. As Graça Aranha says of Brazil, it is "a state of bewitchment in which reality fades away and is transformed into mirages." Manuel Estrada Cabrera (1857–1924), a famous military despot of Guatemala (1898–1920), consulted sorcerers regularly and spent long hours in meditation in front of a mirror wearing the habit of a Dominican monk. Maximiliano Hernández Martínez (1822–   ), a theosophist and healer who seized the government of El Salvador (1931–44), was able to maintain his prestige partly because he kept a medicine chest filled with colored waters that he claimed would cure rheumatism, cancer, and heart disease. Perón exploited the charisma of his wife, Evita (1919-52), who was regarded by the common people of Buenos Aires and Paraguay as a saint. Candles were burned before her image. The dictator of Colombia (1953–57), Gustavo Rojas Pinilla (1900–   ) used to distribute a portrait of himself that had a Sacred Heart in the center, thus imitating Gabriel García Moreno of the preceding century (whose "relics" were stolen from the Vatican, for unknown reasons, late in 1965). If an anthology were made of the speeches delivered by the major despots of America, it would demonstrate that they all made optimum use of Divine Providence as the source of earthly power.

After all, magic is magic! The dark depths in which its ingredients ferment may be found on every continent and in every period of history. Today there is as much magic in the air of Europe, Asia, Africa, and Latin America as in the heyday of witchcraft. But there are other flights of magic, nobler in origin, which cast the musical spell of a poetic imagination, and they achieve their effects merely by loosening the tie of raw reality—on the assumption that man is a rational being—and something more. The knowledge of Latin America in the world of literature and art moves forward partly through magic, which enlaces the European culture with that of the Western hemisphere. After all, reason counts for little in the evocation of the emotions. One of the happy circumstances that has smoothed the way of Jorge Luis Borges in Europe has been his fabulous invention of unrealities. When Borges defines the "Aleph," a usage of his own invention, as a "small, iridescent sphere of almost unbearable brilliance," he calls up a picture of a laboratory in Buenos Aires like the workshop of Dr. Faustus. "The diameter of the Aleph would be two or three centimeters, but it holds cosmic space without any diminution of its size. Each thing (the glass of the mirror, let us say) was infinite things." With such tools as these, Borges set forth to conquer Europe, and discovered the Europe of the magical arts transfigured in the philter of America. Perhaps all the magics take on new dimensions in the New World. Being new is bound to be of some use, as a mere field for experimentation if nothing more. And let it never be forgotten: in the beginning, everything was chaos.

Chronological Table

THE FOLLOWING TABLES WILL SERVE
AS GUIDES AND REFERENCES TO THE
MATERIAL TREATED IN EACH CHAPTER

CHAPTER I: AMERICA'S OLD WORLD

NEW WORLD CHRONOLOGY

5000 B.C. The first signs of corn found in Puebla, Mexico.

2500 B.C. An agrarian society begins in Huaca, Peru.

1500 B.C. El Arbolito civilization in the Valley of Mexico.

900 B.C. Beginning of Mayan civilization. Tlatilco civilization. Pottery of fair women (Mexico).

800–350 B.C. Zenith of Las Ventas.

700 B.C. Great textile art in Peru.

500 B.C. Oldest gold metallurgy in Peru.

400 B.C. Polychrome pottery south of Peru.

300 B.C. Necropolis of Paracas, Peru.

200 B.C.–A.D. 800 The Toltecs set their capital in Teotihuacán.

100 B.C. Civilization of Monte Albán, Oaxaca.

1000 B.C.–A.D. 1521 Civilization on the Pacific coast of Mexico.

A.D. 300 Teotihuacán I, Mexico.

CONTEMPORARY WORLD CHRONOLOGY

3238 B.C. Egypt's prehistoric period ends as the first dynasty begins.

2000 B.C. The first Aegean civilization flowers on Crete.

1400 B.C.–1000 B.C. The Hellenes established on the Peloponnesus, Alba Longa, the capital of Latium, at its zenith.

793 B.C. Founding of Rome.

700 B.C. Homer.

509 B.C. Etruscans expelled from Rome.

467–428 B.C. Age of Pericles in Athens.

429–347 B.C. Plato.

384–322 B.C. Aristotle.

146 B.C. Destruction of Carthage.

49 B.C. Caesar crosses the Rubicon.

A.D. 117–217 Roman Temples built in Baalbek, Lebanon.

A.D. 330 Byzantium capital of an empire.

349 Constantine orders the first Vatican basilica built.

406 The Vandals occupy southwestern Spain.

NEW WORLD CHRONOLOGY
continued

CONTEMPORARY WORLD
CHRONOLOGY *continued*

A.D. 300 Development of gold, silver, copper metallurgy, Moche civilization in Peru.

328 Temple of Uaxactún, oldest discovered in the Mayan region.

400 Classical Teotihuacán.

416 First recorded date of Tikal, largest city in the Mayan Empire.

500–1000 Rise and fall of Tiahuanacu (Upper Peru).

666–829 Teotihuacán II, construction of pyramids and Temple of Quetzalcoatl.

692 Probable date of the Bonampak frescoes.

711–756 Copán Temple with the hieroglyphic staircase.

771 Morning Star Temple consecrated in Tikal (Mexico).

856–1168 Great period of the city of Teotihuacán.

987–1194 Mayapán League, Mayan Empire.

1299–1351 Founding of Tenochtitlán, the Aztec capital.

1300 Beginning of the Incan Empire.

1418–72 Netzahualcóyotl, the poet-king.

1440–1532 Inca Empire's period of greatness.

1440–1519 Apogee of the Aztec Empire.

1469–81 The Aztec calendar stone sculptured in the period of Axayacatl.

456 The Visigoths occupy southern Spain.

585 The Visigoths occupy entire Iberian Peninsula.

713 Caliph of Damascus becomes ruler of Toledo.

714 Zaragoza falls to the Arabs.

800 Charlemagne crowned Emperor in Rome.

827 First Anglo-Saxon king, Egbert, crowned king of England.

1094 Kingdom of Portugal (occupied by the Visigoths 584–712, and by the Moors 712–c. 1000) united with Castile.

1271–95 Marco Polo visits the Orient.

1333–1407 Alhambra Palace and Mosque.

1397–1482 Paolo dal Pozzo Toscanelli.

1434 Brunelleschi completes the dome of the Florence cathedral.

1435 Cosimo de' Medici initiates the Mediçean era in Florence.

1471 Portuguese ships cross the Equator.

CHAPTER II: THE AMERICA OF 1500

WHO WAS RULING IN 1500

Pope Alexander VI; Louis XII of France; Maximilan I of Austria; Ivan III (the Great) of Russia; John I of Poland. Bajazet II of Turkey;

Henry VIII of England; Philip the Handsome, Duke of Burgundy and ruling in Flanders; Ferdinand and Isabella of Aragon, Castile, and León; Frederick the Bastard, King of the Two Sicilies; Manuel I (the Fortunate) of Portugal; John (Hans) of Norway and Denmark. Ahuitzotl (1486–1503), Emperor of the Aztecs; Huayna Capac (1450?–1525), Emperor of the Incas.

EVENTS OF 1500
Machiavelli ambassador from Florence to King Louis XII of France—Fra Giovanni Giocondo of Verona begins the construction of the Bridge of Notre Dame in Paris—Cesare Borgia enters Rome in triumph after seizing Forlì—Columbus returns to Spain in chains—The Florentines lay siege to Pisa—Pedro Álvarez de Cabral arrives in Brazil—Michelangelo is commissioned to sculpture David and Goliath after completing the Pietà.

POPULATION OF VARIOUS EUROPEAN CITIES ABOUT 1500
Paris, 260,000 in 1553; Rome, 40,000; Naples, 110,000; Toledo 200,000 (1550); Lisbon 65,000 (1550); Genoa 50,000 (1550); Florence 59,000 (1561); London 100,000 (1568); Madrid 5,000 (1530). Total population of Spain about 1500 was 9,800,000.

CHAPTER III: WHAT THE SPANIARDS BROUGHT TO AMERICA

1493 On his second voyage, Columbus brings sugar cane, horses, donkeys, oxen, mules, and pigs to Santo Domingo, as well as mirrors, glass beads, and cloth used in barter.

1497 Columbus brings samples of corn back to Spain.

1497 Arrangements are made for Columbus to take to the Antilles wheat and barley seed, pickaxes, hoes, picks, stone hammers, crowbars, mill parts, cows, mares, and mules.

1505 The silkworm is introduced into Spain.

1514 Pedrarias Dávila brings vegetable seeds to Darién.

1514 Oviedo learns that oranges are being grown in Hispaniola.

1516 Peter Martyr refers to caucho in De Orbe Novo; Sahagún, Oviedo, Herrera, and Torquemada mention this plant in their books on America.

1520 Live plants, shoots, or seeds of almond, fig, cherry, pomegranate, and quince trees are sent from Spain.

1530 A planting of corn is recorded in Ávila.

1531 Grapevines and olive trees are prepared to be sent to Mexico.

1531 Francisco Pizarro brings pigs to Peru.

1535 Inés Suárez cultivates the first wheat planting in Lima.

1536 Pedro de Mendoza carries wheat to the Río de la Plata.

1538 Horses, burros, chickens, pigs, and dogs arrive in Sabana de Bogotá with Quesada, Belalcázar, and Federmann.

1559 The botanist Francisco Hernández de Toledo takes back to Spain the first tobacco seeds.

1560 Jean Nicotin, French ambassador to Portugal, sends Francis II and Catherine de' Medici tobacco seeds.

1580 The Spaniards carry the potato to Spain. It is introduced into France under Louis XVI by Parmentier, who makes it fashionable in the court.

1736 La Condamine sends the first specimens of *hevea*, the raw rubber tree, from Ecuador.

1876 Wickham, an Englishman, smuggles 70,000 *caucho* seeds out of Brazil to be taken from London to Ceylon. Eighty years later millions of acres are covered with descendants of those seeds.

CHAPTER IV: THE BIRTH OF A LITERATURE

1228 Marco Polo, a Venetian, dictates in prison *The Million*, an account of his voyage to the Orient.

1492 Christopher Columbus, a Genoese, writes the first pages of Spanish American literature in his diary.

1500 Pedro Vaz de Caminha, a Portuguese, writes the first page of Luso-American literature.

1500–4 Amerigo Vespucci, a Florentine, writes letters on his voyage in Italian.

1523 Antonio Pigafetta, a Venetian, writes the *Primo Viaggio intorno al Mondo*.

1528 Giovanni da Verrazano, a Florentine, writes in French to the king of France, reporting his voyage to North America.

CHAPTER V: DON QUIXOTE AND THE CONQUEST OF AMERICA

1372 Jean de Mandeville dies, leaving his book of fabulous tales of voyages to the Levant, East Indies, Arabia, and the Near East.

1498 Columbus reaches the site of the Earthly Paradise (Venezuela).

1499 Vespucci lands on the Island of Giants (Curaçao).

1508 García Ordóñez de Montalvo publishes *Amadís de Gaula* in Zaragoza.

1510 *Las Sergas de Esplandián*, by Ordóñez de Montalvo, is published in Seville.

1513 Juan Ponce de León sails for Florida in search of the Fountain of Youth.

1519 Gonzalo Fernández de Oviedo publishes *Claribalde*, a novel of chivalry.

1519 Hernán Cortés glimpses the city of Tenochtitlán, which seems to "emerge from a story of *Amadís*."

1520 Magellan finds men with enormous feet (the Patagonians) in the South.

1522 Cristóbal de Olid believes he has come to the Amazons' island, where California reigns, "to the right of the Indies . . . very near the Earthly Paradise."

1529 Ambrosio de Alfinger, a German governor of Venezuela, leaves Coro in search of El Dorado.

1530 Nikolaus Federmann, a German, finds the country of the pygmies, the "Aymanes," six hands tall, in Venezuela.

1533 The *Audiencia* of Santo Domingo authorizes an expedition to look for El Dorado.

1536 Jiménez de Quesada leaves Santa Marta to conquer El Dorado.

1538 Sebastián de Belalcázar leaves Popayán for the kingdom of the Chibchas, where El Dorado was said to be.

1539 Gonzalo Pizarro and Francisco de Orellana leave Quito in search of El Dorado and the Land of Cinnamon. Orellana reaches the country of the Amazons.

1543 Fernández de Oviedo writes to Pietro Bembo concerning the existence of the Amazons in the New World.

1584 Antonio de Berrío, governor of the Orinoco, sets forth in search of El Dorado.

1617 Sir Walter Raleigh obtains his release from the Tower of London to head an expedition to conquer El Dorado (on the Orinoco).

CHAPTER VI: GREEN BRAZIL

1484 Columbus appears before João II of Portugal and solicits ships and men for a voyage to the west. His plan is rejected.

1493 Pope Alexander VI issues the Bull that fixes the Line of Demarcation at a hundred leagues west of the Azores. He grants the Portuguese all lands they may discover east of that line, the Spaniards all lands west of it.

1494 The Treaty of Tordesillas moves farther west the line drawn by Alexander's Bull.

1497 Vasco da Gama rounds the Cape of Good Hope.

1499 Amerigo Vespucci discovers the coast of Brazil.

1500 Pedro Álvarez de Cabral touches the Brazilian Coast. Pedro Vaz Caminha, who accompanies him, writes a description of the land in Portuguese.

1500 July 28, Vespucci writes his letter on the coast of Brazil to Lorenzo di Pier Francesco de' Medici.

1505 Francisco de Almeida appointed Portuguese viceroy of India.

1515 Portuguese ships arrive in Japan.

1531 The first sugar mill is built in Brazil.

1532 Duarte Coelho begins the systematic colonization of Brazil with one of the two captaincies granted by the Crown. In 1534 he founds the city of Olinda.

1548 The slave trade begins.

1549 Tomé de Souza, governor general, brings the first six Jesuits to Brazil (Bahia). Founding of Salvador de Bahia.

1554 The Jesuits establish their secondary school in São Paulo and the city grows around it.

1555 The French knight Nicolas Durand de Villegaignon settles on the island of Coligny, named for Admiral Coligny, in the Bay of Guabanara and calls himself "Rex Americae."

1557 Calvin sends a selected group of Huguenots to reinforce Villegaignon.

1567 Villegaignon returns to France.

1580–1641 Portugal is ruled by the King of Spain.

1567 Rio de Janeiro is founded.

1604 Paul van Caarden, a Dutch pirate, tries to seize Bahia.

1617 Governor Luis de Sousa transfers the capital to Pernambuco.

1621 The Dutch West Indies Company is founded.

1624 Dutch ships land in Bahia.

1625 The Portuguese-Spanish fleet expels the Dutch from Bahia.

1635 The Dutch West Indies Company captures Recife and founds a colony that lasts twenty years.

1637 Maurice of Nassau governs New Holland. The painter Franz Post, the theologian-poet Francis Pante, the Humanist Elias Herchmans, Dr. Willem van Milaem, and the naturalist Willem Piso accompany him.

1640 The Jesuit Antônio Vieira delivers his famous sermon attacking the Dutch.

1700 Word of mines in the interior of Brazil spreads.

1717 The colony becomes a viceroyalty.

1727 Governor Maia da Gama sends Sergeant De Melo Palheta to Guiana to obtain some coffee plants.

1763 The capital moves from Bahia to Rio de Janeiro.

CHAPTER VII: THE SPANISH COLONIES

THE FIVE VICEROYALTIES—*Founding dates*

1509 Viceroyalty of Santo Domingo (ended in 1526 with the death of Diego Columbus, the only viceroy).

1534 Viceroyalty of New Spain.

1543 Viceroyalty of Peru.

1717 Viceroyalty of New Granada (abolished in 1724, restored in 1740).

1776 Viceroyalty of the Río de la Plata.

FOUNDING OF CITIES

1493–4 (La) Isabela, Hispaniola (abandoned shortly afterwards)
1496 Santo Domingo
1508 San Juan, Puerto Rico
1514 Santiago, Cuba
1515 Havana
1519 Veracruz
1521 Panamá
1521 Tenochtitlán becomes capital of New Spain
1524 Guatemala (Antigua)
1525 León, Nicaragua
1525 Granada, Nicaragua
1525 San Salvador
1525 Santa Marta
1527 Coro
1531 Puebla de los Ángeles
1533 Cartagena
1533 Guadalajara
1534 Quito

1535 Lima
1535 Guayaquil
1536 Buenos Aires (first founding did not last and the city was founded the second time in 1580)
1537 Asunción, Paraguay
1538 Bogotá
1539 Chuquisaca (now Sucre)
1541 Santiago, Chile
1541 Valladolid de Michoacán (New Morelia)
1542 Mérida, Yucatán
1545 Potosí
1549 La Paz
1552 Valdivia
1553 Santiago del Estero
1561 Mendoza
1562 San Juan, Argentina
1562 Caracas
1565 St. Augustine, Florida

ROYAL AUDIENCIAS (*dates of establishment*)

1527 Mexico
1535 Panamá
1542 Lima
1543 Guatemala
1548 New Galicia (Guadalajara)
1549 Bogotá

1559 Charcas
1563 Quito
1583 Manila
1609 Santiago, Chile
1661 Buenos Aires
1786 Caracas
1787 Cuzco

CHAPTER VIII: THE CONVENTS AND THE MISSIONS

RELIGIOUS ORDERS OF THE FIRST YEARS OF COLONIZATION

1. Franciscans
1502 Santo Domingo
1509 Darién
1523 México
1534 Quito
2. Dominicans
1510 Santo Domingo

1526 México
1529 Santa Marta and Venezuela
1541 Quito
1549 Bogotá
3. Augustinians
1523 México

1570 Quito
1575 Bogotá
1595 Chile
4. *Jesuits*
1566 Florida
1567 Peru
1572 México
1589 New Granada
1593 Chile

1605 Asunción
1607 The Paraguayan Missions
become independent of
Peru
1628 Venezuela
1650 Santo Domingo
1767 Expulsion of the Company

UNIVERSITIES (*dates of founding*)

1538 Santo Tomás de Aquino
in Santo Domingo
1540 De Santiago de la Paz in
Santo Domingo
1553 Lima and México
1620 San Gregorio Magno,
Quito
1624 San Francisco Javier,
Charcas
1636 Javeriana, Bogotá

1639 Tomista del Rosario, Bogotá
17th Century: San Ignacio de
Loyola, Córdoba, Argentina
1676 San Carlos Borromeo,
Guatemala
1725 Santa Rosa, Caracas
1728 San Jerónimo, Havana

CHAPTER IX: A FIRST INVENTORY OF SPANISH-AMERICAN LITERATURE

HISTORY

*Some Historians Born in Spain who
Wrote on Spanish America During the First Period*

Bartolomé de las Casas (1474–1566)
Hernán Cortés (1485–1547)
Antonio de Herrera (1559–1625) Never visited America.
Antonio de Solís (1610–86) Never visited America.
Francisco López de Gómara (1511–66) Never visited America.
Bernal Díaz del Castillo (1485–1584)
Gonzalo Fernández de Oviedo (1478–1559)
Francisco Fernández de Salazar (1514–75)
Fray Bernardino de Sahagún (1500–90)
Fray Toribio de Benavente (died in 1569)
Fray Juan de Torquemada (c.1536–1624)
Fray Diego Durán (1537–88)
José de Acosta, S.J. (1539–1616)
Fray Antonio de Remesal (Moved to Central America, 1613)
Gonzalo Jiménez de Quesada (1500–79)
Fray Pedro Aguado (died in 1589)
Fray Pedro Simón (1574–1630)

Fray Reginaldo de Lizárraga (1539–1600)
Fray Gasper de Carvajal (1504–84)
Father Manuel Rodríguez (1628–84)
Fray Cristóbal de Acuña (1597–1676)
Francisco López de Xérez (1504–39)
Juan de Betanzos (1510–76)
Pedro Cieza de León (1518–60)
Pedro Sarmiento de Gamboa (1530–92)
Juan Polo de Ondegardo (died in 1575)
Agustín de Zárate (died in 1560)
Diego Rosales (1603–77)
Pero Hernández (born in 1513)
Fray Bernabé Cobo (1528–1627)

Some of the First Writers Born in Spanish America

Juan Suárez de Peralta (1537–91) Mexican
Pedro Gutiérrez de Santa Clara (born in 1570) Mexican
Juan Rodríguez Freile (1566–1640) New Granada
Juan Flórez de Ocariz (died in 1629) New Granada
José Oviedo y Baños (1671–1738) New Granada
Fray Gaspar de Villarroel (1587–1665) Quito
Gaspar de Escalona y Agüero (17th century) Quito
Francisco Núñez de Pineda (1607–80) Quito
Fray Antonio de la Calancha (1584–1654) Upper Peru
Alonso de Ovalle, S.J. (1601–51) Chile

Some American Writers of Indian Blood

Garcilaso de la Vega, Inca (1539–1616) Peru
Hernando Alvarado Tezozómoc (1519–99) Mexico
Fernando de Alva Ixtilxochitl (1568–1648) Mexico
Lucas Fernández de Piedrahita (1624–88) New Granada
Jacinto Collahuaso (16th century) Quito
Felipe Guamán Poma de Ayala (1526–1613) Peru

POETRY

Some of the First Poets Who Wrote in Spanish America

Alonso de Ercilla y Zúñiga (1533–1596?) Spanish-Chilean
Pedro de Oña (1570–1643) Chilean
Hernando Álvarez de Toledo (came to America, 1561) Spanish-Chilean
Martin del Barco Centenera (1544–1605) Spanish-Argentine
Juan de Castellanos (1522–1606) Spanish-Granadine
Bernardo de Balbuena (1568–1627) Spanish-Mexican
Leonor de Ovando (died c.1611) Dominican
Francisco de Terrazas (1525–84) Mexican
Fernán González de Eslava (c.1534–c.1601) Spanish-Mexican

Carlos de Sigüenza y Góngora (1645–1700) Mexican, nephew of Luis de Góngora y Argote
Silvestre de Balboa (1564–1644) Canarian-Cuban
Fray Diego de Ojeda (c.1571–1615) Spanish-Peruvian
Luis Antonio de Oviedo, Count of La Granja (1636–1717) Spanish-Peruvian
Juan de Peralta (1663–1747) Peruvian
Juan Espinosa de Medrano (1632–88) Peruvian
Sor Juana Inés de la Cruz (1648–95) Mexican
Herando Domínguez Camargo (1606–59) Granadine

THEATER

Juan Ruiz de Alarcón (1581–1639) Mexican-Spanish
Juan Espinosa de Medrano (1632–88) Peruvian
Sor Juana Inés de la Cruz (1648–95) Mexican
Juan del Valle Caviedes (1652–97) Spanish-Peruvian
Fernando Fernández de Valenzuela (born in 1616) Granadine
Juan de Cueto y Mena (c.1602–69) Spanish-Granadine
Juan Pérez Ramírez (died c.1545) Mexican
Hernán González de Eslava (1534–1601) Mexican

CHAPTER X: THE ARTS IN THE SPANISH COLONIES

ARCHITECTURE

Religious Architecture

CATHEDRALS

The first cathedrals in America   The oldest are: Quito (started in the middle of the 16th century, consecrated in 1570); Santo Domingo (1573); México (1573–1656); and Puebla (1675–1649). As those in Lima (1746) and Bogotá (1792) stand today, they were built two centuries later. The old cathedral in Santiago, Chile, was destroyed in the earthquake of 1730; rebuilt, it burned in 1769; the new one was consecrated in 1775. The one in Buenos Aires was started during the colony and dedicated during the republic (1753–1822). The old cathedral in Caracas was destroyed in the earthquake of 1641; the second, begun in 1674, was completed in 1713. New earthquakes in 1766 and 1812 necessitated repairs.

Cathedrals contemporary with the first in America   St. Peter's in Rome (1506–1626–colonnade of the Square, 1667); St. Paul's, London (1675–1710).

FAMOUS CHURCHES AND CONVENTS OF THE COLONY
México   San Francisco de Tepeaca (1530–80); San Francisco de Acatepec (18th century); San Agustín, Acolman (1539–60); San

Agustín, Querétaro (18th century); San Martín, Tepoztlán, Dominican (1570); Jesuit convent and church, Tepotsotlán (1606–1762); Church of Saint Sebastián and Saint Prisca, Taxco (1751–58); Sanctuary of Our Lady, Ocotlán (18th century); Churrigueresque churches of Santa Clara and Santa Rosa, Querétaro (18th century); Neoclassic church of Carmen, Celaya (1802–07); Santa María Tonantzintla, Cholula (16th century).

Ecuador   Church and convent of San Francisco (1537–60); Church of San Agustín (1575–1617); Church of the Company (1600–1766); Basilica of La Merced (1700–37).

New Granada   Church of Santo Domingo, Cartagena (1597); Church and convent of the Augustinians, La Popa (1617–22); Church and convent of the Franciscans, Mongui (1702); Church of Santo Domingo, Popayán (1736–41); Church of San Agustín, Bogotá (1637); Church of San Ignacio (1638) Bogotá; Church of San Francisco, Bogotá (1638).

Military Architecture

1589, Bautista Antonelli and Giovanni Bautista Antonelli come to America to plan the fortresses of Portobello; San Juan de Ulúa; Havana; San Juan, Puerto Rico; and Cartagena. San Juan de Ulúa is started in 1590; Havana, 1589; Cartagena required more than a century of work between 1632 and 1741.

Civil Architecture

Some distinguished examples: Palace of Cortés, Cuernavaca (1523–8); House of Tiles, Mexico (1737); Montejo House in Mérida, Yucatán (1549); Torre Tagle Palace, Lima (18th century); Palace of the Inquisition, Cartagena (18th century).

PAINTING

Important Dates in the Early History of Painting

1530 Frescoes in the Franciscan convent at Cholula.
1566 The Flemish painter Simon Pereyns arrives in Mexico and teaches a generation of Mexican painters.
1534 The Flemish painter Fray Pedro Gosseal arrives in Quito.
16th century   The Italian painters Angelino Medoro and Francesco del Pozo arrive in Bogota and go on to Quito and Lima; the Spanish painter Baltasar de Echave (1548–1630) works in Mexico;
1586 Spanish painter Luis de Rivera arrives in Quito.

CHAPTER XI: THE ENLIGHTENMENT

1540 *De Revolutionibus orbium cœlestium* by Copernicus is published.
1633 Galileo is found guilty by the Inquisition.

1637 Descartes publishes his *Discourse on Method*.
1726–60 Feijoo's *El Teatro Crítico* is published in Spain.
1730 Antequera states in Paraguay that the people may oppose the prince.
1743 Muratori's book on the Jesuit missions of Paraguay is published in Venice.
1748 Students of Jesuits in Spain debate the theories of Ptolemy, Descartes, and Copernicus in a competition.
1751 The first volume of the *Encyclopédie* is published.
1759 *Candide* is written by Voltaire.
1762 *Emile* and the *Le Contrat social*, both by Rousseau, are published.
1764 The ideal republic, which would grant the sovereign senate supreme power in place of the monarch, is planned in Chile.
1765 The Economic Society of Friends of the Country founded in Vergara, Spain, by Basques.
1767 The Peruvian Pablo Olavide plans a new course of study for Seville, which inspires changes at Salamanca.
1767 Expulsion of the Jesuits. Decree drawn up by Count Aranda, who reformed Spain's economic system.
1768 Plan for agrarian reform of Andalusia is drawn up by Pablo de Olavide.
1770 *L'Histoire Philosophique et politique des établissements et du Commerce des Européens dans les Indes*, written by Abbé Raynal in collaboration with Diderot, is published.
1772 Bougainville's *Voyage au tour du Monde* is published.
1774 Mutis triumphs over the Inquisition in Bogotá with his defense of the Copernican system.
1775 The Economic Society of Friends of the Country is established in Madrid.
1776 Declaration of Independence of the United States of America.
1780 Martínez y Compañón, Bishop of Trujillo, defends royal authority using the theory of The Social Contract as basis of his arguments.
1782 French *États généraux* condemns Abbé Raynal's book.
1785 Francisco Miranda begins his travels in Europe.
1792 Simón Rodríguez, a disciple of Rousseau, is hired to tutor the young Simón Bolívar in Caracas.
1793 Antonio Nariño translates the *Rights of Man* in Bogotá.
1795 Jovellanos offers his memo on agrarian reform in Madrid.
1797 Juan Bautista Picornell translates the *Rights of Man* in Madrid and writes a preliminary speech addressed to Americans; the work is re-published in Caracas in 1811.
1803 The *Gaceta de México* forbids reading *Le Contrat social*.
1806 Félix Varela lectures at the University of Havana on Descartes, Feijoo, and Copernicus.
1808 The *Gaceta de México* opposes the ideas contained in *Le Contrat social* and *L'Esprit des lois*.

1810 Manuel Belgrano publishes his translation of the *Le Contrat social* in Buenos Aires.
1810 Miguel José Sáenz, writing in the *Semanario de Caracas* bases the revolution on the doctrines of *Le Contrat social* and links it to the *comuneros* of Castile.

CHAPTER XII: THE SCIENTIFIC MISSIONS

1703 The French scientist Father Louis Feuillée initiates botanical studies in Venezuela and Colombia.
1709 The French scientist Le Sieur Bachelier goes to Lima.
1711 Feuillée visits Argentina, Chile, and Peru.
1713 The French scholar Amédée François Frézier goes to Lima.
1735 Linnaeus's system of plant classification is published.
1735 La Condamine and a group of scholars from the Paris Academy of Science leave on an expedition to Ecuador. The Spanish engineers Jorge Juan and Antonio Ulloa go with them.
1754 The Swede Peter Loefling, a pupil of Linnaeus, goes to study the flora of Venezuela.
1755 The Dutch-Austrian botanist Nikolaus Joseph von Jacquin, director of the Botanical Gardens of Vienna, cruises the Caribbean coast.
1763 The Spanish physician José C. Mutis proposes the formation of the Botanical Mission in Bogotá.
1767 Bougainville reaches Montevideo on his tour of the world.
1768 The Royal Society in London sponsors Cook's voyage around the world.
1775 The French botanist Christophe Fusée Aublet publishes book on the flora of Guiana after two years of study there.
1781 Félix de Azara studies the flora of the Río de la Plata.
1784 The Spanish mining engineer Juan José Elhuyar goes to New Granada.
1785 The Spanish botanists Pavón and Ruiz and the Frenchman Dombey study the flora of Chile and Peru.
1786 Le Comte de la Pérouse visits Easter Island.
1789 Alessandro Malaspina, an Italian in the service of Spain, undertakes a scientific expedition and cruises the Pacific Coast to Alaska.
1792 The Spanish mining engineer Fausto de Elhuyar founds the School of Mines in Mexico.
1799 Humboldt and Bonpland start their voyage to South America.
1803 The smallpox vaccination expedition leaves Spain.
1822 The French agricultural chemist Jean-Baptiste Boussingault goes to Colombia, Venezuela, and Ecuador.
1824 The English pedagogue Joseph Lancaster goes to Caracas.
1826 The Italian Agostino Codazzi begins geographical studies that will cover all of Venezuela and Colombia.

CHAPTER XIII: INDEPENDENCE

1592 Uprisings against excises in Quito, Tunja, and elsewhere.
1649 The Paraguayan *comuneros* rise against the Jesuits.
1717–35 Second *comunero* revolution in Paraguay.
1740 Revolt in Vélez, New Granada, headed by Ensign Alvaro Chacón de Luna.
1743 An appeal from Mexico seeks English support for independence.
1749–52 Uprising in Venezuela headed by Juan Francisco León.
1765 Uprising of artisans in Quito.
1767 First reforms in the University of Mexico.
1780 Tupac Amarú uprising in Peru.
1781 *Comuneros* revolt in Socorro, New Granada.
1781 *Comuneros* revolt in Antioquía, New Granada, and Mérida, Venezuela.
1791 Viscardo y Guzmán writes a letter to Spanish Americans.
1792 Espejo begins publication of *Las Primicias de Quito*.
1800 The Mexican Teresa de Mier meets the Venezuelan Simón Bolívar in Bayonne.
1803 Hipólito Unánue publishes his memorandum on *The Climate of Lima*.
1806 The people riot in Buenos Aires, shouting "Let's plant the republican flag!"
1806 Francisco de Miranda leaves Boston with the first freedom expedition.
1808 Francisco José de Caldas begins publication of the *Semanario de la Nueva Granada*.
1809 Camilo Torres presents his List of Grievances in Bogotá.
1809 Independence is proclaimed in Quito.
1810 The cry of independence spreads through the colonies from Buenos Aires to Mexico.
1811 Publication of the *Aurora de Chile*, edited by Camilo Henríquez, is initiated.

CHAPTER XIV: ROMANTICISM AND LIBERALISM

1787 Schiller presents *Don Carlos*.
1797 German Romanticism proclaimed in the review *Athenäum*.
1798 Wordsworth's preface to his and Coleridge's *Lyrical Ballads*—the manifesto of English Romanticism—is published.
1800 Schiller's *Mary Stuart* appears.
1801 Chateaubriand's *Atala* is published.
1801 Simón Rodríguez and Fray Servando Teresa de Mier publish a translation of *Atala* in Paris.

1808 The German poet Kleist publishes his novel *The Earthquakes of Chile.*

1813 Mme de Staël, in exile from France, publishes *De l'Allemagne,* which carries German Romanticism to France in London.

1819 Byron plans to visit Venezuela.

1820 An adaptation of *Atala* and *Guatimoc,* by José Fernández Madrid, is staged in Havana.

1823 Andrés Bello publishes his Address on Poetry in the *Biblioteca Americana* in London.

1825 Esteban Echeverría sails for Europe.

1826 Andrés Bello publishes his "Ode to Agriculture in the Torrid Zone" in *El Repertorio Americano.*

1826 James Fenimore Cooper: *The Last of the Mohicans.*

1827 Alessandro Manzoni: *I Promessi Sposi.*

1830 The battle over *Hernani* in Paris.

1831 Schiller's *Wilhelm Tell* and *Maria Stuart* are presented in Buenos Aires.

1831 Echeverría's first Romantic works published in Buenos Aires.

1833 Debate on Romanticism between Argentines and Chileans starts in Chile.

1833 *Lucrèce Borgia,* by Victor Hugo, is presented in Buenos Aires.

1834 *Antonino,* by Dumas, is presented in Buenos Aires.

1835 Victor Hugo's *Hernani* is banned in Buenos Aires.

1835–7 Larra's complete works published in Madrid.

1837 Sarmiento translates Dumas's *Thérèse* in Santiago.

1838 *Ruy Blas* is presented in Buenos Aires.

1838–9 Translations of *Ruy Blas,* (by Bartolomé Mitre), *Lucrèce Borgia, Angèle, Le Roi s'amuse,* and *Marion de Lorme* are presented in Montevideo.

1839 Larra's complete works are published in Caracas.

1842 Larra's complete works are published in Valparaiso.

1844 *Amalia,* by Marmol, is published.

1852 *Uncle Tom's Cabin,* by Harriet Beecher Stowe.

1859 Juárez promulgates his Reform Laws.

1862 Victor Hugo's *Les Misérables.*

1867 *María,* by Jorge Isaacs.

1878 *Enriquillo,* by Manuel de Jesús Galván.

1879 *Cumandá,* by Juan León Mera.

CHAPTER XV: CIVILIZATION AND BARBARISM

1816–40 Dr. J. G. R. Francia, supreme dictator of Paraguay.

1821–7 Rivadavia founds the University of Buenos Aires, introduces the Lancastrian system, suppresses ecclesiastical law and tithing, confiscates the property of religious orders, and proclaims the land laws.

1829–39 Andrés Santacruz, *caudillo* of Bolivia.
1827–40 Morazán introduces liberal reforms in Honduras, Salvador, Costa Rica, and finally in the United Provinces of Central America. Shot in 1842.
1835–62 The Rosas dictatorship in Argentina.
1837–65 Rafael Carrera imposes his reactionary program in Guatemala.
1847–55 Belzú dictatorship in Bolivia.
1861–75 Dictatorship of García Moreno in Ecuador.
1862–70 Dictatorship of Francisco Solano López in Paraguay.
1864–71 Dictatorship of Melgarejo in Bolivia.
1876–83 Veintemilla dictatorship in Ecuador.
1897–1901 Liberal government of Eloy Alfaro in Ecuador.

CHAPTER XVI: FROM UTILITARIANISM TO POSITIVISM

1789 Bentham's *Principles of Morals and Legislation*.
1821 Rivadavia introduces Bentham in the Argentine.
1821 José María Luis Mora spreads Bentham's teachings in Mexico.
1823 Francis Hall, a disciple of Bentham, founds *El Quiteño Libre* in Quito.
1823 José Cecilio del Valle disseminates Bentham's philosophy in Guatemala.
1825 Santander introduces texts by Bentham in the University of Colombia.
1830–42 Comte publishes his lessons in Positivistic Philosophy.
1837 Alberdi speaks on Social Science in Buenos Aires.
1837 The Colombian philosopher José Eusebio Caro writes *Philosophy of Christianity* following Comte in reconciling Christianity and science.
1842 Francisco Bilbao publishes *La Sociabilidad Chilena*.
1844 Lastarria introduces positivism in Chile.
1862 Salvador Camacho Roldán establishes the chair of Sociology at the University of Bogotá.
1862 Spencer's *First Principles*.
1867 Gabino Barreda, disciple of Comte, secretary of Public Education under Juárez, founds the *Escuela Preparatoria* for Mexican "scientists."
1868 Alberdi expresses his enthusiasm for Spencer in commentaries on the Argentine Civil Code.
1876 Spencer's *Principles of Sociology*.
1880 Positivism takes a Spencerian turn in Mexico with Justo Sierra.
1880 Rafael Núñez proposes the study of Spencer in Colombia.
1882 Camacho Roldán delivers an academic encomium on Spencer in Bogotá.

1883 Hostos publishes his first treatise on sociology in Santo Domingo.
1884 Manuel María Madiedo publishes translations of Comte and Lafitte in Bogotá.

CHAPTER XVII: BRAZIL FROM COLONY TO EMPIRE TO REPUBLIC

1775 The Lisbon Earthquake.
1758 Freedom for the Indians, independent of the missionaries, is extended throughout Brazil.
1758 Brief report on the Republic established by the Jesuits in America.
1759 Pombal's decree expelling the Jesuits from Brazil.
1763 The capital is moved from Bahia to Rio de Janeiro.
1764 The Jesuits are expelled from France.
1767 The Jesuits are expelled from Spain, Naples, and Parma.
1789 The Tiradentes Revolution.
1807 The Portuguese court is transferred to Brazil.
1814 "O Aleijadinho" dies.
1817 Revolt in Pernambuco; the republican flag is flown.
1821 Don João I goes back to Lisbon. Dom Pedro regent of Brazil.
1822 The Liberty Cry at Ipiranga, Independence for Brazil.
1825 The *Diario de Pernambuco*, the oldest daily in America, is founded.
1826 Dom Pedro I is proclaimed king of Portugal. Renounces the crown in favor of his daughter, María Gloria.
1827 The *Journal do Comerico* is founded in Rio de Janeiro.
1831 Dom Pedro I abdicates and returns to Portugal.
1841 Dom Pedro II is declared of age and proclaimed king.
1852 Benjamin Constant teaches in the Military School.
1888 Abolition of slavery.
1889 Parnassians come out against the Romanticists.
1872 *Inocencia*, by Alfredo d'Escragnolle Taunay, is published.
1881 Machado de Assis, *Memorias Póstumas de Brás Cubas*.
1881 *O Mulato*, by Aloísio Azevedo.
1902 *Os Certões*, by *Euclides de Cunha.*
1902 *Canaan*, by Graça Aranha.
1922 Modernist Manifesto.
1933 *Casa-Grande e Senzala*, by Gilberto Freyre.
1948 *Geografía da fome*, by Josué de Castro.

CHAPTER XVIII: HAITI IN BLACK AND WHITE

1492 Columbus founds La Navidad near Cap Haïtien, first Spanish settlement in the New World.

1697 Haiti is ceded to France by the Treaty of Ryswick.
1749 The city of Port-au-Prince is founded.
1791 The Negro insurrection.
1791 Vincent Ogé, leader of the insurrection, is executed.
1800 Toussaint l'Ouverture dictates the first constitution and is proclaimed president.
1802 Toussaint l'Ouverture is captured by General Leclerc and sent to France a prisoner.
1803 Dessalines, Pétion, and Clarvaux in armed rebellion.
1804 The second republic proclaimed; Dessalines appointed governor for life, proclaims himself Emperor Jacques I.
1807 Henri-Christophe is elected president of the republic, proclaims himself King Henri I. Rupture with the Holy See, Christian schism.
1820 Henri-Christophe, defeated, commits suicide; the republic again is proclaimed.
1847 Faustin-Élie Soulouque elected president. Proclaims himself Emperor Faustin I.
1859 Faustin is dethroned.
1860 ⎫
1867 ⎪
1874 ⎬ New constitutions.
1888 ⎪
1918 ⎭
1915 Vilbrun is assassinated; American Marines are landed, remain in occupation until 1934.

CHAPTER XIX: FROM *MODERNISMO*
TO *ANTI-MODERNISMO*

1882 José Martí: *Versos Libres.*
1886 J. A. Silva: *Poesías.*
1888 Rubén Darío: *Azul.*
1890 Julián del Casal: *Hojas al Viento.*
1894 Gutiérrez Nájera founds the *Revista Azul.*
1896 Carrasquilla: *Frutos de mi Tierra.*
1897 Lugones: *Las Montañas de Oro.*
1898 Valencia: *Ritos.*
1898 Nervo founds the *Revista Moderna.*
1899 Jaime Freyre: *Castalia Bárbara.*
1900 Herrera y Reisig: *Las Pascuas del Tiempo.*
1905 Gómez Carrillo: *El Modernismo.*
1908 Luis C. López: *De mi Villorrio.*
1908 Larreta: *La Gloria de Don Ramiro.*
1911 González Martínez: *Los Senderos Ocultos.*
1915 Eduardo Barrios: *El Niño que Enloqueció de Amor.*
1918 Azuela: *Los de Abajo.*

1918 Quiroga: *Cuentos de la Selva.*
1920 Edwards Bello: *El Roto.*
1922 Gabriela Mistral: *Desolación.*
1924 Oliveiro Girondo and Jorge Luis Borges found the Martín Fierro group.
1924 Rivera: *La Vorágine.*
1924 Lynch: *El Inglés de los Güesos.*
1926 Güiraldes: *Don Segundo Sombra.*
1929 Gallegos: *Doña Bárbara.*
1934 Icaza: *Huasipungo.*
1935 López y Fuentes: *El Indio.*
1938 José Rubén Romero: *La Vida Inútil de Pito Pérez.*
1939 Ciro Alegría: *El Mundo es Ancho y Ajeno.*
1941 Asturias: *El Señor Presidente.*

CHAPTER XX: FROM ARIEL TO CALIBAN

1894 González Prada: *Páginas Libres.*
1900 Rodó: *Ariel.*
1903 Theodore Roosevelt: *I Took Panama.*
1904 Rubén Darío: *Ode to Roosevelt.*
1913 José Guadalupe Posada dies, leaving 15,000 engravings, in Mexico.
1909 Ugarte: *El Porvenir de la América Latina.*
1911 Francisco I. Madero starts the Mexican Revolution.
1912 García Calderón: *Les Démocracies Latines de l'Amerique Latine.*
1917 New Mexican constitution is adopted.
1918 University revolution in Córdoba, Argentina.
1920 Vasconcelos becomes Mexico's Secretary of Public Education.
1921 Isidro Fabela: *Los Estados Unidos contra la Libertad.*
1921 Diego Rivera and José C. Orozco initiate the Mexican school of mural art.
1922 The Chilean Communist Party is founded and joins the Third International.
1928 Mariátegui: *Siete Ensayos sobre la Realidad Peruana.*
1930–61 The Trujillo dictatorship in Santo Domingo.
1937–56 The Somoza dictatorships in Nicaragua.
1938 Cárdenas nationalizes the oil fields in Mexico.
1938 The Chilean Falange (the party from which the Christian Democratic Party later emerges) is founded.
1941 The National Revolutionary Movement is established in Bolivia.
1945 Perón's "Shirtless" march in Buenos Aires.
1949 Ospina Pérez suspends the lawful regime in Colombia. (Congress does not hold sessions again until 1958.)
1952–8 The Pérez Jiménez dictatorship in Venezuela.
1954 The Stroessner dictatorship begins in Paraguay.

1956 Fidel Castro lands in Cuba and takes refuge in the Sierra
     Maestra.
1959 The Christian Democratic Party holds its first national conven-
     tion in Chile.
1961 Fidel Castro proclaims the Marxist-Leninist orientation of the
     Cuban revolution.

Bibliography

GENERAL HISTORIES—HISTORIES OF CULTURE

Crow, John Armstrong: *The Epic of Latin America*. Garden City: Doubleday & Co.; 1948.
Crawford, William: *A Century of Latin America Thought*. Cambridge, Mass.: Harvard University Press; 1944.
Herring, Hubert: *A History of Latin America, from the Beginnings to the Present*. New York: Alfred A. Knopf; 1961.
Lanning, John Tate: *Academic Culture in the Spanish Colonies*. New York: Oxford University Press; 1940.
Levene, Ricardo: *Historia de América*, 14 vols. Buenos Aires, 1940, 1942.
Picón-Salas, Mariano: *De la Conquista a la Independencia*. México, D.F., 1944.
Sánchez, Luis Alberto: *Vida y Pasión de la Cultura en América*. Santiago de Chile, 1935.

LITERARY HISTORIES

Anderson-Imbert, Enrique: *Historia de la Literature Hispano-Americana*, 2 vols. 3rd. edn. México, D.F., 1961.
Arrón, José Juan: *Estudios de Literatura Hispanoamericana*. Havana, 1960.
———: *El Teatre en Hispanoamérica en la época colonial*. Havana, 1956.
———: *Esquema generacional de las letras hispanoamericanas*. Bogotá, 1963.
Aubrun, Charles V.: *Histoire des Lettres Hispanoamericaines*. Paris, 1954.
Bazin, Robert: *Histoire de la Littérature Américaine en langue espagnole*. Paris, 1957.
Barbagelate, Hugo: *La Novela y el Cuento en Hispanoamérica*. Montevideo, 1947.
Cambours Ocampo, Arturo: *El Problema de las Generaciones Literarias*. Buenos Aires, 1953.
Carrile, Emilio: *El Romanticismo en la América Hispánica*. Madrid, 1958.

De Onís, Federico: *Antología de la Poesía Española e Hispanoamericana* (*1882–1932*). Madrid, 1934.

De Torre, Guillermo: *Tres Conceptos de la Literatura Hispanoamericana*. Buenos Aires, 1963.

Ferreira, João Francisco: *Capítulos de Literatura Hispanoamericana*. Porto Alegre, 1959.

Gallo, Ugo, and Bellini, Giuseppe: *Storia della Letteratura Ispanoamericana*. Milan, 1958.

García Prada, Carlos: *Estudios Hispano-Americanos*. México, D.F., 1945.

Henríquez Ureña, Max: *Breve Historia del Modernismo*. Mexico, D.F., 1954.

Henríquez Ureña, Pedro: *Literary Currents in Hispanic America*. Cambridge, Mass.: Harvard University Press; 1945.

Leguizamón, S. A.: *Historia de la Literatura Hispanoamericana*, 2 vols. Buenos Aires, 1945.

Knapp Jones, Willis: *Antología del Teatro Hispanoamericano*. México, D.F., 1959.

Leonard, Irving: *Books of the Brave*. Cambridge, Mass.: Harvard University Press; 1949.

Mead, Robert G.: *Breve Historia del Ensayo Latinoamericano*. México, D.F., 1956.

Meléndez, Concha: *La Novela Indianista, 1832–1889*. Madrid, 1934.

Menéndez y Pelayo, Marcelino: *Historia de la poesía Hispanoamericana*. Madrid, 1934.

Menton, Seymour: *El Cuento Hispanoamericano*. México, D.F., 1964.

Montezuma de Carvalho, Joaquim, ed.: *Panorama das Literaturas das Americas*, 3 vols. Angola, 1959.

Queiroz, María José de: *Do Indianismo ao indigenismo nas letras hispanoamericanas*. Belo Horizonte, 1962.

Romero, Francisco: *Sobre la filosofía en América*. Buenos Aires, 1952.

Sánchez, Luis Alberto: *Nueva Historia de la Literatura Americana*. Asunción, 1950.

Solórzano, Carlos: *El Teatro Latinoamericano en el Siglo XX*. Mexico, D.F., 1964.

Torres Rioseco, Arturo: *La Novela Iberoamericana*. Albuquerque, N.M., 1951.

———: *Nueva Historia de la Gran Literature Hispanoamericana*. Buenos Aires, 1960.   .

Uslar Pietri, Arturo: *Breve Historia de la Novela Hispanomericana*. Caracas, 1957.

Vitier, Medardo: *Del Ensayo Americano*. México. D.F., 1945.

Zea, Leopoldo: *América en la historia*. México, D.F., 1957.

Zum Felde, Alberto: *Indice Crítico de la Literatura Hispanoamericana: I. El Ensayo y la Crítica; II. La Narrativa;* 2 vols. México, D.F., 1954–9.

MUSIC—FOLKLORE

Abadía, Julio: *Aires Populares de Colombia.* Bogotá, 1941.
Almeida, Renato: *Historia de la Música Brasileira.* Rio de Janeiro, 1942.
Alvarenga, Oneyda: *Música Popular Brasileira.* Porto Alegre, 1945.
Andrade, Mario de: *Ensaio sobre a música brasileira.* São Paulo, 1928.
Arroyo, César E.: *Romancero del Pueblo Ecuatoriano.* Madrid, 1919.
Berruti, F.: *Manual de Danzas Nativas.* Buenos Aires, 1954.
Cabrera, Lydia: *Les contes nègres de Cuba.* Paris, n.d.
Calcaño, José Antonio: *Contribución al Estudio de la Música en Venezuela.* Caracas, 1939.
Callejo, Fernando: *Música y músicos puertorriqueños.* San Juan, 1915.
Cámara Cascudo, Luis de: *Antologia do folclore brasileiro.* São Paulo, 1945.
Campos, Rubén M.: *El Folklore y la Música Mexicana.* México, D.F., 1928.
Carpentier, Alejo: *La Música en Cuba.* México, D.F., 1946.
Carrizo, Juan Alfonso: *La Poesía Tradicional Argentina.* La Plata, 1951.
Castillo, Jesús: *La Música Maya-Quiché.* Quetraltenango, 1941.
Cevallos, D. F.: *Folklore Hondureño.* Tegucigalpa, 1948.
Coluccio, Félix: *Diccionario Folklorico Argentino.* Buenos Aires, 1950.
Cortázar, Augusto Raúl: *Confluencias culturales en el Folklore Argentino.* Buenos Aires, 1950.
Díez de Medina, Fernando: *Nay Jama.* Bolivia, 1950.
Espinosa, Francisco: *Folklore Salvadoreño.* San Salvador, 1946.
Garay, Narciso: *Tradiciones y Cantares de Panamá.* Brussels, 1930.
García Acevedo, Mario: *La Música Argentina Contemporánea.* Buenos Aires, 1963.
González Sol, Rafael: *Historia del Arte de la Música en El Salvador.* San Salvador, 1940.
Guevara, Tomás: *Folklore Araucano.* Santiago, 1911.
Harcourt, Raoul and Marguerite: *La musique des Incas et ses survivances.* Paris, 1925.
Hogue, Eleanor: *Latin American Music, Past and Present.* Santa Ana, California, 1934.
Houston-Péret, Elsie: *Chants populaires du Brésil.* Paris, 1930.
Izikovitz, Karl Gustav: *Musical and Other Sound Instruments of South American Indians: A Comparative Ethnographical Study.* Göteborg, 1935.
Martí, Samuel: *Canto, Danza y Música Pre-cortesianos.* México, D.F., 1961.

Mayer, Augusto: *Guia do folclore gaucho*. Rio de Janeiro, 1951.
Mayer-Serra, Otto: *Música y Músicos de Latinoamérica*, 2 vols. México, D.F., 1947.
———: *Panorama de la Músicos Mexicana*. México, D.F., 1941.
Mead, Charles W.: *The Musical Instruments of the Incas*. New York: American Museum Press; 1924.
Mejía Sánchez, Ernesto: *Romances y Corridos Nicaraguenses*. México, D.F., 1946.
Melo, Guilherme Teodoro Pereyra de: *A música no Brasil*. Bahia, 1908.
Mendoza, Vicente T.: *El Corrido Mexicano*. México, D.F., 1954.
Mera, Juan León: *Antología Ecuatoriana: Cantares del Pueblo Ecuatoriano*. Quito, 1892.
Moya, Ismael: *El Arte de los Payadores*. Buenos Aires, 1959.
Onís, Harriet de, ed.: *The Golden Land*. New York, 1948.
Ortega, Pompilio: *Folklore Hondureño*. Tegucigalpa, 1946.
Ortiz, Fernando: *La Africanía de la Música Folklorica de Cuba*. Havana, 1950.
———: *Los Bailes y el Teatro de los Negros en el Folklore de Cuba*. Havana, 1951.
———: *Los negroes brujos*. Havana, 1906.
Paredes, Rigoberto: *Mitos, Supersticiones y Supervivencias populares de Bolivia*. La Paz, 1920.
———: *El Arte Folklórico de Bolivia*. La Paz, 1949.
Perdomo Escobar, José Ignacio: *Historia de la Música en Colombia*. Bogotá, 1963.
Prado, Alcides: *Apuntes Sintéticos sobre la Historia y Producción musical de Costa Rica*. San José, n.d.
Quiñones Pardo, Octavio: *Cantares de Boyacá*. Bogotá, 1937.
Ramírez Sendoya, Pedro José: *Refranero del Gran Tolima*. Bogotá, 1952.
Ramón y Rivera, L. F.: *La Música Popular de Venezuela*. Buenos Aires, 1951.
Ramos, Artur: *O Folclore negro do Brasil*. Rio de Janeiro, 1936.
Restrepo, Antonia José: *Cancionero de Antioquia*. Barcelona, 1929.
Romero, Emilia: *El Romance Tradicional en el Perú*.
Romero, Silvio: *Cantos populares do Brasil*. Rio de Janeiro, 1897.
Saldícar, G.: *Historia de la Música en México*. México, D.F., 1954.
Seeger, Charles L.: *Music in Latin America*. Washington: Pan American Union; 1942.
Slonimsky, Nicolas: *Music in Latin America*. New York: Thomas Y. Crowell Co.; 1945.
Vargas, Teófilo: *Aires Nacionales de Bolivia*. Santiago de Chile, 1940.
Vásquez, Santana, H.: *Historia de la Canción Mexicana*. México, D.F., 1931.
Vega, Carlos: *Panorama de la Música Popular Argentina*. Buenos Aires, 1944.

Weinstock, Herbert: *Notes for Concerts Arranged by Carlos Chávez.* New York: Museum of Modern Art; 1940.

Wilkes, J. I.: *Formas Musicales Rioplatenses.* Buenos Aires, 1946.

Zárate, Belisario: *Folklore Boliviano.* Cochabamba, 1938.

ARCHEOLOGY AND ANCIENT CULTURES

Ameghino, Florentino: *La Antiguedad del Hombre en el Plata.* Paris, 1880.

Aubin, J. M. A.: *Histoire de la Nation Mexicaine.* Paris, 1893.

Balliván, Manuel Vicente: *Monumentos prehistóricos de Tiahuanaco.* La Paz, 1910.

Baessler, Arthur: *L'Art précolombien.* Paris, 1928.

Bancroft, Hubert Howe: *History of Mexico.* New York: The Bancroft Co.; 1914.

————: *The Conquest of Mexico.* 6 vols. San Francisco: A. L. Bancroft & Co.; 1883-8.

Barreda Vásquez, Alfredo, and Rendón, Silvia: *El Libro de los Libros de Chilam Balam.* México, D.F., 1948.

Baudin, L.: *L'Empire socialiste des Incas.* Paris, 1928.

Bertoni, M. S.: *La civilizacíon Guaraní.* Asunción, 1922.

Bingham, Hiram: *Machu Picchu, a Citadel of the Incas.* New Haven: Oxford University Press; 1930.

Broadbent, Sylvia M.: *Los Chibchas.* Bogotá, 1964.

Canals Fran, Salvador: *Prehistoria de América.* Buenos Aires, 1955.

Carrillo y Ancona, Crescencio: *Historia Antigua de Yucatán.* México, D.F., 1937.

Caso, Alfonso: *El Pueblo del Sol.* México, D.F., 1953.

Collier, John: *Los Indios de las Américas.* México, D.F., 1960.

Cosío del Pomar, Felipe: *Arte del Perú Precolombiano.* México, D.F., 1949.

Duque Gómez, Luis: *Colombia: Monumentos Historicos y Arqueológicos,* 2 vols. México, D.F., 1955.

————: *Prehistoria,* 2 vols. Bogotá, 1965.

Dupaix, Guillermo: *Antiquités Mexicaines.* Paris, 1834.

Flor y Canto del Arte Prehispánico Mexicano. México, D.F., 1964.

Flórez Guerrero, Raúl: *Historia General del Arte Mexicano. Eposa Prehispanica.* México, D.F., 1962.

Gallenkamp, Charles: *Los Mayas.* México, 1960.

Gamboa, Fernando: *Chefs d'oeuvre de l'art mexicain.* Paris, 1962.

Gamio, Manuel: *La Población del Valle de Teotihuacán.* México, 1922.

Garcilaso de la Vega, Inca: *Historia General del Perú.* Madrid, 1772.

Gostantas, Estanislao: *Arte Colombiano Aborigen.* Bogotá, 1960.

Heyerdahl, Thor: *Kon-Tiki*. London: Penguin Books; 1950.
Imbeloni, José: *Civiltá Andina*. Florence, 1960.
Jijón y Camaño, Jacinto: *Antropología Prehispánica del Ecuador*. Quito, 1952.
———: *La Religión del Imperio de los Incas*. Quito, 1919.
Krickeberg, Walter: *Las Antiguas Culturas Mexicanas*. México, D.F., 1964.
Larco Hoyle, Rafael: *Cronología Arqueológica del Norte del Perú*. Buenos Aires, 1948.
León Postilla, Miguel: *Los Antiguos Mexicanos a través de Sus Crónicas y Cantares*. México, D.F., 1961.
Levillier, Jean: *Paracas, a Contribution to the Study of Pre-Incaic Textiles in Ancient Peru*. Paris, 1928.
Lothrop, S. K.; Foshag, W. F.; Mahler, J.: *Arte Precolombiano*, Milan, 1958.
Markham, Sir Clements Robert: *Cuzco: A Journey to the Ancient Capital of Peru*. London, 1856.
Mason, John Alden: *The Ancient Civilization of Peru*. London: Penguin Books; 1957.
Means, Philip Ainsworth: *Ancient Civilizations of the Andes*. New York: Charles Scribner's Sons; 1931.
Métraux, Alfred: *Les Incas*. Paris, 1962.
Morley, S. G.: *The Ancient Maya*. Stanford: Stanford University Press; 1956.
Nordenskiöld, Erland: *Archéologie du Bassin de l'Amazone*. Paris, 1930.
———: *Orígen de las Civilizaciones en la América del Sur*. Buenos Aires, 1946.
Del Paso y Troncoso, F.: *Descripción Histórica y Exposición del Códice Pictórico de los Antiguos Nauas* (Codex Borbonicus). Florence, 1898.
Pérez de Barradas, J.: *Orfebrería Prehistórica de Colombia*. Madrid, 1954.
———: *Arqueología Agustiniana*. Bogotá, 1944.
Popol Vuh: Las Antiguas Historias del Quiché. México, D.F., 1947.
Posnansky, Arthur: *Tiahuanacú, the Cradle of American Man*, 2 vols. New York: T. T. Agustin; 1946.
Prescott, William Hickling: *History of the Conquest of Peru*. New York: Dutton; 1963.
———: *The Conquest of Mexico*. Garden City: Doubleday, Doran; 1937.
Preuss, K. Th.: *Arte Monumental Prehistórico: Excavaciones en el Alto Magdalena y San Agustin*. Bogotá, 1931.
Rivet, Paul: *Los Orígenes del Hombre Américano*. México, D.F., 1960.
———: *Cités Maya*. Paris, 1934.
Sahagún, Bernardino de: *Historia de las Cosas de la Nueva España*, 5 vols. México, D.F., 1938.

Samayoa Chinchilla, Carlos: *Aproximación al Arte Maya*. Guatemala, 1964.

Séjourné, Laurette: *Palenque, una Ciudad Maya*. México, D.F., 1952.

———: *Un Palacio en la Ciudad de los Dioses*. México, 1959.

Seler, Eduard: *Comentarios al Códice Borgia y Edición Facsimilar del Códice Borgia*. México, D.F., 1963.

Soustelle, Jacques: *La Vie Quotidienne des Aztèques à la Vieille de la Conquête Espagnole*. Paris, 1955.

Spinden, Herbert Joseph: *Maya Art and Civilization*. Indian Hills, Colo.: Falcon Wing Press; 1957.

Thompson, J. Eric: *The Rise and Fall of Maya civilization*. Norman: University of Oklahoma Press; 1954.

Toscano, Salvador: *Arte Precolombino de México y de la América Central*. México, D.F., 1944.

Triana, Miguel: *La Civilización Chibcha*. Bogota, 1922.

Vaillant, George C.: *The Aztecs of Mexico*. Garden City: Doubleday; 1962.

Valcárcel, Luis E.: *Historia de la Cultura Antigua del Perú*. Lima, 1943.

Villacorta, J. Antonio: *Arqueología Guatemalteca*. Guatemala, 1927.

———: *Códices Mayas*. Guatemala, 1930.

Villagra, A.: *Bonampak, la Ciudad de los Muros Pintados*. México, D.F., 1949.

Von Hagen, V. W.: *The Aztec and Maya Papermakers*. New York: J. J. Agustin; 1943.

———: *The Ancient Kingdoms of the Americas—Aztec, Maya, Inca*. Cleveland: World Publishing Co.; 1961.

Westheim, Paul: *Arte Antiguo de México*. México, D.F., 1950.

———: *Ideas Fundamentales del Arte Prehispánico en México*. México, D.F., 1957.

ARCHITECTURE—THE PLASTIC ARTS

Angulo Iñiguez, Diego; Dorta, E. M.: *Historia del Arte Hispanoamericano*. Barcelona, 1945.

Atl, Dr. (Gerardo Murillo): *Las Artes Populares en México*. México, D.F., 1922.

Baxter, Sylvester: *Spanish Colonial Architecture in Mexico*, 10 vols. Boston: J. B. Millet; 1901.

Boulton, Alfredo: *Historia de la Pintura en Venezuela—Epoca Colonial*. Caracas, 1964.

Buschiazzo, M. J.: *Estudios de Arquitectura Colonial Hispanoamericana*. Buenos Aires, 1944.

Cardoza ye Aragón, Luis: *México, Pintura de Hoy*. México, D.F., 1964.

Cossío del Pomar, Felipe: *La Pintura en el Cuzco*. Cuzco, 1921.

Cuoto, José Bernardo: *Diálogo sobre la Historia de la Pintura en México*. México, D.F., 1947.
Diaz, Víctor Miguel: *Las Bellas Artes en Guatemala*. Guatemala, 1934.
Fernández, Justino: *El Arte Moderno en México*. México, D.F., 1937.
Gasparini, Graziano: *Templos Coloniales de Venezuela*. Caracas, 1959.
————: *La Arquitectura Colonial en Venezuela*. Caracas, 1965.
Giraldo Jaramillo, Gabriel: *La Pintura en Colombia*. México, D.F., 1947.
————: *El Grabado en Colombia*. Bogotá, 1960.
Gómez Sirce, José: *La Pintura en Cuba*. New York, 1944.
Goodwin, Philip: *Brazil Builds: Architecture New and Old*. New York: The Museum of Modern Art; 1943.
Hernández de Alba, Guillermo: *Teatro del Arte Colonial*. Bogotá, 1938.
Kubler, George: *Mexican Architecture of the Sixteenth Century*. New Haven: Yale University Press; 1948.
Mariscal, Federico: *Colonial Architecture in Mexico and Central America*. New York, 1928.
Mattos, Anibal: *Arte Colonial Brasileiro*. Belo Horizonte, 1936–7.
Moreno Villa, José: *La Escultura Colonial Mexicana*. México, D.F., 1942.
Nadal Mora, V.: *La Arquitectura Tradicional de Buenos Aires*—1536–1870. Buenos Aires, 1947.
Navarro, José Gabriel: *La Escultura en el Ecuador*. Madrid, 1929.
————: *Artes Plásticas Ecuatorianas*. México, D.F., 1945.
Paredes, Rigoberto: *El Arte de la Altiplanicie*. La Paz, 1912.
Revilla, Manuel G.: *El Arte de México en la Epoca Antigua y durante el Gobierno Virreinal*. México, D.F., 1923.
Rojas, Pedro: *Historia General del Arte Mexicana: Epoca Colonial*. México, D.F., 1963.
Sandford, Trent Elwood: *The History of Architecture in Mexico*. New York: W. W. Norton; 1947.
Sola, Miguel: *Historia del Arte Hispanoamericano*. Barcelona, 1935.
Tibol, Raquel: *Historia General del Arte Mexicano: Epoca Moderna y Contemporánea*. México, D.F., 1964.
Toussaint, Manuel: *Arte Colonial en México*. México, D.F., 1962.
Vargas, José M.: *Arte Quiteño Colonial*. Quito, 1944.
Velarde, Héctor: *Arquitectura Peruana*. México, D.F., 1946.
Villanueva, Emilio: *Disquisiciones sobre el Arte Colonial*. La Paz, n.d.
Wethey, Harold E.: *Colonial Architecture and Sculpture in Peru*. Cambridge: Harvard University Press; 1949.
Wolfe, Bertram D.: *The Fabulous Life of Diego Rivera*. New York: Stein & Day; 1963.

ARGENTINA

Arrieta, R. A.: *La Literatura Argentina y sus Vínculos en España.* Buenos Aires, n.d.

Babini, José. *Historia de la Ciencia Argentina.* México, D.F., 1949.

Berenguer Carisomo, Arturo: *Teatro Argentino Contemporáneo.* Madrid, 1960.

Blanksten, G. I.: *Perón's Argentina.* Chicago: University of Chicago Press; 1953.

Carilla, G. I.: *Literatura Argentina 1800–1950 Esquema Generacional.* Tucumán, 1954.

Beltrán, O. R.: *Orígenes del Teatro Argentino.* Buenos Aires, 1941.

Canal-Feijoo, Bernardo: *Alberdi, Proyección sistemática del Espíritu de Mayo.* Buenos Aires, 1961.

Castaguino, R. H.: *Esquema de la Literatura Dramática Argentina (1717–1949).* Buenos Aires, 1950.

Echeverría, Estéban: *Los Ideales de Mayo y la Tiranía.* Buenos Aires, 1927.

Foppa, Tito Livio: *Diccionario Teatral del Río de la Plata.* Buenos Aires, 1962.

García, Germán: *La Novela Argentina: un Itinerario.* Buenos Aires, 1952.

García Velloso, Enrique: *Historia de la Literatura Argentina.* Buenos Aires, 1914.

Ghiano, Juan Carlos: *Poesía Argentina del Siglo XX.* Buenos Aires, 1957.

Giménez Pastor, A.: *Historia de la Literatura Argentina,* 2 vols. Buenos Aires, 1945.

Ingenieros, José: *Evolución de las Ideas Argentinas.* Buenos Aires, 1951.

Kirpatrick, F. A.: *A History of the Argentine Republic.* Cambridge: Harvard University Press; 1931.

Levene, Ricardo: *Historia del Derecho Argentino.* Buenos Aires, 1945.

——: *Orígenes de la Democracia Argentina.* Buenos Aires, 1942.

——: *A History of Argentina.* Chapel Hill: University of North Carolina Press; 1937.

Korn, Alejandro: *Influencias Filosóficas en la Evolución Nacional,* 3 vols. La Plata, 1940.

Mallea, Eduardo: *Conocimiento y Expresión de la Argentina.* Buenos Aires, 1935.

Moya, Ismael: *El Arte de los Payadores.* Buenos Aires, 1959.

Nichols, Madaline W.: *The Gaucho.* Durham, N.C.: Durham University Press; 1942.

Ordaz, L.: *El Teatro en el Río de la Plata.* Buenos Aires, 1946.

Rojas, Ricardo: *La Literatura Argentina.* Buenos Aires, 1947.

Romero, José Luis: *La Ideas Políticas en la Argentina*. México, D.F., 1946.
Sarmiento, Domingo Faustino: *Life in the Argentine Republic in the Days of the Tyrants*. New York, 1868.
Sánchez Viamonte, Carlos: *Historia Institucional Argentina*. México, D.F., 1948.
Suárez Calimano, E.: *Directrices de la Novela y el Cuento Argentinos*. Buenos Aires, 1933.
Verdevoye, Paul: *D. F. Sarmiento éducateur et publiciste entre 1839 et 1852*. Paris, 1965.
Williams Alzaga, Enrique: *Dos Revoluciones* (10. de Enero de 1809–25. de Mayo de 1810). Buenos Aires, 1963.

BOLIVIA

Alexander, Robert: *The Bolivian National Revolution*. New Brunswick, N.J.: Rutgers University Press; 1958.
Argüedas, Alcides: *Historia General de Bolivia*, La Paz, 1922.
Diez de Medina, Fernando: *Literatura Boliviana*. Madrid, 1954.
Finot, Enrique: *Historia de la Literatura Boliviana*. México, D.F., 1943.
Francovich, Guillermo: *El Pensamiento Boliviano en el Siglo XX*. México, D.F., 1956.
Guzmán, Augusto: *Historia de la Novela Boliviana*. La Paz, 1938.
Guerra, José Eduardo: *Itinerario Espiritual de Bolivia*. Barcelona, 1936.
Molins, Wenceslao Jaime: *La Ciudad Única: Potosí*. Potosí, 1961.
Osborne, Harold: *Bolivia, a Land Divided*. London: Royal Institute of International Affairs; 1954.
Quirós, Juan: *Indice de la Poesía Boliviana Contemporánea*. La Paz, 1964.
René Moreno, Gabriel: *Ultimos Días Coloniales en el Alto Perú*. La Paz, 1940.
Vaca Guzmán, Santiago: *La Literatura Boliviana*. Buenos Aires, 1884.
Villalobos, Rosendo: *Letras Bolivianas*. La Paz, 1936.
Vizcarra Fabre, G.: *Poetas Nuevos de Bolivia*. La Paz, 1941.

BRAZIL

Azevedo, Fernando de: *A Cultura Brasileira, Introdução ao estudo da Cultura no Brasil*. São Paulo, 1944.
———: *Brazilian Culture: an Introduction*. New York: The Macmillan Co.; 1950.
Bandeira, Manuel: *Brief History of Brazilian Literature*. New York: Frank; 1964.

————: *Obras Primas de Lirica Brasileira*. São Paulo, 1943.

Besouchet, Lidia, and Freitas, Newton: *Literatura del Brasil*. Buenos Aires, 1947.

Andrade, Muricy: *A Nova Literatura Brasileira*. Porto Alegre, 1936.

Calmon, Pedro: *História do Brasil*, 7 vols. Rio de Janeiro, 1961.

Capistrano de Abreu, João: *O Descobrimento do Brasil pelos Portugueses*. Rio de Janeiro, 1900.

Carvalho, Ronald de: *Pequena história da literatura Brasileira*. Rio de Janeiro. 1938.

Colgeras, João Pandiá: *A History of Brazil*. Chapel Hill, N.C., University of North Carolina Press, 1939.

Costa, Benedicto: *La roman au Brésil*. Paris, 1918.

Cruz Costa, J.: *O Positivismo na república*. São Paulo, 1956.

————: *Esbozo de una Historia de las Ideas en el Brazil*. México, D.F., 1957.

Cunha, Euclides da: *Os Sertões*. Rio de Janeiro, 1908.

Domingues, Mario: *O drama e gloria do padre Antônio Vieira*. Lisbon, 1961.

Ferreira Carrato, Jose: *A crise dos costumes nas Minas Gerais do Seculo XVIII*. Assis, 1962.

Freyre, Gilberto: *The Masters and the Slaves (Casa Grande y Senzala)*. New York: Alfred A. Knopf; 1956.

————: *Interpretación del Brasil*. México, D.F., 1945.

Goldberg, Isaac: *Brazilian Literature*. New York: Alfred A. Knopf; 1922.

Griego, Agrippino: *Evolução da poesia brasileira*. Rio de Janeiro, 1933.

Lira, Heitor: *História de D. Pedro II*. São Paulo, 1938–40.

Niello Morales Filho, Alexandre: *Poetas brasileiros contemporáneos*. Rio de Janeiro, 1903.

Oliveira Torre, João Camilo de: *O Positivismo no Brasil*. Rio de Janeiro, 1943.

Putnam, Samuel: *Marvelous Journey: Four Centuries of Brazilian Literature*. New York: Alfred A. Knopf; 1948.

Ramos, Arthur: *O Folclore Negro do Brasil*. Rio de Janeiro, 1954.

————: *Culturas Negras: Las poblaciones del Brasil*. México, D.F., 1944.

Rocha Pombo, José Francisco de: *História do Brasil*, 10 vols. Rio de Janeiro, 1905.

Romero, Sylvio: *História da Literatura Brasileira*, 2 vols. Rio de Janeiro, 1902.

Smith, T. Lynn: *Peoples and Institutions of Brazil*. Baton Rouge, La.: Louisiana University Press; 1946.

Verissimo, Erico: *Brazilian Literature*. New York: The Macmillan Co.; 1945.

Verissimo, José: *História da Literatura Brasileira de Benito Texeira (1601) a Machado de Assis (1908)*. Rio de Janeiro, 1916.

CHILE

Alegría, Fernando: *La Poesía Chilena: Orígenes y Desarrollo: del Siglo XVI al XIX.* México, D.F., 1953.

Amunátegui Solar, Domingo: *Bosquejo Histórico de la Literatura Chilena.* Santiago, 1920.

Barros Arana, Diego: *Historia General de Chile,* 16 vols. Santiago, 1884–1902.

Díaz Arrieta, Hernán (Alone): *Panorama de la Literatura Chilena en el Siglo XX.* Santiago, 1930.

———: *Historia personal de la Literatura Chilena.* Santiago, 1962.

Donoso, Armando: *Nuestros Poetas: Antología Chilena Moderna.* Santiago, 1924.

Edwards, Alberto: *La Fronda Aristocrática.* Santiago, 1945.

Encina, Francisco A.: *Historia de Chile desde la prehistoria hasta 1891.* 20 vols. Santiago, 1940–52.

———: *Resumen de la Historia de Chile,* 3 vols. Santiago, 1959.

Evans, Henry Clay: *Chile and Its Relations with the United States.* Durham, N.C.: Durham University Press; 1927.

Fergusson, Erna: *Chile.* New York, 1943.

Galdames, Luis: *A History of Chile.* Chapel Hill, N. C.: University of North Carolina Press; 1941.

Guilisasti-Tagle, Sergio: *Partidos Políticos Chilenos.* Santiago, 1964.

Latorre, Mariano: *La Literatura de Chile.* Buenos Aires, 1941.

Lillo, Samuel: *Literatura Chilena.* Santiago, 1938.

McBride, George: *Chile: Land and Society.* New York, 1936.

Medina, José Toribio: *Historia de la Literatura Colonial Chilena,* 3 vols. Santiago, 1878.

Merino Reyes, Luis: *Panorama de la Literatura Chilena.* Washington: Pan-American Union; 1959.

Montes, Hugo: *Antología de Medio Siglo.* Santiago, 1956.

Silva Castro, Raúl: *Panorama Literario de Chile.* Santiago, 1961.

———: *Panorama de la Novela Chilena.* México, D.F., 1955.

Solar, Hernán del: *Índice de la Poesía Chilena Contemporánea.* Santiago, 1937.

COLOMBIA

Academia Colombiana: *Poemas de Colombia.* Bogotá, 1959.

Academia Colombiana de Historia: *Historia Extensa de Colombia,* 23 vols. Bogotá, 1965.

Arango Ferrer, Javier: *La Literatura de Colombia,* Buenos Aires, 1940.

———: *2 Horas de Literatura Colombiana.* Medellín, 1963.

García Prada, Carlos: *Antología de Líricos Colombianos,* 2 vols. Bogotá, 1937.

Gómez Restrepo, Antonio: *Historia de la Literatura Colombiana*, 4 vols. Bogotá, 1945–7.

Groot, José Manuel: *Historia Eclesiástica y Civil de la Nueva Granada*, 4 vols. Bogotá, 1956–7.

Henao, J. M., and Arrubla, G.: *A History of Colombia*. Chapel Hill, N.C.: University of North Carolina Press; 1938.

Jaramillo Uribe, Jaime: *El pensamiento Colombiano en el Siglo XIX*. Bogotá, 1964.

López de Mesa, Luis: *Introducción a la Historia de la Cultura en Colombia*. Bogotá, 1930.

——: *De cómo se ha formado la nación Colombiana*. Bogotá, 1934.

Maya, Rafael: *Los Orígenes del Modernismo en Colombia*. Bogotá, 1961.

Nieto Arteta, Luis E.: *Economía y Cultura en la Historia de Colombia*. Bogotá, 1942.

Ortega Ricaurte, José V.: *Historia Crítica del Teatro en Bogotá*. Bogotá, 1927.

Otero Muñoz, Gustavo: *La Literatura Colonial y la Popular en Colombia*. La Paz, 1928.

Ospina, Eduardo: *El Romanticismo, Estudio de Sus Caracteres Esenciales en Colombia*. Bogotá, 1952.

Pachón Padilla, Eduardo: *Antología del Cuento Colombiano*. Bogotá, 1959.

Romoli, Kathleen: *Colombia, Gateway to South America*. Garden City: Doubleday, Doran & Co.; 1944.

Sanín Cano, Baldomero: *Letras Colombianas*. México, D.F., 1944.

Veintiseis Cuentos Colombianos. Bogotá: El Tiempo; 1959.

Vergara y Vergara, J. M.: *Historia de la Literatura en la Nueva Granada*. Bogotá, 1905.

COSTA RICA

Borges Pérez, Fernando: *Historia del Teatro en Costa Rica*. San José, 1942.

Fernández, Maximino: *Lira Costarricense*. San José, 1890–1.

Fernández Guardia, Ricardo: *Historia de Costa Rica: El Descubrimiento y la Conquista*. San José, 1933.

Jones, Chester Lloyd: *Costa Rica and the Civilization in the Caribbean*. Madison: University of Wisconsin; 1935.

Monge y Wender: *Historia de Costa Rica*. San José, 1947.

Ory, Eduar de: Los mejores poetas de Costa Rica. Madrid, 1929.

Sotela, Rogelio: *Literatura Costarricense*. San José, 1920.

——: *Escritores de Costa Rica*. San José, 1942.

CUBA

Bachiller y Morales, Antonio: *Apuntes para la Historia de las Letras y la Instrucción en la Isla de Cuba*, 3 vols. Havana, 1859–61.
Bueno, Salvador: *Antología del Cuento en Cuba*. Havana, 1953.
———: *Historia de la Literatura Cubana*. Havana, 1963.
Chacón y Calvo, José María: *Ensayos de Literatura Cubana*. Madrid, 1922.
———: *Las Mejores Poesías Cubanas*. Madrid, 1922.
Fernández de Castro, José A.: *Esquema Histórico de las Letras de Cuba, 1548–1902*. Havana, 1949.
———: *Medio siglo de Historia Colonial de Cuba*. Havana, 1923.
González Freire, Natividad: *Teatro Cubano*. Havana, 1961.
Guerra y Sánchez, Pérez Carera; Remos y Santovenia: *Historia de la Nación Cubana*, 10 vols. Havana, 1952.
Guirao, Ramón: *Órbita de la Poesía Afrocubana*. Havana, n.d.
Lizaso, Félix: *Panorama de la Cultura Cubana*. México, D.F., 1949.
Martí de Cid, Dolores: *Teatro Cubano Contemporáneo*. Madrid, 1959.
Mitjans, Aurelio: *Estudio sobre el Movimiento Científico y Literario de Cuba*. Havana, 1890.
Phillips, R. Hart: *Cuba: Island of Paradox*. New York, 1959.
Portuondo, J. A.: *Cuentos Cubanos Contemporáneos*. México, D.F., 1946.
Remos y Rubio, Juan José: *Historia de la Literatura Cubana*, 3 vols. Havana, 1925.
Saco, José Antonio: *Historia de la Esclavitud*, 7 vols. 1875.
Varona, Enrique José: *De la Colonia a la República*. Havana, 1919.
Vitier, Cintio: *Cincuenta Años de Poesía Cubana* (1902–52). Havana, 1952.
Vitier, Medardo: *La Filosofía en Cuba*. México, D.F., 1947.
Wilcox, Marrion: *A Short History of the War with Spain*. New York, 1898.
Wright, I. A.: *The Early History of Cuba, 1492–1586*. New York.

DOMINICAN REPUBLIC

Balaguer, Joaquín: *Letras Dominicanas*. Santo Domingo, 1944.
Bazil, Osvaldo: *Parnaso Dominicano*. Barcelona, 1915.
Fernández Spencer, A.: *Nueva Poesía Dominicana*. Madrid, 1953.
Galíndez, José de Jesús: *La Era de Trujillo*. Santiago de Chile, 1956.
Henríquez Ureña, Max: *Panorama Histórico de la Literatura Dominicana*. Rio de Janeiro, 1945.
Henríquez Ureña, Pedro: *La Cultura y las Letras Coloniales en Santo Domingo*. Buenos Aires, 1936.
Hicks, Albert C.: *Blood in the Streets: the Life and Rule of Trujillo*. New York: Creative Age Press; 1946.

Mejía, Abigail: *Historia de la Literatura Dominicana*. Santo Domingo, 1936.
Mejía Ricart, Gustavo A.: *Historia de Santo Domingo*, 2 vols. Ciudad Trujillo, 1948–52.
Rodman, Selden: *Quisqueya: a History of the Dominican Republic*. Seattle: University of Washington Press; 1960.
Welles, Sumner: *Naboth's Vineyard: the Dominican Republic, 1844–1924*, 2 vols. New York: Payson & Clarke Ltd.; 1928.

ECUADOR

Academia del Ecuador: *Antología Ecuatoriana*. Quito, 1892.
Andrade y Cordero, C.: *Ruta de la Poesía Ecuatoriana Contemporánea*. Cuenca, 1951.
Arias, Augusto: *Panorama de la Cultura Ecuatoriana*. Quito, 1936.
Barrera, Isaacs: *La Literatura del Ecuador*. Buenos Aires, n.d.
Benites, Leopoldo: *Ecuador, Drama y Paradoja*. México, D.F., 1950.
Blanksten, George: *Ecuador: Constitutions and Caudillos*. Berkeley: University of California Press; 1951.
Blomberg, R.: *Ecuador: Andean Mosaic*. N.p., 1952.
Carrera Andrade, Jorge: *Galería de Místicos y de Insurgentes*. Quito, 1959.
————: *El Camino del Sol*. Quito, 1959.
Carrión, Benjamín: *El Nuevo Relato Ecuatoriano*. Quito, 1958.
Franklin, Albert B.: *Ecuador: Portrait of a People*. Garden City: Doubleday, Doran; 1943.
González Suárez, Federico: *Historia General del Ecuador*, 8 vols. Quito, 1890–1903.
Lasso, Raphael V.: *The Wonderland of Ecuador*. New York: Alpha-Ecuador; 1944.
Linke, Lilo: *Ecuador, Land of Contrasts*. London: Oxford University Press; 1960.
Orellano, Gonzalo J.: *El Ecuador en Cien Años de Independencia, 1830–1930*. Quito, 1930.
Pareja Diezcanseco, Alfredo: *Historia del Ecuador*, 2 vols. Quito, 1958.
Reyes, Oscar Efrén: *Historia de la República*. Quito, 1949.
Rojas, Ángel F.: *La Novela Ecuatoriana*. México, D.F., 1947.
Vascónez, Francisco: *Historia de la Literatura Ecuatoriana*. Quito, 1919.
Von Hagen, Víctor Wolfgang: *Ecuador, the Unknown*. New York: Oxford University Press; 1939.

GUATEMALA

Cardoza y Aragón, Luis: *Guatemala: las Líneas de Su Mano*. México, D.F., 1955.

Contreras, R.: *Breve Historia de Guatemala*. Guatemala, 1951.

Díaz Vasconcelos, L. A.: *Apuntes para la Historia de la Literatura Guatemalteca: Épocas Indígena y Colonial*. Guatemala, 1942.

Jones, C. L.: *Guatemala, Past and Present*. Minneapolis: University of Minnesota; 1940.

Mencos Franco, A.: *Literatura Guatemalteca en el período de la Colonia*. Guatemala, 1937.

Milla, José: *Historia de la América Central*, 2 vols.; and Gómez Carrillo, Agustín: *Continuación de la Historia de Milla*, 3 vols. Guatemala, 1879–97.

Porta Mencos, Humberto: *Parnaso Guatemalteco*. Guatemala, 1928.

Salazar, Ramón A.: *Historia del Desenvolvimiento Intelectual de Guatemala*. Guatemala, 1897.

Solórzano, Carlos: *Teatro Guatemalteco Contemporáneo*. Madrid, 1964.

Vela, David: *La Literatura Guatemalteca*, 2 vols. Guatemala, 1947.

HAITI

Cabon, A.: *Histoire d'Haiti*, 4 vols. Port-au-Prince, 1927–37.

Davis, H. P.: *Black Democracy*. New York: The Dial Press; 1936.

Bellegarde, Dantés: *La nation haïtienne*. Paris, 1938.

————: *Haïti et son peuple*. Paris, 1953.

Cook, Mercer: *Education in Haiti*. Washington: Federal Security Agency; 1948.

Leyburn, James G.: *The Haitian People*. New Haven: Yale University Press; 1941.

Madion, T.: *Histoire d'Haïti*, 3 vols. Port-au-Prince, 1847–8.

Rodman, Selden: *Haiti: The Black Republic*. New York: Devin-Adair Co.; 1954.

————: *Renaissance in Haiti: Popular Painters in the Black Republic*. New York: Devin-Adair Co.; 1948.

Scharon, Faine: *Toussaint L'Ouverture et la Revolution de St. Domingue*. Port-au-Prince, 1957.

HONDURAS

Barrera, C.: *Antología de Poetas Jóvenes de Honduras*. Tegucigalpa, 1950.

Castro, J. L.: *Antología de Poetas Hondureños*. Tegucigalpa, 1939.

Chamberlain, Robert S.: *The Conquest and Colonization of Honduras*. Washington, D.C.: Carnegie Institution of Washington; 1953.

Durón, Rómulo Ernesto: *Bosquejo Histórico de Honduras*, 1502–1921. San Pedro Sula, 1927.

————: *Honduras Literaria: Escritores en Prosa*. Tegucigalpa, 1896. 1896.

————: *Honduras Literaria: Escritores en Verso*. Tegucigalpa, 1899.
1899.
Valle, Rafael Heliodoro: *Las Ideas Contemporáneas en Centro América*. México, D.F., 1960.

NICARAGUA

Ayón, Tomás: *Historia de Nicaragua*, 2 vols. Granada, 1882.
Cardenal, E.: *Introducción a la Nueva Poesía Nicaragüense*. Madrid, 1949.
Cox, Isaac: *Nicaragua and the United States*. Boston: World Peace Foundation Pamphlets; 1927.
Gámez, José Dolores: *Historia de Nicaragua desde los Tiempos Prehistóricos hasta 1860*. Managua, 1889.
Sánchez, María Teresa: *Poesía Nicaragüense*. Managua, 1948.
Ortiz, Alberto: *Parnaso Nicaragüense*. Barcelona, 1912.
Tweedy, M.: *This Is Nicaragua*. Ipswich, 1953.

MEXICO

Aguayo Spencer, R.: *Flor de Moderna Poesía Mexicana*. México, D.F., 1955.
Carballo, E.: *Cuentistas Mexicanos Modernos*, 2 vols. México, D.F., 1956.
Castro Leal, Antonio: *Las Cien Mejores Poesías Líricas Mexicanas*. México, D.F., 1945.
————: *La Poesía Mexicana Moderno*. México, D.F., 1953.
Chávez Orozco, Luis: *Historia Social y Económica de México*. México, D.F., 1938.
Crow, John Armstrong: *Mexico To-day*. New York: Harper; 1957.
Fernández Arias Campoamor, J.: *Novelistas de México*. Madrid, 1952.
González Obregón, Luis: *Breve Noticia de los Novelistas Mexicanos en el Siglo XIX*. México, D.F., 1889.
González Peña, Carlos: *Historia de la Literatura Mexicana*. México, D.F., 1954.
Jiménez Rueda, Julio: *Antología de la Prosa en México*. México, D.F., 1938.
————: *Historia de la Cultura en México: El virreinato*. México, D.F., 1950.
————: *Letras Mexicanas del Siglo XIX*. México, D.F., 1944.
Leal, L.: *Antología del Cuento Mexicano*. México, D.F., 1957.
Leiva, Raúl: *Imagen de la Poesía Mexicana Contemporánea*. México, D.F., 1959.
Martínez, José Luis: *Literatura Mexicana del Siglo XX*, 2 vols. México, D.F., 1949–50.
————: *El Ensayo Mexicano Moderno*, 2 vols. México, D.F., 1958.

Maples Arce, Manuel: *Antología de la Poesía Mexicana Moderna.* Rome, 1940.

Méndez Plancarte, A.: *Poetas novo-hispánicos*, 3 vols. México, D.F., 1943–5.

Mendoza, V. T.: *El Corrido Mexicano.* México, D.F., 1954.

Monterde, Francisco; Magaña Esquivel, Antonio; and Gorostiza, Celestino: *Teatro Mexicano del Siglo XX*, 3 vols. México, D.F., 1956.

Navarro, Bernabé: *La Introducción de la Filosofía Moderna en México.* México, D.F., 1948.

Olavarría y Ferrari, E.: *Reseña Histórica del Teatro en México.* México, D.F., 1895.

Parkes, Henry Bamford: *A History of México.* Boston: Houghton Mifflin; 1960.

Pereyra, Carlos: *Historia del Pueblo Mexicano.* 2 vols. México, D.F., n.d.

Ramos, Samuel: *Historia de la Filosofía en México.* México, D.F., 1943.

Reyes, Alfonso: *Letras de la Nueva España.* México, D.F., 1948.

Ricard, Robert: *La "Conquête Spirituelle" du Mexique.* Paris, 1933.

Sierra, Justo: *Juárez, Su Tiempo y Su Obra.* México, D.F., 1950.

Tannenbaum, Frank: *México: The Struggle for Peace and Bread.* New York: Alfred A. Knopf; 1950.

Usigli, Rodolfo: *México en el Teatro.* México, D.F., 1932.

Vasconcelos, José: *Breve Historia de México.* Madrid, 1952.

PANAMA

Biezanz, John and Mavis: *The People of Panama.* New York: Columbia University Press; 1955.

Castillero Reyes, E. J., and Arce, Enrique J.: *Historia de Panamá.* Panamá, 1949.

Garay, Narciso: *Tradiciones y Cantares de Panamá.* Brussels, 1930.

Karsi, Demetrio: *Antología de Panamá: Poesía y Prosa.* Barcelona, 1926.

Mack, Gerstle: *The Land Divided: A History of the Panama Canal.* New York: Alfred A. Knopf; 1944.

Méndez Pereira, Octavio: *Parnaso Panameño.* Panamá, 1916.

Miró, Rodrigo: *El Cuento en Panamá.* Panamá, 1950.

————: *La Literatura Panameña. Breve Recuento Histórico.* Panamá, 1946.

————: *La Cultura Colonial de Panamá.* México, D.F., 1950.

Ruiz Vernacci, Enrique: *Introducción al cuento panameño.* Panamá, 1946.

PARAGUAY

Benz, Cecilio: *Historia del Paraguay*. Asunción, 1919.
Bertoni, Moisés S.: *La Civilización Guaraní*. Puerto Bertoni, 1922.
Centurión, Carlos R.: *Historia de las Letras Paraguayas*, 3 vols. Buenos Aires, 1947–51.
De Vitis, M. A.: *Parnaso Paraguayo*, Barcelona, 1925.
Elliot, Arthur E.: *Paraguay: Its Cultural Heritage, Social Conditions and Education*. New York, 1931.
Godoi, Juan Silvano: *Monografías Históricas*. Buenos Aires, 1893.
González, Natalicio: *Proceso y Formación de la Cultura Paraguaya*. Buenos Aires, 1938.
———: *Geografía del Paraguay*, 2 vols. México, D.F., 1963–5.
Koebel, William Henry: *Paraguay*. London: T. F. Unwin Ltd.; 1917.
Lozano, Pedro: *Historia de las Revoluciones del Paraguay, Tucumán, y Río de la Plata*. n.d.
Maldonado, Silvio: *El Paraguay*. México, D.F., 1951.
Wey, Walter: *La Poesía Paraguaya*. Montevideo, 1951.
Warren, W. G.: *Paraguay: an informal History*. Norman, Okla., 1949.
Washburn, C. A.: *History of Paraguay*, 2 vols. Boston, 1871.

PERU

Barrera Laos: *Vida Intelectual del Virreinato del Perú*. Buenos Aires, 1940.
Basadre, Jorge: *Historia del la República del Perú*. Lima, 1946.
———: *Perú: Problema y Posibilidad*. Lima, 1931.
Bazán, Armando: *Antología del Cuento Peruano*. Santiago, 1942.
Belaúnde, Victor Andrés: *El Perú Antiguo y los Modernos Sociólogos*. Lima, 1908.
Beltroy, Manuel: *Las Cien Mejores Poesías Líricas Peruanas*. Lima, 1921.
Cossío del Pomar, Felipe: *Víctor Raúl: Biografía de Haya de la Torre*. México, D.F., 1951.
Defourneaux, Marcelin: *Pablo de Olavide, ou L'Afrancesado (1725–1803)*. Paris, 1959.
Eguiguren, Luis Antonio: *La Universidad Nacional de San Marcos*. Lima, 1951.
García, José Uriel: *El Nuevo Indio*, Lima, 1949 (?).
García Calderón, Ventura: *Del Romanticismo al Modernismo. Prosistas y Poetas Peruanos*. Paris, 1910.
———: *Parnaso Peruano*. Barcelona, 1914.
Haya de la Torre, V. R.: *Treinta Años de Aprismo*. México, D.F., 1936.
Hesse Murga, José: *Teatro Peruano Contemporáneo*. Madrid, 1959.
Karsten, Rafael: *A Totalitarian State of the Past: The Inca Empire*. Leipzig, 1949.

Lohman Villena, Guillermo: *El Arte Dramático en Lima durante el Virreinato*. Madrid, 1945.

Mariátegui, José Carlos: *Siete Ensayos de interpretación de la Realidad Peruana*. Lima, 1928.

Markham, Clements R.: *A History of Peru*. Chicago: C. H. Sergel & Co.; 1892.

Mason, John Alden: *The Ancient Civilisations of Peru*. London: Penguin Books; 1957.

Monguió, Luis: *La Poesía Modernista Peruana*. México, D.F., 1954.

Paz Soldán, Mariano Felipe: *Historia del Perú Independiente*. Lima–Buenos Aires, 1868–88.

Porras Barranechea, Raúl: *Los Viajeros Italianos en el Perú*. Lima, 1957.

————: *Pequeña Antología de Lima*. Madrid, 1953.

Riva Agüero, José de la: *Carácter de la Literatura del Perú Independiente*. Lima, 1906.

Sáenz, Moisés: *Sobre el Indio Peruano*. México, D.F., 1933.

Sánchez, Luis Alberto: *La Literatura Peruana*, 6 vols. Asunción, 1950–1.

————: *Índice de la Poesía Contemporánea*. Santiago, 1938.

Universidad Nacional de Córdoba, Argentina: *César Vallejo. Simposium para Estudiar Su Vida*. Córdoba, 1962.

Valcárcel, Luis E.: *Ruta Cultural del Perú*. México, D.F., 1945.

Sancho de la Hoz, Pedro: *Relación para S. M. de la Sucedido en la Conquista y Pacificación de Estas Provincias de la Nueva Castilla*. Lima, 1917.

PUERTO RICO

Angelis, María Luisa de: *Poetas Puertorriqueños*. Guayana, 1912.

Babín, María Teresa: *Panorama de la Literatura Puertorriqueña*. San Juan, 1956.

Brau, Salvador: *Historia de Puerto Rico*. New York, 1944.

Cabrera Manrique, Francisco: *Historia de la Literatura Puertorriqueña*. San Juan, 1956.

Gontán, José A.: *Historia Político-Social de Puerto Rico*. San Juan, 1945.

Hernández Aquino, Luis: *Poesía Puertorriqueña*. México, D.F., 1954.

Hostos, Eugenio María de: *Reseña Histórica de Puerto Rico*. Santiago de Chile, 1872.

Labarthe, Pedro Juan: *Antología de Poetas Contemporáneos de Puerto Rico*. México, D.F., 1946.

Meléndez, Concha: *Figuración de Puerto Rico*. San Juan, 1958.

Peñaranda, Carlos: *Cartas Puertorriqueñas, 1878–1880*. Madrid, 1885.

Ribera Chevremont, E., and Alegría, J. S.: *Antología de Poetas Jóvenes de Puerto Rico*. San Juan, 1918.

Rivera de Álvarez, Josefina: *Diccionario de Literatura Puertorriqueña*. Río Piedras, 1956.

Rosa-Nieves, Cesáreo: *La Poesía en Puerto Rico.* México, D.F., 1943.
Sánez, Antonia: *El Teatro en Puerto Rico.* Río Piedras, 1950.
Torres Rivera, E.: *Parnaso Puertorriqueño.* Barcelona, 1920.

EL SALVADOR

Barberena, Santiago Ignacio: *Historia del Salvador,* 2 vols. San Salvador, 1914–17.
Dueñas, Ricardo: *Biografía del General Francisco Morazán.* San Salvador, 1961.
Gallegos Valdés, Luis: *Panorama de la Literatura Salvadoreña.* San
———: *.El Teatro del Salvador.* San Salvador, 1961.
López Jiménez, Ramón: *José Matías Delgado y de León.* San Salvador, 1961.
Martin, Percy F.: *El Salvador of the Twentieth Century.* New York: Longmans, Green Co.; 1911.
Mayorga Rivas, Román: *Guirnalda Salvadoreña,* 3 vols. San Salvador, 1884–6.
Montes, Arturo Humberto: *Morazán y la Federación Centroamericana.* México, D.F., 1958.
Toruño, Juan Felipe: *Desarrollo Literario del Salvador.* San Salvador, 1958.

URUGUAY

Ardao, Arturo: *Espiritualismo y Positivismo en el Uruguay.* México, D.F., 1950.
———: *La Filosofía en el Uruguay en el Siglo XX.* México, D.F., 1956.
Blanco Acevedo, Pablo: *Historia de la República Oriental del Uruguay,* 6 vols. Montevideo, 1910.
Bollo, S.: *El Modernismo en el Uruguay.* Montevideo, 1951.
Caillava, Doimgo A.: *Historia de la Literatura Gauchesca en el Uruguay, 1810–1940.* Montevideo, 1945.
Dibarboure, J. Alberto: *Proceso del Teatro Uruguayo, 1808-1883.* Montevideo, 1940.
Falcao-Espalta, M.: *Antología de Poetas Uruguayos.* Montevideo, 1922.
Fitzgibbon, R. H.: *Uruguay, Portrait of a Democracy.* New Brunswick: Rutgers University Press; 1954.
Hudson, W. H.: *The Purple Land.* New York: The Modern Library; 1927.
Koebel, W. H.: *Uruguay.* London: T. F. Unwin; 1911.
Lasplaces, Alberto: *Antología del Cuento Uruguayo,* 2 vols. Montevideo, 1943–4.
Montero Bustamente, Raúl: *El Parnaso Oriental.* Montevideo, 1905.
Rodó, José Enrique: *Obras Completas,* 4 vols. Montevideo, 1956.

Roxlo, Carlos: *Historia Crítica de la Literatura Uruguaya*, 7 vols. Montevideo, 1912.

Silva Valdés, Fernán: *Teatro Uruguayo Contemporáneo*. Madrid, 1959.

Zum Felde, Alberto: *Proceso Intelectual del Uruguay y Crítica de Su Literatura*. Montevideo, 1930.

————: *La Literatura del Uruguay*. Buenos Aires, 1939.

————: *Índice de la Poesía Uruguaya Contemporánea*. Santiago de Chile, 1934.

VENEZUELA

Acosta, Cecilio: *Estudios sobre la Sociología Venezolana*. Caracas, 1908–9.

Angarita Arévalo, Rafael: *Historia y Crítica de la Novela en Venezuela*. Berlin, 1938.

Arcaya, Pedro: *Estudios en Sociología Venezolana*. Madrid, 1916.

Baralt, Rafael María: *Resumen de la Historia de Venezuela*. Paris, 1841.

Barrios Mora, José R.: *Compendio Histórico de la Literatura Venezolana*. Caracas, 1948.

Cortés, P.: *Contribución al estudio del Cuento Venezolano*. Caracas, 1945.

D'Sola, Otto: *Antología de la Moderna Poesía Venezolana*, 2 vols. Caracas, 1940.

De Grummond, Jane Lucas: *Envoy to Caracas*. Baton Rouge: Louisiana State University; 1951.

Díaz Seijas, Pedro: *Literatura Venezolana*. Caracas, 1952.

Febres Cordero, G.: *Tres Siglos de Imprenta y Cultura Venezolanas*. Caracas, 1959.

Fombona Pachano, Jacinto: *Poetas Venezolanos*. Buenos Aires, 1951.

Gil Fortoul, José: *Historia Constitucional de Venezuela*. Caracas, 1930.

Marsland, W. D. and A. L.: *Venezuela Through Its History*. New York, 1954.

Olivares Figueroa, R.: *Nuevos Poetas Venezolanos*. Caracas, 1939.

Picón Febres, Gonzalo: *La Literatura Venezolana en el Siglo XIX*. Caracas, 1940.

Picón-Sales, Mariano: *Formación y Proceso de la Literatura Venezolana*. Caracas, 1940.

————: *Antología de Costumbristas Venezolanos del Siglo XIX*. Caracas, 1940.

Planchart, Julio: *Tendencia de la Lírica Venezolana*. Caracas, 1940.

Semanario de Caracas (Edición facsimilar). Caracas, 1959.

Torrealba Lossi, Mario: *Diez estudios sobre Literatura Venezolana*. Caracas, 1950.

Uslar-Pietri, Arturo: *Letras y Hombres de Venezuela*. México, D.F., 1948.

Uslar-Pietri, A., and Padrón, J.: *Antología del Cuento Moderno Venezolana*, 2 vols. Caracas, 1940.
Venegas Filardo, Pascual: *Novelas y Novelistas de Venezuela*. Caracas, 1955.

SPECIAL BOOKS AND SOME BOOKS REFERRED TO IN THE TEXT

Bello, Andrés: *Obras Completas*, 16 vols. Caracas, 1952–64.
Bolívar, Simón: *Obras Completas*, 3 vols. Havana, 1950.
Bougainville, Louis-Antoine de: *Voyage au Tour du Monde*. Paris, 1958.
Chardon, Carlos E.: *Boussingault*. Ciudad Trujillo, 1953.
Codazzi, Agostino: *Le Memorie—a cura di Mario Longhena*. Milan, 1959.
Colombo, Fernando: *La Storia della vita e dei fatti di Cristoforo Colombo*. Milan, 1957.
Del Mazo, Gabriel: *La Reforma Universitaria*, 3 vols. La Plata, n.d.
Del Río, Ángel: *El Mundo Hispánico y el Mundo Anglosajón en América*. Buenos Aires, 1960.
Diderot, Denis: special number of the magazine *Europe*, January–February, 1963.
García Mercadal, J.: *Lo que España Llevó a América*. Madrid, 1959.
Gómez Robeldo, Antonio: *Idea y Experiencia de América*. México, 1958.
Hanke, Lewis, ed.: *Do the Americas Have a Common History?* New York: Alfred A. Knopf; 1964.
Henríquez Ureña, Pedro: *Seis Ensayos en Busca de Nuestra Expresión*. Buenos Aires, 1928.
Humboldt, Alexander von: *Viaje a las Regiones Equinocciales del Nuevo Mundo*, 5 vols. Caracas, 1940.
———: *Essai Politique de la Nouvelle Espagne*. Paris, 1811.
———: *Examen Critique de l'Histoire de la Géographie du Nouveau Continent*. Paris, 1814–34.
Leturia, Pedro de: *Relaciones Entre la Santa Sede e Hispanoamérica*, 3 vols. Rome, 1959–60.
Martí, José: *Obras Completas*, 2 vols. Havana, 1939.
Medina, José Toribio: *Biblioteca Hispanoaméricana*, 7 vols. Santiago de Chile, 1898–1908.
Montaigne, M. de: *Oeuvres Complètes*. Paris, 1962.
Morley, Sylvanus Griswold: *The Ancient Maya*. Stanford: Stanford University Press; 1956.
Péret, Benjamin: *Anthologie des Mythes et Légendes d'Amérique*. Paris, 1960.
Presencia de Rousseau. Universidad Nacional Autónoma: México, D.F.; 1962.

Ramos, Arthur: *Las Culturas Negras del Nuevo Mundo*. México, D.F., 1943.

Ribadeau Dumas, François: *Histoire de la Magie*. Paris, 1963.

Salas, Alberto M.: *Crónica Florida del Mestizaje en las Indias, Siglo XVI*. Buenos Aires, 1960.

Sarrailh, Jean: *L'Espagne éclairée de la seconde moitié du XVIIIᵉ. siècle*. Paris, 1954.

Schumacher, Hernán Albert: *Biografía del General Agustín Codazzi*. Bogotá, 1913–14.

Spell, Jefferson Rea: *Rousseau in the Spanish World before 1833*. Austin: University of Texas Press; 1938.

Vespucci, Amerigo: *Él Nuevo Mundo: Cartas Relativas a Sus Viajes y Descubrimientos*. Buenos Aires, 1951.

Whitaker, Arthur P.: *Latin America and the Enlightenment*. New York: D. Appleton Century Co.; 1942.

Zavala, Silvio: *América en el Espiritu Francés del siglo XVIII*. México, D.F., 1949.

Zea, Leopoldo: *Dos Etapas del Pensamiento en Hispanoamérica: Romanticismo y Positivismo*. México, D.F., 1949.

Index

by Mary H. Waters

Abakuá African Society, 548

Aberdeen Law, 421

Abrantès, Duc d' (General Junot), 412

Abrantès, Duchesse d' (Laure Permon Junot), 306

Abreu, Capistrano de, 117

Acatepec, 195

Acero de la Cruz, Antonio, 223, 229

Achá, Dr. José M. de, 376

Acolman, 197, 212, 214; convent of, 221

Acosta, Cecilio, 398

Acosta, Joaquín: *History of Colombia*, 284

Acosta, José de, 148; *Historia . . . de las Indias*, 171; *Doctrina Cristiana . . .*, 264–5

Acosta, Miguel, 42, 43

Actopan, 196

Acuña, Fray Cristóbal de: *Nuevo descubrimiento del Río Amazonas*, 172

Acuña, Manuel, 462

Adams, John, xiii *n.*, xvi, 336

Africa, 6, 37, 79, 94–5, 99, 108, 117, 125, 238, 444, 451–2, 488; *see also* magic, mysticism

Agramonte, Roberto: *Sociología Latina Americana*, 520

agrarian reform: *see* land tenure and reform

agriculture: Indian, 22–6; horticultural exchanges, 38–47, 57–62; 93; *see* land tenure and reform; *see also under names of countries*

Aguado, Fray Pedro, 85; *Conquista de la Nueva Granada*, 146; *Historia de Santa Marta . . .*, 171

Aguiguren, Luis Antonio, 295

Aguirre, Lope de, 36, 48, 73, 82, 84, 138, 172, 176

Aguirre, Nataniel: *Juan de la Rosa*, 478

Aguirre, Pedro, 223

ahuacpintas (textile shops), 34

Ahumada, Agustín de, 84

Alaska, 270

Alberdi, Juan Bautista ("Figarillo"): *Bases y Puntos de Partida para la organización política de la República* and *Argentina*, 324; 326, 328–9, 359, 379, 385, 393–5

Alberti, Rafael, 477

Albertus Magnus, 530

albinagio, 368

Albizzi, Francesco degli, 70

Albuquerque, Alfonso de, 95

Alcedo y Herrera, Antonio de: *Diccionario Histórica Geográphico de las Indias Occidentales o América*, 304

Alegría, Ciro: *Los Perros Hambrientos*, 481–2

"Aleijandinho, O": *see* Lisboa, António Francisco

Alemán, Mateo, 191

Alemán, Miguel, 497

Alembert, Jean Le Rond d', 336, 380

Alencar, José Martiniano de: *O Guaraní*, 432

Alexander the Great, 5

Alexander VI, Pope (Roderigo Borgia), 138

Alexandre, Maxime, 322

Alfaro, Eloy, 367

Alfonso, Martín, 99
Alfonso the Wise: *History of Spain*, 128
Almafuerte (Pedro B. Palacios), 462–3
Almagro, Diego de, 36, 172, 194
Almeida, Francisco de, 95
Alone: *see* Díaz Arrieta, Hernán
Alonso, Amado, 480
Altenberg, Peter, 473
Altuna, Manuel Ignacio, 245
Alva Ixtlilxóchitl, Fernando de: *Historia Chichimeca*, 182
Alvarado, Alonso de, 35, 146
Alvarado, Doña Beatriz de, 160
Alvarado, Don Pedro de, 48, 160, 171
Alvarado Huanitzin, Diego, 182
Alvarado Tezozómoc, Hernando: *Crónica Mexicáyotl*, 182
Álvares, Diego, 99
Alzaga, Martín de, 299–300, 340
Alzate Ramírez, José Antonio: *Observaciones meteorológicas* and *La Noticia sobre las minas de azogue que hay en la Nueva España*, 277; 296
Amadís de Gaula, 28, 76, 77
Amado, Jorge, 440
amansaguapos, 533
amautas, 33
Amazon, river, region, xx, 13, 36, 48, 73, 88, 267, 536
"Amazons," the, 70, 77, 78, 80–2, 526
Ameghino, Florentino, 395
"America," xii–xxiii, 68–9, 103, 280
America: cultural subdivisions and evolutionary contrasts, xiv, xix–xxii, 3, 21, 27–8, 35–6, 50, 98, 123–5, 127, 287, 461–3, 466; world contributions, xv–xvii, 58–63, 233–4, 238–50; dawn of Christian era, 3, 308–9; first bonds with Spain, 37–57, Portugal, 88–122; mystique, 461–3, 525–8, 548–50; *see also* pre-Columbian America; Portuguese America; Spanish America

American Argus (newspaper), 297, 329
American Popular and Revolutionary Alliance (APRA), 491–3
Anacaona, Queen, 537
Anacreon, 239
Anáhuac, Valley of, 29, 144, 199, 316, 499
Anchieta, Father José de: *De Beata Virgini* and *De Gestis Mendi de Sáa*, 116
Ancizar, Manuel: *Peregrinación de Alpha*, 284
Anderson Imbert, Enrique, 80, 180, 184, 520
Andes, the, xxi, 15, 16, 35, 41, 85, 89
Andrada e Silva, José Bonifácio de: *Poesias avulsas*, 415–16; 418, 427
Andrade, Raúl, 333
Anglo-Saxon, the, xi, xxi, 354–5, 395
Antequera, José de, xvi
anticlericalism, 344, 347–8, 362, 396
anti-Semitism, 370, 410, 502; *see also* Jews
Antilles, the, 79, 107, 129, 141
Antolínez, 220
Antropofagia (review), 435
Apollinaire, Guillaume, 435, 476, 495
APRA: *see* American Popular and Revolutionary Alliance
aprismo, 493
Aquaviva, Father, 105
Arabia, 79, 108–9
Arago, François, 281, 284
Aragon, Louis, 476
Aranda, Conde de, 399
Arango Ferrer, Javier, 537
Aranha, Osvaldo, 438
Araucanians, 158–9, 173–6
Araucos (Arawaks), 89
Araujo Porto-Alegre, Manuel de: *A Estátua Amazônica*, 421
Arbeláez, Enrique Pérez, 274
architecture, Portuguese American: *Manuelino*, 96; Brazilian plantation, 111; Baroque, 411; *modernismo*, 436–7

architecture, Spanish American: Indian, 51, 147–50 (*see* Aztec; Inca;
Maya; pre-Columbian America);
colonial, 126, 131, 193–211, 216;
plateresque, 193–4, 197–8, 212;
translation, blending of styles,
193–203; Church, 195–204; Moorish, Oriental influence, 194–5,
200–3, 205; Churrigueresque, 198,
204; materials, 199–208; rural
church, 203–4; civil, 204–10; furniture, decoration, 207–8; military,
210–11; influence of engraving,
224–7; modern, 497, 517
Arcos, Santiago, 386
Ardouin, Corolian, 459
Areco, Sergeant-Major de, 40
Arenas Betancourt, José, 502
Arequipa, 194, 197–8
Arequipan style, 198
Argentina: dance, 53; name, 96; 106;
agriculture, 108; colonial, 126, 129,
133, 208–9 (*see* viceroyalties);
Paraguay, 157; architecture, 208–
9, 517; independence, 208–9, 254,
287, 299–300, 341, 343; Enlightenment, 232, 253–5; letters, 255,
323–8, 358–9, 462, 475–7, 481–2,
513; education, 255, 282, 290, 324,
395, 489–91, 513, 520; scientific
missions, 266, 270; press, 295, 297,
299–300, 504; dictatorships: see
caudillos; constitution, 324, 355;
flag, 340; monarchy vs. republic,
340–2; Church, 347–8; land reform, 356–7, 359; immigration,
359, 395–6; Utilitarianism, 380;
Positivism, 393–6; racism, 394–5;
Socialist Party, 396; slavery, 423;
World War I, 489; university revolution, 490–1; Nazism, 502–3
Argentine University Federation, 491
Argüedas, Alcides: *History of Bolivia,* 370; 375–7; *Pueblo Enfermo,*
504–5
argüedismo, 504
Aristarchus of Samos, 236

Aristotle, 265, 530
Arkansas, 228
armaments: *see* military, Spanish
American; Brazil
Armas, Castillo, 363
Arraiz, Antonio: *Puros Hombres,* 511
art, Portuguese American: Indian,
89, 93; introduction of oil painting, 119; colonial, 119–20; sculpture, 411; European influence,
411–15; patronage, 419; *modernismo,* 435–8; painting, 437; collections, museums, 440
art, Spanish American: pre-Columbian: *see* pre-Columbian America, Aztec, Inca, Maya; Exposition, 1950, 4, 5, 497–8; birth
of, 46–9; 51, 126, 131–2; decoration, furniture, 46–7, 194–5, 200–
2, 206–8; *mestizo,* 49, 193–5,
211–12; Indian, 147–50, 193–5,
198–200, 202, 211–12, 216–18,
221, 225–6, 229; sculpture, 162,
211–18, 215–16; painting, 167,
204, 218–29, 344, 462, 494–5;
Moorish, Oriental influence, 194,
200–3, 205; mural, fresco, 197–8,
221–4, 344–5, 390; materials, 211–
15, 221–2, 227; religious, 215–20;
education, 217, 277; galleries,
museums, 218–21; collections of
European, 218–21; influence of
engraving, 221–7, 483; early masters, 227–9; scientific missions,
272, 282, 284; modern, 462, 494–
5, 497–8, 502 (see *modernismo*)
Artigas, José Gervasio, 248, 288,
356
Asentzio, Manuel, 277
Asia, 6, 21, 37, 68, 69, 94–7, 108,
117, 238
Assyria, 3
Astorquiza, Eliodoro, 479 *n.*
astronomy, 9, 10, 233–6, 264–8, 271,
277, 284
Asturias, Miguel Ángel: *El Señor
Presidente,* 481–2

Asunción, 74, 131, 138
Atahualpa, 134
Athenäum, 314–15
Atlantis, 78
Atlixco, 219
Atotonilco, 196
Atzacoalco, 212
audiencia, the, 84, 130–1, 180, 222,
    250, 254, 298, 300, 313
Augustín I, Emperor: *see* Iturbide,
    Augustín de
Augustine, Saint, 131
Augustinian Order, 113, 145, 150,
    153, 197
auquénidos, 34
Aurora de Chile (newspaper), 301
Aury, Louis, 283
Austin, John, 336, 380
Australia, 6
Austria, 268, 310
Aviles, Viceroy, 126, 134
Avispa de Chilpancingo (newspa-
    per), 296
Ayachucho, 311, 349, 398
Azara, Félix: *Viaje a . . . la Amér-
    ica Meridional . . .* and *Apuntia-
    mentos . . . del Paraguay y Río
    de la Plata*, 274–5
Azcoitia, 245
Azcurra, Doña Encarnación, 358
Azevedo, Aluizo de: *O Mulato*, 434
Azpilcueta Navarro, João de, 116
Aztec civilization, xiv, 3, 5, 21; cal-
    endar, 22; 27, 28; capital: *see*
    Tenochtitlán; culture, art, archi-
    tecture, 29–30, 197, 199, 221–2,
    225; religion, 31, 148, 534–6 (*see*
    religion, pre-Christian); 36, 37, 45,
    80, 85, 88, 128, 131–2; early lit-
    erature, 145–6; post-conquest, 193,
    197, 277, 295
Azuela, Mariano: *Los de Abajo*, 390,
    483
Azuero, Vicente, 381

Baal, Roberto, 210
Baalbek, temples of, 5

Bachelier, Dr. Le Sieur, 213
Bachué, 148
Bacon, Francis, 232–3
Baerle, Caspar van, 120
Bagatelle, The (Colombian gazette),
    311
Bahamas, the, 65
Bahia: date founded, xiv; xv, 103,
    106, 113, 119, 406, 412, 545
Balboa, Vasco Núñez de, 39, 48–9,
    73, 138, 244, 251
Balbuena, Bernardo de: *Grandeza
    Mexicana* and *Siglo . . . las selvas
    Erífile*, 176–7; *Bernardo . . .* , 185
Ballivián, José, 372, 374
Balmis, Francis Xavier, 293
Bandeira, Manuel, 440–1
bandeirantes, 98, 102, 105, 109, 111,
    113, 116, 428–9, 432–3
bangüê, 112
Banville, Theodore de, 472
Baquijano y Carrillo, José, 232, 293
Baralt, Rafael María, 284
Barba Jacob, Porfirio, 501
Barbusse, Henri: *Le Feu*, 483
Barco Centenera, Martín del: "Ar-
    gentine Epic," 175
Barredo, Gabino, 385, 389, 394
Barreto, Isabel, 60
Barrios, Eduardo: *Gran Señor y
    Rajadiablos*, 210, 480
Barrios, Justo Rufino, 362–3
Bartolache, José Ignacio, 296
Basadre, Jorge, 134
Bascoco, Antonio, 207
Bashkirtsev, Marie, 463, 468, 472
Basques, 244–5, 247, 276–7, 299
Batista y Zaldívar, Fulgencio, 507,
    510, 513–14
Bautista Antonelli, Juan, 210
beatas; beatos, 140
Beaumont, Élie de, 284
Beckett, Samuel, 476
Bécquer, Gustavo Adolfo, 465, 467–
    8
Beethoven, Ludwig van: *Eroica*, 315
Belalcázar, Miguel de, 222

Belalcázar, Sebastián de (Sebastián Moyano), 36, 38, 125, 131

Belaúnde Terry, Fernande, 493

Belgrano, Manuel, 253, 340–1, 343, 357

Bellegarde, Dantès, quoted, 448 and n.

Bello, Andrés, 256–7, 280, 282, 292, 315; "Alocución a la Poesía," 320; "A la Agricultura de la Zona Torrida," 321; 322, 328–33, 353, 355, 379, 380–1, 388, 463

Bello, José Luis, collection of, 219

Beltrán, Luis, Saint, 163

Belzú, Manuel Isidro, 374–6

Benavente, Fray Toribio de (Motolinía): Historia de los Indios de la Nueva España, 145, 171, 221

Benedictine Order, 406

Benitez, Jaime, 522

Bennett, Wendell C., 13–14

Benot, Yves, 252

Bentham, Jeremy, 307, 320, 336, 355, 357, 379; Introduction . . . Principles of Morals and Legislation, 380; 382–3, 393

Bergeaud, Éméric: Stella, 459

Berkeley, George, 320

Berlanga, Fray Tomás de, 41

Bernadelli, Rodolfo: Christ and the Woman Taken in Adultery and The Mourning of the Tribe, 419

Bernardin de St. Pierre, Jacques Henri, 319

Berney, Antoine, 250

Berrío, Antonio de, 87

Berruguete, Alonso, 215

Berthelot, Pierre Eugène Marcelin, 284

Betancourt, Rómulo, 514

Betanzos, Domingo de, 149

Betanzos, Juan de: Suma . . . de los Incas, 172

Bible, the, 5, 70, 538

Biblioteca Americana (anthology), 320

Bilac, Olavo Bras Martins dos Guimarães: O Caçador de Esmeraldas, 428; 433

Bilbao, Francisco, 379; Sociabilidad chilena, 386; 387

Bimini, island of, 82

Bingham, Hiram, 15

Björnson, Björnstjerne, 472

"Black Legend," the, xii, 72

Blanco, Andrés Eloy, 202, 502

Blanco, Pedro, 372–3

Blanco Fombona, Rufino: see Fombona, Rufino Blanco

Blanco White, Joseph: see White, Joseph Blanco

Blest Gana, Alberto: Durante la Reconquista, 478–9

Bocachica, 211

Boccaccio, Giovanni: Decameron, 70

Bogotá: Gold Museum, 20; 197, 199, 206, 209, 212–13; Seminary Museum, 220; Bolívar estate, 225; 261; botanical library, 272; 296–7, 344, 381; University of, 391

Bolívar, Simón, xiv, xix, xx, 225, 251, 254; education, 256–7, 259; Memorandum of Cartagena, 258; Venezuela, Peru, 258–9, 282–3, 292–4, 307; Humboldt, 280–2; 288–9, 309, 353, 315, 319; Bolivian constitution, 324, 338; 330, 334; vs. Church, 344–50; 352; exile and death, 356; on United States, 379; Utilitarianism, 380–1; Comte, 386; 505, 541

Bolivia, 13, 15–16; dance, 53; colonial, 125, 129, 131 (see viceroyalties, Peru); art, 13–16, 19, 35, 211, 218; independence, 289, 301, 353–4, 356, 371–2; constitutions, 324, 338, 372–3; dictatorships: see caudillos; letters, 371, 374, 478, 512–13; education, 374; socialism, 375; Nazism, 503; Chaco War, 512; mines, 513

Bonafoux, Louis, 398

Bonampak, 10, 12, 45, 93, 221, 495, 535

Bonaparte, Pauline, 456
Bonifácio, José: *see* Andrada e Silva, José Bonifácio de
Bonpland, Aimé-Jacques-Alexandre, 278–9, 368
Bopp, Raul, 436
Borda, José de la, 207
Borges, Jorge Luis, 359; *Fervor de Buenos Aires*, 476–7; 513, 550
Borgia, Francisco, 138, 153
Borgia, Roderigo: *see* Alexander VI, Pope
Borgraf, Diego, 228
Boston, 131, 307
botánicas, 533
botany, botanical missions: *see* rediscovery
Botelho de Magalhães, Benjamin Constant, 423–5
Botero, José María, 382
Botticelli, Sandro: *Primavera*, 70, 240
Bougainville, Louis de, 59, 252, 268–9, 278, 410
Bouguer, Pierre, 266
Bourbon dynasty, 232, 266
Bourdelle, Émile, 517
Bourdon, James, 281
Boussingault, Jean-Baptiste, 280–2, 284
Braganza, House of, xiv, xviii
Brandão, Ambrosio Fernandes: *Diálogos das grandezas do Brasil*, 117
Brasilia, xv, 432, 436
Brasílica dos Renascidos (literary group), 406
Brazil: United States of, xiii, 129; colonial: *see* Portuguese America; independence, xvii–iii, 288, 341, 412, 415–17; 27; rubber, 59–60; 70; coast, 94; name, 96; military, 102, 413, 423–5; Mamelukes, 105–6, 157; music, 114, 410–11, 413, 419, 421, 429, 436, 438; dance, 114; art, 226, 419 (*see* art, Portuguese American); 328; constitution, 355;

Positivism, 387, 389, 423–7; economy, 410, 430, 439; press, 416 435, 440; jurisprudence, 417; constitutional monarchy, 417–23, 425 Freemasonry vs. Church, 417–18 422; letters, 420, 432 (*see* literature, Portuguese American); abolition of slavery, 421–3, 425 republic, 423–4; education, 423–5 436; flag, 425; Indians, 427 (*see* Guaranís); Germans, 427, 429 frontier, 428–34: agriculture, 435–6, 439; nationalism, 435–6; industry, cities, 436; political revision, Communist Party, 438 social structure, 439, 532, 545–6 mystique, 549 (see *macumba*); *see also* Portuguese America
brazilwood (*brasil*), 96–7
Breton, André, 476
British Museum, 219
Brooklyn, 466
Brown, Thomas, 320
Brueghel, Pieter, 221
Brughetti, Bishop Romualdo, 411, 417
Brull, Mariano, 527–8
Brunelleschi, Filippo, 199
Bruno, Giordano, 234–5
Bry, Théodore de: *Collectiones . . . Peregrinationum in Indiam . . .*, 226
Buenos Aires: colonial, 40, 129, 131, 141, 208–9, 266, 241; Enlightenment, 254–6, 270; independence, 295, 299–300; Romanticism, 323–4; liberalism, 347–8; Patriotic Society of, 371; growth, 396, 517; Negro, 444, 539
bullfights, 136, 354
Bunge, Carlos Octavio, 394; *Nuestra América*, 395; 396
Buñuel, Luis, 498
Busch, Germán, 507
Butantan Institute, 440
Byron, George Gordon, Baron, 269, 316, 319–20, 322, 324, 327

Byron, John, 269

Caballero, José Agustín, 233, 399
Caballero Calderón, Eduardo: *Tío Pancho*, 511
Caballero y Góngora, Antonio, 220, 291, 371
Cabello y Mesa, Francisco Antonio, 299
Cabeza de Vaca, Álvar Núñez, 49; *Los Naufragios* and *Comentarios*, 73; 74–5, 138, 244
Cabot, John, xv, 99
Cabral, Pedro Álvarez, 79, 89, 95
Cabrera, Lydia, 545, 548
Cabrera, Manuel Estrada, 363
caciques, 32
Cadamosto, Alvise da, 97
Cádiz, 219, 267, 287, 400
Caesar, Julius: *Commentaries*, 306
Cajamarca, 134
Calancha, Fray Antonio de la: *Crónica . . . del Orden de San Augustín en el Perú*, 127, 180–1
Calaumana, Juana Basilia, 373
Caldas, Francisco José de, 15, 272–4, 280, 285; *Memorias Científicas* and *Diario Político*, 297
Caldera, Rafael, 516
Calderón de la Barca, Pedro: *La Vida es Sueño*, 190–1
Caldwell, Erskine, 481, 511
Cali, 131
California, xx, 78, 79, 81, 83, 109, 197, 522
Caligula, 250
Calima, 20
Callao, 270
Callasaya, Thomás, 19
Calles, Plutarco Elías, 495–6
Calmón, Pedro, 96, 103–4, 106, 117, 119; *História do Brasil*, 407 n.; 410, 413, 434
Calpán, chapel of San Miguel, 224
Calvin, John, 103
Camões, Luis Vaz de: *The Lusiads*, 118

Campeche, 8
Campo, Estanislao del: *Fausto*, 462
Campoamor y Campoosorio, Ramón de, 465
Campomanes, Conde de, 336
Campos, Canon Batista de, 417
Can, Diego, 94
Canada (Anglo-French America), xiv, xv, xvii, xxii–iii, 21, 129, 268
cancha, 34
Candelaria, chapel of the (Tunja), 229
candombé, 539
cannibalism, 51, 93, 95–6, 110, 119, 149, 226
Cano, Alonso (El Granadino), 217, 220
Cano, Fidel: *Pastoral Laica*, 333–4
canoa, 28
Cantinflas, 498
Canto, Francisco de, 295
Cantuña, church of, 216
Cap-Haïtien, 443, 445–6, 454, 457
capital punishment: Colombia, 333; Guatemala, 361
capitalism, 506
captaincies: *see* Portuguese America
Capuchin Order, 106, 431, 444
Caracas, 129–31, 256–7, 295, 339, 396
Caracas, Semanario de (periodical), 248–9
Cárdenas, Juan de: *Primera Parte de los Problemas y Secretos . . . Indias*, 171
Cárdenas, Lázaro, 495–6
Cardoza y Aragón, Luis, 24–5, 37
Carías Andino, Tiburcio, 363
Caribbean, the, 27, 48, 72, 85, 87, 89, 125, 141, 195, 197, 204, 210–11, 227, 268, 289, 489
Caribs, 89
Carlos, Father (sculptor), 217
Carlota, Empress (Mexico), 339
Carlota, Princess (Portugal), 340
Carmelite Order, 84, 106, 139, 162, 218, 219, 406, 444
Caro, Don José Eusebio, 382

Caro, Miguel Antonio, 381–2, 392–3
Carolinas, the, 111
Carpentier, Alejo: *Los Pasos Per-didos*, 515
Carranza, Ángela, 140
Carranza, Venustiano, 494
Carrasquilla, Tomás: *Homilías*, 484; *La Marquesa de Yolombó*, 485; 547–8
Carreño de Miranda, Juan, 220
Carrera, Rafael, 354, 360–3
Carrera Andrade, Jorge: *Galería de Místicos y de Insurgentes*, 162 *n.*, 172; 180
Carrión, Benjamín: *El Santo del Patíbulo*, 366
Cartagena, 125, 131, 141, 163–5, 170, 195, 197, 205, 209–10, 258, 260, 295, 444
Carteret, Philip, 269
Cartesians, 232–3; *see also* Enlightenment
Carthage, 6
Cartier, Jacques, xv
Carvajal, Don Gabriel de, 82
Carvajal, Fray Gaspar de, 39; *Relación del Descubrimiento del . . . Amazonas*, 172
Carvalho, Vicente Augusto de, 433
Carvalho e Mello, Sebastião de: *see* Pombal, Marquês de
Casa, Alfonso, 501
Casa de España: *see* Mexico, College of
Casa del Alfeñique, 207
Casal, Julián del: *Nostalgias* and *Neurosis*, 446–7
Casals, Pablo, 522
Casaus, Archbishop, 361
Caspicara: *see* Chili, Manuel
Cassini, Jacques, 266
Cassini, Jean-Dominique, 266
Castelar, Emilio, 390
Castellanos, Juan de: *Elegías de Varones Ilustres* and *Historia de la Nueva Granada*, 176, 188
Castellanos, Rosario: *Balún Canán*, 499

Castile, xii, 6, 68, 88, 94, 137
Castillo, Antonio del, 220
Castillo, Mother: *Afectos espiritu-ales*, 161, 163
Castlereagh, Viscount, 301
Castro, Alonso de, 155
Castro, Don Joaquín, 262
Castro, Fidel, 508, 510, 513–15, 549
Castro, Josué de: *Geografía da Fome*, 108, 439
Castro Alves, Antônio de: *Os Es-cravos*, "A Cachoeira de Paulo Alfonso," and "Navio Negreiro," 422
Catari, Tomás (Francis I, the Powerful), 304
Catherine II, 306, 380
Catherine of Siena, Saint, 162
Catholic Institute of Paris, 464
Catholicism: *see* Roman Catholic Church; Inquisition; Portuguese America; *see also under names of religious orders*
Cauca, Valley of the, 19
caucho, 108
caudillos, 257, 351–7, 465; Argentina, 357–60, 503–4; Bolivia, 370–7, 503; Chile, 348, 388, 503–4; Colombia, 274, 297, 345, 504; Ecuador, 333, 363–7; El Salvador, 363; Guatemala, 360–3; Honduras, 363; Mexico, 494; Nicaragua, 363; Paraguay, 367–70; Peru, 507; Spain, 503–4; Venezuela, 284, 355, 398, 482, 507; post-World War II, 507–10; as magic, 548–9
Cavendish, Thomas, 102
Central America, 353; United Provinces of, 360–1; federation vs. fragmentation, 361–3; Utilitarianism, 380; *see also* Spanish America
Cepeda, Lorenzo de: *Vida . . . de Doña Juana de Fuentes*, 162
Cepeda, Rodrigo de, 84
Cepeda, Teresa de, 162
Cerezo, Mateo, 220
Cervantes de Salazar, Francisco, 131,

Cervantes de Salazar (*cont.*) 151, 170; *Chronicle of New Spain*, 171

Cervantes Saavedra, Miguel de: *Don Quixote de la Mancha*, 76, 77, 85–6, 170, 177, 185, 528

Céspedes, Augusto: *Sangre de Mestizos*, 513

Céspedes, Pablo de, 220

Cetina, Gutiérrez de: *Paradoja en la alabanza de los cuernos*, 178

Ceylon, 5, 59, 60

Chabaneau, M., 276

Chaco War, 370, 512

champi, 34

Champlain, Samuel de, xv

Champollion, Jean-Jacques, 401

Charcas, 129

Chardon, Carlos A., 282

Charles I of Spain: *see* Charles V, Holy Roman Emperor

Charles III of Spain, 154, 232–3, 236, 259, 268, 278, 302, 390

Charles IV of Spain, 257, 270, 274, 320, 341, 412

Charles V, Holy Roman Emperor, xii, 74, 80–1, 85, 137–8, 212–14, 220, 244, 292, 528–9, 531–3

Charles IX of France, 239

Charleston, 246, 253

Chateaubriand, Francisco Assis, 440

Chateaubriand, François-René de: *Le Génie du Christianisme*, 247; *Atala*, 309, 316; 313, 317, 319, 322, 325, 327

Chavannes, Jean-Batiste, 454

Chavín de Huántar, 12, 13

Chavín style, 13

Cheops, 9

Cheppe, Abbot, 277

Chiapas, 8

Chibchas, the, 20, 54, 129, 148, 535

chicha, 536

Chichén-Itzá, 9, 10

Chilám Balám, 9, 56, 536

Chile, xx, 21, 36, 44, 118, 180; agriculture, 45, 160; dance, 53; colonial, 126, 129–30, 140, 160 (*see* viceroyalties, Peru); Jesuit experiment, 158–9; letters, 173–6, 181, 210, 218, 476, 477–9, 481, 515 (*see* literature, Spanish American); independence, 250–2, 255–6, 288, 301–2, 303–4, 344, 353, 356; Church, 255–6, 348; scientific missions, 266, 270; education, 282, 330, 521; press, 295, 301–2; Romanticism, 328–33, 379; civil code, 330; dictatorships: see *caudillos*; Positivism, 384–8; abolition of slavery, 422–3; music, 491; Nazism, 503–4; Christian Democracy, 516

Chili, Manuel (Caspicara), 215–16

Chiloé, 270

Chilpancingo, Constitution of, 344

Chimborazo, Mt., 270

China, 41, 91, 117, 514

Chinchón, the Countess of, 60

chinchona, 60, 274

Chiquinquirá, Virgin of, 148, 343

Chocano, José Santos, 463

Choco, 276

cholo, 493, 504

Cholula: pyramid of, 9; Franciscan convent of, 221

Chorographic Commission, Album of the, 284

Christian Democracy, 515–16

Christophe, Henri, 451, 454, 456–7

Chuquisaca, 180, 254, 371, 374

Churriguera, José, 198

Churrigueresque, 198, 204

Ciborium, chapel of the (Sagrario), Mexico, 200, 214

Cieza de León, Pedro: *Crónica del Perú*, 172–3

Ciguatán, 81

cimarrones, 40

Cisneros, Cardinal: see Jiménez de Cisneros, Francisco

Clare of Assisi, Saint, 163

Clare Order, 163–5

Claver, Pedro, Saint, 163, 204, 539

Clavigero, 45
Clavijero, Father Francisco Javier: *Physica Particularis, Historia Eclesiástica de México*, and *Historia Antigua de México*, 302–3
Cobo, Fray Bernabé, 44; *Historia del Nuevo Mundo*, 173
coca leaf, 110, 538
Codazzi, Agostino, 15, 283–5
Coelho Pereira, Duarte, 97–8
coffee, 57, 62; Brazil, 108–9, 510; Venezuela, 284; Central America, 363
Coimbra, University of, 405–6, 420
Coleridge, Samuel Taylor: *Lyrical Ballads*, 315
Coleti, José Domingo: *Dizionario . . . dell'America Meridionale*, 304
Coligny, island of, 103
Collaert, Johannes, 224
Collahuasco, Jacinto: *Guerras Civiles del Inca . . .* , 182
Colombia, xiv; art, 15, 16, 19, 35, 211–12, 215, 224–5, 228–9, 502; 41, 146, 148; colonial: *see* viceroyalties, New Granada; independence, 62, 261, 274, 280–1, 301, 343–4; letters, 187–8, 391–3, 462, 472–3, 475, 477, 481–2, 484–5, 501, 511–12, 520, 544 (*see* literature, Spanish American); architecture, 195, 197, 199, 201–6, 209–11; Enlightenment, 235, 260; scientific missions, 266, 268, 284; education, 281, 291, 391, 491, 520; press, 295–7, 504; flag, 307; Romanticism, 333–4; monarchy vs. republic, 339–40, 345; first president, 349; Utilitarianism, 380–2; Positivism, 391–3; abolition of slavery, 422; Nazism, 504–6; National University, 512; witchcraft, 547–9
colonialism: *see* Spanish America; Portuguese America; viceroyalties; *see also under names of countries*

Colorado, 228
Coluccini, Father, Juan Bautiste, 199
"Columbia"; "Colombia"; "Great Colombia," xiii, xiv, 307
Columbia University, 509, 512
Columbus, Bartholomew, 153
Columbus, Christopher, xii, xiii, xix, 3–6, 22, 27, 42, 48; journals, 64–8, 72; *Book of Prophecies*, 69; 73, 79–80, 83, 88–9, 94, 128, 152, 168, 176, 181, 226, 231, 238, 240, 279, 442–3, 526
Columbus, Diego, 128, 204
Columbus, Ferdinand: *La Vida . . . de Cristóbal Colón*, 153
Communism, 438; Peru, 492–3; Mexico, 495, 501; Cuba, 509, 513–15; 510, 516, 548–9
Company of Jesus: *see* Jesuit Order
Company of Jesus, Church of the (Quito), 197, 200
Comte, Auguste, xviii, 369, 378, 384; *Cours de Philosophie Positiviste*, 385; 386–91, 402, 424–7, 488
comuneros, 62, 138, 156–7, 240–2, 244, 248, 255, 261, 313
Concolorcorvo (Alonso Carrión de la Vandera): *Lazarillo de Ciegos caminantes*, 41, 209; 254, 371
Condillac, Étienne Bonnot de, 357, 400, 410
Condorcanqui, José Gabriel: *see* Tupac Amaru
Congress of Cardinals, 236
conquest: *see* Spain; Spanish America
Constant de Rebecque, Benjamin: *Adolphe* and *Journal Intime*, 319
Constantinople, 28, 380
convent, the, 53, 141, 145; Quito, 161; Mexico, 161–2; life, 163; education, 163, 167; laxity, 163–7, 266, 268; architecture, 197; art, 162, 200, 218, 221; independence, 294

Cook, James, 269–70

Cooper, James Fenimore: *The Last of the Mohicans*, 337

Copacabana (Brazil), 545

Copacabana, island of (Lake Titicaca), 19, 218

Copacabana, sanctuary of the Virgin of, 218

Copán, 8, 9

Copernicus, Nicolaus: *De Revolutionibus orbium* . . . , 233–6; 264

Coppée, François, 459

Córdoba, 28, 140, 295

Córdoba, Gonzalo de, 128

Córdoba, University of, 290

Córdoban manifesto, 490–1

Coricancha, Palace of, 34–5

Coriche, Christoval Mariano: *Oración vindicativa* . . . , 246

corihuayrachinas (smithies), 34

corn, pre-Columbian importance of, 6, 22–6, 45

Coro, 131

corregidores, 156

Correia, Raymundo da Mota Azevedo, 433

Correo Literario y Político de Londres (review), 320

Cortés, Hernán, xix, 28; on Tenochtitlán, 30; 32, 35, 36, 41, 44, 48, 51, 73, 80–2, 85, 124–5, 130, 132, 144, 168–70, 178; houses of, 204; 213, 225–6, 244

Cortés, Martín, 179

Cortés de Madariaga, José, 344

Coruña, Fray Agustín de la, 153

Coruña, Fray Martín de la, 147

Cos, José María, 296

Cosío Villegas, Daniel: *Historia Moderna de México*, 496–7, 499

Costa, Claudio Manuel da (Glauceste Satúrnio): *Canto to the Vila Rica* and *Ribeirão do Carmo*, 407; 409

Costa, Lucio (architect), Ministry of Education building, Brazil, 437

Costa, Pereira da, 114

Costa Rica, xi, 356, 362, 513

Coutinho, Azeredo, Bishop of Olinda, 410

coxilhas (militia), 106

Creole, 55, 178, 181, 200, 236; vs. Spaniard, 299–300, 311–13, 340

Crete, 4

Croce, Benedetto, 128

Cruz, Oswaldo, 439

Cruz, Sor Juana Inés de la, 122, 161–3; *Los Empeños de una casa* and *Sueños*, 186–8; 526, 544

Cruz e Sousa, João da: *Protissão de Fé*, 433

Cuadernos Americanos (review), 497, 499

Cuatrocasas, José, 274

Cuauhtémoc, 32, 316, 499

Cuautitlán, Franciscan church of, 220

Cuba, xviii, 80, 129–30, 141; letters, 184, 316, 365–7, 474, 478, 515; architecture, 211; Enlightenment, 233, 235, 399; independence, 289, 398, 466; press, 295; United States, 398; developmental influences, 399; Freemasonry, 399; Varona, 400–2; Positivism, 403; Negroes, 423, 539, 542; Batista, 507; Castro, 508, 513–15, 549; African subreligion, 539, 542, 545, 548

cueca, 536

Cuernavaca, 12; convent of, 221

Cueto y Mena, Juan de: *La Competencia en los Nobles* . . . , 190

Cueva, Juan de la, 178

Cundinamarca, 311

Cunha, Euclides da: *Os Sertões*, 431–2

Cunha, Flores da, 438

Curaçao, 79, 443

Cuvier, Baron Georges, 281, 401

Cuzco, xi, 16, 28, 32–5, 44, 51, 83, 91, 129–31, 202, 227, 229, 238–9

Dabry, Pierre: *La Vie Catholique*, 464

Dahomey, 451, 543

D'Alembert, Jean le Rond: *see* Alembert, Jean le Rond d'

Damascus, 195

dance, 53, 91, 114, 453, 536–7, 539, 542–6

D'Annunzio, Gabriele, 463; *Il Trionfo della Morte*, 468; 472–3

Dante, 70; *Divine Comedy*, 327

Dardim, Father Fernão: *Do . . . Origem dos Indios do Brasil* and *Do Clima e Terra do Brasil*, 116

Darién, 20, 170

Darío, Rubén, 398, 435, 464–5; *Azul*, 469; *Los Raros* and *Prosas Profanas*, 470; *Responso* and *Canto a la Argentina*, 471; 487, 526

Darwin, Charles, 280, 359, 391

Dávalos, Sister Magdalena, 162

David d'Angers, Pierre-Jean, 382

De Soto, Hernando, 37, 82

Debussy, Claude, 472

Declaration of the Rights of Man, 260–1, 298, 311

Delacroix, Eugène, 467, 472

Delavigne, Casimir, 325

Delgado, José Matías, 350

Della Robbia family, 216

Democritus, 233

descamisados, 417

Descartes, René: *Discourse on Method*, 232–6, 248

Despertador Americano, El (newspaper), 296

Desportes, Alexandre-François, 120

Dessalines, Jean-Jacques, 451, 456–8

Diario Curioso (Lima newspaper), 299

Diario de Mexico (newspaper), 416

Diario de Pernambuco (newspaper), 416

Diário do Rio de Janeiro, 433

Dias, Antônio Gonçalves: *Primeiros Cantos, Patkull, Beatriz Cenci, Vocabulario da . . . Alto Amazonas*, and *Dicionário da Lingua Tupi*, 420

Dias, Bartolomeu, 94

Dias, Diego, 91

Días, Porfirio, 389–91, 494

Días, Ramón, 284

Díaz Arrieta, Hernán (Alone), quoted, 175

Díaz de Gamarra, Juan Benito: *Errores del Entendimiento Humano*, 232

Díaz del Castillo, Bernal, 28–9; *Verdadera Historia de la conquista . . .*, 44; 51–2, 76–7, 80, 132, 169–71, 526

Díaz Mirón, Salvador, 463

Díaz Rodríguez, Manuel: *Sangre Patricia*, 480

dictatorships: see *caudillos;* law, government, Spanish American

Dictionary of the Spanish Academy, xii

Diderot, Denis: *Encyclopédie, ou Dictionnaire . . .*, 251–3; 268–9, 315, 319, 336

Diego, Juan, 308

Diez Canseco, Alfredo Pareja, 458

Diez de Medina, Fernando, 521

Dique Canal, 211

discovery, voyages of, xvi, 63–75, 442–3; motivation for, 76–87; *see also* rediscovery

Domínguez Camargo, Hernando, 187–8

Dominican Order, 106, 113, 147; first American university, 150; 153; Mexico, 198; architecture, 198; Guatemala, 361–2; Haiti, 444

Dominican Republic, 399, 507, 512; *see also* Santo Domingo

Dominici, Pedro César: *Dyonysos*, 480

Don Quixote, 76–7, 83, 85–7, 170

Doret, Fédéric, 448

Dostoevski, Fëdor Mikhailovich, 333

Drake, Sir Francis, 125; *History of the Incas*, 173; 176, 210, 227

Dresden Codex, 8

Dresden Museum, 9

Ducange, Victor: *Thirty Years, or The Life of a Gambler*, 325; 326

Ducasse, Isidore-Lucien: *see* Lautréamont, Count de

Duende de Santiago, El (newspaper), 301

Dumas, Alexandre, 324; *Antonino*, 325; 326; *Thérèse*, 330

Dumont, René, 539

Dumouriez, Charles-François, 305

Durán, Fray Diego: *Historia de las Indias* . . . , 171, 264

Durand, Oswaldo, 459

Durão, Jose de Santa Rita: *Caramuru*, 408

Dürer, Albrecht, 221–2, 224, 226

Dutch, the, 101–2; in Brazil, 118–22; 129, 210

Dutch Guiana (Surinam), 108–9, 241, 532

Dutch West India Company, 119

Dutra, Eurico Gaspar, 438

Duvalier, François, 458, 460

Easter Island, 211, 269

Echave Ibía, Baltasar, 228

Echave Ibía, Manuel, 228

Echave Orio, Baltasar de, 228

Echegaray y Eizaguirre, José, 465

Echeverría, Esteban, 323–5; *Elvira* . . . , *Jóven Argentina, Asociación de Mayo*, and *El Matadero*, 326; *El Dogma Socialista*, 326, 384; 359, 394

Eckourt, Albert, 119

Economic and Social Council, Inter-American, 519

economy: Brazil, 438–40; Mexico, 494–7; post-World War II, 506–10; *see* land tenure and reform; *see also under names of countries*

Ecuador, xiv, 19; colonial, 129 (*see* viceroyalties, New Granada; Quito); missions, 154; architecture, 154, 155 n., 172, 200–1, 204; agriculture, 155 n., 364; letters, 172, 180, 481, 512–13, 543; art,

212, 214–16, 218, 222, 228; scientific missions, 267; education, 281, 364, 491; independence, 288–9, 301, 304, 353–4; press, 295, 297–9, 366; flag, 307; dictatorships: see *caudillos;* Romanticism, 334–5; monarchy vs. republic, 342; first president, 342; immigration, 365; railroads, 367; Utilitarianism, 383

Édouard, Emmanuel, 459

education, Spanish American: College for Indians, 131; 136, 139; Church: *see* Roman Catholic Church; missions; *see also under names of religious orders;* universities, 150–3, 280–2, 289–94, 344, 355, 399, 489–1; women, 163, 294; theater, 188–9; arts, 217; Enlightenment, 254–5; reform, 256–6, 281, 289–94, 297, 310, 324, 336–7, 402–3, 489–91, 494; Lancastrian system, 282–3, 347, 355, 361; student revolutionaries, 489–91; educators, 519–22; *see* Portuguese America; *see also under names of countries*

Edwards Bello, Joaquín, 481

Egaña, Mariano, 388

Egypt, 3, 5

Eisenhower, Dwight D., 509

Eisenstein, Sergei, 498

El Dorado: seat of, 19; 35, 71, 79, 81, 83–7, 98, 126, 129, 177, 198, 241

El Lunarejo: *see* Espinosa de Medrano, Juan

El Salvador, 8, 350; Central American Federation, 354, 363; magic, 549

Elhuyar, Fausto, 276–7

Elhuyar, Juan José, 272, 276–7

Eliot, T. S., 476

Emerson, Ralph Waldo: *English Traits*, xii

Encina, Francisco A., 303–4

encomienda; encomenderos, 52, 100, 105–6, 123–8, 143, 156, 160–1, 166, 206, 208

Encyclopédie, 240–1, 245, 250, 257, 264, 276, 343; *see also* Diderot, Denis
Encyclopedists, 232, 236, 238, 251–3, 256, 259, 260, 262, 268, 280, 287, 410; *see also* Enlightenment
Ender, Thomas, 413
England, xvi, 6, 282, 310, 312; Romanticism, 315, 320, 332; 343; influence, 319–20, 354–5, 378–9, 381, 488; Industrial Revolution, 336, 378; Falkland Islands, 359; Brazil, 412, 421; imperialism, 488; Mexico, 496
English, the, 83, 86–7; Brazil, 101–2; colonies, 124, 129, 312; 299, 302; Cuba, 399
Enlightenment, xiii *n.*, 159, 166; prelude, 230–1 (*see* Spanish America, ideological evolution); physics vs. metaphysics, 232–7; America's "noble savages," 238–43, 253, 407; Rousseau and colonialism, 243–53; *Rights of Man* revolutionaries, 253–63; educational reform, 290–4; fruits of: *see* rediscovery; Independence; Romanticism; Positivism; *see also under names of countries*
Enriquillo, 72
Epazoyucan, 222
Epicurus, 233
Erasmus, 71, 151, 231
Ercilla y Zúñiga, Alonso de, 118; *La Araucana*, 173–4, 176
Escalona y Agüero, Gaspar de: *Gazophilatium Regium Pervianum; Ordenanzas . . . para los Oficiales de las Indias*, 180
Escobar, Father Sancho de, 298
Escorial, 196, 198, 231
Esmeraldas River basin, 19, 365
Espada, Bishop, 400–1
Espectador, El (Colombian newspaper), 333–4
Espejo, Francisco Javier Santa Cruz y (Marco Porcio Catón): *La*

Ciencia Blancardiana, and *El Nuevo Luciano*, 297–9; 311
Espejo, Luis, 298
Espinosa de Medrano, Juan (El Lunarejo): *El Auto Sacramental del Hijo Pródigo, Amar su Propia Muerte*, and *Apologético . . . de Góngora*, 185, 189–90
Espíritu de los Mejores Diarios, El (Madrid review), 260, 295
Estaing, Count Jean-Baptiste d', 454–5
Esthetic Investigations, Institute for (Mexico), 501
Estrada Cabrera, Manuel, 549
Eugénie, Empress (Eugénie de Montijo de Guzmán), 339
Europe, 5–6, 20; America's contribution to, xv–ii, 58–63, 233–4, 238–50; revolutionaries in, 302–8; 315; democracy, 351–2; post-World War II, 507; 1500 populations of, 553; *see also under names of countries and monarchs*
Europe (review), 252
exploration: *see* discovery; rediscovery; *see also under names of countries*

Fabela, Isidro: *Los Estados Unidos contra la Libertad*, 489
Fabregat, José Joaquín, 227
Falkland Islands, 359
Fals Bord, Orlando, 512
Faria e Sousa, Manuel de, 185
farrapos, 288, 417
Farrell, Edelmiro, 503
Fascism, 397, 438, 502–8
Faubert, Pierre: *Ogé et le Préjuge . . .*, 459
Faulkner, William, 481, 511
Faust, Johann, 528–9
Federmann, Nikolaus, 35, 38, 68, 79, 81, 82
Feijoo y Montenegro, Benito Jerónimo, 235, 246, 336
Felipe, León, 477

Fenton, Edward, 102
Ferdinand V of Castile and Aragon, 42, 137, 238
Ferdinand VII of Spain, 320, 338, 340–1, 345–6; encyclicals on behalf of, 348–9; 357, 400
Fernández, Carmelo, 284
Fernández, Gregorio, 215
Fernández de Lizardi, José Joaquín: El Periquillo Sarniento, 131, 233; Don Catrín de la Fachenda, 337, 483; 527
Fernández de Navarrete, Martín: El Libro de la Primera Navegación, 65
Fernández de Oviedo y Valdés, Gonzalo: see Oviedo y Valdés
Fernández de Piedrahita, Lucas: Historia . . . del Nuevo . . . Granada, 182
Fernández de Valenzuela, Fernando: Laurea Crítica, 190
Fernández Madrid, José: Atala and Guatimoc, 317
Ferreira Xarrato, José: see Xarrato
Ferri, Enrico, 394
Féry, Alibée, 459
Feuillée, Father Louis, 266 and n.
Fierro, Martín, 476–7
"Figarillo": see Alberdi, Juan Bautista
Figaro: see Larra, Mariano José de
Figueroa, Baltasar de, 223, 229
Figueroa, Gaspar de, 223, 229
Flores, Cirillo, 362
Flores, Gaspar, 43
Flores, Juan José, 289, 301, 342, 353, 363–4, 383
Flórez, Julio, 462
Flórez de Ocariz, Juan: Genealogías . . . de Granada, 179
Florida, 37, 49, 73–4, 79, 82–3, 131, 154, 522
Floridablanca, Count of (José Moñino y Redondo), 260–1, 336
Fogazzaro, Antonio: Il Santo, 464
Fombona, Rufino Blanco, 467

Fondo de Cultura Económica (Mexico), 497, 521
Fonseca, Antônio Isidoro da, 406
Fonseca, Manuel Deodoro da, 423
Foronda de Vergara, Valentín, 276
Foscolo, Ugo, 316
Fountain of Youth, the, 82–3, 177, 526
France: Romanticism, 315, 318, 324–5; Republic, 338, 343; Mexico, 339, 342, 365, 496; Argentina, 340–2, 359; Ecuador, 342; influence, 378 (see Enlightenment; rediscovery; Romanticism); modernismo, 398, 463–74, 487; World War I, 489–90; see also French, the; French Revolution; Haiti
France, Anatole, 488
Francia, Dr. José Gaspar Rodríguez, 157, 279, 367–9, 386–7
Francis of Assisi, Saint, 107, 163
Francis I of Austria, 268
Francis I of France, 85, 102
"Francis I, the Powerful": see Catari, Tomás
Francis II of France, 103
Franciscan Order, 106–7, 113, 145, 147, 150, 153; vs. Clares, 163–5; Mexico, 197; architecture, 199; Guatemala, 361–2; Brazil, 406
Franco, Francisco, 503–4, 507, 509
Francovich, Guillermo, 521
Franklin, Benjamin, xii n., 262, 336
Freemasonry: Chile, 255; independence, 302, 343; first lodges, 307; future Pope enrolled, 347; 349, 381; Venezuela, 396–7; Cuba, 399; Brazil, 413–17; Haiti, 453; 506
Frei, Eduardo, 516
Freire, Ramón, 348
French, the: in Portuguese America, 101–3; in Spanish America, 129, 210, 232, 266, 339; see also Haiti; Mexico
French Guiana, 108–9, 241, 417–18

French Revolution, the, xv, 248, 253, 259–61, 269, 299, 305–6, 337, 423

Fretes, Juan Pablo, 344

Freyre, Gilberto, 99, 102, 104, 107, 112, 117; *Casa Grande e Senzala*, 439

Freyre, Ricardo Jaimes: *Castalia Bárbara* and *Russia*, 472

Frézier, Amédée François, 134, 266

Frondizi, Risieri: *Las Universidades . . . Perón*, 513

Fuenleal, Bishop Ramírez de, 151

Fuentes, Carlos, 499

Fuentes, Doña Juana de, 162

Funes, Gregorio: *Methodus practica . . . Thomas de Kempis de Imitatione Christi*, 155, 232

Furlog, Guillermo, 347

Gaceta de Buenos Aires, 300

Galápagos Islands, 270

Galaup, Jean-François de, 269

Galberi, M. Segundo, 223

Galileo, 233–6

Galíndez, Jesús de: *La Era de Trujillo*, 512

Gallardo, Guillermo, 40

Galle, Philippus: *Venationes ferrarum . . .*, 224

Gallegos, Rómulo: *Reinaldo Solar* and *Doña Barbara*, 482; 502, 547

Galván, Manuel de Jesús: *Enriquillo*, 72, 478

Gálvez, José, 491

Gálvez, Manuel, 366, 502

Gama, José Basílio da: *O Uruguai*, 407–8

Gama, Maia da, 109

Gama, Vasco da, 95–6, 168

Gamboa, Fernando, 497

Gamboa, Silvestre de: *Espejo de Paciencia*, 184

Garcés, Enrique, 299

García Calderón, Francisco: *La Creación de un Continente*, 489

García, Manuel José, 341

García, José Uriel: description of

Cuzco, 34–5

García, Juan Augustín: *La Ciudad Indiana*, 208–9

García, Rodolfo, 117

García del Río, Juan: *Meditaciones Colombianas*, 329

García Icazbalceta, Joaquín, 534

García Lorca, Federico, 477

García Mercadal: *see* Mercadal

García Monge, Joaquín: *Repertorio Americano*, 521

García Moreno, Gabriel, 333–4, 342, 360, 363–7, 392–3, 502, 549

Garcilaso de la Vega ("El Inca"): *La Florida del Inca*, 39, 82–3; 180–1, 240, 242; *Los Comentarios Reales*, 293

Garibaldi, Anita, 328

Garibaldi, Giuseppe, 328

Garofalo, Raffaele, 394

Garrido, Juan, 45

Gasparini, Graziano: *Templos Coloniales de Venezuela*, 204

Gassendi, Pierre, 232–3

Gassendists, 233

gaucho, 106, 248, 288, 323, 328, 357–8, 462, 480

Gauguin, Paul, 472

Gay-Lussac, Joseph-Louis, 281–2, 401

Gazeta do Rio de Janeiro, 413

Gazette of Mexico (newspaper), 253, 295

geography, 265–8, 283–5, 304

George, Stefan, 473

Gerchunoff, Alberto: *Los Gauchos Judíos*, 532

Germans, 35, 38, 68, 79, 80–3, 196, 272; Venezuelan colony, 284; Paraguayan colony, 370; Brazil, 427, 429; *see also* rediscovery

Germany: Romanticism, 314–15, 318, 322–3; World War I, 490, 503; World War II, 502–4, 511; witchcraft, 528–9

Gersón, Juan, 222

Giants, Island of: *see* Curaçao

Gibbon, Edward: *The Decline and Fall of the Roman Empire*, 306

Gil-Fortoul, José: *Julián, Pasiones, El Hombre y su Historia*, and *Historia . . . de Venezuela*, 397–8

Giordano, Luca, 220

Giraldo Jaramillo, Gabriel: *Historia del Grabado en Colombia*, 223; 224, 229, 226 *n.*, 304

Girondo, Oliverio, 476

Goa, 95

Gobineau, Comte Joseph-Arthur de, 419, 505

Godin, Louis, 266–7

Godoy, Manuel de, 270, 300, 341

Goethe, Johann Wolfgang von, 318, 322, 324

gold, 19, 20, 29; Peru, 33–4, 127–8, 133–5, 198; 67, 70, 83; Brazil, 109; 126, 198, 201, 275; *see also* El Dorado

Gold Museum, Bank of the Republic, Bogotá, 20

Goldoni, Carlo: *La Peruviana*, 242

Gómara, Francisco López de, 39; *Historia General de las Indias*, 169–70; 227

Gomes, Carlos: *O Noite no Castelo*, 419; *O Guaraní*, 420

Gómez, Juan Vicente, 355, 397, 482, 505, 511–12

Gómez, Laureano, 504; *Interrogantes . . . el Porvenir de Colombia*, 505; 511

Gómez Carillo, Enrique, 398; *Literatura Extranjera*, 470–2

Gómez de Alvarado, María (Amaryllis), 177

Gómez de Avellaneda, Gertrudis: *Sab*, 478; 485

Gómez de la Serna, Ramón, 476

Gómez Jurado, Father Pedro Severo: *Vida de García Moreno*, 366

Góngora y Argote, Luis de, 161, 183, 185–6, 216

Gongorism, 183–8, 216

Gonzaga, Tomaz Antônio: *Marilia de Dirceu*, 408

González, Joaquín V., 489

González, Juan Vicente: *Historia . . . civil en Venezuela*, 398

González, Natalicio, 368

González de Ávila, Gil, 533

González de Eslava, Fernán: *Spiritual . . . Conversations, Canciones Divinas*, and *Interlude of the Two Ruffians*, 183; *Coloquio III*, 190–1

González de Santa Cruz, Father, 157

González Martínez, Enrique, 474

González Prada, Manuel, 491–3

González Prada Popular Universities, 491

Gorki, Maksim, 463

Goseal, Fray Pedro, 196, 228

Goudot, Justin, 281–2

Gourmont, Rémy de, 480

Gouveia, Diogo, 104

government: *see* law, government

Graça Aranha, José Pereira da: *Canaan*, 429; 434–5, 549

Grafigny d'Issembourg, Mme Françoise de: *Lettres Péruviennes*, 242–3

Gramusset, Antoine, 250

Granada, 137, 168

Grandmaison (Casamayor), Isabel, 267

Gray, Thomas, 327

Greco, El, 228

Greece, 3, 79, 319

Gregory XIII, Pope, 8

Greiff, León de, 477

Gromberg, Johann, 294

Groot, Piet de, 119

Grotius, Hugo, 119

Grur, Anakasius, 468

Guachay, Isabel, 172

Guadalajara, 129–31, 219; Museum, 220; 295–6

Guadalupe, Virgin of, 148, 308–9, 343; Order of, 339

Guamán Poma de Ayala, Felipe: *Nueva Crónica y Buen Gobierno*, 537–8

Guanahaní, 65, 67
Guaranís, the, 79, 88, 103, 106–8, 111, 157, 239–40, 370, 407, 536, 538
Guarionex, Chief, 153
Guatavita, Lake of, 20
Guatemala, 8, 9, 35, 37, 44, 48, 131; colonial, 160 (*see* viceroyalties, Mexico); letters, 170–1, 481–2; architecture, 203; art, 211; education, 282, 361–3; press, 295–6; schism, 350; reform, reaction, 360–3; immigration, 363; magic, 549
Guatemala City, 361
Guatemala Gazette, 296
Guatemalteco, El (newspaper), 301
Guayaquil, 126, 131, 270, 295
Guercino (Giovanni Francesco Barbieri), 220
Guernica, 244
Guevara, Ernesto (Ché), 510, 514
guilds, 214–15
Guillén, Jorge, 477
Guillén, Nicolás, 459; *Songoro Cosongo*, 515; quoted, 543–4
Guimarães, Alphonsus de: *Pauvre Lyre* and *Setenario das Dores* . . . , 433
Guinea, 41, 94
Guipuzcoan Company, 236
Güiraldes, Ricardo: *El Cencerro de Cristal* and *Don Segunda Sombra*, 480
gunpowder, 28, 75
Gutiérrez, Juan María, 134, 329
Gutiérrez de Santa Clara, Pedro: *Historia . . . guerras civiles del Peru*, 179
Gutiérrez Nájera, Manuel: *Cuentos Frágiles* and *Cuentos de Color de Huma*, 466–7
Guzmán, Antonio Leocadio, 397
Guzmán, Monsignor Germán, 512
Guzmán, Martín Luis: *The Eagle and the Serpent*, 390, 483
Guzmán Blanco, Antonio, 396–7

Habanero, El (gazette), 400
Haenke, Thaddeus, 269
Haiti: independence, 343, 399, 448, 451, 456, 540; 442–3; slavery, 443–5, 455; Spain, France, 443–4, 456; socio-economic evolution, 443–7; Catholicism, 444–5, 450–3; theater, 445, 459; press, 446, 459–60; education, 448, 459–60; language, 448–50; letters, 448, 459; Freemasonry, dance, music, 453; monarchy vs. republic, 456–8; Duvalier, 458–9; mysticism: *see* magic, mysticism; *see also* voodoo
Hall, Colonel Francis, 363, 383
Hambriento, El (Chilean newspaper), 388
Hamilton, Alexander, 262, 306, 336
hanpicoc, 537
Harlem, 533
Hartzenbusch, Juan Eugenio, 468
Hauptmann, Gerhart, 472
Havana, 130, 141, 232, 235, 295, 444, 548
Hawaii, 416
Hawkins, Sir Richard, 102, 125, 210
Haya de la Torre, Victor Raúl, 491–2
health, medicine: Spanish America, 52, 102, 111–12, 152, 271–2, 291–3, 298, 538; Brazil, 406, 409, 439–40
Hearn, Lafcadio, 473
Hegel, Georg Wilhelm Friedrich, 463
Helvétius, Claude-Adrien, 336, 410
Hemingway, Ernest, 481; *The Old Man and the Sea*, 486
Henríquez, Camilo, 301
Henríquez Ureña, Max, 161
Henríquez Ureña, Pedro, 151, 501, 521
Henry VII of England, xv
Henry VIII of England, 529
Henry the Navigator, 79, 94, 97
Heredia, José María de: "Ode to Niagara," 316; "En el Teocali de

Cholula," 316–17; 321, 475, 485, 501

Hernández, José: *Martín Fierro*, 462

Hernández, Pedro: *Comentarios al viaje de . . . Cabeza de Vaca al Paraguay*, 173

Hernández de Avilés, Pedro, 210

Hernández de Toledo, Francisco, 61

Hernández Martínez, Maximiliano: *see* Martínez

Herrera, Francisco de, 220

Herrera, Juan de (architect), 196, 198, 224; *Construction of the Escorial*, 225

Herrera y Reissing, Julio: *La Torre de las Esfinges*, 473–4

Herrera y Tordesillas, Antonio de: *Decades . . .* , 169; 227

Herskovits, Melville J., 539

Heyerdahl, Thor, 48

Heyse, Paul von, 472

Hidalgo y Costilla, Miguel, 41, 287, 296, 344, 356

Hinojosa, Doña Inés de, 179

Hispaniola: *see* Haiti; Santo Domingo

Hitler, Adolf, 438, 502–4, 507

Hobbes, Thomas, 336

Hobhouse, John, 319

Hofmannsthal, Hugo von, 473

Holbach, Paul Henri Dietrich d': *Système de la Nature*, 336

Holbein, Hans: *Icones historiarum . . .* , 222

Hollanda, Sergio Buarque de: *Raízes do Brazíl*, 439

Holy Alliance, 342

Homer, 21, 78–9, 259

Honduras, 8, 9; independence, 354; dictatorship, 363; letters, 501

Hostos, Eugenio María de: *La Peregrinación de Bayoán*, 402; *Moral Social*, 403; 522

Houssay, Bernardo, 513

Huaca, 12

huamanga stone, 212

Huancavelica, 267

Huaraz, 12

Huastecs, 5

Huayna Cápac (Incan emperor), 32, 172

hucuchoca, 39

Hudson, William Henry: *Green Mansions*, 87, 274, 485–6

Huejotzingo, convent of (Mexico), 197, 221

Huerta, Victoriano, 494

Hughes, Langston, 459

Hugo, Victor: *Marion de Lorme*, 323, 327; *Hernani*, 323, 325, 330; 324; *Cromwell*, 325; 326; *Lucrèce Borgia, Angelo, La Roi s'amuse*, and *Ruy Blas*, 327, 331, 352; *Prayer for Everyone*, 330; *Les Misérables*, 333; 478

Huguenots, 103

Huidobro, Vicente, 476

Huitzilopochtli, 148, 535

Humanism, 69, 131, 231

Humboldt, Alexander von, 57, 62, 131, 206, 248, 257, 269, 271–2, 277–80; *Voyage . . . the Southern Regions of the New Continent, Political Essay . . . the Kingdom of New Spain, On the New Conditions . . . Guatemala, On . . . Antioquia and . . . Deposits of Platinum, Observations . . . Little-known Phenomena, Goiter in the Tropics . . .* , and *The Possibility of Connecting the Two Oceans . . .* , 279; 284–5, 297, 304, 322–3, 401

Humboldt, Karl Wilhelm von, 278, 318

Hume, David, 320, 336

Huysmans, Joris Karl, 472

Ibsen, Henrik, 472

Icaza, Jorge: *Huasipungo*, 481

Ihering, Dr. Hermann, 427

ilacates, 373

Ilustrador Nacional (Mexican newspaper), 296

Incan empire: Machu Picchu, 15;
founding of, 16; 21; calendar, 22;
27–9; architecture, 32; government, 33, 156; art, 34–5; 36, 44–5,
48, 51; music, 53–4; 82–3, 88, 91,
128; religion, 149, 535; historical
references, 172–3, 240–3; post-
conquest, 193, 240, 287, 293, 338,
341, 373–4; medicine, 538
"Incanate" monarchy, 338, 341, 373
Independence, Spanish American,
62, 167; intellectual beginnings,
230–63 (see Enlightenment);
champions of, 286–313 passim,
335–6; Memorandum of Grievances, 287, 311–13; non-national-
istic character of, 288–9, 353;
ideal of revolution, 294; press as
weapon, 294–302; Spaniard vs.
Creole, 299–300, 311–13; exiled
Jesuit vanguard, 302–5; United
States, England, France, 305–8,
343; final battle, 311, 349; Church,
the, 343–50; see law, government,
Spanish American; see also under
names of countries
India, 37, 41–2, 59, 95, 98, 117, 488
indiano; derecho indiano, xii, 55, 67
Indians, Spanish American, 71–4,
82, 84–5; abuses, 124–7, 136, 144,
156, 166, 209, 238, 395, 443, 504–
5; rebellions, 127, 173, 247, 287,
293; College for, 131; Church, the,
139–40, 147–50, 166, 194, 268,
533 (see also religion, pre-Christian; magic, mysticism); languages, 144–5, 167, 171; education: see under missions and
names of religious orders; women,
160; communes: see Paraguay,
Jesuits, comuneros; France, 239–
40; protection, reforms, 292 (see
Laws of the Indies); contributions: see Enlightenment; art;
magic; see also Portuguese America; pre-Columbia America; Aztec;
Inca; Maya; Guaraní

Indies, the, xii, 52, 67, 72, 78
Industrial Revolution, 135, 336, 378
Infantado, Duque del, 64
Ingenieros, José: Evolución de las
Ideas Argentinas, El Hombre
Mediocre, and Evolución socioló-
gica argentina . . . , 394; 395, 491,
502
Iñiguez, Don Diego Angulo, 219
Innocent VIII, Pope, 238
Inquisition, the, 122, 139–41, 194;
palaces of, 204–5; 226; Human-
ism, 231–3; Scholastics vs. Car-
tesians, 235–7; social contract,
247–50, 253–6; revolution, 260,
306, 344; 308; witchcraft, 528–34
Irigoyen, Hipólito, 489
Irisarri, Antonio José de, 282, 301–
2; El Cristiano Errante; Historia
del Períndito . . . ; Cuestiones
Filológicas, 302; 315, 353
Isaacs, Jorge: María, 317, 532
Isabel the Catholic, Order of, 346
Isabella I of Castile, 137
Italy, 71, 196; Romanticism, 318,
328; Risorgimento, 328; influence,
394, 397; fascism, 394–5, 503
Iturbide, Augustín de (Emperor
Augustín I), 338–40, 354, 364
Ituri Patiño, Simón, 513

Jacquin, Nikolaus Joseph von: Se-
lectarum Stirpium Americanum
. . . , 268
Jamaica, 70, 443
James I of England, 86
James the Hermit: Voyages of
L'Hermite, 227 and n.
Jamestown Colony, xv
Japan, xiii, 67, 91, 95, 118, 472
Jefferson, Thomas, 258, 336, 400
Jérez, Francisco López de: Verda-
dera Relación de la Conquista del
Peru y . . . Cuzco, 172
Jesuit Letters, 117
Jesuit Order, 60, 100–2; founding
of, 104, 150, 153; Brazil, 105–17,

Jesuit Order (*cont.*)
   404–7; Spanish America, 145, 150,
   153–6; expulsion, 154, 157, 159,
   167, 260, 289–91, 404–7; 155;
   Paraguay, 105–8, 156–7, 252, 255;
   Ecuador, 154, 333, 365; Chile,
   158–9, 181, 301; laxity, 166–7;
   Mexico, 197, 294; architecture,
   198–9; art, 223; Enlightenment,
   236, 245, 252; independence, 302–
   5, 344; Guatemala, 362–3; Colom-
   bia, 392; Haiti, 444–5
Jesus, Church of (Rome), 198–9,
   201
Jesús, Felipe de, Saint, 163
Jesús, Sor Catalina de: *Secretas
   entre el alma y Dios*, 162
Jesús, Sor Mariana de (Lily of
   Quito), 161–2
Jews, 98–9, 110, 118–19, 122, 137,
   139, 182, 419, 525–6, 531–2; *see
   also* anti-Semitism
Jiménez, Juan Ramón, 463, 467;
   Platero y Yo, 474; 477, 522
Jiménez, Francisco: *Historia de . . .
   Guatemala*, 171
Jiménez de Cisneros, Francisco, 138,
   147
Jiménez de Quesada, Gonzalo, 35,
   38, 51–2, 73, 84–7; *Anti-Giovio*,
   86; 125, 130, 138; *Epitome de la
   Conquista del Nuevo . . . Granada*,
   171, 244; 179
Jiménez López, Miguel: *¿Nuestras
   razas decáen?*, 506
jitanjáfora, 527–8
João II of Portugal, 94, 104
João III of Portugal, 103
João IV of Portugal, 122
João VI of Portugal, 412, 414–15
John XXIII, Pope, 516
John the Troublemaker, Saint, 532–3
Jornal do Comercio (Brazilian news-
   paper), 416
Jotabeche (José Joaquín Vallejo),
   330–1
Jovellanos, Gaspar Melchor de, 247,
   301, 336

Juan, Don Jorge: *Memorias Secretas*, 127, 166–7; 236–7, 267–8,
   323; *see also* Ulloa, Don Antonio
Juárez, Benito, 283, 339, 344, 352,
   385, 389–90, 392
Juárez, José, 228
Julián, Father Antonio: *La Perla
   de América*, 304
Junot: *see* Abrantès, Duc d', Duchesse d'
Jussieu, Joseph, 267
Justo, Juan B.: *Teoría y Práctica de
   la Historia*, 394, 396

Kabah, 10
Kafka, Franz, 322
Kamehameha II of Hawaii, 416
Karnak, Temple of, 14
Karsten, Rafael, 32
Kennedy, John F., 519
Kepler, Johannes, 234, 292
Khanti, Vicente Pazos, 371–2
Kleist, Heinrich von: "The Nun of
   Santiago in Paris," 322; "The
   Sweethearts of Santo Domingo,"
   322–3
Kondori, 202
Korn, Alejandro: *La Libertad Crea-
   dora*, 520
koyem, 25
Kundt, Hans, 503

La Condamine, Charles Marie de,
   59, 108, 266–8, 278
La Gasca, Licentiate, 44, 160, 173
La Guayana, 129
La Moda (gazette), 326
La Moneda (palace), 200
La Paz, 14, 371–2, 374, 376
La Plata, University of, 489
Lafayette, Marquis de, 262, 383–3
Laffite, Pierre, 425
Laforgue, Jules, 467, 485
Lagarrigue, Jorge, 387
Lamartine, Alphonse-Louis de Prat
   de, 316, 324–5, 335

Lamennais, Félicité-Robert de: *Pa-roles d'un croyant* and *De l'escla-vage modern,* 386
Lancaster, Joseph, 282–3, 307, 320, 347
land tenure and reform, 52, 100, 105–6, 123–8; Mexico, 126, 494, 496; Argentina, 357, 359; Cuba, 515; 247, 287, 516–17; see also *encomienda; repartimiento*
Landivar, Rafael: *Rusticana Mexicana,* 321
languages, 49, 50, 68, 70; Indian, 143–6, 374, 536–7; Creole, 448–50
Lanuza, D. Juan, 250
Lanuza, José Luis: *Victor Hugo y los Románticos argentinos,* 325
Laplace, Marquis Pierre-Simon de, 281
Lapland, 266
Larra, Mariano José de (Figaro), 320, 324, 329
Larreta, Enrique: *La Gloria de Don Ramiro,* 479–81
Las Casas, Fray Bartolomé de, xii; *Historia de las Indias,* 64; 65; *Brevísima relación . . . Destruc-ción de las Indias,* 71; 72, 110, 127, 170, 238, 240, 280, 443, 478, 499, 525–30, 548–9
Las Ventas, the heads of, 211, 498
Lastarria, José Victorino: *Investiga-ciones sober la(s) influencia(s) social(es) . . . en Chile,* 384–6; 388, 391
latifundia, 112, 496
Latin America: see America; pre-Columbian America; Portuguese America; Spanish America
"Latin America"; "Latins," xi
Latin-American Union, 491
Lattes, César, 440
Lautréamont, Count de (Isidore-Lucien Ducasse), 210, 485
Lavapatas, 15
law, government, Spanish American: colonial, 51–2, 67, 127–30, 137–8,

142–3, 156–9 (*see* viceroyalties; *encomienda; audiencia;* Laws of the Indies); ideological revolution, 238–43, 343–4 (*see* Enlighten-ment; Independence); birth of con-stitutional, 248–51, 355; federal-ism, 258–9, 337, 351–5; central-ism, 311–13, 352, 354–5; codifica-tion, 280; conservative vs. liberal, 335–7, 502–8 (*see* Romanticism); republic vs. monarchy, 338–43, vs. Church, 343–50; rise of national-ism, 351–77 (*see* caudillos); search for form, 378–403, 465–6, 487–8; revolution, reform, 489–500; democracy vs. dictatorship, 502–22; post-World War II crisis, 507–8; economic fulcrum, 508–10; Christian Democracy, 515–16
Laws of the Indies, xii, 52, 67, 72, 138, 238
Le Corbusier: *Vers une Architec-ture,* 437, 517
Leclerc, Charles, 456
Legardo, Bernardo, 217
Leibnitz, Baron Gottfried Wilhelm von, 232–3, 292
Leite, Cassiano Ricardo, 436
Lemos, Miguel, 425–6
Lemos de Faria, Francisco de, 406
Lenin, Nikolai, 494
Leo X, Pope, 224
Leo XII, Pope, 348–50
Leo XIII, Pope, 366
León, Fray Luis de, 151, 532
León Abrabanel, Judah (León He-breo): *Diálogos sobre el Amor,* 182
León Mera, Juan: *Cumandá,* 318
León y Gama, Antonio de, 277
Leonard, Irving A.: *Books of the Brave,* 77; 83–4, 87
Leopardi, Giacomo, 463, 468
Lerdo de Tejada, Miguel, 126
Lerminier, Eugène, 324 and *n.*
Léry, Jean de: *L'Histoire d'un Voy-age . . . dit l'Amérique,* 102

Leturia, Father Pedro de, 346–8
Lewin, Boleslao: *Presencia de Rousseau*, 254 n.
Leyburn, James G., 445, 451
Lezo, Blas de, 210–11
Liberdade do Ventre (law), 421–3
Lillo, Eusebio (Rouget de L'Isle), 386
Lima, xiv, 39, 87, 131, 213, 247, 517; opulence of, 133–5, 215, 266; School of Medicine, 291–2; aristocracy, 293–5, 344
Lima, Jorge de: *Essa Negra Fulo, Medicina e Humanismo, Calunga,* and *A Mulher Obscura,* 440
Linares, José María, 375–6
Lincoln, Abraham, 337
Linnaeus, Carolus, 61, 264, 268, 270–3
Lisboa, Antônio Francisco (O Aleijadinho), 411
Lisbon, xiv, xviii, 95–6, 110, 404–5
Literary Gazette (Mexico), 277
literature, Portuguese American: birth of, 89–94; frontier, 113; theater, 114–16, 410, 413, 420–1, 436; poetry, 116, 407–9, 415, 420, 422, 428, 436; history, 116–17; Renaissance academy, 406–7; patronage, 420; antislavery, 422; novel, 429, 431–4, 436, 440; Parnassians vs. Romantics, 432–4; Symbolists, 433; Naturalists, 434; *modernismo,* 434–8, 440–1
literature, Spanish American: language, 49–50, 68, 70, 168, 243–4; birth of, 64–75, 168–70; Medieval vs. Renaissance, 70–1, 177; fantastic vs. realistic, 76–87, 461–3 (*see* magic, mysticism); of discovery, 117 (*see* Columbus; Cuzco; Tenochtitlán; rediscovery); missions, 144–6; theater, 145, 188–92, 256, 317, 325–8, 336; Indian manuscripts, 147–50, 533 (*see* pre-Columbian America); poetry, 161, 173–8, 183–8, 216,

277, 316, 318, 321, 336, 338, 461–7, 499, 543–5; history, 169–73, 183, 302–5, 500; novel, 177, 180, 210, 233, 318, 336–7, 390, 397, 402, 478–83, 498–9, 510–13; Creole, 177–81, 183–8; *mestizo,* 181–2; Enlightenment, 232–3, 236–7, 242–8, 254, 262, 274; revolution, 260, 277, 294–302, 304–5, 308–13, 337; Romanticism, 316–17, 320–1, 323–8, 335–7, 461–3; modern movement, 317–18, 398 (see *Modernismo*); contemporary fiction, 322, 380–1, 498–9, 510–13; anti-modernism, 474–7, 484; modern fringe, 484–5; political essayists, 502; Negro contribution: *see* Negro; *see also* magic, mysticism
Littré, Maximilien-Paul-Émile, 425
Livingston, Edward, 362
Lizárraga, Fray Reginaldo de: *Descripción . . . de las Indias,* 171
Lizaso, Felix, 233
Lleras Camargo, Alberto, 518
Locke, John, 233, 292, 336, 357, 400
Loefling, Pieter: *Iter Hispanicum,* 268, 271
Loisy, Alfred Firmin, 464
Lombardo Toledano, Vicente: *see* Toledano, Vicente Lombardo
Lombroso, Cesare, 394
London, 59, 319–20, 329
Longfellow, Henry Wadsworth, 327, 401
Lopes Neto, João Simões: *Contos Gauchescos,* 434
López, Carlos Antonio, 369
López, Estanislao, 359
López, Francisco Solano, 369–70
López, Luis Carlos: *De Mi Villorrio,* 475
López, Vicente Fidel: *La Novia . . . La Inquisición de Lima,* 324; autobiography, 325; 328–9
López de Jérez, Francisco: *see* Jérez
López de Mesa, Luis, 521

López Mateos, Adolfo, 497
López y Fuentes, Gregorio: *El Indio*, 481–2
Lorrain, Jean, 472
Loti, Pierre, 472
Louis XIV of France, 120
Louisiana, 111, 267, 522
Louvre, the, 119
Louÿs, Pierre, 473, 480
Loyola, Ignatius, Saint, 104–5, 187
Lozano, Father, xvi, 244–5
Lucca, Duke of, 341
Ludovico, Father, 295
Lugo, Cardinal Juan de, 60
Lugones, Leopoldo, 322; *Odas Seculares* and *La Guerra Gaucha*, 475–6; 502
Luther, Martin, 147, 529, 531
Lutheran Church, 139, 235, 532
Luz y Caballero, José de la, 401
Lynch, Benito: *El Inglés de los güesos*, 481–2
Lynch, Eliza, 369

Mabille, Dr. Pierre, 452
Machado, Manuel, 463
Machado de Assis, Joaquim Maria, 408, 435; *Dom Casmurro, Resureição, Memórias Póstumas de Braz Cubas*, and *Quincas Borba*, 434
Machado Ruiz, Antonio, 463, 478
Machiavelli, Niccolò: *The Prince*, 137; 393, 397
Machu Picchu, 15, 16, 35
Maciel, Antônio Vicente Meudes (the "Prophet"), 431–2
Mackandal, 540–1
macumba, 452, 545–6
Madariaga, Salvador de, 139; *El Corazón de Piedra Verde*, 486; 496
Madeira, 97
Madeiros, José, 545
Madero, Francisco I, 390, 483, 493–4
Madison, James, xiii n., 262
Madrid, Botanical Gardens, 272,

274, 518
Magalhães, Domingo José Gonçalves de: *Confederação dos Tamoios*
Magalhanes Gandavo, Pero de: *Tratado da Terra do Brasil*, 117
Magdalena River, xx, 71, 73
Magellan, Ferdinand, 73, 79, 168, 231
magic, mysticism: 9, 71, 76–87, 139, 152, 179; as vital force, 461–3, 525–8, 548–50; of three worlds, 523–5, 546–8; European, 528–34, 540; Indian, 534–8 (*see* religion, pre-Christian); African, 538–46; *see* voodoo; *macumba;* Roman Catholic Church; *see also under* names of countries
maicero, 25
maiohanan, 152
Malacca, 95
Malaspina, Alessandro, 269–70
Maldonado, Fray Severo, 296
Malfatti, Anita (painter): *The Yellow Man*, 435
Mallea, Eduardo: *Historia de una Pasión argentina*, 517
Malvinas Islands, 268
Mamelukes, 105–6, 157
Mañach, Jorge, 515
Manco Capac, 341
"Mandeville, Sir John" (Jehan de Bourgogne), 79–80
Manhattan Island, 231
Mann, Horace, 336, 355
Mañozca, Juan de, 540
Manuel I of Portugal, 96, 224
Manuelino, 96
Manzanillo, 211
Manzoni, Alessandro: *I Promessi Sposi*, 324; *Giovine Italia*, 326
Mapuches, 158–9
Maracaibo, 131
Marcelin, Philippe-Thoby, 459
Margallo, Father, 381
Maria I of Portugal, 406, 412, 414
Maria II of Portugal, 417
María Cristina of Spain, 342

María Luisa Teresa of Spain, 270, 341

Mariátegui, José Carlos, 492

marijuana (*Cannabis Sativa*), 538

Marinello, Juan, 515

Marinetti, Emilio Filippo Tommaso, 435

marinheiro, 414

Mariquito, 277

markets, Aztec, 30–1; colonial Mexico City, 132

Marmol, José: *Amalia*, 327; *El Poeta*, 328

Marquesas Islands, 60

marranos, 532

Martí, José, xxiii, 398, 435; *El Presidio Político in Cuba*, 465; *Los Pinos Verdes*, 466; 487, 501

Martin of Porres, Saint, 127, 216

Martínez, Dean Francisco: *Historia de las Ciencias Naturales*, 223

Martínez, Maximiliano Hernández, 363, 549

Martínez de la Rosa, Francisco, 318

Martínez Estrada, Ezequiel: *La Cabeza de Goliath*, 517

Martínez y Compañón, Bishop, 247, 249, 272

Martinique, 447

Martir o Libre (Argentine newspaper), 371

Martyr, Peter: *De Orbe Novo Decadas*, 42, 79, 168

Marx, Karl: *Das Kapital*, 396, 438

Marxism, 438, 492–3

Mary, Queen of Scots, 101–2

Mary Tudor, 173

Mascarenhas, José, 406–7

Mason, John Alden, 14, 18

Masonic lodges: see Freemasonry

Mastai-Ferretti, Gian Maria: see Pius IX, Pope

Meta, Andrés, 462

mate, 536

Matins, Father Almeida, 422

Matisse, Henri, 472

Matiz, Francisco Javier, 272

Matosinhos, Church of Good Jesus of, 411

Matthews, Herbert, 515

Matto de Turner, Clorinda: *Aves sin Nido*, 478

Mauricio, Miguel, 217

Maurras, Charles, 472

Maximilian I of Mexico, 339, 365

Maya civilization, xiv, 5; birth and duration of, 6–7; territory, 8; art, architecture, learning, cities, 8–12, 221; corn-centered society, 22–4; religion, 22–5; 88; post-conquest, 193, 197; 534–6

Mayflower, the, xv, xix, xxi

mayomberos, 542, 544–5

mazorcas, 358, 375

mechanistic philosophy, 233

Medici, Lorenzo di Pierfrancesco de', 68, 70, 89

medicine: see health, medicine

Medoro, Angelino, 223, 229

Mejía Vallejo, Manuel: *El Día Señalado*, 512

Melgarejo, Mariano, 370, 374, 376, 392

Melo, Pereira, 114

Melo Franco, Francisco de: *Reina da Estupidez*, 409

Memorandum of Grievances, 287, 311–13

Mena, Pedro de, 215

Mendaña, Alvaro de, 60

Méndez, Briceño, 340

Méndez, Diego, 71

Mendieta, Jerónimo de: *Historia Eclesiástica . . .* , 171

Mendoza, Antonio de, 129, 143

Menéndez Pidal: see Pidal, Menéndez

Menéndez y Pelayo, Marcelino: *Antología de la Poesía Hispanoamericana*, 329

Mercadal, García: *Lo Que España Llevó a America*, 42

Mercier, Sebastián: *L'an 2240*, 252

Mercurio Chileno (newspaper), 329

Mercurio de Lima (newspaper), 292, 298

Mercurio Volante (newspaper), 296

Mercury of Mexico (newspaper), 295

Mercy, Brothers of, 150

mestizo, 55, 83, 140, 193–5, 202, 298, 363

metalwork, 46–7, 206, 213

Metropolitan Museum of Art, 440

Metsys, Quentin: "Virgin at Prayer," 219

Mexia, Pedro: *Historia Imperiale*, 83

Mexican War, 496

Mexico: United States of, xiii, xx, xxi; pre-Columbian: *see* Aztec, Maya; colonial, 28–9, 40–1, 48, 51, 78, 107, 123, 126, 143–4, 213 (*see* viceroyalties); education, 131, 150–53, 217, 283, 290, 389–90, 489, 491, 494, 497, 520; letters, 170–1, 176, 178–9, 182–3, 186, 189–91, 390, 462–3, 467, 474, 481–3, 497–502, 520; architecture, 131, 193–7, 199–200, 203–5, 207, 497; art, 211, 216–18, 221–4, 227–8, 494–5, 497–8, 501; Enlightenment, 232, 256; constitution, 256, 296, 355, 494, 497; independence, 260, 287–8, 308–10, 343–4, 356; scientific missions, 270, 277; press, 294–6; 1822 Congress, 338; civil wars, 339, 482–3; monarchy, 339, 342, 265, 496; first president, 349; Utilitarianism, 380; Positivism, 385, 388–91; Porfiriate, 389–91, 496; slavery, 423; 1910 revolution, 482–3, 390, 493–7; 1917 reforms, 493–7; Church, the, 494–5; Communist Party, 495; United States, 495–6; dance, cinema, 498; Cuba, 513–14; see also *caudillos*; law, government, Spanish American

Mexico City, xiv, 4, 9, 12, 21, 29, 74; Hotel del Prado, 12, 345; Cathedral, 31, 131, 199–200, museum, 220; colonial, 131–2, 135, 217–18, 230–33, 235–8, 250–63; Plaza Mayor, 131, 200, 205; Reforma, Paseo de la, 132, 205, 344–5; School of Medicine, Treasury building, 204–5; School of Mines, Botanical Gardens, Academy of Fine Arts, 277; 1921 student congress, 491; Preparatoria, 495; artists, intellectuals, 501–2; 517

Mexico, College of (Casa de España), 496, 499

Mexico, Gulf of, 8, 12, 514

Mexico, University of, 113, 131, 151, 170, 489

Michelangelo, 198–9, 220, 225

Michelet, Jules, 386

Michoacán, 147, 151

Mier, Servando Teresa de, 248, 308–10; *Las Cartas de un americano a un español*, *La Historia de la Revolución . . .* , *El Manifesto apologético*, and *Memorias*, 310; 315–16, 337, 339, 344, 533

military, Spanish American, 352; vs. civilian, 354–6, 503, 506, 510; political ascendency, 503–10; budget expenditures, 508; United States aid for, 509–10

Mill, James, 320, 336, 380

Mill, John Stuart, 320, 336, 380

Milton, John, 382

Minas Gerais, 407–8

mines, mineralology, 126–7, 133, 267–8, 275–7, 281–2, 297, 513; *see also* Portuguese America; rediscovery

minga, the, 13

Miramón, Alberto, 467

Miranda, Francisco de, xiv, 282, 287, 293, 305–8, 311, 313, 315, 319, 330, 338, 380

missions: Guaraní, 106–8, 111; language, printing, 144–6, 167; theater, 145, 188–9; education, 145–6; universities, 150–3; conversion,

missions (*cont.*)
  destruction, 147–50; orders, 150;
  laxity, 163–7, 266, 268; art, 223;
  independence, 294
Mississippi, the, xx, 37, 74
Mistral, Gabriela, 476, 501, 532
mita, the, 126
Mitre, Bartolomé: *Memorias de un
  Botón de Rosa, Las Ruinas de
  Tiahuanacu, Ollantay*, and *His-
  toria de la Independencia Argen-
  tina*, 327; 328, 360
Mixtecs, 5
Moche, 16
Moctezuma II, 31, 37, 52, 80, 131–2,
  182, 225
Modernismo: roots of, 317–18, 398,
  461–3; Church and, 464; political
  expression, 465–6, 487, 491; Sym-
  bolists, 433, 464–74; exoticism,
  472–4; Ultraism, Futurism, Da-
  daism, Creationism, 476–8; Im-
  pressionism, 480; Surrealism, 485;
  Cubism, 495
Modigliani, Amedeo, 495
Mogrovejo, Toribio Alfonso de,
  Saint, 163
Molien, Comte François-Nicolas, 259
Molina, Wenceslao Jaime, 202
Molina y González, José Ignacio:
  Storia Natural de Cile, 303–4
Mompox, Fernando, xvi, 244, 248
Monagas, José Tadeo, 284
Monardes, Nicolás, 61
monetary system, Aztec, 31; Incan,
  33; 54
Monitor Araucano (Chilean news-
  paper), 301
Monroe, James, 306
Monroe Doctrine, 306, 518
Montaigne, Michel Eyquem de:
  Essais, 89, 102, 169, 227, 238–
  41, 253, 315, 408
Montalvo, García Ordóñez de: *Ama-
  dís de Gaula* and *Las Sergas de
  Esplandián*, 77–8
Montalvo, Juan: *Mercurial Eclesi-

ástica, Las Catilinarias, and *Capí-
  tulo que se le olvidaron a Cervan-
  tes*, 334–5
Montaña, Juan, 217
Montañés, Piedro, 215, 217
Monte Albán, 501
Monte Caseros, Battle of, 359
Monteagudo, Bernardo, 371
Monteiro Lobato, José Bento de:
  Urupês, 435
Montesinos, Fernando, 238
Montesquieu, Baron de la Brède et
  de: *Encyclopédie*, xv, 157, 240;
  L'Esprit des Lois, 253, 258; 262,
  309, 315, 336, 391
Monteverde, Giulio, 419
Montevideo, 141, 269–70, 295, 326–
  8, 347–8, 517, 546
Montjoie, Galart de: *History of the
  Constitutional Assembly*, 260–1
Montt, Manuel, 388
Moore, Henry, 4
Moors, the, 41, 99, 124, 137, 194,
  238
Mora, José Joaquín, 320, 328–30,
  353
Mora, José María Luis: *Catecismo
  . . . La Revolución Mexicana*, 380
Moraes Silva, Antônio da: *Diccion-
  ario da Lingua Portugueza*, 409
Morais Andrade, Mario de, 436
Morales, Luis de (El Divino), 220
Morand, Paul, 476
Morazán, Francisco, 354, 356, 360–3
More, Thomas: *Utopia*, 101, 151
Moréas, Jean, 472
Moreau, Gustave, 467
Morelos y Pavón, José María, 251,
  256, 287, 296, 344, 356
Moreno, Mariano: *Memorial de los
  Hacendados*, 253–5; 287, 300, 311,
  371, 413
Moreno Villa, 212
Moreno y Escandón, Francisco An-
  tonio: *History of the New King-
  dom of Granada*, 291
Morgan, Sir Henry, 210

Morgrovejo, Archbishop Tomás de, 106
Morillo de Cartagena, Pablo, 274, 297, 345
Morison, Samuel Eliot, 65, 66 n.
Morley, Sylvanus G., 8 n.
Mormonism, 452
Morning Star Temple, 9
Mosquera, Don Joaquin, 382
Mosquera, Tomás Cipriano de, 301
"Motolinía": see Benavente, Fray Toribio de
Moxo, Benito María: Cartas Mexicanas, 371
Moya de Contreras, Bishop, 190
Muñoz Marín, Luis, 522
Muratori, Lodovico Antonio, 223; Il cristianesimo felice . . . nel Paraguai, 240–1
Muriel, Domingo, 304
Murillo, Bartolomé Esteban, 218–20, 224, 226
Murillo, school of, 219, 229
Murillo Toro, Manuel: see Toro
Musée de l'Homme, 19, 24
Museo de Ambas Américas, 329
Museo Universal de Ciencias y Artes (review), 320
music: Brazil, 114, 410–11, 413, 419, 421, 429, 438; Spanish America, 131, 152, 157, 239, 491, 535, 539
Mussolini, Benito, 397, 438, 503, 507
Mutis, José Celestino, 60, 235, 237, 270–4, 284, 292
Muzafar of Cambay, Sultan, 224
Muzi, Monsignor Giovanni, 255–6, 346–8
Muzo, 277
Mycenae, 4

Nabuco, Joaquím: O Abolicionismo, 422
Nahuatl, 144–5, 171
ñanduti, 370
Napoleon I, xv, 63, 257, 259, 278, 289, 315, 412, 414–15

Napoleon III, 339, 342, 387
Nariño, Antonio, 57, 62, 260–1, 298, 311, 315, 380
Narváez, Alonso de: Our Lady of Chiquinquiró, 228
Narváez, Pánfilo de, 74
Nassau-Siegen, Count Joan Mauritz van, 119
National Preparatory School (Mexico), 389–90
nationalism: see law, government; caudillo
Naudet, Paul: Justice Sociale, 464
Navarro, Gaspar: A Tribunal of Crafty Superstition . . . , 540. . .
Navidad, La, 442–3
Nazca, 16
Nazism: Argentina, 502–3; Germany, 503; Bolivia, Chile, 503–4; Colombia, 504–6
Necropolis: see Paracas
Nees, Louis, 269
Negro: introduction of, 54, 97–100; Brazil, 110–12, 122, 439; cultural contribution, 114–15, 323, 401, 422, 433, 478, 544–5 (see magic, mysticism); United States, 352; see slavery; Haiti; see also under names of countries
Negroes of Lubola, Society of, 546
Neruda, Jan, 515
Neruda, Pablo (Neftalí Ricardo Reyes): Canto a Stalingrado, 515
Nervo, Amado, 398; Poemas Interiores, 474
Nevada, xx; Tule Springs, 21
New England, xvi
New Granada: xiv, 52, 62, 96; colonial, 123, 125–6, 129–30, 146 (see viceroyalties); territory, 129, 353; missions, 153–4; letters, 168, 171, 173, 176, 179; art, 194, 215, 228; architecture, 194, 209–10; Enlightenment, 235; independence, 255; scientific missions, 270–4, 281
New Mexico, 522
New Orleans, xi, 444

"New Spain," 29, 73, 168

"New World," 3, 5

New York, xx, 131, 466, 487–8, 533, 546–7

New York Public Library, 226

New York Times, The, 515

newspapers, 294–302, 328–9, 460; *see* printing press; *see also under names of countries*

Newton, Sir Isaac: *Philosophiae* . . . , 233, 237, 277, 292

Nicaragua, 131, 294; dictatorship, 363; slavery, 423; letters: *see* Darío, Rubén

Niemeyer, Oscar (architect), 437

Nietzsche, Friedrich Wilhelm, 370, 463–4; *Also Sprach Zarathustra,* 468

Niños Expósitos (Foundlings) Press, 255, 300

Niterói (magazine), 420–1

Nobel Prize, 476, 513, 520

"noble savage," the, 62, 103, 227, 238–43, 253, 309, 315

Nobrega, Father Manuel de, 117

Nolasco, Fray Juan, 223

Norderflycht, Baron Furchtegott Leberecht, 277

North America: *see* America; pre-Columbian America; Spanish America; Mexico; United States; Canada

Núñez, Rafael, 391–3

Núñez de Arce, Gaspar, 318

Núñez de Pineda, Francisco: *Cautiverio Feliz* . . . , 180

Nuremberg Chronicles, 224

Oaxaca, 208, 295

Obeso, Candelario, 544

Obregón, Álvaro, 494

Ocampo, Victoria, 513

Ocotlán, sanctuary of the Virgin of, 195, 214

Ocuituco, convent of, 221

Odrí, Manuel, 507, 510

Ogé, Vincent, 454–5

O'Gorman, Edmundo: *Invención de América,* 501

O'Higgins, Bernardo, 126, 251, 307, 315, 356, 371

oidor, 180

oil, petroleum: Venezuela, 396, 510; Argentina, 489; Mexico, 494, 496; Chaco War, 512–13

Ojeda, Fray Diego de: *La Cristiada,* 184

Oklahoma, xx

Olavide, Pablo de, 247, 307

Olid, Cristóbal de, 77, 78, 81

Olinda, Bishop of: *see* Coutinho, Azeredo

Olinda, Seminary of, 425

Oliveira, Antônio Mariano Alberto de, 433

Oliveira, Artur de, 433

Oliveira, João Fernandes de, 429–30

Oliveira de Torres, Jaçinto Camilo, 424, 427

Oliveira Viana, Francisco José de: *Evolucão do Povo Brasileira,* 439

Olmecs, 5, 8, 12

Olmedo, José Joaquín: "Oda a la Victoria de Junín," 338

Olmos, Fray Antonio, 146

Omaguas, 89

Oña, Pedro de: *Arauco domado* and *El Vasauro,* 175–6

O'Neill, Eugene: *The Emperor Jones,* 459

Ordóñez de Montalvo, García: *see* Montalvo, García Ordóñez de

Orejuela, Manuel José de, 250

Orellana, Francisco de, 36, 48, 172, 182

Organization of American States, the, 508, 518–19

Orinoco River, 73, 88

Orizaba, 214

Ormuz, 95

Orozco, José Clemente, 221, 494–5; Juárez, portrait, 344; National Preparatory School, fresco, 390

Ortega y Gasset, José: *La Misión de la Universidad,* 490–1

Ortiguera, Toribio: *Noticia* . . . *Quito y del río* . . . *Amazonas*, 172

Ortiz, Adalberto: *Juyungo*, 543

Ortiz, Fernando, 539, 543, 545

Ortiz, Fray Tomás, 149

Ortiz, Juan, 223, 227

Otamendi, Juan, 363

Otavalo, xi

Otero Silva, Miguel: *Fiebre*, 511

Ouro Prêto, 407

Ovalle, Alonso de: *Histórica Relación*, 181

Ovando, Doña Leonor de, 161

Oviedo, Luis Antonio de (Count of La Granja): *Vida de Santa Rosa de Lima*, 185

Oviedo y Baños, José: *Historia de la Conquista y Poblaciones* . . . *de Venezuela*, 179

Oviedo y Valdés, Gonzalo Fernández de: *Claribalde*, 80; *Historia* . . . *de las Indias*, 170; 478, 537

Pachacámac, 270

Pacheco, Juan Manuel, 154

Páez, José Antonio, 301, 339–40, 353, 381

Paine, Thomas, 262

Pais, Fernão Dias, 428

Palacios, Alfredo L., 491

Palafox, Juan de, Saint, 163

Palenque, 10, 35, 211, 535

Pales Matos, Luis: *Tuntún* . . . , 544

Palheta, De Melo, 109

Palma, Ricardo: *Tradiciones en salsa verde* and *Ropa Vieja*, 484

Pampulha, 437

Pan American Conference, the Ninth, 518

Pan American History and Geography, Commission on, 521

Pan American Union, 518

Panama, 41, 73, 125; scientific missions, 270; Congress of, 350; emergence of, 353; United States, 322, 353, 489

Panama Canal, 211, 279, 281, 322, 383, 522

Panama City, 125, 131, 141

Pane, Fray Román, 152–3

Panidas movement, 477

panopticon, 367, 380

Papel Periódico (Bogotá newspaper), 296–7, 399

Papini, Giovanni, xv

Paracas, 12, 16, 18

Paraguay: independence, 62, 354; colonial, 68, 74, 89, 106, 129, 138, 244 (*see* viceroyalties); Jesuit, Indian communes, 105–8, 138, 156–7, 240–2, 244–5, 248, 252, 255; Argentina, 157; architecture, 197, 199; art, 223; Enlightenment, 239, 244–5; scientific missions, 269; dictatorships, 279, 507 (see *caudillos*); press, 295, 299; *albinagio*, 368, 369; Chaco War, 370, 512; military, 507–8; mysticism, 549

Paraguay River, 81, 274

Paraná River, xx

Pardo García, Germán, 501

Parisiense, Guillermo, 534

Parmentier, 58

Pasto, 225

Patagonia, 22, 27, 79, 129, 269–70

Pater, Adrian Juanes, 210

Patria (Cuban newspaper), 466

Pátzcuaro, xi

Pau Brasil (review), 435

Paul III, Pope, 104

Paulistas, 157

Pavón, José Antonio, 60, 274

Paz, Octavio: *El Laberinto de la Soledad*, 499

Pedregal, the, 497

Pedro I of Portugal, xviii, 410, 414–17, 421

Pedro II of Brazil, 417–24, 425

Pedroso, Regino: *El Ciruelo* . . . , 473

Peixoto, Afranio, 117, 408; *Fruta do Mato*, 434
Pellicer, Carlos, quoted, v; 216, 501
Pentecostal Churches, 546–7
Peralta, Gastón de, 134, 228
Peralta, Juan de: *Tres Jornadas al Cielo*, 185
Pereira Ramos, Juan, 406
Pereyns, Simon, 217, 228
Pérez Arbeláez, Enrique, 533
Pérez Holguín, Melchor, 229
Pérez Jiménez, Marcos, 398, 507, 509–10, 511
Pérez Triana, Santiago, 398
pericón, 536
pericotes, 39
Per me Reges Regnant, 250
Pernambuco, 98, 113–14; 1817 revolt, 414
Pernaty, Dom, 269
Perón, Eva María Duarte de, 549
Perón, Juan Domingo, 358, 503–4, 507–8, 510, 513, 549
Perret, Pedro, 225
Peru: pre-Columbian: *see* Incan Empire; social structure, 127, 194 (*see* Lima); colonial, 127–9, 133–5, 141, 162, 213 (*see* viceroyalties); education, 134, 282, 291–2; missions, 153–4, 156, 266, 294; letters, 172–3, 184, 463, 497, 481–2, 491–3, 512–13; architecture, 197, 202–3; art, 212, 215, 223, 229; Enlightenment, 232, 246–7; independence, 259, 287–8, 293–4, 301, 344, 353; scientific missions, 266–8, 270; first governors, 289; press, 292, 294–5; Incanate proposal, 338; university revolution, 491–3
Peter of Ghent, 131, 147, 155
Petit, Andrés Facundo Cristo de los Dolores, 548
Petrarch, 71
Philadelphia, 131, 262, 305, 379, 400
Philip II of Spain, 61, 119, 124, 153, 162, 173, 196, 225, 231
Philippines, the, 44, 200
Piçanco, José Correia, 406
Picasso, Pablo, 6, 495
Picchia, Paulo Menotti del: *Inca Mulato*, 435–6
Picón-Salas, Mariano: *De la Conquista a la Independencia*, 139, 321, 521, 540
Picornell, Juan Bautista, 261
Pidal, Menéndez, 68
Pigafetta, Antonio: *Primo Viaggio intorno al Mondo*, 79
Pilgrims, the, xv, xix, xxi, 124
Pintó, Bento Texeira, 116
Pinto, Francisco Antonio, 348
Pinzón, Martín Alonso, 65
"pipiolo," 348
piracy, 97, 101–3, 119, 129, 141, 179, 210–11, 227, 399, 443–4
piratini, 418
Pitt, William, 306
Pius VII, Pope, 345
Pius IX, Pope (Gian Maria Mastai-Ferretti), 346–8, 368
Pius X, Pope, 464
Pius XI, Pope, 157
Pizarro, Francisco, xix, 28, 29, 32, 48, 79, 172–3, 82, 125, 134, 144, 194, 226
Pizarro, Gonzalo, 82, 172, 194
Pizarro, Hernando, 29, 32, 82, 194
Plácido: *see* Valdés, Gabriel de la Concepción
plantations: *see* Portuguese America
plateresque, 193–4, 198
platinum, 267, 276, 281
Plato: *Republic*, 77, 103, 157, 240
plaza, 135–6
Pliny the Elder, 78–9
Pocaterra, José Rafael: *Memorias* ..., 511
Poe, Edgar Allan, 463, 467
Politian, 70, 240
Polo, Marco: *The Million*, 27, 95; 69, 73, 78
Polo de Ondegardo, Juan: *Infor-*

Polo de Ondegardo, Juan (*cont.*)
  mación . . . Religión de los Incas,
  172
Polynesia, 21
Pombal, Marquês de (Carvalho e
  Mello, Sebastião de), 404–7
Ponce, Aníbal, 502
Ponce de León, Juan, 37, 73, 82
Pontins, Baron de, 210
Popayán, 131, 153, 473
Popocatépetl, 31
Popul Vuh, 9, 22–4, 536
Porras Barrenechea, Raúl, 237,
  242–3
Porres, Martín de, Saint, 163
Portales, Diego, 301, 330, 388
Port-au-Prince, 444–5, 457, 541
Portinari, Cándido, murals, 437
Portugal: xiv, xv, 88, 94; Africa,
  Asia, 94–6; 99; Jesuits, 104, 404–
  7; 1755 earthquake, 404–5; court
  in Brazil, 411–15
Portuguese America: arrival of Portuguese, xiii–iv, 88, 95; Indians,
  xiv, 21–2, 87–94, 99–100, 110–11,
  114, 119, 122; plantations, 97–
  101, 111–13, 409, 412, 428;
  slavery, 97, 100, 110–12, 421;
  natural products, 97, 108; mines,
  97, 109, 405, 428–9; social structure, 98–103, 429, 439; peaceful
  evolution, 98, 414–17, 421–4;
  captaincies, 98–102, 130, 428;
  monasteries, 98, 409; cities, 98,
  428, 436; frontier, 98, 100–1, 428–
  30; Catholicism, 99–100, 107, 112,
  114, 150 (*see* Jesuits); Spanish,
  the, 101; French, the, 101–4, 417;
  Dutch, the, 101–2, 108–9, 118–
  22; English, the, 101–2, 410, 412,
  417; agriculture, 102, 109–10, 410;
  education, 113, 405–6, 413; monarchy, 338, 340, 342, 411–17; industry, 406, 410, 412–13; Enlightenment, Romanticism, 406–
  9, 410, 412–16, 420, 425, 427;
  independence: *see* Brazil

Posada, José Guadalupe, 227, 483,
  494, 501
posadas, 189
Positivism: roots of, 335–7; Comte's
  stages of history, 378, 385; religious outgrowth, 387, 391, 425–
  7; Spencer's peaceful evolution,
  391–8; *see also under names of
  countries*
Post, Franz, 119
Potosí, 36, 41, 127, 133–5, 194, 197,
  202, 218, 276
pottery, 3–5, 10, 14–19, 208, 498,
  501
Pound, Ezra, 476
Pozo, Francisco del, 223, 228
Pozo, José del, 304
Pradt, Dominique de, 349
pre-Columbian America, xiv, 3–6;
  surviving codices, 8–9, 22–4, 147,
  225, 536–7; communication, 16,
  19; characteristics, 20–6, 28, 33,
  35–6; art, 497–8, 501; *see also*
  Aztec; Inca; Maya; religion, pre-
  Christian
Prescott, William H., 337, 401
Prester John, 78–9, 94
Prestes, Luiz Carlos, 438, 440
Preto, Manuel, 106
Preuss, K. H., 15
printing press: Mexico, 131, 294–
  6; playing cards, 223; 225; first
  print shop, 294–5; vehicle of in-
  dependence, 294–302, 312, 329;
  Central America, 296; Brazil, 406
"Prophet, the": *see* Maciel, Antônio
  Vicente Mondes
Protestantism, 139, 343, 347, 349–
  50, 354, 364–5, 367, 506
Ptolemy, 236
Puebla, 25, 195, 198, 201, 207, 219,
  228, 295
Puerto Cabello, 141, 160
Puerto Rico, 130, 141; press, 295;
  independence, 398; determining
  influence, 399; Hostos, 402; letters,
  education, 521, 544; heritage, 522

pulque, 536
Punta del Este charter, 519
Pushkin, Aleksander Sergeevich, 472
pyramids, 9, 10, 31, 535
Pythagoras, 236

Quadros, Janio, xviii
Quebec, xv
Quechidona, 172
Quechuas, xiv, 34
"Quenti-Cancha," 34
Querétaro, 339
Quesada: see Jiménez de Quesada
Quesada, Cristobal, 228
Quesada, Manuela, 267
Quevedo y Villegas, Francisco Gómez de, 185; El Buscón, 337
Quiche Maya, 22
Quimbaya, 20
Quinche, Virgin of, 360
Quinet, Edgar, 386-7
quintados, 134
Quintana, Manuel José, 293
Quintana Roo, 8
quipus, 19, 242-3
Quiroga, Facundo, 359
Quiroga, Horacio: Anaconda and Cuentos de la Selva, 274; 481-2
Quiroga, Vasco de, 151
Quitan style, school, 198, 214-17, 222, 272
Quiteño Libre, El (newspaper), 383
Quito: 48, 84; colonial, 125-6, 129-31, 162; convent, 161, 166-7; letters, 172; 180; architecture, 196; art, 212, 214-16, 218, 222, 228; science, 267; press, 297-9; "Francis I," 304; 363-4
Quito, Cathedral of, 216

Rabelais, François, 227
racism, 394-5, 504-6
Raleigh, Sir Walter, 58; History of the World, 86; 87
Ramírez, Ignacio ("the Necromancer"), 345, 390

Ramírez, Pedro, 228
Ramírez de Fuenleal: see Fuenleal
Ramos, Arthur: Introdução a Antropologica Brasileira, 114, 439, 546
Ramos, Graciliano: Memórias do Cárcere, 440
Raphael, 224, 228
Ratzel, Friedrich, 505
Ravel, Maurice-Joseph, 472
Raynal, Abbot: Histoire . . . des éstablissements . . . dans les Indes, 251-2, 318
Reader's Digest, 295
Reconquest and Pacification: see Spain
rediscovery (scientific missions): 236, 260; La Condamine, rubber, platinum, 266-8; Malaspina, floating laboratories, 269-70; Botanical Missions, 270-4, 281, 297; Azara, rivers Plata and Paraguay, 274-5; Basques, mineralogy, 275-7; Humboldt, first, second trips, 278-9; Boussingault, chemistry, 280-2; Codazzi, first atlas, 283-5
Reid, Thomas, 320
religion, pre-Christian, 3, 4, 13-15, 19-20; corn, significance of, 22-6; 31, 50-1, 56; missions, impact of, 147-50; 152, 154, 308-9; surviving, 534-8; see also magic, mysticism
Remesal, Antonio de: Historia de . . . Guatemala, 171
Remón, José Antonio, 507
Renaissance, the, 69-71, 77, 177, 196, 230-2
Renan, Joseph-Ernest, 488, 491
René-Moreno, Gabriel: Los últimos días . . . del Alto Perú, 371
Reni, Guido, 221, 224
repartimiento, 52, 123-5, 143
Repertorio Americano (anthology), 320-1
Restrepo, Don Camilo, 57
Restrepo, José Manuel: History of

Restrepo, José Manuel (*cont.*)
the Revolution in . . . *Colombia*, 288

Revillagigedo, Viceroy, 270

Revista de Valparaíso (newspaper), 329

"*Rex Americae*": *see* Villegaignon, Nicolas Durand de

Reyes, Alfonso, 176, 183, 186, 190–1, 303, 399, 520

Reyes Marrero, Baltasar de los, 232

Reyles, Carlos: *Gaucho Florido*, 480

Ribera, Francisco de, 84

Ribera, José (El Españoleto), 220, 228

Ricard, Robert, 144, 147–8

Ricardo, Antonio, 294

Ricke de Marselaer, Jodoko, 155 and *n;* 196, 228

Rigaud, André, 455

Rimsky-Korsakov, Nikolai, 472

Rio, Andrés del, 277

Rio Branco, Viscount of (José da Silva Paranhos), 421–2

Rio de Janeiro, xiv, 113, 338, 406, 410, 412, 415, 422, 436–7, 439–40, 545–6

Rio de Janeiro Pact, 514

Río de la Plata, xx, 68, 81, 84, 96, 133, 162, 274; United Provinces of, 341; *see also* viceroyalties

Rio Grande, 353

Rio Grande do Sul, 288, 417–18

Riquelme, Pedro, 159

Rivadavia, Bernadino, 282, 341, 347–8, 356–9, 380, 382, 423

Rivadeneira, Manuel, 329

Rivera, Diego, 221, 494–5, 501; Hotel del Prado, mural, 12, 345; National Palace, mural, 344; National Preparatory School, mural, 390

Rivera, Don Antonio de, 45

Rivera, José Eustacio: *The Vortex*, 85, 481–2

Rivero, Mariano de, 281

Roa, Raúl, 549

Robbia: *see* Della Robbia

Roberto, José, 537

Robertson, William, 336

Robespierre, 306

Rocafuerte, Vincente, 364–5

Rochambeau, Donatien, 456

Rodin, François Auguste René, 517

Rodó, José Enrique: *Ariel*, 470, 487–9

Rodrigues, Simão, 104

Rodríguez, Francisco, 140

Rodríguez, Manuel: *El Marañón y el Amazonas*, 172

Rodríguez, Manuel del Socorro, 296–7

Rodríguez, Simón, 256–7, 308–10; *Sociedades americanas en 1828*, *El Liberator . . . de la causa social*, and *Educación Popular*, 310; 315–16, 374

Rodríguez Francia, José Gaspar: *see* Francia, Dr.

Rodríguez Freile, Juan: *Historia . . . de la Nueva Granada* and *El Carnero*, 179

Rodríguez y del Castillo, Father, 157

Röhm, Ernst, 503

Rojas, Fernando de, 532

Rojas, José Antonio de, 250–1, 336

Rojas, Pedro, 207, 212, 222, 224

Rojas, Ricardo: *Ollantay*, 190, 536

Rojas Pinilla, Gustavo, 507, 510, 549

Roland, Mme, 360

Roldán, Salvador Comacho, 391

Román, Doña Soledad, 392

Roman Catholic Church, 3; education, 50–1, 53, 83–4, 139, 145–6, 150–3, 344; art, architecture, 51, 126, 147–50, 195–204, 215–20, 226; properties, 126, 159, 220, 343–4; Reform, 138–9, 216, 231–3 (*see* Inquisition); orders, 150; laxity, disputes, 162–7, 266, 268, 445; slavery, 238; independence, 247–50, 253–6, 258, 308–9; monarchy vs. republic, 341, 343–50; Muzi mission, 346–8; Central

Roman Catholic Church (*cont.*)
American Federation, 361–3; García Moreno, 366; Utilitarianism, 381–2; Positivism, 392; *modernismo,* "Americanism," 464; racism, Nazism, 502–3; magic, 533–4; *see* missions; Portuguese America; Catholicism; *see also under names of orders*
Romano, Giulio, 221
Romanticism: 292–3, 310; European roots, 314–16, 318–23 (*see* Enlightenment); American, 314, 316–28, 461–3; Hugo, 323, 325–7, 330, 333–5; vs. Classicism, 324–6, 330–3, 432–4; political outgrowth, left, right, 324, 326–37 (*see* law, government); Realism, 337
Rome, 5, 29, 198, 257
Romero, Francisco, 520
Romero, José Rubén: *La Vida inútil de Pito Pérez,* 483
Romualdo, Bishop: *see* Brughetti, Romualdo
Roosevelt, Franklin D., 507
Roosevelt, Theodore, 489
Rosales, Diego: *Historia . . . de Chile,* 159, 173
Rosary Chapel (Tunja), 202
Rosas, Juan Manuel de, 324, 326–9, 352, 355, 357–60, 366
Rose of Lima, Saint, 43, 161
Rosillo, Canon, 344
Roulin, François Désiré, 281–2
Rousseau, Jean-Jacques: *Confessions,* xv; *Le Contrat Social,* 243–56 *passim,* quoted, 251; *Essai sur l'origine des langues, Discours . . . l'inegalité, Julie . . . , Émile . . . , Pygmalion,* and *Discours sur les Arts . . . ,* 246; 262, 309–10, 315, 322, 336, 408, 410, 425
Rouvroy, Claude-Henri de: *see* Saint-Simon, Comte de
Rozo, Rómulo, 502
rubber, 10, 59, 60, 108, 267
Rubens, Peter Paul, 221

Ruiz, Hipólito, 60, 274
Ruiz de Alarcón, Juan: *La Verdad Sospechosa,* 191–2, 485
Rulfo, Juan: *Pedro Páramo,* 499
Russia, 310, 380, 390, 395, 438, 472, 482–3, 494–5, 497; socialist empire, 507; Cuba, 508, 514

Sá, Mem de, 102
Sabana de Bogotá, 38
Sabès Pétion, Alexandre, 457, 541
Saco, José Antonio: *Historia de esclavitud . . . ,* 401
Sagasta, Juan, 126
Sagrario: *see* Ciborium, Chapel of the
Sahagún, Bernardino de: *Historia General de las cosas de la Nueva España* and *Pláticas de los ancianos,* 146, 171, 536
Saint-Dié, the canons of, xii, 69, 101, 279
St. Francis, Church of (Mexico City), 229
St. Francis, Church of (Quito), 216
St. Gertrude, Church of (Orizaba), 214
St. James, Palace of, 219
St. Maurice, Jacques, 97
St. Peter's Church (Rome), 199
Saint-Simon, Comte de (Claude-Henri de Rouvroy), 323, 383–4, 385
St. Thomas Aquinas, University of, 151–2
Sainte-Beuve, Charles-Augustin, 325
saints, American, 163
Salamanca, 28, 30; University of, 236, 247, 253, 508
Salas, Father Manuel de, 301, 304
Salavarrieta, Policarpa, 328
Salazar, Antonio de Oliveira, 438
Salgado, Plínio, 435
Salinas, Pedro, 477, 522
Sallusti, Giuseppi, 347
Samuel Zacuto, Abraham ben, 526
San Agustín, 15, 16, 19, 35, 211, 285

San Augustín, Church of (Acolman), 197–8, 214
San Diego, Church of, 212
San Felipe de Barajas, castle of, 210–11
San Fernando, castle of, 211
San Francisco, Church of (Acatepec), 195
San Francisco, Church of (Quito), 196
San Ignacio, Church of (Bogotá), 197, 199, 201
San Ildefonso, Colegio de, 180
San Jorge, Marquis de, 209
San Jorge de Mina, 94
San José, castle of, 211
San Juan (Argentina), 347
San Juan (Puerto Rico), 130, 141, 295
San Lorenzo, Church of (Potosí), 202–3
San Marcos, University of, 180, 232, 293–4
San Martín, José de, 250, 282, 287–9, 193–4, 329, 343, 353, 356, 371
San Miguel el Grande (Allende), 208
San Salvador, 131
San Sebastián del Pastelillo, 211
Sánchez, Luis Alberto, 492, 520
Sánchez de Tejada, Ignacio: see Tejada
Sancho, Hipólito, 184
Sancho, Pedro, 32–3
Sand, George, 325
Sanfuentes, Salvador de, 331
Sangro, Raimundo di: Lettera apologetica . . . , 243
Sanguily, Manuel, 549
Sanín Cano, Baldomero, 467–8, 520
Santa Catalina, 407
Santa Cruz, 211
Santa Cruz, Marshal Andrés, 301, 372–4
Santa Cruz y Espejo, Francisco Javier: see Espejo

Santa Fe de Bogotá, 87, 129, 131, 163
Santa María, Domingo, 387
Santa María de Ora, Fray Justo, 311
Santa Maria del Fiore (Florence), 199
Santa Maria Itaparica, Manuel de, 407
Santa María Tonantzintla, Church of, 201
Santa Marta, 35, 130–1, 138, 149, 165, 304
Santa Mónica, convent of, 195
Santander, Francisco de Paula, 281, 288, 349, 380–2
Santiago (Chile), xxi, 38, 44, 73, 129, 140, 160, 163, 218, 295, 329
Santiago (Cuba), 130, 211
Santiago, Miguel de, 228
Santo Cristo del Buen Viaje, Institución, 548
Santo Domingo: colonial, 41, 128–30, 204, 399; schools, 150–2, 399; letters, 161, 399; architecture, 195, 204, 211; press, 295; France, 307; Haiti, 398–9; United States, 399; influences, 399, 443, 460; witchcraft, 533–4; negro, 539
Santo Domingo (city), 130, 195, 444
Santos, 113
Santos, Eduardo, 509–10
Sanuto, Martino, 96
Sanz, Miguel José, 248–50
São Paulo, 105–6, 113, 157, 230, 235–7, 415–16, 428; University of, 439
Sargasso Sea, 78
Sarmiento, Domingo Faustino, 324, 330–3, 352; Recuerdos de Provincia, 328; Facundo, 329, 355, 359, 360, 379, 384
Sarmiento de Gamboa, Pedro: Historia . . . de las Incas, 172–3
Sartre, Jean-Paul, 514
Sassoferrato, Il (Giovanni Battista Salvi), 224
Sastre, Marcos, 324

Satúrnio, Clauceste: see Costa, Claudio Manuel da
Savannah, Battle of, 454–5
Scharon, Faine, 445–6, 450–1
Schiller, Johann Christoph Friedrich von, 324; *William Tell* and *Mary Stuart*, 325; *The Bride of Messina*, 420; 463, 467–8
Schlegel, August Wilhelm von, 315, 318
Schlegel, Friedrich von, 315, 318
Schmidt, Ulrich, 68, 79, 81–2
Schneider, Herbert W.: *History of American Philosophy*, xiii *n*.
Schneider, Johann Gottlob, 323
Scholasticism, 70, 232–3, 248, 287, 289, 302, 378
Schongauer, Martin, 222
Schopenhauer, Arthur, 463–4
Schumacher, Bishop, 367
Science, Royal Academy of (Paris), 266, 284
scientific missions: see rediscovery
Scott, Sir Walter: *Ivanhoe*, 316; *The Talisman*, 329; 401
Sebastián, Santiago, 225
Seghers, Gerard, 223, 229
Seixas, Maria Dorotea Joaquina de, 408
Semanario Republicano (Chilean newspaper), 301
Seniegues, Jean, 267
Serlio, Sebastiano, 225
sertanistas, 430
Servando, Fray: see Mier, Servando Teresa de
Seven Cities of Cibola, 228
Shakespeare, William, 488
Sierra, Don Justo, 283; *Evolución Política . . . Mexicano*, and *Juárez*, 390; 466
Sierra Morena, 247
Siglo, El (Colombian newspaper), 504
Sigüenza y Góngora, Carlos de: *Belerofonte Matemático, Triunfo Parténico*, and *Infortunios de Alonso Ramírez*, 183

Silva, Antônio José da: *Historia do . . . don Quichote . . .* and *Encantos de Medeia*, 410–11
Silva, Diego de, 83
Silva, José Asunción: *Nocturne*, 467–8; *De Sobremesa*, 468, 480; *Día de Difuntos*, *El Recluta*, and *Vejeces*, 469
Silva, Manuel Inácio da, 409
Silva, Xica da, 429–30
Silva Herzog, Jesús, 499
Silva Paranhos, José Maria da: see Rio Branco, Viscount of
Silva Xavier, Joaquím José da: see Tiradentes
silver, 133–4, 277
Simón, Pedro: *Noticias . . . de las Conquistas*, 171, 223
Singerman, Berta, 532
Sinú, 20
Siqueiros, David Alfaro, 221, 494–5
Sismondi, Jean Charles Simonde de, 318
slavery: Brazil, 97–100, 110, 421–3, 429, 439; Spanish America, 125, 141, 163, 203–4, 209, 211, 422–3, 538–9; Jesuits, 166; Declaration of Human Rights, 238–9; literature, 336–7; abolition, 352; markets, 399, 444; see Negro; see also under names of countries
Smith, Adam: *Wealth of Nations*, 409, 413
smuggling, 141, 231, 399, 421, 429
Soares de Sousa, Gabriel: *Tratado . . . do Brasil en 1578*, 107–8, 117
social contract: see Rousseau, Jean-Jacques; Sanz, Miguel José
Socialism, 326, 330–3, 378, 383–4, 386–7
Societies of Friends of the Country, 245, 247, 275–7, 292, 295–8, 399
Socorro, 261
Socorro Rodríguez, Manuel del: see Rodríguez
Soderini, Piero, 68

Sogamoso; Sogamuxi, 19, 20
Solano, Francisco, Saint, 163
Sole de Chile (newspaper), 329
Solís y Ribadeneira, Antonio de:
   Historia . . . Conquista de Mexico,
   169, 227
Solomon Islands, 50, 173
Sombra, Severino, 424
Somoza, Anastasio, 363, 509–10
Soro, Enrique, 491
Soulouque, Faustin-Élie, 451–2, 458
Sousa, Fray Luis de, 103
Sousa Andrade, José Oswald de,
   435
South America: *see* America; pre-
   Columbian America; Portuguese
   America; Spanish America
Souza, Tomé de, 102–3, 150
"sovereign"; sovereign people," 248–
   51, 353
Spain: colonialism, xxi, 47, 57, 71,
   123–41; contributions, 38–41, 46–
   57, 41–5; medieval, Renaissance,
   71, 76–87, 231–2; motivation for
   conquest, 76–87; pre-American
   poverty, 127–8; territories, 129–
   30; New World literature, 168–
   70, 174; art, architecture, 194, 196;
   Enlightenment, 235–7, 259–61;
   scientific missions, 266, 269–70;
   wars of independence, 287, 293,
   308–9, 345; *Memorandum of
   Grievances*, 311–13; Reconquest,
   311, 313, 345–50, 364; expulsion,
   349–50; Republic, 496; Falange,
   502; mysticism, 528, 530, 540
Spanish America: embryo, xiv, 27–
   8, 36, 38–63, 123–8; conquest, exploration, xx, xxi, 9, 20, 38, 76–
   87, 123–8, 146, 168, 213, 230, 330
   (*see* discovery; rediscovery); colonial, xxi, 6, 47, 57, 71, 123–41,
   230–3, 235–8, 250–3, 267–8, 330
   (*see* viceroyalties); religion, xxx,
   50–1, 125, 137–41, 143–67 (*see*
   religion, pre-Christian; Roman
   Catholic Church; magic, mysti-

cism); social structure, 54–6, 124–
   7, 135–6, 351–2, 516–17, 538–9;
   ideological evolution, 62–3, 70–1,
   76–87, 137–8, 244, 288–9, 294,
   335–7, 378–403, 461–3 (*see* America; Enlightenment; Romanticism;
   Positivism); communication, 129–
   30, 299; cities, 129–37, 516–18;
   women, 160–3, 267; political evolution, 351–61, 378–403, 506–10,
   548–50 (*see* Independence; law,
   government); de-Hispanicizing,
   354–5, 378–9; style, mystique,
   461–3, 517, 521, 523–50
Spanish Civil War, 477
Spanish-Mexican style, 198
Spencer, Herbert, 378, 391–8, 488
Spock, Dr. Benjamin, 409
Staden, Hans: *Viagem ao Brasil*,
   118
Staël, Mme de, 307; *De l'Allemagne*,
   318; 319, 325
Stalin Peace Prize, 515, 520
Steinbeck, John, 481, 486
Stewart, Dugald, 320
Stewart, George, xiii
Stowe, Harriet Beecher: *Uncle
   Tom's Cabin*, 337, 422
Stradanus, Giovanni, 224, 226
Stradanus, Samuel, 227
Stroessner, Alfredo, 370, 507
Suárez, Inéz, 44, 160, 218
Suárez, Marco Fidel, 381, 393
Suárez de Peralta, Juan: *Tratado
   del descubrimiento de las Indias
   . . .*, 178
Sucre, Antonio José de, 289, 353,
   356, 372–3
sugar, 41, 57, 97–8
Sur (Argentine review), 513
Suster, Adrián, 217
Swinburne, Algernon Charles, 472

Tabasco, 8, 501
Tablada, José Juan: *Li-Po* and *En
   el País del Sol*, 473
Tahiti, 252, 269, 472

Taine, Hippolyte: *Les Origines de de la France Contemporanée*, 398
Tairona, 20
Tajimarca, 212
Talavera, Father Ramón, 370
Talavera ware, 208
Tamayo, Franz, 521
Tamayo, Rufino, 498
Taunay, Alfredo d'Escragnolle: *The Retreat from Laguna* and *Inocência*, 432–3
Tavora, family of, 404–5
Tecamachalco, church of, 222
Tejada, Ignacio Sánchez de, 345, 348–50
Telégrafo . . . , El (Argentine newspaper), 299, 329
Téllez, Hernando: *Cenizas . . .* , 512
Tello, Julio C., 13
Teniers, David, 221
Tenochtitlán, 9, 21, 28–31; 17th-century Europe contrasted, 28, 35; 33, 35, 37, 48, 73, 77, 91, 132, 146, 227, 238–9
teocalli, 131
Teotihuacán, 5, 9, 10, 535
Tepeaca, 197
Tepozotlán, Dominican church of, 198
"Tequitqui Art," 212
Teresa of Jesus, Saint, 83–4, 139; *Moradas*, 162; *Vida*, 162, 170; 532
Terrazas, Francisco de, 178, 191
Terrazas, Matías, 254
Teteoinan, 148
Texas: Lewisville, 21; 522; Austin, 534
Texcoco, 171
Texeira Mendes, Raimundo: *Life of Benjamin Constant*, 425–7
Texeira Pintó, Bento: *see* Pintó, Bento Texeira
textiles, 18, 19, 34, 370
tezontle, 200, 205
Theophrastus: *Historia Plantorum*, 78
Thevet, André: *Cosmographie Uni-*

verselle and *Les Singularités de la France Antarctique*, 102
Thiry, Leonard, 224
Thomas, Henry, 77
Thomas, Saint, legend of, 308
Thompson, James, 282
Thoreau, Henry David, 337
Tiahuanacu, 13–16, 19, 35, 211, 535
Ticunas, 535
Tierra del Fuego, 22, 270
Tikal, 9, 535
Tilcara, Tomás, 223
tin, 513
Tinoco, Diogo Grasson: *A Relação . . . em Oitava Rima . . . das Esmeraldas*, 428
Tiradentes (Joaquím José da Silva Xavier), 408–9
Tirso de Molina (Gabriel Téllez), 177, 191
Titian: *Charles V*, 220; 221
Titicaca, Lake, 13, 48, 218, 295
Tlalmanalco, convent of, 221
Tlatilco, 3–6
Tlaxcala, 144, 195, 219, 221
tobacco, 41, 58, 103–4, 276, 536–7
Tobar Colony, 284
Toledano, Vicente Lombardo, 495
Toledo, Francisco de, 129, 143
Tolima, 20
Tolsa, Manuel: *Charles V*, 132, 213–14
Tolstoy, Leo Nikolaevich, 333, 436, 468
Toltecs, 5
Tolú, 538, 540
Tonantzin, 148
Topa Inca, 48
Torah, the, 532
Toro, Manuel Murillo, 62
Torquemada, Juan de: *Monarquía Indiana*, 171; 217–8, 533
Torre Tagle, Marquis of, 205
Torres, Camilo: *Memorandum of Grievances*, 287, 311–13
Torres Bodet, Jaime, 497
Tortuga, 443

Toscanelli, Paolo del Pozzo, 64, 231

Toscano, Salvador, 498

Toussaint, Manuel, 195, 217–19, 221, 227, 501

Toussaint L'Ouverture, Pierre-Dominique, 386, 446 *n.*, 448, 451, 455–6, 541

Toxcatle, 535

Treaty of 1821, 82

Treaty of Ryswick, 443

Treaty of Tordesillas, 95

Trinidad, 240, 401

Tristán, Teresa, 257

Trujillo, 247, 249, 272, 294

Trujillo Molina, Rafael Leonidas, 399, 507, 509–10, 512

Tucumán, 41; Bishop of, 105; Congress of, 341

Tula, 211, 535

Tumaco, 19

tumbaga, 20

Tunja, 176, 194, 202, 223–5

tunjos, 20, 85

Tupac Amaru (José Gabriel Condorcanqui), 19, 173, 247, 287, 293

Tupa-Mbae, 156

Tupinambas, 107

tzenzontle, 132

Tzinzuntzan, 147

tzité, 24

Uaxactún, temple of, 10

Ugarte, Manuel, 489

Ulloa, Don Antonio: *Memorias Secretas*, 127, 166–7; 236–7, 267–8, 323

Ulloa, Francisco, 140

Umaña Luna, Eduardo, 512

Unamuno, Miguel de: *¡Adentro!*, 474, 508

Unanue, Hipólito: *The Climate of Peru*, 291–2

United Fruit Company, 42

United Nations: building, 437; Food and Agriculture Organization (FAO), 439; Educational, Scientific, and Cultural Organization, 497; Charter, 519

"united states," xiii

United States, the, xii, xviii, xix, xx, 21, 73, 62, 78, 129, 131, 135, 263; Constitution, xiii and *n.*, 258, 260, 262, 361; independence, 246, 257–8, 287, 383, 454; aid, 306, 507–10; Panama, 322, 353, 489; imperialism, 337; government, 338, 352, 354; Negro, 352, 421–3; Falkland Islands, 359; penal code, 362; influence, 378–9, 408–9; Cuba, 398, 466, 514–15; Utilitarianism, 487–8; aggression, 489, 518; World War I, 489–90; Mexico, 495–6, 499; World War II, 507; "mutual security" program, 509–10; territories, 522; Puerto Ricans, 533, 546–7

Upper Peru, 13–16, 19, 35, 41, 254, 262, 288

Upsala, 273, 277

Urabá, 138

Urdaneta, Luis, 363

Urquiza, Justo José de, 359–60

Urrutia, Manuel, 514

Ursúa, Pedro de, 172

Urubamba River, 15

Uruguay, 105–6; colonial, 129, 141 (*see* viceroyalties); Paraguay, 157; independence, 248, 288, 354, 356; scientific missions, 269–70; press, 295; Romanticism, 326–7; Church, 347; education, 491, 520; letters, 520; Negro, 546

Usigli, Rodolfo, 189

Uslar Pietri, Arturo, 521

Utilitarianism, 320, 378–83

Uxmal, 10, 35

Valde Hoyos, Marquis de, 209

Valdés, Gabriel de la Concepción (Plácido), 401, 544

Valdivia, Pedro de, 36, 44, 73, 158–60, 218

Valdivieso, 360

Valencia, Guillermo: *Ritos,* 472;
"Los Camelos," 473
Valentín Gómez, José, 341
Valenzuela, Don Mario, 382
Valera y Alcalá Galiano, Juan, 469–70
Vallalpando, Cristóbal de, 228
Valle, José Cecilio del, 380
Valle, Rafael Heliodoro, 501
Valle Caviedes, Juan del: *Entremés del Amor Alcalde, Baile del Amor Médico,* and *Baile del Amor Tahur,* 190
Valle de Orizaba, Count del, 207
Valle Inclán, Ramón del, 463
Vallejo, Francisco Antonio, 228
Vallejo, José: see Jotabeche
Vallenilla Lanz, Laureano: *Cesarismo Democrático,* 397; 398, 505
Vallenilla Lanz, Laureano, Jr.: *Escrito de Memoria,* 398
Valparaíso, 270, 301
Valverde di Hamusco, Giovan, 223
Varela, Felix, 231, 399–401
Varela, Luis V.: *Historia . . . de . . . Argentina,* 341
Vargas, Getulio, xviii, 438, 440
Vargas, Juan de, 224
Vargas Vila, José María, 398
Varnhagen, Francisco Adolfo de: *Historia . . . do Brasil,* 421
Varona, Enrique José: *Con el Eslabón,* 402
Vasconcelos, José: *La Raza Cósmica,* 109; *Estudios Indostánicos* and *History of Mexico,* 483; 491, 494–5, 501, 506
Vásquez, Francisco: *Crónica de . . . Guatemala,* 171
Vásquez Arce y Ceballos, Gregorio, 223, 229
Vaupés, 536–7
Vaux, Clotilde de, 387, 391, 425–7
Vaz de Caminha, Pedro, 89–91, 95
Vaz Ferreira, Carlos, 520
Vega, Lope de: *La Dragontea,* 177; 184, 191

Vega, Pedro: *Flos Sanctorum,* 224
Veintemilla, Ignacio de, 366–7
Velasco, Juan de, 182; *History of Quito,* 304
Velázquez, Diego, 80
Velázquez, Diego Rodríguez de Silva y, 220, 228
Velásquez de Cárdenas, Joaquín, 277
Vélez Sarsfield, Dalmacio, 394
Veloso, José Mariano da Conçeicão: *Flora Fluminense,* 409
Venezuela: United States of, xiii; colonial, xiv, 35, 38, 68, 81, 129, 146, 150 (*see* viceroyalties); missions, 154; architecture, 196–7, 204; independence, 256–9, 262, 288, 301, 305, 307–10, 343–4, 353–4, 356; scientific missions, 266, 268, 283–5; education, 281–2, 491, 521; 284; press, 295; 307, 319; monarchy vs. republic, 339–40; Constitution, 355; Positivism, 396–8; letters, 397–8, 463, 480, 482, 511; military, 505; 507; Cuba, 513; Christian Democracy, 516; see also *caudillos*
Venus of Tlatilco, 3, 4, 6, 22
Vera Cruz (Brazil), 95
Vera Cruz, Alonso de la: *Recognitio Summularum, Physica Speculatio,* and *Dialectia Resolutio,* 151
Veracruz, 36, 125, 129–30, 138, 141, 295
verde-amarelismo, 435
Vergara, 276
Verissimo, Erico, 436–7
Verlaine, Paul, 463, 467, 470–2
Vernon, Admiral Edward, 211
Verrazano, Giovanni da, xx, 68, 231
Vespucci, Amerigo, xii; *New World,* 3; 5, 22, 27, 67–70, 72, 79, 80, 89–93, 95, 109, 168, 181, 226, 231, 238, 240, 280, 526
Vespucci, Simonetta, 70
viceroyalties, 70, 344; Mexico (Mexico, Central America, United States), 29, 128–9, 143, 205, 217,

viceroyalties (*cont.*)
228, 270, 295; New Granada (Colombia, Venezuela, Ecuador), 129, 270, 296; Peru (Peru, Bolivia, Chile), 128–9, 266, 293–4; Plata, the (Argentina, Uruguay, Paraguay), 129, 208, 299–300, 340; Santo Domingo, 128, 204; dissolution of, 353–4
Victoria, Guadalupe, 349
Vicuña Mackenna, Benjamín: *Historia . . . de Santiago*, 388
Vieira, Antônio, 110, 120–2, 186
Vienna, 268
Vignola, Giacomo da, 225
Vikings, the, 5
Villa, Pancho (Doroteo Arango), 390, 438, 494
Villa-Lobos, Heitor: *Magdalena*, 438
Villamil de Rada, Emeterio: *La Lengua de Adán*, 374
villamiserias, 516
Villarroel, Gaspar de: *Govierno Eclesiástico Pacífico . . .*, 180
Villavaleix, Charles-Seguy, 459
Villaverde, Cirillo: *Cecilia Valdés*, 478
Villegaignon, Nicolas Durand de ("*Rex Americae*"), 101–4
Vilumilla, 159
La Violencia en Colombia (sociological study), 512
Vitoria, Francisco, 127, 151
Vitruvius Pollio, Marcus: *On Architecture*, 306
Vivero, Rodrigo, 207
Vives, Juan Luis, 151, 532
Vizcardo y Guzmán, Juan Bautista: *Letter to the American Spaniards*, 304–5; 311
Vogel, Henriette, 322
Volney, Comte de: *Voyage en Égypte . . .*, 401
Voltaire, 234, 316; *Candide*, 240–2, 404, 408, 524
voodoo, 448, 450–5, 458, 540–1
Vos, Marten de, 220

Wagener, Zachariah, 119
Wagner, Richard, 420
Walker, William, 423
Wallis, Samuel, 269
Wallis Island, 269
Warren, H. G., 370
Washington, D.C., 131
Washington, George, xx, 262
Welsers of Augsburg, 81
wheat, 44–5, 108, 155 *n.*
White, Joseph Blanco, 320
"White King, the," 129, 133
Whitman, Walt, 463, 465, 472
Wickham, Sir Henry, 59
Wilde, Oscar, 465, 472
Wilder, Thornton: *The Bridge of San Luis Rey*, 486
Williams Alzaga, Enrique, 340
Wilson, Sir Robert Thomas, 259
Wimpffen, Baron de, 445
witchcraft: *see* magic, mysticism
Wittenberg Bible, 222
Wordsworth, William: *Lyrical Ballads*, 315
World War I, 489–90, 502
World War II, 503, 507–8
Wright, Colonel, 363, 383
Wright, Richard, 481, 511

Xala, Count Bartolomé de, 207–8
Xarays, 81
Xarrato, José Ferreira, 429–30
Xavier, Francis, 104

yabas, 533
Yáñez, Agustín: *Al filo del Agua*, 499
Yáñez, Francisco Javier: *Manual Político del Venezolano*, 262–3
Yáñez, Vicente, 65
Yaparí, Juan, 223
Ydigoras Fuentes, Miguel, 363
Yecapixtla, 195–6
yerba maté, 111
ypaca'a, 275
Yucatán, 8, 10, 12, 70, 220

Yupanque, Tito, 218
Yurupary, 536–7

Zalamea, Jorge: *El Gran Brundum*
    . . . , 511
zambo, 140, 543
Zangurima, Gaspar, 216
Zapata, Emiliano, 390, 494
Zapotecs, 5
Zárate, Agustín de: *Historia . . .*
    conquista del Peru, 172
Zavala, Silvio: *La Utopia de Tomás*
    Moro, 501
Zea, Francisco Antonio, 281
Zea, Leopoldo, 500
zócalo, 132

Zonda, El (Argentine newspaper),
    328
Zorrilla de San Martín, Juan: *Ta-*
    baré, 318; 462
Zulueta, Luis de, 467
Zum Felde, Alberto: *Índice Crítico*
    . . . , 504, 520
Zumárraga, Archbishop Juan de,
    145, 147, 533
Zumeta, César: *El Continente En-*
    fermo, 505
Zurbarán, Francisco de: *Jesus at*
    Emmaus, 219; 224, 228–9
Zurriago, El (Ecuadorian newspa-
    per), 366

A Note About the Author

Germán Arciniegas was born in Bogotá, Colombia, in 1900. He was educated at the National University of Colombia. At various times he has been Colombian Vice-Consul in London, Counselor of the Colombian Embassy in Buenos Aires, a deputy in the Colombian Congress, and his country's ambassador in Rome. He has taught sociology in both the Free University and the National University of Colombia; in the United States he has been visiting professor at the University of Chicago, the University of California, Mills College, and Columbia University. He has served twice as Colombian Minister of Education, has been a member of the editorial board of Bogotá's distinguished newspaper *El Tiempo*, a contributor to *La Prensa* and *La Nación* of Buenos Aires, and editor of the *Revista de América* and of *Cuadernos*. Among the books by Germán Arciniegas which have been published in the United States are *The Knights of El Dorado* (1942), *Germans in the Conquest of America* (1943), *Caribbean: Sea of the New World* (1946), *The State of Latin America* (1952), and *Amerigo and the New World* (1955). He also edited the well-known anthology *The Green Continent: A Comprehensive View of Latin America by Its Leading Writers*.

A Note on the Type

The text of this book is set in Monticello, a Linotype revival of the original Binny & Ronaldson Roman No. 1, cut by Archibald Binny and cast in 1796 by that Philadelphia type foundry. The face was named Monticello in honor of its use in the monumental fifty-volume *Papers of Thomas Jefferson*, published by Princeton University Press. Monticello is a transitional type design, embodying certain features of Bulmer and Baskerville, but it is a distinguished face in its own right.

The book was composed, printed, and bound by The Haddon Craftsmen, Inc., Scranton, Pa. Illustrations printed by Halliday Lithograph, Corp., West Hanover, Mass.

Typography and binding designed by Vincent Torre